THE SERPENT
SYMBOL IN TRADITION

THE SERPENT SYMBOL IN TRADITION

DR. CHARLES WILLIAM DAILEY

A study of traditional serpent and dragon symbolism, based in part upon the concepts and observations of René Guénon, Mircea Eliade, and various other relevant researchers

ARKTOS
LONDON 2022

Copyright © 2022 by Charles William Dailey and Arktos Media Ltd.

All rights reserved. No part of this book may be reproduced or utilised in any form or by any means (whether electronic or mechanical), including photocopying, recording or by any information storage and retrieval system, without permission in writing from the publisher.

ISBN	978-1-914208-68-3 (Paperback)
	978-1-914208-69-0 (Hardback)
	978-1-914208-70-6 (Ebook)
EDITING	Jason Rogers
	Constantin von Hoffmeister
COVER & LAYOUT	Tor Westman

Arktos.com | fb.com/Arktos | @arktosmedia | arktosmedia

CONTENTS

Introduction   xv
Tradition, Symbols, and the Metaphysical xvii
The Concepts of "the Indefinite Series of Cycles of Manifestation"
and *Samsara*.. xxv
'Enlightenment' and the Equivalency of 'Chaos' and "the Indefinite
Series of Cycles" xxx
'Transcendence,' *Matter*, and the New Man... xxxiv
'Symbolic Modifications,' 'Spiritualization,' and Outline of the Project...... xxxviii

PROLEGOMENA

1. **René Guénon**   1
   The Man and His Thought..1
   The Question of Mastery and Other Criticisms 11

2. **Mircea Eliade**   25
   The Man and His Thought..25
   The Function of Symbols 39
   Symbols and Reductionism...44
   Some Criticisms of Eliade, and Responses...47
   The Continuing Importance of Eliade's Approach...................................54

3. **Symbolism, 'Tradition,' and Universalism**   59
   Symbols and Symbolism in Guénon and Eliade 59
   The Idea of 'Tradition' in Guénon and Eliade..68
   Universalism 76

4. **The Symbolism of the Serpent/Dragon in the Context of Guénon's 'Hindu Doctrines' and Eliade's Interpretation of the Traditional Idea of Chaos**   93
   Traditional Metaphysics and Epistemology in the Hindu *Vedanta*........93
   The *Samkhya* Concept of *Tamas* 99
   'Slaying' the Serpent/Dragon: 'Realization' in the Chaos of *Matter*......102
   Eliade's 'Extraterrestrial Archetypes' and 'Creation'................................110

THE SERPENT/DRAGON SYMBOL

5. **'Modifications' of the Serpent/Dragon Symbol: 'Spiritualization' and 'Materialization'**   **114**
   Heroic 'Transcendence' and 'Symbolic Modifications' of the Serpent/Dragon..114
   Manifestation and Creation as 'Realization' of the New Man 121
   'Chaos,' the Serpent/Dragon Symbol, and the Combat Myth 123
   The 'Thunderweapon' and the World Axis/*Axis Mundi*...............................127
   'Duality,' 'Spiritualization,' and 'Materialization'..129

6. **The Serpent Symbol, the World Axis, and 'Duality' and Its Variations in Ancient Egypt and Genesis 3**   **139**
   The World Axis or *Axis Mundi* in Guénon and Eliade 142
   The Serpent, 'Duality,' and Dichotomy in Genesis 3 and
      Ancient Egyptian Myth..147
   'Duality' and Dichotomy Imply the Ideas of Formlessness,
      Indefinitude, and Potentiality..154
   The 'Traditional' Interpretation of Genesis 3 from the Perspective
      of *Advaita Vedanta*..157
   Samsara and the Serpent Symbol in Genesis 3...163
   Samsara and *Maya* in Genesis 3 165
   The 'Fascination' of the Serpent 168

7. **Migration of the 'Self' in the Bible**   **170**
   'Migration' and Axial Symbols in Jewish and Christian Tradition 170
   'Involution,' 'Evolution,' 'Redemption,' and Dichotomies............................173
   Maya and the Manipulative *Nachash* in Genesis 3 176
   Migration of the 'Self' in Genesis 3 and *Advaita Vedanta*............................179
   Dichotomies and 'Migration' in Numbers 21 and John 3 183
   The Use of Snake Imagery to Represent 'Migration' 185

8. **The Guardian of Immortality/*Moksha***   **188**
   Ancient Greek Guardians 191
   The Serpent as 'Guardian' in Genesis 3..198
   The Metaphysical Symbolism of the Cross, the 'Ways' of Islam, and
      the *Gunas* of *Samkhya* in Relation to Genesis 3 201
   The Guardian of Immortality/*Moksha* in *The Epic of Gilgamesh* 207
   Guardian of *Moksha*, Not of Physical Life: A Critique of James Frazer's
      Interpretation of Genesis 3 211

9. **The *Ouroboros* and the *Anima Mundi***   **216**
   The *Ouroboros*..216
   Anima Mundi, the 'Soul of the World'...230

10. Symbols of 'Duality' in Unity   244
The Double Spiral and the Androgyne...245
Yin-Yang, 'World Egg,' 'Word' and *Tao* in Connection with Serpent/Dragon
    Symbolism...249

11. The Serpent as 'Mediator' and 'Messenger'   263
The Caduceus and Hermes/Mercury: 'Messenger' and 'Mediator'
    of the Divine...265
Hermes/Mercury and Other Traditional 'Mediators'/'Messengers'
    of the Divine...267
'Creation'/'Manifestation' and 'Reactualization'...................................272
Healing as Re-'Creation,' 'Mediation,' Resurrection,
    and Reincarnation/Rebirth..275
The 'Mediation' of 'Contrariety'..280
The *Amphisbaena* and the 'Plumed Serpent' Quetzalcoatl 284

12. The 'Risen' Serpent: The Conjunction of Wisdom and 'Healing' in *Kundalini*, the *Uraeus*, the Bible, and Buddhism   293
Kundalini as 'Mediator' and 'Messenger'...293
The Serpent, 'Healing,' and Knowledge/Wisdom 302
Kundalini, *Uraeus*, Circle and Sun..306
'Copper Serpent' and Crucified Christ in Connection with the
    Uraeus and *Kundalini*..322
The Buddhist Variation of Wisdom and 'Healing' as 'Enlightenment':
    The 'Risen' Serpent in Buddhist Art and Myth 328
The Symbolism of the Buddha with *Naga* 337

13. The Serpent and Sacred Stones   342
Shesha/Ananta and the *Devas* and *Asuras*: The 'Churning of the Sea'
    in the *Ramayana*..342
The Serpent, the Mountain, the *Omphalos*, and Sacred Stones 350
The *Beith-El*, the *Omphalos*, and the Oracle of Delphi 354
Serpents, 'Angels,' and 'Polarized Currents'...360
Sacred Stones Considered Transculturally...370

14. The Symbolism of the Serpent in Menhirs and Mounds   378
Megaliths as 'Sacred Stones' and the Element of Time..............................379
Serpent Symbolism in the Megaliths: The Avebury Cycle of Wiltshire,
    England...385
The Ohio Serpent Mound 402

15. The Dragon and the Orb — 423

The East Asian, or 'Far-Eastern,' Dragon 423
General Relationship between the Serpent/Dragon and the Circle/Sphere 425
'Polarization' of the Principle and Symbolic Differentiation
  of Circle/Sphere Symbolism 429
The Serpent/Dragon and the Moon 434
The Serpent's/Dragon's Traditional Association with the Control of 'Water' 436
East Asian Dragon, South Asian *Naga*, and Moon/Ball/Pearl/Spiral 442
To Control 'Water' Is to Control 'Possibilities' 455
The Dragon: 'Water,' 'Possibility,' 'Chaos,' *Matter* 460
The Symbolism of the Spiral, and the Chinese *Wang* as Mediator of
  'Possibilities' 466

16. The Spiral, the 'Thunderweapon,' and the *Swastika* — 475

'Spiraled Orb,' *Wang*, and 'Thunder' 475
The Meaning of the 'Thunderweapon' and the Gods Who Wield It 485
'Sky Gods' and the 'Thunderweapon' 497
The 'Spiraled Orb' and the *Swastika* 506

Conclusion — 516

The Serpent Symbol's Identification with 'Life' 516
The 'Overcoming' of Cyclicity: The Redefining of 'Life' 522
The Management and Control of 'Life' 528
The Serpent Symbol, Shamanism, DNA, and 'Duality' 537
'Life' Is Something to Be Transcended... and 'Controlled and Managed' 556

Bibliography — 573

Index — 591

LIST OF ILLUSTRATIONS

5.1	Zeus against Typhon	126
5.2	Asklepios	137
5.3	Façade of the Temple of the Tigers, Chichen Itza, Yucatan, Mexico	138
6.1	Temptation and Fall of Adam and Eve	149
6.2	The Cosmic Serpent 'Provider of Attributes'	153
8.1	Hercules in the Garden of the Hesperides with a Serpent in the Tree	193
8.2	Medea and Jason with the guardian serpent	194
9.1	The black and white ouroboros of alchemy	217
9.2	Double-headed serpent forming a bowl	220
9.3	Cosmic Spirit	238
10.1	Lady of Pazardzik	246
10.2	The Double Spiral	248
10.3	The Hermetic androgyne	248
10.4	Yin-yang	250
10.5	Plate, Ch'ing Dynasty	259
11.1	The Caduceus or serpent-staff of Mercury	266
11.2	Seal Cylinder of King Gudea	271
11.3	Libation vase of Gudea	271
11.4	Asklepios in the guise of a youth	277
11.5	Amphisbaena	286
11.6	Double-headed serpent	288
11.7	Untitled (Plumed Serpent)	289
11.8	Double-headed serpent forming a bowl	290
11.9	Two-headed Dragon, Copan, Honduras	290

12.1	The cakras	296
12.2	The Chakras	298
12.3	The Mask of Tutankhamen	309
12.4	The Uraeon (Egyptian)	311
12.5	From the ruins of Naki Rustan	311
12.6	A Chinese Uraeon	311
12.7	Azon, the Persian god (After Kaempfer)	311
12.8	Azon, the Persian god	312
12.9	Thothmes III. Wearing the sacred crown of Osiris	313
12.10	The Brazen Serpent	323
12.11	Buddha Meditating on the Naga Mucalinda	331
13.1	The Omphalos of Delphi	358
13.2	Four-winged serpent, Chnuphis or Bait	361
13.3	Jacob's Dream	365
13.4	The Crowned Virgin: A Vision of John	368
14.1	Engraving of Avebury	386
14.2	Plan of Avebury	389
14.3	Ohio Serpent Mound	403
14.4	Untitled (Crucified Serpent)	411
14.5	The Rearing Vision Serpent	420
14.6	K'awil merged with a Vision Serpent	420
15.1	Plate, Ch'ing Dynasty	425
15.2	Imperial court robe, Qing dynasty	446
15.3	Tray, Ming Dynasty	447
15.4	Bronze, the Forbidden City, China	449
15.5	Stone carving, the Forbidden City, China	450
15.6	Pendant, Middle Chou Dynasty	462
15.7	The character *wang*	469
16.1	The Double Vajra	491
16.2	Japanese statuette, with pedestal	493
16.3	Tibetan thunderweapon (*dorje*) of bronze	493
16.4	Classical Greek Thunderweapon (*keraunos*)	494
16.5	Thor Battering the Serpent of Midgard	504

16.6	The Two Directions of the Rotation of the Swastika	508
16.7	The Double Spiral	510
16.8	The Two Directions of the Rotation of the Swastika	510
C.1	Snake Goddess, Marble sculpture	519
C.2	Snake Goddess, Clay figurine	519
C.3	Snake Goddess, Terracotta	520
C.4	Snake Goddess	520
C.5	Neolithic painted terra-cotta figurine of seated mother with child	521
C.6	Serpent-headed goddess with child	521
C.7	Lord Krishna Dancing with Seven-Headed Cobra	527
C.8	Hagesander, Polydorus, and Athenodorus, The Laocoon Group	532
C.9	Moses and Aaron Before Pharaoh	536
C.10	The Rearing Vision Serpent	540
C.11	K'awil merged with a Vision Serpent	540
C.12	Untitled (The Double Helix)	550
C.13	The DNA double helix represented as a pair of snakes	550
C.14	Ornamental niche on façade, Uxmal, Yucatan, Mexico	552
C.15	Façade of the Temple of the Tigers, Chichen Itza, Yucatan, Mexico	553
C.16	Two-headed Dragon, Yaxchilan, Chiapas, Mexico	554
C.17	The Cosmic Serpent 'Provider of Attributes'	555

This book is dedicated, first of all, to my mother Candee McBride Dailey, who, with her unique poetic observations on life and regular encouragement during my period of writing, provided me, as has often been the case in other of my ventures, with an enduring emotional strength and many asymmetrical moments of reflection that allowed for the cultivation of insights and lines of investigation that I probably would not have otherwise perceived as I ultimately did. From the beginning of my life, she has been the primary wellspring of my love of South Asian and other non-Western cultures, and generally of epic tales and sagas the world over. Decades of watching films and reading books together about traditional India and China, the indigenous cultures of North America and Africa, and the experiences of Europeans and Americans in all of these wonderful places, has exercised an incalculably positive influence on both the shaping of my character and my great loves in life, as well as on the direction of my thought and research.

My second dedication is to my loyal border collie, Hank, or Hankston Sr. as I often call him. Hank has, nearly every day without fail, chosen to lie quietly (for the most part) close by, sometimes awake, sometimes asleep, while I worked during the days, months, and years required to complete the project that has culminated in the production of the present book. Although I have had the honor to befriend and live my life with many great dogs and cats — all wonderful, eternally luminous, beings wherever they may now be — Hank was the one destined to be consistently there with me, from the beginning of my notes to the words that I am now writing, on the great adventure of which the present work is the manifestation.

My final dedication is to Professor George Alfred James, my dissertation supervisor at the University of North Texas in Denton, Texas. This book is based upon that work. Dr. James, along with one other individual, has been the greatest *academic* teacher in my life. This was not so much because of his classroom instruction in the courses that I took from him, but because of the dedication that he persistently exercised, after some initial disagreements concerning argument forms and tone, in coaxing me to modify certain elements of my grammatical construction style and diction, of which I was once told many years previously, by a professor who taught me at another university, that it was "stodgy and Germanic." Being who I am, I of course took that as a compliment, for being described as 'Germanic' or compared to the Germans is nearly always a compliment in my view. I began to see, however, that one need not write like Kant or Hegel in order to emulate their genius. Over several months, Dr. James aided me in weeding out or improving unnecessary phrases, usages, and constructions in my writing. I am forever grateful for that and intend to try to remember everything that he taught me on that count. He should receive that gratitude and pledge as the greatest form of respect that I can repay him for his efforts, as it shall last me my life long.

Introduction

As the skin of a snake is sloughed onto an anthill, so does the mortal body fail; but the Self, freed from the body, merges in Brahman, infinite life, eternal light.

— Brihadaranyaka Upanishad IV: 4:7

In serpent iconography, humans, since 40,000 BCE, have found a way of finding the self.

— James H. Charlesworth, *The Good and Evil Serpent: How a Universal Symbol Became Christianized*

Serpent and dragon symbolism, taken together or separately, is present in the art and mythology of nearly all of Earth's cultures, figuring prominently in European, Egyptian, Near Eastern, Asian, African, Australian, and North and South American cultural artifacts. Various interpretations of both symbols have been proposed over the centuries. The serpent and dragon have both been associated with the ideas of: wisdom and knowledge; healing and renewal; life and fertility; immortality and time; chaos and creation; and evil, sin, and death, among others. To the philosophically curious, to the active intellect searching for universals in a landscape of particulars, the question arises as to whether there is some one idea underlying this diversity. I argue that, in what the symbolist René Guénon and the historian of religions Mircea Eliade have termed 'traditional,' or 'premodern,' or 'archaic,' art and mythology, both serpent and dragon symbolize the *state of existence* that I term *matter*. More specifically, the serpent/dragon symbolizes the 'traditional' experience of 'cyclicity' or the cyclical nature of the physical (or 'natural') world, and what I term 'symbolic modifications' of the serpent/dragon, such as the serpent with rod or the dragon with 'orb,' symbolize what I shall call the 'Spiritualizing' of *matter*. 'Spiritualizing' in this book denotes the act of forming, defining, and 'actualizing,' by means of a specific potentiality of human being, 'nature' or the physical world as it is *perceived* in its cyclical aspect, what Guénon describes as "the indefinite series of cycles of manifestation." The perception by some humans which I shall call New Men of the *limitedness* of "the indefinite series of cycles of manifestation," the physical world in its cyclical aspect, is what constitutes, from the 'traditional' perspective according to Eliade, 'chaos.' The mentioned state of *matter*, therefore, is a 'new' state of awareness in some humans that consists in the *perception* of "the indefinite series of cycles of manifestation" — the cyclical aspect of 'nature' — *as* 'chaotic.' This perception is made possible by what I shall call human 'realization,' the experience of *direct awareness of* ('intuition' of) a meta-physical Reality. Both this experience and this Reality were, according to Guénon and Eliade, known to 'traditional'/archaic peoples around the world. 'Realization' of the metaphysical, a *relative* form of 'enlightenment' for the individual experiencing such 'realization,' allows that individual to 'realize,' specifically, that the cyclical aspect of existence or 'nature' is *derivative of*, and substantially *lesser than*, a 'higher,' meta-physical, order. 'Realization' 'creates' the New Man and allows him/her to *reconceive* 'life' by perceiving the 'old' human 'identification' with what *was* seen by humans, from a less 'realized' level of consciousness, as 'life' — the cyclical aspect of 'nature' — to be 'chaotic.' Thus does 'realization' allow the New Man, by means of conceiving of the old 'life' as merely *one* possible state of 'human being,' to 'problematize' that idea of 'life' and, thereby, distance himself from it in order to, as I say, 'overcome' or 'Spiritualize' it. In making my argument, I employ a large variety of myths, legends, and artworks from, or referring back to, the 'traditional' cultures of the world, as Guénon and Eliade define the latter. I also rely on Guénon and Eliade, as well as many other nineteenth- and twntieth-century symbolists, religious scholars, archaeologists, and historians, for substantial considerations.

Tradition, Symbols, and the Metaphysical

In *The Myth of the Eternal Return*, Eliade states that "premodern or 'traditional' societies include both the world usually known as 'primitive' and the ancient cultures of Asia, Europe, and America."[1] In *Rites and Symbols of Initiation*, he adds that 'premodern societies' are "those that lasted in Western Europe to the end of the Middle Ages, and in the rest of the world to World War I."[2] As his biographer Robin Waterfield notes in *René Guénon and the Future of the West*, Guénon's understanding of what he terms the 'Primordial Tradition' is somewhat more "elusive and shadowy and…very difficult to find a definition [for] in his writings."[3] Waterfield summarizes, however, that, for Guénon,

> Tradition was essentially that body of knowledge and self-understanding which is common to all men of all ages and nationalities. Its expression and clarification forms the basis of all traditional wisdom and its application the basis of all traditional societies. It is supra-temporal in origin, the link which unites man as manifestation to his unmanifest origin.[4]

---

1   Mircea Eliade, *The Myth of the Eternal Return*, trans. Willard R. Trask (New York, NY: Bollingen Foundation Inc., 1954), 3.

2   Mircea Eliade, *Rites and Symbols of Initiation: The Mysteries of Birth and Rebirth*, trans. Willard R. Trask (Putnam, Connecticut: Spring Publications, 1994 [originally published in 1958]), 18.

3   Robin Waterfield, *René Guénon and the Future of the West: The Life and Writings of a 20th-Century Metaphysician* (Hillsdale, New York: Sophia Perennis, 1987), 80.

4   Robin Waterfield, *René Guénon and the Future of the West*, 80.

For Guénon and Eliade both, Tradition, although it is in its present day form only a shadow of its former self that has been, due to the effects of modernity, relegated largely to the peoples of South American jungles, South Asian villages, the Siberian tundra, and the Australian desert, *was* an ancient and *global* phenomenon, which transcended separating oceans, continental divides, and the superficial differences of regional cultures, and that always professed the unwavering belief in the existence of a meta-physical Reality considered 'more real' than the physical, or so-called 'natural,' world.

Eliade's and Guénon's understandings of Tradition are, for the most part, consonant. According to Eliade, however, 'ordinary language,' and especially Western philosophical terminology, must be problematized in order to comprehend the traditional/archaic symbolic worldview. In *The Myth of the Eternal Return*, Eliade explains that

> [o]bviously, the metaphysical concepts of the archaic world were not always formulated in theoretical language; but the symbol, the myth, the rite, express, on different planes and through the means proper to them, a complex system of coherent affirmations about the ultimate reality of things, a system that can be regarded as constituting a metaphysics. It is, however, essential to understand the deep meaning of all these symbols, myths, rites, in order to succeed in translating them into our habitual language. If one goes to the trouble of penetrating the authentic meaning of an archaic myth or symbol, one cannot but observe that this meaning shows a recognition of a certain situation in the cosmos and that, consequently, it implies a metaphysical position. It is useless to search archaic languages for the terms so laboriously created by the great philosophical traditions: there is every likelihood that such words as "being," "nonbeing," "real," "unreal," "becoming," "illusory," are not to be found in the language of the Australians or of the ancient Mesopotamians. But if the word is lacking, the thing is present; only it is "said" — that is, revealed in a coherent fashion — through symbols and myths.[5]

---

5   Mircea Eliade, *The Myth of the Eternal Return*, 3.

Eliade identified the 'primitive' perspective of Tradition as a variety of Platonic metaphysics, stating in *The Myth of the Eternal Return* that

> "primitive" ontology has a Platonic structure; and in that case Plato could be regarded as the outstanding philosopher of "primitive mentality," that is, as the thinker who succeeded in giving philosophic currency and validity to the modes of life and behavior of archaic humanity.[6]

For Eliade, so-called 'primitive' peoples believe(d) that physical beings of all kinds are only imperfect embodiments of eternal 'archetypes' ('Forms') that only 'become real' when they 'participate in' a 'transcendent' (metaphysical) reality.[7] In a similar fashion for Guénon, traditional peoples believe(d) that 'the World,' 'nature,' was derived from, and eternally dependent upon, a metaphysical 'Principial' Reality. The most faithful remaining expression[8] of this belief, accord-

---

6   Mircea Eliade, *The Myth of the Eternal Return*, 34.

7   In "Plato's Metaphysical Epistemology," Nicholas P. White states that "[t]he Forms are central to Plato's metaphysics and epistemology. So is the distinction between them and the objects of perception in the natural world around us....Reality for him is indissolubly linked to...the Forms." Nicholas P. White, "Plato's Metaphysical Epistemology," in *The Cambridge Companion to Plato*, ed. Richard Kraut (Cambridge: Cambridge University Press, 1992), 280 and 298.

8   I say here 'most faithful remaining expression' because Guénon accepted a form of 'catastrophism' in his writings on this subject — very much consistent with Hindu tradition — in which civilization is regularly disrupted or destroyed by various kinds of catastrophes and much is lost in the forms of knowledge and tradition. The Hindu myth of the 'seven sages' is based upon the paradigm of 'catastrophism' for its understanding of the long-term development of humanity on earth. According to Guénon, because of the pattern of catastrophes that punctuate the long course of human history, traditional knowledge is not always preserved equally by all of the cultures/societies that survive catastrophes. What this implies for the purposes of this book is that, for the *current* 'age' of the world, what Guénon terms 'Tradition' has been *best* preserved in the specific form of what Guénon refers to as the 'Hindu Doctrines,' the *darshana* of *Vedanta* most clearly and completely, but also the *darshana* of *Samkhya*, and others.

ing to Guénon, is the Hindu system of thought called *Vedanta*[9], one of several orthodox Hindu *darshanas* ('points of view') that Guénon collectively calls the 'Hindu Doctrines.'[10]

For Guénon and Eliade, *symbols* are the most common means by which: 1) 'traditional' doctrines, such as the 'Hindu Doctrines,' are

---

9   In *The System of the Vedanta*, scholar Paul Deussen says of the Sanskrit term '*Vedanta*' that it refers, in a literal sense, to "the end of the Veda[s]," with the term Veda(s) referring to, according to Ramakrishna Puligandla in his *Fundamentals of Indian Philosophy*, "the oldest and most sacred scriptures of the Hindus." Paul Deussen, *The System of the Vedanta*, trans. Charles Johnston (Chicago: The Open Court Publishing Company, 1912), 3. Ramakrishna Puligandla, *Fundamentals of Indian Philosophy* (New Delphi: D. K. Printworld Ltd., 1994 [originally published in New York in 1975]), 10. For Guénon, as for many Hindus, *Vedanta* means *both* "the end of the Vedas"—that section of the Vedas called the Upanisads—*and*, according to Puligandla, "the various elaborations and interpretations of the Upanisads." Ramakrishna Puligandla, *Fundamentals of Indian Philosophy*, 209. In *A Source Book in Indian Philosophy*, Radhakrishnan and Moore state that "The Upanisads are the concluding portions of the Vedas and the basis for the Vedanta philosophy." Sarvepalli Radhakrishnan and Charles Moore, eds., *A Source Book in Indian Philosophy* (Princeton, New Jersey: Princeton University Press, 1957), 37.

10 "The Sanskrit word *darshana*," according to Guénon in his *Introduction to the Study of the Hindu Doctrines*, "properly speaking denotes nothing more or less than 'sight' or 'point of view,' for the principal meaning of the verbal root *drish*, from which it is derived, is 'to see.'" For Guénon, "The *darshanas* are really therefore 'points of view' within the doctrine, and not, as most orientalists imagine, competing or conflicting philosophical systems; insofar as these points of view are strictly orthodox [accepting of the authority of the Vedas], they naturally cannot enter into either conflict or into contradiction with one another." René Guénon, *Introduction to the Study of the Hindu Doctrines*, trans. Marco Pallis (Hillsdale, New York: Sophia Perennis, 2001 [originally published in 1921 as *Introduction générale à l'étude des doctrines hindoues*]), 162-163. In his *Fundamentals of Indian Philosophy*, Ramakrishna Puligandla defines *darsana* as "vision of truth and reality." Ramakrishna Puligandla, *Fundamentals of Indian Philosophy*, 4. Although Puligandla employs the term '*darsana*' without the letter 'h,' I will generally use the spelling to be found in all of the translated works of Guénon: '*darshana*' *with* the letter 'h.' It should also be noted that Guénon's use of 'doctrines,' rather than 'philosophies' or 'religions,' would be considered, by many, the more accurate appellation.

communicated and 2) the meta-physical realm is accessed. In *Yoga: Immortality and Freedom*, Eliade states that "[i]n general, symbolism brings about a universal 'porousness,' 'opening' beings and things to transobjective meanings."[11] In *Symbols of Sacred Science*, Guénon remarks that "the essential role that we have ascribed to symbolism" is "a means of raising ourselves to the knowledge of divine truths."[12] For both authors, a 'symbol' in traditional art and myth is something that conveys insight into the meta-physical order of being, the latter of which Eliade sometimes refers to as 'Reality.' For both authors, the traditional worldview recognizes multiple 'levels' of existence, of which the purely metaphysical level is the 'highest' in terms of its being the 'most real.' The physical world, or 'nature,' is, in the traditional worldview as defined by Guénon and Eliade, a 'lower' level of existence (or 'Being') that is 'less real' than the metaphysical level of Reality. Traditional symbols are, for both authors, one means by which the metaphysical level of existence, the source of *all other* levels of existence (including the grossly material level that modern humans are most interested in), is 'realized' by traditional peoples. Traditional symbols can be thus thought of as a kind of 'device,' since all devices are developed in order to either facilitate regular and dependable access to a specific phenomenon or to make a uniform product. The device that we call a microscope, for example, facilitates for humans regular and dependable access to microscopic phenomena, just as the device that we call a window facilitates for humans one form of regular and dependable access to the world outside of a building without their actually having to go outside of the building. Of all of the kinds of devices that exist, however, the device that is called a 'key' is most similar to the device of the language of traditional symbols.

---

11   Mircea Eliade, *Yoga: Immortality and Freedom*, (New York, NY: Bollingen Foundation, Inc., 1958), 250–251.

12   René Guénon, *Symbols of Sacred Science*, ed. Samuel D. Fohr, trans. Henry D. Fohr (Hillsdale, NY: Sophia Perennis, 2001 [originally published in 1962 as *Symboles fondamentaux de la science sacrée*]), 10.

This is because, for traditional peoples according to Guénon, symbols 'unlock,' in the minds of those who are capable of 'using' them, a level of understanding physical, or 'natural,' phenomena that transcends both the theoretical and practical meanings that are, from the 'materialist' perspective, assigned to these phenomena.[13] A *physical* key, it is known, provides its user access to physical places and physical objects: a room, an automobile, a safe box, etc. A *symbolic* key, however, provides its user access to ideas or concepts that, according to Eliade and Guénon, provide a 'bridge' to a meta-physical understanding of existence. Eliade's 'trans*objective* meanings' and Guénon's 'divine truths' are both references to a meta-physical level of existence since, in Eliade's case, only the physical level of existence is understood in terms of *objects* and, in Guénon's case, the terms 'divine' and 'truth' are only meaningful when referring to, or describing, the metaphysical level of existence that is 'occupied' by 'the gods.'

As a hammer and chisel revealed to the Renaissance sculptor Michelangelo the idea of *Moses* in a piece of marble, the traditional symbol is able to reveal to those who, like Michelangelo, understand their 'tools,' a metaphysical level of existence within the 'material' of the physical/'natural' world. Those individuals who *do* understand their tools, who understand the language of traditional symbolism, are those humans who have, according to Guénon and Eliade, been initiated into Tradition. The meaning of every tool, however, the meaning of every device, is its function. The meaning of a microscope is its function of revealing the structure of microscopic phenomena, the meaning of a window is its function of revealing the world outside

---

13 In *The Book of Certainty*, Abu Bakr Siraj Ed-Din (the traditional name of Martin Lings, specialist in Islamic art and esoterism and formerly Keeper of Oriental Manuscripts and Printed Books at the British Museum) similarly states that "a symbol is something in a lower 'known and wonted' domain which the traveler considers not only for its own sake but also and above all in order to have an intuitive glimpse of the 'universal and strange' reality which corresponds to it in each of the hidden higher domains." Abu Bakr Siraj Ed-Din, *The Book of Certainty* (New York: Samuel Weiser Inc., 1970), 50–51.

of a building/auto/ship while still maintaining a certain degree of strength and cohesiveness against the affronts of weather. The meaning of *every* symbol, likewise, is to reveal and express those ideas that are of importance to the culture within which that particular symbol exists and has significance. Specific symbols have specific meanings and specific functions. Cultural meanings, however, are not always limited to *particular* geographical regions or to relatively short periods of time. They can, on the contrary, be *global* in extent and last for very long periods of time.[14] Because of this, it is reasonable to postulate that certain specific symbols had *specific* meanings not merely for relatively circumscribed groups of humans inhabiting tiny locales for relatively short periods of time, but for humans existing across vast swaths of the globe for very long periods of time.

Eliade, in *The Myth of the Eternal Return*, states that "the serpent symbolizes chaos, the formless and nonmanifested."[15] Guénon, in *The Symbolism of the Cross*, argues that "the serpent will depict the series of the cycles of universal manifestation,"[16] "the indefinitude of universal Existence,"[17] and "the being's attachment to the indefinite series of cycles of manifestation."[18] In all of these statements, Eliade and Guénon

---

14 For example, there are various iterations of the tool that we term a 'saddle' throughout history and around the globe. Saddles have been created for various beasts — horses, oxen, and camels — and even within horseback riding, specifically, there are many variations on the saddle. All have the same function, just as a single symbol may have the same meaning over very long periods of time and in widely separated places around the globe. See, for example, Deb Bennet, *Conquerors: The Roots of New World Horsemanship* (Amigo Publications Inc., 1998) and Susan McBane, *The Essential Book of Horse Tack and Equipment* (Devon, England: David & Charles, 2002).

15 Mircea Eliade, *The Myth of the Eternal Return*, 19.

16 René Guénon, *The Symbolism of the Cross*, trans. Angus Macnab (Hillsdale, NY: Sophia Perennis, 2001 [originally published in 1931 as *Le symbolisme de la croix*]), 122.

17 René Guénon, *The Symbolism of the Cross*, 123.

18 René Guénon, *The Symbolism of the Cross*, 124.

both are referring to the *traditional* meaning(s) of the serpent/dragon symbol, thus contending that the symbolism of the serpent/dragon, as they have analyzed it, possessed a transcultural meaning that lasted for millennia. Eliade and Guénon are also implying in these statements, and directly state elsewhere, that those artifacts that describe or depict the traditional serpent/dragon symbol may be discovered in very widespread, and *apparently* culturally diverse, regions of the world. Although Guénon employs the term 'depict' in the above quotations instead of 'symbolize,' he means for the reader to think of the two terms as synonyms, as he affirms in the same sentence as the one that the above relevant quotation is drawn from that "the tree symbolizes the 'World Axis.'" Although Eliade and Guénon employ different terminologies in the above quotations concerning the meaning of the traditional symbolism of the serpent/dragon, I argue that both authors refer to, in these and other statements on the subject, the same reality that is symbolized by the serpent/dragon in traditional art and myth. I furthermore contend that the serpent/dragon symbol in Tradition, in both its pictorial and narrative forms, is a means of expressing a juxtaposition of concepts that are inductively derivable from the nature of the snake as observed in its habits and environments. For, in its very being, the snake is preeminently *cyclical* in its skin-shedding, relatively *formless* in its monomorphic anatomy, and reminiscent of the separate and 'alien' nature of the divine (the *metaphysical*) in its unsocial behavior and simple 'otherness.'

Divine truths, doctrinal teachings (of the specifically 'traditional' variety like those included in the Vedas), and 'transobjective' meanings are all, from the perspective of Tradition, expressions of metaphysical knowledge, knowledge of a 'Principle' that exists beyond ('meta') the physical/'natural' world. Knowledge of the metaphysical 'Principle' is sometimes traditionally expressed, in a more superficial sense, as knowledge of 'the gods.' It is the function of symbols in the traditional sense of the term, according to both Eliade and Guénon, to bring humans to a comprehension of the gods or the Principle that is both depicted and described in the various forms of traditional doctrinal teachings. The metaphysical Principle that is, as I say, superficially described and depicted as 'the gods' is, according to Guénon, referred to in the 'transmission' of Tradition as having been *experienced*, not inferred, under such names as 'God' (Yahweh), '*Brahman*,' *Tao*, and various other titles encapsulating the Principle's monistic *and* pluralistic (such as 'the gods' or Plato's 'Forms') expression. The 'metaphysical' is, thus, in Tradition, interchangeable with the 'divine.'

The Concepts of "the Indefinite Series of Cycles of Manifestation" and *Samsara*

According to Guénon, the expression "the indefinite series of cycles of manifestation" encapsulates an idea that is intrinsic to *all* traditional metaphysical systems, all systems of thought that recognize the existence of a metaphysical source of the physical/'natural' world. During the present age of the world, it is for Guénon the South Asian concept of *samsara* that most faithfully conceptualizes the traditional idea of an "indefinite series of cycles of manifestation."[19] In his translation of the Hindu classic the Bhagavad Gita, the spiritual teacher, author, and translator Eknath Easwaran translates *samsara* as "the world of flux, the round of birth, decay, death, and rebirth."[20] For Guénon, the

---

19   See footnote 8 concerning Guénon's interpretation of the Hindu idea of 'ages of the world.' In *The Hindu Religious Tradition*, scholar Thomas J. Hopkins defines *samsara* more generally as 'passage.' Thomas J. Hopkins, *The Hindu Religious Tradition* (Belmont, California: Wadsworth Publishing Company, 1971), 50. Guénon says of "the indefinite series of cycles of manifestation" that "[t]his is the Buddhist *samsara*, the indefinite rotation of the 'round of existence,' from which the being must liberate himself in order to attain *Nirvana*." René Guénon, *The Symbolism of the Cross*, 124. As Guénon seems to imply, this idea of *samsara* is the *same* as that discussed in the *Vedanta* and in the orthodox 'Hindu Doctrines' generally. It constitutes an idea of, as I put it, the 'cyclicity' of 'nature' that transcends any particular South Asian philosophy or religion.

20   Eknath Easwaran, trans., The Bhagavad Gita (Tomales, California: Nilgiri Press, 2007), 285.

ancient Hindu perspective presented in The Bhagavad Gita constitutes an excellent example of traditional knowledge, although it is not for him as faithful an expression of Tradition as the Vedas (inclusive of the Upanishads). The perspective presented in the BG,[21] as well as that presented in many other Hindu, Jain, and Buddhist texts, is, however, pervaded by an ancient, transcultural, belief in *cyclical existence*, and that on various levels. It is a belief that is not entirely absent in the modern outlook since *any* being that is capable of empirical observation of the physical/'natural' world, and of discerning pattern there, realizes that 'nature' resolves itself into various kinds of cycles, whether these be cosmological, biological, microscopic, or subatomic. *Samsara*, defined by Easwaran as the "round of birth, decay, death, and rebirth" in South Asian expressions of Tradition, conceptually crystalizes the, for Guénon, traditional idea of a *generalized* "indefinite series of cycles of manifestation" that is not merely limited to 'life'-cycles. In the R. E. Hume translation of the Maitri Upanisad, for example, *samsara* is translated simply as "cycle of existence."[22] The concept of *samsara* constitutes a *general* idea of the 'cyclicity' of the emergence and destruction of beings in the physical universe, of which the events of the births and deaths of living beings constitutes only a subset. What is called 'birth,' therefore, in the context of this broader idea of *samsara*, refers to the event in which particular 'individuals' of the subset of beings called 'living' *emerge*; what is called 'death' refers to the event in which particular 'individuals' of the subset of beings called 'living' are *destroyed*. The use in the BG of a *limited* set of beings, living beings — humans, specifically — to exemplify a more expansive cosmic cyclical process is, I argue, among other things, a pedagogical tool that is employed in other expressions of the Hindu Doctrines, such as the Upanishads. It is a tool that reveals how a 'higher,' metaphysical,

---

21 I shall sometimes abbreviate The Bhagavad Gita as BG.

22 Maitri Upanisad 4, R. E. Hume, *The Thirteen Principal Upanishads* (London: Oxford University Press, 2nd ed., rev., 1931) in Sarvepalli Radhakrishnan and Charles Moore, eds., *A Source Book in Indian Philosophy*, 93.

Reality is imperfectly mirrored in "the indefinite series of cycles of manifestation" that goes to constitute 'nature,' but is only mirrored for those beings that are *consciously aware* of the 'system of cycles': humans that have, in other words, achieved a certain level of 'enlightenment.' When more expansively considered, *samsara* refers to what might be called the "round (the cycles) of *emergence and destruction*," rather than referring only to the 'smaller' cyclical system constituted by the "round (the cycles) of birth, decay, death, and rebirth." This interpretation of *samsara* constitutes an application of the concept of 'indefinite cyclicity' to the physical/'natural' world *in general* rather than only to the living beings that exist *within* that world.

Guénon and Eliade, respectively, employ the terms 'manifestation' and 'creation' to describe the 'emergence' of *all* beings (not just living beings) in the physical universe, with Guénon's use of 'creation' not implying the production of the physical universe 'out of nothing.' 'Manifestation'/'creation'/'emergence' occurs, however, and always has occurred, according to Guénon's and Eliade's interpretations of Tradition, *constantly* in the physical/'natural' world by means of an *indefinite* number, and wide variety, of *cycles*. The menstrual cycle of women that is connected with birth and life, the cycle of the rejuvenation of cells in living organisms, the recurring cycles of subatomic particles' interactions, the lunar cycle (the phases of the moon), the solar cycles (the movement of the sun throughout the year from the perspective of earthly observation *or* the cycles of 'sun spots' and the sun's movement through the galaxy — examples of 'subjective' *or* objective cycles, in other words), the cycles of the seasons, the cyclicity of the tides of the seas, the cycles of the growth and shedding of hair, fur, and shells by animals — *all of these, together*, and along with innumerable other cycles both discovered and yet to be discovered, constitute a magnificent *indefinite*, returning, *series of cycles* that has no obvious beginning *or* end in the experience of observers capable of discerning universals in the midst of particulars. This, to use Guénon's phrase, "indefinite series of cycles of manifestation" is a cyclical series in which beings are manifested — 'created' or 'born' into the physical/'natural' world — and then become *non*-manifest: they are destroyed; they die; they 'exit' the physical/'natural' world.[23] 'Manifestation,' therefore, from the 'traditional' perspective, according to Guénon and Eliade, is an *essentially* metaphysical idea, as it describes the expression, or revelation, of a *non*-physical reality *in* the physical/'natural' world. The physical/'natural' world *itself*, and all physical/'natural' beings that together 'constitute' that world, are, according to Guénon's and Eliade's interpretations of Tradition, therefore, ultimately 'manifestations' of either: 1) a singular metaphysical Reality that Guénon terms the 'Principle,' or, equivalently, 2) plural metaphysical realities that Eliade refers to as 'archetypes,' 'the gods,' or Plato's 'Forms.' I describe the 'action' of the Principle, or of the archetypes/gods/Forms, as the forming, defining, and 'actualizing' — 'Spiritualizing' — of: 1) what Guénon calls, in a general sense, "the indefinite series of cycles of manifestation," *samsara* in South Asian tradition, and 2) what Eliade calls 'chaos' or "the formless and nonmanifested."[24]

What is called 'nature,' or the physical world, by those New Men who are aware of their *essential* 'separateness' from it, is the human *perception* of *samsara*/"the indefinite series of cycles of manifestation." The physical/'natural' world *appears*, to such 'enlightened' humans,

---

23 As is pointed out by Samuel D. Fohr, the editor of Guénon's *Studies in Hinduism*, "the word 'creation'...is not suitable from the point of view of Hindu doctrine" in translating the idea of the coming-into-being of beings of all orders (the 'manifestation' of beings), although Guénon "frequently uses — and in particular to translate the term *srishti* — the word 'creation.'" René Guénon, *Studies in Hinduism*, ed. Samuel D. Fohr, trans. Henry D. Fohr and Cecil Bethell (Hillsdale, New York: Sophia Perennis, 2001 [originally published in 1966 as *Études sur l'Hindouisme*]), 16. Eliade also employs the term 'creation' to describe the simple event of "the coming-into-being of beings," as we have seen above. 'Production,' too, is a term used by Guénon in a similar, although not entirely justified, sense. The reader should not infer from such usages, however, that Guénon is trying by means of his diction to 'smuggle into' his analyses of 'manifestation' the argument for intelligent design by a 'divine maker.'

24 Mircea Eliade, *The Myth of the Eternal Return*, 19.

a 'chaos' because they have achieved that state of being that I term the state of *matter*, and are thus directly aware of, or 'intuitive' of, to some degree, a 'higher' meta-physical Reality. What is called the physical/'natural' world is, therefore, according to Guénon's and Eliade's understandings of Tradition, from the perspective of enlightened, 'new,' humans, I argue: 1) formless in comparison with the, as perceived by them, *essentially* formative character of the metaphysical Principle/archetypes/gods/Forms that provides for the revelation of forms in the physical/'natural' world, and 2) nonmanifest because it is that which is, from the perspective of 'enlightened' humans, the field *for* 'manifestation' of a meta-physical Reality (the Principle/archetypes/gods/Forms). Narrowly construed, *samsara* expresses the idea of a 'chaotic' "indefinite series of cycles of manifestation" of, and later destruction of, *living* things in the physical/'natural' world. For those beings, therefore, that have become 'enlightened' to the metaphysical Source of "the indefinite series of cycles of manifestation"/*samsara*, and thus of the physical/'natural' world, the latter *appears* relatively 'formless' or 'chaotic.' Guénon interprets the serpent/dragon symbol in Tradition to symbolize "the indefinite series of cycles of manifestation" *and* its South Asian expression *samsara*, both of which I shall sometimes refer to as the 'series of cycles.' 'Unenlightened' humans, because they are, as is sometimes said in South Asian tradition, 'trapped' in the series of cycles, that is, in the relatively unformed 'confusion and obscurity' of the physical/'natural' world, require, for the most part according to Guénon, *symbols* to 'lift' them up out of the *oubliette*[25] that they have constructed by means of their own lack of 'Self'-awareness. 'Self,' as I employ it, refers to the *Atman* that is in *Vedanta* the ultimate and eternal 'ground' of the individual 'ego' and other ideas of 'individuality.' From the perspective of those individuals who cannot see the 'series of cycles' that they are 'trapped' within as something *separate* from their true 'Self,' and who, thus, cannot see

---

25 *oubliette*: "A secret dungeon with access only through a trapdoor in its ceiling." https://enoxforddictionaries.com

samsara as derivative from a 'higher' Reality, the existence of a metaphysical order is 'naturally' a dubious proposition. It is only, therefore, in accordance with traditional doctrine, by means of a direct *experience* ('intuition') of the meta-physical Reality itself, or by means of an indirect experience of the metaphysical by using the 'device' of *symbols*, that this doubt can be remedied. The former of the two means, however, according to the scriptures of many religions, seems to be possible only for a very small minority of individuals.

'Enlightenment' and the Equivalency of 'Chaos' and "the Indefinite Series of Cycles"

In *The Myth of the Eternal Return*, Eliade defines the traditional idea of 'chaos' as the "formless and nonmanifested" aspect of existence and employs that term to refer to the cyclical character of what he calls 'profane time.'[26] 'Profane time,' according to Eliade, is what modern people think of as the 'ordinary' passage of events. From the perspective of traditional/archaic peoples, however, it is a kind of time that lacks ritual significance and objective meaning and is, therefore, 'chaotic.' As such, 'profane time' is, according to Eliade, something that traditional/archaic peoples believe must be 'overcome.' Eliade argues that traditional/archaic peoples have generally sought, and still seek, to 'abolish' the cyclical reality that constitutes 'profane time' in order to "participate…in mythical time" and live "over and over again in the atemporal instant of the beginnings."[27] The 'time of the beginning' (*in illo tempore*) is, according to Eliade, for traditional/archaic peoples, an *a*temporal Reality that exists 'beyond' the influences of the 'chaotic' cyclical system of 'nature' which he argues is symbolized for them by the serpent/dragon.

In *The Sacred and the Profane*, Eliade states that

---

26 Mircea Eliade, *The Myth of the Eternal Return*, 19.
27 Mircea Eliade, *The Myth of the Eternal Return*, 36 and 117.

the dragon is the paradigmatic figure of the marine monster, of the primordial snake, symbol of the cosmic waters, of darkness, night, and death — in short of the amorphous and virtual, of everything that has not yet acquired a 'form'. The dragon must be conquered and cut to pieces by the gods so that the cosmos may come to birth. It was from the body of the marine monster Tiamat that Marduk fashioned the world. Yahweh created the universe after his victory over the primordial monster Rahab.[28]

According to Eliade's interpretation of traditional cosmology, the cosmos 'comes to birth' by means of the imposition, from a divine or transcendent source, of 'form' on 'chaos.' The definition of 'chaos' that Eliade attributes to the traditional mindset seems very intuitive even today, for *what else* is 'chaos' but, as Eliade states, "the amorphous and virtual…everything that has not yet acquired a 'form'"? The divine imposition of form is, from the traditional perspective according to Eliade, the act of 'creation,' what I shall term in this book 'Spiritualization,' or the defining, forming, and 'actualizing' of the state of being that I term *matter*. As Eliade relates, in ancient Babylonian myth, the divine creator, or 'imposer' of form, is the god Marduk; in the Hebrew Torah, He who 'separates' the 'waters,' thus *forming* them in their 'separateness,' is Yahweh. (Genesis 1:6) Synthesizing Guénon's and Eliade's interpretations of traditional/archaic thought on this subject, Eliade's 'creation' and Guénon's 'manifestation' 'each' constitutes, for traditional peoples, the 'infusion' of the meta-physical that 'manifests' or 'creates' — forms, defines, and 'actualizes' — physical boundaries and possibilities. What Guénon describes from the traditional *metaphysical* perspective as "the indefinite series of cycles of manifestation" constitutes a 'blurring' of boundaries that is equivalent to Eliade's 'chaos.'

One could say, in response to the traditional idea of chaos presented by Eliade, that the physical/'natural' world *cannot* be an *absolute* chaos, for, obviously, there are observable patterns and physical

---

28 Mircea Eliade, *The Sacred and the Profane: The Nature of Religion*, trans. Willard R. Trask (Orlando, Florida: Harcourt, Inc., 1957), 48.

'laws' in the physical/'natural' world. This, however, would be to project a 'strawman' onto Eliade's interpretation of chaos, for it would be to presume that 'absolute chaos' *can* exist, or that the concept even makes sense. 'Nature' itself *does* have its own intrinsic kind of order that distinguishes it from pure flux. However, from the *traditional* perspective, this is a 'lower,' *more* 'chaotic,' form of order that is clearly recognized as such from the state of enlightened metaphysical awareness. According to Eliade, the traditional conception of 'chaos,' which I argue characterizes a certain *perception* of 'nature,' is not 'absolute' but rather equivalent to the traditional concept of 'nature' *absent* the infusion of eternal, immutable, and meaningful 'archetypes.' From the traditional perspective, according to Eliade, the absence of eternal archetypes *in itself* constitutes 'chaos.' I say, however, that the traditional symbolism of the serpent/dragon symbolizes the traditional idea of 'chaos' as Eliade presents it *as well as* Guénon's understanding of the traditional idea of an "indefinite series of cycles of manifestation" that is the transcultural expression of the Hindu concept of *samsara*. This equivalency between these two conceptions exists because both conceptions refer to the essence of the physical/'natural' realm, as traditional peoples understand it, *insofar as* is absent the 'infusion' of a metaphysical Reality, or realities, whether this be *a singular* metaphysical 'Principle' or *plural* 'gods'/'archetypes'/'Forms.' In either case, "the indefinite series of cycles of manifestation," the cycles *themselves*, are the means by which the metaphysical Principle/gods/archetypes/ Forms 'manifests'/'creates.' *Equivalently*, *'chaos'* as defined by Eliade is the means by which the metaphysical Principle (gods/archetypes/ Forms) manifests/'creates.' For, in the traditional worldview, it is, according to Eliade, only by means of the *contrast* provided by the physical/'natural' 'chaos' that the gods/archetypes/Forms 'manifest' *in*, or 'create,' that the *meta*-physical 'order' may be discerned: 'chaos' is only revealed once 'order' (the 'Principle'/'the gods') has 'infused' it. *Symbolically*, only when the serpent/dragon has been "cut to pieces by the gods" is their presence revealed/'manifested'/'created.'

Because of traditional peoples', according to Eliade, emphasis on 'forming' chaos, on what I have termed 'Spiritualizing' their *perception* of the 'cyclical system' of the physical/'natural' world that is symbolized by the serpent/dragon, traditional peoples by necessity see the serpent/dragon as symbolizing that which must provide the 'material' for the gods'/Principle's 'action.' According to Guénon, the 'cyclical system' of 'nature' is seen by traditional peoples to be 'indefinite' and, therefore, *requiring* definition. The necessary 'defining' series of events that is, for Guénon, manifested as "the indefinite series of cycles of manifestation" *of* the Principle is, I argue, equivalent to what Eliade calls 'creation' of the cosmos. This is because in traditional thought 'creation' is an indefinitely *ongoing series* of events. Both 'manifestation' and 'creation' are, therefore, symbolized in Tradition by the 'slaying' of the serpent/dragon which must occur *indefinitely*. My unique contribution in this book is that the serpent/dragon symbolizes, in Tradition, Guénon's "indefinite series of cycles of manifestation" (*samsara* in South Asian tradition) *and* Eliade's 'chaos' because both concepts imply the existence of a metaphysical 'Principle,' or 'gods,' that manifests *as* the 'particulars' of the physical ('natural') world and that forms, defines, and 'actualizes'—Spiritualizes—those 'particulars' and 'nature' itself. In traditional thought, the 'chaotic' "indefinite series of cycles of manifestation" is the, from the perspective of 'enlightened' New Humans, imperfect 'reflection' of the metaphysical Principle (gods) *in* the 'lower' terrestrial, physical/'natural' world. The serpent/dragon is thus, for 'traditional' peoples, the best means of symbolizing the particular *way* in which the metaphysical Principle (the gods) *manifests in*, and is *corrupted by*, the 'lower' (from the perspective of an ontology that recognizes non-physical existence) order of things. In the words of the, according to Eliade, preeminently traditional philosopher Plato in his *Timaeus*, the traditional serpent/dragon symbol symbolizes a 'moving image of eternity.'[29] Since Plato finds this expres-

---

29 Plato, *Timaeus* 37d in *Plato: Complete Works*, ed. John M. Cooper (Indianapolis/Cambridge: Hackett Publishing Company, 1997), 1241.

sion descriptive of the nature of time, it is appropriate to also employ it to describe the *temporal nature* of the physical/'natural' world. Based upon these considerations, the serpent/dragon, in addition to its symbolizing the 'chaotic' "indefinite series of cycles of manifestation," also symbolizes for traditional peoples that aspect of human being, the 'individual' ego, that is *conditioned by time* insofar as this conditioning is equivalent to embeddedness in the 'cyclical system,' since the ego is that which is, unlike the transcendent 'Self'/*Atman* that exists 'beyond' cyclical existence, a *product* of cyclical existence. The 'individual' ego, however, as an *apparently separate* being from the perspective of *Advaita Vedanta*, only represents the 'Self'/*Atman* in the sense that it is an incomplete expression of the 'Self.' For, to 'represent' something, whatever it may be, is merely to present it *again* in a somehow less perfect or reduced fashion. The relationship, therefore, by which the *physical* ego represents the *meta*-physical 'Self'/*Atman* is analogous to the relationship by which physical symbols 'represent,' in traditional societies, meta-physical realities. In both cases, the method of analogy elucidates the relationship in question because it is the method by which the imperfections of the physical world, the world captured by imagination, are made to serve as best as they can in expressing the perfection of the meta-physical world, the world revealed directly only by what Guénon calls 'intellectual intuition.'

'Transcendence,' *Matter*, and the New Man

The serpent/dragon in Tradition symbolizes, represents, and 'points to' that aspect of the physical/'natural' world that the Hindu concept of *samsara* abbreviates: Guénon's "indefinite series of cycles of manifestation." This broad idea of *samsara* is equivalent in Tradition to the physical/'natural' world insofar as the latter is *perceived* to be *absent* a meta-physical element. This makes *samsara*, from the traditional perspective, an 'illusion,' an empty concept, since, traditionally speaking, there can be no physical/'natural' world *without* the 'infusion' of a meta-physical Reality. From the perspective of Guénon, and perhaps of Eliade, this outlook is more 'enlightened' than the modern materialistic outlook because it recognizes the *dependency*, and so 'unreality,' of the physical/'natural' world. Only, however, from the perspective of observers who have 'transcended' — seen 'beyond' — the physical/'natural' world to a 'higher' (*meta*) level of existence, can this 'chaotic' 'unreality' be recognized. According to Guénon, the rituals ('rites of passage'), initiations, and disciplinary paths (such as the *yogas*) of traditional societies allow for such 'transcendence,' or 'enlightenment,' or 'realization.' The various *yogas*, for example, represent in South Asian tradition different 'paths' to 'realization' or 'transcendence.' *Karma yoga* emphasizes the path of 'action,' *bhakti yoga* emphasizes the path of 'devotion,' and *jnana yoga* emphasizes the path of 'knowledge.' For Guénon, however, all such initiatory disciplines, and therefore 'enlightenment,' are nearly impossible for moderns to, respectively, *properly* practice and 'attain' because of the almost total lack in the current 'age' of the world of what Guénon calls a 'spiritual influence.'

Whenever I interpret the serpent/dragon as symbolizing in Tradition both Eliade's 'chaos' and Guénon's "indefinite series of cycles of manifestation," and whenever I state that both are, roughly and from a certain perspective, equivalent to the physical or 'natural' world, the latter is *not* to be defined in the modern sense of a collection of physical objects or subatomic particles. Rather, 'nature' (the physical world) is, as traditional peoples thought of it according to Guénon and Eliade, a *state of being* that I term *matter*. Matter is, as I define it, the 'state,' or condition, of the 'Self'/*Atman in* its ego experience of the 'chaotic' "indefinite series of cycles of manifestation." More specifically, *matter* consists of: 1) a *particular* state of awareness by a *particular* kind of human, which I shall term the New Man, that consists in his/her *perception* of the limitedness and dependency of the 'cyclical system' (which, along with the 'cyclical system' itself, constitutes the physical world/'nature'); 2) the New Man's awareness of his/her *particular* embeddedness *in*, and separateness *from*, the 'cyclical system'; and 3) the New Man's conscious striving to 'overcome' — Spiritualize — both the 'cyclical system' itself and his/her *awareness of* the cyclical system, by treating the cyclical system *and* his awareness of the cyclical system as a *potentiality* to be formed, defined, and 'actualized': in a word, Spiritualized. The term *matter*, therefore, and the expression 'state of matter,' as it is employed in this book, is not to be thought of in the modern sense of a 'state of energy' or as the 'totality' of all physical objects or subatomic particles, but rather as "the indefinite series of cycles of manifestation" *as they are perceived by* the New Man *in* their 'chaotic' aspect. This state of being in which such perception is possible, one which is, according to Guénon, the product of traditional rituals, initiations, and disciplinary practices, 'sees' the "indefinite series of cycles of manifestation" *as* a 'chaos' in comparison with a 'higher,' metaphysical, order of being. *Matter*, as defined in this book, therefore, is, from the traditional perspective, 'real' only from the 'confused and obscure,' although 'enlightened' compared to 'less aware' states of existence, *perspective* of beings in a particular state of being of the 'Self'/*Atman*. This is the state in which the individual's ego has not yet been *completely* 'enlightened' to the metaphysical order of things from which the state of *matter* ultimately derives. *Matter* is, then, within the bounds just set, equivalent to Eliade's 'chaos' *and* Guénon's "indefinite series of cycles of manifestation," the latter of which appears 'chaotic' to any 'finite aspect' of *Brahman* (to any 'individual' being, that is), to the extent that the 'individual' being has become aware of its metaphysical nature. 'Traditional' man in general *was*, to different degrees in different persons, so 'aware' — as a result of the above-mentioned initiations, rituals, and disciplinary practices. What Guénon calls 'modern' humans, however, are, according to him, rarely capable of learning from such initiations, rituals, and disciplinary practices, even in the unlikely event that 'moderns' discover authentic versions of them. As modernity is, for Guénon, an essentially physicalist or materialist paradigm, modern humans are, in their essential comportment toward reality, disposed to disregard metaphysical reality. Since such humans are 'unenlightened' to the existence of a meta-physical level of existence, 'nature,' or the physical world, *cannot* be seen as 'chaotic' because, in the modern paradigm, there is nothing of a more encompassing order — a, literally, meta-physical order — that exists for moderns to contrast 'nature' with. The physical, or 'natural,' world, from the modern, and not only the modern-*scientific*, perspective, is *all that there is*, and its physical 'laws' are the only things that *can* count, for moderns, as 'order.' Therefore, when the physical world (the 'cyclical system') *as a whole* appears 'chaotic' to an individual, I argue that this experience *indicates* that the individual in question has become aware of a 'higher' order of existence, since 'chaos' only makes sense in the context of an imagined (however vaguely or unconsciously) 'higher' order. The reality of the 'natural'/physical "indefinite series of cycles of manifestation," then, only takes on a 'chaotic' aspect to that 'new' being that has become aware of the existence of something 'beyond' the physical/'natural' world (level of existence).[30] This 'new' and *necessarily* meta-physical awareness is what allows for the 'problematization' of the older idea of 'life,' the 'identification' by humans with pure

---

30 As the Christian writer and philosopher C. S. Lewis pointed out, there are those who claim to be complete nihilists and complete materialists, and who, therefore, *claim* that the world is both without meaning and without metaphysical order. As Lewis also noted, however, the dictates of logic necessitate asking of such individuals, *where* do you *get* your idea of 'unmeaning' and your idea of a 'lack of transcendent order' in the universe that, within the limits of reason, allows you to classify *all* of existence as being without meaning and without absolute order? Even in his works of fiction, such as in *The Chronicles of Narnia*, Lewis was a stickler for logical thinking, and realized that, for those individuals who have become attached to the notions of nihilism and materialism, there is, sadly, no answer to his question other than that kind of answer that is determined by the constraints of emotion. See, for example, Professor Digory Kirke's remarks on logic in Chapter 5 of *The Lion, the Witch, and the Wardrobe* in *The Chronicles of Narnia* (New York, New York: Barnes & Noble, Inc., 2010), 131. As Guénon similarly points out, the essentially 'sentimental' nature of modern man's form of awareness generally prevents his appreciating the emotionalism inherent in his dearly held, but ultimately irrational, beliefs.

cyclical existence, *as matter* and its symbolization as a serpent/dragon to be 'slain.'

'Symbolic Modifications,' 'Spiritualization,' and Outline of the Project

In the art and myth of Tradition, there are a variety of what I shall call 'symbolic modifications' of the 'simple' serpent/dragon symbol. The 'simple' serpent/dragon is just as it sounds: a representation of an 'unadorned' or 'plain' snake or dragon. The 'modified' serpent/dragon, however, can be found in traditional art and myth in various combinations. These include: 1) the serpent or dragon coiled around a rod or tree or cross, 2) the serpent or dragon juxtaposed with an 'egg' or 'orb,' or other circular/spherical object, 3) the serpent or dragon possessed of wings, and 4) the serpent or dragon in 'combat' with a 'god' or 'hero,' as well as other 'modifications.' Such 'symbolic modifications' symbolize what I have termed the 'Spiritualizing' (forming, defining, and 'actualizing'), or 'overcoming,' of the 'chaotic' cyclical system of 'nature,' the "indefinite series of cycles of manifestation" perceived by the 'enlightened' New Man as *matter*. They symbolize, in general, two things: 1) the New Man's 'struggle,' or 'combat,' with an older idea of 'life' that becomes first problematized and then defined by the New Man under the conceptual apparatus of 'chaos'/ *samsara* (cyclical existence) and 2) the possibility of 'life's' — 'chaos's/ *samsara*'s — 'management and control.' The juxtaposition of what Guénon calls 'axial symbols,' such as the tree, rod, staff, cross, and variations of the 'thunderweapon,' which we shall discuss later, or other traditional symbolic expressions of metaphysical Reality, such as wings, birds, the circle/sphere and the 'world egg,' with the serpent/dragon communicates a concern in traditional societies — by the New Man in particular, who first, in some cases, *founded* such societies by means of his problematization of the old idea of 'life' — with 'going beyond' the physical/'natural' world that the serpent and dragon traditionally symbolize. Examples of the Spiritualizing of 'chaos'/*samsara* (the 'state' of *matter*) in 'traditional' art and myth include: 1) the Mesoamerican 'plumed serpent' (Quetzalcoatl/Kukulcan), 2) the serpent entwined around a rod/tree/cross found in various ancient Near Eastern and Mediterranean iterations, 3) the dragon/serpent with circle/sphere/'orb'/egg in its mouth or in one of its (the dragon's, specifically) claws, or nearby the beast, found in Asia and the Americas, and 4) 'combats' or 'struggles' described and illustrated between 'the gods' (representing the metaphysical), such as the Greek Apollo and the Vedic Indra, and serpents/dragons such as the Greek Python and the Vedic Vritra. All of these cases from both art and myth symbolize what I term the Spiritualizing of *matter*, where 'Spiritualizing' refers to: 1) the forming of the unformed (the clarifying and distinguishing of the 'confused and obscure'), 2) the defining of the indefinite, and 3) the 'actualizing' of potential, all by means of a meta-physical Source or 'Principle' called *Brahman* in the *Vedanta*, God/Yahweh in the Bible, and *Tao* in East Asian tradition. Spiritualizing is, thus, equivalent to both what Guénon terms 'manifestation' (as a verb) and what Eliade terms 'creation.' 'Manifestation' and 'creation' both, therefore, express the idea of the imposition of form, definition, and 'actuality' onto something that is *relatively* formless, undefined, and potential. Both terms express the idea of Spiritualizing or 'overcoming' (as in a 'struggle' or 'combat') because they express the idea of 'transcendence.' In symbolic terms, the Spiritualizing of *matter*, the forming, defining, and 'actualizing' of the New Man's experience of the 'chaotic' "indefinite series of cycles of manifestation" that was 'identified' with by an older, 'less aware,' kind of human, is the 'slaying' of the serpent/dragon.

In order to more clearly flesh out, and provide deeper theoretical foundations for, the above-presented argument, I begin this book with a series of *prolegomena* that provide: 1) the background, influences, and some criticisms, of René Guénon and Mircea Eliade (Chapters 1 & 2); 2) a detailed examination of these two authors' understandings of 'Tradition,' traditional symbolism, and universalism (Chapter 3);

and 3) a detailed examination of Guénon's particular understanding and use of 'metaphysics' in the context of his appropriation of what he calls the 'Hindu Doctrines,' the *Vedanta darshana* in particular (Chapter 4). The body of my book (Chapters 5–16) consists of my interpretations of prominent traditional examples of the 'simple' symbolism of the serpent/dragon, as well as prominent cases of its 'symbolic modifications' in Tradition. A synthesis of Guénon's and Eliade's understandings of the symbolism of the serpent/dragon in Tradition largely provides the theoretical basis for my thesis, with Guénon's interpretive approach being the more privileged. I also, however, consider the important perspectives of other researchers of serpent and dragon symbolism in the context of Guénon's and Eliade's observations, and *all* within the context of what Guénon and Eliade define as 'Tradition.' The conclusion of my book, beyond mere summary, includes a brief discussion of what I call the 'categories of Spiritualization' that are revealed in the history of traditional serpent and dragon symbolism. My conclusion also serves, however, as a *prolegomenon* to an historical evaluation of the development, or 'evolution,' of human awareness of the 'cyclical system,' the 'state of matter,' as I have defined it. It, therefore, addresses two interconnected topics: 1) three major kinds of 'hosts' of Spiritualization and 2) a proposed 'history of consciousness' of what was a three-stage historical 'evolution' in human awareness of the *samsaric* nature of the physical world (the 'cyclical system'). The three major kinds of 'hosts' of Spiritualization are: a) Spiritualizing *professions and personalities* (e.g., healers, shamans, priest-kings, Emperors, 'enlightened' individuals, and prophets); b) *places* of Spiritualization (e.g., temples, henges, and mounds); and c) *events* of Spiritualization (e.g., 'healings' and 'enlightenment experiences'). The three-stage historical evolution of human awareness consists of: a) unconscious 'identification' with an older idea of 'life,' conceptualized by the New Men as *samsara*/"the indefinite series of cycles of manifestation"/'chaos'; b) dawning awareness of, and psychological 'struggle' or 'combat' *against*, this older idea of 'life' that is conceptualized as *samsara*/'cyclical existence'/'chaos'; and c) the believed-in 'management' or 'control' of 'life' *considered as samsara*/'cyclical existence'/'chaos.' Examples of 'Spiritualizing professions' (such as king or Emperor), 'Spiritualizing personalities' (such as Jesus or Siddhartha), 'Spiritualizing places' (such as Avebury or the 'Ohio Serpent Mound'), and 'Spiritualizing events' (such as 'shamanic journeys' or the metaphysical 'healings' effected by Jesus and Siddhartha) will have already been considered at length in the body of the book, but I will use the conclusion to remark upon the 'evolving' idea of 'life' in general from the perspective of the particular 'Spiritualizing profession' known as shamanism.

CHAPTER 1

René Guénon

The Man and His Thought

René-Jean-Marie-Joseph Guénon was born in Blois, France, 'the town of the wolves,' the 'town of kings,' on November 15, 1886 to, as his first biographer Paul Chacornac described them, "staunch Catholics."[1] Robin Waterfield, another of Guénon's biographers, states that Guénon "came from a family of small landowners, whose property consisted mainly of vineyards and who can be traced back to a Jean Guénon born in Saumur in 1741."[2] Guénon was, according to Chacornac, of delicate health from birth and his health was to remain 'fragile' throughout his life, although he eventually "overcame his weakness."[3] Guénon began his formal education at age eleven at the secondary school of Notre Dame des Aydes, according to Waterfield "a school with a religious foundation staffed by secular priests, the syllabus being identical with that of a minor seminary."[4] Perhaps attempting to explain by means of biography Guénon's later scholarly

---

1   Paul Chacornac, *The Simple Life of René Guénon* (Hillsdale, New York: Sophia Perennis, 2001), 7.
2   Robin Waterfield, *René Guénon and the Future of the West*, 11.
3   Paul Chacornac, *The Simple Life of René Guénon*, 9.
4   Robin Waterfield, *René Guénon and the Future of the West*, 12.

1

interests, Waterfield remarks in *René Guénon and the Future of the West* that

> [c]oming from the heartlands of France gave Guénon a strong sense of being rooted and of belonging to a given place and a given culture which, as it has been for many Frenchmen, was an almost mystical source of confidence for him.[5]

Chacornac and Waterfield reveal the atmosphere within which Guénon grew up as one of commitment to religious tradition and a sense of cultural rootedness, both characteristics perhaps conducive to the development of a conservative mindset, although not of course constituting proof as to why Guénon developed an abiding interest in Tradition[6] and ancient belief systems — countless other humans rejective of such influences have experienced the same sort of upbringing and education.

"Open-minded and intelligent," Chacornac notes of the young Guénon that he "rapidly assimilated and mastered his subjects and became a brilliant student, often standing first in his class."[7] In January of 1902, Guénon entered the College Augustin-Thierry as a student of rhetoric and, after a few months according to Chacornac, "was considered an excellent student in every respect by all his teachers," although his health often prevented his regular class attendance.[8] In general, Guénon's religious and conservative upbringing did nothing to make him a dogmatic pedant in the sense of many of those other famous literary figures of his era, such as Hegel and the Hegelians, or Marx and the Marxists, who sought to reduce all knowledge to a particular universalizing system. As his thought matured, Guénon always railed against systematization. As we shall see in later chapters, he argued that such a perspective was essentially at odds with a truly

---

5 Robin Waterfield, *René Guénon and the Future of the West*, 11.
6 See the *Introduction* for an overview of Guénon's idea of Tradition.
7 Paul Chacornac, *The Simple Life of René Guénon*, 13.
8 Paul Chacornac, *The Simple Life of René Guénon*, 15.

metaphysical understanding, in his mind the only *complete* understanding, of reality. The anti-systematic character of Guénon's understanding of metaphysics is important to note. Waterfield, referring in *René Guénon and the Future of the West* to Guénon's study of Taoism (one of many cultural expressions for Guénon of what he termed the 'Primordial Tradition'), states:

> Guénon's writings do not provide a rigid, all-embracing system into which we have somehow to cram ourselves, accepting it all passively without contributing our own personal understanding and experience. Guénon believed that living by the Tao meant rejecting all notions of systematization:
>
> > The highest good is like water.
> >
> > Water gives life to ten thousand things and does not strive,
> >
> > It flows in places men reject and so is like the Tao.
>
> This adaptability and fluidity Guénon believed was characteristic of what he called the Primordial Tradition, which can be equated with the Tao.[9]

Such an approach to 'enlightenment,'[10] in which systematic 'rigor' is absent, often seems at odds with the methodology embraced by modern anthropologists and historians of religion, making Guénon's writings sometimes seem to be lacking in their idea of 'scholarship.' Guénon frequently, however, pointed out the limitations of the essentially inductive method that lies at the heart of such modern 'systematic' scholarship, saying for example that

> [t]hese experimental methods will never reveal anything other than simple phenomena, on which it is impossible to construct any kind of metaphysical

---

9   Robin Waterfield, *René Guénon and the Future of the West*, 5–6.
10 'Enlightenment' is employed here in the general sense of a greater, or deeper, awareness. The terms 'scholarship' and 'education' are insufficient to describe the purpose of study and concentration in 'traditional' (the Primordial Tradition) societies, since both scholarship and education (in the modern sense), although they may increase an individual's store of information, usually, from the perspective of Tradition, leave him/her in the same *state of being*.

theory, for a universal principle cannot be deduced from particular facts. Moreover, the claim to acquire knowledge of the spiritual world through physical methods is obviously absurd; it is only within ourselves that we can find the principles of this knowledge, not in external objects.[11]

What Guénon calls a 'universal principle' in this quotation, which we shall later define more thoroughly, he believes can *never* be derived from the essentially limited nature of empirical experiences. For Guénon, the *general* laws that are discovered through the scientific method are not equivalent to *universal* principles discerned spiritually through direct intuition of metaphysical reality. Those familiar with the arguments of the eighteenth-century Scottish philosopher David Hume, as well as those who wish to separate *certain* knowledge from *probable* hypotheses and theoretical constructs, will appreciate the truth of Guénon's claims concerning what can and cannot constitute universal, rather than simply general, principles.

On the relationship between Guénon the man and Guénon the thinker and writer, Waterfield states that

> [l]ike all great teachers his approach is essentially supra-personal. The facts of his life, the sources of his knowledge, the historical and personal factors which encouraged him to write and say what he did, are of interest, particularly to the modern Western mind, which is obsessed with the personal. But ultimately they are irrelevant. What matters most is the message he transmitted.[12]

Waterfield notes that Guénon's "impersonality and authority" are "baffling and repellent" to many today because modern readers and critics are accustomed to judge an author's work, at least in part, by

> his 'personal slant,' as we call it, [which] enables us to agree or disagree with him on personal grounds and to justify our attitude by a variety of

---

11 Found in Paul Chacornac, *The Simple Life of René Guénon*, 23–24, from 'Gnosis and the Spiritual Schools,' Miscellanea, pt. 3, chap. 6.

12 Robin Waterfield, *René Guénon and the Future of the West*, 4.

intellectual tricks. These tricks include what may be called psychological reductionism...or a more general relativization that considers a writer predominantly in his historical and cultural setting and as the product of a continuing stream of ideas that will inevitably be superseded by fresh thoughts and newer ideas and can therefore be disagreed with. Such judgments are made on the basis of a strong presumption that what is new is better than what is old—an evolutionary theory that Guénon constantly rebutted.[13]

James R. Wetmore, the series editor of the *Collected Works of René Guénon*, provides the following summary of Guénon's perspective and project:

> His works are characterized by a foundational critique of the modern world coupled with a call for intellectual reform; a renewed examination of metaphysics, the traditional sciences, and symbolism, with special reference to the ultimate unanimity of all spiritual traditions; and finally, a call to the work of spiritual realization.[14]

To appreciate Guénon, then, the modern thinker must be prepared to doubt many cherished, and often little analyzed, notions that buttress his confidence in the idols of modernity. S/he must be willing to entertain criticism of the modern idea of 'criticism' itself, and of the, according to Guénon, limited perspective that it promotes. The belief in 'progress,' the presumed positivistic undoing of metaphysics, and the widespread sentimental obsession with the presumed success of physical/material 'explanations,' are but a few of the major 'axioms' of modernity that Guénon criticizes from the perspective of Tradition.

In *René Guénon and the Future of the West*, Waterfield writes that "what [Guénon] consciously or unconsciously was undertaking was the radical re-orientation of the prevailing trend of Western thought and its common mental outlook, deriving ultimately from Greek

---

13 Robin Waterfield, *René Guénon and the Future of the West*, 4–5.
14 René Guénon, *The Symbolism of the Cross*, xiii.

Aristotelian ways of thinking."[15] "Guénon's message," according to Waterfield, "was to deny [the] one-sided approach" of Western philosophy that ultimately culminated, in the modern world, in a "scientific materialism that maintains that the way to grasp reality is to break it up into pieces."[16] To convey this 'message' of denying the analytical materialist paradigm, Guénon concentrated in many of his works on what he believed to be the most faithful remaining expression of what he called Tradition: according to Waterfield, "a special form of Hindu thought, the Advaita Vedanta."[17] Although *Advaita Vedanta* is, perhaps, that expression of Tradition that Guénon was most knowledgeable in, it must be understood that Guénon's interest and expertise in this area constitutes only one example of his understanding of a 'primordial' traditional knowledge that he believed transcends *particular* cultures and 'philosophies.' In *The Simple Life of René Guénon*, Chacornac opines that Guénon

> was not an orientalist, although — or perhaps because — no one knew the East better than he; he was not an historian of religions, although no one knew better than he how to illustrate their common basis, as well as the differences in their perspectives.[18]

Guénon was not so much what is today thought of as a 'scholar,' in the sense of one who studies in order to make 'original' contributions to a 'field of research,' but, as he felt, a 'medium' or 'transmitter' of the Primordial Tradition.[19] For Guénon, the modern obsession with making an 'original contribution' to the understanding of the fundamental structure of reality is a vanity and a waste of time, for the fundamental structure of reality was *already* 'discovered' by traditional peoples from time immemorial.

---

15   Robin Waterfield, *René Guénon and the Future of the West*, 56.
16   Robin Waterfield, *René Guénon and the Future of the West*, 57–58.
17   Robin Waterfield, *René Guénon and the Future of the West*, 57–58.
18   Paul Chacornac, *The Simple Life of René Guénon*, 1.
19   Robin Waterfield, *René Guénon and the Future of the West*, 52.

One objection that Waterfield notes concerning Guénon's idea of Tradition (the 'Primordial Tradition') "is [that it is] elusive and shadowy and…very difficult to find a definition [for] in his writings."[20] As Waterfield observes, "Even in the chapter entitled 'What is meant by Tradition?' in his *Introduction to the Study of the Hindu Doctrines*, we find a baffling series of generalizations."[21] It is true that, as Waterfield states, Guénon "was reluctant to provide clear definitions for any of the major concepts with which he was concerned."[22] What Guénon *meant* by 'Tradition,' however, was, as Waterfield puts it

> that body of knowledge and self-understanding which is common to all men of all ages and nationalities. Its expression and clarification forms the basis of all traditional wisdom and its application the basis of all traditional societies. It is supra-temporal in origin, the link which unites man as manifestation to his unmanifest origin.[23]

In *Introduction to the Study of the Hindu Doctrines*, for example, Guénon states that "social institutions, to be considered traditional, must be effectively attached in their principle to a doctrine that is itself traditional, whether it be metaphysical or religious or of any other conceivable kind."[24] 'Traditional,' in other words, for Guénon, describes those societies and social norms that are based upon an *essentially* metaphysical understanding of reality.

Guénon was aware from an early age of how perennial forms of wisdom could easily be appropriated or pigeon-holed by the prevailing cultural forces of any given time. An example of this, for Guénon, was the newly emergent school of 'theosophy.' About a decade before Guénon's birth, the Theosophical Society was founded in 1875 by

---

20   Robin Waterfield, *René Guénon and the Future of the West*, 80.
21   Robin Waterfield, *René Guénon and the Future of the West*, 80.
22   Robin Waterfield, *René Guénon and the Future of the West*, 80.
23   Robin Waterfield, *René Guénon and the Future of the West*, 80.
24   René Guénon, *Introduction to the Study of the Hindu Doctrines*, 55.

Madame H. P. Blavatsky[25] and Colonel Olcott in New York and, as Waterfield states, "soon reached France."[26] For Guénon, theosophy was permeated with both error and charlatanry and represented a glaring case of how traditional knowledge can be greatly perverted and propagandized by individuals with ulterior motives. Along with several essays, Guénon wrote two books critical of the school. Yet, as Waterfield points out, theosophy was in France at the time "the main vehicle for the dissemination of the idea that secret wisdom was available from the East, and its teachings were no doubt one element among those that led Guénon to study Eastern philosophy and religion."[27]

In addition to theosophy's influence on Guénon's thought and writings, there were other currents of Eastern thought swirling through the air of late nineteenth-century France. According to Waterfield, "mainly due to the activities of Swami Vivekananda," the Hindu *darshana* of "Vedanta was very much in the air at that time."[28] And, as we have noted, it was the concepts of *Vedanta* that later served Guénon as the primary means for his understanding of both Tradition and the *symbols* of Tradition. In his very first article on *Vedanta*, Guénon, according to Chacornac,

---

25 According to *Merriam-Webster*, "The word *theosophy*, combining the roots meaning 'God' and 'wisdom,' appeared back in the 17th century, but the well-known religious movement by that name, under the leadership of the Russian Helena Blavatsky, appeared only around 1875. Blavatsky's theosophy combined elements of Plato's philosophy with Christian, Buddhist, and Hindu thought (including reincarnation), in a way that she claimed had been divinely revealed to her." https://www.merriam-webster.com.

26 Robin Waterfield, *René Guénon and the Future of the West*, 23.

27 Robin Waterfield, *René Guénon and the Future of the West*, 23.

28 Swami Vivekananda was an influential disciple of the nineteenth-century Indian mystic Ramakrishna Paramahansa. Robin Waterfield, *René Guénon and the Future of the West*, 30.

evinces already...an unerring knowledge of Hindu metaphysics, the essential themes of which are brought to light and supported by citations from Shankaracharya.[29]

It is rather mystifying that Guénon knew so much about Hindu metaphysics at the age of 22 or 23, unless we take seriously Waterfield's observation that Guénon "always claimed that he received his teachings orally from Hindu and other masters and there certainly were Hindu teachers in Paris about this time."[30] While Waterfield admits that "it has not been possible to establish from which, if any of them, Guénon actually received his teaching,"[31] Chacornac provides the following statement of one Roger du Pasquier on the matter:

> It was not until 1949, while staying in Benares, that I came to read Guénon's work. It had been recommended to me by Alain Danielou, who had shown Guénon's books to the orthodox Pandits. Their verdict was unequivocal: of all the Westerners who have studied Hindu doctrines, only Guénon, they said, has really understood their meaning.[32]

A Frenchman named André Préau published the following on this perplexing subject in the review *Jayakarnataka* in 1934:

> This author [Guénon] presents the very rare case of a writer who expresses himself in a Western language, and whose knowledge of Eastern philosophy has been direct, that is to say derived essentially from the masters of the East. It is in fact to the oral teaching of these masters that Guénon owes his knowledge of the doctrines of India, of Islamic esoterism, and of Taoism, as well as of the Sanskrit and Arabic languages; and this sufficiently distinguishes him from European and American orientalists, who have no

---

29 Shankaracharya are the teachers of the 'way,' or philosophy, of Shankara, the eighth-century Indian thinker who brought together as one doctrine what is now called *Advaita Vedanta*. Paul Chacornac, *The Simple Life of René Guénon*, 28.
30 Robin Waterfield, *René Guénon and the Future of the West*, 30.
31 Robin Waterfield, *René Guénon and the Future of the West*, 30.
32 Paul Chacornac, *The Simple Life of René Guénon*, 59.

doubt worked with Asians, but have asked only for help to facilitate the bookish research characteristic of Western erudition.[33]

Waterfield further adds that Guénon was always

> noticeably reticent about his sources, but we learn of discussions held in his little flat late into the night in which his closest friends regularly took part, along with a stream of passing visitors of all kinds, Muslims, Hindus, and others. But there were two French contemporaries, and friends, who also no doubt influenced him. One was Sedir (Yvon Le Loup)…who had made a deep study of Vedanta philosophy….The other influence was… Alexandre St Yves d'Alveydre…who…had written a number of philosophical and kabbalistic works.[34]

Based upon the testimonies of the mentioned experts, it would appear that Guénon's knowledge of Tradition was acquired by him in what he himself would describe as an authentically 'traditional' fashion: by means of *oral transmission* from one, or many, 'masters' of the relevant subject matters. According to Guénon, comprehending Tradition requires *living* the content of sacred texts that have been, for at least a part of their history, *orally* preserved. Such preservation, however, entails more than simple remembrance and conveyance of the appropriate information. It requires that the master of the relevant subject matter has achieved a certain state of being that allows the qualified pupil, by being under the master's tutelage for a specified period of time, to himself achieve this state of being, one which is necessary to unlock the essence of Tradition. The 'living' of Tradition, then, from the perspective of Tradition, usually requires the 'transmission,' from master to pupil, of a 'spiritual influence' that is embodied in the *total life* of the master. Waterfield states that

---

33 André Préau, "Connaissance orientale et recherche occidentale," *Jayakarnataka* (April 1934).

34 Robin Waterfield, *René Guénon and the Future of the West*, 30–31.

Guénon's message is not the dry statement of a set of intellectual propositions, to which we can assent or not as we wish, but a challenge to a new way of life, which if accepted will affect every aspect of our thinking and acting. The truths that Guénon enunciated can only be understood by being lived, *crede ut intellegas*; they are what the French call *vérité vécue* — lived truth.[35]

According to Guénon's understanding of traditional wisdom, academic degrees and honors are no proof that a person has 'lived truth.' As Waterfield states, "For Guénon, as for all traditional wisdom, truth has to be lived by the whole man, which explains his frequent dismissals of the inadequacy of rational thought, of thinking about things."[36] There is an emphasis in Guénon's works, as in the Hindu Upanishads which Guénon took to be a standard of traditional knowledge, on intuition or intellection, as opposed to pure rationality combined with empirical observation. According to Guénon, the latter combination can actually stand in the way of appreciating the perspective of the Primordial Tradition, if it is overemphasized. This is because, once one believes with all of his/her being that rationality plus empirical observation is the *only* way to acquire real knowledge, any other methodology will be dogmatically opposed without trial.

The Question of Mastery and Other Criticisms

The manner in which Guénon apparently mastered various subjects is not always clear. But his verified knowledge of numerous languages is perhaps more mysterious than his mastering of Tradition, the *Vedanta*, and the other *darshanas* of the 'Hindu Doctrines.' Concerning the subject of Guénon's facility with languages, François Bonjean, one of Guénon's friends, spoke confidently on Guénon's behalf. Bonjean often held gatherings at his home in Paris that Guénon and his wife would often attend. Bonjean describes the attendees of these parties as "people interested in past, present, or future relations between

---

35 Robin Waterfield, *René Guénon and the Future of the West*, 5.
36 Robin Waterfield, *René Guénon and the Future of the West*, 91.

East and West....With rare exceptions these gatherings would attract Muslims, Hindus, Jews, and Christians."³⁷ Observing Guénon carefully at such gatherings, Bonjean states that he frequently noted, among Guénon's other talents, his exceptional linguistic facility:

> His knowledge of Sanskrit and Hinduism prevailed, I believe, over classical Arabic and Islam. An expert linguist, he knew also Latin, Greek, and Hebrew, as well as English, German, Italian, Spanish, Russian, and Polish. He could easily reply to questions in any of these languages, and could therefore converse with most interlocutors in their native tongue.³⁸

Chacornac also writes of Guénon's knowledge of Arabic in particular, observing that "it seems likely that he perfected his knowledge of Arabic" while he lived in Setif, Algeria,³⁹ and that, during his stay in Egypt, "Guénon contributed some articles to a journal printed entirely in Arabic, *Al Marifah* ('Knowledge')...These two articles demonstrate to what extent Guénon has mastered Arabic."⁴⁰

On the important subject of the language of symbolism, in particular, there is also no *official* record of the degree of Guénon's mastery. Waterfield defers to the archaeologist Louis Charbonneau-Lassay, who is best known for his monumental *The Bestiary of Christ*, on this point. Charbonneau-Lassay was both a friend of Guénon and a frequent contributor to *Regnabit*, a journal with which Guénon was affiliated for a time. Waterfield notes in *René Guénon and the Future of the West* that Charbonneau-Lassay "was for Guénon the final authority on all matters relating to symbolism."⁴¹ In *The Bestiary of Christ*,

---

37 'Souvenirs et réflexions sur René Guénon,' *Revue de la Méditerranée*, March — April 1951, 214–220. Reproduced in Paul Chacornac, *The Simple Life of René Guénon*, 68.

38 'Souvenirs et réflexions sur René Guénon.' Reproduced in Paul Chacornac, *The Simple Life of René Guénon*, 68.

39 Paul Chacornac, *The Simple Life of René Guénon*, 43.

40 Paul Chacornac, *The Simple Life of René Guénon*, 79.

41 Robin Waterfield, *René Guénon and the Future of the West*, 41.

Charbonneau-Lassay explains the principle reasons for the ancient use of symbolism. He provides there the following quotation attributed to St. Dionysius the Areopagite:

> Take care, above all, not to reveal the secrets of the holy mysteries, and do not allow them to be indiscreetly exposed to the daylight of the profane world....Only the saints—not everyone—may lift a corner of the veil which covers the things which are holy....Our most saintly founders... charged the celebration [of the mysteries] with so many symbolic rites that what is in itself one and indivisible can appear only little by little, as if by parts, and under an infinite variety of details. However, this is not simply because of the profane multitude, who must not glimpse even the covering of holy things, but also because of the weakness of our own senses and spirit, which require signs and material means to raise them to the understanding of the immaterial and the sublime.[42]

Charbonneau-Lassay concludes that

> [t]hese words...are a very exact statement of the principal reasons for the use of symbolism. It is to remedy the weakness of our nature and to satisfy its need that all religions and mysteries have felt the obligation to create for themselves codes of symbols kept secret by a strict discipline of caution.[43]

Charbonneau-Lassay's statement that "[o]nly the saints—not everyone—may lift a corner of the veil which covers the things which are holy" accords with Guénon's general contention that it takes more than a great facility for acquiring and synthesizing facts to grasp metaphysical truths; it takes a change of perspective and lifestyle. To describe such a perspective as 'saintly' may not be exactly what Guénon

---

42 Louis Charbonneau-Lassay, *The Bestiary of Christ*, trans. D. M. Dooling (New York, New York: The Penguin Group, Viking Penguin, Arkana Books, 1992 [originally published in 1940 by Desclée, De Brouwer & Cie, France]), vii. Taken from *Le Traité de la Hierarchie* (English: *Celestial Hierarchies*), attributed to St. Denis (Dionysius the Areopagite). Cf. Lecornu, "La mystique de la Messe," in Revue du Monde Catholique, 1866, 14: 115, 226.

43 Louis Charbonneau-Lassay, *The Bestiary of Christ*, vii.

had in mind, but it does reveal how radical a change he believed is necessary from the average person's consciousness to comprehend traditional symbolism. Also, the idea that "the weakness of our own senses and spirit...require signs and material means to raise them to the understanding of the immaterial and the sublime" is in accord with Guénon's statement in *Symbols of Sacred Science* that "the essential role that we have ascribed to symbolism" is "a means of raising ourselves to the knowledge of divine truths."[44] It is consonant also with Guénon's statement in *Introduction to the Study of the Hindu Doctrines* that "symbolism...is...the natural language of metaphysics"[45] and "is but the employing of forms and images as signs of ideas or of suprasensible things."[46] Although, according to these statements, it would seem that Guénon is largely in agreement with Charbonneau-Lassay's conception of symbolism and, thus, also the idea of symbolism that Charbonneau-Lassay attributed to St. Dionysius the Areopagite, there is no apparent *specific* inspiration for Guénon's devotion to the study of symbolism other than his belief that symbolism is the only means, other than oral transmission, for expressing traditional metaphysical truths. We shall address this topic in much greater depth later.

Beyond the objections to Guénon's *manner* of learning, whether this concerns languages or the other subject matters germane to his life's work, there are, of course (as with any thinker or scholar), a wide range of objections to his *corpus*, some of which should be mentioned here. Guénon's most famous 'follower,' in terms of the thinker who most recognizably and famously continued to perpetuate, and elaborate on, the Primordial Tradition (Tradition) as Guénon understood it, was the German traditionalist Frithjof Schuon (1907–1998). In a small book entitled *René Guénon: Some Observations*, Schuon articulates some of the academic objections to Guénon's arguments.

---

44 René Guénon, *Symbols of Sacred Science*, 10.
45 René Guénon, *Introduction to the Study of the Hindu Doctrines*, 86–87.
46 René Guénon, *Introduction to the Study of the Hindu Doctrines*, 86.

He notes what is, perhaps, the most common objection to Guénon's understanding of Tradition when he states that Guénon "overestimates Eastern man as such and underestimates Western man."[47] More specifically, Schuon argues that, while Guénon extolls the diversity of Eastern (Asian) manifestations of Tradition, he "leaves the West nothing except Freemasonry" and a "conjectural Christianity." Schuon also contends that Guénon, in general, reduces "Western intellectuality" to Aristotelian Scholasticism.[48] While it is certainly true that Guénon is constantly expounding the virtues of 'Eastern metaphysics' in his books, while at the same time harping on the shortcomings of Western thought, he did, in fact, appreciate that the West could, and should, look to its own version of Tradition for recreating what he considered a proper civilization. As to Guénon's stance on Christianity, although he often claimed that only a form of Catholicism could seriously be considered as a means for forging a new instantiation of Tradition in the West, Schuon's reaction to Guénon's stance on what constitutes 'Christian tradition' is a bit of an *over*reaction. Guénon has certainly underappreciated great thinkers of the West, such as Plotinus and Eckhardt, but the recreation of a traditional society has no need for an awards ceremony dedicated to the West's 'greatest.' The point, for Guénon, is not to recognize geniuses and their impact (which is a particularly modern proclivity, in any case) but to revive a way of life and being.

Another criticism of Guénon, which comes from an entirely different misgiving, is the claim that Guénon was introducing a 'new religion' when he attempted to elaborate on his so-called 'Tradition.' Waterfield notes that "Guénon has naturally enough been accused of preaching a new religion and some may draw back for fear that their

---

47 Frithjof Schuon, *René Guénon: Some Observations* (Hillsdale, New York: Sophia Perennis, 2004 [originally published as 'Quelques critiques' in *René Guénon: Les Dossiers H*, 1984]), 20–21.

48 Frithjof Schuon, *René Guénon: Some Observations*, 20–21.

religious faith will be weakened."[49] On the contrary, according to Waterfield, "Guénon always maintained [that] it is absolutely necessary to be an active participant in one of the [already extant] great traditional religions,"[50] showing that Guénon had no desire to undermine the faith of any particular religions, but rather to *clarify* the most fundamental principles that, in his view, support *all* religious faith. These, however, are not, for Guénon, strictly speaking *religious* principles, but what Guénon calls *metaphysical* principles. Guénon thought there to be many valid 'great religions' capable of propelling an individual to an understanding of the esoteric truths underlying the orthopraxy and dogma that are often believed to completely constitute religion. From Guénon's perspective, there was no need to "preach a new religion," since there are already several available which, if adhered to properly by the believer, will accomplish the task of spiritual realization and the birth of a 'new man,' which is, for Guénon, the goal of all religions.

Clarifying the differences between religion and metaphysics was a task that Guénon often returned to, possibly in part because of the above confusion. This clarification bears upon Guénon's understanding of traditional symbolism, specifically, because for Guénon *traditional* symbolism is not of religious truths but of metaphysical truths. Guénon repeatedly states in his works that: 1) religion is *not* metaphysics and 2) religion is a corruption of metaphysical knowledge in the sense that each religion's means of expression is, unlike the means of expression employed in metaphysics, adulterated by the realm of manifestation (the physical world). Symbols are indeed employed by religions, according to Guénon, but what they *express* is the metaphysical, or intellectual, core of religions that transcends their historical exigencies. Concerning the relationship among the descriptions 'metaphysical,' 'intellectual,' 'religious,' and 'traditional,' Guénon states in *Introduction to the Study of the Hindu Doctrines* that

---

49   Robin Waterfield, *René Guénon and the Future of the West*, 66.
50   Robin Waterfield, *René Guénon and the Future of the West*, 94.

[t]hose institutions are traditional that find their ultimate justification in their more or less direct, but always intentional and conscious, dependence upon a doctrine which, as regards its fundamental nature, is in every case of an intellectual order; but this intellectuality may be found either in a pure state, in cases where one is dealing with an entirely metaphysical doctrine, or else it may be found mingled with other heterogeneous elements, as in the case of the religious or other special modes which a traditional doctrine is capable of assuming.[51]

Bhakti Yoga, for example, is not *itself* a pure 'metaphysical doctrine' because it is not, itself, the Primordial Tradition (Tradition) but only an expression of Tradition. Neither, for Guénon, are, for example, any particular form or branch of Christianity or Islam. Neither, for Guénon, is *any* religion, since *all* religions for Guénon are but *particular manifestations* of the *one* 'metaphysical doctrine' (Tradition) that are, according to him, "mingled with other heterogeneous elements."[52] It is the empirical element, specifically, the sentimental or emotional element and the historical embeddedness of the prophets and promulgators of religions in the empirical world that, for Guénon, constitutes these 'heterogeneous elements.' In any given religion, for Guénon, there is always an 'intellectual element,' a metaphysical element; in metaphysics, however, there is *only* the intellectual element. Waterfield explains Guénon's position by referring to the Hindu *Vedanta*, specifically, when he states that "metaphysics in the Vedantist meaning of the word is the basis on which all true religion must be built and has nothing to do with the doctrines or dogmas of the various religions as we know them today."[53] Since, according to Guénon, metaphysics "is essentially knowledge of the Universal" and "is entirely detached from all relativities and contingencies,"[54] the 'heterogeneous elements' of all

---

51 René Guénon, *Introduction to the Study of the Hindu Doctrines*, 55–56.
52 René Guénon, *Introduction to the Study of the Hindu Doctrines*, 55–56.
53 Robin Waterfield, *René Guénon and the Future of the West*, 66.
54 René Guénon, *Man & His Becoming According to the Vedanta*, trans. Richard C. Nicholson (Hillsdale, NY: Sophia Perennis, 2001 [originally published in 1925

religions play for Guénon the part of 'Particulars,' in the terms of the Platonic distinction between 'Universals' (the Platonic 'Forms') and 'Particulars.' As we have noted in the *Introduction*, Eliade too sees the Platonic metaphysics as a, historically late, expression of Tradition. Particulars are, thus, for Eliade and Guénon as for Plato, the empirical objects, beings, and events of the physical world. Universals, for all three thinkers, are the eternal and immutable patterns by which, from the perspective of Tradition, Particulars have their very being. Plato's overriding contention in many of his works, in line with the traditional mindset described by Guénon and Eliade, was that a metaphysical source (the 'Forms') is the cause of all *physical* existence. According to Guénon, therefore, historical religions, because they *are* historical, must superimpose the historical, and thus physical, Particulars of their time upon the ahistorical and immutable Universal principles that are the meta-physical foundations of all religions. Although there exist historical tales of the lives of Moses and Jesus, Krishna and Siddhartha, and other religious founders, the details of these tales (events, places, and times) are, for Guénon, only "relativities and contingencies" involving the Particulars of the physical world. Opposed, for Guénon, to such Particulars are the Universal *principles* of the traditional doctrine that underlies all of these "relativities and contingencies." *Symbols* are, for Guénon, the prime traditional means by which the Universal (intellectual) principles of all religions are expressed.

Knowing this, we may enumerate what Guénon is, and is not, doing in his *corpus* in the following terms: 1) Guénon is *not* 'preaching' because he is not attempting to proselytize but, rather, *transmit*; and 2) Guénon is *not* introducing a 'new religion' because his work is a process of transmitting Tradition, that which, he holds, has always existed and which presents a more fundamental account of Reality than any religion. In order to more clearly understand what Guénon means by Tradition, it is useful to compare Tradition to the science

---

as *L'Homme et son devenir selon le Vêdânta*]), 9.

of mathematics. By considering how mathematics is related to the various special sciences, such as physics, chemistry, and sociology, we may more clearly understand how Tradition is related to the various religions of the world. Mathematics, as the science of measurement, has been called the 'language' of all of the special sciences—physics, chemistry, sociology, etc.—insofar as these sciences produce *quantitative* information. And it is, in fact, quantitative information that truly makes the various special sciences scientific, since without quantitative information the sciences must devolve into mere lists of imprecise observations. The scientific elements of predictability and measurability are both based upon the ability to quantify. Without mathematics, however, without quantification, there is neither measure nor predictability in the special sciences. Time, for example, cannot be measured without mathematics, without number, and predictions cannot be made without references to time and quantity. Insofar, then, as science *requires* both measurement and predictability, there is no 'science' in the special sciences without mathematics. This relationship between mathematics and the special sciences is similar to Guénon's understanding of the relationship between Tradition (metaphysics) and the various religions of the world that have a metaphysical basis. For, as mathematics serves as the language of the special sciences, Tradition (metaphysics) serves as the language of all authentic religions, all religions that are based upon intuitive or revealed knowledge of the meta-physical. Examples of such religions, for Guénon, include Judaism, Christianity, Islam, Hinduism, Buddhism, Jainism, and Taoism, as well as others. For Guénon, there is no *authentic* religion that does not appeal to a metaphysical reality. There may be, according to Guénon, systems of ethics, or systems of rituals and ceremonies, that have been *termed* 'religions,' but these are *not* traditional, they are not based upon Tradition, since they do not appeal to a metaphysical reality.

Traditional metaphysics, by means of its symbols, is, like mathematics by means of its symbols, a language that transcends all *particular* 'applications' of it. As we will consider in more depth later, traditional symbols, for Guénon and Eliade both, are a means, a 'device,' for becoming aware of, and interacting with, the metaphysical. For both Guénon and Eliade, 'encountering' the metaphysical is the ultimate reason for the existence of religion(s). Analogously, quantitative understanding of phenomena, which requires measurement and thus mathematics, is the ultimate reason for the existence of the special sciences. The quantitative understanding of phenomena is the ultimate reason for the existence of the special sciences insofar as the goal of the special sciences is *not* to merely accumulate observations and facts but to *measure* those observations and facts and then *predict* (which requires quantifying time) future observations and facts. Mathematics is, thus, the 'device' for 'encountering,' becoming aware of, the quantitative aspect of reality in an analogous fashion to how, for Guénon, Tradition (metaphysics) is the device for encountering the metaphysical or 'divine.' Without the quantitative element, the special sciences are merely banks of trivia without a 'higher' framework (mathematics) for understanding them. Analogously, without the Universal element, the various religions of the world are merely collections of Particular historical events, ceremonies, and rituals without a higher framework (metaphysics) for *understanding* them. In discussing Tradition, therefore, Guénon is not "preaching a new religion" but rather asserting that there is a structure of reality that can only be described by a specific language, the language of traditional symbolism, that is more comprehensive than the language of any particular religion, just like the 'language' of mathematics is more comprehensive than the language of any particular special science. Particular religions, like particular sciences, are rooted in *particular* facts, observations, and revelations. Christ rose from the dead according to Christianity, but not according to Islam; subatomic reality 'behaves' in a certain way according to quantum physics, but not according to General Relativity.⁵⁵ Mathematics, however, describes a layer of reality that is common to both quantum physics *and* General Relativity, although the two disciplines may apply different mathematical *methods* in understanding that reality. Similarly, for Guénon, traditional metaphysics describes a layer of reality that is common to both Christianity *and* Islam, although the historical texts of those two religions may interpret that layer of reality in somewhat different ways. Because of this, the language of traditional symbols is, according to Guénon, applicable to a level of reality that is more fundamental than that level of reality described by the religious language of any particular religion, such as Christianity or Islam. The language of mathematical symbols is, likewise, I argue, applicable to a level of reality more fundamental than the language of quantum physics or General Relativity, or biology or chemistry, or sociology, etc. Traditional symbolism is the language of Tradition like mathematical symbolism is the language of mathematics. Many mathematicians contend that mathematics, at least potentially, holds within itself a complete understanding of the physical structure of the universe that *underlies* the particular phenomena of the universe, the latter of which are described by the various special sciences. For Guénon, the same may be said of Tradition, as it also potentially holds within itself a complete understanding of the metaphysical structure of Reality that underlies the particular discoveries that have been made by the various religious founders and leaders of history, the discoveries documented in the particular religious texts of the world's religions.

One roadblock that is to be met with in appreciating Guénon's accomplishment consists in the dubiousness of his actual knowledge of what he terms Tradition. We mentioned earlier that the source(s) of Guénon's knowledge of Tradition and of the 'Hindu Doctrines,' *Vedanta* specifically, is somewhat mysterious, although Guénon does provide in his books copious references to the various classics

---

55 Corey S. Powell, "Relativity versus Quantum Mechanics: The Battle for the Universe," *The Guardian* (Nov 4, 2015).

of Hinduism and other traditions. As for his particular *interpretation* of the sources that he used, there is confirmation and adulation from other Traditionalists such as Frithjof Schuon, whom we have already mentioned, Ananda Coomaraswamy, Seyyed Hossein Nasr, Huston Smith, and others. Coomaraswamy, for example, has remarked that

> [n]o living writer in modern Europe is more significant than René Guénon, whose task it has been to expound the universal metaphysical tradition that has been the essential foundation of every past culture, and which represents the indispensable basis for any civilization deserving to be so called.[56]

In *Knowledge and the Sacred*, Seyyed Nasr states that

> Guénon, as he is reflected in his writings, seemed to be more of an intellectual function than a "man." His lucid mind and style and great metaphysical acumen seemed to have been chosen by traditional Sophia itself to formulate and express once again that truth from whose loss the modern world was suffering so grievously [sic].[57]

On the subject of Guénon's criticisms of the modern faith in the power of 'science,' Nasr adds:

> Guénon was also thoroughly critical of modern science not because of what it has accomplished but because of the reductionism and also pretensions which have been associated with science in the modern world. His greatest criticism of modern science was its lack of metaphysical principles and its pretension, or rather the pretension of those who claim to speak from the "scientific point of view," to be *the* science or *the* way of knowing, whereas it is *a* science or *a* way of knowing concerned with a very limited domain of reality.[58]

---

56 Roger Lipsey, *Coomaraswamy, Vol. 3: His Life and Work* (Princeton, New Jersey: Princeton University Press, 1977), 169.

57 Seyyed Hossein Nasr, *Knowledge and the Sacred: The Gifford Lectures, 1981* (Chowk Urdu Bazar, Lahore, Pakistan: Suhail Academy Lahore, 1988), 101–102.

58 Seyyed Hossein Nasr, *Knowledge and the Sacred*, 103.

Guénon's extensive criticisms of modern science have caused some to conjure a convenient caricature of him that is not only critical of modernity but inflexible and combative. In *Journeys East*, however, Harry Oldmeadow states that

> Guénon's "inflexibility" is nothing other than an expression of his fierce commitment to the truth and it is precisely his refusal to compromise first principles which gives his work its power and integrity.[59]

Huston Smith seems to sum up the general impression left by Guénon on these authors as well as others in his comments on the *Sophia Perennis* edition of Guénon's writings. He states, "The *Collected Works of René Guénon* brings together the writings of one of the greatest prophets of our time, whose voice is even more important today than when he was alive."[60]

Tradition, according to Guénon, can only be transmitted orally or symbolically from the lips or pen of one who has completely, as we stated earlier, 'lived' its truth. Today, 'standardized education,' 'delivery methods,' and 'instructional pedagogy' determine and define what moderns call teaching. In *Man & His Becoming According to the Vedanta*, however, Guénon uses the term 'teaching' in a different sense. He states that

> [i]n the East the traditional doctrines always employ oral teaching as their normal method of transmission, even in cases where they have been formulated in written texts; there are profound reasons for this, because it is not merely words that have to be conveyed, but above all it is a genuine participation in the tradition which has to be assured.[61]

---

59 Harry Oldmeadow, *Journeys East: 20th Century Western Encounters with Eastern Religious Traditions* (New Delhi: Pentagon Press, 2005), 192.
60 René Guénon, *Man & His Becoming According to the Vedanta*, back cover review by Huston Smith.
61 René Guénon, *Man & His Becoming According to the Vedanta*, 17.

If we are to have any hope of fathoming Guénon's understanding of what, according him, is the more holistic method of teaching of traditional societies, the 'lived' education that removes the pupil from Plato's 'cave' of ignorance by means of his comprehending his complete Self rather than only his rationality and aptitude for empirical science, then we must first begin by understanding the traditional language of symbols. For, according to Guénon, the language of traditional symbolism is the only written means of communication that can validly transmit the intellectual, not the rational, spirit that is so often smothered by the modern reliance on induction, systematization, historization, and vague scientism. The subject of our book, the meaning of the serpent/dragon symbol in Tradition is, for Guénon as well as for Eliade, one example of the traditional means of transmitting an idea that transcends all particular religions and their 'heterogeneous elements' and, therefore, all historical manifestations of the metaphysical.

CHAPTER 2

Mircea Eliade

The Man and His Thought

Mircea Eliade was born in Bucharest, Romania on March 9, 1907, the son of a Romanian army officer who traveled often (both with and without the family) and "never rose above the rank of captain," and a mother who, as Eliade states, "always gave me as much money as I wanted whenever I asked to buy books... [She] had always liked to read" herself.[1] From an early age, Eliade was studious, eclectic, and devoted to his interests. In *Seven Theories of Religion*, Professor of Religious Studies at the University of Miami Daniel Pals remarks, for example, on how "as a boy [Eliade] loved quiet places, science, stories, and writing."[2] In his *Autobiography*, Eliade recalls that, when he was around eleven years of age, "I discerned what later proved to be characteristic of my temperament: that it was impossible for me to learn something on demand; that is, to learn as everyone else does, in conformity with an academic schedule."[3] From his earliest years,

---

1   Mircea Eliade, *Mircea Eliade: Autobiography, Volume I: 1907–1937, Journey East, Journey West*, translated by Mac Linscott Ricketts (Chicago and London: The University of Chicago Press, 1981), 3 and 17.
2   Daniel L. Pals, *Seven Theories of Religion* (New York, New York: Oxford University Press, 1996), 159.
3   Mircea Eliade, *Mircea Eliade: Autobiography, Volume I: 1907–1937*, 41.

Eliade was an autodidact and a rebel against academic uniformity, and he generally questioned the modern notion of 'education.' This questioning, however, never inhibited Eliade's academic productivity, which was constant and vast. Pals notes, for example, that "at the age of eighteen, [Eliade] celebrated with friends the appearance of his one-hundredth published article! Already at this young age, he was hired by a newspaper to write feature stories, opinion columns, and book reviews."[4]

In *Volume 1* of his *Autobiography, Journey East, Journey West*, Eliade tells of experiences that he began to have from an early age that developed in him an awarenss of, and ever growing interest in, something that for him was much more profound than the stuff of opinion columns, book reviews, and 'feature stories': the existence of a world 'beyond' the chemical, clock-work, reality that was embraced by the newspaper writers and intelligentsia of the day who were determining the curricula of twentieth-century thought and higher education. According to Eliade, one of the earliest of these experiences occurred when he was three or four years old:

> I remember especially a summer afternoon when the whole household was sleeping. I left the room my brother and I shared...and headed toward the drawing room. I hardly knew how it looked, for we [Mircea and his three siblings] were not allowed to go in except on special occasions or when we had guests. Besides, I believe that the rest of the time the door was locked. But this time I found it open and entered....The next moment I was transfixed with emotion. It was as if I had entered a fairy-tale palace. The roller blinds and the heavy curtains of green velvet were drawn. The room was pervaded by an eerie iridescent light....I don't know how long I stayed there on the carpet, breathing heavily. When I came to my senses, I crept carefully across the floor, detouring around the furniture, looking greedily at the little tables and shelves on which all kinds of statuettes had been carefully placed along with cowry shells, little crystal vials, and small silver boxes. I gazed into the large venetian mirrors in whose deep and

---

4   Daniel L. Pals, *Seven Theories of Religion*, 159.

clear waters I found myself looking very different—more grown-up, more handsome, as if ennobled by that light from another world.

I never told anyone about this discovery. Actually, I think I should not have known what to tell. Had I been able to use adult vocabulary, I might have said that I had discovered a mystery.[5]

According to his *Autobiography*, the episode recounted seems to have been Eliade's first encounter with, to his mind, a reality that requires more to describe it than the everyday 'adult vocabulary' that most humans of the modern world rely upon to communicate their experiences. I would suggest that in this youthful experience we see a spark of Eliade's later interest in what he considered to be a mode of being and a comportment toward the cosmos that is historically prior to the modern mentality. It is also a first glimmer of his realization that an *essentially* different kind of 'vocabulary' is required to adequately communicate that mode of being and its characteristics. In Eliade's *Autobiography*, this vocabulary appears to be equated with the ancient language of traditional symbolism.

Eliade's first composition about an essentially different kind of vocabulary that is capable of, and necessary for, communicating 'more' than the modern human 'adult vocabulary' is capable of communicating, was not a conscious exposition on the subject of symbolism, although symbolism is what Eliade seems to be referring to when he writes of this 'vocabulary.' Because Eliade knew next to nothing about symbols at the time of the referred-to composition, it couldn't have been a conscious examination of symbolism. It was, however, on a subject matter that is replete with symbolism of various kinds, the subject of alchemy. In 1923, Eliade entered a contest for lycée students in which participants were required to write on "a scientific topic to be treated in a literary fashion." Eliade composed "a brief fantasy [as he called it] entitled, 'How I Found the Philosopher's Stone.'"[6] One

---

5 Mircea Eliade, *Mircea Eliade: Autobiography, Volume I: 1907–1937*, 7.
6 Mircea Eliade, *Mircea Eliade: Autobiography, Volume I: 1907–1937*, 55.

wonders whether he could have chosen a more appropriate subject to initiate himself into the mysteries of symbolism, as the search for the meaning of the Philosopher's Stone has come to rival all other esoteric quests in terms of its symbolic depth of meaning. "Decades later," Eliade states, "I realized that it was not without significance. When I wrote it I was enthusiastic about chemistry and knew almost nothing about alchemy....but I was…fascinated by the mystery of chemical structures."[7] Years after composing his 'brief fantasy' on the Philosopher's Stone, Eliade began to publish several articles and book-length treatments of alchemy. Concerning the books, in particular, of which some were finished in the 1930s and one in 1956, Eliade observes that "I tried to demonstrate…that alchemy was not a rudimentary chemistry…but a spiritual technique, seeking…at bottom, the transmutation of man: his 'salvation' or liberation."[8] It would appear that, for his initiation into the world of symbolism, Eliade had stumbled across one of the most profound historic endeavors of the human race to find its 'higher' Self, the study of alchemy. Reflecting on his composition of 'How I Found the Philosopher's Stone' in his *Autobiography*, Eliade exclaimed,

> What I wouldn't give to be able to read that story again now, to find out what that mysterious character revealed to me, what alchemistic operations he had witnessed! I had found, in dreams, the Philosopher's Stone. Only decades later was I to understand, after having read [Carl] Jung, the meaning of that oneiric symbolism.[9]

As in the case of his experience in the drawing room as a boy, Eliade's short story about the Philosopher's Stone was not a rational evaluation or an empirical observation of the, as Eliade called it, 'mystery'

---

7   Mircea Eliade, *Mircea Eliade: Autobiography, Volume I: 1907–1937*, 55–56.
8   Mircea Eliade, *Mircea Eliade: Autobiography, Volume I: 1907–1937*, 56.
9   Mircea Eliade, *Mircea Eliade: Autobiography, Volume I: 1907–1937*, 56. The Swiss psychiatrist and psychoanalyst Carl Jung (1875–1961) is most famous for his theory of the 'archetypes of the collective unconscious.'

that reveals itself in the wonder of a child or in the dreams of an open-minded, or gifted, adult. It was only later, however, that Eliade was capable of consciously reflecting on his childhood experience of the mystery of something 'other,' something *entirely different* from the mechanistic worlds of 'nature' and technology that Eliade lived to see increasingly embraced and marketed in the modern world. When he did achieve conscious realization of his (for moderns) unusual experiences, however, Eliade began to also realize the need for a language that was especially suited to comprehending and communicating those experiences. As he came to discover, such a language already existed, the language of 'traditional' symbolism.

I once read a review on Amazon.com of one of Eliade's books in which the author stated that "Mircea Eliade is a maniac." The evaluation wasn't meant by the reviewer as an insult, but rather as a statement of his incredulity in response to how much Eliade read and wrote on a daily basis. For, from the perspective of the average person, at least in the sense summarized by the mentioned reviewer, Mircea Eliade *was* a maniac. His gusto and endurance were remarkable, to say the least. In his *Autobiography*, Eliade often recounts writing for ten, twelve, or fourteen hours a day—*every day*. He mentions that at one point in his life,

> I accustomed myself to sleeping less and less. Sometimes three or four hours per night sufficed. I arrived at this point only after a long process of self-discipline....Eventually, I accustomed myself to a ration of four hours.[10]

Eliade states in his *Autobiography* that, as a young man, he "came to read a book a day," and these not just fiction or history but of "the natural sciences" as well. "Every morning I was tempted by three or four volumes."[11] These 'testimonials' reveal that, even when compared to other scholars, Eliade's natural curiosity and his passion for

---

10 Mircea Eliade, *Mircea Eliade: Autobiography, Volume I: 1907–1937,* 63.
11 Mircea Eliade, *Mircea Eliade: Autobiography, Volume I: 1907–1937,* 46.

learning were extraordinary. He was a comprehensive *investigator* and he read *everything*: history, science, classics of literature, pulp fiction, technical journals, as well as philosophy and religion. Eliade was a polymath, being extremely erudite in disparate fields of study, fluent in several languages (which will be considered shortly), and, before devoting himself (for the most part) to the history of religions, "convinced that I would major in the physical sciences in the university."[12] Consistent with his eclectic academic interests, Eliade was greatly attracted to what he termed 'universal' authors, such as the eighteenth-century French writer Voltaire, who Eliade writes, "attracted me at first because he wrote everything—novels, pamphlets, historical monographs, letters, philosophy, and literary criticism, with the same unequaled perfection."[13] As Eliade states, he never wanted to 'specialize,' to "be forced to limit myself to science…or literature or history."[14] Let us thank God (or the gods) that he didn't, or we wouldn't have the unique perspective of one who was equal parts philosopher, phenomenologist, and historian of religions, a combination that usually only reveals itself, not in a succession of buried journal articles, but in wide-ranging and controversial books.

One of Eliade's abiding interests was the thought and culture of ancient India. One might suggest 'obsession' rather than 'interest' in describing Eliade's felt connection to India, as he states in his *Autobiography* that he believed there to be a

> mystery that was waiting for me somewhere in India, that mystery of which I knew nothing except that it was there for me to decipher and that in deciphering it I would at the same time reveal to myself the mystery of my own existence; I would discover at last who I was and why I wanted to be what I wanted to be, why all the things that had happened to me had happened to me, why I had been fascinated in turn by material substances, plants, insects, literature, philosophy, and religion, and how I had gotten

---

12   Mircea Eliade, *Mircea Eliade: Autobiography, Volume I: 1907–1937*, 59.
13   Mircea Eliade, *Mircea Eliade: Autobiography, Volume I: 1907–1937*, 70.
14   Mircea Eliade, *Mircea Eliade: Autobiography, Volume I: 1907–1937*, 70.

from the [childhood] games on the vacant lots to the problems that perplexed me now.[15]

Eliade's obsession with the 'mystery' of India is rather similar to Guénon's central focus on what he called the 'Hindu Doctrines,' specifically *Vedanta*, in understanding the idea of Tradition. Eliade had a high opinion of the Hindu Doctrines as well. Perhaps like Guénon's possible chance encounter with some or other Eastern 'master' in early twentieth-century Paris, Eliade's study of ancient India began rather accidentally, or perhaps fortuitously, when he agreed during his sixth year at lycée, and knowing "next to nothing about ancient India," "to give a lecture about...the [Indian] god Rama."[16] For the purposes of the lecture, Eliade, as he states, "extracted entirely" all of his source material from a book entitled *Les grands initiés*, only later discovering that the information presented in the book, which he had taken to be factual, "was a case of a 'mystical' story that Schuré [the author of *Les grands initiés*] himself had invented!"[17] This embarrassing experience ever afterwards catalyzed in Eliade an extreme fastidiousness in research, "a mistrust of dilettantes, a fear of letting myself be duped by an amateur, an increasingly insistent desire to go directly to the sources, to consult exclusively the works of specialists, to exhaust the bibliography."[18]

Eventually leaving Europe by means of a Romanian steamer on November 20, 1928 in order to study Indian philosophy and Sanskrit in Calcutta under the master of Indian philosophy, Surendranath Dasgupta, Eliade did make his way to India to search for, as he said, the "mystery that was waiting for me."[19] Once there, Eliade devoted

---

15   Mircea Eliade, *Mircea Eliade: Autobiography, Volume I: 1907–1937*, 153.
16   Mircea Eliade, *Mircea Eliade: Autobiography, Volume I: 1907–1937*, 68.
17   Mircea Eliade, *Mircea Eliade: Autobiography, Volume I: 1907–1937*, 68.
18   Mircea Eliade, *Mircea Eliade: Autobiography, Volume I: 1907–1937*, 68.
19   Mircea Eliade, *Mircea Eliade: Autobiography, Volume I: 1907–1937*, 150, 154, and 176.

himself to the study of the ancient Sanskrit language and "regularly attended Dasgupta's classes at the University of Calcutta." He mentions in his *Autobiography* being "the only European [in those classes], and [that] for my sake Dasgupta gave his lectures in English for almost two years."[20] Eliade studied *Samkhya* and post-Sankarian *Vedanta* under Dasgupta, and mentions that Dasgupta "concerned himself more with the technical vocabulary of Samkhya-Yoga" for a while in tutoring Eliade individually, and "preferred me to concentrate on the history of the doctrines of yoga, or on the relationships among classical Yoga, Vedanta, and Buddhism."[21] Eliade also remarks in his *Autobiography*, however, that his true interests lay in another direction, that he "felt attracted by Tantrism and the different forms of popular yoga...as [the latter] is found in epic poetry, legends, and folklore."[22] After studying Sanskrit with Dasgupta for a good while, Eliade added Bengali to his repertoire of languages and, much later, in the spring of 1931, began to teach himself Tibetan.[23]

Like Eliade's otherworldly childhood experience in the drawing room of his parents' home, and like the subliminally inspired dreamstate story 'How I Found the Philosopher's Stone' which he composed as a young adult, other of Eliade's later feelings and moods had a great influence on his overall philosophy and scholarship. Even before leaving for India, for example, he writes in his *Autobiography* of suffering from "attacks of melancholia" in which he felt a "terrible sensation of the irremediable — the feeling that I had lost something essential and irreplaceable."[24] In battling these attacks, Eliade recalls that he soon "discovered that my inexplicable sadness sprang from...unsuspected sources: for instance, the feeling of 'the past,' that simple fact that

---

20 Mircea Eliade, *Mircea Eliade: Autobiography, Volume I: 1907–1937*, 160.

21 Mircea Eliade, *Mircea Eliade: Autobiography, Volume I: 1907–1937*, 160 and 175–176.

22 Mircea Eliade, *Mircea Eliade: Autobiography, Volume I: 1907–1937*, 176.

23 Mircea Eliade, *Mircea Eliade: Autobiography, Volume I: 1907–1937*, 178.

24 Mircea Eliade, *Mircea Eliade: Autobiography, Volume I: 1907–1937*, 72.

there have been things that *are* no more, that have 'passed,' such as my childhood or my father's youth."²⁵ In these 'sensations' and 'feelings' is discernible the germ of Eliade's later theory of the 'myth of the eternal return' and his belief that the dearest desire of the peoples of traditional cultures is to *destroy history* and live as much as possible in the 'mythic past.' Expressing his worry concerning what one of his good friends and colleagues, Mircea Marculescu, might think of him should he learn of Eliade's seemingly irrational thoughts and powerful emotional states, Eliade writes,

> I would have been ashamed to have him think that his friend, whom he believed to be so "scientific," could suffer in such an inexplicable way, and for no other reason than the fact that time passes, and in its passing something essential in us is irretrievably lost.²⁶

I would argue that the mood that Eliade expresses in this quotation, and that he experienced from time to time, is in perfect consonance with his understanding of the mood of the 'traditional' or 'archaic' peoples that Eliade wrote of so passionately in *The Myth of the Eternal Return*. It is the very mood that supports the traditional ideas of 'mythic time' and the 'recovery' of the 'time of beginnings,' and that ritualizes the 'destruction' of 'profane' time and the everyday world of change and decomposition. Contained in this 'archaic' mood is the recognition, which cannot be slowly acquired but only suddenly 'realized,' that beyond the apparent meaninglessness of the everyday 'natural' world there lies another level of reality. Eliade believed that a change in the individual's fundamental comportment toward the world is necessary in order to achieve this 'realization.' In his *Autobiography*, he describes an afternoon in which he found himself sitting on a bench in Cişmigiu Park [in Bucharest], contemplating what he thought to be the vanity of Plutarch's *Morals* and of the "mysterious treatise, *De Pythiae oraculis*" [an essay on the oracles

---

25 Mircea Eliade, *Mircea Eliade: Autobiography, Volume I: 1907–1937*, 73.
26 Mircea Eliade, *Mircea Eliade: Autobiography, Volume I: 1907–1937*, 74–75.

at Delphi] contained therein, the vanity of *all* of the other books that he had loved in his life.[27] Of his experience of that moment, Eliade states that "it was as if the whole world had suddenly turned to ashes and I found myself in a universe of shadows and vanities, without meaning or hope, where all things are essentially vain and empty."[28] After unsuccessfully trying to reason himself out of the despair that he felt sitting there on the park bench, Eliade states that he *suddenly decided* — after quickly observing the everyday events and beauties of the park around him — that "I had been wrong: that, although I didn't know the answer, the world *does* have a meaning, Plutarch deserves to be read, and *De Pythiae oraculis* was a true discovery."[29] At that moment, there occurred what might be termed Eliade's 'alchemical transmutation,' which seems to have been more a revelation based upon an instantaneous change of perspective than a product of careful reasoning. Sometime after this, Eliade says of himself that "I found myself becoming estranged from my beloved natural sciences, physics, and chemistry, and increasingly fascinated not only by literature, which I had loved since childhood, but also by philosophy, Oriental studies, and the history of religions."[30] He remarks that

> [d]uring those years of almost mystical admiration for the ancient Orient, when I believed in the mysteries of the Pyramids, the deep wisdom of the Chaldeans, and the occult sciences of the Persian magi, my efforts were nurtured by the hope that one day I would solve all the 'secrets' of religions, of history, and of man's destiny on earth.[31]

---

27 Mircea Eliade, *Mircea Eliade: Autobiography, Volume I: 1907–1937*, 81. More specifically, "De Pythiae oraculis" is Plutarch's essay on the change in presentation of oracles at Delphi from verse to prose.

28 Mircea Eliade, *Mircea Eliade: Autobiography, Volume I: 1907–1937*, 81.

29 Mircea Eliade, *Mircea Eliade: Autobiography, Volume I: 1907–1937*, 81.

30 Mircea Eliade, *Mircea Eliade: Autobiography, Volume I: 1907–1937*, 84.

31 Mircea Eliade, *Mircea Eliade: Autobiography, Volume I: 1907–1937*, 85.

Eliade's interest in ancient mysteries was very personal at this time in the sense that he came to believe that he had experienced, in his own feelings and reflections, what lay *beyond* the limitations of modern nihilism, the latter of which seemed to him to be the final result of the modernist reduction. Eliade's initial embarrassment over his "inexplicable sadness" at the mere fact that history 'moves on' had been transmuted by his experience on the park bench and turned into an awareness that this 'moving on' characterizes the nature of only *one* level of existence. We may say that Eliade had experienced on that park bench something akin to the process by which the Philosopher's Stone of old burned away the impurities of the questing 'hero's' soul and prepared him to see deeper into the folds of reality.

As we mentioned briefly earlier, Eliade was not only a polymath in academic disciplines but in the acquisition and employment of various languages. Much of this was self-taught, as was the case with René Guénon. Early on, however, Eliade made choices that took him away from the study of languages or that prevented his mastering them. In 1921, for example, he entered the fifth year of lycée and chose, of three available paths of study, the one that "included a considerable amount of mathematics and no Latin."[32] Eliade states of this choice that "it didn't take me long to realize that I was mistaken and had been wrong in my choice" to give up studying Latin.[33] Somewhat later in his life, but before leaving for India, Eliade began to study Hebrew independently from a textbook, stating in his *Autobiography* that "[a]s was my habit, I studied several hours per day."[34] Again, however, Eliade says that in spite of his curiosity he wasn't really focused on acquiring a new language, remarking that "Hebrew did not appeal to me" and that he "did not make much progress." Not discouraged by these setbacks, Eliade recalls that he then "plunged into Persian and Sanskrit," although he

---

32 Mircea Eliade, *Mircea Eliade: Autobiography, Volume I: 1907–1937*, 59.
33 Mircea Eliade, *Mircea Eliade: Autobiography, Volume I: 1907–1937*, 59.
34 Mircea Eliade, *Mircea Eliade: Autobiography, Volume I: 1907–1937*, 85.

admits in his *Autobiography* that he didn't get "very far."[35] All of this stopping and starting was just a preliminary phase in Eliade's path to acquiring several languages, a phase that primarily only revealed his great *interest* in learning multiple languages, as he was eventually to return with gusto, as we have already seen, to the successful study of various ancient languages, Sanskrit in particular.

About this time, the time in which he was trying out Hebrew and Persian, Eliade also discovered James Frazer's monumental works *The Golden Bough* and *Folklore in the Old Testament*, which, as Eliade relates, "revealed to me the inexhaustible universe of primitive religions and folklore."[36] Eliade actually learned English simply "in order to be able to read Frazer,"[37] and his interest in ancient and 'traditional' belief systems only grew after this. He records that, in the winter of 1926, he "felt himself increasingly drawn to the history of religions," having

> discovered at the library of the Institute of Ancient History…the five volumes of *Cultes, mythes et religions* by Salomon Reinarch, Frazer's annotated translations from Pausanias and *Fasti* by Ovid, and the works of Ridgeway and Jane Harrison.[38]

Again in his *Autobiography*, Eliade states that he "read breathlessly" of these works, at the same time still keeping to his schedule of sleeping only four or five hours each night. On this fascinating subject of Eliade's disciplining himself to always read and study more, while sleeping very little, he records that

> I had been convinced that a human being could do anything, provided he *wanted to*, and *knew how* to control his will….I believed that such self-discipline was the gateway to absolute freedom. The struggle against sleep, like the struggle against normal modes of behavior, signified for me a heroic

---

35 Mircea Eliade, *Mircea Eliade: Autobiography, Volume I: 1907–1937*, 85.
36 Mircea Eliade, *Mircea Eliade: Autobiography, Volume I: 1907–1937*, 85.
37 Mircea Eliade, *Mircea Eliade: Autobiography, Volume I: 1907–1937*, 93–94.
38 Mircea Eliade, *Mircea Eliade: Autobiography, Volume I: 1907–1937*, 109–110.

attempt to transcend the human condition. I did not know then that this is precisely the point of departure of the techniques of yoga.[39]

By his own observations, Eliade's overall lifestyle and emotions, or 'feelings'[40] as he called them, most directly and compellingly led him to his study of ancient Indian thought and culture. "Even in adolescence," he notes, "I had tried to suppress normal behavior, had dreamed of a radical transmutation of my mode of being. My enthusiasm for yoga and Tantra was due to the same Faustian nostalgias."[41] At one point, Eliade even reflected that "it is quite probable that my interest in yoga, which three years later was to lead me to India, stemmed from my faith in the unlimited possibilities of man."[42]

More generally, Eliade confessed that "the freedom I thought I could obtain by doing the opposite of the 'normal' signified the surpassing of my historical, social, and cultural condition…Basically, I instinctively resisted any attempt to be molded according to current patterns."[43] This confession again expresses Eliade's general attitude toward existence that is consonant with his later interpretation of the traditional outlook and its emphasis, according to Eliade, on 'mythic time' and the 'overcoming' of history. Most fundamentally, for Eliade, the traditional outlook is based upon a desire to 'transcend' the 'profane' realm and to ritualize everyday actions by imbuing them with the 'sacred.' There is, however, a strong parallel to this traditional outlook in Eliade's own *personal* desire to, similarly, 'transcend' the 'normal' "social, historical, and cultural condition" that he found himself within. Daniel L. Pals expresses the 'traditional' sentiment that is the subject of Eliade's *The Myth of the Eternal Return*. In his *Seven Theories of Religion*, he states:

---

39 Mircea Eliade, *Mircea Eliade: Autobiography, Volume I: 1907–1937*, 110.
40 Mircea Eliade, *Mircea Eliade: Autobiography, Volume I: 1907–1937*, 73.
41 Mircea Eliade, *Mircea Eliade: Autobiography, Volume I: 1907–1937*, 256.
42 Mircea Eliade, *Mircea Eliade: Autobiography, Volume I: 1907–1937*, 110.
43 Mircea Eliade, *Mircea Eliade: Autobiography, Volume I: 1907–1937*, 110–111.

> The one theme which dominates the thought of all archaic peoples is the drive to abolish history—all of history—and return to that point beyond time when the world began. The desire to go back to beginnings…is the deepest longing, the most insistent and heartfelt ache in the soul of all archaic peoples.[44]

All 'current patterns,' as Eliade calls them, are, from this archaic perspective according to him, to be conformed to, and understood in terms of, the 'eternal archetypes'[45] for human existence. The latter are the mythic 'gods' and ancestors of the time of the 'beginning' and their perfect virtues. Eliade adds, however, the condition that "if the fantastic or the supernatural or the supra-historical is somehow accessible to us, we cannot encounter it except camouflaged in the banal."[46] It is easy to see in his 'quest for freedom' a major influence on Eliade's later scholarly works concerning 'traditional' societies and Indian thought in general—and on his dissertation on *yoga*, in particular. Even in his fiction, Eliade remains fascinated with the possibility of an 'added dimension' of existence that lies beyond the 'everyday world.' In his novel *Sarpele*, Eliade writes of a set of 'banal characters' who "find themselves" in a "fantastic world" which

> is the same as the everyday one—with the single difference that it discloses now an added dimension, inaccessible to profane existence. It is as if the everyday world camouflages a secret dimension which, once man knows it,

---

44 Daniel L. Pals, *Seven Theories of Religion*, 179.

45 As Eliade scholar Douglas Allen points out in *Structure and Creativity in Religion*, "Eliade defines 'archetype' as 'exemplary model' or 'paradigm' and explicitly distinguishes it from the Jungian meaning. This is Eliade's main sense of archetype. However, in a few of his works, he uses the term in a manner quite similar to Jung's concept." Douglas Allen, *Structure and Creativity in Religion: Hermeneutics in Mircea Eliade's Phenomenology and New Directions* (The Hague, the Netherlands: Mouton Publishers, 1978), 145.

46 Mircea Eliade, *Mircea Eliade: Autobiography, Volume I: 1907–1937*, 274.

reveals to him simultaneously the profound significance of the Cosmos and his authentic mode of being.[47]

The question for Eliade is, how does one 'access' this 'secret dimension' that is 'camouflaged' and, thereby, "go back to beginnings"?

The Function of Symbols

The question of how to "go back to beginnings" and "access a secret dimension" beyond the "everyday world of profane existence" is the question of what a *symbol* is, a question most pertinent to this book. In *Patterns in Comparative Religion*, Eliade states that "symbolic thought makes it possible for man to move freely from one level of reality to another," and "whatever its context, a symbol always reveals the basic oneness of several zones of the real."[48] As I stated with respect to Guénon, one may conceive of a 'traditional' symbol as a sort of 'device' that has the explicit function of revealing and providing connection with a 'higher' metaphysical reality that exists 'beyond,' and is the source of, the physical/'natural' world. This is one of the functions of traditional symbols that Eliade refers to, and for Guénon the most important function of traditional symbols. For Eliade, however, it is also true that a traditional symbol can reveal "the...oneness of several zones of the real." These 'zones of the real' are not, for Eliade, equivalent to 'levels' of the real. In *Patterns in Comparative Religion*, Eliade discusses the "'unifications' effected by the symbols of water or of the moon, whereby so many biological, anthropological, and cosmic zones and levels are identified along various lines."[49] Although Eliade uses the terms 'zones' and 'levels' together in this statement, he means different things by the two terms. 'Zones' refers to different 'areas' of

---

47 Mircea Eliade, *Mircea Eliade: Autobiography, Volume I: 1907–1937*, 322.
48 Mircea Eliade, *Patterns in Comparative Religion*, trans. Rosemary Sheed (Lincoln and London: University of Nebraska Press, 1996 [originally published in 1958 by Sheed & Ward, Inc.]), 455 and 452.
49 Mircea Eliade, *Patterns in Comparative Religion*, 452.

human experience in the physical world that humans may focus on or be concerned with. These include: 1) natural/biological phenomena, such as water or fertility; 2) anthropological realities, such as initiation; and 3) basic cosmic realities, such as the moon or death. The 'levels,' however, are only two: the physical and the metaphysical or, metaphorically, Earth and Heaven, the terrestrial and the celestial. We observe that the last given example of what, for Eliade, is a 'zone' of 'cosmic reality,' death, overlaps with a metaphysical *level* of reality because death is the most common form of transition from the physical level of reality to the metaphysical level of reality.

In a chapter in *Patterns in Comparative Religion* entitled 'The Moon and Its Mystique,' Eliade discusses the symbolism of the moon as the point of focus of one 'zone' or 'area' of traditional/archaic human experience. There are several sections of 'The Moon and Its Mystique' that refer to 'zones'/'areas' of human experience that are related to the 'powers' or 'values' of the Moon, with titles as follows: 'The Moon and Time'; 'The Moon and the Waters'; 'The Moon and Vegetation'; 'The Moon and Fertility'; 'The Moon, Woman, and Snakes'; 'The Moon and Death'; 'The Moon and Initiation'; and 'The Moon and Fate.'[50] These section titles of 'The Moon and Its Mystique' refer, for Eliade, to the symbolism of various 'zones' or 'areas' of human experience, and not to 'levels' of reality. As Eliade reiterates, not only does a symbol serve the function of "[making] it possible for man to move freely from one level of reality to another," but "every symbolism aims at integrating and unifying the greatest possible number of zones and areas of human and cosmic experience."[51] We refer in this book primarily to traditional symbols' function of providing access to the metaphysical 'level' of reality. It is, however, relevant to refer to the various 'zones' of human experience described in Eliade's section titles of 'The Moon and Its Mystique' because many of the ideas encompassed in those

---

50 Mircea Eliade, *Patterns in Comparative Religion*, 154–185.
51 Mircea Eliade, *Patterns in Comparative Religion*, 455 and 452.

titles are intimately connected to traditional serpent/dragon symbolism. As we shall see, serpent/dragon symbolism was connected in Tradition not only to moon symbolism, but also to the symbolisms of time, water, vegetation, fertility, and death.

I suggest that the function of traditional symbolism as a device for accessing a 'higher' level of reality is, for traditional or archaic humans, more important than its function of revealing the interconnections among Eliade's various 'zones' of reality, although the symbolism relating to any of these zones — water, fertility, etc. — may indeed help to facilitate an individual's access to the various 'levels' of reality in Tradition. It is difficult to determine whether an awareness by traditional or archaic peoples of the interconnectivity of zones of the real was more or less efficacious in "giving meaning," as we might say today, to existence than was the accessing of other 'levels' of reality. The modern pragmatic goal of 'giving meaning' to existence was not, however, the purpose of symbols for traditional peoples. In *The Sacred and the Profane*, Eliade states that "[traditional/archaic] man desires to have his abode in a space opening upward, that is, communicating with the divine world."[52] Eliade employs the terms 'space' and 'upward' in this statement metaphorically in order to describe the traditional/archaic human desire to communicate with, or access, another 'level' of reality that entirely transcends (is 'above') the profane, physical, world. This 'space,' which is 'upward' of (transcendent of) the profane world, Eliade terms the "divine world." 'Upward,' therefore, is the *symbolic* direction of the 'divine world.'

According to Eliade, the desire by traditional/archaic humans to communicate with another, 'higher,' level of reality is shown in the culturally pervasive "symbolism of the center" that may be found in traditions around the world. We shall later address this idea more fully, but suffice it to say here that, according to Eliade, traditional peoples commonly believed there to be, rather than a merely *physical*

---

52 Mircea Eliade, *The Sacred and the Profane*, 91.

center of the world, a *metaphysical*, or spiritual, center of the world. Guénon also discusses this concept at length in several of his books. For both authors, traditional peoples built *each* of their cities, temples, and houses around a metaphysical or spiritual 'center' that indicated to them the 'nearness' of the presence of the divine. As Eliade states, "to live near to a Center of the World is, in short, equivalent to living as close as possible to the gods."[53] The divine presence of 'the gods,' however, according to traditional/archaic peoples, derived from another 'level' of reality that is separate from the physical/'natural' world. "To live near to a Center of the World," therefore, for Eliade, brought such peoples as near as possible to the 'sacred space' and 'sacred time' of a 'divine level' of reality that is 'beyond' physical space and time. As Eliade states in *The Sacred and the Profane*,

> The intention that can be read in the experience of sacred space and sacred time reveals a desire to reintegrate a primordial situation — that in which the gods and the mythical ancestors were *present*, that is, were engaged in creating the world, or in organizing it, or in revealing the foundations of civilization to man. [However,] this primordial situation is not historical, it is not calculable chronologically; what is involved is a mythical anteriority, the time of origin, what took place 'in the beginning,' *in principio*.[54]

The "primordial situation…in which the gods and the mythical ancestors were present" is for Eliade equivalent to a 'level' of reality the access of which requires the use and understanding of traditional *symbols*. This 'primordial situation' or 'level' of reality is, for Eliade, 'beyond' the descriptive capacity of those languages that are based exclusively upon the experience of the physical dimensions of space and time and the 'contents' of those dimensions. When Eliade thus completes his book *Patterns in Comparative Religion* by concluding that "[f]or, thanks chiefly to his symbols, the real existence of primitive man was not the broken and alienated existence lived by civilized

---

53 Mircea Eliade, *The Sacred and the Profane*, 91.
54 Mircea Eliade, *The Sacred and the Profane*, 91–92.

man to-day,"⁵⁵ he is therefore saying that, *only because* 'primitive' (traditional/archaic) man was able to 'access' a 'higher' (metaphysical/spiritual) level of reality (the 'primordial situation'), was s/he capable of living a life that is meaningful and 'whole,' as opposed to the "broken and alienated" existence characteristic of beings that have no contact with a 'transcendent' reality. The concluding sentence of *Patterns* reveals Eliade's emphasis on the greater importance, out of the two functions that we mentioned earlier, of symbols in aiding traditional/archaic peoples in effecting 'realization' of the 'level' of the 'primordial situation' that exists beyond physical space and time. Examples of such 'events of realization,' I contend, or as I shall more generally term them, 'events of Spiritualization' *of* the state of *matter* that characterizes 'life' at the physical/'natural' 'level' of existence include, among others: 1) shamanic 'flight' and 2) the communication by the heroes and gods of world mythology with a 'higher' level of reality ('the gods'). It should be noted that my first usage of 'heroes and gods' refers to those individuals who have achieved a certain, exceptional, level of 'realization' whereas my second usage of 'the gods' refers to the metaphysical, 'Principial,' level of reality *in general*.

It is not obvious, based upon his extant writings, what *exactly* inspired Eliade's interest in symbols. It is reasonable to presume that Eliade's experiences of a "camouflaged secret dimension" at different moments in his life inspired him to investigate the means by which this 'dimension' was 'opened' to him. Since, according to Eliade, "symbolic thought [is that which] makes it possible for man to move freely from one level of reality to another," it would appear that a 'symbol' is that which allowed Eliade to 'move freely' into that "camouflaged secret dimension" that he experienced briefly at different moments in his life.⁵⁶ A symbol (a 'traditional' symbol specifically) is that 'device' that "opens a window" into what Eliade has described as a "camouflaged

---

55 Mircea Eliade, *Patterns in Comparative Religion*, 456.
56 Mircea Eliade, *Patterns in Comparative Religion*, 455 and 452.

secret dimension." In *Symbolism, the Sacred, and the Arts*, Eliade remarks that "the symbol reveals a pre-systematic ontology to us, which is to say an expression of thought from a period when conceptual vocabularies had not yet been constituted."[57] Based upon this statement, it is difficult to understand a symbol as constituting a 'conception' of a 'higher reality' because concepts are elements connected within *specific* 'conceptual vocabularies' that, Eliade argues, "had not yet been constituted" in the times or places of Tradition. More generally, if, as Eliade states, traditional symbolism is revelatory of a 'pre-systematic ontology,' then traditional symbols are a kind of 'device' that can be neither conceptually nor systematically understood in the sense that moderns understand 'natural' languages and their 'concepts.'

Symbols and Reductionism

There is, of course, academic disagreement on the definition of 'symbol' as well as the ultimate meanings for traditional/archaic peoples of such terms as 'sacred' and 'profane.' Many famous twentieth-century scholars are at odds with Eliade over his definitions of 'symbol,' 'religion,' and his favorite dichotomy, 'sacred and profane.' According to Daniel L. Pals, when for example the early twentieth-century French sociologist Emile Durkheim "speaks of the sacred and profane, he is always thinking of society and its needs. The sacred for him is the social—that which matters to the clan; the profane is the opposite—that which matters to the individual."[58] Similarly, for Durkheim, "the purpose of symbols is simply to make people aware of their social duties by symbolizing the clan as their totem god."[59] As Eliade notes in *The Sacred and the Profane*, "Durkheim...believed that he had found the sociological explanation for religion in totemism." Durkheim

---

57 Diane Apostolos-Cappadona, ed., *Symbolism, the Sacred, and the Arts* (New York: Crossroad, 1986), 3 ff.
58 Daniel L. Pals, *Seven Theories of Religion*, 164.
59 Daniel L. Pals, *Seven Theories of Religion*, 164.

observed that "among the Ojibwa Indians of North America the term *totem* designates the animal whose name a clan bears and which is regarded as their ancestor."[60] For Durkheim, totemism is the essence of religion. The deity is actually the clan and the 'sacred' is simply the clan writ large. For Eliade, however, the sociological 'explanation' is a reduction of religious and ritual phenomena to temporal dimensions of society. As Eliade scholar Douglas Allen remarks in *Structure and Creativity in Religion*, "by insisting [in contrast to such reductions as Durkheim's] on the irreducibility of the sacred, Eliade attempts sympathetically to place himself within the perspective of *homo religiosus* [traditional man] and to grasp the meaning of the religious phenomena."[61] In his methodology, Eliade did not simply *suppose* that modern methods of discovery are objective means of knowledge acquisition that can be applied to ancient practices and thought-patterns in order to discern their deep reasonings and meanings. Rather, in order to understand the perspective of traditional/archaic societies, he attempted to see the cosmos, and the nature of these societies' religions, from *within* the paradigm of their own practices and thought-patterns. Such a methodology, in contrast to Durkheim's reductionist approach, takes seriously the metaphysical/spiritual perspective of traditional peoples, and does not actively seek to reduce this perspective to an epiphenomenon of what's 'actually' real: physical, social, and kinship relationships. As Daniel L. Pals remarks in *Seven Theories of Religion*,

> From the outset Eliade announces his strong dissent from the reductionist approaches favored in his day and still attractive in ours. In opposition to Freud, Durkheim, and Marx, he strongly asserts the independence of religious ideas and activities. He accepts that psychology, society, economics, and other forces have their effects on religion, but he refuses to see their influence as determining or even dominant. Religion, he insists, can be understood only if we try to see it from the standpoint of the believer. Like

---

60 Mircea Eliade, *The Sacred and the Profane*, 231.
61 Douglas Allen, *Structure and Creativity in Religion*, 115.

Roman law, which we can grasp only through Roman values, or Egyptian architecture, which we must see through Egyptian eyes, religious behaviors, ideas, and institutions must be seen in the light of the religious perspective, the view of the sacred, that inspires them. In the case of archaic peoples, especially, it is clearly not profane life—social, economic, or otherwise—that controls the sacred; it is the sacred that controls and shapes every aspect of the profane.[62]

To understand that symbols are a special form of 'device' that allows access to a 'higher' level of reality that is, for traditional/archaic peoples, independent of the physical/'natural' level, differs radically from the reduction of symbols to socio-materialistic signs of social, or kinship, relations. As scholar in religious studies and Professor Emeritus of the University of Chicago Divinity School Joseph M. Kitagawa points out in his article "Primitive, Classical, and Modern Religions,"

> Mircea Eliade rightly reminds us that "to try to grasp the essence of such a [religious] phenomenon by means of physiology, psychology, sociology, economics, linguistics, art or any other study is false; it misses the one unique and irreducible element in it—the element of the Sacred."[63]

'Historicism' is, in a general sense, the modern perspective that encompasses such psychological, sociological, economic, etc. reductions. It constitutes a viewpoint that believes that it already knows the large-scale structure of reality, and, therefore, only needs in its academic work to recognize a similar, although perhaps unconscious and vaguely expressed, knowledge in the religious traditions of traditional/archaic peoples. It is, according to Pals, "a type of thought that

---

62 Daniel L. Pals, *Seven Theories of Religion*, 186–87.
63 Joseph M. Kitagawa, "Primitive, Classical, and Modern Religions: A Perspective on Understanding the History of Religions," in *The History of Religions: Essays on the Problem of Understanding*, ed. Joseph M. Kitagawa (Chicago: University of Chicago Press, 1967), 40; Eliade, *Patterns in Comparative Religion*, xvii.

recognizes only things ordinary and profane while denying any reference at all to things supernatural and sacred."[64]

Some Criticisms of Eliade, and Responses

It is possible for the reader to infer that, because Eliade criticized modern reductionist attempts at explaining 'the Sacred' and the purpose of symbolism for traditional/archaic peoples, he must have believed traditional peoples incapable of the sort of thinking and analysis that is common to modern man. One major criticism of Eliade has been, as scholar Bryan Rennie points out in *Reconstructing Eliade*, that "Eliade utilizes [Lucien] Levy-Bruhl's discredited theory that non-literate peoples lack the scientific attitude because their mental structure and logical thought differs fundamentally from that of modern Western people."[65] Levy-Bruhl had famously observed in his book *Primitive Mentality* that "the linear and unrepeatable nature of time was a feature of the modern, 'civilized' time consciousness."[66] This, of course, sounds similar to Eliade's near constant promotion of his argument that 'archaic' peoples wished to 'destroy history' in order to 'return' to 'mythic time,' "the time of origin." As Rennie remarks, however, Eliade never accepted Levy-Bruhl's theory and, in his "Notes on the Symbolism of the Arrow," Eliade states of so-called 'primitive men' (archaic peoples) that

> [t]heir mind was neither "pre-logical" nor paralyzed by a participation mystique. It was a fully human mind. But this also means that every significant act was validated and valorized both on the level of empirical experience and in a Universe of images, symbols and myths. No conquest

---

64 Daniel L. Pals, *Seven Theories of Religion*, 184.
65 Bryan S. Rennie, *Reconstructing Eliade: Making Sense of Religion* (Albany: State University of New York Press, 1996), 180.
66 Bryan S. Rennie, *Reconstructing Eliade: Making Sense of Religion*, 79.

of the material world was effected without a corresponding impact on human imagination and behavior.[67]

Eliade clearly argues in the above quotation that the "fully human mind" is a mind that is *both* logical *and* symbolical in the sense that it is both a problem-solving apparatus *and* a discoverer and realizer of meaning. Rennie further points out Eliade's awareness of Levy-Bruhl's theory's limitations when he states that,

> Eliade's criticism of Levy-Bruhl seems to be that there is some kind of alternative mentality [possessed by traditional peoples]: an ability to grasp a coherence in a system of symbolism prior to its logical or verbal extrapolation. However, this mentality, this ability, is far from absent in "civilized" peoples. In fact, "every historical man carries on, within himself, a great deal of prehistoric humanity."[68]

For Eliade, both archaic/traditional humans *and* modern humans have the capacities for both symbolic thought and 'logical' thought (as moderns would define this). Modern humans, however, have, according to Eliade, largely lost the traditional person's "ability to grasp a coherence in a system of symbolism prior to its logical or verbal extrapolation." In *The Sacred and the Profane*, Eliade states

> The nonreligious man refuses transcendence, accepts the relativity of 'reality,' and may even come to doubt the meaning of existence....Modern nonreligious man assumes a new existential situation; he regards himself solely as the subject and agent of history, and he refuses all appeal to transcendence. In other words, he accepts no model for humanity outside of the human condition as it can be seen in the various historical situations. Man *makes himself*, and he only makes himself completely in proportion as he desacralizes himself and the world. The sacred is the prime obstacle to

---

67 Mircea Eliade, "Notes on the Symbolism of the Arrow," in *Religions in Antiquity*, ed. J. Neusner (Leiden: E. J. Brill, 1968), 465.

68 Bryan S. Rennie, *Reconstructing Eliade: Making Sense of Religion*, 183; Mircea Eliade, *Images and Symbols: Studies in Religious Symbolism* (London: Harvill Press, 1961. Translated from the French by Philip Mairet), 12.

his freedom. He will become himself only when he is totally demysticized. He will not be truly free until he has killed the last god."[69]

If true, this analysis by Eliade indicates that the modern worldview is not the purely objective attempt to understand the universe that it purports to be, but an *assertion* that the universe is basically constituted, at least in its broad outlines, in such a way that mysticism and an appeal to 'higher' non-human agents are *necessarily* impossible means to 'honestly' comprehend existence.

Another criticism of Eliade is the charge that he has, as Bryan Rennie puts it, a 'hidden theological agenda' with a specifically Christian emphasis.[70] In reading Eliade's books, however, one gets the impression that he is much more fascinated by, and impressed with, the religious traditions of ancient India and of shamanic cultures around the world than by, or with, *any* theology, including Christian theology. If anything, Eliade was fascinated with a sort of 'peasant' "cosmic Christianity" in which, as Pals states in *Seven Theories of Religion*,

> it is accepted that Jesus of Nazareth was a man in history, but that fact virtually disappears from view once it is taken up into the peasants' image of Christ as the great lord of nature, the eternal divinity who, in sacred folklore, continues to visit his people on earth, just as the high god does in the myths of other archaic cultures.[71]

In *Patterns in Comparative Religion*, Eliade discusses the Christian Incarnation of God in Jesus as one of an *indefinite number* of 'hierophanies,' or manifestations of the Sacred within the Profane, that have occurred throughout human history. He states that

> [o]ne *could* attempt to vindicate the hierophanies which preceded the miracle of the Incarnation in the light of Christian teaching, by showing their

---

69 Mircea Eliade, *The Sacred and the Profane*, 202-203.
70 Bryan S. Rennie, *Reconstructing Eliade: Making Sense of Religion*, 191-94.
71 Daniel L. Pals, *Seven Theories of Religion*, 186.

importance as a series of prefigurations of the Incarnation. Consequently, far from thinking of pagan religious ways (fetishes, idols and such) as false and degenerate stages in the religious feeling of mankind fallen in sin, one *may* see them as desperate attempts to prefigure the mystery of the Incarnation. The whole religious life of mankind — expressed in the dialectic of hierophanies — would, *from this standpoint*, be simply a waiting for Christ.⁷² (My emphases)

As is indicated by my italics, Eliade's analysis in this quotation is obviously meant as a purely *imaginative exercise* that is not in any way dogmatic or a statement of theological belief. On the contrary, it epitomizes the kind of exercise required of any serious scholar of religions or belief systems in general. For, in order to *truly* take any religion or belief system seriously, and not to immediately reduce it to another paradigm, one must consider the *possibility* that it is *absolutely* true. Such an exercise is what Eliade performs in the above quotation by means of his careful use of modal verbs ('could' and 'may') as well as the proviso "from this [the Christian] standpoint."

Rennie states that Eliade "is in no way claiming that Christianity is the absolutely highest form of religion, but rather that it has characteristics which have allowed it to be convincingly perceived as such by certain specific people."⁷³ It is, perhaps, the final chapter of Eliade's *The Myth of the Eternal Return* that causes misgivings in some on this point. In "The Terror of History," Eliade writes that

> [w]e may say, furthermore, that Christianity is the "religion" of modern man and historical man, of the man who simultaneously discovered personal freedom and continuous time (in place of cyclical time)....Since the "invention" of faith, in the Judeo-Christian sense of the word..., the man who has left the horizon of archetypes and repetition can no longer defend himself against that terror [of history] except through the idea of God. In fact, it is only by presupposing the existence of God that he conquers, on the one hand, freedom...and, on the other hand, the certainty that

---

72 Mircea Eliade, *Patterns in Comparative Religion*, 30.
73 Bryan S. Rennie, *Reconstructing Eliade: Making Sense of Religion*, 192.

> historical tragedies have a transhistorical meaning....Any other situation of modern man leads, in the end, to despair....In this respect, Christianity incontestably proves to be the religion of "fallen man": and this to the extent to which modern man is irremediably identified with history and progress, and to which history and progress are a fall, both implying the final abandonment of the paradise of archetypes and repetition.[74]

In this passage, Eliade does not contend that Christianity is the 'true' religion *or* the greatest of all religions. Neither does he argue for a theology of history in the manner of Augustine's *City of God*, which claims that all of history has been 'building' towards the Christian revelation. His approach is actually much deeper than that. What Eliade is saying is the following: 1) modern man sees time differently than traditional man: as linear ('continuous') rather than as cyclical; 2) modern humans are unable to conceptualize the world by means of cyclical time and the ancient mythical archetypes, and thus are left to 'defend' themselves against the 'terror of history' ("the idea that the human adventure as a whole might be merely a pointless exercise, an empty spectacle with death as its end"[75]) with *only* that idea of God that originates in the historical, temporally linear, Judeo-Christian tradition; 3) the idea of the existence of the Judeo-Christian God usefully provides modern man with a sense of freedom and of 'transhistorical' meaning, since modern man can no longer comprehend how the old cyclical, archetypal, view did this; 4) *because* of this, Christianity (or a Messianic Judaism) *has to be* (since modern humans don't have the other cyclical/archetypal option anymore) the religion of humans who have identified with linear time, history, and 'progress' — the latter two of which are based on the projection of linear time; 5) the 'identification' by moderns with history and progress is what shows their 'abandonment' of the archetypal/cyclical paradigm for comprehending the universe in the first place; and 6) this means that a linear,

---

74 Mircea Eliade, *The Myth of the Eternal Return*, 161–62.
75 Daniel L. Pals, *Seven Theories of Religion*, 180.

historical, religion is now *necessary* and that Christianity happens to both: a) fit that description and b) be the dominant religion now *most available* to modern humans which fits that description.

Eliade is not promoting Christian dogma but, rather, arguing that Christianity (the Judeo-Christian paradigm in general) *suits* modern humans because of their particular comportment toward reality. *Because* modern humans generally conceive of time linearly and have a sense of historical development ('progress') they are, for Eliade, generally unable to adopt the 'traditional' religions that are based upon the recognition of an immutable cyclical cosmic process and the repetition of eternal archetypes. Instead of having an indefinite cyclical *series* of 'redemptions' like traditional peoples did, modern humans must rely on one 'big' redemption at the end of linear, historical, time: the supposed return of Christ, or of a messiah figure in general. For Eliade, this is just the way things are now. It is the fundamental structure of the modern human psyche. Eliade is saying that, for people of the current world age, Christianity (the Judeo-Christian tradition) is 'what we got.' Because humans now largely identify with a linear conception of time and because we now identify with the idea of historical progression (which is based on the idea of linear time), and insofar as we desire to find 'transhistorical meaning' and defend ourselves against the 'terror of history,' the Judeo-Christian paradigm is our only real option. This doesn't mean, however, that Eliade *likes* the option or wishes to promote it. As Rennie states, Eliade "refuses to share with Tillich the focus of his ultimate concern in the Christian religion."[76] It's just how things are, for Eliade, that Christianity grew to be the historically dominant religion that is most accessible for modern humans who see reality in terms of linear time and a historically progressive pattern of events that, at least ideally, are expected to culminate in some hoped-for eventuality. Actually, for Eliade, as for Guénon, *Eastern* traditions were/are spiritually 'higher' and

---

76 Bryan S. Rennie, *Reconstructing Eliade: Making Sense of Religion*, 192.

'deeper' than Christianity and other Western religions. In *Structure and Creativity in Religion*, Allen argues that, according to Eliade, "the 'highest' or 'deepest' manifestations on the level of mystical experience have a structure more typical of Eastern mysticism" and that "Mircea Eliade could take the very bold step and claim that not he, but the religious data themselves…establish the conclusion that the highest levels of spiritual realizations are more often expressed by Eastern rather than Western phenomena."[77] This, however, does not mean that such traditions present the best means for specifically *modern* humans to stave off the 'terror of history' and feel 'free.'[78]

Along this same line that claims that Eliade had a 'hidden theological agenda,' Allen also notes that

> [m]any interpreters have seized upon Eliade's personal doctrine of a 'fall' as being a pivotal notion in his thought. It is only because of Eliade's 'theological assumptions' [according to these interpreters] that he considers modern secularization to be a 'fall.'[79]

As Allen points out, however, such criticisms come from theologians who, perhaps because of their own focus and interests, take Eliade for a theologian. Eliade, however, purports to be a historian of religions, and, as Allen so eloquently puts it, "his [Eliade's] claim is not that Mircea Eliade is committed to these diverse themes of a 'fall' but that

---

77 Douglas Allen, *Structure and Creativity in Religion*, 222.
78 A similar thesis may be found in the works of Carl Jung, who spoke of the 'dangers' of Westerners seeking spiritual fulfillment in Asian traditions. In submitting this warning, Jung did not mean to imply that Western religious traditions are, because 'less dangerous' to unpracticed Westerners, thereby *objectively superior* to Eastern traditions. It is rather, as both he and Eliade contended, a matter of the psychic 'situation' that the 'seeker' finds him/herself in. If one is drowning in the ocean and a plank from an ancient wrecked ship floats within reach, one reaches for *it* to stave off death, not for the well-made boat that is a hundred yards away.
79 Douglas Allen, *Structure and Creativity in Religion*, 129.

homo religiosus has entertained such beliefs."⁸⁰ In *Seven Theories of Religion*, Pals clarifies that Eliade *did believe* that

> all archaic peoples have a sense of a 'fall,' of a great tragic loss, in history. By this he does not mean only the fall of humanity into sin as told in the biblical story of Adam and Eve, who disobeyed the command of God and were punished accordingly.⁸¹

Rather, as Pals points out,

> [a]rchaic peoples know a fall in the sense of a profound separation. They feel that from the first moment human beings become aware of their situation in the world, they are seized by a feeling of absence, a sense of great distance from the place where they ought to be and truly want to be — the realm of the sacred.⁸²

Allen similarly states that

> Eliade finds that 'paradisiac myths' all speak of a 'paradisiac epoch'...and express a 'nostalgia' for that 'prefallen' Paradise. If history is a 'fall' for *homo religiosus*, it is because historical existence is seen as separated from and inferior to the 'transhistorical' (absolute, eternal, transcendent) realm of the sacred.⁸³

The Continuing Importance of Eliade's Approach

With these thoughts in mind, I find it easy to argue for the continuing importance of Eliade's outlook and theories. This is for the primary reason that Eliade provides an alternative to the modern reductionist-materialist paradigm. There is, as an axiom of the 'scientific method' ostensibly employed by such moderns, always room for error in the construction of hypotheses and theories; and there usually *is* error in

---

80 Douglas Allen, *Structure and Creativity in Religion*, 129.
81 Daniel L. Pals, *Seven Theories of Religion*, 168.
82 Daniel L. Pals, *Seven Theories of Religion*, 168.
83 Douglas Allen, *Structure and Creativity in Religion*, 129–30.

both scientific testing and scientific theory formulation. This acknowledged, any scientist knows well that it is only a matter of time before almost every theory proposed will be either drastically modified to account for new evidence or eventually completely abandoned. The latter has happened many, many times to theories that were proffered by respected and competent researchers, let alone wild independent thinkers and completely unknown savants. Eliade points out that "Hegel believed that he knew what the Universal Spirit wanted."[84] *How* though, he asked, "could Hegel know what was necessary in history, what, consequently, must occur exactly as it had occurred?"[85] Knowing how attached humans become to the products of their labor and to those things that they have generally invested a great deal of time and reputation in, it is always good to allow space for theories that are completely opposed to the variations on a theme that are the various versions of the modern materialist-reductionist paradigm. Eliade notes the dangers of the modern belief in 'historicism' coupled with the human belief in 'necessities.' With respect to the Hegelian model, he remarks that "a century later [after Hegel], the concept of historical necessity will enjoy a more and more triumphant practical application; in fact, all the cruelties, aberrations, and tragedies of history have been, and still are, justified by the necessities of the 'historical moment.'"[86] Eliade's passionate consideration of the traditional/archaic human's understanding of reality in terms of the Sacred and the Profane, in terms of a metaphysical or spiritual reality, is opposed at the most fundamental level to the materialist-reductionist paradigm. In my opinion, the free expression of, and earnest attempt to understand, *especially* those theories of religion that are endorsed by only a minority of scholars should be freely encouraged. It serves as a reminder that there is always something entirely different out

---

84 Mircea Eliade, *The Myth of the Eternal Return*, 148.
85 Mircea Eliade, *The Myth of the Eternal Return*, 148.
86 Mircea Eliade, *The Myth of the Eternal Return*, 148.

there that contradicts the mainstream opinion and that might actually be true. Eliade's works should still be read and taken seriously because, like a true *philosopher* of old, he: 1) emphasizes the possibility that transcendence is a genuine reality, and 2) casts his investigative net *wide* in order to encompass a mass of information that he knows no single human could hope to synthesize with complete scientific exactitude. Heraclitus once said that "men who are lovers of wisdom must be inquirers into many things indeed."[87] This is a *requirement* of a philosopher, I believe, and this designation describes Eliade as much as the designation 'historian of religion' does.

In *Seven Theories of Religion*, in his chapter on Eliade, Daniel L. Pals states that

> [t]he skeptical mind of the scholar is always inclined to think that no two things are ever quite the same; every time, every place is different from the next. Eliade disagrees. He thinks that certain general forms, certain broad patterns of phenomena in religion, can be taken outside of their original time and place to be compared with others. Times and places may differ, he would say, but concepts are often the same. The mathematician Euclid was an ancient Greek, a man of his time; yet we can study his geometry as if he had taught it just yesterday. The man may be historical, but his theorems are timeless. The same would seem to apply to the concepts of religion. The worship of Zeus is in one sense tied to a single time and place in history; it is a belief and practice belonging to ancient Greek religion. But if we notice that, in the Greek stories of the gods, Zeus has a wife, that he lives on Mt. Olympus, and that he is more powerful than other divine beings, it is not hard to see in him certain typical features of the "sky god" as he appears in many different times and places around the world. Zeus may belong to the Greeks, but the phenomenon of the sky god does not. And because such gods appear in many cultures, we can learn a great deal by tracing their patterns—by noticing which features they share with one another and which they do not.[88]

---

87 S. Marc Cohen, Patricia Curd, and C. D. C. Reeve, *Readings in Ancient Greek Philosophy: From Thales to Aristotle* (Indianapolis: Hackett Publishing Company, Inc., 1995), 27.

88 Daniel L. Pals, *Seven Theories of Religion*, 162–63.

The reason I provide this long quotation from Pals is that it: 1) illustrates well a connection between two fields of research, mathematics and religion, that are usually not thought of together and 2) reveals that, for some individuals at least, the compulsion that is usually accepted as an appropriate final cause for a person to become interested and engaged in one of the fields of research (mathematics) is also an appropriate final cause for a person to become interested and engaged in the other field of research (religion). In the passage provided, Pals compares the discoveries of a mathematician (geometrical concepts) with the discoveries of a student of religion (religious concepts). Almost everyone believes that mathematics deals with certainty and with universal claims that can be proven through rigorous mathematical analysis. But do people, in our contemporary world, think the same thing about religion? It is a simple fact that, as Pals says, we may discover 'sky gods' in many cultures around the world and over very long stretches of history. One may also find, as another example that both Eliade and Guénon draw attention to, 'axial imagery' in many cultures around the world and over very long stretches of history. Both of these constitute, within Tradition, universal, or at least pervasive, patterns to be discerned.

The British mathematician G. H. Hardy claimed that "a mathematician...is a maker of patterns" and that mathematics is, therefore, what we may call 'the study of patterns.'[89] In my field of research, the study of 'traditional' symbols, one finds that the very same symbols occur in very many cultural artifacts around the world and over long stretches of human history. There are recurring *patterns* in the use of traditional symbols, in other words. One of the great things about Eliade is that he takes seriously the possibility that, as in mathematics, there *may* be certain patterns in 'religion' (which is, as yet, still an unknown quantity) that are universal, or near-universal, and that these patterns were (and may still be) recognized as constituting a 'universal

---

89 G. H. Hardy, *A Mathematician's Apology* (Cambridge, England: Cambridge University Press, 1940), 84.

language' by traditional/archaic peoples. I believe that this possibility exists as a compulsion (in the positive sense) in the minds of some scholars, such as Eliade, that drives the study of religion in a fashion very similar to the compulsion that drives the study of mathematics. It is a non-pragmatic compulsion to discern greater and greater connectivity, more and more broadly 'universal' instantiations of the same idea(s), and only for *the pure sake of knowledge*. The post-modern obsession with specializations within specializations makes even considering the possibility/potentiality that this compulsion seeks to 'actualize' a near-fantasy for many academics (if we are to judge by Eliade's critics), but for the scholar writing this sentence it is both admirable and fascinating. We must consider very seriously the *possibility* that, for Eliade and Guénon, there are patterns in comparative religion that are pervasive, that have the same or similar meanings, and that are expressed by means of the *same* or similar symbols around the world and over long stretches of time, for that is what the language of traditional symbolism is — a universal language, a universal pattern, at least within the parameters of that which we term 'Tradition.'

CHAPTER 3

Symbolism, 'Tradition,' and Universalism

Symbols and Symbolism in Guénon and Eliade

In *The Good and Evil Serpent*, James Charlesworth remarks that

> [i]f under the influence of Aristotle we can speak about the essence of the serpent, then the symbol of the serpent does not reside in its physicality (*natura sua*). Serpent symbolism derives from what the human imaginatively adds to the concept of the animal: the form. The symbol of the serpent thus represents what cannot be reduced to the formal essence of a snake. The symbol and symbology are what the human perspective adds to nature, creating a meaningful world out of chaotic phenomenology.[1]

Although the material remains of what Guénon and Eliade have termed 'traditional,' or archaic, societies are easily discoverable, these remains can never, by themselves, reveal the thought-world of such societies. Until we have understood, from their own perspective, the 'symbolic language' that is communicated by means of the art, myths, and legends of traditional societies, we must remain as, for example, one who takes a bench for a table or one who takes a pistol for a club.

---

1 James H. Charlesworth, *The Good and Evil Serpent: How a Universal Symbol Became Christianized* (New Haven and London: Yale University Press, 2010), 192–193.

For, although it is true that a bench *may* serve as a table and that a pistol *may* serve as a club, what a thing *may* do compared to what it was *intended* to do are radically different things. Understanding the meanings of traditional symbols is, therefore, not merely a matter of formulating a 'consistent' interpretation of their meanings, but of discerning their *actual* meanings, and this requires understanding the mindset of those who 'created' such symbols.

In this chapter, I provide an overview of three concepts of fundamental importance to my thesis: 1) symbol, 2) Tradition, and 3) Universal. These three ideas are inextricably linked in Guénon's and Eliade's works, even if these authors do not examine the linkage in exactly the same manner or by using the same terminology. Both authors completely agree, however, as we have previously noted, that the traditional/archaic paradigm is *essentially* meta-physical. 'Nature,' or the physical world, is considered to be in traditional/archaic, or 'primitive,' societies a 'manifestation' or 'creation' of a 'higher' meta-physical Reality. As Eliade argues repeatedly, "'primitive' ontology has a Platonic structure."[2] This is to say that the traditional understanding of existence presumes, or *knows*, that the Particulars of 'nature,' whether inanimate objects, animate beings, or physical processes, are, in Platonic fashion, derivative of a Universal meta-physical Reality. Guénon emphasizes the 'unity' of this Universal Reality when he refers to it as *a* meta-physical Principle. Eliade, alternatively, embraces a *plurality* of metaphysical 'archetypes.' For both authors, *symbols* are a common traditional means of understanding or 'accessing' Universal metaphysical Reality.

The term 'context' has a very relative meaning. What we refer to by the term 'human being,' for example, not *a* human being, exists in no particular time or place, but rather in an *indefinite number* (billions, for example) of times and places. 'Human being' is, therefore, a word that expresses a universal idea. A symbol, insofar as it refers to an idea,

---

2   Mircea Eliade, *The Myth of the Eternal Return*, 34.

refers to a metaphysical reality, for an idea *is* a metaphysical reality. To communicate an idea, therefore, a symbol must have the same form across all *physical* 'contexts,' it must be *meta*-physical. According to Guénon, a specifically 'traditional' rendering of, for example, a dragon on a tapestry in Europe and a specifically 'traditional' rendering of a serpent on a drum in Africa are, from the perspective of one initiated into Tradition, particular instantiations of, or variations on, the *same* 'traditional' symbol. A very similar situation holds in the case of the physical sciences, in which generalizations, which are similar but not equivalent to Universals, are often made/discovered. From the perspective of one 'initiated' into the study of Physics, a pencil falling off of a desk conveys the same information as a limb falling from a tree: the presence of *gravity*. A pencil, however, is not a tree limb, just as a European dragon is not an African serpent, and the English word 'human' is not the Italian word 'umano.'

In *The Secret Language of Symbols*, British psychologist David Fontana states that "a symbol can represent some deep intuitive wisdom that eludes direct expression."[3] According to both Guénon and Eliade, this "deep intuitive wisdom," at least in traditional cultures, is knowledge of the meta-physical. The 'indirect expression' required to express such knowledge is the 'language' of traditional symbols. 'Ordinary languages,' such as English or German, are useful in providing information about physical objects, but a cursory glance at the history of Western Philosophy clearly reveals the limits of such 'ordinary languages' when they attempt to provide information concerning meta-physical ideas, such as 'being,' 'goodness,' 'God,' and 'justice.' The endless debates over these terms' 'ordinary language' definitions evidences this. In *The Multiple States of the Being*, by contrast, Guénon states that

---

3   David Fontana, *The Secret Language of Symbols: A Visual Key to Symbols and Their Meanings* (San Francisco: Chronicle Books, 1994), 8.

strictly symbolic representations...are incomparably less narrowly restricted than ordinary language and consequently more apt for the communication of transcendent truths, and so they are invariably used in all truly 'initiatic' and traditional teaching.[4]

'Transcendent truths,' for Guénon, are meta-physical truths. In *The Symbolism of the Cross*, however, Guénon argues that "'metaphysical' is synonymous with 'universal,'" and concludes that

[h]ence no doctrine that confines itself to the consideration of individual beings can merit the name of metaphysics, whatever may be its interest and value in other respects; such a doctrine can always be called 'physical' in the original sense of the word, because it lies exclusively within the realm of 'nature' — that is, of manifestation.[5]

In *Lectures on Ancient Philosophy*, the mystic and student of the occult Manly P. Hall similarly contended that "symbolism deals with universal forces and agencies."[6] A (individual) human being, however, is always embedded in a 'particular' spatiotemporal, *physical*, 'context.' By contrast, the *idea* of 'human being,' because it is not limited to *any* physical context, is a Universal, meta-physical, reality. Although 'ordinary language' is useful in communicating information about individual human beings, 'traditional' symbolism is, according to Guénon, tailored to the purpose of communicating information about 'human being' *itself*, as well as any other aspect of meta-physical reality.

In *Introduction to the Study of the Hindu Doctrines*, Guénon states that "symbolism is but the employing of forms and images as signs of ideas or of suprasensible things....Indeed, symbolism...is as it were

---

4 René Guénon, *The Multiple States of the Being*, ed. Samuel D. Fohr, trans. Henry D. Fohr (Hillsdale, NY: Sophia Perennis, 2001 [originally published in 1932 as *Les États multiples de l'être*]), 2.

5 René Guénon, *The Symbolism of the Cross*, 7.

6 Manly P. Hall, *Lectures on Ancient Philosophy* (New York, New York: Jeremy P. Tarcher/Penguin, 2005 [originally published in 1929]), 1.

the natural language of metaphysics."⁷ In *Symbols of Sacred Science*, he similarly states that "the essential role that we have ascribed to symbolism" is "a means of raising ourselves to the knowledge of divine truths,"⁸ effectively equating 'metaphysical' with 'divine.' Eliade, in *Patterns in Comparative Religion*, argues that a symbol's "function...is to transform a thing or an action into *something other* than that thing or action appears to be in the eyes of profane experience."⁹ In *Yoga: Immortality and Freedom*, he states that "[i]n general, symbolism brings about a universal 'porousness,' 'opening' beings and things to transobjective meanings."¹⁰ For Guénon and Eliade both, symbolism, in the 'traditional' sense, is "a means of raising ourselves to the knowledge of divine truths,"¹¹ a means of seeing the divine, or meta-physical, or transobjective, *in* the physical or 'natural' or 'profane.' In *Dynamics of Faith*, the theologian Paul Tillich similarly argued that symbols are those things that "open...up levels of reality which otherwise are closed for us."¹² Symbols, therefore, as I proposed in the *Introduction*, are a kind of 'device.' Like the device, for example, that is called a key, they 'unlock' a level of understanding that, in the minds of those who 'use' them, 'transcends' the physical (or 'natural') level of existence. This 'unlocking,' in the words of Eliade and Guénon, consists in 'opening,' or 'raising,' humans to a 'higher' level of knowledge or meaning. A *physical* key opens a lock that prevents passage into a physical 'space.' A symbol, however, for 'universalizing' creatures (humans), opens a 'lock' that prevents passage into a *meta-physical* 'space.' Eliade states that "*symbolic thought* makes it possible for man to move freely from

---

7   René Guénon, *Introduction to the Study of the Hindu Doctrines*, 86–87.
8   René Guénon, *Symbols of Sacred Science*, 10.
9   Mircea Eliade, *Patterns in Comparative Religion*, 445.
10 Mircea Eliade, *Yoga: Immortality and Freedom*, 250–251.
11 René Guénon, *Symbols of Sacred Science*, 10.
12 Paul Tillich, *Dynamics of Faith* (New York, New York: Harper & Row, Publishers, 1957), 47–49.

one level of reality to another."[13] To appreciate Eliade's claim, however, one must take seriously the possibility that there *are* multiple 'levels of reality,' and that what we call the 'physical world' constitutes only one of these 'levels.' More than this, the so-called 'physical world' is, according to Guénon and Eliade both, from the perspective of traditional peoples, a 'lower level' of existence that is *derivable from* the meta-physical level. The symbol, for these two authors, is the 'key' that 'unlocks' traditional human awareness *of* the meta-physical level, and that, furthermore, provides traditional humans with the means necessary to formulating a complete conception of existence.

In Eliade's works, the idea of 'hierophany' recurs often and is intimately related to his idea of what a symbol is. In *Patterns in Comparative Religion*, Eliade defines 'hierophany' as a "manifestation of the sacred" that "takes place in some historical situation."[14] In *The Sacred and the Profane*, he states that "[t]he sacred tree, the sacred stone are not adored as stone or tree; they are worshipped precisely because they are *hierophanies*, because they show something that is no longer stone or tree but the *sacred*."[15] "The sacred," for Eliade, is that which "always manifests itself as a reality of a wholly different order from 'natural' realities."[16] "The first possible definition of the sacred," Eliade states, "is that it is the opposite of the profane."[17] "Man becomes aware of the sacred," Eliade contends, "because it manifests itself, shows itself, as something wholly different from the profane."[18] The 'profane,' thus, for Eliade, is that which the 'sacred' manifests *by means of*; it is the 'ordinary object' — "a stone or a tree," or an individual human being — that serves as the 'locale' for "manifestation of

---

13 Mircea Eliade, *Patterns in Comparative Religion*, 455.
14 Mircea Eliade, *Patterns in Comparative Religion*, 2.
15 Mircea Eliade, *The Sacred and the Profane*, 12.
16 Mircea Eliade, *The Sacred and the Profane*, 10.
17 Mircea Eliade, *The Sacred and the Profane*, 10.
18 Mircea Eliade, *The Sacred and the Profane*, 11.

the sacred."[19] In the profane, the sacred show itself as "a reality of a wholly different order" from the 'natural' or 'nature.' This only occurs, however, according to Eliade, in 'historical situations,' meaning that the sacred only 'manifests' as something different from the 'natural' *from the perspective of* a being that exists 'historically.' The human being is the only 'historical' being that Eliade refers to in his works. The sacred, therefore, 'manifests' in the *human interpretation of* 'nature' or 'natural realities.' The latter, *for* 'historical' humans, is the 'profane.'

In *Reconstructing Eliade: Making Sense of Religion*, Bryan Rennie describes Eliade's idea of the relationship between hierophanies and symbols when he states that, "while all hierophanies [for Eliade] are not symbols, all symbols are hierophanies or at least 'carry forward' the hierophanic revelation of the real."[20] Another way of phrasing this, I submit, is that "[w]hile all manifestations of the 'sacred' do not necessarily count as symbols for 'traditional' people, all symbols reveal, for traditional people, the sacred or meta-physical (meta-'natural') order of existence *in* the physical ('natural') world." As I mentioned before, in *essentially* the same way that a hammer and chisel revealed Michelangelo's sculpture *Moses* in a piece of marble, the 'traditional' symbol is able to reveal, from the perspective of the 'enlightened,' or 'initiated,' traditional human, the sacred, or meta-physical, *within* the 'raw material' of "some historical situation" in the physical ('natural') world. The state of 'enlightenment' or 'initiation' that allows for this is, as we discussed before, the product of an essentially 'spiritual transmission' of sacred knowledge from master to pupil. Daniel L. Pals summarizes Eliade's idea of the "manifestation of the sacred" in *Seven Theories of Religion* when he says,

> In all of its beauty and ferocity, its complexity, mystery, and variety, the natural world is continually opening windows to disclose the different

---

19 Mircea Eliade, *The Sacred and the Profane*, 11.
20 Bryan S. Rennie, *Reconstructing Eliade: Making Sense of Religion*, 49.

aspects of the supernatural [the metaphysical] — what Eliade calls 'the modalities of the sacred.'[21]

For moderns, mathematical formulae and equations probably constitute the most familiar examples of what they define as 'symbols.' Even if they don't have much talent for, or understanding of, mathematics, moderns still *believe* in the 'power' of mathematics. Mathematical formulae and equations *do* function quite similarly to 'traditional' symbols, perhaps more so than any modern 'ordinary language' does. For they undeniably provide a means for comprehending what mathematicians, and average people, understand to be 'universal' forms. Beyond the characteristic of being 'universal,' however, the 'forms' described by mathematical language seem to exist, as many mathematicians and average people believe, 'beyond' (*meta*) the particulars of the physical universe. They are, in a word, *meta-physical*. $A=\pi r^2$ is an example of a modern 'compound symbolism' constituted by four 'simple symbols' — A, π, r, and ^{2} — that expresses the area of a circle. It is an 'equation' that expresses, to those capable of understanding the symbols involved in the equation and their relationship, the area of *any* circle *anywhere*, within the content of how Euclidean geometry defines 'circle.' As such, $A=\pi r^2$ expresses, within the language of mathematics, a 'universal' truth. The case is similar, I argue, with the 'traditional' symbolism of the serpent/dragon. For, from the perspective of those 'initiates' or 'enlightened' individuals capable of understanding the language of traditional symbolism, the serpent/dragon symbol has the *same* meaning, in its 'simple' form, in any of its 'manifestations' in traditional *realia* anywhere in the world, whether this be as a European dragon, an African serpent, or some other 'version' of the 'traditional' serpent/dragon symbol. $A=\pi r^2$, therefore, is, like any other mathematical equation, and like the 'traditional' symbolism of the serpent/dragon and other traditional symbols, a 'key' that unlocks aspects of 'universal' reality. It is a 'device' that facilitates

---

21 Daniel L. Pals, *Seven Theories of Religion*, 170.

non-inferential, non-discursive, 'intellectual intuition' of the 'universal,' or metaphysical, realm of being. For, at a certain point in one's mathematical education, one stops applying discursive reasoning in the comprehension of many equations and formulas and, as is the case with those 'initiated' into Tradition, according to Guénon, immediately 'sees' the truth of $A=\pi r^2$.

Let us take the comparison between 'traditional' and mathematical symbolism somewhat further. Any mathematical equation, such as that expressing Newton's 'law of universal gravitation,' is a means for understanding phenomena of a specific kind, and often in the physical world.[22] In the case of the 'law of universal gravitation,' this specific kind of phenomena is the kind of phenomena that is caused by the force of gravity. Like Newton's equation that expresses the 'law of universal gravitation,' the traditional symbolism of the serpent/dragon expresses what I shall call the 'law of universal *manifestation*.' Newton's 'law of universal gravitation' is applicable to 'universal' instantiations of the gravitational force. Similarly, the 'law of universal manifestation' is applicable to 'universal' instantiations of Guénon's 'Principial' metaphysical Reality, Eliade's 'hierophanies.' From the 'traditional' perspective, Newton's 'law of universal gravitation,' symbolized by the equation $F=G*(m_1 m_2)/r^2$, applies to a much smaller set of physical phenomena than the 'law of universal manifestation' symbolized by the 'traditional' serpent/dragon symbol does, since it applies to only a *subset* of all physical phenomena, gravitational 'events' specifically.[23] The 'law of universal manifestation,' by contrast, applies to *all* physical phenomena, all 'natural' events or

---

22   Mathematical equations that apply only to phenomena of the physical world may be opposed to the equations of 'pure' mathematics, such as $A=\pi r^2$, which may also consider the 'phenomena' of 'ideal' geometrical figures. Newton's 'law of universal gravitation' is an equation that is more often employed in 'applied mathematics,' physics specifically.

23   'Newton's law of universal gravitation' is expressed by the equation $F=G*(m_1 m_2)/r^2$, where F symbolizes the gravitational force acting between two objects, m1 and m2 express the masses of the two objects, r is the distance

'manifestations' of the meta-physical Reality that make up the physical world. Every time an object falls to earth due to the influence of gravity, we may describe this event as a 'manifestation' of the principle that we term 'Newton's law of universal gravitation,' expressed by the equation $F=G*(m_1 m_2)/r^2$. This equation *symbolizes*, in physics, the mathematical principle that underlies the indefinite number of manifestations of gravity in 'nature': a falling apple ('all' the falling apples), the orbit of the earth around the sun ('all' orbits of 'all' planets around stars), etc.[24] Analogously, the serpent/dragon symbol symbolizes, in Tradition, the meta-physical 'Principle' that underlies the indefinite number of manifestations of a 'higher,' metaphysical, Reality in 'nature.' This indefinite 'series' of physical manifestations of a 'higher' metaphysical Reality in 'nature' Guénon terms the "indefinite series of cycles of manifestation."

The Idea of 'Tradition' in Guénon and Eliade

As we have seen, Guénon and Eliade both, in their discussions of serpent and/or dragon symbolism, refer to the idea of Tradition and to traditional, or 'archaic,' societies. As noted in the *Introduction*, Eliade contends in *The Myth of the Eternal Return* that "the premodern or 'traditional' societies include both the world usually known as 'primitive' and the ancient cultures of Asia, Europe, and America"[25]; in *Rites and Symbols of Initiation*, he adds that "premodern societies" are "those that lasted in Western Europe to the end of the Middle Ages, and in the rest of the world to World War I."[26] For Eliade, 'traditional' societies are those that look to eternal, metaphysical, 'archetypes' rather than historically contextualized 'laws' to comprehend the manifold

---

between the centers of masses of the two objects, and G is the 'gravitational constant.'

24 We do not know the number of manifestations of gravity in the universe to be *actually infinite* since we cannot observe or measure *all* gravitational events.
25 Mircea Eliade, *The Myth of the Eternal Return*, 3.
26 Mircea Eliade, *Rites and Symbols of Initiation*, 18.

of experience and discover a bearing in life. This does not imply, however, that traditional peoples employed the language of *philosophical* metaphysics to refer to or describe those archetypes. As Eliade states,

> Obviously, the metaphysical concepts of the archaic world were not always formulated in theoretical language…the symbol, the myth, the rite, express, on different planes and through the means proper to them, a complex system of coherent affirmations about the ultimate reality of things, a system that can be regarded as constituting a metaphysics.[27]

Like Eliade, Guénon also contends in many of his works that there existed, and still exists to a certain extent, mostly in what he calls the 'East' (Asia), what he terms a 'Primordial Tradition' that was once global in extent and that reached back in time to a 'Hyperborean Age' of the world.[28] In *Introduction to the Study of the Hindu Doctrines*,

---

27 Mircea Eliade, *The Myth of the Eternal Return*, 3.
28 Guénon adhered to the ancient Hindu concept of various 'ages' of man. In *The King of the World*, he refers to *Manvantaras, Yugas,* and other Hindu concepts designating various periods of time. There, Guénon states that "[t]he *Manvantara*, or era of a *Manu*, also called *Maha-Yuga*, comprises four *Yugas* or secondary periods: the *Krita-Yuga*…, the *Treta-Yuga*, the *Dvapara-Yuga*, and the *Kali-Yuga*, which are identified respectively with the 'age of gold', the 'age of silver', the 'age of bronze', and the 'age of iron' of Greco-Roman antiquity. In the succession of these periods there is a kind of progressive materialization resulting from the gradual distancing from the Principle that necessarily accompanies the development of the cyclical manifestation in the corporeal world, starting from the 'primordial state.'" René Guénon, *The King of the World*, ed. Samuel D. Fohr, trans. Henry D. Fohr (Hillsdale, NY: Sophia Perennis, 2001 [originally published in 1958 as *Le Roi du Monde*]), 49. Guénon also discusses in *The King of the World*, on this general topic, the ancient idea of a 'supreme country' named 'Tula' which name was "given to very diverse regions…[and] from which one must doubtless conclude that in some more or less remote age each of these regions was the seat of a spiritual power that was an emanation as it were of that of the primordial *Tula*." Guénon argues that it is "the Hyperborean *Tula*…[that truly represents] the original and supreme center for the totality of the present *Manvantara*; it was this that was the 'sacred isle' par excellence, having originally been situated quite literally at the Pole." René Guénon, *The King of the World*, 62–63.

Guénon states more specifically that there have existed two fundamental dispositions typifying the human comportment toward existence, one characterizing 'traditional humans,' the other characterizing 'modern' humans. For Guénon, 'intellectuality' is the most significant trait that characterizes the ruling disposition of traditional humans. Moderns, by contrast, according to Guénon, are characterized by the trait of 'sentimentality,' an "emotional element."[29] 'Intellectuality' is a perspective that, for Guénon, consists of non-rational 'intuition' of 'the metaphysical': that which "lies beyond physics."[30] It is a 'direct knowing' that is accomplished, according to him, by means of various special methods or disciplines. Examples of 'intellectual intuition' include, in the Hindu tradition, Arjuna's sudden realization of the divinity of Krishna described in the Bhagavad-Gita[31] and, in the Jewish

---

29 René Guénon, *Introduction to the Study of the Hindu Doctrines*, 81.

30 In *Introduction to the Study of the Hindu Doctrines*, Guénon claims that "[i]t now becomes possible to grasp the profound significance of the distinction between metaphysical and scientific knowledge: the first is derived from the pure intellect, which has the Universal for its domain; the second is derived from reason, which has the general for its domain since, as Aristotle has declared, 'there is no science but that of the general.'" René Guénon, *Introduction to the Study of the Hindu Doctrines*, 76–77. More concisely put, 'metaphysics' for Guénon is the study of the 'universal' and 'natural science' is the study of the 'general.' For Guénon, generalizations are *not* equivalent to universal truths, although they are often considered to be so.

31 "Having spoken these words, Krishna, the master of yoga, revealed to Arjuna his most exalted, lordly form....There, within the body of the God of gods, Arjuna saw all the manifold forms of the universe united as one. Filled with amazement, his hair standing on end in ecstasy, he bowed before the Lord with joined palms and spoke these words. O Lord, I see within your body all the gods and every living creature. I see Brahma, the Creator, seated on a lotus.... You are the Lord of all Creation, and the cosmos is your body....You are the supreme, changeless Reality, the one thing to be known." Bhagavad-Gita 11:9, 13–18. Let it be noted that, even after having interacted and spoken with Krishna for much of the Bhagavad-Gita, it is only through 'revelation'—'intellectual intuition'—that Arjuna realizes the divinity that has been beside, within, and all around him all along. This 'realization' is *sudden* and is transformative of Arjuna's 'individuality,' his body and mind.

tradition, Moses's realization, during his encounter with the 'Burning Bush' described in Exodus 3:2, that he is in the presence of God.[32] Such cases of exceptional human insight into the nature of the metaphysical Principle (*Brahman* and God, respectively) are, according to Guénon, cases of intellectual intuition in which the emotive and discursive faculties of the 'individual' play no part.[33] The above-related experiences

---

32 Exodus 3:2 states, "And the angel of the LORD appeared to him [Moses] in a flame of fire out of the midst of a bush. He looked, and behold, the bush was burning, yet it was not consumed." Now, it could be argued that, in the event of his encounter with the Burning Bush of Exodus 3, Moses *reasons* his way—based upon empirical evidence and a dearth of natural hypotheses that could sufficiently explain the phenomenon to which he has just been subjected—to the conclusion that the Burning Bush is a manifestation of God since, when he first notices that "the bush was burning, yet it was not consumed," he says to himself—rather scientifically, one may note—"why doesn't the bush burn up?". Such a conclusion, however, ignores the *previous* statement of Exodus 3:2 that Moses's *first* perception in the event is not of a burning bush alone but of an "angel of the LORD" *appearing* "in a flame of fire out of the midst of a bush." At the point of Moses's actual curiosity, which occurs *after* he has already experienced the Burning Bush as an 'angel' (read: 'expression') of God, God deigns to speak to Moses directly, saying, "I am the God of your father, the God of Abraham, the God of Isaac, and the God of Jacob." At this point, the text confirms that Moses has *already* decided that this Burning Bush is indeed God—a manifestation, or 'angel,' of God—addressing him, as the text reads, "And Moses hid his face, for he was afraid to look at God." Exodus 3:2–6 [ESV]. My conclusion that is based upon these ruminations and analysis is that, although Moses *did* apply both his imagination and power of reason in order to wonder at the *manner* in which the Burning Bush burned, he had already—and quite directly and *immediately*—experienced the Burning Bush as a manifestation of the divine: "And the angel of the LORD appeared to him in a flame of fire out of the midst of a bush." Therefore, in the account of Moses and the Burning Bush provided in Exodus 3, it is *not* an induction or deduction of divinity that Moses arrives at through his power of reason, but a direct *intuition* of the divine presence.

33 Guénon also distinguishes so-called 'mystical' experiences from events of 'intellectual intuition' when he states that the "emotional element nowhere plays a bigger part than in the 'mystical' form of religious thought." René Guénon, *Introduction to the Study of the Hindu Doctrines*, 81.

attributed to Krishna and Moses are *not*, therefore, from Guénon's perspective, descriptive of the results of: inductive reasoning, deductive logical insight, or heightened emotional sensitivity. 'Intellectual intuition' is, rather, in Tradition, according to Guénon, attributable to that aspect of personhood (the 'Self') that 'transcends' the 'individuality' of the ego *completely*.

In the Bhagavad-Gita, the transcendent *Atman* or 'Self,' symbolized by the divine Krishna, instructs the 'individual,' or 'ego,' that is symbolized by the mortal Arjuna on the latter's ephemerality. Guénon states in *The Great Triad* that "the names *Arjuna* and *Krishna*...respectively represent *jivatma* and *Paramatma*, or the 'ego' and the 'Self,' the individuality and the personality."[34] The purpose of life, from the perspective of the Bhagavad-Gita and other remnants of Tradition, according to Guénon, is to 'intuitively' know the metaphysical (or 'divine') Principle that is the Source and sustainer of the universe. As Guénon notes in *Introduction to the Study of the Hindu Doctrines*, however, "the metaphysical ['traditional'] point of view is purely intellectual" and requires the purging of the 'sentimental element' in each manifested being in order for that being to attain to "an attitude of entirely disinterested speculation," the attitude that is, according to Guénon, required to facilitate knowledge of the Principle of many names (such as *Brahman* or God).[35] In *René Guénon and the Future of the West*, Waterfield describes what Guénon means by 'traditional intellectuality' in the terms of the *Advaitan* interpretation of the *Vedanta darshana* (Guénon's paragon of the 'traditional' mindset) in which *Brahma* is the name for the metaphysical Principle. Waterfield states:

---

34 René Guénon, *The Great Triad*, ed. Samuel D. Fohr, trans. Henry D. Fohr (Hillsdale, NY: Sophia Perennis, 2001 [originally published in 1957 as *La Grande Triade*]), 35.

35 René Guénon, *Introduction to the Study of the Hindu Doctrines*, 81.

The only way *Brahma* can be known is through the experience of direct intellectual intuition. This experience can be achieved by means of strict discipline with the aim of acquiring understanding. This discipline is one of the various *yogas* or paths to *moksha* or deliverance. The particular yoga connected with Advaita Vedanta is *jnana-yoga*, the discipline of knowledge.[36]

If one wishes to 'know,' in the traditional sense, the metaphysical Principle that is sometimes called *Brahma(n)* and sometimes 'God,' among many other appellations, it is, as Waterfield argues, not a matter of academic study, the accumulation of information, or rigorous reasoning, but rather *living* in a particular, disciplined, way.

One example of what Guénon does *not* mean when he speaks of intellectual intuition is what Rudolph Otto described in *The Idea of the Holy* as the 'feeling' of the 'numinous.'[37] In that book, which is about what Otto sees as the unique characteristics of the human experience of the divine, or 'holy,' the author speaks of the 'numinous' as "'the holy' *minus* its moral factor or 'moment', and…minus its 'rational' aspect altogether."[38] The numinous is, Otto contends, *essentially mysterious*, a '*mysterium tremendum*' that is not reasoned to, but *felt*.[39] It "completely eludes apprehension in terms of concepts" and, as what might be called the 'pre-moral' experience of 'the Holy,' it is *not* 'morally good,' for according to Otto, the 'ethical element' is not "original [to it] and never constituted the whole meaning of the word."[40] Nevertheless, according to Otto, the numinous, or 'original' holy, is

---

36 Robin Waterfield, *René Guénon and the Future of the West*, 61. It has often been argued, or presumed, that the Bhagavad-Gita is, primarily, a discourse on *karma* and/or *bhakti yoga*.

37 Rudolph Otto, *The Idea of the Holy: An Inquiry into the Non-Rational Factor in the Idea of the Divine and Its Relation to the Rational*, trans. John W. Harvey (London: Oxford University Press, 1923), 12.

38 Rudolph Otto, *The Idea of the Holy*, 6.

39 Rudolph Otto, *The Idea of the Holy*, 12.

40 Rudolph Otto, *The Idea of the Holy*, 5.

still able to "touch the feelings."[41] It is, for Otto, 'God' as the 'union of opposites'—a God that includes *both* "the morally good" *and* the morally evil in its nature, as humans perceive these attributes.[42] Otto's broad-minded notion of 'the holy' is not, however, what directly concerns us about his work, but only his belief concerning how humans interact with it.

Otto's emphasis on 'feeling' characterizes his interpretation of the human encounter with the divine throughout history. For example, he states,

> When Abraham ventures to plead with God for the men of Sodom, he says....'Behold now, I have taken upon me to speak unto the Lord, which am but dust and ashes.' There you have a self-confessed '*feeling* of dependence'....Desiring to give it a name of its own, I propose to call it 'creature-consciousness' or creature-*feeling*. It is the *emotion* of a creature, submerged and overwhelmed by its own nothingness in contrast to that which is supreme above all creatures.[43] (My emphases)

Continuing with his emphasis on a *felt* connection with God a page later, Otto adds that

> [t]here must be *felt* a something 'numinous', something bearing the character of a 'numen', to which the mind turns spontaneously; or (which is the same thing in other words) these *feelings* can only arise in the mind as accompanying *emotions* when the category of 'the numinous' is called into play.[44]

The numinous is thus, for Otto, "*felt* as objective and outside the self," and "the nature of the numinous can only be suggested by means of

---

41 Rudolph Otto, *The Idea of the Holy*, 15.
42 Otto notes that "[a]nyone who uses [the term 'holy'] to-day [sic] does undoubtedly always feel 'the morally good' to be implied in 'holy.'" Rudolph Otto, *The Idea of the Holy*, 5–6.
43 Rudolph Otto, *The Idea of the Holy*, 9–10, quoting Genesis 18:27
44 Rudolph Otto, *The Idea of the Holy*, 11.

the special way in which it is reflected in the mind in terms of *feeling*."[45] (My emphases.)

As we see, Otto affirms at every turn that the numinous is only truly encountered by means of human *feelings* or emotions. If we may equate, however, Otto's 'pre-moral' idea of 'the holy' with Guénon's 'metaphysical'—both being essentially different from the physical/'natural' world—then Otto's hypothesis of 'feeling' as the primary means of human interaction with the numinous does *not* describe how, according to Guénon, the peoples of traditional societies interacted with the divine/metaphysical. It is, according to Guénon, non-emotive 'intellectual intuition' that provides such a means. As implied earlier, the traditional idea of intellectual intuition discussed by Guénon is not the popular idea of 'following one's intuition' or having a 'hunch' or 'gut-feeling' about something or other, but is, rather, the direct and *exact* knowing of eternal truths, such as may be found for example, according to Guénon, in the Hindu Vedas. Otto's notion of a subjective human 'creature-feeling' towards 'the holy' or 'numinous' is, therefore, like these popular ideas of 'intuition,' according to Guénon, at odds with the traditional perspective.

Otto considers the subject of symbolism in *The Idea of the Holy* when he claims that the 'religious bliss' inspired by human contact with the 'numen' is "purely a felt experience only to be indicated symbolically by 'ideograms.'"[46] According to Guénon, however, this thesis is not consonant with the traditional outlook. For, just as 'feelings' are, from the traditional perspective, *not* a validation of contact with metaphysical Reality, symbols are *not* a means to 'indicate' a presumed 'felt experience' of the 'numinous.' On the contrary, according to Guénon, the modern attachment to 'sentiment' that Otto seems to extol usually serves as an epistemological impediment to understanding or accessing 'the holy'—the meta-physical. The ecstatic 'trance states'

---

45 Rudolph Otto, *The Idea of the Holy*, 11–12.
46 Rudolph Otto, *The Idea of the Holy*, 59.

experienced by the shamans of traditional societies, for example, that allow their 'flights' to, what they see as, other 'levels' of existence are, from the traditional perspective that Guénon discusses, neither the products of their great 'love' for the divine nor of their hyper-attuned sentiments or exemplary sympathy for human suffering. They are rather, in Tradition, only the products of long and arduous training, method, and *discipline*.

Universalism

According to Guénon and Eliade, although they are quite rare in the modern world, traditional societies remain an eternal potentiality. This is because their existence is, for these authors, essentially *not* the product of transient 'economic forces,' 'ecological pressures,' or other supposed 'historical' or physical 'causes,' but rather the consequence of 'transmission,' by qualified 'initiates,' of a 'higher' knowledge of a meta-physical, or 'spiritual,' Reality. The ideas of 'transmission' and 'initiation' are, for Guénon, central to an understanding of the Primordial Tradition. Traditional knowledge, for Guénon, derived by means of what he calls intellectual intuition, is, according to him, potential in *all* human beings, and must be consciously cultivated by humans in order to be 'realized.' This 'cultivation,' as I call it, may be accomplished, according to Guénon, by means of either: 1) specific disciplinary methods, such as the Hindu *yogas*, or 2) social forms of 'initiation.' Guénon states in *The Reign of Quantity & the Signs of the Times*, however, that "there is nothing and can be nothing truly traditional that does not contain some element of a supra-human order."[47] The discovery of that 'supra-human' knowledge that, according to Guénon, constitutes Tradition is, therefore, the exclusive product of those methods of *conscious effort* that lead to a 'realization'

---

[47] René Guénon, *The Reign of Quantity & the Signs of the Times*, trans. Lord Northbourne (Hillsdale, NY: Sophia Perennis, 2001 [originally published in 1945 as *Le Règne de la quantité et les signes des temps*]), 211.

of, or 'union' with —*yoga*—the 'supra-human.' The disciplinary path of *jnana-yoga* that is emphasized in the *Advaita Vedanta darshana* is an example of a means of both initiation and transmission by which 'union' with the supra-human is made possible.[48] Concerning the idea of 'transmission,' specifically, Guénon states in *Perspectives on Initiation* that "initiatic transmission...is essentially the transmission of a spiritual influence,"[49] by which he means a meta-physical influence that cannot be quantified or expressed fully by means of 'ordinary' communication. Transmission of the 'spiritual influence,' according to Guénon, is ideally *spoken* by master to student throughout a lineage of masters and students over long periods of time, hundreds or thousands of years. Combined with other initiatic elements, this continuing action constitutes what Guénon terms 'regular conditions.' Absent these 'regular conditions,' the written language of traditional symbolism approximates the 'influence' of Tradition that is carried by traditional initiates. In the latter case, however, the student who 'studies' written symbols must *already* be especially receptive to the power of such symbols in order to have any chance of 'absorbing' the spiritual influence that they are meant to transmit. Guénon states that

> the complete knowledge of a rite [ritual] is entirely devoid of any effective value if it has been obtained outside of regular conditions. It is for this reason...that in the Hindu tradition a *mantra* learned otherwise than from the mouth of an authorized *guru* [spiritual teacher] is without effect because it is not 'vivified' by the presence of the spiritual influence whose vehicle it is uniquely destined to be. This...is why, even where traditional teachings are more or less completely available in written form, they still continue to be transmitted orally, for this is indispensable for their full effect.[50]

---

48 Robin Waterfield, *René Guénon & the Future of the West*, 61.
49 René Guénon, *Perspectives on Initiation*, ed. Samuel D. Fohr, trans. Henry D. Fohr (Hillsdale, NY: Sophia Perennis, 2001, [originally published in 1946 as *Aperçus sur l'initiation*]), 26.
50 René Guénon, *Perspectives on Initiation*, 53–54.

While Guénon focuses mostly in his books on Eastern (Asian) forms of initiation, such as those related to the admittance of new members into the Hindu *Brahmin* and *Kshatriya* castes,[51] he also discusses what he describes as the "possible survivals of certain rare groups of medieval Christian Hermeticists [,]…the Compagnonnage and Masonry" in the West, describing these groups as those that "can claim an authentically traditional origin and a real initiatic transmission."[52]

Guénon and Eliade both argue for versions of what is called 'universalism,' the philosophical perspective that contends that particular objects, events, and thoughts are 'instantiations' of universal 'forms' or (for Eliade) 'archetypes' that exist 'beyond' the sensible, physical, universe. Plato's so-called Theory of Forms is, as we mentioned in the *Introduction*, for Eliade the most thorough exposition in Western history of metaphysical universalism, but variations on Plato's speculations concerning non-physical ideas have arisen time and again throughout the history of Western philosophy. As Alfred North Whitehead wrote in *Process and Reality*, "The safest general characterization of the European philosophical tradition is that it consists of a series of footnotes to Plato."[53]

In modern times, the philosophical perspective known as 'structuralism' presents yet another variation on 'universalism.' It argues that the many similarities discovered worldwide among both human minds and human artifacts can be accounted for by appealing to fundamental 'structures' that are common to *all* human minds and cultures. One could say that structuralism is simply a 'modern twist' on

---

51 René Guénon, *Perspectives on Initiation*, 94.

52 The editor of *Perspectives on Initiation*, Samuel D. Fohr, notes that "[t]he Compagnonnage is closely related to Freemasonry, but is largely restricted to France, where it is still an active presence….The word 'Compagnonnage' itself, of course, derives from the Latin *cum panis*, 'sharers of the bread', as does its English cognate 'companion.'" René Guénon, *Perspectives on Initiation*, 34.

53 Alfred North Whitehead, *Process and Reality* (New York, New York: Free Press, 1979), 39.

Plato's Theory of Forms, and that Guénon's and Eliade's insights into traditional societies are 'structuralist' in the sense that they both often discuss the 'universal' traits of traditional, or archaic, societies as well as of the humans that constitute those societies. British social anthropologist Edmund Leach states in his essay "Structuralism" that "the term *structuralism* was not used before 1950,"[54] but Guénon published nearly all of his books *before* that year. Of course, the simple failure to use, or to record for posterity, a *word* is no proof that the *idea* was not already in circulation. More important are the substantial differences that divide the perspective of modern structuralism from the perspective that constitutes what Guénon and Eliade call Tradition. In the *Oxford Dictionary of Philosophy*, the philosopher Simon Blackburn defines 'structuralism,' in its application to human civilizations, as the theory that "behind local variations in the surface phenomena there are constant laws of abstract culture."[55] The phrase 'abstract culture' refers to an *ideal form* that, according to structuralists, all, or most, cultures seem to share. In their attempts to understand this ideal form — the 'constant laws of abstract culture' — in traditional societies, however, some structuralists have, by means of the limitations intrinsic to their sociological and psychological theories, made certain theoretical *reductions* of the traditional worldview that is described by Guénon and Eliade. Although they have ostensibly wished to understand the 'constant laws' of the diverse cultures of the pre-modern, as well as of the modern, world, structuralists have sometimes failed to take into account the *actual beliefs* of traditional/archaic peoples.

---

54 Edmund Leach, "Structuralism," in *The Encyclopedia of Religion*, 16 volumes, ed. Mircea Eliade (New York: Macmillan Publishing Company, 1987), 14:54.

55 Simon Blackburn, *Oxford Dictionary of Philosophy*, second edition revised (Oxford: Oxford University Press, 2008), "structuralism." We make no attempt here to reconcile the many definitions of 'structuralism' floating about. The definitions of, and comments concerning, 'structuralism' that we provide are, however, entirely representative of a great many 'structuralists' past and present, and that is all that is necessary for the purposes of this book.

The primary distinction between modern structuralists and those individuals, such as Guénon and Eliade, who appreciate the commitments of Tradition[56] is that the epistemological axioms of modern structuralists are inevitably *physical* rather than *meta-physical*. In 'Structuralism,' Leach raises the problem of 'context' that we mentioned earlier in this chapter, specifically with regard to the various modern opinions on how comparative mythology 'should' be studied. According to Leach, one approach to the study of mythology understands myth as that which is

> made to serve as a precedent for customary political conventions which are still significant in the societies in question. In this approach to myth, the social context in which the stories are told is fundamental; a myth story isolated from its proper context is devoid of meaning.[57]

---

56 I hesitate to use the term 'traditionalist' to refer to either Guénon or Eliade here, tempting as it may seem to be from the reader's perspective, for the reason that Guénon himself rejects the term. In *The Reign of Quantity & the Signs of the Times*, Guénon states that 'traditionalists' are "people who only have a sort of tendency or aspiration toward tradition without really knowing anything at all about it; this is the measure of the distance dividing the 'traditionalist' spirit from the truly traditional spirit, for the latter implies a real knowledge, being indeed in a sense the same as that knowledge. In short, the 'traditionalist' is and can be no more than a mere 'seeker', and that is why he is always in danger of going astray, not being in possession of the principles that alone could provide him with infallible guidance; and his danger is all the greater because he will find in his path, like so many ambushes, all the false ideals set on foot by the power of illusion, which has a keen interest in preventing him from reaching the true goal of his search." René Guénon, *The Reign of Quantity & the Signs of the Times*, 210. Guénon similarly stands forth on the use of the term 'system' to describe traditional, or 'pure,' metaphysics. According to Guénon, pure metaphysics isn't susceptible of systematization because it is *un*systematic by its very nature. In *Introduction to the Study of the Hindu Doctrines*, Guénon states for example that "[p]ure metaphysics necessarily excludes all systematization, for a system cannot avoid being a closed and limited conception, contained in its entirety within boundaries more or less narrowly defined, and as such is in no wise reconcilable with the universality of metaphysics." René Guénon, *Introduction to the Study of the Hindu Doctrines*, 98–99.

57 Edmund Leach, "Structuralism," in *The Encyclopedia of Religion*, 14: 59.

Leach contrasts this approach with that of the Belgian structuralist Claude Lévi-Strauss, whose work scholars adhering to the first approach would see, according to Leach, "as largely a waste of time, since the whole exercise is devoted to the cross-cultural comparison of abbreviated versions of manifestly untrue stories completely isolated from their very diverse original social setting."[58] By the tone of his comment, it would seem that Leach has played his hand here concerning his own opinion on the matter. He subsequently states, in a rather flippant manner, that

> [s]ome of the myth analyses which Lévi-Strauss published prior to 1962 took note of a functional (contextual) factor, but in his later work, he seems to assume that myth is an undifferentiated, species-wide phenomenon which the human mind is predisposed to generate in much the same way as it is predisposed to generate speech. He seeks to show how the patterning and combination of myth stories are capable of conveying meaning, but the meaning in question is very general and not context-determined. The superficial differences between the myths of various cultures are treated as comparable to the differences of phonology and grammar in different human languages. At the level of innate capacity, the deep structure is always the same. The myths that appear in ethnographic records are all transformations of a single universal myth, which, like phonology, is structured according to a system of distinctive features based on binary oppositions. It follows that the themes with which this mythology is concerned are ultimately human universals of a physiological kind such as sex, metabolism, orientation, and life/death, rather than the solution of local, culturally determined moral issues.[59]

In some ways, Leach's interpretation of Lévi-Strauss's approach to myth, and therefore to the peoples who lived by (the archaic form of) myth, is quite similar to the approaches of both Guénon and Eliade. For example, Guénon and Eliade would agree that myth is a "species-wide phenomenon," that the "differences between the myths of various

---

58 Edmund Leach, "Structuralism," in *The Encyclopedia of Religion*, 14: 59.
59 Edmund Leach, "Structuralism," in *The Encyclopedia of Religion*, 14: 59–60.

cultures" are "superficial differences," that "at the level of innate capacity, the deep structure [of myth] is always the same," and that "[t]he myths that appear in ethnographic records are all transformations of a single universal myth." What Guénon and Eliade would *not* agree with are Lévi-Strauss's contentions, in Leach's words, that "the human mind is predisposed to *generate*" [my emphasis] myth(s) and that "the themes with which...mythology is concerned are ultimately human universals of a physiological kind, such as sex, metabolism... life/death," etc. Here is revealed Lévi-Strauss's commitment to the 'physicalist' axioms of *modern* 'structuralism' that I mentioned earlier, axioms that are opposed, according to Guénon and Eliade, to the essentially *meta*-physical 'traditional' understanding of existence. To the degree, however, that structuralism does *not* attempt to understand traditional/archaic cultures from the perspective of their 'transcendent' *meta*-physical outlook, indicates the degree to which *modern* structuralists differ from Tradition. It is still the case, however, that Guénon and Eliade, in their emphasis on the traditional/archaic belief in 'archetypes' or 'universals,' *are* 'structuralists' of a kind, and perhaps of a more consistent kind than modern structuralists are.

Another kind of difference between Guénon's and Eliade's perspective and the modern structuralists' approach to the study of myth is the structuralist presumption of a significant 'unconscious' element in the traditional/archaic *comprehension* of myth. According to Leach,

> But the structuralists assume that there is always another deeper, unconscious meaning [of myths and rituals] which is of equal or perhaps greater significance [than their 'superficial' meanings]. The structuralist thesis is that such deeper meanings are apprehended by the listener to a myth, or by the participant-observer in a ritual situation, at a subliminal, aesthetic or religious level of consciousness. Structuralist analytical procedures are supposed to make such hidden meanings explicit.[60]

---

60 Edmund Leach, "Structuralism," in *The Encyclopedia of Religion*, 14:60.

This statement outlines the 'psychological' approach to understanding mythological archetypes that may be found, most prominently, in the works of C. G. Jung. It is an interpretive approach to the study of myth that Eliade, specifically, attempts to distance himself from when he defines the 'archetypes' of Tradition as, properly understood, *metaphysical*. The problem, from Guénon's perspective, with appealing to 'unconscious' meanings of myths and rituals, and to a 'subliminal' or 'religious' level of consciousness where such meanings may be 'apprehended,' is that it is an appeal to a 'lower' level of consciousness or being, rather than to a 'higher' level of consciousness or being. Such an appeal, according to Guénon, betrays a view of the nature of existence that is in *diametrical opposition* to the methods and goal of traditional initiation, which consists of cultivating 'higher' levels of consciousness or awareness in, as Leach calls them, 'participant-observers.' From the perspective of Tradition, for Guénon, it is the function of myths, as well as the symbols that constitute and convey them, to aid traditional peoples in achieving such 'higher' levels of consciousness, for this is what is required for the successful 'transmission' of Tradition. Guénon argues in *The Reign of Quantity & the Signs of the Times* that "the truly traditional spirit…implies a real knowledge, being indeed in a sense the same as that knowledge."[61] This 'real knowledge' is, according to Guénon, that which in traditional societies results from an *increase* in consciousness, not a decrease. For it is only, from the perspective of Tradition, in the *increase of awareness* of the authentic 'Self' (*Atman* in *Vedanta*) that an 'individual,' as Guénon says, becomes 'the same as knowledge,' or, more specifically, becomes 'intellectual intuition' *itself*, which is the ultimate goal of Tradition.

Guénon's understanding of Tradition, as opposed to the modern structuralist position, can perhaps best be expressed metaphorically in the terms of the following conditional statement: *if* one wishes to understand, and not to merely describe or explain, how children play,

---

61 René Guénon, *The Reign of Quantity & the Signs of the Times*, 210.

one must first *believe* in the fantasy world that children often live in, as well as in the beings that inhabit that world. For, it is essential to note, if one does not so *believe*, then one does not truly *understand* how children play. One, perhaps unconsciously, rather *projects* a 'model' in order to predict how children 'behave' in such and such situations and under such and such circumstances. This example is not meant to persuade the reader that traditional peoples are like children compared to modern people, nor that they live in a 'fantasy world,' although in my own mind the fantasy world of children is perhaps *more real* than the 'real world' that adults often refer to so menacingly and seriously. The essential point to be made is that, if one attempts to understand a phenomenon through the lens of one's *own* notions rather than through the lens of the ideas of those people whose understanding of the phenomenon is the very object of one's pursuit, it is most probable that one will see something *entirely different* from what one actually *wishes* to see. In *Introduction to the Study of the Hindu Doctrines*, Guénon states that

> in fact the metaphysical point of view is itself radically opposed to the historical point of view, or what passes for such, and this opposition will be seen to amount not only to a question of method, but also, what is far more important, to a real question of principle....One might say in fact that metaphysics can only be studied metaphysically. No notice must be taken of contingencies such as individual influences, which are strictly non-existent from this point of view and cannot affect the doctrine in any way; the latter, being of the universal order, is thereby essentially supra-individual, and necessarily remains untouched by such influences. Even circumstances of time and space, we must repeat, can only affect the outward expression but not the essence of the doctrine.[62]

Modern 'structuralism,' at least in many of its forms, does not, from the perspective of Guénon's and Eliade's expositions of Tradition, attempt to understand Reality *as it is experienced by* traditional peoples.

---

62 René Guénon, *Introduction to the Study of the Hindu Doctrines*, 74.

It does not, in other words, make any effort to cultivate the traditionally meta-physical understanding of existence. Rather, it attempts to *project*, along 'physicalist' lines, a linguistic and psychological *reduction of* the traditional perspective *onto* the *authentic* traditional perspective and then pretend that this projection is 'understanding.'

At its *root*, we may say that modern structuralism agrees with the 'traditional' perspective that goes back to Plato and, according to Eliade and Guénon both, *before*. It is that, under superficial differences (Particulars) lie substantial commonalities (Universals, 'archetypes,' or 'Forms'). Leach observes in *Culture and Communication* that structuralists "infer that it is necessary to study a number of contrasted empirical examples…before we can be confident that we know what is the common abstract 'reality' which underlies them all."[63] Such is the essence of empirical science. But what is this "abstract 'reality'" that Leach speaks of? In *Introduction to the Study of the Hindu Doctrines*, Guénon states that scientific knowledge "is derived from reason, which has the general for its domain," whereas metaphysical knowledge "is derived from the pure intellect, which has the Universal for its domain."[64] According to Guénon, empirical science makes 'general' claims about the nature of existence because no "number of contrasted empirical examples," however great, can substantiate Universal claims. The modern generic 'structuralist,' however, if s/he subscribes to the spirit of empirical science, wishes to derive information about what Leach calls the 'collectivity' of 'the human mind.'[65] As a 'modernist,' however, the structuralist must, because s/he does not admit the existence of meta-physical Reality, submit to the limitations of empirical science and not search for the *Universal* 'human mind' but, rather, for the 'general' human mind which, for the modernist, is an *abstraction*. The *modern* structuralist, then, although s/he admits the existence

---

63 Edmund Leach, *Culture and Communication* (Cambridge: Cambridge University Press, 1976), 5.
64 René Guénon, *Introduction to the Study of the Hindu Doctrines*, 76–77.
65 Edmund Leach, *Culture and Communication*, 5.

of abstractions and generalizations, *never* admits the existence of Universals *because* they are meta-physical. S/he appeals to a weak and dissembling idea of 'universal' (the common or 'general') rather than to a strong and consistent idea of Universal. According to Guénon's and Eliade's interpretation of the 'traditional' perspective, however, the so-called "common abstract reality" that Leach says structuralists believe 'underlies' "a number of contrasted empirical examples" is *not* just a generalization or an abstraction. Nor is it, for that matter, something inferred by means of repeated empirical observation. It is, rather, *Real* to the 'highest' degree and accessed only, according to Guénon, by means of that 'highest' mode of knowing in Tradition that is often communicated by means of the 'device' of symbols: 'intellectual intuition.'

Guénon would say that traditional peoples *knew* that metaphysical Reality exists, and Eliade at least admitted this conclusion for the purposes of trying to *actually understand*, rather than 'project' upon, the perspectives of the societies that he studied. If, however, we accept, with the structuralists, that there is a *common* deep 'structure' of 'the human mind' that exists in all *individual* human beings, then it is no great leap to presume that at least some forms of language, and the thoughts behind these forms, are 'universal' to human *societies* as well. A 'universal' (common) mental structure, however, implies 'universal' (common) *ideas*. If this can be shown, then it is eminently reasonable to propose that there are some kinds of human actions and constructions, as well as ideas, that are 'the same' — 'universal' — around the world and throughout time, so that the 'universality' (commonality) of the idea of 'human,' for example, is made entirely plausible. An *idea*, however, is, in its essence, Universal — meta-physical — not *merely* 'universal' (common). But, if one (Universal) idea exists, then it stands to reason that *other* (Universal) ideas exist as well. And this, of course, is what we all find in our daily experience of the world. The Universal idea of 'human,' specifically, is key to Guénon's and Eliade's argument that 'traditional peoples' have existed in different places over very long stretches of time, since Guénon and Eliade both argue that *all* humans who were *truly* part of traditional societies, no matter where or when, are 'the same' in the sense that their comprehension of traditional symbols was/is the same. This is a 'traditional' rewording of, according to Leach, the apparent 'structuralist' thesis that, if there exists a "collectivity — 'the human mind'" that is fundamentally 'the same' among all individual humans, then it stands to reason that each individual example of 'the human mind' must, theoretically at least, have access to the same ideas, and, therefore, to the same *symbols*. For what *is* 'the human mind' if it is not that 'thing' in the universe that ponders and analyzes ideas? And *how* is it that these things called 'ideas' are encapsulated *for* 'the human mind' if *not* by means of those things that we call symbols? All of this said, one could never, strictly speaking, scientifically test whether *all* humans were, and are, capable of using, and understanding in the same way, the same Universal language since Universal does not, and *cannot* as Guénon argues, apply to that which is the object of empirical testing.

The validity of the perspective of *strict* 'Universalism,' and the existence of *absolutely* universal structures, is impossible to prove within the confines of inductive empirical science. I, nevertheless, rely in this book upon inductive reasoning to confirm the existence of ideas and symbols that are, at least on some level according to Guénon and Eliade, 'universal' to cultures around the world and throughout history. In the study of symbols, one can never know whether s/he has accounted for *all* cases ('instantiations') of a particular symbol. In the sciences, however, generalizations are commonly made well before *all* cases of a phenomenon are analyzed or even discovered. In fact, this is always true. When astrophysicists, for example, make claims about the process of star formation, they are generalizing from *particular* observations of *particular* stars to *general* conclusions. It doesn't matter whether they have observed one hundred stars or one hundred million. They can *never* know enough about stars to make *strictly* Universal claims about the process of star formation — from the perspective of inductive science. As in the example considered earlier of Newton's 'law of universal gravitation,' however, the term 'universal' is often employed in a less than absolute sense. Thus, we may note the *many* examples of *apparently* Universal structures that make reasonable the claims of *some* variety of 'universalism,' especially if we specify the boundaries of that universalism. The phrase "from the traditional perspective" outlines the boundaries of 'universalism' as that term is employed in this book. Universalism is, therefore, to be thought of here from the perspective of that particular mode of human experience that Eliade and Guénon term 'traditional.'

There are striking similarities among the artifacts of what Eliade and Guénon term 'traditional' societies or civilizations around the world, whether these be physical objects or *ideas*. These similarities, which are discernible across long stretches of time and vast distances, prompt certain questions among the inquisitive. One cannot help but ask, for example: is it debatable that the things called pyramids were built not only in ancient Egypt, but in ancient Mesoamerica and ancient China in quite different pre-modern historical eras? Or: is it debatable that sea-going vessels were devised and employed by both the Vikings of Scandinavia and the Polynesians of the South Pacific, who had no contact with one another? Further: is it debatable that, from time immemorial, humans in widely different geographical locales have understood the rudiments of arithmetic and have had the capacity for, and use of, language? Again: is there any doubt that tool use among ancient humans, in general, has been revealed in the furthest reaches of the globe, and that this tool use was very similar in all cases? Finally: is it not true that myths of a great flood, creation myths, and myths of 'the gods' descending from 'Heaven' are to be found in *many* cultures around the world, separated by vast distances, and stretching back (at least) thousands of years? Once one begins to examine the 'universal' patterns to be discerned within human societies throughout the ages, one should, I submit, *not* stop with the remnants of their material culture or the languages employed by them, but, rather, continue on to examine the *ideas* underlying the material culture and languages. According to Guénon and Eliade, reverence for the *essentially* meta-physical nature of existence is among these 'universal' ideas.

It would seem that, in order to explain the innumerable similarities of human cultures around the world and throughout the course of history — especially their use of symbols, for our purposes — one has two broad methodological options: 1) 'diffusionism' and 2) 'independent origination.' Either, that is: 1) an idea 'originated' in one place and then 'spread' to other places or 2) 'the same' idea originated independently in many different places. One problem with the first possibility is that it is quite often observed that the same ideas originate on opposite ends of the earth with *no discernible contact* between the originators. If survival mechanisms and survival strategies may be considered 'ideas' of a sort, then this state of affairs goes very far back indeed. For, consider the following variety of 'ideas' that seem to have emerged independently around the globe, rather than being diffused from one central source: 1) the idea of constructing shelters, 2) the idea of tool use, 3) the idea of using beasts of burden, 4) the idea of stock-piling food, and 5) the idea of a 'spirit world' of some kind — all arising in the most widespread locales possible. Recognizing the possibility, then, of the 'independent emergence' not only of artifacts but of *ideas* in various locales and times, we may ask the following questions that are pertinent to the subject matter of this book: 1) When a researcher sees a serpent with wings depicted in both ancient Mesoamerican *and* ancient Egyptian art, and these two examples are separated by thousands of miles and thousands of years, what is s/he to conclude? 2) When a researcher sees a serpent with wings *juxtaposed with a circle* in the art of ancient Egypt, Persia, Greece, Italy, China, and Mexico, what is s/he to conclude? 3) When a researcher sees a snake or a dragon with an egg or an orb, either held in its mouth or in one of its 'claws' or simply nearby the beast, depicted in the art of ancient North America *and* ancient Asia, what is s/he to conclude? There is, again, no empirical evidence of *strict* 'Universalism' in the world of symbols, no absolute proof that every instance of 'traditional' serpent/dragon symbolism, in particular, has the same meaning. Any philosopher knows, however, that *strict* Universality can never be proven by recourse to empirical data because empirical data only support inductive reasoning, and inductive reasoning does *not* support *strictly* Universal claims. More than this, however, anyone who simply understands the *meaning* of 'Universal' knows that even such seemingly pervasive characteristics of the physical universe as the forces of gravity and electromagnetism can never be *proven* as strictly Universal forces. Newton's 'law of gravitation' is not, strictly speaking, a truly *Universal* law; it is merely very pervasive. It is, as Guénon would say, 'general.' In this book, therefore, I do not, and cannot from the perspective of inductive knowledge, make any *strictly* Universal claims. I do *not* argue that every case of serpent and dragon symbolism to be found in the world represents the same thing or has the same exact meaning. And neither did Guénon or Eliade. What I do argue is that in *traditional* cultures around the world, and throughout history, in *many* cases — perhaps most — there is one meaning common to serpent and dragon symbolism. Although they differed, at least in terms of terminology, on what that meaning is, this is what Guénon and Eliade argued for as well.

In *The Abolition of Man*, C. S. Lewis noted, "As Plato said that the Good was 'beyond existence' and Wordsworth that through virtue the stars were strong, so the Indian masters say that the gods themselves are born of the *Rta* and obey it."[66] Ancient cultures around the world have, for millennia, promoted similar paradigms for comprehending the cosmos and for acting 'properly' within it. These cultures differ in their specifics, naturally, but there is, as Lewis illustrates, a level of

---

66 C. S. Lewis, *The Abolition of Man: Reflections on education with special reference to the teaching of English in the upper forms of schools* (New York, New York: HarperCollins, 1944), 17.

'universalism' among their claims that is undeniable. *Of course* there is no apodictic proof, from empirical data, for *absolute* 'Universalism.' In *An Enquiry Concerning Human Understanding*, Hume convincingly argued that, although interesting 'conjoinings' seem to playfully abound for very long periods of time, nothing can 'prove' a *necessary* causal relationship between events. Concerning the idea of causation, specifically, which is perhaps the most beloved 'universal' in human history, Hume states:

> But there is nothing in a number of instances, different from every single instance, which is supposed to be exactly similar; except only, that after a repetition of similar instances, the mind is carried by habit, upon the appearance of one event, to expect its usual attendant, and to believe that it will exist. This connexion, therefore, which we feel in the mind, this customary transition of the imagination from one object to its usual attendant, is the sentiment or impression from which we form the idea of power or necessary connexion.[67]

We live in a universe in which there are a seemingly endless number of things called 'stars' that have many traits in common (but also some different) and which exist at vast distances from one another. It is the same case for those very similar objects (with some differences, admittedly) that humans have termed 'planets.' And it is the same with those things that humans call electrons and protons, quarks and leptons, and all other 'elementary' particles. It is the same with ears, and with noses, with eyes and with mouths, with hands and with feet. It is the same with houses and with temples, with saddles and ropes, and, finally, it is the same with *ideas*, and with those things that, for humans, express certain *kinds* of ideas: *symbols*. The old Aristotelian common sense still holds true: there *are* Universals *in* Particulars, although not all Particulars express these Universals to an equal degree. If there were *not* such things as Universals, then my words and

---

[67] David Hume, *An Enquiry Concerning Human Understanding* (New York: Barnes & Noble, Inc., 2004 [originally published in 1772]), 57–58.

statements and hypotheses written down in this document couldn't even be debated. For how could we debate the idea of 'universal' if we have no examples that seem to illustrate it particularly well, like the serpent/dragon symbol?

CHAPTER 4

The Symbolism of the Serpent/Dragon in the Context of Guénon's 'Hindu Doctrines' and Eliade's Interpretation of the Traditional Idea of Chaos

Traditional Metaphysics and Epistemology in the Hindu *Vedanta*

In *Knowledge and the Sacred*, Seyyed Nasr states that

> Guénon set about to expound metaphysics and cosmology from the traditional point of view and in relation to and as contained in the sapiential [wisdom] teachings of various traditions. His point of departure was Hinduism.[1]

The "traditional point of view," as we noted in Chapter 3, is characterized by what Guénon terms 'intellectuality,' the ruling perspective of traditional peoples that accounts for their ability to appreciate, contemplate, and interact with a 'Principial' meta-physical reality. As Nasr points out, however, the best remaining expression of intellectuality, according to Guénon, is Hinduism, more specifically the orthodox Hindu *darshanas* ("'points of view' within the doctrine") which, as we

---

1   Seyyed Hossein Nasr, *Knowledge and the Sacred*, 104.

noted in the *Introduction*, Guénon refers to as the 'Hindu Doctrines.' Among the Hindu Doctrines, Guénon focuses primarily in his works on the tradition of thought and disciplinary practice that is called *Vedanta*, and even more specifically on that version of *Vedanta* that is known as *Advaita Vedanta*.² Intellectuality, or 'intellectual intuition,' is Guénon's generic name for what is called *paravidya* in *Vedanta*, the 'direct knowing' of the absolute metaphysical Reality ('Principle') and 'ground' of all existence that is called *Brahman*. Intellectuality, as noted in Chapter 3, constitutes for Guénon a *non*-rational, although not *ir*rational, form of knowing, one that is *not* acquired by means of scholarship or discursive reasoning, but rather by means of rituals, initiations, or disciplinary practices, such as the *yogas*, that prepare the individual *in its entirety* for 'realization' of *Brahman*. The example presented previously from the Bhagavad-Gita of Arjuna's sudden 'realization' of the divinity of Krishna is a classic Hindu example of intellectual intuition.³

As *Brahman* is, for Guénon, simply the *Vedantic* concept for the 'Principial' metaphysical Reality that is, according to him, recognized

---

2   *Advaita Vedanta*, as a developed potentiality of the ancient Hindu *Vedanta darshana*, is attributable primarily to the eighth-entury Indian thinker Samkara. In *Fundamentals of Indian Philosophy*, Puligandla states that "Samkara's *Advaita Vedanta* is the most systematic articulation of the Upanisadic insights and vision of man and world; as such, it is the flower of Hindu wisdom, which subsumes under itself the best in all the other orthodox systems....In short, Samkara's *Advaita Vedanta* is the flesh and blood of the Hindu culture." Ramakrishna Puligandla, *Fundamentals of Indian Philosophy*, 275-76.

3   "Having spoken these words, Krishna, the master of yoga, revealed to Arjuna his most exalted, lordly form....There, within the body of the God of gods, Arjuna saw all the manifold forms of the universe united as one. Filled with amazement, his hair standing on end in ecstasy, he bowed before the Lord with joined palms and spoke these words. O Lord, I see within your body all the gods and every living creature. I see Brahma, the Creator, seated on a lotus.... You are the Lord of all Creation, and the cosmos is your body....You are the supreme, changeless Reality, the one thing to be known." Bhagavad-Gita 11:9, 13-18.

by *all* traditional peoples, *paravidya* is, likewise for Guénon, the *Vedantic* concept for the 'intellectual intuition' that all traditionally trained peoples are capable of. The nature of *Brahman* is itself the best explanation for why intellectual intuition is the only form of knowledge capable of 'realizing' the meta-physical. According to Waterfield in *René Guénon and the Future of the West*,

> All begins and ends with *Brahma* [*Brahman*], the Principial Unity, which is beyond all conception and only recognizable as the experience of *saccindananda*, i.e., 'being' (*sac*) [sic], 'consciousness' (*cit*), and 'bliss' (*ananda*). Nothing can be said about *Brahma*, for speech is a function of the world of manifestation, so whatever can be said must therefore be partial and inadequate. The only way *Brahma* can be known is through the experience of direct intellectual intuition.[4]

Puligandla's most succinct definition of *paravidya* in *Fundamentals of Indian Philosophy* is "the higher knowledge…by which the infinite and imperishable *Brahman* is attained."[5] According to Guénon, *all* traditional forms of intellectual intuition are *meta*physics because the absolute Reality is 'Universal' and, as Guénon contends in *Introduction to the Study of the Hindu Doctrines*, "metaphysics…is essentially the knowledge of the Universal, or, if preferred, the knowledge of principles belonging to the universal order."[6] Guénon similarly argues in *The Symbolism of the Cross*, as we noted in Chapter 3, that "no doctrine that confines itself to the consideration of individual beings can merit the name of metaphysics, whatever may be its interest and value in other respects."[7] The methods and practices for 'realization' of *Brahman* in South Asian versions of Tradition (which may collectively be called 'doctrines of the Universal') are anything but a "consideration of individual beings." This makes such methods and practices

---

4 Robin Waterfield, *René Guénon and the Future of the West*, 60–61.
5 Ramakrishna Puligandla, *Fundamentals of Indian Philosophy*, 223–224.
6 René Guénon, *Introduction to the Study of the Hindu Doctrines*, 71.
7 René Guénon, *The Symbolism of the Cross*, 7.

of a fundamentally different kind than those employed in the modern empirical sciences, for, as alluded to in Chapter 3, any field of investigation that is based upon empirical observation of *individual* beings, or 'particulars,' such as the empirical sciences of biology, chemistry, sociology, etc., cannot, for Guénon, 'know' in the 'highest' sense of the term *meta*-physical reality: the Universal. Because of this, all such 'special sciences' are, in total, only *a* way of knowing, and only concerning phenomena of that derivative domain of manifestation that is, in its entirety, for Guénon, but an incomplete reflection of the 'higher' reality of *Brahman*. As noted in Chapter 1, Nasr states that Guénon's

> greatest criticism of modern science was its lack of metaphysical principles and its pretension, or rather the pretension of those who claim to speak from the "scientific point of view," to be *the* science or *the* way of knowing, whereas it is *a* science or *a* way of knowing concerned with a very limited domain of reality.[8]

In sum, the scientific 'general' is, again, not for Guénon equivalent to the metaphysical Universal. Grand generalizations that are, therefore, based in the inductive sciences upon the observation and analysis of 'particular' objects and events are, for Guénon, *not* equivalent to *paravidya* of the Universal. Similarly, as we stated with respect to Rudolph Otto's contentions in *The Idea of the Holy*, the *generally* similar *emotional* reactions of individuals are, for Guénon, *not* revelatory of truth, since truth is a Universal *meta*-physical Reality that is not accessible by means of emotional states which are always reactions to 'particular' *physical* phenomena.

When Guénon gave his only public lecture, in 1925, he spoke, according to Waterfield, of "the metaphysics without a name, since it is neither Eastern nor Western but universal."[9] Unlike what are called human 'inventions,' Guénon often reiterated that 'universal

---

8   Seyyed Hossein Nasr, *Knowledge and the Sacred*, 103.
9   Robin Waterfield, *René Guénon and the Future of the West: The Life and Writings of a 20th-Century Metaphysician*, 41.

metaphysics' is *not* the product of human culture or civilization, but rather exists as an eternal bequest from a transcendent Source to all humans who prove themselves worthy of its admission. As Gai Eaton observed in *The Richest Vein*, Guénon

> believes that there exists a Universal Tradition, revealed to humanity at the beginning of the present cycle of time, but partially lost....[His] primary concern is less with the detailed forms of Tradition and the history of its decline than with its kernel, the pure and changeless knowledge which is still accessible to man through the channels provided by traditional doctrine.[10]

Within the Universal (Primordial) Tradition, according to Guénon, all physical as well as psychological events are believed to be manifestations of the meta-physical Reality that is called *Brahman* in *Vedanta*. Along with the hard sciences of physics, chemistry, and biology, therefore, the disciplines of sociology and psychology are also limited to the study of the particulars of the physical/'natural' level of existence, and in no way constitute studies of that intellectually accessible Reality that is, from the perspective of Tradition, the cause of both living *and* non-living beings. In *The Multiple States of the Being*, Guénon notes, for example, that

> [p]sychology... only concern[s] itself with what we may call 'phenomenal consciousness,' that is, consciousness considered exclusively in its relations with phenomena, and without asking whether or not this is the expression of something of another order which, by very definition, no longer belongs to the psychological domain.[11]

The modern tendency to reduce psychological states to their physical 'causes' in order to purportedly 'explain' those states is, from the

---

10 Gai Eaton, *The Richest Vein* (London: Faber & Faber, 1949), 188–189.
11 René Guénon, *The Multiple States of the Being*, 41–42. On the same page, Guénon adds, "From this it follows that psychology has exactly the same character of relativity as any other special and contingent science, whatever some people claim; nor does it have anything to do with metaphysics."

traditional perspective, according to Guénon, a fruitless endeavor *if* the goal is to truly understand the ultimate organizing Principle behind all such states. This is because, for Guénon, such a tendency merely leads to the imposition of the rubric for perceiving one set of phenomena, the physical, upon the rubric for perceiving another set of phenomena, the psychological. More specifically, for Guénon, it is a tendency that tries to understand one set of phenomena from the perspective of another set of phenomena that are themselves *less* expressive of the nature of their metaphysical (meta-phenomenal or 'noumenal') Source. Simply put, according to Guénon, from the 'traditional' perspective, the modern science of psychology, as long as it attempts to comprehend the nature of psychological states by appeal to purely physical phenomena, will remain, like the overtly physical sciences of physics, chemistry, and biology, a *description of phenomena*, explanatorily *consistent* perhaps, rather than an *understanding* of their ultimate Cause or Source.

In *Fundamentals of Indian Philosophy*, Puligandla states more thoroughly what we have already noted in part:

> The Upanisads ["the concluding portions of the Vedas"[12]] distinguish between two kinds of knowledge: the lower knowledge (*aparavidya*) and the higher knowledge (*paravidya*). The former is the product of the senses and intellect and is accordingly limited to the finite, objective world of change and impermanence. On the other hand, the higher knowledge is that by which the infinite and imperishable *Brahman* is attained.[13]

According to Guénon, *paravidya*, the 'higher knowledge' that we mentioned earlier, is that knowledge that maintains the 'spiritual

---

[12] Sarvepalli Radhakrishnan and Charles Moore, eds., *A Source Book in Indian Philosophy*, 37.

[13] Ramakrishna Puligandla, *Fundamentals of Indian Philosophy*, 223–224. It should be noted that Puligandla employs the term 'intellect' in this quotation to refer to 'rational thought' rather than to refer to that 'intellectual intuition' of the metaphysical Principle that is, according to Guénon, 'beyond' rational thinking.

transmission' of the 'doctrine' of Tradition. *Aparavidya*, by contrast, is the "product of the senses and intellect...[that is] limited to the finite, objective world of change" and, therefore, includes the methods of the empirical sciences. In *Vedanta*, specifically, *paravidya* is purely metaphysical knowledge because it is knowledge of *Brahman* and *Brahman* is meta-physical, "infinite and imperishable," as Puligandla states. *Aparavidya*, by contrast, is the *Vedantic* equivalent to 'natural science': imperfect, finite, and 'perishable.' From the 'traditional' perspective of *Vedanta*, therefore, in the words of Guénon, *aparavidya* ('natural science') can only *infer* the 'general' but not 'realize' the Universal. To be a 'scientist' in the modern sense, therefore, is, according to Guénon, no qualification for transmitting the *paravidya* of Tradition, since the latter requires not an aptitude for empirical confirmation of hypotheses that can *never* be proven to be absolutely true but, rather, the facility for 'realization' of a 'higher' knowledge (*paravidya*) of Reality. We may presume that Guénon believed himself to possess this facility, which, as we noted in Chapter 1, Nasr appears to argue for when he states that

> Guénon, as he is reflected in his writings, seemed to be more of an intellectual function than a "man." His lucid mind and style and great metaphysical acumen seemed to have been chosen by traditional Sophia itself to formulate and express once again that truth from whose loss the modern world was suffering so grievously [sic].[14]

The *Samkhya* Concept of *Tamas*

Along with Guénon's *The Symbolism of the Cross* and *The Multiple States of the Being, Man & His Becoming According to the Vedanta* constitutes his most thorough presentation of what he believed to be the central ideas of Tradition. In the first two works, Guénon does not strictly rely upon, although he often does employ, the terminology of the 'Hindu Doctrines' and *Advaita Vedanta*, specifically. *The*

---

14 Seyyed Hossein Nasr, *Knowledge and the Sacred*, 101–102.

Symbolism of the Cross and *The Multiple States of the Being* are, largely, appeals to a *transcultural* Primordial Tradition of which *Vedanta* is, for Guénon, the best remaining expression in the *current* 'world age.' Guénon's primary purpose in all of his works is to elucidate Tradition *by means of Vedanta*, not to elucidate *Vedanta* in particular. In *The Simple Life of René Guénon*, Paul Chacornac states, for example, that

> [a]fter asserting that the Vedanta represents the purest metaphysics in Hindu doctrine, Guénon acknowledges the impossibility of presenting a comprehensive exposition of it, and announces that the specific object of his study is the nature and constitution of the human being. But, having taken the case of man as point of departure, Guénon goes on to expound the fundamental principles of all traditional metaphysics. Not since the fourteenth century had this doctrine been expounded in the West — and here in a lucid language free of symbolism. By degrees he leads up to the doctrine of the Supreme Identity and its logical corollary — the possibility that the being in the human state might in this very life attain liberation, the unconditioned state where all separateness and risk of reversion to manifested existence ceases....
>
> Although Guénon chose the doctrine of the Advaita [*Vedanta*] school (and in particular that of Shankara[15]) as its basis, *Man and His Becoming* must not be considered exclusively as an exposition of this school and of this master. It is essentially a synthetic account which draws not only upon other orthodox branches of Hinduism, but on occasion also upon the teachings of other traditional forms.[16]

In explicating my thesis concerning the meaning of serpent and dragon symbolism in Tradition, I rely to a large degree upon Guénon's usage of the terminology of *Vedanta*. I also employ, to a much lesser degree, Guénon's interpretations of some of the terms of the *Samkhya darshana*, which is, like *Vedanta*, an 'orthodox' Hindu *darshana* that

---

15 Shankara (or Samkara), referred to earlier, was the eighth-century Indian thinker who brought together as one doctrine what is now called *Advaita Vedanta*.

16 Paul Chacornac, *The Simple Life of René Guénon*, 58–59.

respects the ultimate authority of the Hindu Vedas. I appeal, in a general sense, to the *Samkhya* concept of *gunas*, or, as Guénon defines them, "conditions of Universal Existence, to which all manifested beings are subjected."[17] More specifically, I argue that the *guna* termed *tamas* that, according to Guénon, denotes the condition of "obscurity, assimilated with ignorance... [and that is traditionally] represented as a downward tendency,"[18] characterizes the New Man's experience of the limitedness, or 'chaotic' aspect, of the physical/'natural' world. This condition is experienced only by the 'migrating' ('reincarnating') being as it is partially, although not fully, 'enlightened' to the limitedness of *samsara* ("the indefinite series of cycles of manifestation").[19] Such is the state of the New Man. *Tamas*, therefore, tidily encapsulates what I mean in this book by the *state* of *matter*, the experience, by beings of a certain sufficient level of 'Self'-awareness, of the limitedness of the physical/'natural' world that they find themselves in.[20] My usage of *tamas* in this way is completely consistent, as can be seen from

17 René Guénon, *Man & His Becoming According to the Vedanta*, 44.
18 René Guénon, *Man & His Becoming According to the Vedanta*, 45.
19 'Migration' is the term that Guénon employs to describe the process by which beings (or 'the being,' more accurately) transition from one state of being to another. 'Reincarnation' is only a rough equivalent to 'migration' because it implies 'migration' of the being into a specifically *corporeal* state of existence. Guénon argues that, according to Hindu tradition, before the interjection of *Brahma[n]* (pure Spirit) "at the outset of manifestation," 'Existence' took the aspect of *tamas*. René Guénon, *The Symbolism of the Cross*, 32. This makes the 'condition' of *tamas*, more so than any of the other *gunas*, virtually equivalent to: 1) *samsara*/"the indefinite series of cycles of manifestation" and 2) 'chaos,' as it is described by Eliade in *The Sacred and the Profane* as existing before the time of Creation. For, as long as 'the being' continues to 'migrate' from one state of being/'Existence' to another, it remains, by definition, within the 'confused and obscure' ('chaotic') 'condition' of *samsara*, 'trapped' within "the indefinite series of cycles of manifestation." It follows that *samsara* is not completely itself to the degree to which 'the being' is not *aware* of *samsara*'s, and 'nature's' by extension, limitedness.
20 My employment of *tamas* in this book in no way implies my acceptance of the 'dualism' that many believe is absolute in *Samkhya*.

Chacornac's above quotation, with Guénon's 'synthetic account' of the Hindu Doctrines and Tradition in *Man & His Becoming According to the Vedanta*. The state of "obscurity, assimilated with ignorance" that characterizes the condition of *tamas* is itself characterized, more generally, by its essential *lack* of the three elements of form, definition, and 'actuality' that, I argue, together constitute the metaphysical 'Principial' Reality that 'Spiritualizes' the state of *matter*. Form, definition, and 'actuality' are elements that are, from the perspective of 'realization' of the metaphysical Principle, or gods/Forms/ archetypes, *relatively* absent in *samsara*/"the indefinite series of cycles of manifestation." They are, therefore, also relatively absent in 'nature,' or what people call 'the World,' *as it is experienced* in the state of *matter* by (partially) 'enlightened' beings that are 'migrating' through the "indefinite series of cycles of manifestation." This is because such beings, from the perspective of the state of *matter*, have, *because of* their 'new' awareness of a higher meta-physical order of existence, become aware of the limitations of that which we call 'nature' or the physical world. *Samsara* is thus characterized by *tamas*, the state of "obscurity, assimilated with ignorance," *from the perspective of* those beings 'migrating' through *samsara* that are 'enlightened,' those individuals that I named New Men in the *Introduction*. From the perspective of these New Men who are aware of a 'higher' organizing Principle, the 'flux' of *samsara* prevents *complete* forming, defining, and 'actualization' of 'nature' by the metaphysical Reality which they are now (partially) aware of.

'Slaying' the Serpent/Dragon: 'Realization' in the Chaos of *Matter*

In *The Sacred and the Profane*, as we recounted in the *Introduction*, Eliade states that "the dragon must be conquered and cut to pieces by the gods so that the cosmos may come to birth."[21] In *The Myth of the Eternal Return*, he argues that "the serpent symbolizes chaos, the

---

21 Mircea Eliade, *The Sacred and the Profane*, 48.

formless and nonmanifested"²² and states, in reference to traditional New Year ceremonies, which are symbols of 'creation' or 'beginnings,' that "the ritual combats between two groups of actors reactualize the cosmogonic moment of the fight between the god and the primordial dragon [, with]... the serpent almost everywhere symbolizing what is latent, preformal, undifferentiated."²³ Guénon, as we have also noted, argues in *The Symbolism of the Cross* that "the serpent will depict the series of the cycles of universal manifestation"²⁴; "the indefinitude of universal Existence"; and "the being's attachment to the indefinite series of cycles of manifestation."²⁵ Although expressed differently by the two authors, the traditional symbolism of the serpent/dragon symbolizes for both of them the traditional/archaic idea of how metaphysical Reality (the Principle or 'gods') 'manifests' in (or, more appropriately, *as*) the physical level of existence. For Guénon, the "indefinite series of cycles of manifestation" is an 'indefinite series of cycles' in which each cycle, and each state of being 'within' each cycle, 'manifests,' or reveals, in its own particular way, the metaphysical Principle in the realms of 'formal' and 'informal' manifestation.²⁶ For Eliade, 'creation' is the favored term for describing the process by which the objects and events of the physical world 'become real.' He also sometimes, however, equates 'creation' and 'manifestation,' as when he states that "the act of Creation realizes the passage from the nonmanifest to the manifest, or, to speak cosmologically, from chaos to cosmos."²⁷ With

---

22 Mircea Eliade, *The Myth of the Eternal Return*, 19. See also especially pages 37–42.
23 Mircea Eliade, *The Myth of the Eternal Return*, 69.
24 René Guénon, *The Symbolism of the Cross*, 122.
25 René Guénon, *The Symbolism of the Cross*, 123–124.
26 The Principle may, again, manifest in *other* levels of 'manifestation,' such as the psychic/subtle level.
27 Mircea Eliade, *The Myth of the Eternal Return*, 18. Eliade also refers, in *The Sacred and the Profane*, to the 'creation' of the entire universe as a 'manifestation' when he states that "the cosmogony is the supreme divine manifestation." Mircea Eliade, *The Sacred and the Profane*, 80.

respect to the *human perspective* on 'creation' specifically in Tradition, Eliade states in *The Myth of the Eternal Return* that

> [i]f we observe the general behavior of archaic man, we are struck by the following fact: neither the objects of the external world nor human acts, properly speaking, have any autonomous intrinsic value. Objects or acts acquire a value, and in doing so become real, because they participate, after one fashion or another, in a reality that transcends them.[28]

'Creation' is, therefore, in the traditional worldview according to Eliade, the event of 'becoming real,' the process by which the physical world, a chaos insofar as it does not 'participate' in the eternal archetypes, *becomes ordered* by means of the 'divine manifestation' of the transcendent archetypes.

I argue that the traditional composition of the dragon, specifically, which consists prominently of its characteristic of fire-breathing as well as its multi-fauna nature—part horse in ancient China, for example—is symbolically expressive of the 'ever-changing-ness' of "the indefinite series of cycles of manifestation," *samsara* in South Asian tradition. For Guénon, the 'condition' known as *tamas* in *Samkhya* of the being 'migrating' through the cycles of *samsara* typifies existence in what he calls the 'manifested' world. It also, however, typifies by process of inclusion the condition of beings manifested in the physical world/'nature' because the 'formal manifestation' of 'nature' constitutes, for Guénon, a subset of 'manifestation' in general.[29] Since both Eliade's 'chaos' and Guénon's "indefinite series of cycles of manifestation" are experienced within the context of that state of the 'migrating' being's existence that *recognizes* its own 'obscurity,' assimilated with

---

28 Mircea Eliade, *The Myth of the Eternal Return*, 3–4.
29 René Guénon, *The Symbolism of the Cross*, 7. We will not, in this book, make a strict differentiation between 'manifestation' and 'formal manifestation.' For our purposes, as has already been shown, 'nature' or the physical world will be taken to be roughly synonymous with *samsara*/"the indefinite series of cycles of manifestation," although the prior is, in actuality, a *perception of* the latter by the New Man *in* his state of *matter*.

ignorance,' the *Samkhya* concept of *tamas* provides, within the terminology of the Hindu Doctrines, a rough analogue to what I term the state of *matter*. And since, according to Guénon, the serpent/dragon in Tradition symbolizes "the indefinite series of cycles of manifestation," it also by extension symbolizes *tamas* itself, since *tamas* is that 'condition' that is analogous to the state of *matter* that the traditional serpent/dragon symbolizes. *Tamas/matter*, therefore, is the condition, or 'state,' to which, as Guénon says, "all manifested beings are subjected," but which is only become *aware of* by those beings capable of a level of awareness from which such beings may 'problematize' *tamas/matter*.

'Migrating' beings that experience "the indefinite series of cycles of manifestation" *as a* '*chaos*' exist within a state of relative ignorance that breeds obscurity, the 'condition' of *tamas* described in the *Samkhya darshana*. Those beings, however, that have *not* achieved a level of awareness whereby they may experience 'chaos,' that is, the 'limitedness' of the physical world/'nature,' although they may be thought of as being 'more ignorant' than the first group of beings, cannot 'realize' their condition of ignorance. It is, for example, generally agreed, I think, that a rock, which is one small part of "the indefinite series of cycles of manifestation," is 'un-knowing': the rock *knows nothing*. On the other hand, the rock is *not*, strictly speaking, ignorant because it has not the *capacity* to know, *or* to not know. According to many South Asian versions of Tradition, such as Hinduism and Buddhism, there exist an indefinite number of grades, or levels, of ignorance (lack of awareness) between the state of being of those beings, such as the rock, that have *no* 'Self'-knowledge/awareness and those beings that have 'realized' perfect, or *total*, knowledge/awareness: *paravidya* in *Vedanta*. Synthesizing Eliade's and Guénon's perspectives on Tradition, I argue that only those beings that are, to at least some degree, *aware of* their existence within *samsara* ("the indefinite series of cycles of manifestation")[30] are capable of experiencing 'chaos.' This is because 'chaos,' as Eliade defines it, can only be experienced by beings that have an *idea* of order, and an *idea* of order is a recognition of something meta-physical. From the South Asian perspective, a being is only 'trapped' in *samsara* if it 'knows' that there exists something 'beyond' *samsara*. A 'prison,' that is, is only a prison to s/he who sees it as an obstacle to the fulfillment of his/her desires. If a person desires *nothing* beyond prison life, then the so-called prison is not, in fact, a prison. Similarly, beings that are 'trapped' in *samsara* are trapped only to the extent that they are aware of *samsara*, aware of its limitedness, *and* have a desire to 'escape' *samsara*. In *Maitri Upanisad* XIII: 4 the example of a "frog in a waterless well" is meant to illustrate the condition of beings experiencing *samsara*. The frog feels itself 'trapped' in the well insofar as it recognizes, *by means of its very being*, that there exists 'beyond' the well a watery environment that more adequately suits its particular nature than the well does.[31] In *Vedanta*, the case is the same from the perspective of the 'migrating' being who desires *moksha* — 'escape' or 'deliverance'[32] — from *samsara*. Only *ignorance* (*avidya*[33]) is the cause of the being's 'imprisonment.' It is a form of ig-

---

30 As noted in the *Introduction*, Guénon says that "the indefinite series of cycles of manifestation…is the Buddhist *samsara*, the indefinite rotation of the 'round of existence,' from which the being must liberate himself in order to attain Nirvana." René Guénon, *The Symbolism of the Cross*, 124. I agree with Guénon's implication that *this* idea of *samsara* is the same as that discussed in *Vedanta* and in the other 'Hindu Doctrines' generally. It is the notion of *samsara* that transcends any particular South Asian philosophy or religion.

31 *Maitri Upanisad* 13:4 from Sarvepalli Radhakrishnan and Charles Moore, eds., *A Source Book in Indian Philosophy*, 93–94.

32 Puligandla defines *moksha* as "the state of absolute freedom from ignorance, maya, bondage, and suffering." Puligandla, *Fundamentals of Indian Philosophy*, 251. Guénon defines *moksha* as "that final liberation of the being [,]…which is the ultimate goal toward which the being tends… [,] the attainment of the supreme and unconditioned state." René Guénon, *Man & His Becoming According to the Vedanta*, 153.

33 René Guénon, *Man & His Becoming According to the Vedanta*, 122.

norance, however, that at *some* level, as with the very *being* of the frog, 'knows' that its possessor is ignorant or lacking in some way in its current situation. *Avidya*, however, requires, ultimately, the *possibility* for the acquisition of *paravidya*, 'enlightenment' by 'intellectual intuition' of the 'Principle.' The desire for 'escape' from *samsara*, however, need not be an *explicit* desire in order to exist. At whatever level it is experienced, it implies *some* awareness/knowledge on the part of the being that possesses it that the object of its desire *does* exist, just as the awareness of the 'chaos' of physical existence at various levels implies in those beings that experience it an awareness of a meta-physical order. In *Vedanta*, as in all traditional forms for Guénon, the metaphysical Principle provides, and *is*, this order.

At the moment that the 'migrating' being becomes aware/knowledgeable of the state of being that it exists 'within,' the state that I term *matter*, it becomes capable of 'problematizing' the idea of 'life' that, as I proposed in the *Introduction*, consists of 'identification' with the 'cyclical system' of *samsara*. This 'moment' constitutes the being's first conscious glimpse of a *meta*-physical Reality that is 'beyond' 'nature.' As of that moment, the newly 'enlightened,' or 'realized,' being that I call the New Man begins to 'identify' by means of *paravidya* with the meta-physical (*Brahman* in *Vedanta*). Simultaneously, the being acquires the potential to, first, *increase* its awareness of the limitedness of *samsara*, the 'chaos' of 'nature,' and then, eventually, *diminish* its awareness of 'chaos' as it approaches *complete* 'identification' with its true 'Self'/*Atman*, which it realizes is equivalent to *Brahman*. At all times in the development of the 'realized' being it experiences as 'chaotic' the state of *matter* which is its *perception of* "the indefinite series of cycles of manifestation." This variable, because fluctuating both *within* the 'enlightened' being and *among* 'enlightened' *beings*, experience of the 'chaos' of 'nature' is, I argue, traditionally symbolized by the serpent/dragon. The serpent/dragon is, therefore, symbolically representative of a tenuous condition that holds the potential of leading the 'migrating' being in one of two directions: 1) toward *lesser* awareness of *Brahman* (the metaphysical) or 2) toward *greater* awareness of *Brahman*. Based upon South Asian tradition, if the being moves in the direction of *lesser* awareness of *Brahman*, it becomes increasingly embedded in the purely ephemeral and mindless machinery of its 'body', its instincts and unreflective passions. It is then, in the language of traditional symbolism, *devoured*, or 'materialized', by the serpent/dragon. If, however, the being moves in the direction of *greater* awareness of *Brahman*, again according to South Asian tradition, it 'realizes' that that which it currently *believes* itself to be is only a *particular state* of what it *really* is: 'subjectively', *Atman*, 'objectively', *Brahman*. This 'realization', in *Vedanta*, is the knowledge (*paravidya*) that leads to 'identification' with *Brahman* and is expressed symbolically in traditional art and myth from around the world as the 'slaying' or 'Spiritualizing' of the serpent/dragon.

The state of being that I call *matter* is the state wherein the 'chaos', or limitedness, of *samsara*/"the indefinite series of cycles of manifestation" is perceived by the migrating being that is aware of its current state of 'trapped-ness' within the physical/'natural' world. This state of 'trapped-ness' is only 'made real' by means of the being's recognition of *samsara*/"the indefinite series of cycles of manifestation" as a non-dependent state of existence. This 'trapped' kind of awareness has, perhaps, an indefinite number of degrees between complete 'ignorance' (*avidya*) and complete 'realization' (*paravidya*) of the metaphysical Principle (*Brahman* in *Vedanta*). As a symbol of *matter*/'chaos'/*samsara*/"the indefinite series of cycles of manifestation," in general, therefore, the serpent/dragon in Tradition is a symbol of that which is, ultimately, from the traditional perspective, 'not real.' This is because the state of *matter*/'chaos'/*samsara*/"the indefinite series of cycles of manifestation" only exists for the being *as it* 'identifies' with states of being other than the *only* state of being that is, in *Advaita Vedanta*, completely real: *Brahman*, the absolute Reality. For, from the traditional perspective that is encapsulated, according to

Guénon, in *Vedanta*, it is only from a state of 'obscurity, assimilated with ignorance' (*tamas* in *Samkhya*) that the 'chaotic' "indefinite series of cycles of manifestation" — symbolized traditionally by the serpent/dragon — can be considered 'real.' The state of 'obscurity, assimilated with ignorance' that recognizes the reality of *matter*/'*chaos*'/*samsara*/*tamas*/"the indefinite series of cycles of manifestation" is, however, the very *means* by which metaphysical reality reveals itself to the being that exists in such a state. Only, therefore, by 'slaying' the serpent/dragon which is constituted by 'false identification' with the indefinite number of states of being that are characterized to different degrees by the 'condition' of *tamas* ('obscurity, assimilated with ignorance') may the being 'escape' (*moksha*) such states. As this 'slaying' of the serpent/dragon is symbolic of the destruction of 'false identification' with any state of being that is not completely *meta*-physical, not completely 'spiritual,' it is equivalent to what I call 'Spiritualization.' In the language of traditional symbolism, then, to 'slay' or 'defeat' the serpent/dragon is to *completely transcend* — Spiritualize — the *experience*, by the 'migrating' being, of 'trapped-ness' in the physical world that I term the state of *matter*. What Guénon calls 'the being' is the purely meta-physical, or Spiritual, Reality (called *Brahman* in *Vedanta*) that manifests itself indefinitely as the 'migrating' being that is both the ultimate 'subject' *and* 'object' of the entire process of 'realization.' 'The being,' then, *expresses itself* in all 'states of the being' throughout *all* manifestations of *samsara*/"the indefinite series of cycles of manifestation," as is implied in the title of Guénon's *The Multiple States of the Being*. In *Advaita Vedanta*, therefore, *samsara* is 'the being's' — *Brahman*'s — experience, in a particular limiting state, such as the human state, of a *particular perspective* on its '*Self*.'

Eliade's 'Extraterrestrial Archetypes' and 'Creation'

'Creation,' for Eliade, in a way similar to 'manifestation' for Guénon, is the effect of 'the being' of meta-physical Reality. For Eliade, however, Reality is Realities, something plural in nature which he terms 'extraterrestrial archetypes' that is akin to 'the gods' of ancient mythologies or Plato's 'Forms.' According to Eliade, traditional/archaic peoples believed that *humans*, because of their capacity for 'archetypal' or Universal thought, are those beings in the physical universe through which, and to whom, the true nature of Reality is revealed. Human existence thought of 'traditionally' is, as Eliade illustrates in various examples, the 'conduit' for 'creation.' In *The Myth of the Eternal Return*, for example, Eliade states that

> [t]he…world in which the presence and the work of man are felt—the mountains that he climbs, populated and cultivated regions, navigable rivers, cities, sanctuaries—all these have an extraterrestrial archetype, be it conceived as a plan, as a form, or purely and simply as a 'double' existing on a higher cosmic level. But everything in the world that surrounds us does not have a prototype of this kind.[34]

With these words, Eliade divides existence into two realms: cosmos and 'chaos,' formed and (relatively) form-less, that which has been organized in accordance with the 'extraterrestrial archetypes' by humans and that which has not. According to Eliade, traditional/archaic peoples believed that without the formative influence of extraterrestrial Realities, 'chaos' is the result. Extraterrestrial archetypes, by means of human activity—"the presence and the work of man"—'create,' or form, the physical world by dispelling 'chaos.' Thus for traditional peoples, according to Eliade, do "the objects of the external world… acquire a value, and in so doing become real."[35] 'Creation,' therefore, in Platonic fashion according to Eliade, results for traditional peoples

---

34 Mircea Eliade, *The Myth of the Eternal Return*, 9.
35 Mircea Eliade, *The Myth of the Eternal Return*, 3–4.

from the very *being* of the 'extraterrestrial archetypes' but *acts through human being*.[36] Because of this, the traditional idea of 'creation,' as interpreted by Eliade, is *equivalent to* the metaphysical '*realization*' of *Brahman*/the 'Principle'/'the gods'/'Forms'/'archetypes' discussed earlier.[37] 'Creation,' therefore, *only* exists in the physical world/'nature' (the physical world/'nature' is, equivalently, *only* 'created') *insofar as* there are 'manifested beings' in the physical world that have achieved that level of 'realization' (*paravidya*) that enables them to perceive 'chaos' and, thereby, the 'higher' (meta-physical) order.

Eliade's 'creation,' like Guénon's 'manifestation,' is a 'poking through' of the metaphysical into the physical realm ('nature'). Since, however, 'creation'/manifestation cannot, from the traditional perspective, be the result of a *physical* cause, it must be the result of *meta-physical* 'realization.'[38] In the above quotation, Eliade speaks of various *kinds* of 'creation'/manifestation: the building of a town, the marriage of a man and woman, the initiation of an individual into a new phase of life. All of these cases of, according to Eliade, traditional

---

36 The traditional idea of 'man' that is implied by Eliade here *must* be defined as a *universalizing being*.

37 Possible objections to this usage of the term 'creation' are duly noted. We have already recognized, for example, in the *Introduction*, the argument by Samuel D. Fohr, the editor of Guénon's *Studies in Hinduism*, that "the word 'creation'... is not suitable from the point of view of Hindu doctrine" in translating the idea of the coming-into-being of beings of all orders (the 'manifestation' of beings), although Guénon "frequently uses — and in particular to translate the term *srishti* — the word 'creation.'" René Guénon, *Studies in Hinduism*, 16. In *René Guénon and the Future of the West*, Waterfield contends that Guénon dismisses the notion of 'creation' because it "implies purposive action and is thus anthropomorphic in character, whereas manifestation — the making known to the senses of what is and always has been — can be considered as suprapersonal." Robin Waterfield, *René Guénon and the Future of the West*, 81.

38 For the purposes of my argument in this book, 'creation' and 'manifestation' shall be used interchangeably, both referring to an event in which a metaphysical Reality orders, defines, and 'actualizes' physical reality ('nature') as it *appears as* 'chaos' to beings of a certain stage of awareness/knowledge.

'creation' are, I argue, instances of the *'actualization,' definition, and formation* of, in the terms of *Vedanta*, the 'migrating' being *by way of* its metaphysical realization of *Brahman*. Ultimately, this amounts to 'Self'-realization because 'the being' *is Brahman*. It is *Brahman*, therefore, or the 'archetypes,' the metaphysical in general, that *through* 'man' navigates, populates, cultivates, and generally *orders* the 'chaos' of the 'natural' world of cyclical existence. An unclimbed mountain, an unnavigable river, an uncultivated land—all of these are, from the traditional perspective according to Eliade, 'chaotic' obstacles to 'creation' because they have not yet been assimilated to a 'higher,' or 'new,' order of being—the order of the 'extraterrestrial archetypes.' Each of these obstacles is, therefore, from the traditional perspective according to Eliade, symbolically a 'serpent/dragon' to be 'slain,' since traditionally "the serpent symbolizes chaos, the formless and nonmanifested."[39] Again, as Eliade states, "the dragon must be conquered and cut to pieces by the gods so that the cosmos may come to birth."[40]

The twentieth-century cubist painter Pablo Picasso once said that "Every act of creation is first of all an act of destruction."[41] The 'slaying' of the serpent/dragon in traditional art and myth is, according to Eliade, a symbolic representation of the event of creation. Creation, however, is generally speaking the bringing-into-being of something 'new,' something 'different,' something of a 'different order.' Genesis 1:1 begins with the words "In the beginning, God created the heavens and the earth." [ESV] Eliade often uses the term 'creation' similarly in describing the various ancient Near Eastern accounts of the divine origin of the cosmos.[42] 'The gods' *created* the cosmos, Eliade says, and brought about a *new* 'order' by 'slaying,' or 'conquering,' the

---

39 Mircea Eliade, *The Myth of the Eternal Return*, 19.
40 Mircea Eliade, *The Sacred and the Profane*, 48.
41 *Goodreads: Book Reviews*, "Pablo Picasso quotes." www.goodreads.com
42 Mircea Eliade, *The Myth of the Eternal Return*, 70 and 74.

serpent/dragon. The question *is*, however, what *sort* of 'new order' did these 'gods' bring about and *who were* these 'gods'? The answer to this question must be that the 'new order' was brought about by New Men, *humans* who had 'realized,' to varying degrees, the 'level' of 'the gods' — thus, in a way, *becoming* 'the gods' — and that the 'new order' was, is, and always shall be, from the traditional perspective, that order of being that is constructed upon the dawning 'realization' and development, in *humans* specifically, of meta-physical Reality.[43]

---

43 It is, perhaps, to such 'realization' that Jesus refers in the Gospel of John when, in response to the charge of blasphemy leveled against him, he responds, "Is it not written in your Law, 'I said, you are gods'? If he called them gods to whom the word of God came…do you say of him whom the Father consecrated and sent into the world, 'You are blaspheming,' because I said, 'I am the Son of God'?" [John 10:34–36 English Standard Version] Jesus is here referencing Psalms 82:6 ("I said, 'You are gods, sons of the Most High, all of you.'" [ESV]).

CHAPTER 5

'Modifications' of the Serpent/Dragon Symbol: 'Spiritualization' and 'Materialization'

Heroic 'Transcendence' and 'Symbolic Modifications' of the Serpent/Dragon

In his interpretation of Tradition, Guénon accepts the *Vedantic* distinction between the *Atman* ('Self') and the mind that is only one aspect of the *Atman*. The mind's activity, at any given moment, is describable in one of two ways: rational or irrational. The 'Self's' activity, however, is according to Guénon 'beyond' rationality altogether. It is, in Guénon's terms, 'intellectual.' As noted in Chapters 3 and 4, 'intellectuality' is, according to Guénon, a non-rational, although not irrational, way of 'knowing' that is acquired by traditional peoples by means of appropriate rituals, initiations, or disciplinary practices, such as the *yogas*. Such are the means by which, for Guénon, the 'migrating' being attains *moksha*, or the *complete* 'Self-realization' that consists of 'identification' with the metaphysical 'Principle' called *Brahman* in *Vedanta*. There are, as I noted in Chapter 4, other non-'final' degrees of 'realization' which lie between *complete* ignorance (*avidya*) and *complete* 'Self-realization' (*moksha*) that are also attainable by the 'migrating' being. In *Man & His Becoming According to the*

Vedanta, however, Guénon defines *moksha* as "that final liberation of the being...which is the ultimate goal toward which the being tends... [which] differs absolutely from all states which that being may have passed through in order to reach it, since it is the attainment of the supreme and unconditioned state."[1] In *Vedanta*, the "supreme and unconditioned state" of *moksha* consists of 'escape' from *samsara*, for Guénon "the indefinite series of cycles of manifestation," and, therefore, 'escape' from that state of being in which the physical world or 'nature' is considered 'real.'

Along with Eliade, I employ the term 'transcendence' to describe the *various* states of being in which the 'migrating' being, to greater or lesser degrees, 'goes beyond' physical existence by means of its becoming aware of its dependency upon something existing 'beyond' (*meta*) its physical 'individuality.' *Moksha* describes the case of *complete* transcendence of physical existence because it refers to a state of awareness that is 'unconditioned' by *any* physical constraints. The state of *matter*, however, which according to my argument consists of an awareness of the dependency of the physical world ('nature') upon the metaphysical — in which 'nature' is, more specifically, perceived as 'chaos' — is not a state of being indicative of *complete* transcendence (*moksha*) because the being experiencing it 'feels' 'trapped' within *samsara*/"the indefinite series of cycles of manifestation." However, although not equivalent to the state of *moksha*, the perception of *matter* nevertheless indicates an increase in awareness that is a necessary stage along the path *towards moksha*. For, it is that state of being in which the 'chaotic' aspect of the physical world is first *recognized*, and in which the 'migrating' being no longer 'identifies' with cyclical existence or, to put things simply, the 'biological.' *Matter* is, equivalently, that state in which the physical world has not yet been *completely* 'Spiritualized.'

---

1 René Guénon, *Man & His Becoming According to the Vedanta*, 153. As was said in Chapter 4, Puligandla defines *moksha* as "the state of absolute freedom from ignorance, *maya*, bondage, and suffering." Puligandla, *Fundamentals of Indian Philosophy*, 251.

The levels of transcendence by the 'migrating' being are, thus, equivalent to levels of Spiritualization and constitute levels of *Spiritual*, not physical, 'extrication' of the being's true identity from (perceived) physical determinations. As stated in different terms before, the levels of Spiritualization of 'the being' and, thus, of existence in general, according to *Vedanta*, are equivalent to levels of 'identification' with the *completely* Spiritual reality that is called *Brahman* in *Vedanta*, God/ Yahweh in the Bible, and *Tao* in East Asian thought. This Reality is, as is said of *Brahman* in *Mundaka Upanishad* II: 2-3, "above name and form. He is present in all and transcends all. Unborn, without body and without mind, From him comes every body and mind. He is the source of space, air, fire, water, and the earth that holds us all."[2] 'Transcendence' is, whether in Eliade's usage or as it appears in Easwaran's translation of the Upanishads, like *paravidya*, that 'knowledge' that, rather than consisting of the accumulation of *information* leading to erudition, consists of the accumulation of Spiritual 'realizations' that lead, potentially, to *moksha*.

I suggest that one of the ways in which 'transcendence'/'realization' has been recorded in Tradition is through the depiction and description, in traditional art and myth, of the extraordinary, or 'supernatural,' actions of exceptional individuals. These individuals are widely known today as the 'gods' and 'heroes' of the ancient world. The Greek gods Apollo and Zeus were both 'dragon (or serpent) slayers,' as were the Greek demigods, or 'heroes,' Herakles and Perseus.[3] So, however, were the 'Hindu' gods Indra and Krishna, as well as the Babylonian god Marduk. Such individuals, I argue, were depicted and described in traditional art and myth as serpent/dragon 'slayers' to indicate their transcendence, or *attempted* transcendence, of the state of *matter* — their awareness of 'chaos.' Their 'heroic' actions in doing

---

2 Eknath Easwaran, trans., The Upanishads (Tomales, California: Nilgiri Press, 1987), 188.

3 I shall use 'Herakles' and 'Hercules' interchangeably throughout the present work.

so, I propose, belong within the same category of Spiritualizing actions as the traditional rituals, initiations, and disciplinary practices mentioned earlier. Their depicted 'struggles' with, or 'slayings' of, the serpent/dragon are representations of the struggles, and mastering, of ritual and initiatory, and/or disciplinary, practices. Traditional representations of *only* the serpent/dragon by itself—what I call the 'simple' symbolism of the serpent/dragon—symbolize for traditional peoples *only matter* and, therefore, *only* the awareness by New Men of 'chaos' or, equivalently, their awareness of being 'trapped' in the chaotic "indefinite series of cycles of manifestation" which awareness is the state of *matter*. Traditional representations of 'gods' or 'heroes' 'struggling' with or 'slaying'/'defeating' the serpent/dragon, by contrast, constitute what I call 'complex symbolisms,' symbolisms that consist of two or more 'simple' symbols that each have discrete meanings but which may go to create more complex meanings when combined with other simple symbols. 'Simple' symbols such as the unadorned 'simple' serpent were 'modified' in traditional art and myth by other 'simple' symbols, such as the representation of a god/hero or something indicative of his unique person, to produce 'complex symbols' such as the 'dragon-slaying god/hero.' The 'god'/'hero' counts, in this book, as one example of a 'symbolic modification' of the 'simple' serpent/dragon symbol. The 'god'/'hero' 'struggling' with and/or 'slaying' the serpent/dragon, specifically, is an example of a 'complex symbolism' that symbolizes the general traditional/archaic belief in the possibility of 'transcending' the 'chaotic' "indefinite series of cycles of manifestation" and, by extension, the physical/'natural' world. One critical element of this particular form of 'symbolic modification' consists of the various kinds of weapons employed by ancient 'gods' and 'heroes' to 'combat' and/or 'slay' the serpent/dragon.

To understand the symbolism of the serpent/dragon in traditional art, one must, at least to some degree, understand traditional art itself. In *Knowledge and the Sacred*, Seyyed Nasr states,

Traditional art is concerned with the truths contained in the tradition of which it is the artistic and formal expression. Its origin therefore is not purely human. Moreover, this art must conform to the symbolism inherent in the object with which it is concerned as well as the symbolism directly related to the revelation whose inner dimension this art manifests. Such an art is aware of the essential nature of things rather than their accidental aspects. It is in conformity with the harmony which pervades the cosmos and the hierarchy of existence which lies above the material plane with which art deals, and yet penetrates into this plane. Such art is based on the real and not the illusory so that it remains conformable to the nature of the object with which it is concerned rather than imposing a subjective and illusory veil upon it. ...Traditional art is brought into being through... [sacred] knowledge and is able to convey and transmit this knowledge. It is the vehicle of an intellectual intuition and a sapiential message which transcends both the individual artist and the collective psyche of the world to which he belongs....Knowledge is transmitted by traditional art through its symbolism, its correspondence with cosmic laws, its techniques, and even the means whereby it is taught through the traditional craft guilds which in various traditional civilizations have combined technical training in the crafts with spiritual instruction.[4]

I suggest that, in traditional art of all kinds, the 'symbolic modification' of the serpent/dragon symbol that consists in the hero's/god's weapon symbolizes his capacity to 'transcend' his own experience of the 'chaos' of 'nature' and "the indefinite series of cycles of manifestation": the state of *matter*. The essence of such transcendence, *paravidya* in *Vedanta*, is, as Guénon argues and Nasr affirms in the above quotation, "an intellectual intuition and a sapiential message which transcends both the individual artist and the collective psyche of the world to which he belongs."[5] Beyond this general symbolic function of traditional art, however, the gods'/heroes' 'symbolic weapons,' as Guénon terms them, depicted in such art are symbolic of the metaphysical Source of 'intellectual intuition': the metaphysical 'Principle.'

---

4   Seyyed Hossein Nasr, *Knowledge and the Sacred*, 254 and 258–59.
5   Seyyed Hossein Nasr, *Knowledge and the Sacred*, 258.

Such 'symbolic weapons,' therefore, in the terms of my argument, are 'symbolic modifications' of the serpent/dragon symbol that symbolize the forming, defining, and 'actualizing,' or 'overcoming,' of the 'chaotic' cyclical system of 'nature,' the "indefinite series of cycles of manifestation" *as perceived by* the 'enlightened' New Man.

The New Man, I suggest, *is* the hero/god that is depicted and described in instantiations of the serpent/dragon-slayer motif in traditional art and myth. As I proposed in the *Introduction*, therefore, the traditional 'symbolic weapons' that are depicted in martial engagements between a hero/god and a serpent/dragon, symbolize: 1) the New Man's capacity for 'struggle,' or 'combat,' with an older idea of 'life' that becomes first 'problematized,' and then defined, by the New Man under the conceptual apparatus of 'chaos'/*samsara* (cyclical existence) and 2) the possibility of 'life's' — chaos's/*samsara*'s — 'management and control' by New Humans. More generally, I contend that traditional depictions and descriptions of martial engagements between a hero/god and a serpent/dragon convey to traditional peoples the series of steps involved in the 'enlightened' being's 'realization' of the dependency of the physical world ('nature') upon metaphysical Reality: 1) 'struggling' with 'nature' (perceiving 'nature' as a 'chaos'), 2) 'problematizing' 'nature' ('realizing' ever more clearly the limitedness of 'nature'), and 3) 'managing and controlling' 'nature' (specifically, one's perception of it) by means of disciplining ('managing and controlling') one's states of awareness. In addition to the cases of martial engagements between heroes/gods, with their 'symbolic weapons,' and serpents/dragons, there are other traditional symbolisms that are meant to convey, to those fluent in the 'language' of traditional symbolism, the general idea of overcoming/transcending/Spiritualizing the 'chaos' of 'nature.' As mentioned in the *Introduction*, these include depictions and descriptions of: 1) the winged, or 'plumed,' serpent, 2) the serpent entwined about a rod, staff, tree, or cross, and 3) the serpent/dragon juxtaposed in some way with a circle, sphere, ball, orb, or egg. All of these motifs, which may be found in seemingly distinct cultures from around the world, symbolize the Spiritualizing of *matter* that communicates, to traditional peoples, the process of 'realization' of the metaphysical.

Eliade's 'creation' and Guénon's 'manifestation,' as discussed in Chapter 4, refer in Tradition to the event of 'realization' of the metaphysical in the physical world. All beings that have not *completely* 'transcended' Guénon's 'multiple states of the Being' or, in *Vedantic* terms, achieved *moksha*, continue to perceive 'chaos' because they remain in a state of being that is characterized by *tamas*, "obscurity, assimilated with ignorance." Such 'migrating' beings are, in the slang of the 'Hindu Doctrines,' 'trapped' in *samsara*, Guénon's "indefinite series of cycles of manifestation." They are, in the terms of this book, not yet formed, defined, or, most specifically, 'actualized' because 'migration' implies the failure to completely 'realize' ('actualize') *all potentiality*. As long as *some* potentiality still exists in 'the being,' it remains an 'unrealized' ('non-actualized') 'migrating' being. By extension, however, since complete 'actualization' is contingent upon unambiguous form as well as precise definition — 'actualization,' form, and definition being *interdependent* qualities — 'the being' is only *ambiguously* formed and *imprecisely* defined as long as it is subject to the ever-changing determinations of the flux of *samsara*. This the being *is*, to greater or lesser degrees, in *all* of its 'migrations.' Matter, therefore, is that *general* state which encompasses the plurality of those of the 'multiple states of the being' that are characterized by various levels of *relative* 'Self'-awareness and which, thus, are not *completely* formed, defined, and 'actualized.' These states are all those relatively 'Self'-aware states of 'migration' of 'the being' that are not yet 'identified' with: 1) what I term Spirit, 2) what Guénon calls the metaphysical 'Principle' (*Brahman* in *Vedanta*), and 3) what Eliade refers to as the 'extraterrestrial archetypes' or 'gods.' It is because the 'migrating' being symbolically 'slays' the serpent/dragon that he 'identifies' with 'the gods' and, I argue, can be *known as* a 'god' or 'hero.' Beyond that motif, however, 'symbolic modifications' of the serpent/dragon such as wings, 'axial' symbols (the tree/staff, etc.), and circular/spherical symbols all symbolize the 'migrating' being's 'struggle' to form, define, and 'actualize' its 'Self' by means of 'controlling and managing' both its own awareness of the 'chaos' of 'nature', and, in other cases, the awareness of individuals who fail at the task or never undertake it.

Manifestation and Creation as 'Realization' of the New Man

'Manifestation' is Guénon's term for the process by which the Principial metaphysical Reality is revealed in 'cyclical existence' and, thus, in 'nature.' From the perspective of the 'realization' of the 'migrating being,' 'manifestation' is better understood as the process of 'Self-knowledge' (*paravidya*) whereby 'the being' (*Brahman*) more clearly 'knows' (becomes aware) that the metaphysical Principle (Itself) is *everything* and that his *perception* of *samsara*, 'nature,' is but an incomplete interpretation of Reality that appears 'chaotic' to all aspects of itself (to all 'migrating' beings) that experience 'trapped-ness' and therefore desire 'escape' (*moksha*) from that experience. As noted before, not *all* beings that are part of "the indefinite series of cycles of manifestation" 'desire' *moksha*, only those that have *some* level of awareness, however little, of their own existence. Thus it is that a rock, for example, cannot be ignorant because it cannot be knowledgeable either. It cannot desire because it cannot 'go beyond' desire. Thus it is, also, that the frog in the waterless well that is described in Maitri Upanishad XIII: 4[6] *can* be ignorant, in a comparatively unaware fashion, because it *can*, albeit instinctually, 'know' its purpose or 'nature' and yet still fail to 'realize' that *telos*. The experience of *samsara*, and thus the experience of the state of *matter*, is ultimately the experience *of Brahman by Brahman*, but only in those *particular* states of *Brahman*'s existence from which 'the being' (the metaphysical 'element' of existence) desires 'release'

---

6   *Maitri Upanisad* 13:4 from Sarvepalli Radhakrishnan and Charles Moore, eds., *A Source Book in Indian Philosophy*, 93–94.

or 'escape' from *samsara*. The 'symbolic modifications' that are the serpent/dragon-slayer's weapons, therefore, symbolize *Brahman* as it is being 'used' by the 'struggling' god/hero (who symbolizes a 'lower' state of manifestation, and thus awareness, of *Brahman*) to dispel the illusion of *samsara*.

As we have mentioned, Eliade states in *The Myth of the Eternal Return* that not "everything in the world that surrounds us" has a 'prototype' — an 'extraterrestrial archetype' — only

> the world in which the presence and the work of man are felt — the mountains that he climbs, populated and cultivated regions, navigable rivers, cities, sanctuaries…have an extraterrestrial archetype, be it conceived as a plan, as a form, or purely and simply as a 'double' existing on a higher cosmic level….Desert regions inhabited by monsters, uncultivated lands, unknown seas on which no navigator has dared to venture, do not share with the city of Babylon, or the Egyptian nome, the privilege of a differentiated prototype….All these wild, uncultivated regions and the like are assimilated to chaos.[7]

What Eliade presents in *The Myth of the Eternal Return*, as well as in *The Sacred and the Profane*, as the traditional/archaic viewpoint is, as noted previously, a variety of Platonic Idealism. Another way, therefore, to express the thought that is encapsulated in the above quotation is to say that beings of a 'universalizing' capacity, such as humans, do not *perceive* the metaphysical in *every* aspect of the physical/'natural' world. As also noted previously, Eliade contends that "the act of Creation realizes the passage from the nonmanifest to the manifest, or, to speak cosmologically, from chaos to cosmos."[8] 'Creation,' therefore, for traditional peoples according to Eliade, signifies that inscrutable point where the metaphysical *becomes* physical or, more concretely, where "wild, uncultivated regions" become tame and cultivated. In the terms of this book, 'creation' from the traditional

---

7   Mircea Eliade, *The Myth of the Eternal Return*, 9.
8   Mircea Eliade, *The Myth of the Eternal Return*, 18.

perspective is a 'realization' because it is only defined based upon a *prior perception* of what 'chaos' ('wildness' and 'uncultivated-ness') consists in. Eliade's examples of 'chaos,' such as an unclimbed mountain, an unnavigable river, or an uncultivated land, are only 'uncreated' or 'nonmanifest' *from the perspective of* beings that are capable of the 'higher knowledge' of *paravidya*, awareness of meta-physical Reality. The 'hero' that explores the "wild, uncultivated regions" or the "desert regions inhabited by monsters," or the "unknown seas," is that New Man who has become aware of, to at least some degree, the limitedness of (his perception of) the physical world and, therefore, its 'ripeness' so to speak, for a 'higher' kind of forming, defining, and 'actualizing' — Spiritualizing — and 'controlling and managing.' The New Man's 'weapons' that he employs in the performance of this task, although variable in appearance in ancient art, are all symbolic of his newfound awareness and his means of applying that awareness onto the 'chaos' of his perception of *samsara*: 'nature.'

'Chaos,' the Serpent/Dragon Symbol, and the Combat Myth

The traditional use of the serpent/dragon to symbolize the idea of chaos probably derives from the taxonomical uncertainty presented by the snake to traditional peoples. From time immemorial, the snake was observed to live not only amongst other more 'natural' animals, but in the 'border lands' of the world's 'edge,' a belief popularly illustrated in the depictions of dragons in the corners of old maps. The snake was thus, incredibly to those who knew little about its physiology, well-suited to existing in radically different environments — deserts, grasslands, marshes, swamps, forests, mountains, and waterbodies of various kinds. It could live on the earth, in the air (in trees), *under* the earth (in holes), and in water. In *Lady of the Beasts*, the American painter and animal symbolism researcher Buffie Johnson refers to the serpent's capacity to live in both the "lush valleys of the Tigris and Euphrates rivers" *and* the "wild desert regions" of the ancient Near East, contending that "the serpent was honored for its ability to be at home in either habitat."[9] Ancient Egyptian artifacts also provide copious examples of the believed 'mystery' or 'strangeness' of the snake in comparison to other animals. In *Myth and Symbol in Ancient Egypt*, former lecturer on Egyptian history and language R. T. Rundle Clark summarizes the general impression of the snake in the Pyramid Texts when he states that "having neither arms nor legs they [snakes] do not belong to the animal world but to something primeval."[10] The Egyptian Pyramid Texts themselves describe the snake as "that mysterious and shapeless thing, of whom the gods foretold that you should have neither arms nor legs on which to go following your brother gods."[11]

As I've already emphasized, 'chaos' is a relative term, for it always begs focus on the kind of 'order' with which it is to be contrasted. According to Eliade, ancient creation myths in which a god or hero defeats a serpent or dragon express symbolically the traditional/archaic understanding of 'order' and 'chaos.' In *Python: A Study of Delphic Myth and Its Origins*, classical scholar Joseph Fontenrose analyzed many different versions of what he called 'combat myths' in which ancient gods or heroes "encounter and defeat dragons, monsters, demons, and giants."[12] It was, however, Fontenrose's interest in Greek mythology specifically, and, as he states, "My interest in the Delphic Oracle... [that first] led me inevitably to a study of the combat of Apollo with the dragon Python, the origin myth of Apollo's

---

9   Buffie Johnson, *Lady of the Beasts: The Goddess and Her Sacred Animals* (Rochester, Vermont: Inner Traditions International, 1994), 136.
10 R. T. Rundle Clark, *Myth and Symbol in Ancient Egypt* (London: Thames and Hudson Ltd, 1959), 243.
11 R. T. Rundle Clark, *Myth and Symbol in Ancient Egypt*, 243, quoting Pyramid Texts, edited by Sethe, chapter 664.
12 Joseph Fontenrose, *Python: A Study of Delphic Myth and Its Origins* (Berkeley and Los Angeles, California: University of California Press, 1959), 1.

Delphic shrine."[13] As mentioned previously, and as Fontenrose and Eliade both agree, along with Apollo other non-Greek gods, such as the Babylonian Marduk and the South Asian Indra, had their own 'dragons' to defeat, Tiamat and Vritra, respectively. As Fontenrose states,

> Every god has his enemy, whom he must vanquish and destroy. Zeus and Baal, Coyote and Ahura Mazda, Thor and the Lord of Hosts, are alike in this: that each must face a dreadful antagonist. Apollo's enemy was the great dragon Python, whom he had to fight and kill before he could establish his temple and oracle at Delphi.[14]

For Eliade, each of these instances of Fontenrose's so-called 'combat myth' that may be discerned in the art and myth of ancient societies from around the world symbolically presents the traditional/archaic ideas of 'order' and 'chaos.' The god, or hero, in the various versions of the 'combat myth' symbolizes 'order' and the serpent/dragon, or 'monster,' symbolizes 'chaos.' The 'combat' *itself* symbolizes the 'forming' of 'chaos' that culminates in the 'creation' of a 'new' order of some kind, whether this order be cosmic, personal, or *social*. We've already seen that, for Eliade, the traditional idea of 'creation' encompasses human habitation, cultivation, and navigation of 'wild' or unexplored regions.

One interpretation of the 'combat myth' is that it portrays a struggle between patriarchy and matriarchy or, more specifically, the 'victory' of the masculine-ordered societies of the Vedic Aryans and Homeric Greeks over the, allegedly, older matriarchal societies that worshipped 'Mother' Earth (the 'Goddess') and the powers of fertility. This interpretation is adhered to, for instance, by the mythologist Joseph Campbell in his *Occidental Mythology*.[15] According to Campbell and other like-minded scholars, the masculine gods,

---

13   Joseph Fontenrose, *Python: A Study of Delphic Myth and Its Origins*, vii.
14   Joseph Fontenrose, *Python: A Study of Delphic Myth and Its Origins*, 1.
15   Joseph Campbell, *The Masks of God: Occidental Mythology* (New York, New York: Penguin Group, 1964), 22–25.

such as Indra and Zeus, that are portrayed in the various versions of the combat myth are the purveyors of a new *social* order, wielding weapons representative of the warlike proclivities of 'patriarchy' (see fig. 5.1).

Fig. 5.1. *Zeus against Typhon*, c. 650 BCE, Munich Museum[16]

Guénon and Eliade, however, by contrast, interpret the same portrayals from a less political or 'sociological' perspective. Guénon, specifically, argues, as we have just noted and shall consider in more depth later, that the 'symbolic weapons' employed by ancient gods and heroes to vanquish their serpentine foes are indicators *not* of 'male supremacy' but of the 'manifestation' of the metaphysical 'Principle' in the physical/'natural' world that is the *Source* of the physical/'natural' world. The symbolization of the 'active' Principle as 'male' and the 'passive' 'substance' as other than male (not always explicitly 'female') is yet another transcultural expression of the 'symbolic language' of Tradition, which can also be seen, for example, in the symbology of the Chinese *yin-yang* symbol and in medieval European alchemical manuscripts.

---

16 Joseph Campbell, *The Masks of God: Occidental Mythology*, 23.

The 'Thunderweapon' and the World Axis/*Axis Mundi*

Apollo, Zeus, Indra, Marduk, the Norse god Thor, and other ancient gods and heroes are often represented in traditional art and myth battling serpentine/draconic foes wielding what the archaeologist Christian Blinkenberg has called the 'thunderweapon.' In *The Thunderweapon in Religion and Folklore*, Blinkenberg argues that the power attributed to the thunderweapon derived from a widespread experience of an object that was commonly seen by the peoples of various cultures from around the world: the 'thunderstone.' According to Blinkenberg,

> Over a great part of the globe...the belief in thunderstones is spread.... This popular belief is not limited to any one race; for the same chain of ideas is found in almost the whole of Asia and Africa, in China and Japan, as well as amongst the negroes of the Guinea Coast. The main idea, that the thunderstone comes down with the lightning, is everywhere the same; many secondary ideas attaching to it are also found in remarkably similar forms....The thunderstone falls down from the sky in thunderstorms or, more accurately, whenever the lighting strikes. The stroke of the lightning, according to this view, consists in the descent of the stone; the flash and the thunder-clap are mere after-effects or secondary phenomena.[17]

The power of 'thunderstones' for traditional peoples, I would agree, was undoubtedly centered not in their intrinsic substance or appearance but, rather, in their 'sky origin' and association with sky phenomena, such as lighting and thunder. In *Patterns in Comparative Religion*, Eliade writes of the ancient reception, among the Romans, Carthaginians, and early Muslims, of the object similar, or equivalent, in appearance to the thunderstone that is now called 'meteorite.' Concerning the 'symbolic value' of meteorites in traditional/archaic societies, Eliade observes that "[t]heir sacred character was due

---

17 Christian Blinkenberg, *The Thunderweapon in Religion and Folklore: A Study in Comparative Archaeology* (Cambridge: Cambridge University Press, 1911), 5–6 and 1.

primarily to their heavenly origin....Their sky origin can hardly have been forgotten, for popular belief attributed it to all prehistoric stone implements, which were called 'thunder-stones.'"[18]

Blinkenberg and Guénon both argue that one of the ways in which certain of the ancient gods' 'sky-power' was revealed in traditional cultures was by means of the symbolic 'weaponizing' of the power of 'Heaven.' Guénon states in *Symbols of Sacred Science*,

> It is known that Apollo killed the serpent *Python* with his arrows, just as, in the Vedic tradition, Indra kills *Ahi* or *Vritra*, the counterpart of *Python*, with the *vajra* which represents the thunderbolt; and this comparison leaves no doubt whatsoever as to the original symbolical equivalence of the two weapons in question.[19]

The 'thunderbolt' is Guénon's variation on what Blinkenberg calls the 'thunderweapon.' All of the 'symbolic weapons' listed in the above quotation are, for Guénon, 'symbolically equivalent,' and thus equally representative of the 'thunderbolt,' and also, according to Guénon, of something that he terms the 'World Axis.'[20] Eliade's 'thunder-stones,' similarly, though not always 'thunder*weapons*' per se, are, according to him, traditionally symbolic of the *Axis Mundi*.[21] *Axis Mundi*, being merely the Latinized form of 'World Axis,' is Eliade's equivalent expression for the metaphysical, or 'transcendent,' Reality that, according to both authors, traditional peoples believed exists at the 'center' of the universe. The 'symbolic weapons' of ancient heroes and gods, such as those referred to by Guénon above, are, for Guénon and Eliade both, one group of traditional symbols that represent the World Axis.[22] As listed in the *Introduction*, other traditional 'axial' symbols

---

18 Mircea Eliade, *Patterns in Comparative Religion*, 227.
19 René Guénon, *Symbols of Sacred Science*, 173.
20 René Guénon, *Symbols of Sacred Science*, 173–74 and 317.
21 Mircea Eliade, *Patterns in Comparative Religion*, 227.
22 Since 'World Axis' and *Axis Mundi* are equivalent terms, I will often refer to only one of them.

which are often found in juxtaposition with the serpent/dragon include: the tree, the staff, the rod, and the cross. All of these symbols, according to Guénon and Eliade, symbolize the essence of that which the World Axis/*Axis Mundi* refers to: for Eliade, the 'transcendent' 'extraterrestrial archetypes' or 'gods'; for Guénon, the metaphysical 'Principle'; and, in the terms of this book, 'Spirit.' In addition to these purely 'axial' symbols, there are, as previously stated, other traditional symbols of 'the metaphysical' that, I propose, may be found in combination with the traditional serpent/dragon symbol to indicate a new 'complex symbolism' of the Spiritualization of *matter*. As we've mentioned, these include the symbolism of the circle and its 'variations,' such as the sphere, ball, orb, and 'egg,' but also the symbolism of stones and mountains, and birds and wings. We shall have more to say about the World Axis in Chapter 6, and much more to say about the just-mentioned 'extra-axial' symbols in other chapters.

'Duality,' 'Spiritualization,' and 'Materialization'

What we see symbolized in the various versions of the combat myth is, from the perspective of traditional or archaic humans, a 'Spiritualization' of *matter*, where the first term, as we have noted, entails a forming, defining, and 'actualizing' action, and the second term, in its reference to a state of perceived 'chaos,' entails a *relative* lack of form, definition, and 'actuality.' As is expressed equivalently in the *Vedantic* concept of *paravidya*, Spiritualization is a process of 'Self'-realization, an accumulation of Spiritual 'realizations' (not of mere information) by means of 'intellectual intuition' leading to greater awareness of the 'identity' of *Atman* ('Self') and *Brahman* ('Principle') in *Vedanta*. Spiritualization is a spiritual 'struggle' or 'combat' against the 'chaos' that *samsara* presents to those beings sufficiently aware of the 'natural' condition of *tamas*, "obscurity, assimilated with ignorance," that they are currently 'trapped' within. When Guénon writes of *samsara*, "the indefinite series of cycles of manifestation," or "the series of the cycles of universal manifestation," he is emphasizing 'nature' *in its aspect of* resisting and incompletely expressing the 'Principial,' or metaphysical, Reality—*Brahman* in *Vedanta*. 'Nature' then *still*, for Guénon, as a *state of being*,[23] expresses, in spite of its *samsaric aspect*, to different degrees and to different 'migrating' beings, the metaphysical 'Principle' that is, from the traditional perspective according to Guénon and Eliade, its Source. As Puligandla affirms in *Fundamentals of Indian Philosophy*, in the case of the 'migrating' being *as* human, the *Vedanta* holds that "Man's state of bondage and unfreedom is due to his ignorance of his real being and true nature. By destroying this primordial ignorance, man knows himself as the eternal and infinite *Brahman*."[24] The destruction of this 'primordial ignorance' is, I argue, of the essence of the 'creation' that is symbolized in the traditional 'combat myth' when the god or hero 'slays' the serpent/dragon. It is what I call Spiritualization of the state of *matter*, the forming, defining, and 'actualizing' of the 'obscurity' of the condition of *tamas*.

Guénon's realm of 'manifestation' which is a *plural* expression of the 'unity' of the metaphysical Principle will be sometimes referred to in this book, based upon observations made by Guénon in *The Symbolism of the Cross*, as the realm of 'duality.' 'Duality,' as I employ it, refers simply to 'non-unity' in general and characterizes the state of 'nature' for traditional/archaic humans because it characterizes the state of *matter* within which 'nature' is perceived as dependent (as opposed to independent) and 'chaotic.' 'Manifestation,' as it consists of a *plurality* of beings—all 'manifested' beings—may be referred to

---

23 'Nature,' or the 'physical world,' as noted previously, is not, from the traditional perspective according to Guénon and Eliade, some corporeal 'stuff' like a patch of turf, an animal's body, a collection of atoms, a cluster of nebulae, or even a set of physical 'laws' and 'constants.'

24 Ramakrishna Puligandla, *Fundamentals of Indian Philosophy*, 226. The idea expressed in this quotation is common to all three of the major 'schools of *Vedanta*': *Advaita Vedanta* (Non-Dualism), *Visistadvaita Vedanta* (Qualified Non-Dualism), and *Dvaita Vedanta* (Dualism). Ramakrishna Puligandla, *Fundamentals of Indian Philosophy*, xiii–xiv.

as 'dual' because 'duality' is the first, or most fundamental, expression of plurality.[25] The 'duality' of 'manifestation' is, thus, for Guénon, opposed to the 'unity' of the 'Principial' *Source* of 'duality.' I argue that 'nature,' and the state of *matter* by extension, is also, more specifically, *dichotomous* because, from the perspective of human perception, it is a realm in which 'opposites,' such as good and evil or right and wrong, and their various intermediate grades, may exist. I propose that it is *only* in such a state of being, where 'separation' of qualities is possible, that the discernment of *particular* qualities, or a *plurality* ('duality') of *particular* 'manifested' beings in general, is possible. As stated in Chapter 4, however, the 'cycles of manifestation' in which *particular* beings have their reality cannot be described, according to Guénon, by metaphysics, only by 'physics' in the ancient, more comprehensive, sense of the term. As we quoted Guénon stating in Chapter 4,

> 'metaphysical' is synonymous with 'universal.' Hence no doctrine that confines itself to the consideration of individual beings can merit the name of metaphysics, whatever may be its interest and value in other respects; such a doctrine can always be called 'physical' in the original sense of the word, because it lies exclusively within the realm of 'nature' — that is, of manifestation — with the further restriction that it envisages only formal manifestation, and even more especially one of the states that constitute the latter.[26]

I will return to the ideas of 'duality' and 'dichotomy' as I employ them in connection with traditional serpent/dragon symbolism in Chapter 6.

All cases of symbolic modifications of the simple serpent/dragon symbol in traditional art and myth that I shall consider indicate either Spiritualization or its opposite, 'Materialization.' In the case of the combat myth, the migrating being is depicted and described as a 'god' or 'hero' who is 'struggling' to 'overcome,' and possibly 'control

---

25 The word 'two,' or the numeral '2,' for example, expresses the simplest idea of non-unity, non-'oneness.'
26 René Guénon, *The Symbolism of the Cross*, 7.

and manage,' the state of *matter* which consists of his perception of 'nature' as a 'chaos.' This *potential* 'god'/'hero' is, in the terms of this book, *attempting* to Spiritualize his true 'Self'/*Atman* by 'identifying' with his source, Spirit/*Brahman* (Guénon's 'Principle'). It is possible, however, that he may *not* succeed in his task and be, therefore, subject to what I term 'Materialization.' If 'Spiritualization' describes the act of forming, defining, and 'actualizing' *matter*, 'Materialization,' as I define it, describes the unconscious tendency in the 'migrating' being toward *dissolution* of form and definition, as well as the *increase* of potentiality in the, relatively speaking, less 'Self'-aware migrating being. Materialization, as the opposite of Spiritualization, describes the migrating being's 'descent' into the state of *matter* and its 'fixation' on the flux of *samsara*. It describes the being's 'downward tendency,' which, as Guénon notes, characterizes the condition of *tamas*,[27] its 'descent' into lesser awareness of 'chaos' and, thus, more embeddedness in the unconscious levels of 'nature.' As such, Materialization constitutes the relatively unconscious 'wandering' of the 'migrating' being into an increasing formlessness, indefinitude, and potentiality that separates it ever further from 'realization' — *complete* forming, defining, and 'actualizing' of its metaphysical essence, its *actual* 'Self.' That being which 'descends' further into, or embraces more fully, the state of *matter*, therefore, increases: 1) its relative lack of form, 2) its relative lack of definition, and 3) its relative potentiality (its failure to 'realize' or 'discover' its 'Self') because it moves further away from understanding its 'Self'/*Atman as an expression of* Spirit/*Brahman* (the 'Principle').

Another kind of symbolic modification of the serpent/dragon symbol in Tradition consists in the position or 'placement,' vertical or horizontal for example, of the serpent/dragon in the context of a larger 'complex symbolism.' There are thus, as we shall discuss in later chapters, traditional depictions of what I shall call the 'risen' (or 'ascending') serpent as well as depictions of the 'fallen' (or 'descending')

---

27 René Guénon, *Man & His Becoming According to the Vedanta*, 45.

serpent. The 'risen'/'ascending' serpent is symbolic of the event of Spiritualization (or its possibility); the 'fallen'/'descending' serpent is symbolic of Materialization (or its possibility). In the case of the 'risen' serpent, therefore, the (potential) forming, defining, and 'actualizing' of the 'migrating' being is symbolized; in the case of the 'fallen' serpent, the 'migrating' being's (potential) 'fall' or 'descent' into formlessness, indefinitude, and potentiality is symbolized. Traditional examples of the symbolization of Materialization by means of the 'complex symbolism' of the serpent may be found in Genesis 3, *The Epic of Gilgamesh*, and numerous other traditional myths that describe man's loss of 'immortality' to a serpent. In Genesis 3, for example, which we shall look at in more depth in Chapter 6, Adam and 'the woman' (later to become 'Eve') 'fall,' specifically by means of their interaction with a serpent, into what I have called the realm of 'duality,' 'nature' *perceived as* dependent and 'chaotic' — the state of *matter*. In the symbolic language just proposed of the relative vertical 'placement' of symbols, Adam and 'the woman' 'fall'/'descend' into the state of 'duality' discussed earlier as a result of their interaction with both a 'dual-natured' serpent (which we shall explain later) *and* the 'dual' Tree of the Knowledge of Good *and* Evil, which Guénon argues in *The Symbolism of the Cross* to traditionally symbolize 'duality.' This 'fall' into 'duality,' based upon the equivalences argued for so far, consists of a fall into the state of *matter*, that state of awareness of "the indefinite series of cycles of manifestation"/*samsara* whose object is 'manifestation,' the *plurality* ('duality') of beings. Guénon contends that the Tree of the Knowledge of Good *and* Evil symbolizes 'duality' as an existential 'opposite' of the 'unity' that characterizes the metaphysical Principle, God Yahweh in Hebrew tradition. I add to Guénon's hypothesis, as already stated in part, that the 'duality' thus represented by the Tree of Knowledge,[28] which Guénon associates with "the indefinite series of cycles of manifestation"/*samsara*,

---

28 I will sometimes abbreviate 'The Tree of the Knowledge of Good and Evil' as the 'Tree of Knowledge.'

also symbolizes the state of *matter*, which is not *only* "the indefinite series of cycles of manifestation"/*samsara* but also the 'migrating' being's particular *perception* of 'cyclical existence' *as* a 'chaos.' I argue, similarly, in Chapter 8, that in *The Epic of Gilgamesh* the "well of cool water"[29] that distracts Gilgamesh from his quest for a "plant...which restores his lost youth"[30] symbolizes *his* Materialization, or 'descent,' into the formlessness, indefinitude, and potentiality of the state of *matter*, 'identification' with the flux of *samsara*. This occurs because the 'cool water,' or what it *symbolizes*, interrupts Gilgamesh's 'heroic' 'struggle' against a serpent of 'chaos' that 'steals' the desired plant and, therefore, Gilgamesh's 'immortality.' Gilgamesh's quest to 'restore lost youth' is, in *Vedantic* terms, the struggle to achieve *moksha* or 'identification' with Spirit/*Brahman*/Principle. In Chapter 15, we shall address more completely the traditional symbolism of 'water,' or 'the waters' of 'chaos,' that, I contend, are alluded to in *The Epic of Gilgamesh*, in connection with the symbolism of the East Asian (or 'Far-Eastern,' as Guénon calls it) dragon.

A third kind of traditional 'symbolic modification' of the 'simple' serpent symbol appears in the Classical symbolism of the Rod of Asclepius/Aesculapius/Asklepios, in which a serpent is depicted entwined around a rod. This traditional example of 'complex' serpent/dragon symbolism, like that expressed in the combat myth, depicts a juxtaposition of what Guénon calls 'axial' imagery with the 'simple' serpent symbol. The meaning of the Rod of Asklepios for traditional peoples, as I shall argue in a later chapter, is the potential for 'healing' in the traditional sense, which is equivalent to *meta*-physical rejuvenation, or rebirth — Spiritualization, as I say — of a 'lower' aspect of the 'Self,' the being as it is 'trapped' in the 'chaos' of *samsara*/'nature.' The rod symbolizes Spirit — the metaphysical Principle for Guénon — while the serpent symbolizes the 'sickness' or 'death' of the

---

29 N. K. Sandars, trans., *The Epic of Gilgamesh* (London, England: Penguin Books, 1960), 117.

30 N. K. Sandars, trans., *The Epic of Gilgamesh*, 116.

being that has 'fallen' into the state of *matter*, into awareness of the 'chaos' of being 'trapped' in the dependent "indefinite series of cycles of manifestation" of 'nature.'

Beyond the symbolization of the 'simple events' of Spiritualization and Materialization in traditional narratives, such as in the latter case those described in Genesis 3 and *The Epic of Gilgamesh*, there are symbolizations in traditional artifacts of the further degree of Spiritualization that I term 'management and control' of the state of *matter*. More specifically, as noted in the *Introduction*, I propose that there existed in traditional societies both: 1) *individuals* who were considered capable of 'management and control' of the state of *matter* and 2) *places* built in traditional civilizations intended to facilitate this 'management and control,' or Spiritualization, of *matter*. Examples of such individuals are the shamans, Emperors, priest-kings, prophets, healers, and 'enlightened' persons of ancient civilizations from around the world, traditionally considered to be 'messengers' between the metaphysical (divine) and the physical (mortal) realms: 'managers' or 'controllers' of Spiritualization. Examples of such places include, for example, sacred temples (such as the 'Temple of the Tigers' in Chichen Itza), sacred mounds (such as the 'Ohio Serpent Mound'), and at least some of the great megalithic henges of the ancient world (such as the Avebury Cycle in England). These were traditionally considered liminal places conducive to Spiritualization that connected, in the way that the individual 'messenger' could also, the metaphysical and physical realms (the celestial and terrestrial orders). In the cases of both Spiritualizing individuals and Spiritualizing places, as well as in the case of Spiritualizing events, which we shall discuss, serpent/dragon imagery was combined with 'axial' or positional 'placement' ('fallen'/'descending' versus 'risen'/'ascending') imagery of the various sorts listed above to symbolize the Spiritualization of the state of *matter*, whether on an individual or a societal level. The 'thunderweapon' of 'gods' and heroes, the rod and staff of prophets and healers, the cross of 'saviors,' as well as symbols of 'Heaven' or the 'heavens,' such as birds, wings, and what I shall call the 'risen' (vertical) serpent, as well as other symbols to be considered, symbolized for traditional humans either: 1) the potential for (the 'struggle' for) Spiritualization, 2) its actual occurrence, or 3) its 'management and control.' These symbols represented for traditional peoples (in possibility *or* in actual fact and through the representation of *vertical ascension*) by means of person or place, height or flight, either: the 'struggle'/'combat' with, the 'overcoming' of, or the 'management and control' of, the state of *matter* experienced by beings of a certain level of awareness. A healer, such as the Greek physician Asklepios, who carried the staff-with-serpent (see fig. 5.2), or a temple exhibiting serpent imagery, such as the Temple of the Tigers in Chichen Izta (see fig. 5.3), symbolized in Tradition the *potential* for Spiritualization which was believed to exist in the respective person or place. The *absence*, however, of such symbols, or the indication of 'descent,' or of an association with 'water,' or the ground, or 'earth,' or dust or dirt symbolized, for traditional peoples, the 'failure' of Spiritualization, the 'fall' into *matter* and, thus, 'descent' into the cycles of *samsara*: Materialization. Alternatively, depictions and descriptions of 'gods,' such as Indra, Zeus, Apollo, and Thor, facing with the aid of their 'axial' 'thunderweapons' — *vajra*, lightning bolt, bow and arrow, and hammer, respectively — 'combat' or 'struggle' with serpentine/draconic foes symbolized, depending upon how their particular narratives played out, cases of potential *or* actual Spiritualization. For, as in the case of Thor specifically, which we shall consider in Chapter 16, these narratives sometimes describe conflicts that are *unresolved*, although the presence of axial imagery ('symbolic weapons') perhaps predicts the inevitable 'overcoming' of the 'chaos' of *matter* and the 'realization' of 'immortality'/*moksha*.

Fig. 5.2. *Asklepios*, Museo Vaticano, Rome[31]

---

31 J. Schouten, *The Rod and Serpent of Asklepios: Symbol of Medicine* (Amsterdam New York: Elsevier Publishing Company, 1967), 31.

Fig. 5.3. Façade of the Temple of the Tigers, Chichen Itza, Yucatan, Mexico[32]

---

32 Roman Pina Chan, *Chichen Itza: The city of the wise men of the water* (Merida, Mexico: Editorial Dante, 1980), 53.

CHAPTER 6

The Serpent Symbol, the World Axis, and 'Duality' and Its Variations in Ancient Egypt and Genesis 3

In 1833, the Reverend John Bathurst Deane, cofounder of the British Archeological Association and the Royal Archeological Institute of Great Britain and Ireland, stated in *The Worship of the Serpent Traced Throughout the World* that

> [t]he mystic serpent entered into the mythology of every nation; consecrated almost every temple; symbolized almost every deity; was imagined in the heavens, stamped upon the earth, and ruled in the realms of everlasting sorrow.[1]

In their 1877 book *Serpent and Siva Worship and Mythology in Central America, Africa, and Asia*, Hyde Clarke, philologist and member of the British Association for the Advancement of Science, and C. Staniland Wake, Director of the Anthropological Institute of Great Britain and Ireland, observed that

> [t]he remains of Serpent-worship are to be found in all quarters of the earth, among nations geographically remote from each other, and supposed

---

1   Rev. John Bathurst Deane, *The Worship of the Serpent Traced Throughout the World; Attesting the Temptation and Fall of Man by the Instrumentality of a Serpent Tempter* (London: J. G. & F. Rivington, 1833), 220.

to be distinct in characteristics of race, habitude, intellectual constitution and religious belief.[2]

In 1919, G. Elliot Smith, anatomist and Egyptologist who "established the basis for understanding the mammalian brain,"[3] argued in *The Evolution of the Dragon* that

> [i]n the course of its romantic and chequered history the dragon has been identified with all of the gods and all of the demons of every religion. But it is most intimately associated with the earliest substratum of divinities, for it has been homologized with each of the members of the earliest Trinity, the Great Mother, the Water God, and the Warrior Sun God, both individually and collectively.[4]

In 1940, the symbolist Louis Charbonneau-Lassay opined in *The Bestiary of Christ* that "[i]n the general study of religious or philosophical symbolism of former times, the snake certainly presents the largest and most complex possible subject."[5] And, in 1983, Balaji Mundkur, a biologist who turned later in his career to the study of animal cults and iconography, concluded in *The Cult of the Serpent* that the snake is "the one common, forceful element that surfaces amidst the great variety of animals in Western Hemispheric myths and religions."[6]

---

2 Hyde Clarke and C. Staniland Wake, *Serpent and Siva Worship and Mythology in Central America, Africa, and Asia and The Origin of Serpent Worship* (New York, New York: J. W. Bouton, 1877), v–vi.

3 Malcolm Macmillan, "Evolution and the Neurosciences Down-Under," *Journal of the History of the Neurosciences* April 2009, 18:2, 150. 150–196.

4 Sir Grafton Elliot Smith, *The Evolution of the Dragon* (London, New York, Chicago, Bombay, Calcutta, Madras: Manchester University Press, Longmans, Green & Company, 1919 [republished in 2008 by Forgotten Books]), 89.

5 Louis Charbonneau-Lassay, *The Bestiary of Christ*, 153.

6 Balaji Mundkur, *The Cult of the Serpent: An Interdisciplinary Survey of Its Manifestations and Origins* (Albany, New York: State University of New York Press, 1983), 25.

The history of serpent and dragon symbolism is long and opinions concerning the ancient meaning(s) of this symbolism are many. Since ancient times, the creature that we call 'snake' has exercised a spell over humans. In the nineteenth century, freemason and scholar Albert Pike wrote in *Morals and Dogma* that

> [a]ccording to Sanchoniathon[7], Taaut[8], the interpreter of Heaven to men attributed something divine to the nature of the dragon and serpents, in which the Phoenicians and Egyptians followed him. They have more vitality, more spiritual force, than any other creature; of a fiery nature, shown by the rapidity of their motions, without the limbs of other animals. They assume many shapes and attitudes, and dart with extraordinary quickness and force. When they have reached old age, they throw off that age and are young again, and increase in size and strength, for a certain period of years.[9]

The snake has always seemed 'different': more 'vital' than other creatures, as Sanchoniathon argued, more dangerous or fear-inspiring, as Mundkur goes on about,[10] or somehow more illustrative of the 'divine' for man than anything else in nature, as G. Elliot Smith argued. Interpretations of serpent and dragon symbolism go back to the earliest recorded history, often blending the two apparently different creatures, often referring to them in the same contexts, and often attributing to them the same characteristics. The mass of information that exists today on the complex serpent/dragon symbol is beyond

---

7   Sanchoniathon was a Phoenician philosopher roughly contemporary with the pre-Homeric age of Greece, thought by some to be a mythical or quasi-mythical figure.
8   'Taaut' is another name of the Egyptian god Horus when he was young.
9   Albert Pike, *Morals and Dogma of the Ancient and Accepted Scottish Rite of Freemasonry Prepared for the Supreme Council of the Thirty-Third Degree, for the Southern Jurisdiction of the United States and Published by Its Authority* (Charleston, 1871), 494. See Leslie S. Wilson, *The Serpent Symbol in the Ancient Near East* (Lanham, Maryland: University Press of America, Inc.), 61, for a more complete attribution of this quotation.
10 Balaji Mundkur, *The Cult of the Serpent*, xvi.

the capacity of any individual to sift through, let alone intelligently analyze and synthesize. As James Charlesworth, director and editor of the Princeton Dead Sea Scrolls Project, notes in *The Good and Evil Serpent*, "none of the authors who have worked on ophidian [snake] iconography knows the astronomical number of publications in this field of inquiry."[11] As we discussed in Chapter 3, although any scientific endeavor searches for the Universal, it always makes do, according to Guénon, with the 'general.' Such must be the course set for any empirical investigation, insofar as it can never access or analyze *all* relevant information. The perspectives of Guénon and Eliade, however, illuminate to a particularly high degree of clarity many of the extant historical instances of the serpent/dragon symbol.

The World Axis or *Axis Mundi* in Guénon and Eliade

René Guénon's most sustained discussion of the serpent symbol occurs in *The Symbolism of the Cross*, an interpretation of the traditional 'metaphysical symbolism of the cross' which encompasses much more than that symbol's specifically Christian associations.[12] As we noted in Chapter 5, according to Guénon, the cross is merely one among many 'figurations' of the 'World Axis' that symbolize for traditional peoples the metaphysical, 'transcendent,' or spiritual 'center' of the universe. For Guénon and Eliade both, the World Axis symbolizes in traditional societies that metaphysical 'place' where communication or 'travel' is believed to be possible among the various levels of existence, Guénon's 'multiple states of the being.' In *Patterns in Comparative Religion*, Eliade describes the vicinity around the 'universal pillar' or *Axis Mundi* as "a region impregnated with the sacred, a spot where one

---

11   James H. Charlesworth, *The Good and Evil Serpent*, dust jacket description and 24.
12   René Guénon, *The Symbolism of the Cross*, 16 and 3.

can pass from one cosmic zone to another."[13] In *The Sacred and the Profane*, he states:

> Such a cosmic pillar can be only at the very center of the universe, for the whole of the habitable world extends around it. Here, then, we have a sequence of religious conceptions and cosmological images that are inseparably connected and form a system that may be called the "system of the world" prevalent in traditional societies: (*a*) a sacred place constitutes a break in the homogeneity of space; (*b*) this break is symbolized by an opening by which passage from one cosmic region to another is made possible (from heaven to earth and vice versa; from earth to the underworld); (*c*) communication with heaven is expressed by one or another of certain images, all of which refer to the axis mundi: pillar…,ladder (cf. Jacob's ladder), mountain, tree, vine, etc.; (*d*) around this cosmic axis lies the world (=our world), hence the axis is located "in the middle," at the "navel of the earth"; it is the Center of the World.[14]

The 'sacred' for Eliade, as noted in Chapter 3, corresponds to what Guénon identifies as the 'metaphysical' or 'Universal.' Eliade thus argues that "Man becomes aware of the sacred because it manifests itself, shows itself, as something wholly different from the profane."[15] "The sacred always manifests itself as a reality of a wholly different order from 'natural' realities."[16] The 'natural' reality of a tree is, for example, a 'profane' reality, an 'ordinary object.'[17] It is *through* such 'ordinary objects,' however, that, according to Eliade, "something sacred shows itself to us."[18] This 'showing,' as we stated in Chapter 3, is what Eliade terms a 'hierophany,' an "act of manifestation of the sacred."[19] Because the sacred shows itself as "a reality of a wholly different order" from 'natural' realities, it is essentially 'meta-natural': 'meta-physical.'

---

13   Mircea Eliade, *Patterns in Comparative Religion*, 99–100.
14   Mircea Eliade, *The Sacred and the Profane*, 37.
15   Mircea Eliade, *The Sacred and the Profane*, 11.
16   Mircea Eliade, *The Sacred and the Profane*, 10.
17   Mircea Eliade, *The Sacred and the Profane*, 11.
18   Mircea Eliade, *The Sacred and the Profane*, 11.
19   Mircea Eliade, *The Sacred and the Profane*, 11.

Although any 'ordinary' or 'natural' object can, for Eliade, serve as the means for "an opening...either upward [toward] (the divine world) or downward [toward] (the underworld, the world of the dead)," a means by which "the three cosmic levels — earth, heaven, underworld...[can be] put in communication," it is to our purpose here to discuss only that hierophany that, according to Eliade, is "sometimes expressed through the image of a universal pillar, [the] *axis mundi*."[20]

In *Shamanism: Archaic Techniques of Ecstasy*, Eliade says of the *Axis Mundi* that

> [t]his axis...passes through an "opening," a "hole"; it is through this hole that the gods descend to earth and the dead to the subterranean regions; it is through the same hole that the soul of the shaman in ecstasy can fly up or down in the course of his celestial or infernal journeys.[21]

Eliade adds that

> [i]n the archaic cultures communication between sky and earth is ordinarily used to send offerings to the celestial gods and not for a concrete and personal assent; the latter remains the prerogative of shamans....For the former, the "Center of the World" is a site that permits them to send their prayers and offerings to the celestial gods, whereas...only for the latter is *real communication* among the three cosmic zones [sky/heaven, earth, and the 'subterranean regions'] a possibility.[22]

From Guénon's broadly traditional meta-physical perspective, the designations Heaven, Earth, and Underworld, or celestial, terrestrial, and subterranean/infernal, are metaphorical abbreviations for the *indefinite* number of 'states of the being' in its 'travels' or 'migrations.' Although for Guénon and Eliade both, the *Axis Mundi* serves as that 'place' where a change of 'state' is possible for any appropriately disciplined or 'realized' 'migrating' being, Eliade often focuses most in

---

20 Mircea Eliade, *The Sacred and the Profane*, 12 and 36.
21 Mircea Eliade, *Shamanism: Archaic Techniques of Ecstasy*, trans. Willard R. Trask (Princeton and Oxford: Princeton University Press, 1964), 259.
22 Mircea Eliade, *Shamanism*, 265.

his works on the 'journeys' of individuals initiated into that ancient profession called 'shaman' by the Tungus people of Siberia.²³

In agreement with Guénon, Eliade argues that the *Axis Mundi* is represented in a variety of ways in traditional cultures. In *Shamanism*, he writes that

> [t]he Axis of the World has been concretely represented, either by pillars that support the house, or in the form of isolated stakes, called "World Pillars." For the Eskimo [Inuit], for example, the Pillar of the Sky is identified with the pole at the center of their dwellings. The Tatars of the Altai, the Buryat, and the Soyot assimilate the tent pole to the Sky Pillar.²⁴

Also in agreement with Guénon, Eliade points to the many traditional examples of the *Axis Mundi* that have been discovered in juxtaposition with the serpent/dragon symbol, the latter being depicted or described either near the World Axis or 'coiled' *around* it. According to both authors, along with the 'pillar' or 'pole,' one of the most common representations of the World Axis in traditional art and myth is the tree. In *The Symbolism of the Cross*, Guénon compares the transcultural 'axial' symbolism of the tree specifically with the cross, stating that "[a]nother aspect of the symbolism of the cross identifies it with what various traditions describe as the 'Tree in the Midst' or some equivalent term." Guénon adds that "[i]t has been shown elsewhere that this tree is one of the numerous symbols of the 'World Axis.'"²⁵ In *Patterns in Comparative Religion*, Eliade similarly observes that

> [t]here is a mass of myths and legends in which a Cosmic Tree symbolizes the universe (with seven branches corresponding to the seven heavens), a central tree or pillar upholds the world. Each one of these myths and legends gives its own version of the theory of the "centre", in as much as the tree embodies absolute reality, the course of life and sacred power, and therefore stands at the centre of the world.²⁶

---

23 Michael Harner, *The Way of the Shaman* (New York: Harper & Row, 1980), 25.
24 Mircea Eliade, *Shamanism*, 261.
25 René Guénon, *The Symbolism of the Cross*, 54.
26 Mircea Eliade, *Patterns in Comparative Religion*, 380.

According to Guénon, cross and tree are only symbolically equivalent in Tradition insofar as they each represent the 'manifestation' of the metaphysical Principle in its various 'states of the being.' This 'manifestation' of 'the being' is, according to Guénon, symbolized by the *uniting* of a vertical symbol symbolizing the Principle with a horizontal symbol symbolizing the 'multiple states of the being.' The upper portion of the cross or tree symbolizes 'higher' states of 'the being,' the lower portion symbolizes 'lower' states of 'the being.' From the perspective of the East Asian version of Tradition, according to Guénon,

> The vertical axis [of the cross] thus represents the metaphysical locus of the manifestation of the 'Will of Heaven' [the traditional Chinese expression for the metaphysical Principle's 'action'], and passes through each horizontal plane at its center, that is, at the point where the equilibrium which that manifestation implies is achieved; in other words, the point of complete harmonization of all the elements that go to make up that particular state of the being.[27]

The *two* horizontal arms of the cross, from the perspective of Tradition according to Guénon, are merely simplified or 'stylized' versions of the *many* horizontal limbs of the tree. In both cases, according to Guénon, it is the horizontal component of the overall symbolism that represents the 'multiple states of the being' themselves, *through which* the vertically represented metaphysical Principle, or 'Will of Heaven' in East Asian Tradition, 'passes.' The metaphysical essence or Principle—'the being' *itself*, that is—of all of the horizontally symbolized 'multiple states of the being' is, therefore, symbolized in Tradition vertically by either the trunk of the tree or the vertical bar of the cross, or other axial symbols. This Principle is, according to Guénon, in *Vedantic* terms, the 'subject,' 'Self'/*Atman*, of 'migration' through *samsara*/"the indefinite series of cycles of manifestation"

---

27 René Guénon, *The Symbolism of the Cross*, 109 and 111. The traditional East Asian 'versions' and symbolism of the metaphysical Principle in its connection with the symbolism of the 'Far-Eastern Dragon' will be considered in Chapter 15.

and, therefore, the essentially metaphysical Reality that ties together the indefinitude of the 'multiple states of the being.' Based upon these observations, it can be seen that, whereas the 'oneness' of the vertical bar of the cross corresponds *exactly* to what Guénon refers to as the 'unity' of the metaphysical Principle, the corresponding oneness of the *horizontal* bar of the cross is only an idealized or 'stylized' expression of that which would more accurately, according to Guénon, represent the idea that the horizontal bar symbolizes: an *indefinite* number of horizontal bars.

The Serpent, 'Duality,' and Dichotomy in Genesis 3 and Ancient Egyptian Myth

In *The Symbolism of the Cross*, Guénon discusses the traditional representation of the World Axis that he terms the 'Tree in the Midst,' his appellation for the 'Tree of Life' referred to in Genesis 2–3. According to Guénon,

> This tree stands at the center of the world, or rather of a world, that is, of a domain in which a state of existence, such as the human state, is developed. In biblical symbolism, for example, the 'Tree of life', planted in the midst of the Terrestrial Paradise, represents the center of our world.[28]

In Genesis 2:9, however, there are *two* trees growing "in the midst" of the garden:

> And out of the ground the LORD God made to spring up every tree that is pleasant to the sight and good for food. The tree of life was in the midst of the garden, and the tree of the knowledge of good and evil.[29] [ESV]

---

28 René Guénon, *The Symbolism of the Cross*, 54.
29 The usage "Tree of the Knowledge of good and evil" employed in the English Standard Version of the Bible will be preferred here over "tree of knowledge of good and bad" or other such usages, as it is the same translation used in the English editions of Guénon's works and is more consistent with Guénon's overall investigations.

According to Guénon, only the Tree of Life symbolizes the World Axis in the biblical narrative because only the Tree of Life symbolizes the 'unity' that characterizes the metaphysical Principle of which the Hebrew Yahweh (the 'LORD God') is a variant. According to Guénon,

> The nature of the 'Tree of the Knowledge of good and evil', as its name implies, is characterized by duality, for in this name there are two terms which are not even complementary but in truth opposed; indeed, it can be said that their whole raison d'être lies in this opposition, for once it is transcended there can no longer be any question of good or evil. The same cannot be said of the 'Tree of Life', which on the contrary, in its function of 'World Axis', essentially implies unity.[30]

Since, as Guénon states, "the serpent is most commonly associated with the 'Tree of Knowledge,'"[31] it is "characterized by duality," by good *and* evil rather than by good *alone* (see fig. 6.1).

It seems reasonable to presume that there exists a close association, perhaps causal, between the complex symbolism of the serpent/dragon in Tradition and the basic anatomy of the snake. For, how could the snake's characteristic bifid tongue and 'double penis' *not* be related in some way to the serpent's symbolic association with what Guénon terms 'duality'?[32] More generally, one should think that, un-

---

30 René Guénon, *The Symbolism of the Cross*, 55.
31 René Guénon, *The Symbolism of the Cross*, 57.
32 Emphasis on both the snake's 'forked (bifid) tongue' and 'double penis' (*hemipenes*) is marked in many traditional cultures. In *The Cult of the Serpent*, for example, Balaji Mundkur remarks that "in their art practically all cultures portray the bifid tongue as if it were the quintessential ophidian symbol." Mundkur refers to two examples that are separated greatly by both time and distance: 1) the Egyptian case of the Netjer-ankh (the 'living god') symbolized by a serpent with bifid tongue and 2) "the bifid tongue...motif" which recurs "almost constantly in the elaborately styled art of the Maya." Balaji Mundkur, *The Cult of the Serpent*, 24, 25 and 145. Such representations do not, admittedly, prove the traditional serpent symbol's identification with the abstract concept of 'duality' that Guénon discusses in *The Symbolism of the Cross* in *all* traditional cultures, but they provide fair evidence that the tongue of the snake, specifically, was seen as one of its most interesting or representative features.

less some form of homology existed for traditional humans between the anatomical features of natural beings used by them as symbols and the meanings of such symbols, then the relevant symbols would not have become efficacious in the first place.

Fig. 6.1. *Temptation and Fall of Adam and Eve*, ninth or tenth century CE, Codex Vigiliano y Albeldense, folio 17, Biblioteca del Monasterio de San Lorenzo, El Escorial, Spain[33]

Because this feature is so unusual in the animal kingdom, it is hard to imagine that the snake's bifid tongue is *not* one of the anatomical elements that made it so interesting to traditional peoples.

33 Marilyn Nissenson and Susan Jonas, *Snake Charm* (New York: Henry N. Abrams, Inc., Publishers, 1995), 52.

In *Serpent in the Sky: The High Wisdom of Ancient Egypt*, Egyptologist John Anthony West states that

> [i]n Egypt...the serpent was the symbol for duality...more accurately, for the power that results in duality. And that power is itself dual in aspect; it is simultaneously creative and destructive: creative in the sense that multiplicity is created out of unity, destructive in the sense that creation represents the rupture of the perfection of the Absolute....When it is realized that the serpent bears both a forked tongue and a double penis, the underlying wisdom of the choice [of the snake as a symbol of duality] becomes clear.[34]

In Chapter 5, I suggested that Guénon's realm of 'manifestation' could be referred to as a realm of 'duality' because it is a realm of a *plurality*, or multiplicity, of 'manifested' beings and duality is the first, or most fundamental, expression of plurality (multiplicity). 'Duality' can be seen as a shorthand expression for the plurality/multiplicity of the 'manifested' world which, according to Guénon, 'manifests' the 'unity' of the metaphysical Principle. We may add to this that 'duality' can, more specifically within the traditional perspective, be seen to characterize 'nature' because, as Guénon argues, nature is the realm of 'formal manifestation.' If, however, 'duality' characterizes 'nature,' then it also characterizes *matter* as I define it, for *matter* is the state of being within which 'nature' is first explicitly become aware of by the New Man and *perceived*, in its limitedness, as 'chaotic.' Thus is the traditional idea of 'chaos' intimately connected in traditional art and myth with the idea of 'duality.'

Guénon's contrast in *The Symbolism of the Cross* of the 'duality' of the Tree of the Knowledge of good and evil with the 'unity' of the Tree of Life would seem to indicate that he sees the one as the 'opposite' of

---

34 John Anthony West, *Serpent in the Sky: The High Wisdom of Ancient Egypt* (Wheaton, Illinois: The Theosophical Publishing House, 1993), xiii and 58–59. *Serpent in the Sky* is an introduction to the work of the Alsatian philosopher and Egyptologist R. A. Schwaller de Lubicz, specifically his research on ancient Egyptian symbolism.

the other. More abstractly, it seems that Guénon views the 'duality' of 'manifestation' as the 'opposite' of the 'unity' of the metaphysical Principle. West, in a similar fashion, emphasizes the traditional serpent symbol's association not only with 'duality' but with 'dichotomy' as well. In *Serpent in the Sky*, West presents two 'opposite' ideas of 'duality' that he maintains were represented in Egyptian mythology by two *different* serpents, revealing thereby a connection in Egyptian mythology between 'chaos' and 'duality.' He states:

> Duality [in ancient Egypt] as the call to unchecked chaos and multiplicity is symbolized by the 'serpent fiend, Apop', who devours the souls of the dead and thus denies them reunion with the source [of all being]. Duality [also, in opposition] as higher intellect, duality and the primordial creative impulse, is the serpent in the sky—the cobra, symbol of Lower Egypt, which is synthesis, creation.[35]

In *Myth and Symbol in Ancient Egypt*, Rundle Clark describes 'the serpent fiend, Apop,' 'Apopis,' as that creature that the god Seth "has to ward off" when he "is put at the bow of the sun's boat." He is the 'opposite' of light, "the serpent dragon of darkness, who threatens to overwhelm the divine barque at sunrise and sunset."[36] In this imagery, the dichotomy of darkness and the sun's light is virtually synonymous with the dichotomy of 'chaos' and order.

As with Guénon, West notes the 'dual' nature of the serpent symbol itself (as well as the natural snake) by drawing attention to the equivalency represented in ancient Egyptian art between 'chaos' and multiplicity ('duality') as symbolized by the 'serpent fiend, Apop.' From Guénon's perspective, West's description of the serpent Apop as that which "denies…reunion with the source" shows it to be the traditional 'opposite' of 'unity,' and thus representative of 'duality' in Tradition, because the 'source' of all being in Tradition, according to Guénon, is the *unity* of the metaphysical Principle. West's reference

---

35   John Anthony West, *Serpent in the Sky: The High Wisdom of Ancient Egypt*, 132.
36   R. T. Rundle Clark, *Myth and Symbol in Ancient Egypt*, 209.

to the mythological serpent Apop that in ancient Egyptian myth "devours the souls of the dead and thus denies them reunion with the source [of their being]"[37] provides an illustrative example of the, according to Guénon, traditional belief that it is the 'dual,' or plural/multiple, world of 'formal manifestation' ('nature') that prevents reunion with the 'unity' of the metaphysical 'Principle' that is called *Brahman* in South Asia and Yahweh/God in the Torah.

According to West, 'chaos' and 'multiplicity' go hand in hand in ancient Egyptian thought. 'Chaos,' therefore, appropriately symbolized by the 'dual'/multiple-natured serpent, hinders the reunion of the "souls of the dead" with what Guénon describes as the 'unity' of their 'source.' According to Guénon, this 'source' *was*, for a long period of time, considered by the ancient Egyptians to be a *metaphysical* 'unity,' as it still *is* in Orthodox Judaism and *Advaita Vedanta*, in spite of the many superficial changes in Egyptian religion over that civilization's long history. Rundle Clark draws attention to the Egyptian use of serpent symbolism in connection with 'chaos' in the specific case of the serpent as the protector of the world "against the disintegrating forces of the surrounding chaos."[38] According to Clark,

> [a]ll the peoples of antiquity felt that light and life were constantly threatened by very real cosmic enemies, everywhere beyond their own immediate environment. Hence the need to put a guard around the earth or its symbolic alternative, the Primeval Mound. The world area, usually called Hermopolis in this connection, is surrounded by a monstrous serpent with its tail in its mouth. This creature was called Sito — 'Son of the Earth', i.e., 'the essentially earthy one' — a common expression for snakes....Because [the serpent] surrounds the world it is to be found at the ends of the earth. In a sense, it is the surrounding ocean; but it is also the power which defends the world from water.[39]

---

37 John Anthony West, *Serpent in the Sky: The High Wisdom of Ancient Egypt*, 132.
38 R. T. Rundle Clark, *Myth and Symbol in Ancient Egypt*, 240.
39 R. T. Rundle Clark, *Myth and Symbol in Ancient Egypt*, 240–41.

Clark recognizes in this passage a symbolic connection in Egyptian myth among the symbolisms of serpent, water, and "the disintegrating forces of…chaos" that parallels the relationship that we alluded to in Chapter 5 in our brief discussion of the *Epic of Gilgamesh*. The 'Primeval Mound' that Clark refers to would seem to be a representation of the *Axis Mundi* that symbolizes the metaphysical Principle. The 'surrounding' serpent that Clark describes appears to be the Egyptian version of the transcultural symbolism known in the ancient world as the *Ouroboros*, which we shall investigate in depth in Chapter 9. Both the "real cosmic enemies" referred to by Clark and the 'water' that the world is 'defended' from are, I argue, 'chaotic' elements. This 'chaotic' aspect of the serpent symbol in ancient Egypt is, however, complimented by a 'dual' aspect in the art of the same culture, as Clark draws attention to in an illustration that he provides of a two-headed serpent known in the Pyramid Texts as the 'Provider of Attributes' (see fig. 6.2).[40] The title that is given to the two-headed serpent in this representation buttresses my contention that 'duality' is a short-hand in Tradition for 'multiplicity'/'plurality,' since 'attributes' are the 'opposite' of the 'unity' of whatever *singular essence* they are 'attributed' to.

Fig. 6.2. *The Cosmic Serpent 'Provider of Attributes'*[41]

---

40 R. T. Rundle Clark, *Myth and Symbol in Ancient Egypt*, 52.
41 R. T. Rundle Clark, *Myth and Symbol in Ancient Egypt*, 52.

All of these references suggest that the serpent symbol in Tradition is not a symbol of *either* 'duality' *or* 'chaos' but is symbolically associated with both ideas in various ways, and that, therefore, 'duality' and 'chaos' are related concepts in Tradition. The serpent symbol in Tradition would *appear* to have had, as is shown in the case of ancient Egypt, a 'dual' meaning. In looking deeper, however, the two realities that the serpent symbolized, 'chaos' and 'duality,' served the *same* function: *separating* the 'unity' of the metaphysical 'source' of being that is often symbolized by axial images such as the ('Primeval') 'mound' *from* a 'multiplicity' ('duality') of some kind. The very nature of such multiplicity/'duality' would seem, from the traditional perspective, to designate it as 'chaotic.' The serpent Apop, like the serpent of Eden, causes 'separation' from, as West states, "reunion with the source,"[42] whether this be the 'Primeval Mound' or God Yahweh. The 'monstrous serpent' Sito, according to Clark, separates the 'axial' 'Primeval Mound' from 'water,' the latter of which is, as noted in Chapter 5, symbolically connected in Tradition with both 'chaos' and 'multiplicity' (thus 'duality' as we define it). In both the Egyptian and Hebrew versions of Tradition, therefore, the serpent, whether as 'duality' or 'chaos,' symbolizes that which separates or 'guards' one 'state' of being from another — a more 'unified' state of being, that is, from a more fragmented (multiple, plural, or 'dual') state of being. The subject of the 'guardianship' aspect of the serpent/dragon symbol in Tradition will be taken up in Chapter 8.

'Duality' and Dichotomy Imply the Ideas of Formlessness, Indefinitude, and Potentiality

Although 'duality' is an idea that is commonly integrated into traditional serpent symbolism, it is more accurate to say that 'dichotomy' is, at least on a superficial level, what the serpent symbolizes in Tradition. As noted before, 'duality' is the most basic expression, or

---

42 John Anthony West, *Serpent in the Sky: The High Wisdom of Ancient Egypt*, 132.

first form, of the idea of multiplicity or plurality because it is the simplest expression of the idea of non-unity or 'two-ness.' 'Dichotomy,' on the other hand, expresses *both* two-ness *and* the idea that the two elements involved in a given case of 'duality' are either opposed to, or complimentary with, one another. Prominent examples of the serpent symbol's association with dichotomies in Tradition include not only its association with 'good and evil' in Genesis 3, or 'chaos' and the "primordial creative impulse" (creation/order) in ancient Egyptian myth and art, but also its association with 'life and death' in shamanism and in the symbolism of the Rod of Aesculapius/Asclepius/Asklepios, as well as in the dichotomy of gods (*Devas*) and anti-gods (*Asuras*) in Hindu mythology. The serpent/dragon has been associated with each of these pairs, *together and separately*, in traditional art and myth from around the world.

The serpent/dragon symbol's pervasive association with dichotomies in Tradition serves as a clue to the deeper ideas symbolized by the serpent symbol. As mentioned previously, these are the ideas of *potentiality*, *indefinitude*, and *formlessness* that characterize the state of *matter*. Guénon's definition of *samsara* as an "*indefinite* series of cycles of manifestation" and Eliade's definition of 'chaos' as "the *formless* and nonmanifested"[43] express variations of these three deeper ideas. I propose that the dichotomies symbolized by the serpent/dragon in Tradition imply, first, the idea of *potentiality* because each of the 'opposites' of a dichotomy has, from the perspective of the conscious being evaluating it, the *potential* to transform into its 'opposite.' Evil people, for example, turn into good people; living animals turn into dead animals; happy people turn into sad people; and sick plants turn into healthy ones. The dichotomies symbolized by the serpent/dragon also, however, imply the idea of *indefinitude* because, again, for the conscious being, the desire to discern between 'opposites,' for whatever reason, necessitates an *indefinite* comparison and contrast

---

43 Mircea Eliade, *The Myth of the Eternal Return*, 19.

of those 'opposites' in the being's attempt to understand the identity of each and how they relate to one another. Finally, the dichotomies symbolized by the serpent/dragon imply the idea of *formlessness* because each of the two elements of every dichotomy lacks determinate form, is form-less, *to the extent that* each of the two elements, by its very existence, prevents its 'partner' from manifesting fully and continually. Sickness, for example, prevents wellness from manifesting *once and for all* and completely, and vice versa; good prevents evil from manifesting *once and for all* and completely, and vice versa, etc.

Matter, in this book, is that 'dual' state of *potentiality* (non-actualization), *indefinitude*, and *formlessness* that stands in 'opposition' to the 'unity' of what I term Spirit and what Guénon calls the 'Principle,' what is called in other versions of Tradition *Brahman*, Yahweh/God, etc. The essentially cyclical reality of that state of awareness termed 'nature' — constituted, I argue, by a particular kind of *perception* of what Guénon calls "the indefinite series of cycles of manifestation" — may be described as 'dual' because it is always 'becoming': 1) more or less 'actualized,' 2) more or less defined, and 3) more or less formed. I suggest that these 'states of becoming' are, in traditional art and myth, represented as 'opposites,' *dichotomies*. In the physical/'natural' world, 'things' seem to be always moving away from what they 'are' and transforming into what they 'are not' (e.g., from alive to dead, from ignorant to wise, from hot to cold, from good to evil). What they 'are not,' however, doesn't last either. Death, for example, doesn't last because birth always happens again. Cold doesn't last because there is always a new source of heat originating in the universe. Ignorance doesn't last because curiosity drives those with the capacity to know to seek knowledge. An underlying cyclical, continuous, process of 'actualization,' definition, and formation, which is the 'opposite' of an equally strong 'natural' tendency to potentiality, indefinitude, and formlessness, is reflected in such hypostasized 'opposites.' What are perceived as 'natural' beings, therefore, are always *becoming* something else ('actualizing' but not *actualized*), perpetually changing (*in*-definite) but never defined, form*ing* but unable to maintain a *constant* form (therefore form-less). Always in a state of flux or 'duality,' such 'beings' (which are *not* such in an absolute sense) never, therefore, achieve the fully 'actualized,' defined, and formed 'unity' of Guénon's metaphysical 'Principle.' This is well illustrated by the 'cold-blooded' snake's physiological requirement of absorbing heat from an external source, whether this be the Sun or some other manifestation of a 'heat principle.'[44] This 'natural' example is an excellent metaphor, from the traditional *metaphysical* perspective, for the dependency of the relatively formless, indefinite, potential world of 'nature' on the formed, defined, and 'actualized' metaphysical Principle. Along with its bifid tongue, 'dual penis,' and skin-shedding, the 'cold-bloodedness' of the snake would have provided traditional/archaic peoples a pre-eminent means to convey the dependency of the 'duality' of 'nature' upon the 'unity' of the metaphysical 'Principle' (*Brahman*, Yahweh, etc.).

The 'Traditional' Interpretation of Genesis 3 from the Perspective of *Advaita Vedanta*

The Hindu *darshana* of *Vedanta* is, as we've seen, of the utmost importance to Guénon in defining Tradition. In *Introduction to the Study of the Hindu Doctrines*, Guénon states that

> [t]he *Vedanta*, being a purely metaphysical doctrine, appears essentially as *advaita-vada* [*Advaita Vedanta*] or the 'doctrine of non-duality'; we have explained the meaning of this expression when differentiating between metaphysical and philosophical thought. In order to indicate its scope as far as such a thing is possible, it may now be said that whereas Being is 'one', the Supreme Principle, known as *Brahma*[*n*], can only be described as 'without duality', because, being beyond every determination, even beyond Being, which is the first of all determinations, it cannot be characterized by any positive attribute; such is the consequence of its infinity, which is

---

44 See, for example, Linda Hermans-Killam, "Warm and Cold-Blooded," Cool Cosmos, coolcosmos.ipac.caltech.edu.

necessarily absolute totality, containing in itself all possibilities. Thus, there can be nothing really outside *Brahma*[*n*], since such a supposition would be tantamount to limiting it. It follows immediately that the world, taking the word in its widest possible sense, that is, as universal manifestation in its entirety, is not distinct from *Brahma*[*n*], or, at least, is distinguished from it in illusory fashion only. On the other hand, *Brahma*[*n*] is absolutely distinct from the world, since none of the determinative attributes that belong to the world can be applied to it, the whole of universal manifestation being strictly nil in relation to its infinity.[45]

The school of *Vedanta* known as *Advaita* ('non-dualism'[46]) is, as Guénon states, founded upon the "doctrine of non-duality."[47] According to Guénon, however, *Vedanta* as the 'end of the Vedas' (the Upanishads) *plus* its orthodox interpretations is *already essentially* Advaita Vedanta, 'non-dualism.' In *Fundamentals of Indian Philosophy*, Puligandla agrees when he states concerning the *general Vedantic* view,

> To sum up, there are not two realities, the world of change and the unchanging *Brahman*. Rather, there is one and only one reality, the inexpressible *Brahman*. The world of our senses and intellect is merely a world of names and forms having no reality apart from *Brahman*. It is indeed *Brahman* itself appearing to us through the multiplicity of names and forms....*Atman* ['spirit infinite'] and *Brahman* ['infinite spirit'] do not refer to two different realities, but are two different labels for one and the same unchanging reality underlying the changing world of phenomena, external as well as internal. Here is reached the pinnacle of the Upanisadic wisdom.[48]

Although there is an *emphasis* in Advaita Vedanta on the 'non-duality' of the ultimate Reality, it is still the case, as Puligandla points out, that this view is *already* present in *Vedanta*: namely, "the changing world of phenomena, external as well as internal" is distinct from the 'unity' of

---

45 René Guénon, *Introduction to the Study of the Hindu Doctrines*, 201.
46 Ramakrishna Puligandla, *Fundamentals of Indian Philosophy*, 209.
47 René Guénon, *Introduction to the Study of the Hindu Doctrines*, 201.
48 Ramakrishna Puligandla, *Fundamentals of Indian Philosophy*, 220 and 223.

Atman/Brahman (Guénon's 'Principle') "in illusory fashion only." As Puligandla puts it, *Vedanta*, still as yet undifferentiated into its various schools, *already* holds that "there are no two realities, the world of change and the unchanging *Brahman*. Rather, there is one and only one reality, the inexpressible *Brahman*."[49] According to Guénon, *Brahman*, the South Asian variation of the metaphysical Principle, is distinct from 'the World' ("universal manifestation in its entirety") "in illusory fashion only." Any 'migrating' being that perceives such a distinction, therefore, has, from the perspective of *Vedanta*, not yet 'realized' the 'identity' of its true 'Self' (*Atman*) as *Brahman*. Such a being is 'trapped' or 'lost' in *samsara*, the *Vedantic* equivalent of "the indefinite series of cycles of manifestation." In the terms of my thesis, however, the *perception* of the "indefinite series of cycles of manifestation" from the perspective of the being 'trapped' in the state of awareness termed *matter* appears 'chaotic.' Such a being is inordinately 'fixated' on the multiple or 'dual' *aspect* of 'the World' ("universal manifestation in its entirety"), which aspect consists of "the indefinite series of cycles of manifestation." This 'fixation' occurs, I contend, only because 'the being' has achieved a 'higher' state of awareness wherein it recognizes the dependency of 'the World' ('nature') on a Principle that is 'beyond' ('meta') 'nature.' As long, however, as 'the being' does not completely 'identify' with the metaphysical Principle (*Brahman*) that it has become *partially* aware of, it remains in the state of *matter*. In traditional thought, according to Guénon, only the 'unity' of the metaphysical Principle can provide the 'order' necessary to dispel the 'chaos' that 'the being' in the state of

---

49 Ramakrishna Puligandla, *Fundamentals of Indian Philosophy*, 220. Like Guénon, when he states that *Brahman* "cannot be characterized by any positive attribute," Puligandla emphasizes the 'inexpressibility' of *Brahman*—adding the well-known orthodox view that "the Upanisads exhort us to cut through the cloud of ignorance and discover ourselves to be *Brahman*, infinite, eternal, and immortal." Ramakrishna Puligandla, *Fundamentals of Indian Philosophy*, 227. In sum, Guénon and Puligandla both respect and express the traditional view of *Vedanta* as the 'end of the Vedas,' in which *Brahman* is both one and all.

matter perceives. The 'duality' of 'nature,' therefore, the human *perception* of "the indefinite series of cycles of manifestation" from the state of awareness that I term *matter*, because it is a 'fragmented' state of being torn between complete ignorance of the Principle and complete awareness of the Principle, is 'chaotic.' It exists only to the extent that: 1) the Principle is become aware of, but 2) the Principle is *incompletely* 'identified' with. One way to think about this idea is to imagine that, from the perspective of traditional peoples, there must be something that exists 'beyond' the 'duality' of "the indefinite series of cycles of manifestations" that provides a template, or 'extraterrestrial archetype' as Eliade says, for the interminable 'dividing up' of 'nature' into cycles. If 'nature' is taken to be other than "the indefinite series of cycles of manifestation" *of* the 'unity' of the metaphysical Principle — if, in other words, the physical world is taken as Reality *itself* and as the 'authority' for determining its own order and meaning — this serves, from the traditional perspective, as a barrier or 'guard' to 'realization' of nature's (and, so, duality's) Source.

I argue that 'the serpent' of Genesis 3, as the representative or 'personification' of the Tree of the Knowledge of good and evil, and thus, according to Guénon, of 'duality,' symbolizes in Tradition that which 'separates' or 'guards' the migrating being from 'realization' of the metaphysical Principle — Yahweh/'God' in the Torah. Yahweh or 'God' is symbolized in Genesis 3 by what Guénon describes in *The Symbolism of the Cross* as the 'unity' of the Tree of Life. The 'serpent of Eden' serves in its specified capacity only because its 'perspective' on the nature of the Principle, expressed in its opinion of what God meant in His instructions to 'the woman,' is accepted by one *aspect* of what I argue is a *single* 'dual-natured' 'migrating' being named in Genesis 'Adam and Eve.' This being which engages 'the serpent' in conversation in Genesis 3 has two names, 'Adam' and 'Eve,' because it is, like the serpent and the Tree of Knowledge, I suggest, 'dual'-natured or 'separated' in some way from the 'unity' of its Source. 'Adam and Eve's' 'duality' is first revealed in Genesis 3:6 when, after being instructed by God in Genesis 2:16–17 *not* to eat of the fruit of the Tree of the Knowledge of good and evil, 'the woman' (later to become Eve) takes the serpent's *conflicting* advice and eats of the fruit of that tree.[50] In so doing, 'the woman'/Eve: 1) *literally* takes the serpent as an independent authority separate from the authority of God, and 2) *symbolically* takes 'duality' (symbolized by the serpent and the Tree of Knowledge) as independent or 'separate' from 'unity' (symbolized by the Tree of Life). Since 'duality' is, as I have argued, shorthand for the multiplicity/plurality of 'manifestation' or 'nature,' 'Adam and Eve,' in taking the 'dual'-natured serpent's advice by means of its specifically 'Eve' aspect, takes 'nature' to exist independent of metaphysical 'unity' and, thus, to have a 'separate' and independent authority. This 'mis-take' originates only in 'the woman'/Eve *aspect* of the 'migrating' being.

'Adam and Eve's' subsequent actions, as recorded in Genesis, reveal that it has not only entertained the advice, or rhetoric, of 'the serpent' but *believed* it. It has, therefore, 'accepted duality' and, thus, 'fallen' into the state of being that is typified by multiplicity and dichotomies, such as good *and* evil, instead of 'identifying' with the 'unity' of the metaphysical Principle that is called 'God' in the Bible and that is symbolized there most directly by the 'unity' of the Tree of Life. This 'fallen' state of being I have termed *matter*. 'Adam and Eve's' newfound awareness of its own 'nakedness' referred to in Genesis 3:7 — "Then the eyes of both were opened, and they knew that they were naked" [ESV] — symbolizes the being's newfound awareness of *limitation*, specifically the limitation of 'nature' as perceived from the perspective

---

50 Genesis 2:16–17: "And the LORD God commanded the man, saying, 'You may surely eat of every tree of the garden, but of the tree of the knowledge of good and evil you shall not eat, for in the day that you eat of it you shall surely die.'" Genesis 3:6: "So when the woman saw that the tree was good for food, and that it was a delight to the eyes, and that the tree was to be desired to make one wise, she took of its fruit and ate, and she also gave some to her husband who was with her, and he ate." [ESV]

of the state of *matter*.[51] From the perspective of 'identification' with the metaphysical 'unity' (God), such 'nakedness' (such limitation) is non-existent. 'Identification,' however, is presumably the state of being that 'Adam and Eve' enjoyed previous to its interaction with 'the serpent.' From 'Adam and Eve's' 'fallen,' 'lower,' perspective, 'nakedness' (limitation) 'became,' as 'natural' things do, *apparently* real. This moment of 'nakedness'/limitation in 'Adam and Eve's' 'migration' process illustrates, I would suggest, that point in 'the being's' migration at which it (falsely) becomes aware of its own limitations (its 'nakedness') and begins to define its 'Self' in terms of its new cyclical, 'natural,' state. This condition is describable as the *Samkhyan tamas*, the condition of "obscurity, assimilated with ignorance" discussed in Chapter 4. For, from within the condition of *tamas*, what *appears* to be 'knowledge' only appears as such because 'the being,' exemplified as 'Adam and Eve,' has 'fallen' out of the state of 'identifying' its 'Self' (*Atman*) with the metaphysical Principle (*Brahman* or God/Yahweh in the Torah). It has, in the terms specified at the end of Chapter 5, 'Materialized' or decreased the resolution of its form, definition, and 'actuality' and 'descended' ('fallen') into a relatively unconscious state of 'wandering' in ever-increasing formlessness, indefinitude, and potentiality that separates it ever further from 'realization' of its metaphysical essence, its *actualized* 'Self.'

We have seen that Guénon associates the serpent of Eden with the idea of 'duality' because he associates The Tree of the Knowledge of good and evil with 'duality,' stating that, since "the serpent is most commonly associated with the 'Tree of Knowledge,'" it is "characterized by duality."[52] It is 'duality' for Guénon that, in the 'person' of the

---

51 See also Genesis 3:10: "I heard the sound of you in the garden, and I was afraid, because I was naked, and I hid myself." [ESV]. The structure of this proclamation indicates 'separation' from God by means of both the reference to 'You,' rather than 'I,' and the implication that 'hiding' is a possibility. One cannot hide from that which one is a part of.

52 René Guénon. *The Symbolism of the Cross*, 57.

serpent, obstructs 'Adam and Eve's' access to what Guénon terms the 'sense of unity' and the 'sense of eternity.' Both of these 'senses' are, according to Tradition for Guénon, what makes the 'center of the world,' represented by the Tree of Life in Genesis, 'accessible,' and the loss of which indicates its 'inaccessibility.'[53] The 'center' is, as mentioned earlier, like the World Axis, a traditional symbolism of the metaphysical Principle which, in the Torah, is God/Yahweh. As a symbolic figuration of 'duality,' I contend that the serpent *specifically* obstructs 'Adam and Eve's' 'identification' with the 'unity' of the Principle (God), and thus with 'Adam and Eve's' true 'Self,' by: 1) persuading 'Adam and Eve,' by means of its 'Eve' aspect, to disregard God's directive to *not* eat of the Tree of Knowledge and 2) causing 'Adam and Eve' to ignore the Tree of Life, and thus to ignore the metaphysical Principle (God/Yahweh). In *Patterns in Comparative Religion*, Eliade describes the serpent of Eden as "the obstacle in man's search for the source of immortality, for the Tree of Life."[54] Although alluded to briefly before, I shall argue in Chapter 8 that the so-called 'search for immortality' that is often seen in much traditional art and myth is more accurately thought of, from the perspective of Tradition, as the 'struggle' for metaphysical 'realization' and 'identification' with the Principle, what is called *moksha* in *Vedanta*.

Samsara and the Serpent Symbol in Genesis 3

Formlessness, indefinitude, and potentiality are the primary characteristics of *matter*. By extension, they also characterize the 'duality' of 'nature' or the physical world that is constituted, in part, by the 'flux'[55] of *samsara*, "the indefinite series of cycles of manifestation." Inasmuch, however, as it is 'duality' that 'tempts' the being 'Adam and Eve' away from the 'unity' of God, it is 'indefinitude' that characterizes

---

53 René Guénon. *The Symbolism of the Cross*, 56 and 54.
54 Mircea Eliade, *Patterns in Comparative Religion*, 288.
55 Eknath Easwaran, The Bhagavad Gita, glossary, 285.

that being's doubt and indecision which is inculcated in its 'Eve' ('the woman') aspect by the serpent. 'The woman'/Eve aspect of 'Adam and Eve' is that aspect of the 'migrating' being that is initially receptive to both: 1) the *bifid*-tongued, '*dual*'-penis serpent and 2) the 'dual' Tree of the Knowledge of good *and* evil, as it is 'she' whom the serpent first addresses in Genesis 3:1. Both 1) the doubt and indecision inculcated in 'the woman' that contribute to 'Adam and Eve's' progressive lack of definition ('indefinitude') of its 'Self' and 2) the plurality ('duality') of the 'manifested' realm of 'nature' that 'Adam and Eve' begins to 'fixate' on, characterize *samsara*. The same is the case with *matter*'s two other characteristics of potentiality and formlessness. For anything that is indefinite cannot take on form or 'actualize,' since only that which is definable can *have* form and *be* 'actualized.' Form, in other words, *is* definition and that which is 'actualized' *is* defined.

According to Guénon in *The Symbolism of the Cross*,

> [t]he dual nature of the 'Tree of Knowledge'...appears to Adam only at the very moment of the 'Fall', since it is then that he becomes 'knowing of good and evil.' It is then too that he finds himself driven out from the center which is the place of the primal unity to which the Tree of Life corresponds.[56]

In other words, 'Adam and Eve' loses its 'primal unity' with God and its 'sense of eternity' when the 'center' (God) "become[s] inaccessible to fallen man."[57] This happens from the very moment that 'Adam and Eve' becomes 'knowing of good *and* evil.' The 'duality' of 'Adam *and* Eve's' nature, again, reflects the 'duality' of that which it succumbs to: 'knowing good and evil.' Genesis 3, therefore, describes the dynamism of 'Adam and Eve's' (the 'migrating' being's) 'dual' nature in a 'moment of crisis' in its migration through the "indefinite series of cycles of manifestation." This 'moment of crisis' is constituted by 'Adam and Eve's' being distracted by 'duality' ('nature'/*samsara*), in the specific

---

56 René Guénon, *The Symbolism of the Cross*, 56.
57 René Guénon, *The Symbolism of the Cross*, 56

form of 'the woman's' decision to listen to the 'dual'-natured serpent's 'advice.' In taking seriously the serpent's words, 'Adam and Eve' 'becomes' 'dual' by 'actualizing,' in a negative sense, an aspect of its nature (the Eve aspect) that 'separates' it from the 'primal unity' of God. 'Adam and Eve' thereby succumbs to the tendency of the 'migrating' being to mistake "the indefinite series of cycles of manifestation" that it is migrating *through* for Reality (the 'Principle'/*Brahman*/God). This 'tendency' to misinterpret Reality I shall call 'the serpent's allure.' It is the cause of the Materialization of the 'migrating' being, the being's 'fall' or 'descent' into *samsara* and greater formlessness, indefinitude, and potentiality. This 'deep' interpretation of the travails of the 'migrating' being recounted in Genesis 3 is, I argue, an expression of the same ubiquitous two-part message that may be discovered in nearly all traditional serpent/dragon symbolism: 1) the 'migrating' being can 'achieve' a state of awareness (*matter*) of the 'chaotic' nature of *samsara*/"the indefinite series of cycles of manifestation" but 2) this 'series of cycles' may either: a) 'allure' 'the being' to 'descend'/'fall' further into *samsara* by embracing the state of *matter*, like 'Adam and Eve' did, or b) be 'ascended' out of by the means of succeeding in the 'struggle' to 'identify' one's 'Self' with the metaphysical 'unity' of the Principle (God/*Brahman*), thereby 'realizing' the actualized 'Self.'

Samsara and *Maya* in Genesis 3

Another *Vedantic* concept that aids in explicating the meaning of Genesis 3 and of traditional serpent/dragon symbolism in general is *maya*. According to Puligandla in *Fundamentals of Indian Philosophy*, "[p]sychologically speaking, *maya* is our persistent *tendency* to regard appearances as reality and vice versa....From an epistemological point of view, *maya* is our *ignorance* (*avidya*) as to the difference between appearance and reality."[58] In the terms of this book, *maya* is that 'tendency' to 'misinterpret Reality' which I call 'the serpent's allure.'

---

58 Ramakrishna Puligandla, *Fundamentals of Indian Philosophy*, 237.

Maya is, thus, the *Vedantic* term for the cause of the Materialization (or 'fall') of the 'migrating' being that is called 'Adam and Eve' in Genesis 3. Genesis 3 is a broadly traditional account of the effects of *maya*. 'Adam's' perception of 'his' 'nakedness' described in Genesis 3:10 is, in the terms of *Vedanta*, a sign of the efficaciousness of *maya*, a sign that 'Adam and Eve' is 'misinterpreting Reality,' becoming ignorant (*avidya*) "as to the difference between appearance and reality."[59] 'Adam' denotes that aspect of the 'dual' being 'Adam and Eve' that takes note of this change in the 'migrating' being's level of *paravidya*, "the higher knowledge…by which the infinite and imperishable *Brahman* is attained."[60] From the perspective of the Torah and the Judaic version of Tradition, *avidya* amounts to 'separation' from God/Yahweh. According to Genesis 3:10, 'Adam' says to God "I heard the sound of you in the garden, and I was afraid, because I was naked, and I hid myself." [ESV] This self-evaluation occurs, however, only *after* 'the woman' aspect of 'Adam and Eve' succumbs to the 'allure' of the serpent's rhetoric. 'Adam's' fear, therefore, is, I argue, 'his' (the 'Adam' aspect's) awareness of a loss of some degree of 'identity' with—that is, 'separation' from—God/Yahweh (the 'Principle'/*Brahman*). 'He' only feels 'naked' because 'Adam and Eve' is no longer 'clothed' in the garb of complete 'identification' with God. The lingering *partial* 'identification' with God that allows 'Adam' to be still somewhat aware of that which 'he' has lost manifests itself as 'Adam and Eve's' ability to contrast its 'fallen' state of being with the 'higher' state that it once enjoyed near the 'unity' of the Tree of Life. This lingering awareness of the contrast between God's instructions (complete 'identity' with the metaphysical Principle) and the 'serpent's allure' (increasing 'identity' with *samsara* and 'nature') is what allows 'Adam and Eve' (the 'migrating' being) to perceive chaos and, thus, that which thrusts 'the being' into the state of *matter*. For it is only, I suggest, because 'Adam and

---

59 Ramakrishna Puligandla, *Fundamentals of Indian Philosophy*, 237.
60 Ramakrishna Puligandla, *Fundamentals of Indian Philosophy*, 223-224.

Eve' still has some partial awareness of the 'freedom' of metaphysical 'identification' (*moksha* in *Vedanta*) that it can perceive the limitations of *samsara* and, also, its *perception* of *samsara*, 'nature.' As 'the being' continues its fall into the state of *matter*, however, it is increasingly less able to discern its actual 'identity.' For the spell of *maya* unceasingly inculcates the 'descending' being's "persistent tendency to regard appearances as reality and vice versa."[61]

It is specifically the serpent's rhetoric of doubt, and thus of 'indefinitude,' that causes 'Adam and Eve's' feeling of nakedness and its fall into *avidya*. This is because doubt is that which destroys the metaphysical *certainty* manifest in 'the being' while in the state of *paravidya*. In Genesis 3, this 'metaphysical certainty,' I argue, takes the form of faith in God's inerrancy, specifically the inerrancy of his instructions concerning which trees to eat from and which not to eat from. The serpent's inducement of a state of *un*certainty in 'Adam and Eve' catalyzes the process of Materialization discussed above and in Chapter 5. The serpent symbolizes *samsara* and its 'rhetoric of doubt' symbolizes *maya*. Its rhetoric is the *means* by which it misleads 'Adam and Eve,' just as *maya* is the means by which *samsara* inculcates the 'migrating' being's "persistent tendency to regard appearances as reality and vice versa." Among all of the punishments meted out by God to 'Adam and Eve' after that being's fall, that of "returning to the ground" would seem to be the most representative of all of those states of *avidya* in which the being is separated from its *meta-physical* Source and becomes but the *physical* 'dust' of the 'ground.'[62] The 'return to the ground' is, therefore, the return to *samsara*, "the indefinite series of cycles of manifestation," the situation of *cyclically* returning, again and again, to those states in which 'the being' maintains a "persistent tendency to regard appearances as reality and vice versa." The

---

61 Ramakrishna Puligandla, *Fundamentals of Indian Philosophy*, 237.

62 "By the sweat of your face you shall eat bread, till you return to the ground, for out of it you were taken; for you are dust, and to dust you shall return." Genesis 3:19, ESV.

narrative of 'Adam and Eve' is, therefore, I suggest, a cultural variant of the broadly traditional belief in (experience of?) the human tendency to 'return' to *samsara, as a result of* "our persistent *tendency* to regard appearances as reality and vice versa."[63] It is a broadly traditional 'tale' that was once, perhaps, commonly told among traditional peoples far in advance of ever being associated with what came to be called 'Judaism' and 'Christianity.'

The 'Fascination' of the Serpent

In *The Encircled Serpent: A Study of Serpent Symbolism in All Countries and Ages*, M. Oldfield Howey states,

> It is said that one of the reasons why the serpent was selected as the special symbol of Divinity was its power of fascination: for under the spell of its gaze human beings, beasts and birds may lose their self-control so as to become unable to move, resist, or flee the death awaiting them.[64]

The special state of *avidya* that is called *maya* in *Vedanta* is appropriately inculcated in 'Adam and Eve' by a being whose natural counterpart, the snake, was thought in many ancient cultures to 'fascinate' its prey. The 'fascination' by the snake of a bird or mouse in order to consume it has now been scientifically discredited as a physiological mechanism. It was, nevertheless, *long believed in*. Under the spell of 'fascination,' it was thought that the snake's prey lost its natural capacity to defend itself; it was, in effect, 'spellbound.' It is possible that this belief found its way into many traditional serpent/dragon myths. If so, 'fascination' could have served, for traditional peoples in general, as an analogue to the specifically *Vedantic* concept of *maya*. For, a 'fascinated' creature has lost its 'higher' awareness, its ability to discern *appearance* from *Reality*. *If* this belief in the snake's power of

---

63 Ramakrishna Puligandla, *Fundamentals of Indian Philosophy*, 237.

64 M. Oldfield Howey, *The Encircled Serpent: A Study of Serpent Symbolism in All Countries and Ages* (New York City: Arthur Richmond Company, 1955), 192.

'fascination' was widespread in ancient times, whether snakes *actually* have such a power or not, it is reasonable to conclude, in line with my above interpretation of Genesis 3, that what 'Adam and Eve' perceived in the serpent of Eden's rhetoric is something analogous to what the snake's prey was believed to perceive when it was 'fascinated.' If so, the Genesis 3 narrative would be, traditionally speaking, a timeless story of the manner in which humanity is 'fascinated,' again and again, by 'the serpent' of *samsara* into a 'return' to the 'ground,' an *ignorant* 'return' to that state of being in which credence is given to the perception of *death*.

CHAPTER 7

Migration of the 'Self' in the Bible

'Migration' and Axial Symbols in Jewish and Christian Tradition

As noted in previous chapters, the 'migration' of 'the being' referred to in South Asian forms of Tradition expresses the manner in which 'the multiple states of the being' are revealed in "the indefinite series of cycles of manifestation." 'The being,' from this perspective, is *Brahman*. As Puligandla states in *Fundamentals of Indian Philosophy*, "*Brahman* is the unity of the different selves and material objects of the phenomenal world. *Brahman* as the identity of these different constituents is the underlying substratum."[1] It is also true in *Vedanta*, however, that while "*Brahman* is the substance of all existence — the unchanging reality of which the world of change is a mere manifestation through names and forms [,]...*Atman* is the eternal, silent witness in all beings."[2] *Atman*, thus, in *Vedanta*, is that 'interpretation' of *Brahman* that actually 'experiences' the 'multiple states of the [its] being.' If this is so, then it is slightly more accurate to say that 'the being' that undergoes 'migration' is *Atman* rather than *Brahman*. For it is *Atman*, the Self that "exists not just in man but in all beings," and which is "not to be confused with the empirical ego," which is the

---

1 Ramakrishna Puligandla, *Fundamentals of Indian Philosophy*, 257.
2 Ramakrishna Puligandla, *Fundamentals of Indian Philosophy*, 222.

specifically *perceptive* aspect of *Brahman* that 'migrates' through the 'multiple states' and 'manifests' in "the indefinite series of cycles."[3]

According to Guénon and Eliade both, the most conspicuous 'place' at which 'migration' ('transcendence' for Eliade) occurs is the World Axis or *Axis Mundi*, the 'center' of the world. As we have noted, there are various traditional symbols that represent the *Axis Mundi*, including the tree, the cross, and the rod/staff. All of these symbolize the, as I describe it, Spiritualizing Reality that Guénon calls the 'Principle' and Eliade terms the 'Sacred.' The tree is a particularly common representation in shamanic societies of, as Joan M. Vastokas says in "The Shamanic Tree of Life," that "aperture through which the shaman penetrates the Underworld or Sky, by means of which he transcends the physical universe."[4] The figuration of the tree, however, also appears, as we have seen, in the narratives and art of the ostensibly non-shamanic religions of Judaism and Christianity, sometimes related to other axial symbols.

In discussing "the dual nature of the 'Tree of Knowledge'" in *The Symbolism of the Cross*, Guénon relates the 'primal unity' of the Tree of Life to the specifically Christian symbolism of the cross. He states:

> Moreover, we know that the Cross of Christ is itself symbolically identified with the 'Tree of Life' (*lignum vitae*) but according to a 'legend of the Cross' current in the Middle Ages, the cross was made of the wood of the 'Tree of Knowledge', so that the latter, after being the instrument of the Fall, thus became that of Redemption. Here we find expressed a connection between the two ideas of 'fall' and 'redemption' which are in some respects opposed to each other, and there is also an allusion to the re-establishment of the primordial state; in this new guise, the 'Tree of Knowledge' is in a certain sense assimilated to the 'Tree of Life', duality being effectively reintegrated into unity.[5]

---

3   Ramakrishna Puligandla, *Fundamentals of Indian Philosophy*, 222 and 221.
4   Joan M. Vastokas, "The Shamanic Tree of Life," *Artscanada* 184–187 (1973/1974): 137.
5   René Guénon. *The Symbolism of the Cross*, 56.

Guénon follows this brief historical exegesis with the age-old comparison between the cross of Christ and the "'brazen serpent' which was raised by Moses in the desert," according to Guénon "also known to be a symbol of Redemption." Guénon states that "in this case the rod on which it was placed is equivalent to the cross and also recalls the 'Tree of Life.'"[6] Moses's *copper* serpent' rod/staff (as I shall translate the Hebrew)[7] is, as Guénon notes, a symbol or 'type' of redemption that, from the Christian perspective, prefigures Christ's crucifixion. The idea is most famously expressed in John 3:14–15:

> And as Moses lifted up the serpent in the wilderness, so must the Son of man be lifted up, that whoever believes in him may have eternal life. [ESV]

For Guénon, since: 1) Moses's rod is "equivalent to the cross," 2) the cross is "made of the wood of the 'Tree of Knowledge,'" 3) the cross symbolizes redemption, and 4) the serpent is 'lifted up' on Moses's

---

[6] René Guénon. *The Symbolism of the Cross*, 57.

[7] The Hebrew word that is translated as 'brazen' by Guénon (found in the Douay-Rheims Version of the Bible) is translated, variously, as 'copper' by some scholars and in some editions of the Torah and Tanakh, 'bronze' in the English Standard Version of the Bible, and 'brass' in the King James Version. In *The Serpent Symbol in the Ancient Near East*, Leslie S. Wilson states that "traditional scholarship has treated" the Hebrew term translated as 'serpent' ('seraph serpents') in Numbers 21 "as four separate roots" with four separate meanings. These meanings are: 1) "serpent," 2) "to practice divination, divine, observe signs," 3) "copper, bronze," and 4) "meaning uncertain, perhaps lust, harlotry?" Depending upon the passage from the Tanakh or the Old Testament that the term is drawn from, one of these meanings prevails over the others. I have followed Wilson in choosing 'copper' to translate the term used in Numbers 21 for the following reasons: 1) there exists, according to Wilson, a closer etymological link in the Hebrew between 'serpent' and 'copper' than between 'serpent' and 'bronze' or 'brazen' or 'brass,' and 2) I personally suspect that, during the Bronze Age, the period of time in which Moses is alleged to have lived, any implement that was not expressly intended for use in warfare had a greater chance of being made of copper than of bronze in order to preserve tin. Leslie S. Wilson, *The Serpent Symbol in the Ancient Near East* (Lanham, Maryland: University Press of America, Inc., 2001), 66–71 and 75.

rod (a traditional symbol of the *Axis Mundi*), 'duality' *itself*, symbolized by the serpent, is 'redeemed' or 'fixed' in the unity of the axial symbol. Moses's rod and Jesus's cross are both versions of the latter. In the language of Tradition, as Guénon understands it, duality is thus *re*-integrated, because it is derivative, into the 'primal unity' of the Principle (God or Christ in the Bible) *both* when Moses lifts his rod *and* when Christ is crucified.[8] From the broadly traditional perspective of this book, this symbolism indicates the reintegration of the state of *matter* into the state of 'identity' with ('realization' of) Spirit ('Principle'/*Brahman*/God). Spiritualization is, therefore, in the two mentioned cases, traditionally symbolized as the 'lifting up'/crucifixion *process* itself, the 'ascent' (reintegration or redemption) of that which has become 'manifested' in the duality of 'nature' *back* into the 'primal unity' of its metaphysical Source, God/Christ.

'Involution,' 'Evolution,' 'Redemption,' and Dichotomies

In *The Great Triad*, Guénon argues that one of the primary uses of the serpent symbol in Tradition is to represent a 'dual cosmic force' that is constituted by the 'evolution' and 'involution' of the metaphysical Principle 'into' and 'out of' the "indefinite series of cycles of manifestation." According to Guénon, this 'dual force' is related to

> the inverse and complementary phases of all manifestation, phases which are due, according to the Far-Eastern tradition[9], to the alternating pre-

---

[8] We shall discuss the symbolism of Christ on the cross more thoroughly in a later chapter. In short, I shall argue that the body of Christ is symbolic of the state of *matter* and, thus, symbolically equivalent, from a broadly traditional perspective, to the serpent on Moses's rod. This equivalence is indicated often in the alchemical literature of the Renaissance and early modern periods.

[9] When Guénon refers to the 'Far-Eastern tradition,' he normally has in mind Taoism, but Taoism as the 'esoteric' complement to Confucianism, its 'exoteric' expression. For Guénon, Taoism and Confucianism are not two separate 'philosophies' but, rather, represent two aspects of the same particularization of Tradition that occurred in East Asia millennia ago.

dominance of *yin* and *yang*: 'evolution' or development, unfolding, and 'involution' or envelopment, enfolding; or again, 'catabasis' or descending movement, and 'anabasis' or ascending movement, entry into the manifested, and return to the non-manifested. This double 'spiration' (and one will notice the very significant kinship between the name 'spiral' and that of *spiritus* or 'breath'...) is the universal 'expiration' and 'inspiration' by which are produced, according to Taoist terminology, the 'condensations' and 'dissipations' resulting from the alternate action of *yin* and *yang*, or according to Hermetic terminology, the 'coagulations' and 'solutions'; for individual beings, these are births and deaths, what Aristotle calls *genesis* and *phthora*, 'generation' and 'corruption'; for worlds, they are what Hindu tradition calls the days and nights of *Brahma*, like the *Kalpa* and the *Pralaya*; and at all degrees, in the 'macrocosmic' order as well as in the 'microcosmic' order, there are corresponding phases in every cycle of existence, for they are the very expression of the law that governs the sum total of universal manifestation.[10]

'Evolution' in the realm of 'formal manifestation' ('nature') for Guénon, refers to the unfolding of the process of 'manifestation' which consists of the particularization ('instantiation') of the metaphysical Principle into those 'multiple states of the being' that constitute the physical/'natural' "indefinite series of cycles of manifestation." As Guénon importantly notes, "Needless to say, we take the word 'evolution' in its strictly etymological sense, which has nothing in common with its use in modern 'progressivist' theories."[11] 'Involution,' by contrast, is opposite in action and effect from 'evolution.' It is, in the realm of 'nature,' the process whereby the metaphysical Principle, having already become manifest through 'evolution,' 'withdraws' from manifesting itself in the physical/'natural' "series of cycles of manifestation." Creation and birth, destruction and death: these are, respectively, particular instantiations of the 'evolutive' and 'involutive' processes. 'Redemption,' as Guénon refers to it in *The Symbolism of the Cross*, is an instantiation of the force of 'involution' because it refers to 'the

---

10   René Guénon, *The Great Triad*, 36–37.
11   René Guénon, *The Great Triad*, 36.

being's' 'withdrawing' from "the indefinite series of cycles of manifestation" 'back to' its metaphysical Source: the Principle/*Brahman*/God/Christ. As with all forms of 'involution,' redemption is, in the terms of this book, equivalent to the 'dissipation' or 'solution' (to employ the Taoist and Hermetic terms) of the state of *matter*. The serpent's 'redemption' that is, according to Guénon, symbolized in Moses's raising of the 'copper serpent' is the Hebrew cultural variant on the broadly traditional idea of the 'involution' of "the indefinite series of cycles of manifestation" back to their 'Principial' Source. In Numbers 21, this takes the form of a 'return' by the Hebrews to the 'way' of God outlined in the Torah. In theological language, being 'redeemed' is "going back to God." Jesus's crucifixion similarly symbolizes, in a broadly traditional fashion, 'involution' back into the state of Christ, at which point Jesus is no longer *both* God and man but *only* God. I, equivalently, speak of *matter*'s 'involution' back into pure Spirit at that moment at which 'realization' is achieved by the 'migrating' being. 'The being's' partial awareness of chaos which constitutes the state of *matter* is, at that moment, 'dissipated' into a pure awareness of *only* metaphysical order: Spirit. Guénon's 'evolution' of the Principle into "the indefinite series of cycles of manifestation" is equivalent, I argue, in the cases of beings that have achieved a particular level of awareness, to the eruption of the awareness of chaos that constitutes the state of *matter*. *Matter*'s 'redemption' or reintegration into Spirit is the 'solution' (in Hermetic terms) of the awareness of chaos. It is equivalent to, in *fully* 'aware' states of being (*moksha* in *Vedanta*), 'involution' of the Principle.

The association of the serpent symbol in Tradition with the processes of 'evolution' and 'involution' corresponds, for Guénon, to its association with the idea of duality, and, more specifically, its association with *dichotomies* such as 'good and evil.' Just as the serpent, according to Guénon, broadly symbolizes evolution in some examples of traditional art and myth and involution in others, so it, more particularly, symbolizes 'life' in some cases of traditional art and myth and 'death' in others, 'evil' in some cases and 'good' in others, Satan in some cases and Christ in still others. In *The Symbolism of the Cross*, Guénon states that "in fact symbols often have two opposed meanings....The serpent that represents life must not be confused with the one representing death, nor the serpent that is a symbol of Christ with the one symbolizing Satan."[12] Guénon reveals what he believes to be another example of the traditional serpent symbol's 'opposed meanings,' as well as its transcultural hegemony, when he notes concerning the idea of 'reintegration' of duality into the 'primal unity' of the Principle that "[t]he staff of Aesculapius has a similar meaning; in the caduceus of Hermes, we see the two serpents in opposition, corresponding to the double meaning of the symbol."[13] This Greek variant on the traditional juxtaposition of serpent and axial symbolism, along with its Roman kin, will be examined in depth in a later chapter.

Maya and the Manipulative *Nachash* in Genesis 3

At that moment at which "[t]he dual nature of the 'Tree of Knowledge'...appears to Adam" and 'Adam and Eve' "becomes 'knowing [of] good and evil,'"[14] three things are, according to Guénon, made "inaccessible to fallen man": 1) the 'center' or "place of the primal unity," 2) the 'sense of eternity,' and 3) the 'sense of unity.'[15] The dual-natured (as indicated by its two names) 'Adam and Eve' possesses both of these two 'senses,' I contend, insofar as it is not 'fascinated' by that which the serpent represents: the duality of 'formal manifestation,' the physical/'natural' world that is constituted, in part, by "the indefinite series of cycles of manifestation." As noted, however, it is just this 'fascination' that 'Adam and Eve' succumbs to in Genesis 3 when it falls under the serpent's 'spell' into what I call the state of *matter*. Since,

---

12 René Guénon. *The Symbolism of the Cross*, 57.
13 René Guénon. *The Symbolism of the Cross*, 57.
14 René Guénon. *The Symbolism of the Cross*, 56.
15 René Guénon, *The Symbolism of the Cross*, 56.

according to Guénon, 'Adam and Eve' is not aware that the Tree of Knowledge "is characterized by duality"[16] until the very *moment* that it eats of it, it is accurate to say, as is enshrined in the theological language, that the being fell, rather than 'leapt,' to eat of that tree's fruit, for this term indicates the relatively unconscious nature of the event. It is also consistent with the event being the result of *maya*, "our persistent *tendency* to regard appearances as reality and vice versa."[17] For, a tendency, like a true habit, although perhaps the consequence of *earlier willful actions*, is itself a form of *unconscious behavior*. Based upon this interpretation of 'Adam and Eve's' fall, therefore, that being, in its new state of 'fascination' with the serpent and its subsequent eating of the Tree of Knowledge, did not actually *know* that it, at that moment, embraced duality. It did not 'realize' at that moment that it was falling out of its state of consciousness of 'identity' with the 'primal unity' of God (the 'Principle'). Like the bird or mouse once thought to be 'fascinated' by the snake, 'Adam and Eve' was, I suggest, 'fascinated' with *samsara through maya*, its *two* names reflective of this dual state of being.

The serpent, by means of its rhetoric, fascinates 'the woman'/Eve aspect of 'Adam and Eve' because that aspect of 'the being' is most susceptible to the influence of *maya* and 'nature.' When, therefore, the serpent inspires 'the woman' in Genesis 3:6 to see that "the tree [of Knowledge] was good for food and that it was a delight to the eyes, and that the tree was to be desired to make one wise" [ESV], I argue that this event symbolizes the developing 'tendency' in 'the woman'/Eve aspect of the 'migrating' being to "regard appearances as reality and vice versa." The Hebrew word that is translated as 'serpent' in Genesis 3 is *nachash*. According to Charlesworth in *The Good and Evil Serpent*, however,

---

16   René Guénon, *The Symbolism of the Cross*, 55.
17   Ramakrishna Puligandla, *Fundamentals of Indian Philosophy*, 237.

[i]n Hebrew, the root *nhs* denotes not only snake (*nahas* [with accent on the second syllable]) but also "divination" or "magic curse" (*nahas* [with accent on the first syllable])....Some, maybe many, Hebrews, Israelites, and Jews imagined the "serpent" to be related to divination. Evidence of ophiomancy, divination through serpents, was well known in the ancient world and no doubt was practiced by many in Israel since passages in both the Law and the Prophets repeatedly condemn such practices.[18]

In *Magic, Witchcraft, and Religion*, Moro and Myers state,

> In its strictly etymological sense the term "divination" denotes inquiry about future events or matters, hidden or obscure, directed to a deity who, it is believed, will reply through significant tokens. It usually refers to the process of obtaining knowledge of secret or future things by mechanical means or manipulative techniques.[19]

Merriam-Webster defines 'manipulation' as the capacity "to control or play upon by artful, unfair, or insidious means especially to one's own advantage."[20] If one has the capacity to manipulate reality, then one also has the capacity to obscure or redefine reality in an insidious way. 'Divination,' the 'diviner's' capacity to predict the future, is fundamentally founded upon the presumption that that individual can discern, in its 'divining' process, appearances from reality, since predicting the future consists of predicting not what *appears* might happen but what actually *shall* happen. In order to 'divine' such a thing, however, the very fabric of existence must be 'manipulated' in order to 'see through it.' The throwing of a 'magic curse,' similarly, presumes the capacity of the 'curser' to either manipulate reality *directly* or to manipulate an individual's *perception* of reality, in effect either: 1) *actually* 'cursing'

---

18 James H. Charlesworth, *The Good and Evil Serpent: How a Universal Symbol Became Christianized*, 438.

19 Pamela A. Moro and James E. Myers, *Magic, Witchcraft, and Religion: A Reader in the Anthropology of Religion*, eighth edition (New York, New York: McGraw-Hill, 1985), 145.

20 *Merriam-webster.com*, definition of 'Manipulate,' May 23, 2019 9:03 pm.

the individual or 2) making the individual *believe* that s/he is 'cursed.' Divination and 'magical cursing' are both, therefore, forms of either: 1) manipulating reality or 2) manipulating the *perception* of reality.

According to *Vedanta*, samsara affects, by means of *maya*, a *pervasive* form of 'manipulation.' It is a form of manipulation that, I suggest, is akin to magical 'cursing,' and that, therefore, creates, like 'cursing' can, an *"ignorance (avidya)* as to the difference between appearance and reality."[21] I contend that the serpent, specifically as a symbol in Genesis 3 of that 'state of the being' that consists of fascination with *samsara*, inculcates an ignorance (*avidya*) of Reality (God) in 'the woman'/Eve aspect of 'Adam and Eve' by means of its dishonest, 'manipulative,' rhetoric. This dishonesty consists most visibly in the serpent's use of the word 'like' when, in pontificating on the merits of the Tree of Knowledge, it informs 'the woman' that "God knows that when you eat of it your eyes will be opened, and you will be like God, knowing good and evil." [Genesis 3:5, ESV] 'Like,' however, is not 'is,' but because 'the woman'/Eve aspect of 'Adam and Eve' lacks the divine omniscience necessary to contextualize the serpent's opinion, 'she' does not comprehend the *actual* meaning of the serpent's message: 'Adam and Eve' will be *like* God, but not *equal to* God.

Migration of the 'Self' in Genesis 3 and *Advaita Vedanta*

My interpretation of Genesis 3 includes the contention that 'Adam' and 'the woman' ('Eve') are names that refer *not* to two separate individuals but, rather, to the 'migrating' being undergoing a change of 'state,' a 'fall' into a 'lower' state of being, that is caused by the susceptibility of 'the being's' 'Eve' *aspect* to 'fascination' with *samsara*, "the indefinite series of cycles of manifestation." By this interpretation, Genesis 3 is a broadly traditional account of how the 'allure of the serpent,' the 'fascination' with 'duality' and the 'chaos' of 'nature' that occurs at a

---

21   Ramakrishna Puligandla, *Fundamentals of Indian Philosophy*, 237.

particular stage in 'the being's' (the Principle's) 'evolution,' separates or 'guards' the 'migrating' being, 'Adam and Eve,' from 'realization' of the 'unity' of the Principle (God/*Brahman*/Spirit). Along with contending that the serpent symbol in Tradition symbolizes "the indefinite series of cycles of manifestation" or the "series of the cycles of universal manifestation," Guénon also argues that "the traversing of the different states is represented in some traditions as a migration of the being in the body of the serpent."[22] The serpent is, therefore, according to Guénon, symbolic in Tradition not only of "the indefinite series of cycles of manifestation" but of the 'migrating,' or 'traversing,' of the 'states of the being' that are manifested *in* "the indefinite series of cycles of manifestation." In Genesis 3, therefore, the serpent is symbolic not only of *samsara* but of 'Adam and Eve's' 'traversing'/'migrating' *through samsara*. The serpent symbolizes, therefore, from this perspective, both the cause *and* the fact of 'Adam and Eve's' 'fall' into a 'lower' 'state of the being,' a state of hazier 'realization' of, and 'identification' with, that which 'they' truly are: *Atman*/*Brahman*/God/Spirit.

Based upon this true 'identity' of the migrating being 'Adam and Eve,' the Genesis 3 narrative can be interpreted as a tale of *Atman*/*Brahman* (God) as it perceives itself 'descending' ('falling') from consciousness of its 'higher' 'Self' (*Atman*) to a 'lower' state of consciousness that consists of 'fascination' with "the indefinite series of cycles of manifestation" and residual awareness of its metaphysical Source. In Guénon's terminology, this is 'evolution.' In my terminology, it is Materialization, the 'tendency' towards formlessness, indefinitude, and potentiality—stunted 'actualization' of 'the being's' 'Self' (*Atman*). When Guénon writes of the 'primal unity' of the Principle that is represented in Genesis 3 by the Tree of Life, this 'unity' consists not 'only' of *Brahman* (God) but of *Brahman*/God *as Atman*, *Brahman*/God as the ultimate 'subject' of the migration of 'the being.' According to the *Brhadaranyaka Upanishad*, "This Self is *Brahman*";

---

22 René Guénon, *The Symbolism of the Cross*, 122.

"Pure Consciousness is *Brahman*"; "Where there is consciousness of the Self, individuality is no more." (*BU* I. 4: 10, *BU* II. 5, and *BU* II: 4:12). According to the *Kena Upanishad*, "I am *Brahman*." (*KU* I). All of these statements specifically describe the 'Self'/*Atman* of *Advaita Vedanta*, the 'non-dualism' that was popularized ('founded,' according to Puligandla[23]) by the c. eighth- or ninth-century Indian thinker Samkara.[24] According to Puligandla, "Samkara's *Vedanta* is absolute and unqualified non-dualism, according to which reality (*Brahman, atman*) is pure identity (identity-without-difference)."[25] As I have already argued, however, Samkara's interpretation of *Vedanta* as 'non-dualism' is already implicit in the Upanishads, as can be clearly seen in the above quotations. The following is one of Guénon's arguments in *The Symbolism of the Cross* for the essential 'non-dualism' of *Vedanta*:

> The 'Self'...is the transcendent and permanent principle of which the manifested being, the human being for example, is not more than a transient and contingent modification, which moreover can in no wise affect this principle. Immutable in its own nature, the Self develops its possibilities in all the modalities of realization, indefinite in their multitude, which for the total being amount to so many states, each of which has its limiting and determining conditions of existence, and only one of which constitutes the portion—or rather particular determination—of this being that is the 'ego' or human individuality. Again, this development is only such, in reality, when viewed from the standpoint of manifestation, outside of which everything must necessarily be in perfect simultaneity in the 'eternal present'; on that account the 'permanent actuality' of the Self is not affected thereby. The Self is thus the principle by which all the states of the being exist, each in its own proper sphere, which may be called a degree of existence....[T]his Self subsists by itself alone, for in the total and indivisible unity of its innermost nature it has not, and cannot have, any principle external to itself.[26]

---

23 Ramakrishna Puligandla, *Fundamentals of Indian Philosophy*, 216.
24 Ramakrishna Puligandla, *Fundamentals of Indian Philosophy*, 227.
25 Ramakrishna Puligandla, *Fundamentals of Indian Philosophy*, 272.
26 René Guénon, *The Symbolism of the Cross*, 8–9.

The narrative of 'Adam and Eve' in Genesis 3 is, I contend, a traditional exposition of the *Atman's* ('the being's') 'migration' through the 'multiple states.' As stated in the first paragraph of this chapter, it is more accurate to say that 'the being' undergoing 'migration' is *Atman* rather than *Brahman* because *Atman* is, in *Vedanta*, that 'interpretation' of *Brahman* that actually 'experiences' the 'multiple states of the [*its*] being.' 'Adam and Eve' is the name given in Genesis 3 to what is there called Yahweh or 'God' *when* that Reality is considered from the perspective of *viewing itself* within any state of its being that is 'falling' out of metaphysical 'unity' and 'evolving' into the (physical) 'duality' of 'manifestation.' In *Vedantic* terms, 'Adam and Eve's' awareness of its so-called 'nakedness' is a metaphor for the *Atman's* awareness of its new lack of 'unity' with *Brahman*. 'Fascination' with *samsara* which is brought on by the influence of *maya* is the cause of this state. As long as 'fascination' persists, the 'Self'/*Atman* 'migrates' as a 'duality' (multiplicity/plurality) of (apparent) beings, abbreviated in Genesis 3 as the 'couple' 'Adam' *and* 'Eve.' The reference in Genesis 3:14–15 to the mutual 'bruising' of 'Adam and Eve's' and the serpent's 'offspring' is, I suggest, symbolic of the 'migrating' being's continual 'struggle' with existence in the serpentine 'flux' of *samsara*.[27] Furthermore, Guénon's statement that "the traversing [migration] of the different states is represented in some traditions as a migration of the being in the body of the serpent"[28] means that as long as the 'struggle' between the metaphysical Principle (God) *as* the migrating being and the flux of *samsara* (the serpent) continues, and the 'identity' of *Brahman* and *Atman* is, therefore, not 'realized,' the 'migrating' being is still 'trapped' in "the body of the serpent" (i.e., in *samsara* or "the indefinite series of cycles of manifestation"). 'God,' in other words, is still 'trapped' in

---

27 Genesis 3:14–15: "The LORD God said to the serpent, Because you have done this...I will put enmity between you and the woman, and between your offspring and her offspring; he shall bruise your head, and you shall bruise his heel." [ESV]

28 René Guénon, *The Symbolism of the Cross*, 122.

the state of *matter*. This is an idea that was later developed in great detail in Western alchemy, which we shall consider to some degree in Chapter 9.

Dichotomies and 'Migration' in Numbers 21 and John 3

Guénon argues in *The Symbolism of the Cross* that

> [a]s the traversing [of the being] can be envisaged in two opposite directions, either upward toward the higher states or downward toward the lower, the two opposed aspects of the serpent symbolism, one benefic and the other malefic, thereby explain themselves.[29]

In this statement, Guénon synthesizes three ideas that are, according to him, symbolized by the serpent in Tradition: 1) 'migration'/'traversing,' 2) dichotomies, and 3) *moral/religious* dichotomies, such as 'benefic' and 'malefic.' In *The Symbolism of the Cross*, Guénon refers to Moses's bronze/copper 'serpent rod' in Numbers 21:9 to argue for the 'benefic,' and specifically 'healing,' aspect of the serpent symbol in Tradition. In Numbers 21:6, however, a 'malefic' symbolism is already attributed to the serpent symbol, for "the LORD sent fiery serpents among the people, and they bit the people, so that many people of Israel died." It is only *after* this event that the LORD says to Moses

> "Make a fiery serpent and set it on a pole, and everyone who is bitten, when he sees it, shall live." So Moses made a bronze [copper] serpent and set it on a pole. And if a serpent bit anyone, he would look at the bronze [copper] serpent and live. [Numbers 21:8–9, ESV]

The 'fiery' serpents *kill* and the 'risen serpent,' as I shall call it, *heals*. From the specifically Christian perspective, which is primarily built upon the earlier Jewish perspective, Moses' 'serpent rod' is 'benefic' because of its 'redemption' component discussed earlier in

---

29 René Guénon, *The Symbolism of the Cross*, 122.

this chapter: "And as Moses lifted up the serpent in the wilderness, so must the Son of Man be lifted up, that whoever believes in him may have eternal life." [John 3:14–15, ESV] The crucified Jesus of John 3 and Moses's 'serpent rod' in Numbers 21 are symbolically similar because both are 'raised' 'axial' symbols and both provide 'healing' of a kind. In Numbers 21, Moses's 'copper serpent' *physically* heals those Israelites who look upon it and recognize its power; in John 3, the crucified Christ *spiritually* heals (gives 'eternal life' to) those who look upon Jesus's sacrifice and recognize *its* power. From a broadly traditional perspective, both are, in Guénon's language, symbols of 'beneficence' because both are symbolic of 'rising' out of the 'lower' states of 'the being.' As Guénon might say, both 'ascend' "upward toward the higher states."[30]

Both Moses's 'serpent rod' and the crucified Christ are, I argue, traditionally symbolic figurations of the serpent and the World Axis, overtly in the first case. The crucified *body* of Christ is, furthermore, from the traditional point of view, an acceptable 'symbolic synonym' for the serpent because *physicality* in general is, just like the serpent in some strains of Tradition such as Western alchemy, representative of the *samsaric* flux or physical world of 'nature.'[31] In the Bible, the *Axis Mundi* takes the form of the Tree of Life (in Genesis 3), Moses's rod (in Numbers 21), and Christ's cross (in John 3), all 'Judeo-Christian' versions of Guénon's transculturally recognized Principle. More specifically, however, when associated with the serpent considered under its 'benefic' aspect, these 'axial' symbols represent the 'Self's' (*Atman's*) 'migration' 'upward' out of *samsara* and the state of *matter* to 'identification' with God/Yahweh/Christ (*Brahman*). In Guénon's terms, the 'lifting up' of Moses's 'copper serpent' in the wilderness and the 'lifting

---

30 René Guénon, *The Symbolism of the Cross*, 122.

31 In Chapter 14, we shall discuss the traditional symbolism in Western alchemy of the crucified Christ as the "Mercurial elixir" or "powerful king of nature." Alexander Roob, *The Hermetic Museum: Alchemy & Mysticism* (Los Angeles: Taschen, 2006), 329.

up' of the 'Son of Man' on the cross are both cases of 'involution,' the process by which 'the being,' having become 'manifest' by means of 'evolution,' returns back to the 'unity' of the metaphysical Principle. Moses and Jesus are both, therefore, from a broadly traditional perspective, employed in the Bible to symbolize 'reconciliation' of that aspect of God as pure Spirit that has been fragmented in the physical realm (by means of 'evolution') *with* the 'unity' of its metaphysical source: God/Yahweh or God/Christ. In Numbers 21, 'reconciliation' is between the Israelites (the 'chosen people') and God; in John 3, it is between "whoever believes in him" and God. We shall consider the traditional 'healing' that constitutes this 'reconciliation' in more depth in a later chapter.

The Use of Snake Imagery to Represent 'Migration'

It is easy to imagine how traditional peoples saw in the snake's shedding of its skin the ideas of 'migration' and 'manifestation.' For in this process, it is clear to see that 'something moves on' while 'something is left behind.' The snake 'moves on' and the snake's *skin* is 'left behind.' That which is 'left behind' greatly *resembles* that which 'moves on' and would seem to be an 'expression of' the latter. Because of this resemblance, it is easy, from the right perspective, to confuse the two: snake and snake *skin*. Through the lens of *Advaita Vedanta*, I have argued that the Genesis 3 narrative of 'Adam and Eve' constitutes a traditional illustration of the, according to Guénon, transcultural belief in the 'migration' of 'the being' (the 'Self'/*Atman*) from a 'higher' state of existence in which it is formed, defined, and 'actualized' (because it completely 'identifies' with, and therefore 'realizes,' *Brahman*) to a 'lower' state of existence in which it 'identifies' with its 'natural' ego. This process constitutes a 'migration' from a state of 'unity,' as Guénon calls it, to a state of multiplicity or 'duality.' The snake's shedding of its skin constitutes a *similar* process, a process in which, from a certain 'lower' perspective, 'one thing' *seemingly* 'becomes' 'two things': one snake 'becomes' a snake and its skin. From another, 'higher,' perspective, however, there is, after the skin-shedding, *truly* and *only* one 'real' thing left: *the snake*, which has merely undergone a change of 'state.' The snake 'moves on' while the snake's skin, which is merely 'part' of the snake and *not* 'real' on its own, is 'left behind.'

So it is with the traditional understanding of the 'migrating' being, the 'Self'/*Atman* that is symbolized in Genesis 3 as 'Adam and Eve.' The *Atman*, in its 'multiple states,' may, according to Guénon's understanding of Tradition, 'migrate' in either of two 'directions': it may 'ascend' to 'higher' states of 'the being' or it may 'descend' to 'lower' states. When the *Atman* 'descends' ('falls' in Genesis 3) into the 'dual' being 'Adam and Eve,' its 'reality,' *Brahman*, 'moves on,' like the serpent shedding its skin. Its *illusory* 'dual' 'part,' however, is 'left behind.' This 'dual part' is symbolized in Genesis 3 by 'Adam and Eve.' From the perspective of that *aspect* of God/*Brahman* that is still embedded in its 'fallen' 'dual' manifestation of 'Adam and Eve,' we may say, although it sounds brutal, that God/*Brahman* has 'collected' a skin. For, instead of 'ascending' to a 'higher' state of being, or 'moving on' like the serpent and 'shedding' its skin, the *Atman as* 'Adam and Eve' 'descends' to a 'lower' state of being and, therefore, like a snake moving backwards into itself, 'collects' a 'skin.' The metaphor of 'collecting a skin' is borne out in Genesis 3:21: "And the LORD God made for Adam and for his wife garments of skins and clothed them." [ESV] In this verse, as well as in Genesis 3:14 when God informs the serpent that "on your belly you shall go," are to be recognized by the 'traditional' reader examples of an 'evolutive' process of Materialization that consists of the 'migrating' being's drawing ever further away from Spirit (God/*Brahman*) and ever deeper into awareness of the 'chaos' of "the indefinite series of cycles of manifestation" that constitutes *matter*. Since the Genesis 3 narrative is, as we have proposed, a broadly traditional tale of the 'migrating' being's 'descent' into "the indefinite series of cycles of manifestation" and its 'identification' with its 'natural' ego rather than with its metaphysical 'Self'/*Atman*, it is a tale of *God*'s, from a 'lower' perspective of its 'Self'-awareness, 'identification' with *God*'s 'skin.' In other words, it is a tale of God's 'identification' with a physical *appearance* of itself rather than with its meta-physical *Reality*.

CHAPTER 8

The Guardian of Immortality/*Moksha*

In *The Symbolism of the Cross*, Guénon states:

> There is yet another aspect of the general symbolism of the serpent in which it appears, not precisely as malefic...but at any rate as to be dreaded, insofar as it represents the being's attachment to the indefinite series of cycles of manifestation. This aspect belongs for instance to the function of the serpent (or the dragon which is then an equivalent of it) as the guardian of certain symbols of immortality, the approach to which it forbids.[1]

If the serpent/dragon *as* "the guardian of certain symbols of immortality" symbolizes attachment to "the indefinite series of cycles of manifestation," it must be concluded that that which 'guards immortality' *is* "the indefinite series of cycles of manifestation," what is called *samsara* in *Vedanta*. This follows because 'immortality' is but a broadly 'traditional' idea that translates the *Vedantic* concept of *moksha*, or 'escape' from *samsara*. According to *Vedanta*, it is only by 'realizing' *moksha* that the 'migrating' being attains that state of being that, I argue, is called 'immortality' in other variants of Tradition. The condition of 'attachment' to "the indefinite series of cycles of manifestation," therefore, is symbolized by the serpentine or draconic 'guardian' in Tradition because that creature 'guards' the migrating

---

1   René Guénon, *The Symbolism of the Cross*, 124.

188

being's 'escape' (*moksha*) from *samsara*.² The 'treasure' that is often 'guarded' by a serpent or dragon in traditional art and myth, in consequence, symbolizes 'immortality' as the short-hand for, or broadly traditional understanding of, *moksha*. In this chapter, I shall interpret the transcultural, traditional idea of 'immortality' that is depicted and described in traditional art and myth from around the world as but an imprecise, broadly traditional, synonym of *moksha*.

In the long quotation that begins this chapter, Guénon states that the serpent/dragon, insofar as it symbolizes the "attachment to the indefinite series of cycles of manifestation," is "to be dreaded" because it 'forbids' the 'approach' to immortality.³ For the Hindu or Buddhist who has been given to believe that *karmic* 'entrapment' stands in the way of his/her 'release' (*moksha* or *nirvana*) from *samsara*, this 'dread' can be real. The case is similar for all traditional people who are aware of 'nature's' deceptive power of 'fascination' that 'guards' against 'the being's' return to what Guénon calls the 'unity' of the metaphysical Principle and what Eliade calls communion with the 'gods' or 'extraterrestrial archetypes' *in illo tempore*.⁴ The serpent/dragon, however, symbolizing 'the being's' awareness of the 'chaos' of *samsara* and thus of 'nature,' only appears as 'guardian,' I suggest, insofar as the 'migrating' being has become a *seeker* of *moksha* ('immortality') and, therefore, *desires* that which the serpent/dragon 'guards.' In reality, then, the 'migrating' being, once it has achieved a certain state of awareness, which I call *matter*, 'makes' the serpentine or draconic 'guardian.' The migrating being 'makes' the serpent/dragon 'guardian' by means of its 'attachment' to, or 'fall' into, "the indefinite series of cycles of manifestation." In South Asian philosophy and religion, this event is due to *karma*, the actions of any *particular* 'state of being' of 'the being'

---

2   See Chapter 4.
3   René Guénon, *The Symbolism of the Cross*, 124.
4   *In illo tempore*: "In those days," the days of 'the gods.'

(*Brahman*).⁵ Consistent, therefore, with Guénon's statements in the above quotation, I argue that the 'guardianship' of the serpent/dragon that is represented and described in much traditional art and myth symbolizes the 'migrating' being's *experience* of 'separation' from the 'unity' of Guénon's metaphysical Principle (*Brahman*/God/Spirit)⁶ that is brought on by its 'fall' into the state of *matter*. I furthermore suggest that, in order to extricate itself from this state, the 'migrating' being must, metaphorically, 'defeat' the serpent/dragon. It must, literally, 'overcome' its new state of awareness by forming, defining, and actualizing, in accordance with the 'unity' of the metaphysical Principle, its awareness of *samsara*/'nature.' It must, in a word, *order* 'nature.' As a corollary to this, it should be noted that the serpent/dragon may, then, symbolize in Tradition *any* aspect of *samsara* or "the indefinite series of cycles of manifestation" that, from the *perspective* of the 'migrating' being seeking *moksha*/immortality, 'guards' or serves as an obstacle to that goal. For it is because "the indefinite series of cycles of manifestation" is that which, in one way or another, *always appears* to 'guard' the way to the being's attainment of *moksha*/immortality that the serpent/dragon as 'guardian' symbolizes, for Guénon, "the being's *attachment* to the indefinite series of cycles of manifestation." This 'attachment' is a characteristic of that 'state of the being' that is only 'realized' by what I have described as the *partially* 'enlightened' New Man: the state of *matter*. For, 'attachment' to *samsara* requires a greater level of 'Self'-awareness than complete 'identification' with *samsara*/'nature.'

---

5 Guénon says of *karma* that "in a general sense, it means action in all its forms." René Guénon, *Man & His Becoming According to the Vedanta*, 11. Guénon believes that the more specific idea of the actions of 'previous lives' that is sometimes connected to the idea of *karma* is a bastardization of the concept and an inauthentic expression of the South Asian variation of Tradition.

6 Or 'separation' from 'the gods' *in illo tempore*. This may be translated to also mean 'separation' from *becoming* a 'god.'

Ancient Greek Guardians

In *The Symbolism of the Cross*, Guénon observes that there are "symbolic legends which in numerous traditions represent the serpent or dragon as the guardian of 'hidden treasures.'"[7] He states, for example, that "we find [the serpent/dragon] coiled around the tree with the golden apples in the garden of the Hesperides, or the beech tree in the wood of Colchis on which the 'golden fleece' hangs."[8] In both of the Greek myths, a 'hero' seeks a 'golden' object of some power guarded by a serpent/dragon residing near a notable tree. In *The Greek Myths*, Robert Graves states that retrieval of the 'golden apples' of the Hesperides is the purpose of the hero Herakles' 'Eleventh Labor': "to fetch fruit from the golden apple-tree, Mother Earth's wedding gift to Hera," around which the goddess Hera had "set the ever-watchful dragon Ladon to coil."[9] (See fig. 8.1.) Similarly, according to Graves, the legendary 'golden fleece' that hung from an oak tree and that was also guarded by a dragon was desired by the hero Jason and his Argonauts. As Graves puts it, the fleece "hung, guarded by a loathsome and immortal dragon of a thousand coils, larger than the Argo [Jason's ship] herself, and born from the blood of the monster Typhon."[10] According to the myth, Medea, daughter to the owner of the fleece, King Aeetes, aided in Jason's retrieval of the fleece as "she soothed the hissing dragon with incantations and then, using freshly-cut sprigs of juniper, sprinkled soporific drops on his eyelids."[11] (See fig. 8.2.)

The narratives of Herakles' quest to retrieve the 'golden apples' and Jason's quest to obtain the 'golden fleece' contain many elements in common: a dragon, a prominent tree, a 'golden' object, and the idea

---

7   René Guénon, *The Symbolism of the Cross*, 124.
8   René Guénon, *The Symbolism of the Cross*, 124.
9   Robert Graves, *The Greek Myths: 2* (New York, New York: Penguin Books, 1955, 1977), 145.
10 Robert Graves, *The Greek Myths: 2*, 238–39.
11 Robert Graves, *The Greek Myths: 2*, 238.

of 'guardianship.' In *Python*, Joseph Fontenrose discusses the close relationship that may have existed in antiquity between the two *apparently* different 'golden' objects that are described in the aforementioned myths. He states, for example, that "there were already men in antiquity who, pointing to the homonymy of *melon* 'apple' and *melon* 'sheep,' maintained that the golden apples were originally beautiful sheep of golden fleece."[12] Even, however, if the 'golden apples' and the 'golden fleece' are *not* the same object, they were, I propose, given their 'golden' aspect under the same 'traditional' perspective in order to indicate their value as 'treasure' of a certain, very specific, kind. Since the treasures described in most legends and myths nearly always include copious amounts of gold, and since Guénon sees many of these 'traditional' treasures as symbolic, the symbolism of their 'golden' aspect is relevant.

---

12   Joseph Fontenrose, *Python: A Study of Delphic Myth and Its Origins*, 346.

CHAPTER 8

Fig. 8.1. *Hercules in the Garden of the Hesperides with a Serpent in the Tree*, Early Roman Period, Courtesy of the Trustees of the British Museum[13]

---

13   James H. Charlesworth, *The Good and Evil Serpent*, 148.

Fig. 8.2. *Medea and Jason with the guardian serpent*, c. 50 CE, Basilica de Porta Maggiore, Rome, Italy[14]

In *Classical Mythology*, Harris and Platzner relate the mythic belief that the 'golden apples' of the Garden of the Hesperides bestow and preserve immortality.[15] What *exactly*, however, is it about the apples that does this? In *Patterns in Comparative Religion*, Eliade states that

> [t]he Tree of Life, or the tree with the golden apples, or the golden fleece, which symbolized a state of *absoluteness* (gold meant "glory", immortality, etc.) — became a golden "treasure" hidden in the ground and guarded by dragons or serpents.[16]

---

14 Buffie Johnson, *Lady of the Beasts*, 162.

15 Stephen L. Harris and Gloria Platzner, *Classical Mythology: Images & Insights* (Mountain View, California: Mayfield Publishing Company, 1995, 2001), 281 and 283.

16 Mircea Eliade, *Patterns in Comparative Religion*, 442.

Eliade indicates that the 'goldness' of the mentioned apples, fleece, and 'treasure' symbolizes the *same thing* in all three cases: 'glory,' immortality, or a state of 'absoluteness.' At least the last two qualities, however, are, in Tradition, only associated with divinity, the metaphysical, or with that which is closely related to them. As we have already seen, the Tree of Life, and the traditional symbolism of the 'tree' in general, is connected by Eliade and Guénon both to the *Axis Mundi* or World Axis that is itself a symbol of the divine or meta-physical. Guénon states of the tree in the garden of the Hesperides and the tree with the 'golden fleece' that both are "clearly further forms of the 'Tree of Life' and accordingly they also represent the 'World Axis.'"[17] As we discussed previously, however, it is only near the World Axis, which symbolizes the metaphysical Principle, that the 'sense of eternity' required for achieving immortality is assimilable. Eliade, referring in *Patterns in Comparative Religion* to "the expedition to get the golden apples from the garden of the Hesperides, or to get the golden fleece of Colchis," concludes that "each of these trials is basically a victorious entry into a place hard of access, and well defended, where there is to be found a more or less obvious symbol of power, sacredness and immortality."[18] Earlier in *Patterns*, he more generally states that

> [t]here are serpents "guarding" all the paths to immortality, that is, every "centre", every repository where the sacred is concentrated, every *real* substance. They are always pictured round the bowl of Dionysos, they watch over Apollo's gold in far-off Scythia, they guard the treasure hidden at the bottom of the earth, or the diamonds and pearls at the bottom of the sea — in fact, they guard every symbol embodying the sacred, or able to bestow *power*, *life* or *omniscience*.[19]

---

17 René Guénon, *The Symbolism of the Cross*, 124.
18 Mircea Eliade, *Patterns in Comparative Religion*, 381; also see Mircea Eliade, *The Sacred and the Profane*, 135–36.
19 Mircea Eliade, *Patterns in Comparative Religion*, 291.

The serpent or dragon of ancient art and myth that Eliade and Guénon both describe as a 'guardian' is more accurately thought of as an *obstacle*. For, the serpent/dragon 'guardian' of Tradition is, I argue, symbolic of that obstacle to *moksha* that consists in awareness of the 'chaos' of what Guénon calls "the indefinite series of cycles of manifestation," or *samsara* in *Vedanta*, the reflection upon which, by the New Man, I term *matter*. The serpent's/dragon's 'guardianship,' therefore, consists in the maintenance of the state of *tamas* that characterizes *samsara* and thus characterizes the state of *matter in* the 'migrating' being (the 'hero,' in the present cases). This 'guardianship,' I hold, acts to *obscure*, by means of *ignorance* (*avidya*), the being's 'identity' with, and to prevent its 'realization' of, *Brahman*/God/Spirit. In the terms of the Hindu Doctrines, what I shall call the 'active' element of the serpent's/dragon's 'guarding' (of 'treasure') is equivalent to the *maya* aspect of *samsara*. Maya encompasses, in *Vedanta*, the misleading surface appearance of *samsara*, or, as Puligandla puts it, "our persistent tendency to regard appearances as reality and vice versa... our ignorance (*avidya*) as to the difference between appearance and reality."[20]

Just as the 'golden treasure' is only 'guarded,' or obstructed, by means of the particular state of awareness 'fallen' into and experienced by the 'seeker' (the 'hero' such as Herakles or Jason), it is only 'golden' or 'treasure' *because* of its location near to the World Axis. The latter is symbolized by the apple, beech, or oak trees in the two mentioned Greek myths, and the Tree of Life in Genesis 3. The 'golden apples' and the 'golden fleece' are, in other words, only worthy of attainment by the 'hero' because they are near to the World Axis that symbolizes the metaphysical Principle. Their golden quality is, perhaps, reflective of their nearness to the 'Pole' that is sometimes also symbolized by the Pole Star, with all of the golden radiance that that celestial object contains. Acquisition of these 'golden' objects, in their connection to

---

20 Ramakrishna Puligandla, *Fundamentals of Indian Philosophy*, 237.

the metaphysical Principial Reality symbolized by the World Axis or 'Pole,' symbolizes a *Spiritual* (meta-physical) reward. When, therefore, 'the being' attains the 'treasure' that 'hangs' from the 'tree'—when it 'realizes,' in other words, the Principle that is represented by variations of the World Axis—I argue that *it itself becomes* 'treasure' because it now occupies the 'center' *like* the 'treasure.' In *The Symbolism of the Cross*, Guénon states,

> For the being to realize itself totally, it must escape...cyclic concatenation and pass from the circumference to the center, in other words to the point where the axis meets the plane representing the state in which it is at present situated; the integration of this state having first been thus achieved, the totalization will thereafter take place, starting from that plane as basis, in the direction of the vertical axis.[21]

The 'realization' that Guénon refers to is the 'Self' (*Atman*)-realization expressed in *Chandogya Upanishad* VI: 10: 1–3 when the pupil Svetaketu is told by his master "[t]hat art thou, Svetaketu," that he, in other words, is *essentially equivalent to* "that which is the finest essence...Reality...*Atman*."[22] In this moment, the 'migrating' being (Svetaketu, in this case) 'realizes' that it is identical with the 'Self' (*Atman*) that is *Brahman*. This is the true object of the so-called 'hero's' quest, as it is instantiated in the above narratives of Herakles and Jason, and as it appears in its various iterations in most other traditional myths and artworks. For, 'realization' of 'Self' *is* the 'gold' or 'treasure' that serpents and dragons in Tradition are depicted as 'guarding' from any being that desires to pursue *moksha*/immortality. It is the completion of the 'quest' of *every* being that is (*feels*) 'trapped' in "the indefinite series of cycles of manifestation"/*samsara*/matter.[23]

---

21 René Guénon, *The Symbolism of the Cross*, 124–25.
22 From Sarvepalli Radhakrishnan and Charles A. Moore, eds., *A Source Book in Indian Philosophy*, 69.
23 In a future work, we hope to address the specific symbolism of the so-called 'Holy Grail' that is, as we shall argue, a refinement of the earlier symbolism

The Serpent as 'Guardian' in Genesis 3

'Attachment' to *samsara* is attachment to multiplicity/plurality or 'duality.' The seeker of the 'golden fleece' or the 'golden apples,' like the 'migrating' being that desires *moksha*, is the being that has (to some degree) 'realized' its 'attachment' to multiplicity or *samsara*. In *The Symbolism of the Cross*, Guénon states that "attachment to multiplicity is also, in one sense, the Biblical 'temptation' [of Genesis], which drives the being away from the original central unity and prevents him from attaining the fruit of the 'Tree of Life.'"[24] Upon achieving *partial* 'realization' of the Principle (God), which is to say 'realization' of the 'chaos' of 'nature' in comparison to the 'unity' or completeness of metaphysical Reality, the 'migrating' being strives to slack off 'attachment' (to 'shed' it, like a snake sheds its skin) and to achieve 'unity' with its metaphysical Source. Adam and 'the woman,' according to Guénon, are 'driven away' from the Tree of Life—the 'unity' of the World Axis—because of their attachment to multiplicity or 'duality,' represented by the 'dual nature' of the Tree of the Knowledge of good and evil.[25] 'Duality,' as we have argued, is merely the simplest form of multiplicity. As Adam and 'the woman'—the *singular* being with two natures named 'Adam and Eve'—become(s) enamored of the Tree of the Knowledge of good and evil, that being ('they') simultaneously becomes enamored of the 'duality'/multiplicity of *samsara*. The 'duality'/multiplicity of *samsara*, because it provides apparent 'alternatives' to the present state of being that the being 'Adam and Eve' finds itself in, promotes the *absence of certainty* and the intrusion of apparent 'choice.'[26] 'Duality,' then, is accompanied by *indefinitude*, as noted in

---

of 'Self'-realization that is depicted and described in various versions of the Indo-Aryan *mythos*, such as the Greek myths just considered.

24 René Guénon, *The Symbolism of the Cross*, 124.
25 René Guénon, *The Symbolism of the Cross*, 56.
26 'Certainty' is a term that perhaps best describes the kind of awareness a being acquires upon achieving *moksha*.

Chapter 6, because it invites the apparent 'choice' that makes two (or more) 'options' endlessly evaluable. I suggest that this is represented in Genesis 3 by the serpent's *promotion* of the Tree of the Knowledge of good *and* evil: the promotion of apparent 'choice.' The indefinitude that the serpent promotes to 'Adam and Eve' characterizes the state of *matter* which that being 'falls' into: awareness of the 'chaos' of "the *indefinite* series of cycles of manifestation."

I suggest that what specifically 'tempts' the being 'Adam and Eve' in Genesis 3 is the indefinitude of 'choice,' the being's uncertainty and doubt concerning whether or not to eat of the fruit of the Tree of the Knowledge of good and evil. This indefinitude of 'choice' characterizes the flux of *samsara* or "the indefinite series of cycles of manifestation" because *samsara* generates endlessly varied 'options.' As 'duality' is shorthand for the multiplicity or plurality or *samsara*, however, it is the 'dual' snake and the 'dual' tree that initially represent the indefinitude of 'choice.' The particular kind of 'knowledge' that is referred to in the title 'Tree of the Knowledge of good and evil' is, therefore, a 'lower' form of knowledge (*aparavidya* in *Vedanta*) that is constituted by acute *perception* of 'duality'/multiplicity. The 'higher' knowledge of 'intellection,' according to Guénon, is, by contrast, of the 'unity' of the metaphysical Principle. The latter is symbolized, as we have said before, by the Tree of Life. In *Fundamentals of Indian Philosophy*, Puligandla defines the 'lower' knowledge of *aparavidya* as a perceptual *and* conceptual form of knowledge.[27] Both perception and conception, however, are in Tradition 'lower' than *intellection*. The Tree of the Knowledge of good and evil might, therefore, have been better named the "Tree of the Greater Awareness of 'Duality'/Indefinitude and Lesser Awareness of Unity/Definition."

Guénon states in *The Symbolism of the Cross* that

> [t]he dual nature of the 'Tree of Knowledge' moreover appears to Adam only at the very moment of the 'Fall', since it is then that he...finds himself

---

27 Ramakrishna Puligandla, *Fundamentals of Indian Philosophy*, 223-224.

driven out from the center which is the place of the primal unity to which the Tree of Life corresponds....This center has become inaccessible to fallen man, who has lost the 'sense of eternity', which is also the 'sense of unity'.[28]

Because the serpent in Genesis 3 facilitates 'Adam and Eve's' 'fall' from the 'primal unity' of the 'center,' I argue that it serves as the 'guardian' of these things. For, a 'guardian' is above all else that which *obstructs* passage, or stands between, a 'seeker' and that which it seeks. In the context of this chapter, what is sought by the 'migrating' being is the 'gold' or 'treasure' that symbolizes *moksha* or the broadly traditional idea of 'immortality.' The serpent of Eden, therefore, like the dragons encountered by Herakles and Jason in Greek myth, serves as a 'guardian' when it obstructs passage to the 'unity' of the 'center' that symbolizes the metaphysical Principle—'God' in the Torah. For here, according to Guénon, is the 'place' of the 'sense of eternity,' and only in eternity may immortality be found. As with the narratives of Herakles and Jason, a great tree, the Tree of Life in Genesis 3, symbolizes the World Axis that marks the 'center.' In the Genesis 3 narrative, the serpent 'guards' the 'unity' of the World Axis, represented by the Tree of Life, by *diverting attention away from it*. And this, as we discussed previously, the serpent accomplishes by 'promoting' (speaking for) 'duality' and indefinitude, both symbolized by the Tree of the Knowledge of good and evil. In essence, the serpent makes 'duality' and indefinitude more appealing than 'unity' and eternity to 'Adam and Eve' by characterizing them as 'choices.' Its 'guardianship,' therefore, as is expressed in the first statement describing the serpent in the Bible, consists of 'crafty'[29] misdirection.

---

28 René Guénon, *The Symbolism of the Cross*, 56.
29 Genesis 3:1, ESV.

The Metaphysical Symbolism of the Cross, the 'Ways' of Islam, and the *Gunas* of *Samkhya* in Relation to Genesis 3

In Chapter 6 we discussed Guénon's interpretation of the traditional symbolism of the cross, which according to him is a traditional figuration of the World Axis and a transcultural symbol of the metaphysical Principle. Unlike the symbolism of the tree, for Guénon, the symbolism of the cross allows for a more streamlined visual comprehension of traditional metaphysics. In Chapter 6, we observed that the upper portion of the cross or tree traditionally symbolizes, according to Guénon, the 'higher' states of 'the being,' the latter of which he says 'migrates' through the 'multiple states' of existence. The lower portion of the cross or tree for Guénon symbolizes the 'lower' states of existence 'migrated' through by 'the being.' In Guénon's 'symbolism of the cross,' therefore, what he terms the 'migrating' being may be represented as either: 1) 'ascending' to 'higher' states of existence (higher states of 'the being'), 2) 'descending' to 'lower' states of existence (lower states of 'the being'), or 3) simply remaining in the same state of existence (the same state of the 'multiple states of the being') that it is currently in. The 'vertical movements' of the migrating being along the vertical arm of the cross, whether 'upward' or 'downward,' symbolize, according to Guénon, the being's 'migrations' *through* the 'multiple states of the being.' From the perspective of the Principle, the enlightened perspective of *Brahman* in *Vedanta*, such 'movements' equate to changes in the *level* ('state') *of awareness of Atman/Brahman* of its *own* being. 'Lateral movements' of the 'migrating' being, by contrast, along the *horizontal* bar of the cross, symbolize for Guénon 'expansion' of the migrating being *in a particular state* of 'the being' (*Brahman*). From the enlightened perspective of *Brahman*, such 'lateral movements' equate to those changes in awareness of *Brahman* that *Brahman* experiences while confining itself to *one particular* state of being—such as the human state.

One way in which Guénon articulates the migrating being's relationship to the Principle/*Brahman*/God in *The Symbolism of the Cross* is by applying the symbolism of the cross to the first *Surat* of the Koran, the *Fatihah*, and to the threefold division of human 'ways' of existing that Guénon argues is delineated there. Guénon states in *The Symbolism of the Cross* that, in Islamic esoterism specifically, there are three possible 'paths,' or 'ways,' for 'the being' to take in any particular manifestation which define its relationship in that manifestation to "the divine Will" of Allah. These are: the 'heavenly way,' the 'infernal way,' and the way of 'those who are in error.'[30] In Abdullah Yusuf 'Ali's translation of the *Fatihah*, the 'infernal way' is the way of 'wrath' whereas the way of 'those who are in error' is the way of those who go 'astray,' as may be seen in the last sentence of the *Fatihah*:

> In the name of Allah, Most Gracious, Most Merciful. Praise be to Allah, The Cherisher and Sustainer of the Worlds; Most Gracious, Most Merciful; Master of the Day of Judgement. Thee do we worship, and Thine aid we seek. Show us the straight way, The way of those on whom Thou has bestowed Thy Grace, Those whose (portion) is not wrath, And who go not astray.[31]

The 'heavenly way,' as Guénon observes, is the path of authentic Islam, or "submission to the divine Will," and is the "'straight path' ['straight way']... spoken of in the *Fatihah*."[32] In the terms of *The Symbolism of the Cross*, the 'heavenly way,' Guénon argues, is "the same thing as the vertical axis taken in its upward direction." It is the path of "those who directly receive the influence of the 'Activity of Heaven' and are led by it to the higher states and to total realization."[33] According to Guénon, the migrating being that 'chooses' this 'way' receives the

---

30 René Guénon, *The Symbolism of the Cross*, 125–126.
31 *The Meaning of The Holy Qur'an*, trans., Abdullah Yusuf 'Ali (Beltsville, Maryland: Amana Publications, 1989), Surah 1 (*Al Fatihah*), 14.
32 René Guénon, *The Symbolism of the Cross*, 125–126.
33 René Guénon, *The Symbolism of the Cross*, 125–126.

"divine 'grace'" of Allah.³⁴ In "direct opposition to 'grace,'" however, according to Guénon, is the path of 'anger' — also called the 'infernal way' in Islam.³⁵ Of the 'infernal way,' Guénon states that "'anger' being in direct opposition to 'grace', its action must be exerted along the vertical axis [of the cross], but with the opposite effect, which makes it travel downwards, toward the lower states."³⁶ By 'lower states,' Guénon means those states of being that are 'furthest' from the 'migrating' being's "total realization" — the attainment of *moksha* in *Vedanta*.

The third path or 'way' that is, according to Guénon, described in esoteric Islam as being available to the 'migrating' being is termed in Islam the path of 'error.' According to Guénon,

> [t]hose who are in 'error', in the proper etymological sense of the word, are those who, as is the case with the vast majority of men, drawn and held fast by multiplicity, err or wander indefinitely in the cycles of manifestation, represented by the con-volutions of the serpent coiled around the 'Tree in the Midst'.³⁷

Those beings who, according to Guénon, have taken the path of 'error' are, as he states, neither on the 'upward' path to 'realization' *nor* are their actions "in direct opposition to 'grace'" — 'downward,' in other words. Such beings, one may say, are neither actively promoting *or* dissolving their possibilities for 'ascension' to 'higher' (symbolized by the *upper* vertical arm of the cross) states of being. They are merely, as Guénon states, 'wandering indefinitely,' expressed symbolically by their 'traversing' the *lateral* (or horizontal) bar of the cross. According to Guénon, this 'wandering' is the case for any being, such as the human being, that only actualizes its potentialities within *one particular* state of being. The *particularly human* possibilities of the migrating being that is *currently* in the 'human state,' for example, are thus

---

34 René Guénon, *The Symbolism of the Cross*, 126.
35 René Guénon, *The Symbolism of the Cross*, 126.
36 René Guénon, *The Symbolism of the Cross*, 126.
37 René Guénon, *The Symbolism of the Cross*, 126.

symbolized by means of the lateral/horizontal bar of the cross. As I shall discuss below, however, 'indefinite *wondering*' in a *single* cycle of manifestation, rather than "wandering indefinitely in the cycle*s* of manifestation," better describes the plight of those who are "in 'error.'" In either case, whether through 'wandering' or through 'wondering,' the 'migrating' being is obstructed or 'guarded' from the truth of the metaphysical 'unity' of the Principle by means of its focus on the 'error' of multiplicity ('duality').

Making use of Islamic concepts and beliefs, Guénon connects in the above quotation the allure of 'multiplicity' ("the vast majority of men, drawn and held fast by multiplicity") with the symbolism of the serpent coiled around what he terms the 'Tree in the Midst.' At the same time, however, by employing the traditional symbolism of the cross, he promotes a symbolic connection between axial imagery and levels of 'actualization' as the latter is defined in the Hindu Doctrines. This promotion is consistent with, and further cements, his understanding of Tradition as that which pervades and transcends seemingly opposed religions or cultures. Guénon continues his appeal to an underlying 'Tradition' when he describes the three 'paths' mentioned in the *Fatihah* by means of *Samkhya* terminology, specifically the three *gunas* which we referred to in Chapter 4. Guénon argues that "these three categories of being [the 'heavenly way,' the 'infernal way,' and the path of 'error']...correspond exactly to the three *gunas*: the first to *sattva*, the second to *tamas*, and the third to *rajas*."[38] They are, then, respectively: 1) "conformity to the pure essence of Being (*Sat*), which is identical to the light of knowledge (*jnana*)"; 2) "obscurity, assimilated to ignorance (*avidya*), the dark root of the being considered in its lower states"; and 3) "the urge that provokes the being's expansion in a given state."[39] Those who are in 'error,' or "held fast by multiplicity," therefore, exist according to Guénon within the state

---

38 René Guénon, *The Symbolism of the Cross*, 126.
39 René Guénon, *The Symbolism of the Cross*, 31.

of *rajas*. They 'expand' "in a given state." *Symbolically* speaking, they 'wander indefinitely' on the *horizontal* bar of the cross and are, thus, 'guarded' from either 'ascent' to *jnana* or 'descent' to *avidya*.

Puligandla observes that "in man *rajas* is the cause of activity, restlessness, and pain."[40] I argue, more specifically, that *rajas*, in its equivalency to the Islamic path of 'error,' is the path that the singular being 'Adam and Eve' *initially* 'chooses' in Genesis 3 which ultimately leads to that being's particular varieties of "activity, restlessness, and pain." This occurs as soon as 'the woman' aspect of 'Adam and Eve' begins to seriously consider the serpent's 'promotion' of the fruit of the Tree of the Knowledge of good and evil. For, the serpent's promotion of that 'dual' tree's fruit is equivalently a promotion, in Guénon's terms, of the path of 'indefinite wandering in the cycles of manifestation,' which is really a path of indefinite *wondering* since it is a path taken due to the *doubt* inspired by the serpent in 'Adam and Eve.'[41] We may infer from this that, just as 'wandering' (or 'wondering') generally implies a kind of nervous 'directionless-ness,' some sort of 'restlessness' led the being 'Adam and Eve' to eat of the fruit of a tree that was forbidden to it. At the very least there seems to have been an emergent state of *curiosity* in 'the woman' aspect of 'Adam and Eve' that compelled that being to try something 'new.' Curiosity is a form of restlessness, a form of desiring to go somewhere *other than* where one presently is, either physically or mentally, but without knowing *where* that 'somewhere' is. Inevitably, this 'restless activity' of 'Adam and Eve' leads the being to the 'path' of the *pain* of childbirth, the *activity* of manual labor, and the *restlessness* that comes from separation from God.

For Guénon, "attachment to multiplicity is…, in one sense, the Biblical 'temptation,' which drives the being away from the original central unity."[42] I stated earlier that what 'tempts' the being 'Adam and

---

40 Ramakrishna Puligandla, *Fundamentals of Indian Philosophy*, 122.
41 René Guénon, *The Symbolism of the Cross*, 126.
42 René Guénon, *The Symbolism of the Cross*, 124.

Eve' in Genesis 3 is the indefinitude of 'choice,' manifested in that narrative as the being's uncertainty and doubt concerning whether to eat of the fruit of the Tree of the Knowledge of good and evil. *Because of* 'Adam and Eve's' "attachment to multiplicity," because of, in other words, its 'restlessness' and its 'fascination' with the *indefinitude* of 'choice,' I suggest that 'Adam and Eve' is, from a broadly traditional perspective, described in Genesis 3 as 'coagulating' (in Hermetic terms)[43] into the sedentary state of *rajas*, destined therefore, at least for a time, to "wander [wonder] indefinitely in the cycles of manifestation"/*samsara*. This condition is, however, only temporary. For, the 'contrary' stance represented in Genesis 3 of the 'dual' serpent towards the 'unity' of God/*Brahman*/the Principle only *initially* leads 'Adam and Eve' into the condition of *rajas* or the Islamic path of 'error.' *Immediately afterward*, 'Adam and Eve,' as well as its 'progeny' (later iterations of the 'migrating' being) 'descend' ('fall') into the condition called *tamas* in *Samkhya*: the Islamic 'infernal way' of "obscurity, assimilated to ignorance" (*avidya*). 'Adam and Eve' is no longer, at this point in its 'migration,' directly 'guarded' by the serpent from 'ascending' to 'higher' states of being, but neither is it in a condition to prevent its further 'descension.' We may thus speculate that, had 'Adam and Eve' remained 'faithful' to the 'divine will,' rather than receptive to the serpent's rhetoric concerning 'choice,' its actions may have been less in line with behavior consistent with the conditions of *rajas* and *tamas* and more in line with the condition of *sattva*, "conformity to the pure essence of Being (*Sat*)."[44] For, from a broadly traditional perspective, *Sat* is *Brahman* or 'God.'

---

43 René Guénon, *The Great Triad*, 36–37.
44 René Guénon, *The Symbolism of the Cross*, 31.

The Guardian of Immortality/*Moksha* in *The Epic of Gilgamesh*

Another traditional example of the serpent/dragon-as-'guardian' appears in *The Epic of Gilgamesh*, the Sumero-Akkadian account of the eponymous hero-king of ancient Uruk. The *Epic of Gilgamesh* serves as a very ancient example of serpent symbolism in mythology since, according to one of its translators, N. K. Sandars, it is based upon a cycle of poems which "were already written down in the first centuries of the second millennium B.C., and that...probably existed in much the same form many centuries earlier."[45] Among the many other adventures told of the 'half-divine' Gilgamesh in the *Epic*[46] is that describing his search for a plant or herb that, like the golden apples sought by Herakles in the Garden of the Hesperides, brings immortality to him who consumes it. It is Utnapishtim, the 'Akkadian Noah,' who reveals to our hero the existence of this unusual plant and sets him upon his quest with the following words:

> Gilgamesh, you came here a man wearied out, you have worn yourself out; what shall I give you to carry back to your own country? Gilgamesh, I shall reveal a secret thing, it is a mystery of the gods that I am telling you. There is a plant that grows under the water, it has a prickle like a thorn, like a rose; it will wound your hands, but if you succeed in taking it, then your hands will hold that which restores his lost youth to a man.[47]

Resolving to procure the plant that 'restores lost youth,' Gilgamesh enlists the services of the ferryman Urshanabi in order to cross the unnamed sea that separates him from the location described by Utnapishtim. After a time, Gilgamesh reaches his destination and his objective, at which point he tells Urshanabi,

---

45 N. K. Sandars, trans., *The Epic of Gilgamesh*, 7–8.
46 N. K. Sandars, trans., *The Epic of Gilgamesh*, 30.
47 N. K. Sandars, trans., *The Epic of Gilgamesh*, 116.

> Come here, and see this marvelous plant. By its virtue a man may win back all his former strength. I will take it to Uruk of the strong walls; there I will give it to the old men to eat. Its name shall be 'The Old Men Are Young Again'; and at last I shall eat it myself and have back all my lost youth.[48]

Gilgamesh successfully retrieves the "marvelous plant...that grows under the water," and he and Urshanabi journey away from its source. Before long, however, a rest is needed for the night, and, as the *Epic* describes it,

> Gilgamesh saw a well of cool water and he went down and bathed; but deep in the pool there was lying a serpent, and the serpent sensed the sweetness of the flower. It rose out of the water and snatched it away, and immediately it sloughed its skin and returned to the well. Then Gilgamesh sat down and wept, the tears ran down his face, and he took the hand of Urshanabi; 'O Urshanabi, was it for this that I toiled with my hands, is it for this I have wrung out my heart's blood? For myself I have gained nothing; not I, but the beast of the earth has joy of it now.'[49]

The serpent, the 'beast of the earth,' as Gilgamesh laments, has *stolen immortality* from him and taken it for itself.

There are obvious thematic similarities between *The Epic of Gilgamesh* and Genesis 3. The actuality, or possibility, of immortality and its association with a plant or tree, as well as the conditionality of immortality upon the actions of a 'serpent,' are important elements in both narratives. In Genesis 3, however, the fruit of the Tree of Knowledge appears to *take* immortality from whoever eats of it, while the herb/plant described in *The Epic of Gilgamesh* appears to *give* immortality. In *Patterns in Comparative Religion*, Eliade also observes that "[t]he Tree of Life...is 'hidden' — like the herb of immortality which Gilgamesh went to find at the bottom of the sea."[50] Presumably, this 'hidden' quality of the Tree of Life refers to 'Adam

---

48 N. K. Sandars, trans., *The Epic of Gilgamesh*, 116.
49 N. K. Sandars, trans., *The Epic of Gilgamesh*, 117.
50 Mircea Eliade, *Patterns in Comparative Religion*, 287.

and Eve's' ignorance, or apparent disinterest, in that tree as compared with the being's 'fascination' (as I have described it) with the Tree of Knowledge. Unlike Genesis 3, however, in which it may be presumed that 'Adam and Eve' has no interest in immortality, since none is stated in the text, in *The Epic of Gilgamesh* the protagonist goes *in search of* immortality.

In Chapter 7, I argued that God's giving 'skins' to the being 'Adam and Eve' in Genesis 3:21 traditionally symbolizes, in Guénon's terms, the 'evolutive' process of 'identifying' *less and less* with the metaphysical Principle/God/*Brahman*/Spirit. For, instead of 'ascending' to a 'higher' state of being and, therefore, 'shedding' its old state of being like a snake sheds its skin, in Genesis 3 'Adam and Eve,' the *Atman*, 'descends' to a 'lower' state of being and, like a snake moving backwards into itself, 'collects' a 'skin.' This 'collection of a skin' by the 'migrating' being 'Adam and Eve,' I suggested in Chapter 7, traditionally symbolizes what Guénon calls an 'evolutive' path into "the indefinite series of cycles of manifestation"/*samsara* — into the state of *matter* — and is diametrically opposed to the symbolic 'shedding' of a skin that indicates, by contrast, in Guénon's terminology, the 'involutive' process of 'identifying' ever more closely with the metaphysical Principle (God in Genesis; *Brahman* in *Vedanta*).

When the serpent "sloughs its skin" in *The Epic of Gilgamesh* immediately after consuming the 'marvelous plant' so recently discovered and then lost by the eponymous hero of that tale, this would appear to illustrate the cause of the serpent's 'immortality.' Although in many traditional tales from around the world, it is told that the serpent 'steals immortality' from humans, from Gilgamesh's perspective the serpent is less a thief than an *opponent* to Gilgamesh, more a rival to him than a robber, more an *obstacle* to Gilgamesh's goal of 'having back all of his lost youth' than that which actually takes that youth. Eliade states that "Gilgamesh, like Adam, has lost immortality because of his own stupidity and a serpent's trick."[51] From our perspective, however, this 'trickster' interpretation of the serpent is wrong because it identifies the serpent as a *conscious agent*—a 'thief.' As I have argued, however, the serpent/dragon in Tradition symbolizes *not* a conscious force, but rather a *state of being*: "the indefinite series of cycles of manifestation" in its 'chaotic' perspective: *matter*. The interpretation of the serpent-as-trickster does reveal, however, that there is something about Gilgamesh *himself*—"his own stupidity," according to Eliade—that costs him his prize. It is not, however, so much a lack of *intelligence* but, rather, a lack of *knowledge*—*avidya* as the state of 'original ignorance' which is built into the very nature of human being—that is Gilgamesh's problem.[52] For, the lack of interest by the being 'Adam and Eve' in the Tree of Life as well as the 'hiddenness' "under the water" of Gilgamesh's plant of immortality both imply the presence of *ignorance* in these beings, not stupidity. It is, in both cases, these characters' *avidya*, specifically, that is responsible for their incapacity to discern the 'hidden treasure' that is 'waiting' for them if they but knew how to 'conquer' their *avidya*.[53] In the case of 'Adam and Eve,' this 'treasure' is the fruit of the Tree of Life; in Gilgamesh's case, it is the plant/herb of immortality. In *both* cases, it is the 'Self' (*Atman*) as that which is *known* (*paravidya*) to be equivalent to *Brahman*/God/ Spirit/the Principle by any being that has attained *moksha*. As Eliade states in *Patterns in Comparative Religion*, however, Gilgamesh's herb of immortality is not only "hard of access" but is a "'*thorny*' herb."[54] It is, in other words, not merely some stolen item, but by its very nature

---

51 Mircea Eliade, *Patterns in Comparative Religion*, 290.
52 Ramakrishna Puligandla, *Fundamentals of Indian Philosophy*, 251 and René Guénon, *Man & His Becoming According to the Vedanta*, 122 and 158.
53 As Puligandla states, "it is by conquering this ignorance [*avidya*] by the knowledge of reality—the identity of *atman* and *Brahman*—that man attains *moksha*, the state of absolute freedom from ignorance, *maya*, bondage, and suffering." Ramakrishna Puligandla, *Fundamentals of Indian Philosophy*, 251.
54 Mircea Eliade, *Patterns in Comparative Religion*, 289.

a dangerous thing that can be painful to acquire. *And so it is as well with the state of being called moksha ('immortality') and the process of 'realization' of 'Self' (Atman) as Brahman that is described in the Vedanta.*

Guardian of *Moksha*, Not of Physical Life: A Critique of James Frazer's Interpretation of Genesis 3

Since the only trees that are named in Genesis 3 are the Tree of Life and the Tree of the Knowledge of good and evil, it is reasonable to infer that these two trees are, in some sense, 'opposites.' It is a quick and easy step, however, from identifying the two trees as 'opposites' to reasoning that, 'therefore,' the Tree of Knowledge is 'really' the Tree of *Death*. One could imagine a defender of this interpretation pointing out that 'Adam and Eve's' eating of the Tree of Knowledge eventually leads to that being's *physical death* outside of the Garden of Eden. Such a defender might muse that *if* 'Adam and Eve' had only followed God's command *not* to eat of the Tree of Knowledge, *then* that being would still enjoy 'immortality' in the Garden of Eden. This interpretation would, in the terms of my argument, make the serpent of Eden a 'guardian' not of *moksha*, as I have contended, but rather of *physical life*, the 'opposite' of physical death.

James Frazer, famous for his monumental *The Golden Bough*, makes the interpretive mistake just outlined in his *Folk-Lore in the Old Testament*. He does so in the context of arguing that the depictions of the serpent in Genesis 3 and *The Epic of Gilgamesh* are both examples of a transcultural class of stories that he calls "The Story of the Perverted Message."[55] In *Folk-Lore in the Old Testament*, Frazer observes, "In these stories a single messenger is engaged to carry the...message" of immortality to humankind, but the mission of the messenger fails due

---

55 Sir James George Frazer, *Folk-Lore in the Old Testament: Studies in Comparative Religion, Legend and Law, Vol. 1* (London, England: Macmillan and Co., Limited, 1918 [published by Forgotten Books 2012]), 52.

to either "the carelessness or malice of the missionary."[56] According to Frazer, the narrative of Genesis 3 is a variation of a story the 'true' message of which Genesis 3 does not clearly express. He states:

> These parallels…suggest, though they cannot prove, that in the original of the story, which the Jehovistic writer has mangled and distorted, the serpent was the messenger sent by God to bear the glad tidings of immortality to man, but that the cunning creature perverted the message to the advantage of his species and to the ruin of ours.[57]

The conclusion of traditional peoples, according to Frazer, is that

> [i]f only the serpent had not perverted God's good message and deceived our first mother, we should have been immortal instead of the serpents; for like the serpents we should have cast our skins every year and so renewed our youth perpetually.[58]

Frazer's interpretations of both Genesis 3 and *The Epic of Gilgamesh* are greatly colored by his classification of the two narratives under his rubric of 'The Story of the Perverted Message,' and, more generally, his emphasis on the idea that ancient man had a burning need to explain physical mortality:

> The gist of the whole story of the fall [of mankind] appears to be an attempt to explain man's mortality, to set forth how death came into the world. It is true that man is not said to have been created immortal and to have lost his immortality through disobedience; but neither is he said to have been created mortal. Rather we are given to understand that the possibility alike of immortality and of mortality was open to him, and that it rested with him which he would choose; for the tree of life stood within his reach, its fruit was not forbidden to him, he had only to stretch out his hand, take of the fruit, and eating of it live for ever.[59]

---

56   Sir James George Frazer, *Folk-Lore in the Old Testament*, 55.
57   Sir James George Frazer, *Folk-Lore in the Old Testament*, 51.
58   Sir James George Frazer, *Folk-Lore in the Old Testament*, 52.
59   Sir James George Frazer, *Folk-Lore in the Old Testament*, 47.

Since 'Adam and Eve's' eating of the fruit of the Tree of Knowledge seemed to result in various activities and processes associated with mortality, Frazer concludes:

> This suggests that the forbidden tree was really a tree of death, not of knowledge....Accordingly we may suppose that in the original story there were two trees, a tree of life and a tree of death; that it was open to man to eat of the one and live for ever, or to eat of the other and die... [and] that man, misled by the serpent, ate of the wrong tree and so forfeited the immortality which his benevolent Creator had designed for him.[60]

For Frazer, then, Genesis 3 is simply a skewed version of a near-universal allegory that answers the perennial existential question: Why is there death in the world?

As mentioned, Frazer's renaming of the Tree of Knowledge with the title 'tree of death' is simply an interpretive mistake, a reduction in which Frazer focuses on only one of the possible effects of 'Adam and Eve's' eating from that tree. Other possible effects include: expulsion from the Garden of Eden, tilling the earth, childbirth, the raising of three sons to near adulthood or beyond, and Adam's hundreds-of-years-long life span.[61] Frazer's labeling the Tree of Knowledge the 'tree of death,' therefore, to wax poetic, 'misses the journey' by myopically focusing on what *Frazer* sees as the destination. For, the Tree of Knowledge is not, as Frazer believed, *inaccurately* named, it is merely *ironically* named. It is not a 'tree of death,' but, rather, a tree of *ignorance (avidya)*. What the serpent of Genesis 3 'guards,' therefore, is not physical immortality but, rather, *knowledge*: specifically, the 'migrating' being's 'higher' knowledge (*vidya*[62]) that consists of 'realization'

---

60 Sir James George Frazer, *Folk-Lore in the Old Testament*, 48.
61 Genesis 3:16–19; 5:3–5. We presume that 'Eve' has the exact same life-span as 'Adam,' since, in our interpretation, 'she' is but *an aspect of* the singular being 'Adam and Eve.'
62 Guénon describes *vidya* as "the flash of lightning [that] illumines the darkness; the latter is the symbol of ignorance (*avidya*) while knowledge is an inner

of the being's 'identity' with *Brahman* (God, in the Torah) and the 'identity' of its true 'Self' (*Atman*) and *Brahman*. This 'realization' *does lead* to 'immortality,' but of a more profound variety than merely everlasting *physical life*.

Frazer's error, therefore, is really only one of emphasis, and his interpretation only becomes attractive when one believes that *physical* death is the worst of all possible punishments. I criticize his interpretation, in particular, because it is a well-known example of what I believe to be a common and easy way of trying to understand Genesis 3, that is, as a story of the punishment of mankind by means of taking away his physical immortality. As Guénon and others have pointed out, however, the worst of punishments for traditional or 'archaic' peoples is not physical death but, rather, *avidya*, ignorance of *Brahman* and of its 'identity' with the *Atman*. Frazer's misinterpretation of Genesis 3, as revealed by his misunderstanding of the 'traditional' place of death, is therefore a misinterpretation of the traditional meaning of 'Life,' specifically as it is used in the expression 'Tree of Life.' Frazer projects the modern obsessive concern over physical life onto Genesis 3 and, thereby, interprets 'Life' in 'Tree of Life' according to what he thinks is its literal sense: *physical* life. The serpent in Genesis 3 does serve, of course, in part, as an obstruction or 'guardian' of physical life, since after 'Adam and Eve' 'falls' from the presence of God physical *death* awaits that being. *Essentially*, however, the serpent of Eden symbolizes, I contend, the 'guardian' of *meta*-physical 'Life,' with an uppercase 'L,' that state of existence that is called *moksha* in *Vedanta*, 'escape' from the concern *with* physical life. I suggest that the serpent, like the Tree of Knowledge, 'guards' access to the *actual* Tree of Knowledge, which is the Tree of Life, by means of purveying ignorance, or a 'lower' form of knowledge, *disguised as* the 'higher' traditional knowledge that Guénon calls 'intellectuality,' non-rational 'intuition' of 'the metaphysical.' The serpent of Eden is, therefore, a symbol of ignorance

---

'illumination.'" René Guénon, *Man & His Becoming According to the Vedanta*, 143.

(*avidya*) or 'lower' knowledge just as the Tree of Knowledge ironically is. More specifically, of course, the serpent is a symbol of that *particular level* of ignorance (lack of knowledge) or 'realization' that I term *matter*. This is indicated, as we have discussed, by the 'dual' nature of the serpent and the Tree of 'Knowledge,' both 'opposites' to the 'unity' of the 'sense of eternity' that is present, according to Guénon, near the axial Tree of Life. Both serpent and Tree of 'Knowledge,' in their different ways, distract the 'migrating' being 'Adam and Eve' away from the 'higher' knowledge of Life called *moksha* when they distract 'the being' away from the Tree of Life — away from the 'migrating' being's actual(-ized) 'Self' (*Atman*). For, 'higher' knowledge *just is* 'higher' Life from the perspective communicated in the Genesis 3 narrative. This implies that understanding the symbolism of the serpent in Genesis 3 is not, as Frazer seems to argue, a question of what comes *after* the serpent 'fascinates' 'Adam and Eve,' but, rather, a question of the serpent's (*samsara*'s) 'fascinating' quality itself. For, it is this 'fascination' that accounts for 'Adam and Eve's,' as well as Gilgamesh's, 'evolution' (in Guénon's terms) from the metaphysical Reality that is symbolized by the Tree of Life *into* the less 'realized' and more physical state that is symbolized by the serpent and by the ironically named Tree of 'Knowledge.' This 'fascination' comes, in Genesis 3, through the serpent's rhetoric; in *The Epic of Gilgamesh*, it comes by means of an enticing "well of cool water."[63] We shall have more to say about the symbolism of 'water' in general in a later chapter.

---

63   N. K. Sandars, trans., *The Epic of Gilgamesh*, 117.

CHAPTER 9

The *Ouroboros* and the *Anima Mundi*

The *Ouroboros*

An extremely common traditional figuration of the serpent symbol that Guénon connects with the symbolism of "the serpent coiled round a tree" is the *ouroboros* (see fig. 9.1), "a snake curled in a complete circle and holding the end of its tail in its mouth."[1] In *The Bestiary of Christ*, symbolist Louis Charbonneau-Lassay observes that "in Greek *oura* signifies 'tail,' and *boros* means 'devouring,' or 'that which devours.'"[2] Charlesworth reiterates this in *The Good and Evil Serpent*, where he states that "Ouroboros is a Greek noun that means 'devouring its own tail'"[3] In this chapter, I shall examine the transcultural symbolism of the *ouroboros* in the context of Guénon's and my own interpretation of traditional serpent symbolism, expanding the definition of *ouroboros* to include other traditional figurations that, although fairly different in appearance to the *ouroboros*, are, I contend, equivalent to it in terms of symbolic value. In the second section of this chapter, based upon observations made by the traditionalist Julius Evola and the psychologist Carl Jung that are consonant with Guénon's idea of Tradition, I explore the *ouroboros*'s connection in

---

1   Louis Charbonneau-Lassay, *The Bestiary of Christ*, 427.
2   Louis Charbonneau-Lassay, *The Bestiary of Christ*, 427.
3   James H. Charlesworth, *The Good and Evil Serpent*, 155.

Western alchemy (the 'hermetico-alchemical tradition') to the symbolism of the *anima mundi* or 'soul of the world.'

Fig. 9.1. *The black and white ouroboros of alchemy*[4]

Like many examples of traditional serpent symbolism, the *ouroboros* is both ancient and widespread. Its origin, according to some researchers, is tied to ancient observations of the heavens and celestial movements as well as ancient peoples' understanding of time in that context. Marinus Anthony van der Sluijs and Anthony L. Peratt have argued, for example, in "The *Ouroboros* as an Auroral Phenomenon" that "as the emblem of regularity and the cyclicity of stellar movements, the circular snake personified time itself in several cultures," and "the active consumption by the ouroboros of its own hind parts — which involves contortions that suggest perpetual motion — corresponds to the apparent cyclical revolution of heavenly bodies."[5] In *The Good and Evil Serpent*, Charlesworth both agrees with, and provides literary

---

4   Louis Charbonneau-Lassay, *The Bestiary of Christ*, 431.
5   Marinus Anthony van der Sluijs and Anthony L. Peratt, "The *Ouroboros* as an Auroral Phenomenon," *Journal of Folklore Research* 46, no. 1 (2009): 17.

context to, these generalizations in terms of the specifically Greek and Roman mythological context of the *ouroboros*. He states:

> Ouroboros did not necessarily denote only repetitiousness or repetitive time. There was movement and progression. While the tail ended up in the mouth, it completed the circle of being because the tail had reached the mouth....The perception that Ouroboros denoted the completion of time and the cosmos, or at least that the serpent symbolized the cosmos, at times, in Greek and Roman mythology is enhanced by a study of Ovid's *Metamorphoses*. He [Ovid] occasionally mentions the constellation of the serpent. Referring to the cosmic serpent or the constellation of the serpent, Ovid has Titan advise his son, Phaethon, about driving the celestial chariot so as not to burn up the heavens or the earth and avoid the "writhing Serpent (Anguem)." Subsequently, Ovid explains that "the serpent (Serpens), which lies nearest to the icy pole, once harmless because it was formerly sluggish with the cold, now grew hot, and conceived great frenzy from that fire."[6]

Both the cyclical idea of time and the symbolism of the *ouroboros* are far older and more widespread than the Greeks and Romans. In *Myth and Symbol in Ancient Egypt*, R. T. Rundle Clark observes with respect to the idea of time that

> underlying all Egyptian speculation is the belief that time is composed of recurrent cycles which are divinely appointed: the day, the week of ten days, the month, the year — even longer periods of 30, 400 or 1460 years, determined according to the conjunctions of sun, moon, stars and inundation.[7]

With respect to the antiquity of the *ouroboros*, van der Sluijs and Peratt note that "the earliest known examples of the ouroboros, which are purely artistic, antedate the age of writing and are concentrated in China and the ancient Near East."[8] In speaking to the *ouroboros*'s

---

6   James H. Charlesworth, *The Good and Evil Serpent*, 156, quoting Ovid, *Metamorphoses*, 2 vols., ed. Miller, vol. 1, *Metamorphoses*. 2.138, 68–69 and an 'idiomatic translation' of *Metamorphoses* 2.173–75, ed. Miller, vol. 2, 72–73.

7   R. T. Rundle Clark, *Myth and Symbol in Ancient Egypt*, 246.

8   van der Sluijs and Peratt, "The *Ouroboros* as an Auroral Phenomenon," 4.

widespread geographical presence as well as its antiquity, the same authors add that

> [t]he motif is also found on a significant number of other objects from... Siberia...and the Crimea... [and] has been discovered on a prehistoric Egyptian ring. In scattered places around the world, the ouroboros occasionally appears in petroglyphs and on pottery....Within the Old World [, however], the oldest historical examples of the ouroboros motif are Egyptian.⁹

Referring to an early first millennium Egyptian funerary papyrus, the 'Chantress of Amun Henuttawy,' van der Sluijs and Peratt observe, for example, that a 'tail-biting snake'

> is placed in the right hand of Geb, the personification of the earth, over whose body the star-spangled torso of the anthropomorphic sky goddess is extended. Although the exact significance of the ouroboros in this image is elusive, the arrangement leaves little doubt that the Egyptians conceived of it as a prominent phenomenon in the space between heaven and earth — either as a manifestation of the journeying sun or a repetition of the pattern of the enclosing union of earth and sky.¹⁰

Similar 'New World' cases of serpent symbolism the meaning of which, I argue, is equivalent to that of the 'Old World' *ouroboros* can be found in many ancient Mesoamerican cultural artifacts. In *Maya Cosmos: Three Thousand Years on the Shaman's Path*, Maya archaeologist David Freidel, Maya writing and art expert Linda Schele, and writing instructor Joy Parker argue that, among the ancient Maya of Central America, so-called 'Vision Serpents' "were symbols of the path along which supernaturals traveled on their way to being manifested in this world [and]...also [symbolized] the path of the sun and the planets as they moved through their heavenly cycles."¹¹ The same

---

9   van der Sluijs and Peratt, "The *Ouroboros* as an Auroral Phenomenon," 4–5.
10 van der Sluijs and Peratt, "The *Ouroboros* as an Auroral Phenomenon," 5–6.
11 David Freidel, Linda Schele and Joy Parker, *Maya Cosmos: Three Thousand Years on the Shaman's Path* (New York, New York: Perennial, An Imprint of HarperCollins Publishers, 1993), 195–196

authors contend, more specifically, that "the [Mayan] Double-headed Serpent Bar...symbolized...the ecliptic,"[12] the

> line of constellations in which the sun rises and sets throughout the year. We divide this band into twelve zones that gives us our zodiacal birth signs. At night, these ecliptic constellations create a path across the sky which marks the track of the sun in its daily and yearly movement. The planets and moon also follow this path, which snakes from north to south and back again as the year proceeds. In the tropics [where the Maya lived], the ecliptic actually crosses directly overhead and occupies the zenith position of the sky.[13]

The 'Double-Headed Serpent Bar' referred to by Freidel et al. is not visually equivalent to the symbolism of the *ouroboros*; and neither is the *ouroboros*, at least apparently, employed in its Old World form by the Maya to represent cyclicity or cyclical time (see fig. 9.2).

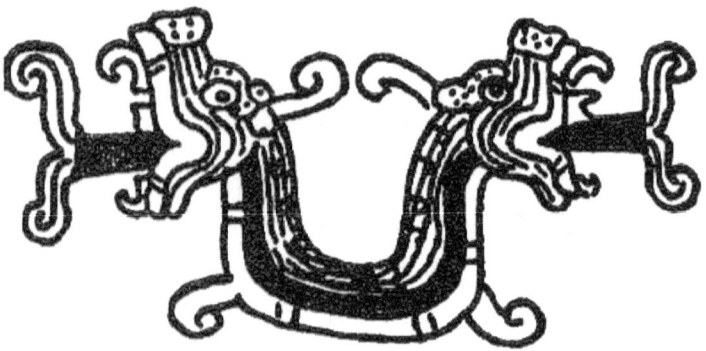

Fig. 9.2. *Double-headed serpent forming a bowl*, Mayan, Codex Vaticanus, 3773, p. 55[14]

However, it is easy to imagine the 'snaking,' as Freidel et al. describe it, of the ecliptic constellations from north to south across the night sky

---

12 Freidel, Schele and Parker, *Maya Cosmos*, 196.
13 Freidel, Schele and Parker, *Maya Cosmos*, 78.
14 Herbert J. Spinden, *A Study of Maya Art: Its Subject Matter and Historical Development* (New York, N.Y.: Dover Publications, Inc., 1975), 224.

creating a pattern in the ancient Mesoamerican's mind that expresses the content, if not the outward form, of the *ouroboros*'s configuration. Otherwise put, the imagined pattern of the movement of the ecliptic constellations in the night sky need not have been translated, representationally, in the exact same fashion in both Old World and New World cultures in order for the symbolisms of the Old World *ouroboros* and the New World 'Double-Headed Serpent Bar' to be equivalent in their meanings. From the perspective of *any* earth-bound observer who enjoys a clear view of the night sky, the band of zodiacal zones (along with its 'components' — stars, planets, and moon) that Freidel et al. describe as constituting the ecliptic would 'disappear' from sight 'into' the horizon each morning only to 'reappear' the next evening 'from' the opposite horizon. How this 'cycle' is, or was, represented may vary greatly. We may reasonably presume, however, that humans that have observed this phenomenon in ancient Mesoamerica could, by means of the human capacities of active imagination and abstraction, have inferred the completion of a great ellipse or 'circle' each time that another 'cycle' of 'disappearance' and 'reappearance' occurred, just as humans did in the Old World cultures, for instance, of Egypt and Greece. To the ancient Maya, such an on-going process could have appeared to mimic a two-headed serpent 'regurgitating,' at one end of its body, and 'consuming,' at the other end, the band of the ecliptic and its contents, rather than appearing as the Old World *ouroboral* 'serpent in the sky's' 'devouring of its own tail.'[15] In the Mayan 'double-headed serpent,' however, in contrast to the *ouroboros*, I argue that only the *processes* of 'regurgitation' and 'consumption' are represented, without any clear indication that it is the serpent that is the *object* of these two processes.

---

15 In further corroboration of such a symbolic identification between celestial events and the snake among the ancient Maya, Freidel et al. relate that in two of the Mayan languages, Cholan and Yukatekan, "the glyphs for…'sky'…and 'snake'…freely substitute for each other in the ancient writing system." Freidel, Schele and Parker, *Maya Cosmos*, 57.

It would appear that in the Old World, as well as in the New, traditional people interpreted time as essentially cyclical. Charbonneau-Lassay observes in *The Bestiary of Christ* that

> the ancient Greeks borrowed this symbol [the *ouroboros*] from the Egyptians who had connected it, according to Olympiodorus and Plutarch, with planetary movements...[and] the most familiar meanings given the ouroboros by the Ancients is that which associates it with Time — time, which alone with God has had no beginning, and will have no end since it is the thread on which eternity is woven....However, it seems that the original meaning of the ouroboros symbol related primarily to cyclic perpetuity, this inescapable, orderly renewal of cycles whose uninterrupted succession constitutes eternity.[16]

As paradigms of the cosmos 'shifted,' however, the ancient symbolism of the *ouroboros* in the Mediterranean region was appropriated to represent such 'evolving' paradigms. Van der Sluijs and Peratt note, for example, that

> [f]rom the sixth century BCE onward, cultures that had adopted a spherical model of the cosmos, such as Greece and India, carried over the notion of the world-surrounding serpent into the new cosmology and portrayed it as the perimeter of the outermost sphere of the material cosmos, universe, or sky, as opposed to the chaotic world that both preceded and surrounded it.[17]

Although the idea of time seems to be inextricably linked with celestial cycles by traditional peoples of both the Old World and the New, these cycles were often understood by such peoples to be caused by something 'beyond' themselves. The ancient Egyptians, for example, according to Rundle Clark, believed that "time is composed of recurrent cycles which are divinely appointed," entailing that they are in some sense *derivative* phenomena and a manifestation of an unseen

---

16 Louis Charbonneau-Lassay, *The Bestiary of Christ*, 428.
17 van der Sluijs and Peratt, "The *Ouroboros* as an Auroral Phenomenon," 16.

factor or factors.[18] The inference to a 'divine,' or metaphysical, cause of such 'recurrent cycles' is later in history explained systematically in the works of Aristotle, the most famous student of Plato, the latter of whom Eliade, as I said earlier, believed to be the last great systematizer of the traditional outlook. In *The Dream of Reason: A History of Philosophy from the Greeks to the Renaissance*, Anthony Gottlieb points out that "Aristotle was struck by the fact that nobody had ever noticed any significant change in the heavens, just an endless revolving of bright, distant objects."[19] This quotation is useful in pointing out how, generally speaking, for Aristotle, as for the ancient Egyptians who preceded him by millennia, the 'endless revolving' referred to by Gottlieb only existed *because of* the eternal existence, and complete 'actuality,' of something that Aristotle termed the 'Prime (or Unmoved) Mover.' Aristotle's 'Prime Mover' serves, from a broadly traditional perspective, just like Guénon's 'Principle,' as a meta-physical explanation for 'nature' and the cosmic system of 'recurrent cycles.' In this sense, Aristotle, in spite of his failure to assimilate his teacher Plato's more esoteric wisdom, also belongs to Tradition.

The "endless revolving of bright, distant objects," as Gottlieb describes it, that is the observed progression of the constellations of the ecliptic in the night sky can also be described as an "*indefinite* revolving of bright, distant objects," since 'indefinite' more accurately describes the only *apparent* endlessness of this progression. This latter expression may be still further translated into the Guénonian description "indefinite series of cycles of manifestation," since the 'endless revolving' is itself a process of 'indefinite' *disappearances and manifestations* of the heavenly bodies. We may imagine, however, that if humans were capable in ancient times of conceiving of the imminent 'return' of the 'snaking' ecliptic into the night sky every evening, then they

---

18 R. T. Rundle Clark, *Myth and Symbol in Ancient Egypt*, 246.
19 Anthony Gottlieb, *The Dream of Reason: A History of Philosophy from the Greeks to the Renaissance* (New York London: W. W. Norton & Company, 2000), 244.

were equally capable of separating, in their 'mind's eye,' as I have said, one *particular* such 'cycle' from its embeddedness in the 'indefinite' series of cycles. In *The Symbolism of the Cross*, Guénon argues that "the *ouroboros* represents the indefinitude of *a* [single] cycle considered in isolation." In his stating this, we may interpret Guénon to mean that the *ouroboros* symbolized, for traditional peoples, something that is in its essence an *abstraction*, since any *specific* cycle, whether of the indefinitely observed 'return' of the ecliptic every evening, *or* of the *samsaric* "indefinite series of cycles of manifestation," cannot *actually* exist 'in isolation' but can only be considered as such by beings existing in a particular 'state' of mind that can conceive of a cycle's existing 'separately.' In symbolic terms, when Guénon asserts that "the *ouroboros* represents the indefinitude of a cycle considered in isolation," he connects the symbolism of the *ouroboros* to the symbolism of the 'coiled serpent' that, for him, represents "the indefinite series of cycles of manifestation."[20] The *ouroboros*, therefore, for Guénon, is but a special case of the symbolism of the 'coiled serpent' since it symbolizes "the indefinitude of *a* cycle considered in isolation" in an analogous fashion to that in which the 'coiled serpent' symbolizes "the indefinite *series* of cycles of manifestation." One may, perhaps, imagine the example of a set of Russian nesting dolls in order to understand this relationship, in which any of the 'individual' dolls can be, from a certain perspective, *considered* 'in isolation' although that doll is *actually* only an integral part of something larger than itself which, in order to exist as that which it *actually* is, must include what may be *interpreted*, from a certain point of view, as 'separate' parts — 'individual' dolls. Along similar lines, that which the *ouroboros* symbolizes as a 'special case' of the 'natural' "indefinite series of cycles of manifestation" is but an abstraction insofar as it cannot exist 'in isolation' except from the perspective of a being that has the capacity to conceive of such 'isolation.' Because of this subjective component, the description "the

---

20 René Guénon, *The Symbolism of the Cross*, 122.

indefinitude of *a* cycle considered in isolation" could, for Guénon, be more accurately phrased as "the *appearance* of the indefinitude of a cycle considered in isolation," since only beings existing in a particular 'state' of being—the human state—are capable of considering a cycle "in isolation." Guénon appropriates the term 'perpetuity' to refer to this appearance, from the perspective of beings ('the being,' more properly) existing in the human 'state,' of "the indefinitude of *a* cycle considered in isolation." For Guénon, 'perpetuity' is what the *ouroboros* more specifically symbolizes to beings in the 'human state.'

Cyclic 'perpetuity,' as one mode of 'indefinitude' according to Guénon, is experienced only by beings ('the being') that have 'migrated' into a certain state of being—the *human* state, specifically. Humans can, and perhaps must, insofar as they are 'trapped' in the *samsaric* "indefinite series of cycles of manifestation," subjectively experience *as* 'perpetuity' the quality of 'indefinitude' that objectively characterizes *samsara* from the 'enlightened' perspective of *Atman/Brahman*. Though Guénon does not explain this, I argue that what he has in mind here is that a 'reduction' or 'transformation' of 'indefinitude' to 'perpetuity' occurs, for humans, due to the essentially *temporal* bearing of their particular 'state of existence,' from within which they tend to 'project' a framework of, shall we say, 'chronological measurement' onto their experiences of *samsara*. By means of this 'reduction' or 'projection,' humans *innately* interpret the particular 'cycle' of existence that they currently exist within as being 'perpetual' rather than 'indefinite.' As Guénon states, the "indefinitude of a cycle *for* the human state, and owing to the presence of the temporal condition, *assumes the aspect of* 'perpetuity.'"[21] (My emphasis) Because they exist *within* the flux of *samsara*, one might say that humans are 'constrained' by *samsara*'s inherent 'temporality,' as well as their inherent 'measuring' (rational) nature, to *interpret* the 'indefinitude' of existence through the 'lens' of 'perpetuity.' In perceiving the 'indefinitude'

---

21 René Guénon, *The Symbolism of the Cross*, 122.

of *a* 'cycle of manifestation' or of *a* particular procession of the ecliptic across the night sky, the 'migrating' being *as human* can only perceive what *seems to be* 'perpetuity,' but which, from the perspective of *Atman/Brahman*, is *actually* 'indefinitude,' since, from the latter perspective, time does not exist. Beings in the 'human state,' therefore, subjectively, and as a species, identify the 'indefinitude' of "the indefinite series of cycles of manifestation" with the 'perpetuity' of *abstract time*, even though the meanings of 'indefinite' and 'perpetual' are not objectively equivalent. In other words, the 'indefinite' aspect of the "indefinite series of cycles of manifestation" *seems* a 'perpetual duration' to beings ('the being') existing in the human 'state.'

To comprehend 'perpetuity,' I would argue that it is necessary for a 'migrating' being to enter a state in which it innately abstracts 'temporal moments' from the fluid continuum of "the indefinite series of cycles of manifestation." Such a being would be 'naturally' capable of 'isolating' *a* cycle from its embeddedness in the undifferentiated 'stream' of "the indefinite series of cycles." Thus isolated and 'frozen in time,' so to speak, that *single* cycle would be 'perpetual.' The human experience of the planetary and astral movements, as the Egyptians had recognized early on, is of a 'perpetual,' 'snake-like,' celestial progression of the 'renewing' 'consumptions' and 'regurgitations' — disappearances and appearances — of the heavenly bodies in their courses. As Charbonneau-Lassay has said, "Probably to the Ancients these renewals were represented by the snake's characteristic of periodically changing its skin; for it was thought that in thus creating a new skin, the reptile also renewed its life."[22] These celestial movements, *as* a progression of such 'conjunctions,' appear 'perpetual' from the perspective of a time-oriented being like the human. Based upon this reasoning, the *ouroboros* symbolized, for the Egyptians and other traditional peoples, what appears to humans to be a 'perpetual' cyclical process by which the sky 'consumes' itself, insofar as it consumes

---

22 Louis Charbonneau-Lassay, *The Bestiary of Christ*, 428.

its 'parts' (the stars and planets), only to 'regurgitate' itself again, and again, at discrete, measurable intervals. More generally, however, it must be pointed out that *any* cycle, whether it be planetary, astral, biological, or 'migratory,' when "considered in isolation," is an *abstraction*. For example, any *one* solar, or lunar, cycle, by itself, only incompletely represents the entirety of the 'snaking' of the ecliptic of constellations across the night sky. Likewise, any given 'state of being' (the 'human' state, for instance) only abstractly and incompletely represents *Atman/Brahman*. Any being, therefore, that 'identifies' with its current 'unrealized' bodily or psychic situation is 'identifying' with an *abstraction* of the 'Self' that is the *Atman*.[23] In previous chapters, I argued that the 'fall' by the 'migrating' being called 'Adam and Eve' in Genesis 3 into *avidya* and *tamas* resulted from its *previous* 'fall' into *rajas*, "the urge that provokes the being's expansion in a given state." I add here that, like the snake that is represented in the *ouroboros*, the being that is called 'Adam and Eve' 'fell' into a state of 'Self-devouring' in the sense that it progressively 'ate away' at the 'sense of unity' with *Atman/Brahman* that it had enjoyed while existing near the 'center' of the Garden of Eden. In so doing, 'Adam and Eve' became an 'abstraction' of its *complete* 'Self' in the same sense that the *ouroboros* represents an abstraction of the *entire* "indefinite series of cycles of manifestation."

---

23 "The 'indestructible' is *Atma* [*Atman*] considered as the personality, permanent principle of the being through all its states of manifestation." René Guénon, *Man & His Becoming According to the Vedanta*, 46. In interpreting a passage from the *Brahma-Sutras*, Guénon expands on how the "'living soul' (*jivatma*)… is…compared to the image of the sun in water, as being the reflection (*abhasa*) in the individual realm, and relative to each individual, of the Light, principially one, of the 'Universal Spirit' (*Atma*)." René Guénon, *Man & His Becoming According to the Vedanta*, 49. It is the *jivatma*, in South Asian tradition, as "the particularized manifestation of the 'Self' in life (*jiva*)" that 'migrates' through the "indefinite series of cycles of manifestation." René Guénon, *Man & His Becoming According to the Vedanta*, 33.

In the terms of Guénon's understanding of the symbolism of the cross, and from the perspective of a particular 'migrating' being such as 'Adam and Eve,' the *ouroboros*, like the horizontal bar of the cross, and like the Mayan 'Double-headed Serpent Bar,' symbolizes a 'perpetual wandering,' or 'expansion,' of the being in one state of 'the multiple states of the being.' It is to be noted, however, that the 'migrating' being in the particularly human state's mode of 'wandering' is, from *its* perspective, 'perpetual' *not* 'indefinite,' as we have already remarked on. The *ouroboros* is, therefore, symbolically equivalent to the horizontal bar of the cross *and* the Mayan 'Double-headed Serpent Bar' in terms of Guénon's understanding of the first two traditional, transcultural, symbols. All three symbols, the *ouroboros*, the horizontal bar of the cross, and the Mayan 'Double-headed Serpent Bar,' symbolize the at least temporary impossibility of a 'migrating' being's 'ascension' to 'higher states' or 'descension' ('fall') to 'lower states.' In *Maya Cosmos*, Freidel et al. argue that, among the Maya, 'Vision Serpents' "were symbols of the path along which supernaturals traveled on their way to being manifested in this world," *as well as* being symbols of "the path of the sun and the planets as they moved through their heavenly cycles."[24] As symbols of the "path along which supernaturals traveled," in particular, I argue that Maya Vision Serpents were, in a broadly traditional sense, symbols of the South Asian conception of the 'migration' of the being into different states of being. I further contend that, since a 'supernatural' being is one that exists, in its completeness, beyond ('super' or 'meta') the 'natural' order, such a being, in this context, is equivalent to the 'migrating' being, the *Atman* in *Vedanta*, that may, as Freidel et al. say, 'manifest in this world' but also in many other 'worlds' ('states of being'). The initial situation of 'Adam and Eve' in Genesis 3, when that being first 'falls' into the state of *rajas* but has yet to begin its further 'descent' into *tamas* allegorizes the 'perpetual wandering' in one state of being that is part of the symbolism of the

---

24 Freidel, Schele and Parker, *Maya Cosmos*, 195–196.

ouroboros. In modern parlance, one could say that, by 'falling', 'Adam and Eve' 'loses consciousness' in the sense that that being 'loses' its prior state of *complete* awareness of, and thus metaphysical 'identity' with, *Atman/Brahman*.

As a contrast to my expansion of Guénon's interpretation of the *ouroboros*, the Jungian psychologist Erich Neumann contends in *The Great Mother: An Analysis of the Archetype* that "the uroboros...is the symbol of the psychic state of the...original situation, in which man's consciousness and ego were still small and undeveloped."[25] Neumann's perspective is opposed to both my, and Guénon's, understanding of the symbolism of the *ouroboros* in relation to the 'psychic development' of man because he interprets the "psychic state of the original situation" as one of 'undevelopment,' whereas Guénon and I understand it as one of 'realization' of a 'sense of unity' with the metaphysical Principle. Neumann takes a 'progressive,' or 'evolutionary,' view of consciousness, in the modern sense of the word, as opposed to a traditional view, in which "man's consciousness and ego *begin* as "small and undeveloped" and later 'develop' into something more complex or 'complete.' In opposition to this, the traditional perspective that both Guénon and I defend understands the 'original situation' of man to be *already* one of (what I term) 'realization' of his 'actualized' 'Self'/ *Atman*, a perspective that I see as being embodied in the symbolism of Genesis 3. In Genesis 3, the 'migrating' being 'Adam and Eve' *begins* its existence, according to Guénon, with a 'sense of unity' with its metaphysical Source (God) — what I describe as 'realization' — and only *later* 'falls' into a state of being that Neumann might describe as "small and undeveloped." For Guénon, as for myself, it is only in 'man's' ('Adam and Eve's) *later* 'situation,' which is provoked by that being's 'fascination' with *samsara*, that its consciousness, though *not* its ego (since the two are not necessarily connected), becomes increasingly "small and undeveloped," as Neumann puts it. I argue that it is only

---

25 Erich Neumann, *The Great Mother: An Analysis of the Archetype* (New York, N.Y.: Princeton University Press by Bollingen Foundation, Inc., 1955, 1963), 18.

in this 'fallen' state of *rajas*, "the urge that provokes the being's expansion in a given state," that 'Adam and Eve' begins to 'wander,' and also to 'wonder,' as I previously suggested, who or what it is. Here in its 'evolved,' in Guénon's *traditional* understanding of the term, state of *rajas* does 'Adam and Eve,' like the *ouroboros*, "feed on its own flesh"[26] by way of looking neither to states of being that are 'above' nor 'below' its new, and narrowly interpreted, 'self' for sustenance. For the being 'Adam and Eve' in this 'fallen' state has become, like the *ouroboros*, *consumed with* (a lesser manifestation of) *itself* as a thing reduced to focusing on 'perpetuity'—on *time*. It thus comes to consider its current 'state,' in Guénon's terms, "in isolation."

Anima Mundi, the 'Soul of the World'

Among its many traditional associations, the symbolism of the *ouroboros* figures prominently in the alchemical, or 'hermetic,' tradition that, according to twentieth-century 'traditionalist' Julius Evola in *The Hermetic Tradition*, substantially originates in "the teachings comprising the Alexandrian texts of the Corpus Hermeticum."[27] This 'hermetico-alchemical tradition,' although having its roots, as Evola points out, in a "secret doctrine…that has been faithfully transmitted from the Greeks, through the Arabs, down to certain texts and authors at the very threshold of modern times," achieved maturity in the alchemical manuscripts of medieval and Renaissance Europe.[28] 'Medieval Hermeticism,' as Guénon refers to it in *The Great Triad*, is for Guénon and Evola, as well as for Eliade, an authentic expression of Tradition.[29] Evola affirms, for example, in accord with Guénon's exultation of the *unity* of the metaphysical Principle in Tradition as the

---

26 Louis Charbonneau-Lassay, *The Bestiary of Christ*, 430.
27 Julius Evola, *The Hermetic Tradition: Symbols & Teachings of the Royal Art*, trans. by E. E. Rehmus (Rochester, Vermont: Inner Traditions International, 1995; Edizioni Mediterranee, 1971), xv.
28 Julius Evola, *The Hermetic Tradition*, xv.
29 René Guénon, *The Great Triad*, 73.

'first cause' of everything, that "the first principle of the true hermetic teaching...is unity, and the formula that expresses it can be found in the [alchemical manuscript] *Chrysopoeia of Cleopatra*: 'One the All.'"[30] Such unity, however, is, according to Evola, "an actual *state* brought about by a certain suppression of the law of opposition between I and not-I and between 'inside' and 'outside,'" what Evola calls the 'subjective' and 'objective.'[31] In this statement, Evola employs language that, although superficially different, is an equivalent means of expressing the same idea that Evola's fellow 'traditionalist,' Guénon, articulates when the latter argues that, from the perspective of *Advaita Vedanta*, the 'Principle' is not a principle as law or rubric but a 'state' of 'identity' between *Brahman* and *Atman*. Evola adds, however, that

> the alchemical ideogram of 'One the All,' is O, the circle: a line or movement that encloses within itself and contains in itself both its end and beginning. In Hermeticism this symbol expresses the universe and, at the same time, The Great Work [of alchemy]. In the Chrysopoeia it takes the form of a serpent—Ouroboros—biting its own tail.[32]

The symbolism of the serpent, and especially of the *ouroboros*, is often connected in the hermetic tradition with something called the *anima mundi*. The *anima mundi* has been addressed by scholars from the Middle Ages to modern times. As an illustration in the modern world, the analytical psychologist C. G. Jung defined *anima mundi* in his last work on 'philosophical alchemy,' *Mysterium Coniunctionis*, as "the oneness and essence of the physical world," arguing that "the *anima mundi* was conceived as that part of God which formed the quintessence and real substance of Physis [nature]."[33] In his *Alchemical*

---

30 Julius Evola, *The Hermetic Tradition*, 20.
31 Julius Evola, *The Hermetic Tradition*, 20.
32 Julius Evola, *The Hermetic Tradition*, 21.
33 C. G. Jung, *Mysterium Coniunctionis*, trans. by R. F. C. Hull (Princeton, N.J.: Princeton University Press, 1970; Bollingen Foundation, New York, N.Y., 1963), 505 and 280.

Studies, Jung makes note, however, of "the perfect spherical form of the *anima mundi*," observing that "according to an old alchemical conception [it] surrounds the cosmos."[34] In *The Great Triad*, Guénon similarly contends that "as symbol of the *Anima Mundi*, the serpent is most commonly depicted in the circular form of the *Ouroboros*."[35] This connection between the symbolism of the *anima mundi* and the element of circularity reveals that the *anima mundi* should not be interpreted as symbolizing that which the *simple* serpent symbolizes in Tradition because the 'modification' of 'circularity' in the 'compound' symbol creates a different meaning. We must remember here Evola's claim that "the alchemical ideogram of 'One the All,' is... the circle." By its containing the symbolic element of circularity, the *ouroboros* symbolizes, for Evola, the 'One the All' or, equivalently, Guénon's 'Principle.' However, by containing the symbolic element of the serpent, the *ouroboros* symbolizes, for Guénon, a particularization of "the indefinite series of cycles of manifestation," or *samsara*. To understand, therefore, how the *ouroboros*, as the *compound* symbol that it is, symbolizes both the 'Principle' and *samsara*, it must be understood how the elements of circle and serpent relate in that symbol.

Evola claims in *The Hermetic Tradition* that "the closed line O, the circle of the Ouroboros, also has another meaning: it alludes to the principle of *exclusion* or 'hermetic' sealing that metaphysically expresses the idea of a unilaterally conceived transcendence being extraneous to this tradition."[36] In stating this, Evola means that 'exclusion,' or 'hermetic' sealing, signifies, in the 'hermetico-alchemical' tradition, 'transcendence' as *including* immanence. In other words, in the 'hermetico-alchemical' tradition, for Evola, there is no 'unilateral' idea of transcendence as a *complete* 'going beyond' in God's (the metaphysical) 'animating' of the world because God's 'soul' (though

---

34 C. G. Jung, *Alchemical Studies*, trans. by R. F. C. Hull (Princeton, N.J.: Princeton University Press, 1967, Bollingen Foundation, New York, N.Y.), 77 and 197.

35 René Guénon, *The Great Triad*, 73.

36 Julius Evola, *The Hermetic Tradition*, 21.

not His spirit) must be immanent in the world in order, *as* the *anima mundi*, to 'animate' the world. In *Mysterium Coniunctionis*, Jung contends that, "for all the alchemists [,]...God was imprisoned in... [what the alchemists called 'matter'] in the form of the *anima mundi*."[37] This 'imprisonment' is equivalent to God's *soul*'s immanence in the world. For the alchemists, however, quite logically, such 'imprisonment' did not prohibit God's *essential* transcendence of the world.

I contend that Evola and Jung are, essentially, making the same claim in their respective interpretations of the idea of God or metaphysical transcendence as it was understood in the 'hermetico-alchemical' tradition with respect to the metaphysical reality's relationship to the world. This is because both Evola's terms 'exclusion' and 'sealing,' as well as Jung's term 'imprisonment,' all refer to forms of 'separation' that indicate the simultaneous transcendence *and* immanence of God (the metaphysical) in the world as both what He is in his *essence* and what He is as *anima mundi*. God (the metaphysical in general), as we will discuss more when we interpret the symbolism of the *uraeus*, is traditionally symbolized by the circle. In the symbolism of the *ouroboros*, however, I argue that the metaphysical, although it is *revealed* by the symbolism of the serpent, is not *symbolized* by the serpent. On this interpretation, the 'hermetic sealing' referred to by Evola expresses, by means of the *ouroboros*, 'imprisonment' of God (the metaphysical) in 'nature'/*samsara*/"the indefinite series of cycles of manifestation." This is because the circle (the metaphysical/God) takes the *form* of the serpent (*samsara*/'nature'/*matter*) in that symbolism. Otherwise stated, the serpent in the *ouroboros* 'seals,' or 'imprisons,' the *pure* circle that symbolizes the metaphysical/God because when one looks at the symbolism of the *ouroboros* s/he does not see just a circle but an *en-circled serpent*.

Jung argues in *Alchemical Studies* that "the goal of the [alchemical] opus was to deliver the *anima mundi*, the world-creating spirit of

---

37 C. G. Jung, *Mysterium Coniunctionis*, 537.

God, from the chains of Physis [nature]."[38] Because of this, and based upon both Evola's and Jung's remarks that we have considered, the *ouroboros* in Tradition symbolizes, in its 'encircling' or 'sealing' function, that 'chaos' which, for the alchemists, 'imprisoned,' or inhibited the expression of, the "world-creating spirit of God" that is the *anima mundi*. Eliade similarly remarks in *The Sacred and the Profane* on the "chaotic space…peopled by ghosts, demons, [and] 'foreigners'" that lies 'outside' of the cosmos.[39] The 'chaos' that I refer to is, in line with my overall argument, 'nature,' or *samsara* as it is perceived by the *relatively* 'unenlightened' 'migrating' being. Evola's claim that the "'all' has also been called *chaos*…because it contains the undifferentiated potentiality of every development or generation" points to a confusion that may be cleared up by appealing to the traditional perspective presented by Guénon.[40] The point is that Evola is stating that the 'All' has been *called* 'chaos,' not that it really *is* 'chaos.' Otherwise stated, from the traditional perspective, the 'migrating' being often *confuses* 'chaos' ('nature') with that which 'animates' nature; equivalently, s/he confuses the 'All' or metaphysical 'Principle' with the 'chaos' of 'nature' insofar as s/he sees 'nature' as 'self-governing.' The 'All' that Evola refers to is, however, I argue, synonymous with, and but another name for, Guénon's metaphysical 'Principle,' and this means that it cannot actually be 'chaos' and nor can it be understood to be, in its essence, 'imprisoned' in 'nature.' The 'All,' therefore, has only been, as Evola claims, 'called chaos' insofar as those calling it 'chaos' are 'unenlightened' in the sense that they are unable to distinguish the 'All' from the 'matter'[41] (*samsara* or "the indefinite series of cycles of manifestation") that the 'All' 'animates' to create 'nature.' Using Evola's words, therefore, I argue that it is *not* the 'All' that "contains the undifferentiated

---

38 C. G. Jung, *Alchemical Studies*, 307.
39 Mircea Eliade, *The Sacred and the Profane*, 29.
40 Julius Evola, *The Hermetic Tradition*, 21.
41 'Matter' is used here in the alchemical sense, not in the sense of the 'state' of being that I argue for in my thesis.

potentiality of every development or generation," but, rather, *samsara*: 'nature,' that is, from the perspective of the 'migrating' being. In contrast to 'containing undifferentiated *potentiality*,' the 'All,' or 'Principle,' as a metaphysical reality, 'contains' *complete actuality*. The 'unenlightened' 'migrating' being referred to before — s/he who does not yet see the distinction between the 'All'/Principle (the metaphysical) and that which it 'animates' (the physical) — is, from the perspective of alchemy, s/he who has not yet completed the transmutation process of the alchemical 'Great Work.' S/he is also that 'individual' who has not yet, from the perspective of Tradition generally, 'realized' and 'identified' with *Brahman* (the 'Principle').

In order to understand the *ouroboros* as the compound symbol that it is we must distinguish between the 'All' — God *Itself* or Guénon's metaphysical 'Principle' — and the "world-creating spirit *of* God" that is but an expression of the 'All'/'Principle' *in* the 'chaotic' world of 'matter,' as the alchemists defined it — what I have termed *samsara* or 'nature' or "the indefinite series of cycles of manifestation." Guénon clarifies this distinction in *The Great Triad* when he argues that the *anima mundi*, symbolized by the *ouroboros*, represents a "'demiurgic' role in the strictest sense of the word in the elaboration of the Cosmos from the primordial hyle."[42] By 'primordial hyle,' Guénon has in mind that aspect of the universe that is 'pure potentiality' in the Aristotelian sense of that which must be 'formed' by the 'pure actuality' of God or the 'Prime Mover.' From the traditional perspective, only the latter, as a metaphysical cause, is sufficient to provide *ultimate* order, as Aristotle confirms in *Metaphysics* XI when he rhetorically asks the question "How is there to be order unless there is something eternal and independent and permanent?"[43] The same idea is expressed in anthropomorphic terms in the *Timaeus* that is attributed to Aristotle's

---

42 René Guénon, *The Great Triad*, 69.
43 Aristotle, *Metaphysics* XI 1060a:25, in *The Complete Works of Aristotle, Volume Two*, ed., Jonathan Barnes (Princeton, New Jersey: Princeton University Press, 1984), 1675.

teacher Plato, where the latter argues that the *kosmos* is not created *ex nihilo* but 'fashioned' by a 'maker.'[44] In the traditional cosmogony expressed in the *Timaeus*, Plato's divine 'maker,' or 'craftsman,' plays the 'demiurgic' role of 'elaboration' because he 'makes' the *kosmos* not 'out of nothing' but by means of 'looking at' an 'eternal model' and 'making' "an image of something else."[45]

For Guénon, the *anima mundi* is, in Aristotelian terms, an 'actualizer' of "pure potentiality."[46] The identification of the symbolism of the *anima mundi* with the idea of 'actualization' may, at first, seem to contradict my thesis in this book that the serpent in Tradition symbolizes potentiality, indefinitude, and formlessness (the 'opposites' of actualization) because the *anima mundi* is represented in Tradition by the *ouroboros* and the *ouroboros* is an example of serpent symbolism. It must be remembered, however, that the symbolism of the *ouroboros* is not that of a *simple* serpent but that of an *encircled* serpent. The *ouroboros* is, therefore, a *compound* symbolism that represents not what the simple serpent symbolizes in Tradition but what the *combination* of the simple serpent *and* the circle symbolize in Tradition. As Evola notes, the *ouroboros* is but one expression of "the alchemical ideogram of 'One the All'" that is symbolized by the circle, and, as I stated earlier, the circle is a traditional symbol of divinity and the metaphysical.[47] It is, therefore, the case that the circularity *element* of the *ouroboros*, insofar as it symbolizes the 'One' (the 'Principle') that is 'All,' also symbolizes that which, in traditional thought, 'actualizes' potentiality, whereas the serpent *element* of the *ouroboros* symbolizes the 'pure potentiality' of 'matter,' or *samsara*, that 'imprisons' God (the 'Principle'). From the traditional perspective, the only thing that can, at the most fundamental level, provide form and 'actualize' potentiality

---

44 Plato, *Timaeus* 28b-29a in *Plato: Complete Works*, ed. John M. Cooper, 1235.
45 Plato, *Timaeus* 29a-b in *Plato: Complete Works*, ed. John M. Cooper, 1235.
46 René Guénon, *The Great Triad*, 69.
47 Julius Evola, *The Hermetic Tradition*, 21.

is a completely actual and, as Guénon calls it, metaphysical 'Principle' of some kind. Aristotle expresses the thinking behind this perspective in *Metaphysics* XII when he argues, in discussing the cause(s) of the 'movement' of substances, that

> there should be an eternal unmovable substance. For substances are the first of existing things, and if they are all destructible, all things are destructible...There must, then, be such a principle, whose very substance is actuality. Further, then, these substances must be without matter; for they must be eternal, at least if anything is eternal. Therefore they must be actuality.[48]

Aristotle goes on to trace the cause of the plural 'substances' that he refers to in this quotation to *one* 'eternal unmovable substance': the 'Prime (Unmoved) Mover,' noting that "[i]f, then, there is a constant cycle, something must always remain, acting in the same way. And if there is to be generation and destruction, there must be something else which is always acting in different ways."[49] That 'something,' from a larger perspective, is the metaphysical 'Principle' of Tradition.

In alchemical manuscripts from the Renaissance and early Modern period, one finds the serpent of the *ouroboros* symbolically 'modified' not only by means of a circularity element but also by means of its depicting a serpent that possesses wings or 'wears' a crown. In *Alchemy & Mysticism*, Alexander Roob includes an illustration of an *ouroboros*-style *pair* of serpents 'eating' one another's tails, the top serpent having wings and 'wearing' a crown and the bottom serpent lacking both (see fig. 9.3). Roob quotes the eighteenth-century alchemist A. Eleazar's comment on the representation that "the top snake is the cosmic spirit

---

48 Aristotle, *Metaphysics* XII 1071b:4–6; 20, in *The Complete Works of Aristotle, Volume Two*, ed., Jonathan Barnes, 1693.

49 Aristotle, *Metaphysics* XII 1072a:9–10, in *The Complete Works of Aristotle, Volume Two*, ed., Jonathan Barnes, 1693.

which brings everything to life, which also kills everything and takes all the figures of nature."[50]

Fig. 9.3. *Cosmic Spirit*[51]

This short statement encapsulates the essential function, in the 'hermetico-alchemical' tradition, of the *anima mundi* as the 'animating' aspect of God: 'actualization' of the 'pure potentiality' of the 'primordial hyle' in order to 'make' the *kosmos* by means of the processes of both 'creation' and 'destruction,' since *both* 'creation' *and* 'destruction' are forms of the 'actualization' of the potentiality of 'matter.' Furthermore, the symbolic elements of circularity, wings, and crown to be found in Renaissance and early Modern alchemical representations of the

---

50 Alexander Roob, *The Hermetic Museum: Alchemy & Mysticism*, 331, quoting A. Eleazar, *Donum Dei, Erfurt*, 1735.

51 A. Eleazar, *Donum Dei, Erfurt*, 1735 in Alexander Roob, *The Hermetic Museum: Alchemy & Mysticism*, 331.

ouroboral anima mundi, like the rod or tree or cross in other traditional figurations of the compound serpent symbol, symbolize the source of this 'actualization': the divine, or metaphysical, 'Principle'/'All' that is the 'actualizer' of the alchemical 'matter' that I contend is equivalent to the *samsaric* "indefinite series of cycles of manifestation."[52]

In reflecting on the meaning of the alchemical symbolism of the *anima mundi* as a 'modified' form of the *ouroboros*, which latter is itself a 'modified' form of the simple serpent symbol, it must be emphasized that the *anima mundi* does not, properly speaking, symbolize God or the Principle *Itself*, but, as Jung describes it, the "world-creating spirit *of* God." What Jung refers to as 'spirit,' however, is, from Guénon's perspective, more accurately called 'soul.' In comparing spirit to soul in *The Great Triad*, Guénon states that "the spirit is the light directly emanating from the Principle whereas the soul is only a reflection of this light."[53] What Guénon refers to as 'spirit' in that text is, thus, the unadulterated *essence* of the Principle (God), whereas the *anima mundi*, or 'soul of the world,' is only that particular aspect of God-as-spirit that acts in what Guénon calls "the 'intermediary world', which can also be called the 'animic' domain."[54] The 'animic domain,' or 'animic world,' for Guénon, is constituted by those states of being of what he terms the 'subtle order' that lie between pure corporeality and pure spirit (the metaphysical unity of the Principle), and is the "meeting place of both celestial and terrestrial influences."[55] Guénon argues, therefore, that the serpent symbol in Tradition, since it also sometimes symbolizes the 'cosmic forces' that connect the celestial and terrestrial realms, is "one of the most common" symbols of the *anima mundi* "by reason of the fact that the 'animic' world is the proper domain

---

52 It bears repeating that this *alchemical* 'matter' is *not* equivalent to the *matter* that is central to my thesis.
53 René Guénon, *The Great Triad*, 72.
54 René Guénon, *The Great Triad*, 72.
55 René Guénon, *The Great Triad*, 73; Guénon uses 'animic domain' interchangeably with 'animic world.'

of cosmic forces, which although also acting in the corporeal world, belong in themselves to the subtle order."[56] Since, for Guénon, the *simple* serpent symbol represents the 'cosmic forces' of 'involution' and 'evolution' in traditional art and myth, it is appropriate, from his perspective, that a 'modified' form of the simple serpent symbol, the *ouroboros*, represents the *anima mundi*. This is because, for Guénon, the *anima mundi* symbolizes the action ('animating' influence) of the two 'cosmic forces' *in* the 'intermediary world,' or 'subtle order' of being, that lies between pure corporeality and pure spirit.

Guénon also contends, however, we must recall, that: 1) "the *ouroboros* represents the indefinitude of a cycle considered in isolation" and 2) the "indefinitude of a cycle for the human state, and owing to the presence of the temporal condition, assumes the aspect of 'perpetuity.'"[57] The first of these claims finds equivalent expression in Evola's contention that "the closed line O, the circle of the Ouroboros… alludes to the principle of *exclusion* or 'hermetic' sealing"[58] as well as in Jung's contention that "for all the alchemists…God was imprisoned in… ['matter'] in the form of the *anima mundi*." For both of these authors, as for Guénon, there is an element of 'separation' in the hermetico-alchemical symbolism of the *ouroboros* that I argue is represented by means of the element of circularity expressed in the *ouroboros*. For Guénon, that which is represented in the *ouroboros* as being 'separated,' or 'isolated,' is the "indefinitude of a cycle." Evola states, however, in *The Hermetic Tradition*, that the kind of 'transcendence,' or 'separation,' characteristic of the 'exclusion' or 'hermetic' sealing that is symbolized by the *ouroboros* is an "overcoming of itself" by 'matter' as 'nature.' As Evola states, "one of the most ancient hermetico-alchemical testaments is the saying that…:'Nature rejoices in nature,

---

56 René Guénon, *The Great Triad*, 72.
57 René Guénon, *The Symbolism of the Cross*, 122.
58 Julius Evola, *The Hermetic Tradition*, 21.

nature triumphs over nature, nature dominates nature.'"[59] As we have stated before, this 'overcoming,' this 'exclusion' or 'hermetic sealing,' that is spoken of by Evola, implies, by means of the symbolism of the *ouroboros*, the 'imprisonment' of an aspect of God/the metaphysical in 'nature'/*samsara*/"the indefinite series of cycles of manifestation" (the alchemists' 'matter'). What is, therefore, represented for Evola as being 'separated' in the *ouroboral anima mundi* is 'nature' as that which is *animated* by God/the metaphysical but not 'identified' with God/the metaphysical. From a Guénonian perspective, this state of affairs is characteristic of the 'indefinite' aspect of 'nature': *samsara* ("the indefinite series of cycles of manifestation"). Guénon's "indefinitude of a cycle considered in isolation" is, thus, a way of describing 'nature' *from the perspective of* a being that is *not* 'trapped' in 'nature'/*samsara*. It is a way of describing 'nature' from the 'enlightened' perspective of *Brahman*. For Jung, since "the goal of the [alchemical] opus was to deliver the *anima mundi*, the world-creating spirit of God, from the chains of Physis [nature]," it is God/Spirit/the metaphysical *as* the 'animating' spirit, or *anima mundi*, that is held by the "chains of Physis" that is 'separated' in the alchemical 'Great Work.'[60] Looked at from the opposite perspective, however, the perspective of *samsara*, the 'animating' *aspect* of God/the metaphysical is 'separated' by "the chains of Physis" from the *entirety*, or *essence*, of God/the metaphysical. For the 'chains' of Physis, the chains of 'nature' that is, are only the *samsaric aspect* of 'nature' — 'nature' thought of without the animating presence of God (the metaphysical). The goal of the alchemical opus, as Jung reveals, is thus to reunite God's (the metaphysical's) 'animating' aspect with God's *complete, spiritual*, reality.

I argue that 'nature,' as the human abstraction of *samsara* that is 'created' by means of the universalizing tendency of humans, is what the *ouroboros* symbolizes. 'Nature' is, as Guénon puts it, "the

---

59 Julius Evola, *The Hermetic Tradition*, 21.
60 C. G. Jung, *Alchemical Studies*, 307.

indefinitude of *a* cycle considered *in isolation*." Otherwise put, what we call 'nature' is only 'real' and distinct from the *samsaric* flux of cycles because the flux of *samsara* is 'animated' by God/the metaphysical from 'beyond' what is interpreted by humans *as* 'nature'; but it is only a "part of God," as Jung states, that provides this 'animation.' When we speak of 'nature' as equivalent to the *samsaric* "indefinite series of cycles of manifestation," therefore, this is only a rough equivalency; for it is only the "indefinitude of *a* cycle considered in isolation" that is what we call 'nature.' The *ouroboral anima mundi*, therefore, symbolizes 'nature' as that reality that is 'separated' or 'sealed' from both: 1) the 'entirety' of God (the metaphysical) and 2) the 'entirety' of "the indefinite series of cycles of manifestation" (*samsara*). Thus does the 'animic domain,' or 'subtle order,' for Guénon, exist as a "meeting place of both celestial and terrestrial influences," for 'nature' is more than simply flux or corporeality.[61] Guénon's second contention that I listed above, that the "indefinitude [of a cycle], for the human state, and owing to the presence of the temporal condition, assumes the aspect of 'perpetuity,'" expresses, in my estimation, a *further* 'separation' of beings in the human state from the 'entirety,' or essence, of God *and* the 'entirety' of "the indefinite series of cycles of manifestation."[62] This further 'separation,' I argue, is due to the particularly human experience of 'perpetuity' that is based, according to Guénon, upon "the presence of the temporal condition." The human experience of this 'temporal condition' I term 'temporality.' 'Temporality' is what makes beings existing in the 'human state' 'separated' from both the spiritual realm of God *and* the corporeal realm of *samsara*. Although 'temporality' is, I hold, indicative of a 'higher' form of spiritual awareness that 'lifts' human experience above the purely 'bodily,' it also prevents beings in the 'human state,' for the most part, from experiencing the 'timelessness' of God/the metaphysical in its *essence*. This 'higher' form of spiritual

---

61 René Guénon, *The Great Triad*, 73.
62 René Guénon, *The Symbolism of the Cross*, 122.

awareness that is manifested in 'the temporal condition' is, I argue, projected by beings in the human 'state' onto the corporeality/flux of *samsara*, thereby revealing an 'intermediary world' that humans call 'nature'. This 'world' of 'nature' is neither fully spiritual nor fully corporeal, just like the *anima mundi*.

In *Aion: Researches into the Phenomenology of the Self*, Carl Jung argued that "[a]s the *anima mundi*, the soul revolves with the world wheel, whose hub is the Pole....The *anima mundi* is really the motor of the heavens."[63] Although the *anima mundi* is the 'motor of the heavens' in Jung's metaphor, it should be emphasized that the 'Pole' that Jung refers to in the same metaphor represents the irreplaceable and sufficient energy that *fuels* that motor: the metaphysical 'Principle' that 'animates' the 'soul of the world.' This is the metaphysical Principle/God that is often symbolized in Tradition by the *Axis Mundi*. The *anima mundi* is derivative of the *Axis Mundi* just as the soul is derivative of the Spirit. The *ouroboros*, therefore, insofar as it represents the *anima mundi*, symbolizes God/Spirit/the metaphysical in its *relatively* actualizing, defining, and forming ('animating') aspect because the *anima mundi* is not the soul that is pure of Spirit but the soul *of the world* (of 'nature'). It is, as such, *not* equivalent to Spirit/God Itself. From this perspective, the *ouroboros* that represents the *anima mundi* is seen as it should be, as "the indefinitude of a cycle considered in isolation" that beings in the human state experience as 'nature,' or *the* 'world' in its 'perpetuity,' the 'place of becoming' where potentiality is never *completely* actualized, indefinitude is never *completely* defined, and the formless is never *completely* formed because God/Spirit/the metaphysical is, as Evola might say, 'sealed' from complete 'realization' there.

---

63 C. G. Jung, *Aion: Researches into the Phenomenology of the Self*, trans. R. F. C. Hull (Princeton, New Jersey: Princeton University Press, 1969 [originally published in 1959 by Bollingen Foundation, New York, New York]), 136.

CHAPTER 10

Symbols of 'Duality' in Unity

Any multiplicity, or 'duality,' is always a trait or aspect of some more fundamental unity. In order to understand the relationship holding among a multiplicity of 'things,' whether inanimate objects, animate beings, humans, cities, or stars, for example, one must understand the unifying element that in each case allows the multiplicity to be perceived as a separate category or 'thing.' The 'dual' forked tongue and hemipenes of the snake are, in the realm of appearances, expressions of the more fundamental unity that is the snake's monomorphic body, in the sense that, whereas the snake's tongue and hemipenes only *sometimes* 'emerge,' its body is 'always' there. I have argued that, in symbolizing "the indefinite series of cycles of manifestation" (*samsara*), the traditional serpent symbol represents a 'fascinatingly' 'dual,' because indefinite and multiple, expression of the 'unity' of Guénon's metaphysical 'Principle' (*Brahman*). Guénon's contention that there are "two opposed aspects of...serpent symbolism," as well as his claim that the 'coiled serpent' represents the 'migration' of 'the being' into either 'higher' *or* 'lower' states of being, places the serpent symbol within the category of what he deems to be traditional symbols of 'duality.' By examining such symbols in this chapter — specifically, the 'double spiral,' the 'Androgyne,' the 'World Egg,' and the *yin-yang* — we shall learn more of the serpent/dragon symbol itself.[1]

---

1   René Guénon, *The Symbolism of the Cross*, 122.

The Double Spiral and the Androgyne

In *The Great Triad*, Guénon examines the 'double spiral,' a symbol that has been closely associated with the serpent symbol from time immemorial. Remarking upon the age of the relationship between the serpent symbol and the 'single' spiral, former professor of European archaeology at UCLA Marija Gimbutas observed in *The Language of the Goddess* that

> [s]pirals appear in Upper Paleolithic [50,000–10,000 BP] caves in association with serpentine forms....Horn, snake, and spiral signs are virtually inseparable, the latter being both an artistic geometrization and a symbolic abstraction of the dynamic snake.[2]

In *Lady of the Beasts*, Gimbutas's friend, the American painter and independent researcher Buffie Johnson, similarly observes that

> [t]he spiral, one of the most conspicuous motifs in prehistoric art, often covers the breast or sex of a divinity. As noted, it is as old as the Siberian Aurignacian era [43,000–28,000 BP, generally] and appears throughout the world on tomb and threshold stones. Doubled it means rebirth or renewal. It conveys the movement of the winding and unwinding labyrinth, the serpentine path to consciousness.[3]

Johnson states, for example, that the mid-third millennium BCE *Lady of Pazardzik* discovered in the Balkans (see fig. 10.1) "displays a double spiral on her vulva."[4] Describing the spiral in ophidian terms and noting its presence on ancient European megaliths, specifically, Johnson remarks that "like paths into and out of the womb, such spirals are also found engraved on stone at the entrance of the mound at New Grange, Ireland, and at the entrance to the altars of the stone temples of Malta in the Mediterranean."[5] We shall look at examples of

---

2   Marija Gimbutas, *The Language of the Goddess* (New York, New York: Thames & Hudson, Inc., 1989), 279.

3   Buffie Johnson, *Lady of the Beasts: The Goddess and Her Sacred Animals*, 130.

4   Buffie Johnson, *Lady of the Beasts: The Goddess and Her Sacred Animals*, 130.

5   Buffie Johnson, *Lady of the Beasts: The Goddess and Her Sacred Animals*, 130.

serpent symbolism as it relates to megalithic monuments, as well as the purported connection between the serpent, spiral, and sex and/or birth and renewal argued for by Johnson, in future chapters.

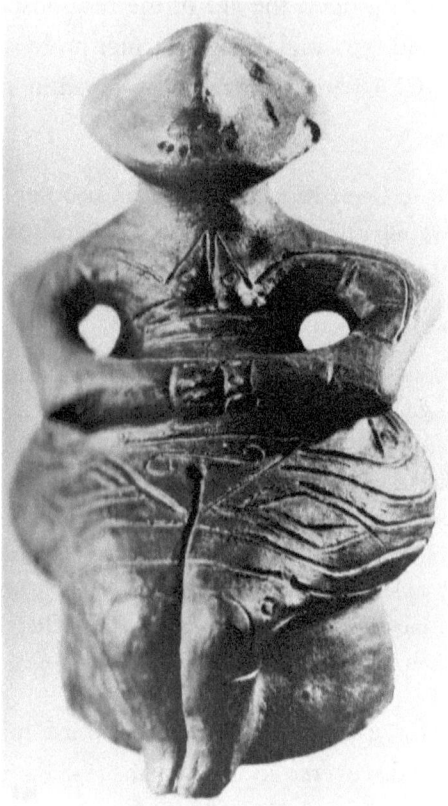

Fig. 10.1. *Lady of Pazardzik*, mid-third millennium BCE, Museum of Natural History, Vienna[6]

In *The Great Triad*, Guénon remarks that the traditional symbolism of the 'double spiral' "plays an extremely important role in the traditional art of the most diverse countries,"[7] quoting Elie Lebasquais's contention in "Tradition hellénique et art grec" that it "offers an image of the alternating rhythm of evolution and involution, of birth and death,

---

6 Buffie Johnson, *Lady of the Beasts: The Goddess and Her Sacred Animals*, 131.
7 René Guénon, *The Great Triad*, 31–32.

and in a word portrays manifestation in its double aspect."[8] (See fig. 10.2.) More concisely, Guénon argues that the double spiral symbolizes in Tradition "the dual action of a single force," thereby categorizing it with other traditional symbols of 'duality,' such as the Androgyne, a symbol of the unity of the masculine and feminine principles, the 'World Egg,' and the *yin-yang*, all of which are, according to Guénon, closely connected symbolically to the symbolism of the serpent.[9] The Androgyne, for example, symbolizes the 'dual action' of a single 'cosmic force,' as Guénon terms it, by representing the feminine and masculine 'sides' of human nature that are present to varying degrees in any given human being. The specifically "Hermetic androgyne — king and queen at the same time" of the 'hermetico-alchemical' tradition that we discussed in Chapter 9 is, according to Titus Burckhardt in *Alchemy: Science of the Cosmos, Science of the Soul*, one example of the Androgyne in which "the androgyne has wings and carries in its right hand a coiled snake and in its left hand a cup with three snakes."[10] (See fig. 10.3.) In the same illustration, the Androgyne "stands on the dragon of Nature," showing the close connection between traditional serpent and dragon symbolism as well as the symbolic 'modification' of wings that I mentioned before in connection with the eighteenth-century alchemist A. Eleazar.[11] Again quoting Lebasquais, Guénon ties the symbolism of the Androgyne to that of the double spiral by noting that the latter "can be regarded as the planar projection of the two hemispheres of the Androgyne."[12] In contrast, however, to the possibly

---

8   Elie Lebasquais, "Tradition hellénique et art grec," in the December 1935 issue of *Études Traditionnelles* quoted in René Guénon, *The Great Triad*, 31.

9   It may be helpful to note that, while 'androgynous,' or 'androgyny,' refers to the *state* of being 'partly male' and 'partly female' in a variety of ways, 'Androgyne,' according to Guénon, is the name for the *being* that combines masculine and feminine principles. René Guénon, *The Great Triad*, 29.

10 Titus Burckhardt, *Alchemy: Science of the Cosmos, Science of the Soul*, trans. William Stoddart (Louisville, Kentucky: Fons Vitae, 1997 [originally published by Walter-Verlag Ag, Olten, 1960]), 150.

11 Titus Burckhardt, *Alchemy: Science of the Cosmos, Science of the Soul*, 150.

12 René Guénon, *The Great Triad*, 31.

distracting gender component of the Androgyne, the double spiral provides a more succinct means of symbolizing 'duality' as the expression of a preexisting unity, Guénon's "dual action of a single force."

Fig. 10.2. *The Double Spiral*[13]

Fig. 10.3. *The Hermetic androgyne,* manuscript of Michael Cohen (c. 1530), Vadian Library, St. Gallen[14]

---

13 René Guénon, *The Great Triad,* 31.
14 Titus Burckhardt, *Alchemy: Science of the Cosmos, Science of the Soul,* 150.

Yin-Yang, 'World Egg,' 'Word' and *Tao* in Connection with Serpent/Dragon Symbolism

Also to be found, according to Guénon, among those traditional symbols representing "the dual action of a single force" is the 'Far-Eastern' (East Asian) symbolism of *yin* and *yang*.[15] Although the *yin-yang* symbol is not directly related to the symbolism of the serpent, it perhaps provides a more familiar expression of unity in 'duality' than does the Androgyne or double spiral and a less jarring transition from South Asian terminology to the Far-Eastern symbolism of the dragon and the Far-Eastern concept of *Tao*, both of which will be important to our efforts in this section and in later chapters. Guénon writes in *The Great Triad* that

> [i]n its properly cosmological part the Far-Eastern tradition attributes capital importance to two principles, or if one prefers, to two 'categories', which it designates *yang* and *yin*. All that is active, positive, or masculine is *yang*; all that is passive, negative, or feminine is *yin*. These two categories are associated symbolically with light and darkness; in all things the light side is *yang*, the dark side is *yin*; but, as one can never be found without the other, they appear much more frequently as complementaries than as opposites.[16]

Guénon goes on to provide the equation that "insofar as the *yang* and the *yin* are already differentiated while still being united…it is the symbol of the primordial 'Androgyne', since its elements are the masculine and feminine principles."[17] Later in the same book, Guénon appeals to the Genesis account of God's (*Elohim*'s) creation of the first human in comparing the Androgyne to the *yin-yang* when he remarks that

---

15 As mentioned in a previous chapter, 'Far-Eastern' is equivalent to 'East Asian,' for Guénon. I prefer his usage.
16 René Guénon, *The Great Triad*, 26.
17 René Guénon, *The Great Triad*, 29.

the Androgyne [is] constituted by the perfect equilibrium of *yang* and *yin*, according to the very words of Genesis (1:27): '*Elohim* created man in his own image..., in the image of *Elohim* created He him; male and female created He them.'[18]

Guénon here identifies the "male and female" that is created, according to Genesis 1, in the image of Elohim (God) with the *single* being referred to in the 'hermetico-alchemical' tradition as the Androgyne. This is, of course, consistent with *my* contention, previously discussed, that 'the being' that is superficially referred to in Genesis 3 as two beings, 'Adam' and 'Eve,' is 'actually' *one being* with *two* primary *aspects*: 'Adam and Eve.'

Relating the *yin-yang* to the double spiral, Guénon similarly observes that

[i]t is easy to see that in the symbol of the *yin-yang* the two semi-circumferences that form the line dividing the light and dark sections of the figure correspond exactly to the two spirals, and that their central points — dark in the light part, light in the dark — correspond to the two poles (see fig. 10.4).[19]

Fig. 10.4. *Yin-yang*[20]

---

18 René Guénon, *The Great Triad*, 61.
19 René Guénon, *The Great Triad*, 32.
20 René Guénon, *The Great Triad*, 29.

In both the symbolisms of the double spiral and the *yin-yang*, Guénon argues that "we may...speak either of the dual action of a single force... or of two forces produced by its [the single force's] polarization."[21] This 'polarization,' however, is not, for Guénon, of 'opposites,' because "the two principles *yin* and *yang* must in reality always be considered as complementaries, even if their respective actions in the different domains of manifestation appear outwardly to be contrary."[22] Such "domains of manifestation," as I have argued, include the *samsaric* world of 'nature' that is characterized by (apparent) dichotomies.

Although the double spiral, Androgyne, and *yin-yang* symbols well illustrate the interconnectedness of Guénon's 'dual action,' it is the symbolism of the 'World Egg' that, specifically for Guénon, illustrates the *potentiality* of the 'single force's' 'polarization' into its 'dual action.' The natural egg is widely seen as a *unity* that is, nevertheless, known by experience to be *potentially* something far more complicated and 'multiple' ('dual') in its traits: the 'hatched' life form. In comparing the symbolism of the *yin-yang* to that of the World Egg, Guénon argues that

> [w]e may thus speak either of the dual action of a single force...or of two forces produced by its polarization and...producing in turn, by its actions and reactions that result from their very differentiation, the development of the virtualities enshrouded in the 'World Egg,' a development that includes all the modifications of 'the ten thousand beings.'[23]

---

21 René Guénon, *The Great Triad*, 32.
22 René Guénon, *The Great Triad*, 32.
23 René Guénon, *The Great Triad*, 32. Guénon's reference to 'the ten thousand beings' is taken from the first chapter of the Tao Te Ching. The Tao, to be discussed further below, "is the Nameless [that] is the origin of Heaven and Earth; The Named is the mother of all things ['the ten thousand beings']." Tao-Te Ching in Wing-Tsit Chan, trans., *A Source Book in Chinese Philosophy* (Princeton, New Jersey: Princeton University Press, 1963), 139. The 'ten thousand beings' only originate *after* the 'polarization' of the singularity of the Tao.

This quotation may be translated to say that, although the *yin-yang* symbolizes the single force that 'divides' itself into a 'dual action' in order to 'produce' the distinctions of actual 'manifestation' — the indefinite 'multiplicity' of 'nature' — it is the World Egg that symbolizes the potential (or 'virtualities') *of* that 'single force.' The symbolism of the World Egg thus provides more information concerning the particular *being* of the 'single force' than do other, more limited, symbols of duality-in-unity such as the *yin-yang*, double spiral, and Androgyne.

The apparently 'dual' forces that emerge from the World Egg might be compared, in biological terms, to 'symbiotic' life forms or, in the jargon of modern physics, to 'alternating currents.' Like the 'dual' forked tongue and hemipenes of the natural snake that are, so to speak, 'manifested' out of its monomorphic body, the double spiral, *yin-yang*, and Androgyne symbolize the process of 'manifestation'/creation as an emergence of 'duality' *from* unity — an emergence, in Guénon's terms, of 'manifestation' by the Principle and, more generally, of the physical by the metaphysical. As Eliade states in *The Myth of the Eternal Return*, "the act of Creation realizes the passage from the nonmanifest to the manifest."[24] Guénon notes, however, that it is the World Egg in particular, among the other listed symbols of duality-in-unity, that "in various traditions…is frequently related to the symbolism of the serpent."[25]

The symbolism of the World Egg is intimately tied to that of the serpent *and* dragon in Tradition, as well as expressive of the traditional idea of 'creation'/'manifestation.' E. G. Squier, a one-time 'Foreign Member of the British Archaeological Association' and 'Member of the American Ethnological Society,' has observed, for example, in *The Serpent Symbol, and the Worship of the Reciprocal Principles of Nature in America* that

---

24 Mircea Eliade, *The Myth of the Eternal Return*, 18.
25 René Guénon, *The Great Triad*, 33.

[w]e have seen in a previous connection how naturally and almost of necessity the *Egg* became associated with man's primitive idea of a creation. It aptly symbolized that primordial, quiescent state of things which preceded their vitalization and activity, — the inanimate chaos, before life began, when 'the earth was without form and void, and darkness was upon the face of the deep.' It was thus received in the early cosmogonies, in all of which the vivification of the *Mundane Egg* constituted the act of creation; from it sprung the world resplendent in glory, and teeming with life.[26]

Squier adds later in the same book that

according to the mystagogues, [the Egyptian deity] KNEPH, the Unity of Egypt, was represented as a serpent thrusting from his mouth an egg, from which proceeds the divinity *Phtha*, the active, creative power — equivalent, in all his attributes, to the Indian *Brahma*. In the Orphic Theogony a similar origin is ascribed to the egg, from which springs the 'Egg-born *Protogones*,' the Greek counterpart of the Egyptian *Phtha*.[27]

Guénon similarly remarks in *The Great Triad* that "the 'World Egg'... in various traditions...is frequently related to the symbolism of the serpent; one will recall here the Egyptian *Kneph*, represented in the form of a serpent producing an egg from its mouth."[28]

Although both Squier and Guénon argue in these quotations that the serpent symbolizes a 'vitalizing' or 'productive' power, I contend, on the contrary, that the serpent in Tradition symbolizes that *through which* such power 'manifests.' Guénon himself often argues, albeit in an abstract and rather inconsistent way, for this position when he contends more generally that the traditional symbolism of the serpent symbolizes "the indefinite series of cycles of manifestation" and that

---

26 E. G. Squier, *The Serpent Symbol, and the Worship of the Reciprocal Principles of Nature in America* (New York: George P. Putnam, 1851 [reprinted by Forgotten Books in 2012]), 146. The 'Mundane Egg' is, of course, equivalent to the 'World Egg.'

27 E. G. Squier, *The Serpent Symbol, and the Worship of the Reciprocal Principles of Nature in America*, 150.

28 René Guénon, *The Great Triad*, 33.

the latter is that *through which* the unity of the metaphysical Principle acts. Squier also comes close to this way of seeing things in his interpretation of the serpent-with-'egg' when he states that the "divinity *Phtha*, the active, creative power—equivalent...to...*Brahma*" 'proceeds' from the 'egg' held in the serpent's mouth. For in making this statement, Squier allows that it is not really the case that the serpent 'thrusts' the 'egg' from its mouth but rather that the egg, as 'holder' of the 'creative power,' 'presents itself,' so to speak, by *means of* the serpent, proclaiming in effect, "Behold, I am the serpent's origin!" One need only remember that a snake is hatched from—*originates from*, that is—an egg in order to understand this, my, interpretation. That which is interpreted by Squier and his Egyptian 'mystagogues' as "a serpent thrusting from his mouth an egg" is, therefore, *actually* the 'egg' 'presenting' itself as the underlying *cause* of the serpent. Although Guénon does not directly argue for this interpretation of the serpent-with-egg figuration, he does argue for the theoretical substructure of my interpretation of that figuration when he states, more generally, that the *samsaric* "indefinite series of cycles of manifestation" is that through which the 'manifesting' Principle 'presents' ('creates'/'manifests') itself. From the traditional perspective, therefore, I am applying this idea (although Guénon does not) to the figuration of the serpent-with-egg and saying that, although *samsara* holds the capacity to 'create,' in the sense of *create an awareness of* in some 'migrating' beings, the Principle that is its cause, it does not hold the capacity to *actually* create the Principle. In the case of a sword created by a blacksmith, for example, the sword (*samsara*) may 'create an awareness' of the blacksmith (the Principle) who forged it in the mind of the swordsman (the 'migrating' being) who later uses the sword, but this by no means implies that the sword (*samsara*) itself *actually* created the blacksmith (Principle). The physical 'nature' of *samsara*, like that of the sword, is therefore 'productive' or 'creative' only insofar as it provides the *means* by which the Principle, or the blacksmith in my example, is able to 'manifest' itself in the being of the swordsman (the 'migrating' being). It is debatable, therefore, in those representations of the 'egg' that are depicted as partially inside, and partially outside, of the mouth of the serpent-as-Kneph, whether the serpent is indeed "*thrusting* from his mouth an egg," as Squier puts it. For this 'thrusting' assumes that the serpent, rather than the 'egg,' represents the "active, creative power" in the symbolism; and even if the serpent in such symbolisms does represent *some* kind of 'active' element in the overall 'compound symbol' of serpent-with-'egg,' this does not imply that the serpent 'produces' the 'egg' in an *active*, 'creative,' sense. It is more likely, again, that what the symbolism of the serpent-with-'egg' represents in such 'compound symbols' is the serpent's capacity to 'manifest' (reveal) that which 'produces,' or *actually* creates, the serpent: the metaphysical 'Principle' that is represented by the 'egg.' We shall examine another traditional example of this symbolic figuration in Chapter 14 when we look at the so-called Ohio Serpent Mound.

Guénon argues in *Perspectives on Initiation* that what he describes as the 'production' of the 'World Egg' from the serpent's mouth "implies an allusion to the essential role of the Word as producer of manifestation."[29] Rundle Clark, in *Myth and Symbol in Ancient Egypt*, states that "the serpent is...a symbol for creation by word, the belief that the universe in its variety is based on the realization of the commands of a designing and conscious mind."[30] The traditional conception of the 'Word' as some kind of facilitator of 'production' or 'creation' is perhaps most familiar from John 1:1–3: "In the beginning was the Word, and the Word was God....All things were made through him, and without him was not any thing made that was made." [ESV] The idea of the 'Word' as that which 'orders' the world, or expresses the 'sense' of the world, finds its earliest clear expression in the ancient Greek idea of the *Logos*, perhaps most familiarly expressed in the

---

29 René Guénon, *Perspectives on Initiation*, 296.
30 R. T. Rundle Clark, *Myth and Symbol in Ancient Egypt*, 51.

fragments of Heraclitus of Ephesus.[31] Though both Guénon and Rundle Clark directly connect the Word as the force of 'creation'/'production' with the serpent/dragon symbol in Tradition, I argue, in opposition, that the serpent/dragon is *not* directly representative of such a force. For, in arguing that the Word is a "producer of manifestation," Guénon defines 'production' as the "development of…virtualities," since the egg that the serpent 'holds' in its mouth symbolizes 'virtualities' (potentiality) for him.[32] This implies, however, that the Word (and thus, the serpent/dragon) does *not* 'create' or 'produce,' because 'developing' is not creating or producing but merely *cultivating* that which already exists. The 'Word,' and thus the serpent/dragon that symbolizes it in Tradition, is therefore a means or 'tool' of 'creation'/'production' and *not*, in Squier's language, "the active, creative power — equivalent… to…*Brahma*." The latter is rather, as Squier also admits, represented in some way by the 'egg.'

Guénon's remarks in *The Multiple States of the Being* and *The Reign of Quantity & the Signs of the Times* more clearly reveal how the serpent-*as-dragon* can be a symbol of the 'Word' while *not* being a symbol of 'production'/'creation' itself. In *The Multiple States*, Guénon argues that the "Far-Eastern [East Asian] symbolism of the Dragon…correspond[s] in a certain way to the Western theological conception of the Word as the 'locus of possibles,'"[33] and in *The Reign of Quantity & the Signs of the Times*, he notes that "the Far-Eastern Dragon…[is] really a symbol of the Word."[34] For Guénon, the dragon specifically, in representing the Word in Tradition, does not symbolize 'production'/'creation' *itself* but the *conditions*, the 'locus of possibles,' necessary for the act of 'production'/'creation' to take place. As possibility does not *imply* actuality, the serpent-as-dragon in Tradition does

---

31 Heraclitus, widely identified as a 'Pre-Socratic' philosopher, flourished between the late 6th and early 5th centuries BCE.

32 René Guénon, *The Great Triad*, 32.

33 René Guénon, *The Multiple States of the Being*, 68.

34 René Guénon, *The Reign of Quantity & the Signs of the Times*, 205.

not, for Guénon, symbolize that which *actualizes* 'possibles.' "Creation is the work of the Word," according to Guénon in *Symbols of Sacred Science*, but this 'work,' insofar as it is 'done' by the Word, is the *gathering* of 'virtualities' (potentialities), not the *actualizing,* or *manifesting,* of them.[35] Such 'work' only *circumscribes* a 'locus of possibles' 'where' 'creation' ('manifestation') *can* occur. This is exactly the function of the "indefinite series of cycles of manifestation," a framework *within which* the metaphysical Principle may 'manifest'/'create' itself. It is also the function of 'chaos' as that *perspective* of beings that allows 'order' to emerge, since there cannot be order without chaos to set it apart. We may say that, if a being has become 'trapped' in the 'chaos' of *samsara*, it is only because that being may yet become 'free' *beyond samsara*, beyond 'chaos.' To 'free' something, however, implies the application of a 'higher' ordering principle, and this implies that there is an element of the trapped being that *transcends* its 'prison' of *samsara*, since otherwise there would be no explanation for the being's perception of 'chaos,' its 'feeling' of being 'trapped.' I argue that the serpent-with-egg is symbolically equivalent to the *modified* "Far-Eastern symbolism of the Dragon…[that Guénon contends] correspond[s] in a certain way to the Western theological conception of the Word as the 'locus of possibles.'"[36] The symbolic correspondence between the 'simple' serpent and the non-modified ('simple') 'Far-Eastern' dragon exists insofar as both serpent and dragon symbolize the 'locus of possibles' that is the *context* within which the 'trapped' being can be 'freed,' or, equivalently stated, in which the 'Principle'-as-*Atman* can achieve *moksha* in the midst of *samsara*. The serpent/dragon thereby symbolizes the Word which, if 'read' correctly, 'produces' or 'creates,' *in the sense of REVEALS,* the 'migrating' being to be *actually* the *Atman* that is *Brahman*.

---

35 René Guénon, *Symbols of Sacred Science*, 9.
36 René Guénon, *The Multiple States of the Being*, 68. The dragon may be symbolically 'modified' just as the serpent is.

In analyzing the symbolism of the Far-Eastern dragon, it is useful to consider that which in East Asian thought, according to Guénon, is equivalent to the metaphysical Principle and thus merely another name for that which is the source of "the indefinite series of cycles of manifestation"/*samsara*. This is the *Tao*. For Guénon, just as *Brahman* is equivalent to the metaphysical Principle in South Asian thought, *Tao* is equivalent to the metaphysical Principle in East Asian thought. Like *Brahman*, *Tao* is another description for that reality that underlies the flux of 'nature' and that which all traditional peoples, according to Guénon, are aware of to different degrees. As we have stated, Guénon argues that the "Far-Eastern symbolism of the Dragon…correspond[s] in a certain way to the Western theological conception of the Word as the 'locus of possibles.'"[37] I contend, however, that insofar as the Far-Eastern Dragon symbolizes the 'locus of possibles' that the Principle may act through, it also symbolizes the 'possibles' (potentiality) that the *Tao* 'acts' through. The Word, insofar as it serves as the means of revealing the metaphysical Principle in the symbolism of the *modified* serpent-with-'egg,' and insofar as the serpent and the dragon are roughly equivalent symbolisms, which Eliade explicitly affirms, also serves by means of the *modified* Far-Eastern dragon-*with*-orb/spiral/pearl/ball to reveal the *Tao* (see fig. 10.5).[38] This is because the *Tao* is the Far-Eastern version of the Principle and the dragon-*with*-orb/spiral/pearl/ball is the Far-Eastern version of the serpent-*with*-'egg.'

---

37 René Guénon, *The Multiple States of the Being*, 68.

38 Apparently, it is not clear to anyone exactly what the 'Far-Eastern,' or 'East Asian,' dragon is so often depicted with, though it has been *interpreted* as an 'orb,' 'spiral,' 'pearl,' and 'ball.'

Fig. 10.5. Plate, Ch'ing Dynasty, Yung-cheng period, 1723–1735, Mr. and Mrs. Myron S. Falk, Jr.[39]

In East Asian thought, the *Tao* only 'acts' according to the logic of what Taoists call *wu-wei*. *Wu-wei* literally translated means 'inactivity,' but it is more accurately thought of, according to Wing-Tsit Chan in *A Source Book in Chinese Philosophy*, as "'taking no action that is contrary to Nature'...[and] letting Nature take its own course."[40] For Guénon specifically, *Tao* and *Brahman* are both the *source* of action but not the *means* of action; they are the *determinant* of 'manifestation' but not, one might say, its 'apparent' or 'evident' cause. The 'apparent cause' of 'manifestation,' from the perspective of manifested beings is, I would argue, 'manifestation' *itself* because those (manifested) beings that are 'trapped' in *samsara* only *perceive* and search for 'manifested' (physical) causes, to greater or lesser degrees. Beings

---

39 Hugo Munsterberg, *Dragons in Chinese Art: March 23 through May 28, 1972* (New York, New York: China House Gallery, China Institute in America, 1972), 58.

40 Wing-Tsit Chan, trans., *A Source Book in Chinese Philosophy*, 136.

'migrating' through the 'cycles,' therefore, generally perceive 'nature' to be the 'cause' of 'nature,' *samsara* to be the 'cause' of *samsara*, and the generalities described by physical laws to be the 'cause' of particular physical events and physical beings — in general, symbolically speaking, the serpent/dragon is considered to be the 'cause' of itself. But all of these perceptions are from that 'unenlightened' perspective that characterizes beings that have not achieved 'identity' with *Atman/Brahman*. The Real cause lying 'behind' all of this, according to Guénon, is the metaphysical 'Principle' that is called *Brahman* by the South Asians and *Tao* by the East Asians.

I argue that the 'Word' as the 'locus of possibles,' that for Guénon is symbolized by the Far-Eastern dragon in Tradition, is an incomplete expression of *Tao* just as "the indefinite series of cycles of manifestation" is an incomplete expression of the Principle/*Brahman*. The Word, in this sense, is *not Tao/Brahman*/Principle/Spirit *itself* because, as the Tao Te Ching states, "The Tao...that can be told of is not the eternal Tao"[41]: the *Tao cannot* be verbalized. As with human speech, in which the spoken word is an incomplete expression of human thoughts and the human mind, so is the 'Word' the incomplete *means* by which the 'Principle' — *Tao, Brahman*, Spirit — is 'manifested.' As Guénon states, however, "In Itself, [the Word]...is the Divine Intellect...; [although] in relation to us, It manifests and expresses Itself by Creation."[42] This is to say that, in its *essence*, in its *cause*, the Word is the Principle ('Divine Intellect'). In its role as that which best expresses the Principle to finite beings, however, the Word is *not* the Principle, for "[t]he Tao...that can be told of is not the eternal Tao." I add to this that, therefore, in terms of the *cause* of its essence, *samsara* (the serpent/dragon) *is* the 'Word' *as* 'Principle' because the 'Principle' is the *cause* of *samsara's* being. For 'migrating' beings, thus, and symbolically speaking, the 'Word' — the 'Divine Intellect'/'Principle' — *looks like* the 'dragon' of 'nature's' laws that *incompletely express* the 'Principle.' *In reality*, in its

---

41 Tao-Te Ching in Wing-Tsit Chan, trans., *A Source Book in Chinese Philosophy*, 139.

42 René Guénon, *Symbols of Sacred Science*, 9.

cause, the 'Word' *is* the metaphysical 'unity' of the serpent's 'egg' (or the dragon's orb/spiral/pearl/ball) that symbolizes the Principle in its essence. Both serpent and dragon, I contend, represent the 'dual' (*samsaric*) 'locus' of 'possibles' 'where' the 'egg'/orb/spiral/pearl/ball representing the 'Principial' *unity* in its *essence* is 'produced'/'created' by being *revealed*. That which the serpent/dragon symbolizes is, therefore, the 'place' 'where' *potential becomes actualized*, the *indefinite becomes defined*, the *formless becomes formed*, and unity is revealed *by* 'duality.'

According to Guénon, Squier, and Squier's Egyptian 'mystagogues,' the 'World Egg' is a symbol of passivity and potentiality, and is 'incubated,' or 'brooded upon,' by what these researchers interpret as the 'active,' 'creative,' serpent. This event leads, according to these researchers, to the 'Egg's' symbolic 'hatching,' which symbolizes the event of 'manifestation.' As I have argued, however, it is rather the serpent/dragon that is 'passive' and 'potential' and the 'egg' (or Chinese 'orb,' etc.) that is 'active' or 'actualizing.' It seems likely, though, that in some cases serpent and 'egg' both may symbolize potentiality. In such cases, neither the 'egg'/orb *nor* the serpent/dragon would symbolize the 'creative' power of the 'Word' as 'Divine Intellect' or as Guénon's 'Principle' (*Brahman*/*Tao*/Spirit). Rather, the serpent/dragon would symbolize an *aspect*, or characteristic, of potentiality and the 'World Egg'/orb would symbolize potentiality *itself*. On this interpretation, the combination of 'egg'/orb and serpent/dragon symbolizes, respectively, potentiality and potentiality's *characteristics* of chaos and indefinitude. If the 'creative' or 'productive' power of the 'Word' *as* 'Divine Intellect' ('Principle') is still to be symbolized in such cases, a *third* symbol is required to represent the 'acting' of this 'productive'/'creative' power on *both* serpent/dragon *and* 'egg'/orb. In line with our previous remarks, one would expect this third symbol to be a version of the 'World Axis' that so often symbolizes the source of 'creation'/'production'/'manifestation.'

In *Symbols of Sacred Science*, Guénon answers the need for an axial symbol representing the 'active' power of 'creation'/'production' in certain figurations of the symbolism of the serpent-and-'World Egg' by means of differentiating between the traditional symbolisms of the 'egg' and the *sphere*. In that book, Guénon argues that the symbols of the sphere and the 'egg' symbolize "two successive phases of the cosmogonic process," with the spherical form being "truly the primordial form, while the egg corresponds to a state already differentiated, deriving from the preceding form by a sort of 'polarization' or splitting of the center."[43] As Guénon observes, this admits that "the 'World Egg' is the figure, not of the 'cosmos' in its state of full manifestation, but of that from which the development of the cosmos will be effected."[44] More to the point, however, Guénon implicitly admits that neither the serpent, as some believe, nor the 'World Egg,' represents the 'active' power in symbolisms of the serpent and World Egg, but that the World Egg *does* serve as an *allusion to* the 'active' power insofar as the 'egg' is "derived from" the "truly primordial form" that is, Guénon argues, represented by the *sphere*. This 'derivation,' according to Guénon, is revealed symbolically by means of the 'egg's' possessing an *imperfectly spherical*, or ovoid, form. This, as well as Guénon's reference to the World Egg's originating "by a sort of 'polarization' or splitting of the center," is a reference to the 'primordial state,' or 'center,' that is represented for Guénon *by* the sphere. As a symbol of the 'center,' or 'primordial state,' the sphere thus serves as a symbolic equivalent to other traditional symbols of the 'center' such as the various figurations of the World Axis—the tree, the rod, the thunderweapon, etc. The 'egg' only imperfectly *alludes to*, although it can still serve as a rough symbol of, as noted, the World Axis by means of its being a sort of 'degraded' sphere. I would therefore suggest that, when those individuals who are capable of intuiting traditional symbolic correspondences see an 'egg' in a traditional symbolic setting, they *also* see a *sphere* and thus see an *indirect* symbolism of the 'active' metaphysical Principle or 'center.'

---

43 René Guénon, *Symbols of Sacred Science*, 212.
44 René Guénon, *Symbols of Sacred Science*, 211.

CHAPTER 11

The Serpent as 'Mediator' and 'Messenger'

We've discussed before the association of the serpent symbol in Tradition with what I have called the 'dichotomies of existence' that are commonly accentuated in traditional art and myth. The emphasis on the opposition between 'good and evil' in Genesis 3 is an example of one of these traditionally emphasized dichotomies. In *The Symbolism of the Cross*, Guénon notes the nuanced symbolic expression of such traditionally recognized dichotomies when he contends that, from the perspective of Tradition, "[t]he serpent that represents life must not be confused with the one representing death."[1] In saying this, Guénon simply means that the serpent symbol in traditional art and myth need not represent in any particular case of serpent symbolism both life *and* death. We may extrapolate from this observation, however, that the serpent/dragon symbol in Tradition need not represent both elements of *any* dichotomy, whether it be 'good and evil,' 'life and death,' 'health and sickness,' or any other. However, although the serpent/dragon need not symbolize both of the elements of any given dichotomy in any given case, it is, I argue, *always* associated with the abstract idea of 'duality' in general in all cases of serpent and dragon symbolism in traditional art and myth. One way that the

---

1   René Guénon, *The Symbolism of the Cross*, 57.

serpent/dragon is associated with 'duality,' although not explicitly with dichotomies, is in its symbolizing the 'messenger,' or 'mediator,' between two forces, groups, or ideas.

In Genesis 3, for example, God is the 'creator' of the world; but it is the serpent, as the 'Word' discussed in Chapter 10, that is in a certain sense the *means*, or 'mediator,' or 'messenger,' *of* God's 'creation.' The serpent's *speaking* in Genesis 3 may be an allusion to its function as the 'Word' that 'mediates' and 'messages' between God and 'nature,' the latter being the result of God's 'creation.' This 'nature' would be equivalent to the flux of "the indefinite series of cycles of manifestation"/ *samsara* interpreted as a unified system by means of human perception. By its *speaking to* 'Adam and Eve,' the serpent reveals possibilities and points out alternatives that are *not* already extant in the earlier stages of the 'creation' process instigated by God. An example of this is when the serpent asks 'the woman' in Genesis 3:1, "Did God actually say, 'You shall not eat of any tree in the garden'?" [ESV] By opening up possibilities, pointing out alternatives, and circumscribing the 'locus of possibles,' as Guénon calls it, that may unfold into 'manifested' existence, the serpent serves as a 'mediator' and 'messenger' between: 1) the 'Principle' (God) and His earlier, and more rough-hewn, stages of 'creation' and 2) manifested existence. As the *samsaric* "indefinite series of cycles of manifestation," the serpent thus symbolizes in Genesis 3 the 'messenger' and 'mediator' between the divine 'Principial' (metaphysical) realm and the human perception of *samsara* that we call 'nature' or 'the World.' This sustained perceptive event of human reality, I argue, indicates, from the traditional perspective, the presence of an essentially meta-physical being in the *samsaric* "indefinite series of cycles of manifestation," the state of being that I term *matter*. The serpent serves in the capacity of 'mediator'/'messenger' insofar as it adds, or *allows for the addition of*, by means of its interplay with 'Adam and Eve,' the more intricate details of the 'creation' process which has already been set in motion by God. It is, after all, the serpent in Genesis 3, not God, who *communicates* possibilities of existence to 'Adam and

Eve' that 'Adam and Eve,' apparently, had no notion of before its interaction with the serpent; and this 'communication' of possibilities is what later allows for 'Adam and Eve's' 'expulsion' into a new state of being. The serpent's 'duality' of forked tongue, the instrument used for speech, and hemipenes, the instrument used for the production of the 'duality' (multiplicity) of 'nature,' reflects its role of 'mediator' and 'messenger' between the two realms of metaphysical (God) and physical ('nature' or 'the World').

The Caduceus and Hermes/Mercury: 'Messenger' and 'Mediator' of the Divine

The symbol known as the 'caduceus,' or Rod of Hermes, which is always depicted with two serpents facing each other, is a good example of the serpent symbolizing 'duality' *and* 'mediation' and 'messaging' in Tradition (see fig. 11.1). According to Howey in *The Encircled Serpent*, "In Greece...its origin can be traced to the herald's staff....Later... [it was] assigned by artists and poets to Mercury and Hermes,"[2] with Hermes being the Greek, and Mercury the Roman, version of the same god. Hermes/Mercury is well known for his function as 'mediator' between, and 'messenger' of, 'the gods.' As Howey notes, he was named "the messenger of the gods of Olympus," "lord of commerce" and "God of Twilight,"[3] all titles indicative of a 'mediator'/'messenger.' The traditional explanation for this, according to Howey, is that

> [o]n his travels, the god saw two snakes in deadly combat and placed his staff between them to end the fight. The magic wand so pacified their anger that they embraced one another and clung around it. Hence the caduceus became the symbol of peace, and caduceator the synonym for an ambassador, or any person sent forth from one belligerent to another.[4]

---

2   M. Oldfield Howey, *The Encircled Serpent*, 72.
3   M. Oldfield Howey, *The Encircled Serpent*, 71.
4   M. Oldfield Howey, *The Encircled Serpent*, 73.

Whether as 'ambassador' or existing on the edge of day and night as the "God of Twilight," Hermes/Mercury with his caduceus always performs the function of 'mediating' or 'messaging' between two elements, whether these be individuals, forces, groups, or ideas. J. Schouten states in *The Rod and Serpent of Asklepios* that

> Hermes is, first and foremost, the messenger of the gods and the mediator between the realm of the dead and the kingdom of the living. By virtue of this latter function he guides departed souls along obscure, unknown paths to the underworld and with his magic wand [the caduceus] awakens the sleeping.[5]

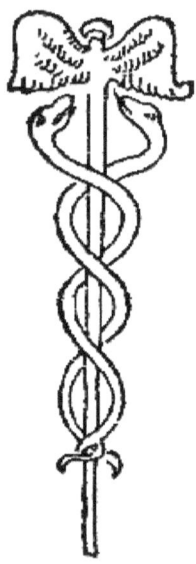

Fig. 11.1 *The Caduceus or serpent-staff of Mercury*[6]

As messenger of the gods in ancient Greece, Hermes connected two specific realms together, the immortal/divine realm of 'the gods'

---

5   J. Schouten, *The Rod and Serpent of Asklepios: Symbol of Medicine*, 117.
6   William Ricketts Cooper, *The Serpent Myths of Ancient Egypt* (Berwick, ME: Ibis Press, an imprint of Nicholas-Hays, Inc., 2005), 11.

and the mortal realm of humans. It seems likely that the wings that are sometimes represented as part of the caduceus, as in Figure 11.1, probably symbolize the 'soul' which was believed to allow a being to 'fly' between the two realms. A. L. Frothingham states in "Babylonian Origin of Hermes the Snake God, and of the Caduceus I" that "it is a well-known fact that in practically the entire ancient world 'soul' and 'breath' were synonymous and also that the soul's emblem was often the butterfly,"[7] a creature known for its light-as-air density, comparatively large wings with respect to its body size, and capacity for nimble flight. 'Spiritual flight' is often represented in traditional art and myth by means of flying creatures *or* their symbolic 'abbreviation,' wings. It may be argued that, as a form of 'mediation' "between the realm of the dead and the kingdom of the living," Hermes' particular version of 'spiritual flight' is one way of describing 'migration' among Guénon's 'multiple states of the being,' the multiple states of *Brahman* in the Hindu version of Tradition.

Hermes/Mercury and Other Traditional 'Mediators'/'Messengers' of the Divine

Like Hermes/Mercury, the figure of Jesus Christ in some passages of the New Testament is also a 'mediator'/'messenger' between the divine and mortal realms, 'Heaven and Earth' specifically. In the case of Jesus, the 'message' is the 'Gospel of salvation.' The 'Spirit of God' that is described in Matthew 3:16 as "descending like a dove" on Jesus is interpreted as indicating the latter's function as that being that is eminently capable of conveying 'Spirit' to 'the world.' As we discussed in Chapter 10, Christ is described in John 1 as the 'Word,' the *means* by which God is 'communicated' into the work of 'creation.' In John 3:14-15, the *crucified* Christ is compared to Moses's 'copper serpent' on a pole that is lifted by the prophet in the wilderness: "as Moses lifted

---

7   A. L. Frothingham, "Babylonian Origin of Hermes the Snake God, and of the Caduceus I," *American Journal of Archaeology*, 20, no. 2 (Apr.-Jun., 1916): 210.

up the serpent in the wilderness, so must the Son of Man be lifted up, that whoever believes in him may have eternal life." The *same* figure, therefore, Christ, is both represented as being descended upon by a dove, a winged creature, *and* compared to the serpent which Moses held in the wilderness. As with Hermes in ancient Greek myth and art, Jesus Christ in the New Testament is closely associated, therefore, with the symbolic elements of serpent, wings, axial imagery (Rod/cross), and 'mediation'/'messaging' between *two* realms, the divine and the mortal ('Heaven and Earth'). In both cases, 'duality' is unified through a 'mediator'/'messenger' of 'the gods'/God.

'Shamanic flight,' an event in which a healer and holy person called a 'shaman' is supposed to 'mediate' and 'message' between 'Heaven and Earth,' or the celestial and terrestrial realms, is sometimes represented in so-called shamanic cultures by birds or the wings of flying creatures. Piers Vitebsky remarks in *The Shaman* that "often shamans use a vehicle such as a bird to fly to the sky."[8] The elements of serpent and axial symbolism, as well as 'mediation' and 'messaging' between the mortal/human/terrestrial and immortal/divine/celestial realms, are common to various versions of 'shamanism' around the world. In *Shamanism: Archaic Techniques of Ecstasy*, however, Eliade seeks to differentiate between shamanic flight and the travels of Hermes, stating that

> Hermes Psychopompos[9]...is far too complex to be reduced to a 'shamanic' guide to the underworld. As for Hermes' 'wing,' symbolic of magical flight, vague indications seem to show that certain Greek sorcerers professed to furnish the souls of the deceased with wings to enable them to fly to heaven. But this is only the ancient soul-bird symbolism, complicated and contaminated by many late interpretations of Oriental origin, connected with solar cults and the idea of ascension-apotheosis.[10]

---

8   Piers Vitebsky, *The Shaman: Voyages of the Soul; Trance, Ecstasy and Healing; From Siberia to the Amazon* (London: Duncan Baird Publishers, 1995), 70.

9   A 'psychopomp,' as Eliade defines it, is one who "conducts the dead person's soul to the underworld." Mircea Eliade, *Shamanism*, 182.

10 Mircea Eliade, *Shamanism*, 392.

Although Eliade does not wish in the above quotation to 'reduce' 'Hermes Psychopompos' (Hermes 'soul-conveyor') "to a 'shamanic' guide to the underworld," he still represents Hermes as a 'messenger' and 'mediator' between 'Heaven and Earth' when he refers to Hermes' 'wing' as "symbolic of magical flight" and states that "certain Greek sorcerers professed to furnish the souls of the deceased with wings to enable them to fly to heaven." In spite of Eliade's reduction of the shaman in this quotation to a 'guide to the underworld,' that figure remains, like Jesus Christ and like Hermes, a 'messenger' and 'mediator' "between the realm of the dead and the kingdom of the living." I argue that, like Hermes' Rod and Christ's cross, the shaman's 'world tree,' which we have previously discussed, is a symbol of the World Axis and serves, along with the Rod and cross, as the 'center' of the world around which all 'manifested' existence, represented by the serpent/dragon in Tradition, 'revolves.' As such, Rod, cross, and tree represent, respectively, Hermes', Christ's, and the shaman's role as 'mediator' and 'messenger' between *two* 'states of being.' This 'mediation'/'messaging' is effected in all three cases by means of the 'mediator's'/'messenger's' acting as the 'center' between the 'state of being' called the physical and that 'state' called the metaphysical.

In "Babylonian Origin of Hermes the Snake God, and of the Caduceus I," A. L. Frothingham discusses the Babylonian 'proto-Hermes'[11] or 'proto-caduceus,' that, according to the author, dates to "at least as early as the millennium between 3000 and 4000 B.C."[12] According to Frothingham, this 'proto-caduceus' was considered by the ancient Babylonians to both represent, as well as actually *be,* the Babylonian god Ningishzida. "Ningishzida was a subordinate deity,"[13]

---

11 A. L. Frothingham, "Babylonia Origin of Hermes the Snake God, and of the Caduceus I", 175.

12 A. L. Frothingham, "Babylonia Origin of Hermes the Snake God, and of the Caduceus I," 180.

13 A. L. Frothingham, "Babylonia Origin of Hermes the Snake God, and of the Caduceus I," 182.

according to Frothingham, an "introducing god"[14] who is sometimes depicted as 'mediating' between gods greater than himself rather than between gods and mortals. Ningishzida was represented, according to Frothingham, as *two* serpents entwined around a rod, similar to the traditional Greek caduceus.[15] An example of Ningishzida's role of 'mediation' between gods and mortals referred to by Frothingham "shows Ningishzida mediating to the Kingdom of Gudea the fertilizing waters that are the gift of Ea, or Shamash or whoever is the main deity."[16] (See figs. 11.2 and 11.3.) Ningishzida, the "secondary deity," is "identifiable by the two snakes that project, one from behind each shoulder."[17] Frothingham argues that Ningishzida was a "messenger and agent primarily of the Mother Goddess and secondarily of the Sun-god," from which we may speculate that the Greek Hermes' function as messenger of 'the gods' in general is but an abstraction from his earlier function presented here by Frothingham as messenger for these *two* particular divinities. If so, we could then perhaps abstract further and conclude that 'mediation' and 'messaging' between 'Mother' Earth and the Sun is the *archetypal case* of the 'two serpents facing one another.' This is of interest because the serpent symbol is often associated, or identified, with both Sun and Earth in various manifestations of Tradition around the world. Regardless, Frothingham's research reveals that the serpent as a symbol of the relationship between gods and humans, or different 'levels' of gods, or *two* 'states' of being, dates to at least 3000 BCE.

---

14 A. L. Frothingham, "Babylonia Origin of Hermes the Snake God, and of the Caduceus I," 183.

15 A. L. Frothingham, "Babylonia Origin of Hermes the Snake God, and of the Caduceus I," 181.

16 A. L. Frothingham, "Babylonian Origin of Hermes the Snake God, and of the Caduceus I," 184.

17 A. L. Frothingham, "Babylonian Origin of Hermes the Snake God, and of the Caduceus I," 183.

Fig. 11.2. *Seal Cylinder of King Gudea*, c. third or fourth millennium BCE, Ward, Fig. 368a, Louvre, Paris[18]

Fig. 11.3. *Libation vase of Gudea*, Sumerian, Lagash, c. 2150 BCE, Louvre, Paris[19]

---

18 A. L. Frothingham, "Babylonian Origin of Hermes the Snake God, and of the Caduceus I," 183.
19 Marilyn Nissenson and Susan Jonas, *Snake Charm*, 34.

'Creation'/'Manifestation' and 'Reactualization'

For Guénon, the "dual action of a single force" that is represented by such symbols as the Androgyne, double-spiral, *yin-yang*, World Egg, and 'coiled serpent(s)' symbolizes what he also terms the forces of 'evolution' and 'involution,'[20] the 'descending' and 'ascending' 'currents' by which the Principle is 'manifested' and then 'withdraws from' 'manifestation.' For Guénon, evolution *is* 'manifestation'/'creation,' the 'descending' of the Principle into "the indefinite series of cycles of manifestation." In *The Sacred and the Profane*, however, Eliade argues that 'creation' is equivalent to 'reactualization,' and that this is exemplified in the ancient Babylonian *akitu* ceremony which "tells how the cosmos came into existence."[21] According to Eliade, the *akitu* "was performed during the last days of the year that was ending and the first days of the New Year" and it "reactualized the combat between [the Babylonian god] Marduk and the marine monster Tiamat" in which "Marduk created the cosmos from Tiamat's dismembered body."[22] This "commemoration of the Creation," Eliade argues, "was in fact a *reactualization* of the cosmogonic act," and both "the combat between Tiamat and Marduk," as well as the 'miming' of this combat by actors in the *akitu* ceremony are, according to Eliade, *repetitions* of "the passage from chaos to cosmos."[23] As for Guénon, 'creation' is, according to Eliade, something that for traditional/archaic peoples occurs *repeatedly* and *indefinitely*. It is *not* a single *ex nihilo* event. The state that *precedes* 'creation,' therefore, *results from* 'creation' as well. This means that not only do the *individual souls of creatures* 'return' indefinitely until they achieve *moksha*, as in the South Asian idea of 'reincarnation,' but that 'chaos' *itself*, "the indefinite series of cycles

---

20 Discussed in Chapter 7.
21 Mircea Eliade, *The Sacred and the Profane*, 77.
22 Mircea Eliade, *The Sacred and the Profane*, 77.
23 Mircea Eliade, *The Sacred and the Profane*, 77.

of manifestation," *as* the perceived 'manifestation' ('evolution') of the Principle as 'nature,' 'returns' indefinitely.

In the terms of Guénon's analysis of Tradition in *The Multiple States of the Being*, 'chaos' denotes 'the totalities of possibilities.'[24] I have spoken of 'chaos' as roughly interchangeable with my notion of *matter*,[25] that is, as the potential, indefinite, formless ('confused and obscure'[26]) aspect of existence—that which *may become* any of the dichotomies, such as 'good' *or* 'evil,' 'benefic' *or* 'malefic,' living *or* dying. 'Creation'/'manifestation,' therefore, is the corresponding event/process of actualization, definition, and formation. The actualization of what is possible though not yet actual is the transition from indefinitude to definition and from formlessness to form *or*, as Eliade would say, "the passage from chaos to cosmos." This process occurs indefinitely at both the 'macrocosmic' and 'microcosmic' levels of reality. It happens in the birth of humans, the fruition of plants, and the building of temples, as much as it does in the creation of a universe. In Eliade's example of the Babylonian *akitu* ceremony, the god Marduk (re-)*actualizes* a 'cosmos' (an 'ordered whole') by *defining and forming* the remnants of Tiamat's body. This is not creation *ex nihilo* but *re*-creation or, I would argue, *regeneration* of that which, as in the case of Tiamat's body, has 'died' in some sense and 'returned' to a state of *potentiality*. In Genesis 1:2, similarly, "the Spirit of God was hovering over the face of the waters," *not* over the face of 'nothing.'

---

24 René Guénon, *The Multiple States of the Being*, 67–68.

25 *Matter* is, more precisely, awareness *of* 'chaos' from a particular level of 'realization.'

26 Again: "Confused and obscure" is used here in the sense of the Hindu concept of *tamas*, which, according to Guénon, is a "condition of universal Existence to which all manifested beings are subjected" and which denotes "obscurity assimilated with ignorance, and [is] represented as a downward tendency." René Guénon, *Man & His Becoming According to the Vedanta*, 44–45. In Hindu tradition, as noted in Chapter 4, before the interference of *Brahma* (pure Spirit) — "at the outset of manifestation" — Existence took the aspect of *tamas*, as Guénon puts it. René Guénon, *The Symbolism of the Cross*, 32.

[ESV] According to Guénon, the symbolism of 'water' or 'the Waters' found in traditional art and myth expresses the idea that 'water(s)' symbolizes not 'nothing' but a 'chaos' of unlimited *potential*. The event/process of 'creation'/'manifestation,' as is illustrated in Genesis 1, *actualizes* this potential. We shall have more to say about this when we discuss the 'Far-Eastern Dragon' in greater depth in Chapter 15.[27]

In all traditional belief systems the individual human is considered a reflection of God, the universe, or the universal process of 'creation'/'manifestation.' It is only reasonable to presume, therefore, that a traditional symbol associated with 'creation' on the macrocosmic scale may also be associated with 'creation' on the microcosmic scale. Specifically, it is reasonable to presume that terrestrial birth and production are associated with the symbolism of the serpent/dragon in Tradition to the same degree that 'creation'/'manifestation'/'reactualization' of the universe is. If all of 'natural' existence is considered to be cyclical for traditional peoples, as Guénon and Eliade affirm, then it is reasonable to presume that such peoples also believe the universe, or universes, to both begin and end again and again in a way parallel to that in which the 'states' of being called human, dog, amoeba, tree, temple, and civilization, for example, begin and end again and again. To speak of 'creation,' therefore, in the traditional sense, is to speak of *re*creation, or 'reactualization,' as Eliade states, or *regeneration*, as I shall put it. 'Creation'/'manifestation'/'reactualization'/'regeneration,' I argue, is a 'mediation' and 'messaging' process/event. In the process/event of 'mediating' or sending

---

27 The reader will recall from Chapter 7 that when Guénon refers to the 'Far-Eastern tradition,' he normally has in mind Taoism and Confucianism, combined with their influences on, and development in, all of the cultures of East Asia. The 'third' Chinese religion, Buddhism, is an interjection from South Asia. The expression 'Far-Eastern Dragon,' therefore, refers to that understanding of the symbolism of the dragon that grew out of the specifically East Asian mindset that was conditioned by Taoism and Confucianism. As was stated in Chapter 7, for Guénon, Confucianism is merely the 'exoteric' complement to an 'esoteric' truth that is more precisely conveyed by means of Taoism.

a message, however, something is *always* 'lost' or 'corrupted.' In any 'translation' or 'transference' of information between two parties, one of the following is imperfectly 'captured': 1) the objective content, 2) the 'mood,' or 3) the intent, of the 'message.' Abstractly stated, the 'message' that is 'sent' by its 'creator' is *always* imperfectly 'manifested.' In Guénon's terms, the 'message' of the 'Principle' is imperfectly 'manifested' in 'migrating' beings by means of what Guénon calls the "indefinite series of cycles of manifestation"/*samsara*. More generally, the 'multiple states of the being' that are described in what Guénon terms the 'Hindu Doctrines' are *limited* 'messages'/'mediations' of *Brahman*. Each particular 'state of being,' therefore, only imperfectly 'sends the message' of what *Brahman* is to each 'state' of *Brahman*.

Healing as Re-'Creation,' 'Mediation,' Resurrection, and Reincarnation/Rebirth

In traditional thought, according to Guénon, Eliade, and others, there is a homology between the human being and cosmic being. Because of this, the idea of 'healing' and medicine was associated by traditional humans with cosmic 'regeneration' itself. Eliade remarks in *The Sacred and the Profane* that "the ritual recitation of the cosmogonic myth plays an important role in healing, when what is sought is the regeneration of the human being."[28] This quotation expresses the idea that the very act of 'returning' to the point of 'creation,' which Eliade states was effected by reciting the 'cosmogonic myth,' as in the Babylonian *akitu* ceremony, was an act of *healing*. Eliade states in *The Sacred and the Profane* that

> by symbolically becoming contemporary with the Creation, one reintegrates the primordial plentitude. The sick man becomes well because he begins his life again with its sum of energy intact.[29]

---

28 Mircea Eliade, *The Sacred and the Profane*, 81–82.
29 Mircea Eliade, *The Sacred and the Profane*, 105.

According to Eliade, 'healing' is, for traditional humans, equivalent to 'beginning again' or becoming part of the re-creation event/process. When the serpentine monster Tiamat is slain by the god Marduk, the cosmos is re-created, which is to say that it "begins its life again," is *re-generated*, as I put it, or 'healed.' This understood, it makes sense to discover the serpent/dragon symbol associated in Tradition not only with the idea of 'creation'/'manifestation' but with the ideas of healing and regeneration (re-creation) as well.

In researching the symbols associated with the great healers of traditional societies, one finds the serpent/dragon. Interestingly, the caduceus that symbolizes 'mediation' and 'messaging' in the ancient Mediterranean world greatly resembles the Rod of Asklepios that symbolizes *healing* in the ancient Mediterranean world (see fig. 11.4).[30] In both cases, a rod/staff/wand is entwined by serpents, or a serpent, respectively. The Rod of Asklepios is named after the Greek god of healing who was son to the god Apollo[31] that, according to Graves in *The Greek Myths*, slew the great serpent Python "beside the sacred chasm" of the Oracle of Delphi.[32] It is interesting, to say the least, that an archetypal healer whose profession is symbolized by the serpent is *also* the son of a famous serpent/dragon slayer.

---

[30] A study of the Asclepian cult that is still considered authoritative by many scholars is E. J. Edelstein and L. Edelstein, *Asclepius: A Collection and Interpretation of the Testimonies*, 2 vols. (Publications of the Institute of the History of Medicine; Johns Hopkins University, Second Series: Texts and Documents 2. Baltimore, Md.: Johns Hopkins Press, 1945).

[31] J. Schouten, *The Rod and Serpent of Asklepios*, 7 and 25.

[32] Robert Graves, *The Greek Myths: 1* (New York, New York: Penguin Books, 1955, 1975), 76. In *Dragons, Serpents, & Slayers*, Daniel Ogden describes the serpent Python as the 'Delphic Dragon.' Daniel Ogden, *Dragons, Serpents, & Slayers in the Classical and Early Christian Worlds: A Source Book* (Oxford: Oxford University Press, 2013), 39.

Fig. 11.4. *Asklepios in the guise of a youth*, c. 140 CE, National Museum, Athens[33]

In the ancient Mediterranean world, both the Rod of Asklepios *and* the caduceus were generally taken to represent the ideas of healing and life in general, though the caduceus was also, as we have seen, a symbol of 'mediation' and 'messaging.' In *The Rod and Serpent of Asklepios*, Schouten affirms that

> the herald's wand of Hermes…is, as a symbol of the life of the earth, essentially the same as the rod of Asklepios. The latter heals the sick with it by, as it was believed, snatching them from death, whereas Hermes with his

---

33 J. Schouten, *The Rod and the Serpent of Asklepios*, 24.

magic wand wafts souls away from the grave and brings the sleeping back to life.³⁴

According to Greek and Roman mythology, the traditional jobs of healing and 'mediation'/'messaging' between the realms/'states' of life and death were *not* of distinct purview but overlapping. The equation between healing and the 'mediation' of the gods, however, went beyond the Classical imagination, as Schouten notes that

> [i]n ancient times, recovery from an illness was regarded as a resurrection from death. Babylonian and Egyptian gods who raised the dead were gods of healing. The sick were in the thrall of death and their liberation from it signified their re-entry into life.³⁵

It was thought in ancient Near Eastern cultures such as the Babylonian and Egyptian, as well as in the more 'Western' cultures of Greece and Rome, that, if only one could 'communicate' and 'negotiate' ('mediate' and 'message') with 'the gods' who were capable of raising the dead, one could possibly 'liberate,' or 'heal,' those "in the thrall of death." Those beings, like Hermes or Jesus Christ, who were capable of 'travel' between 'Heaven' and 'Earth,' between the divine 'state' of 'the gods' and the mortal 'state' of humans, were considered uniquely suited, according to Guénon, Eliade, and others, to this task.

In *Themis: A Study of the Social Origins of Greek Religion*, Jane Harrison describes Hermes as "the very *daimon* of reincarnation,"³⁶ thereby implicitly connecting reincarnation, by way of the ancient idea of healing associated with Hermes, with the symbolism of the *serpent*. It must be recognized that the event of the natural snake shedding its skin does, after all, provide a perfect image of 'reincarnation,' since,

---

34 J. Schouten, *The Rod and Serpent of Asklepios*, 119.
35 J. Schouten, *The Rod and Serpent of Asklepios*, 10.
36 Jane Ellen Harrison, *Themis: A Study of the Social Origins of Greek Religion* (Cambridge: Cambridge University Press, 1912 [Reprinted by Forgotten Books in 2017]), 295.

as we stated in Chapter 7, something is 'left behind' in that process while something else, as Eliade puts it, "begins again." When Eliade states in *The Sacred and the Profane* that "the sick man becomes well because he begins his life again with its sum of energy intact,"[37] he speaks of the traditional idea of healing. For sickness in 'archaic' societies is conceived of not, primarily, as an interference with biological functioning, but as a change in 'state of being.' More precisely, sickness or illness in traditional societies is a *characteristic of* the 'state' of death which signifies that the individual who suffers from a sickness/illness has already *gone beyond* the 'state' of life and needs to be 'reborn' or 'reincarnated' in some sense. By effecting this 'reincarnation' in any given case, as Schouten describes, Hermes 'wafts' a soul "away from the grave" and back to its 'beginning,' where, as Eliade states, "he begins his life again with its sum of energy intact." For traditional peoples, this 'reincarnation'/'rebirth'/'regeneration'/'re-creation' process is 'healing' insofar as it entails a 'return' to the 'Heavenly' realm of 'the gods,' the architects of 'creation.'

Eliade more strongly contends that, according to traditional peoples, the sick man becomes well by "becoming contemporary with the Creation." As we have noted, for Eliade the 'slaying' of the serpent/dragon Tiamat by Marduk symbolizes 're-creation' or 'reactualization' of the cosmos. I argue, however, that because it is the serpent/dragon that is 'slain' in order for the 'Principle' to form, define, and 'reactualize'/'recreate' the cosmos by means of ('mediation' of) the serpent's/dragon's *body*, it is also, due to the ancient belief in the homology between the macrocosmic and microcosmic realms, the serpent/dragon, representing the sick individual's *body*, that is the 'messenger'/'mediator' of *health* to the sick *individual*. In the cases of *both* the sick person's body *and* the body of Tiamat, it is the serpent/dragon that serves as the 'mediator'/'messenger' — potentiality or 'chaos' — that the formative, defining, and actualizing 'Principle,'

---

37 Mircea Eliade, *The Sacred and the Profane*, 105.

symbolized by the rod/staff/wand, 'reactualizes'/'recreates'/'reincarnates'/'regenerates.' The 'body' of the serpent/dragon Tiamat in the Babylonian narrative, like the 'waters' at the beginning of the 'creation' described in Genesis 1, symbolizes the formless, indefinite, potential that is, in the traditional view, 'reactualized' by being 'healed' in the broad sense. The 'body'/'waters' in these cases is, therefore, symbolically equivalent to the 'dual' state of *matter/samsara* which is symbolized by the 'dual' serpent. There is only *one* serpent represented in the Rod of Asklepios, therefore, because that symbol only symbolizes one of Guénon's 'influences,' the 'benefic' influence. The 'benefic' influence, I suggest, corresponds to 'healing' in the broadly traditional sense. With the caduceus, however, the 'movement' to and fro between the "realm of the dead" and the "kingdom of the living" are represented *equally*, as Hermes travels back *and* forth indiscriminately. Because the caduceus, therefore, represents 'movement' from not only the "realm of the dead" *to* the "kingdom of the living" but from the "kingdom of the living" *to* the "realm of the dead," both 'benefic' *and* 'malefic' influences are represented. We may speculate that the caduceus is, therefore, more representative than the Rod of Asklepios of the *complete* traditional conception of healing, since it symbolizes its own potentiality of sickness as well.

The 'Mediation' of 'Contrariety'

In *The Great Triad*, Guénon states that

> [i]t should also be noted that the caduceus (*kerukeion*, insignia of the heralds) is considered the characteristic attribute of the two complementary functions of Mercury or Hermes: on the one hand the Gods' interpreter and messenger, and on the other the 'psychopomp', conducting beings through their changes of state or their passage from one cycle of existence to another; these two functions correspond respectively to the descending and ascending currents represented by the two serpents.[38]

---

38 René Guénon, *The Great Triad*, 33.

From this quotation, Guénon seems to argue that the caduceus portrays two serpents in order to represent Hermes'/Mercury's role as: 1) "the Gods' interpreter and messenger" and 2) 'psychopomp,' or conductor of "beings through their changes of state or their passage from one cycle of existence to another." I contend, however, that, rather than being 'complementary to' the function of "conducting beings through their changes of state," the function of 'interpreting' and 'messaging' for 'the gods' is *equivalent to* such 'conducting.' This is because in Tradition 'the gods,' in their totality, symbolize metaphysical reality, and more specifically the metaphysical reality that Guénon terms the 'Principle.' It is the Principle, however, that, for Guénon, *allows* the 'changes of state' of beings and their 'passage' through the 'cycles of existence.' As I've argued, 'messaging' is equivalent to 'mediation' since the 'messages' of 'the gods' are equivalent to the *means* ('mediation') of a being's 'traversing' the 'states'/'cycles' of being. If this is accurate, then it is incorrect to claim, as Guénon does, that one of the serpents in the caduceus symbolizes the role of "God's interpreter and messenger" whereas the other serpent symbolizes the role of "conducting beings through their changes of state." Guénon also refers in the above quotation to "the descending and ascending currents represented by the two serpents," which may cause some confusion since, as one can see in the representation provided earlier, both serpents of the caduceus are represented as apparently 'ascending' toward the top of the rod/staff that they coil about. I argue, however, that, although the caduceus is meant to *symbolize* in Tradition the 'ascending' and 'descending' currents that Guénon refers to, it is not meant to strictly *represent* the precise directions of the alternating paths of the two currents. Instead, the traditional figure of the caduceus is meant to represent, as it plainly does, two serpents facing one another by facing in opposite directions, one towards the left and one towards the right, from the viewer's perspective, by means of which is symbolized the 'opposition' of the two 'currents,' or directions of movement, of the Principle's influence on "the indefinite series of cycles of manifestation." The fact that both of the two serpents represented in the caduceus face upward is, I suggest, merely a matter of classical stylistic convention meant to preserve the bilateral symmetry required by the Greeks and Romans for an, in their view, overall aesthetically pleasing figure. The same convention explains similar earlier Mesopotamian versions of the caduceus.

The caduceus wielded by Mercury (or Hermes) is a bringer of equilibrium or 'complementarity.' This idea is illustrated in the story of the two fighting serpents that represent contrary forces but yet are made 'complementary' by the 'mediation' of Mercury's rod. When a state of equilibrium is achieved, the elements contained in that state are complementary to a degree not previously extant; when a state of complementarity is achieved, the 'complements' have realized a greater degree of equilibrium. The 'realization' of equilibrium/'complementarity' symbolized by the caduceus is, I argue, the realization of *unity* in the presence of 'duality' thought of as 'contrariety' or 'chaos.' Unity, however, implies 'cosmos' because unity entails an 'ordered whole.' I suggest that Hermes'/Mercury's rod represents the 'unity' of the metaphysical 'Principle' that is 'surrounded by' its 'polarization' into *two* forces, one of which 'ascends' toward its unifying Source and the other of which 'descends' into the realm of 'duality' ('chaos'). The *entire caduceus* symbolizes the transition from a state of 'contrariety' to a state of being characterized by equilibrium/'complementarity.' Such 'transition' is Eliade's idea of 'creation': the 'movement' from 'chaos' to 'cosmos.' The Principle's 'reconciling' of the 'polarization' of the two forces represented by the two serpents in the caduceus is the function represented by the rod about which they coil. The "kingdom of the living" that is represented by the 'descending' serpent must 'complement' the "realm of the dead" that is represented by the 'ascending' serpent in order for 'mediation'/'messaging' to occur. The Rod of Asklepios, in contrast to the caduceus because it portrays only *one* serpent, contains no element that symbolizes a 'contrariety' that needs to be unified or a 'chaos' that needs to be made 'cosmos.' More particularly, the Rod of

Asklepios contains no element that represents *sickness* since, unlike the caduceus I contend, the Rod of Asklepios represents an imagined *future* state in which whatever is 'contrary', 'chaotic', or 'sick' is *already* 'reconciled', ordered, and healed — 'mediated' and 'messaged' in general. Perhaps this is why the Rod of Asklepios became a more popular symbol of healing and medicine than the caduceus: because it optimistically represents only the *healed* state.

When one thinks of 'contrariety' one thinks in terms of dichotomies. Good is contrary to evil, light is contrary to darkness, health is contrary to sickness. In Genesis 3, the 'contrary' serpent manifests its nature as that aspect of reality that allows room for 'alternatives'. The caduceus, by means of its two serpents, similarly represents the "kingdom of the living" as an 'alternative' to the "realm of the dead," for the 'migrating' being. That being may *either* follow the 'current' of 'benefic' influences *or* the current of 'malefic' influences, 'ascending' to *moksha* or 'falling' deeper into *samsara*. In Genesis 3, 'Adam and Eve's' encounter with the 'dual' serpent foreshadows its choice to eat of the Tree of the Knowledge of good *and* evil. The serpent seems to present to 'Adam and Eve', for the first time, the experience of 'contrariety' because it proposes to 'Adam and Eve' ideas that run *contrary to* God's law. The ensuing doubts spawned in 'Adam and Eve' by this experience dissolve its 'unity' with God, a unity symbolized in Genesis 3 by the Tree of Life as that 'Tree in the Midst' that is *contrary to* the 'dual' Tree of Knowledge.

Gregory Mobley states in *The Return of the Chaos Monsters — and Other Backstories of the Bible* that "chaos is the raw material of creation."[39] In *Religion and Monsters*, Timothy Beal states that the chaos "that threatens cosmic and political order is also the source of that order."[40] I have argued that the serpent/dragon in Tradition

---

39 Gregory Mobley, *The Return of the Chaos Monsters — and Other Backstories of the Bible* (Grand Rapids, Michigan/Cambridge, U.K.: William B. Eerdmans Publishing Company, 2012), 19.

40 Timothy Beal, *Religion and Monsters* (New York: Routledge, 2002), 17–18.

symbolizes the 'chaos' of potentiality, indefinitude, and formlessness. It symbolizes that state of *matter* that must be 'resolved' by the actualizing, defining, and forming 'Principle' (Spirit) in order for the 'migrating' being to 'realize' *moksha*/immortality. In order to 'evolve,' it was perhaps necessary that 'Adam and Eve' choose the path of 'chaos' and 'duality' over that of 'order' and 'unity' in Genesis 3. But 'evolution,' in Guénon's sense, is a movement *away from* a being's metaphysical Source. At the same time, however, the serpent of Eden and the 'duality' that surrounds it serves as a 'message' from, and a 'mediation' of, God, just as the "indefinite series of cycles of manifestation" is a 'message' from, and a 'mediation' of, *Brahman*. In this sense, the symbolism of the serpent of Eden is the same as the symbolism of the caduceus. Both examples of traditional serpent symbolism represent 'mediation'/'messaging' of a metaphysical reality by means of an axial symbol and a serpent or serpents. At a certain level, the serpent symbolizes 'contrariety' in both the caduceus and Genesis 3, but it is the 'mediating' and 'messaging' contrariety of 'chaos'/*samsara*/*matter* **to** the force of the Principle/*Brahman*/God(s)/Spirit. It is the 'contrariety' that is the 'complement' of 'healing' not only on the level of eradicating disease, but on that of providing equilibrium in order to form, define, and actualize the *cosmos*.

The *Amphisbaena* and the 'Plumed Serpent' Quetzalcoatl

In *The Great Triad*, Guénon writes that the two forces produced by the 'polarization' of a single force are

> depicted in different though fundamentally equivalent ways in other traditional symbols, particularly by two helicoidal lines [lines forming or arranged in a spiral] coiling in opposite directions around a vertical axis.[41]

---

41 René Guénon, *The Great Triad*, 32–33.

The caduceus, for Guénon, is but one example of "the general symbolism of the serpent in its two opposite aspects" that is a symbolic variant of the "two helicoidal lines coiling in opposite directions around a vertical axis." The symbol known as the *amphisbaena* is another. Guénon connects the *amphisbaena* with both the caduceus and the 'double spiral' in *The Great Triad*, arguing that

> the double spiral can also be seen as representing a serpent coiled around itself in two opposite directions; this serpent is thus an *amphisbaena*, whose two heads correspond to the two poles, and which by itself is equivalent to the two opposite serpents of the caduceus (see fig. 11.5).[42]

An early reference to the *amphisbaena* appears in the works of the first-century Roman author Pliny who stated that "the amphisbaena has a double head."[43] In *The Bestiary of Christ*, Charbonneau-Lassay adds that

> [t]his strange reptile, this impossible creature composed of two bodies joined together and condemned to pull forever against each other, or else to coil one against the other in an inevitable duel, represented among the Alexandrian Neoplatonists the two principles of good and evil which struggle for mastery in the world, the mastery of human souls. With its two parts, it was both the 'agathodaimon,' the spirit of good, and the 'cacodaimon,' the spirit of evil.[44]

---

42 René Guénon, *The Great Triad*, 33.
43 Pliny, *Natural History*, Bk. VIII, quoted in René Guénon, *The Great Triad*, 35.
44 Louis Charbonneau-Lassay, *The Bestiary of Christ*, 437–38.

Fig. 11.5. *Amphisbaena*, detail of archway from St. Cosmus, Narbonne, French (Languedoc), second half of the twelfth century, The Metropolitan Museum of Art, New York[45]

Like a caduceus without its 'rod' of 'mediation,' the *amphisbaena* is a symbol of 'contrariety,' with Charbonneau-Lassay employing the term 'duel' to refer to the struggle between 'good and evil' that the 'strange reptile' represents. This dichotomy of 'good and evil' symbolized by the *amphisbaena* makes it yet another example of the expression of dichotomies by traditional serpent symbolism, and explainable in terms of Guénon's division between 'benefic' and 'malefic' currents/tendencies and his stricture of the 'migration' of the being to 'higher' or 'lower' states. As such, the *amphisbaena* also serves as a symbol of the 'dual' and 'chaotic' state of *matter*, as only a 'chaotic' state that is potential, indefinite, and formless can be *both* 'opposites' of a dichotomous relationship, without 'mediation,' at once.

The symbolism of the *amphisbaena* that is described in the works of both Egyptian Neoplatonists and Imperial Romans is closely paralleled by the symbolism of the Mesoamerican god and cultural hero Quetzalcoatl, a mythological character seemingly originating from

---

45   Marilyn Nissenson and Susan Jonas, *Snake Charm*, 74.

an entirely different culture profoundly separated from the ancient Mediterranean world by both time and distance. In *The Complete Illustrated History: Aztec & Maya*, Charles Phillips notes the connection between 'duality,' serpent symbolism, and the name 'Quetzalcoatl':

> Quetzalcoatl's name has two meanings. In itself, it comprises two Nahuatl words, each of which also has two meanings. *Quetzal* can mean 'green feather' or 'precious' and *coatl* can mean 'serpent' or 'twin.' The elements of the name taken together can therefore mean 'Plumed Serpent' or 'Precious Twin.'....Such dual meaning...demonstrates the concept of duality so characteristic of Mesoamerican deities and religion in general.[46]

In *The Myth of Quetzalcoatl*, Enrique Florescano describes Quetzalcoatl more generally as "one of the most...changeable of characters...reborn during each period of history, but with a different face each time around."[47] The fact that the Nahuatl word *coatl* can mean both 'serpent' *and* 'twin' is obviously an interesting parallel to the ancient Mediterranean association between the serpent symbol and 'duality' that we see in Egyptian myth, Genesis 3, the caduceus, and the *amphisbaena*; and it raises the question of why such a parallel exists in a culture radically separated both in time and distance from the Mediterranean cultures we have been discussing so far. For Guénon and Eliade both, the answer is *Tradition*. Naturally, one might be tempted to explain the commonalities between Central American and Mediterranean serpent symbolism by reference to the snake's anatomy rather than entertaining the hypothesis that there existed a 'perennial philosophy' or transcultural 'wisdom' that united Mesoamerican cultures such as the Maya and Mediterranean cultures such as the Greek, Egyptian, and Judaic. In giving in to this temptation, however, one

---

46 Charles Phillips, *The Complete Illustrated History: Aztec & Maya: The Greatest Civilizations of Ancient Central America with 1000 Photographs, Paintings and Maps* (New York: Ames Publishing Ltd, 2008), 184.

47 Enrique Florescano, *The Myth of Quetzalcoatl*, trans. Lysa Hochroth (Baltimore and London: The Johns Hopkins Press, 1999), 1.

must still explain the transcultural emphasis on this *particular* animal and its particularly 'dual' features. As Mundkur notes in *The Cult of the Serpent*, the snake is "the one common, forceful element that surfaces amidst the great variety of animals in Western Hemispheric myths and religions."[48] Once the South and East Asian connections to the serpent symbol are more fully examined, the denial of Guénon's and Eliade's hypothesis of Tradition becomes even more strained (see fig. 11.6).

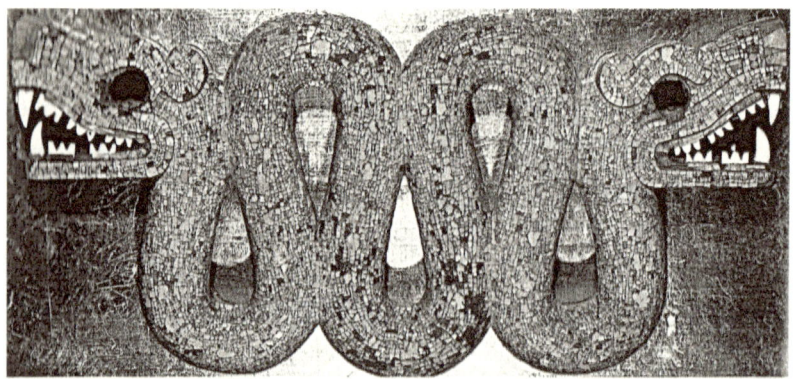

Fig. 11.6. *Double-headed serpent*, Aztec, fifteenth to sixteenth century CE, British Museum, London[49]

Unlike Phillips, Florescano limits his interpretation of the name 'Quetzalcoatl' to "a combination of the Nahua word *quetzalli*, which means 'precious green feather', thereby alluding to a bird with brilliant feathers, and the word *coatl*, which means 'serpent.'"[50] He adds, however, that "in Mesoamerica, the bird and the serpent are symbolic representations of two regions significant to religious and cosmological thought: heaven and earth."[51] The bird's representing 'heaven'

---

48 Balaji Mundkur, *The Cult of the Serpent*, 25.
49 Charles Phillips, *The Complete Illustrated History: Aztec & Maya*, 184.
50 Enrique Florescano, *The Myth of Quetzalcoatl*, 1.
51 Enrique Florescano, *The Myth of Quetzalcoatl*, 1.

and the serpent's representing 'earth' is a common interpretation of the symbolism of both the 'winged' or 'feathered' serpent as well as the *dragon*, which often possesses wings and the capacity for flight in many cultures around the world and throughout history. Phillips states of a "4th-century homage to the Plumed Serpent" that it is "suggestive of the god's possible origins in an ancient dragon deity."[52] (See fig. 11.7.) Whether it is symbolizing 'life and death,' as with the Rod of Hermes/Mercury, 'good and evil,' as with the *amphisbaena*, or 'heaven and earth' or 'twins,' as with Quetzalcoatl (the 'Plumed Serpent'), the serpent is very often explicitly associated with 'duality,' 'opposites,' or 'twins' in many traditional societies (see figs. 11.8 and 11.9). As we have already seen, there are various other less explicit examples as well.

Fig. 11.7. Untitled (Plumed Serpent), fourth century CE, Pyramid of Quetzalcoatl, surroundings of Mexico City[53]

---

52 Charles Phillips, *The Complete Illustrated History: Aztec & Maya*, 184.
53 Charles Phillips, *The Complete Illustrated History: Aztec & Maya*, 184.

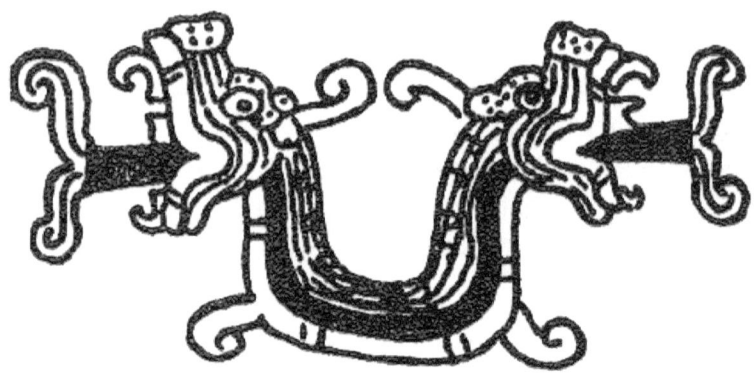

Fig. 11.8. *Double-headed serpent forming a bowl*, Mayan, Codex Vaticanus, 3773, p. 55[54]

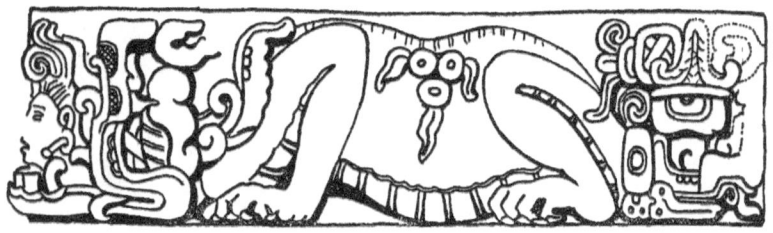

Fig. 11.9. Two-headed Dragon, Mayan, on small rectangular altar, Copan, Honduras[55]

Like Hermes/Mercury, Jesus Christ, and the shaman in many cultures, Quetzalcoatl, the 'Plumed Serpent' and 'Precious Twin,' symbolizes the idea of 'mediation'/'messaging' between 'opposites' such as 'Heaven and Earth,' 'health and sickness,' and 'life and death.' Hermes/Mercury with his caduceus was "the mediator between the realm of the dead and the kingdom of the living"[56] in Greece and Rome just as Moses

---

54   Herbert J. Spinden, *A Study of Maya Art*, 224.
55   Herbert J. Spinden, *A Study of Maya Art*, 53.
56   J. Schouten, *The Rod and Serpent of Asklepios*, 117.

'mediated'/'messaged' between God and the Hebrews by means of his 'copper serpent' staff, just as the crucified Christ 'mediated'/'messaged' between God and *all* humans. Quetzalcoatl served a similarly 'mediating' and 'messaging' role in ancient Mesoamerican myth. As Florescano notes, "the figure of Quetzalcoatl…is linked with the… netherworld…the place of darkness, cold, sacrifice, and death"[57] while *also* being the "double entity [that] is a synthesis of opposites… [which] conjugates the destructive and germinal powers of the earth (the serpent) with the fertile and ordering forces of the heavens (the bird)."[58] In another of his manifestations, Quetzalcoatl is depicted in the ancient city of Teotihuacan as both "the combination of heavenly and earthly forces…in the sculptures of the Temple of the Plumed Serpent"[59] *and* as an agricultural deity "who symbolizes vegetal renewal."[60] Like Hermes/Mercury, Moses, and Jesus, Quetzalcoatl is a 'messenger' and 'mediator' between two dichotomous realms, whether these are described as 'Heaven and Earth,' the "realm of the dead" and the "kingdom of the living," or 'health and sickness.' Similarly, the serpent of Eden 'mediates'/'messages' between the 'Principle' represented by the *unity* of the Tree of Life and the 'dual' Tree of the Knowledge of good *and* evil that represents "the indefinite series of cycles of manifestation." In fact, as I argue, the function of 'mediation'/'messaging' in *all* of these cases is between such physical *samsaric* cycles and a *metaphysical* 'Principle.' Such 'mediation'/'messaging,' however, remains indefinite and, from the human perspective (as discussed in Chapter 9), 'perpetual' until the state of *matter* is completely dissolved by 'realization' of the Principle/*Brahman*/God.

The 'vegetal renewal' symbolized by Quetzalcoatl as an agricultural deity well expresses the *samsaric* flux of "the indefinite series of

---

57 Enrique Florescano, *The Myth of Quetzalcoatl*, 2.
58 Enrique Florescano, *The Myth of Quetzalcoatl*, 1.
59 Enrique Florescano, *The Myth of Quetzalcoatl*, 7.
60 Enrique Florescano, *The Myth of Quetzalcoatl*, 9.

cycles of manifestation" that characterizes *all* life cycles. Like Hermes, Quetzalcoatl is a symbol of 'rebirth,' 'resurrection,' and 'regeneration,' with "vegetal renewal" being the 'message' that he brings to terrestrial mortals just as Hermes brings the 'message' of rebirth into the "kingdom of the living" to those sick souls that have strayed into the "realm of the dead." In six of the cases of transcultural serpent symbolism examined so far that are associated with 'duality' and 'contrariety,' however — the serpent in Genesis 3, the 'copper serpent' staff of Moses, the cross of Christ, the Rod of Hermes/Mercury, the *amphisbaena*, and Quetzalcoatl the 'Plumed Serpent' — the serpent symbolizes not only 'mediation' and 'messaging,' but the more abstract idea of a transition between two particular 'states of being,' a transition that is variously described as 'resurrection,' 'rebirth,' 'reincarnation' as Jane Harrison discusses, 'reactualization' as Eliade puts it, and simple healing.

CHAPTER 12

The 'Risen' Serpent: The Conjunction of Wisdom and 'Healing' in *Kundalini*, the *Uraeus*, the Bible, and Buddhism

Kundalini as 'Mediator' and 'Messenger'

The traditional representation of a coiled snake juxtaposed with an 'axis' of some sort, such as a rod, staff, or wand, finds its overtly Hindu expression in the South Asian symbolism of *Kundalini*. In this case, as in the Greek and biblical cases already considered, serpent-with-axis serves as a symbol of regeneration, re-creation, 'mediation and messaging,' and 'healing' in a 'holistic' sense. The 'rising' of *Kundalini*, however, is described in South Asian traditions as an 'awakening,' or 'enlightening,' in the 'migrating' being of a 'higher' awareness, wisdom, or knowledge (*vidya*). In *The King of the World*, Guénon defines *Kundalini* as

> a form of *Shakti* considered as immanent in the human being. This force is represented by the figure of a coiled snake in a region of the subtle body corresponding precisely to the base of the spinal column; this at least is the case in ordinary man, but by means of practices such as those of *Hatha-yoga*, it is aroused, uncoils, and ascends through the 'wheels' (*chakras*) or

'lotuses' (*kamalas*) that correspond to the 'third eye', that is, the frontal eye of *Shiva*.[1]

In *Introduction to the Study of the Hindu Doctrines*, Guénon defines *Shakti* as the "power or energy [of the 'divine aspects' of *Brahman*]… which is represented symbolically under a feminine form: the *Shakti* of *Brahma* [not *Brahman*] is *Sarasvati*, that of *Vishnu* is *Lakshmi*, and that of *Shiva* is *Parvati*."[2] According to Guénon, each of the 'divine aspects' of the 'Supreme Principle,' *Brahman*, "are…regarded as being endowed with…*Shakti*."[3] Guénon argues in *Man & His Becoming According to the Vedanta* that "in itself, the *Shakti* can only be an aspect of the Principle, and, if it is distinguished from the Principle in order to be 'separatively' considered, it is then nothing but…*Maya* in its inferior and exclusively cosmic sense."[4] This is only to say that *Kundalini*, in its *essence*, is derived from and dependent upon the metaphysical 'Principle' called *Brahman* in *Vedanta*.

Eliade states in *Yoga: Immortality and Freedom* that *Kundalini* "is described at once under the form of a snake, of a goddess, and of an 'energy'" and that it "dwells in the midpoint of the body (*dehamadhyaya*) of all creatures."[5] This, as Guénon points out in the above quotation, is the 'subtle' body, of which Eliade remarks that

> we must not forget that the yogins performed their experiments on a 'subtle body' (that is, by making use of sensations, tensions, and transconscious states inaccessible to the uninitiated), that they became masters of a zone infinitely greater than the 'normal' psychic zone, that they penetrated into the depths of the unconscious mind and were able to 'awaken' the archaic

---

1 René Guénon, *The King of the World*, 47.
2 René Guénon, *Introduction to the Study of the Hindu Doctrines*, 160. It is important to remember that *Brahma* is one among many Hindu 'gods,' whereas *Brahman* is the *ultimate* divine 'Principle.'
3 René Guénon, *Introduction to the Study of the Hindu Doctrines*, 160.
4 René Guénon, *Man & His Becoming According to the Vedanta*, 76–77.
5 Mircea Eliade, *Yoga: Immortality and Freedom*, 245.

strata of primordial consciousness, which, in other human beings, are fossilized.⁶

The 'midpoint' of the 'subtle body' referred to by Eliade is the 'starting point,' so to speak, of the *yogins*' 'experiments.' In both the 'ordinary man' as well as in other terrestrial life forms, *Kundalini* 'sleeps' at 'the base of the spinal column' for the entire expanse of the individual's life and seldom 'awakens.' In some individuals, however, the 'serpent energy' is destined to stir and, as Guénon states, "by means of practices such as those of *Hatha-Yoga*, it is aroused, uncoils, and ascends through the 'wheels' (*chakras*)...to reach finally the region corresponding to the 'third eye.'"⁷ (See fig. 12.1.) This "frontal eye of *Shiva*" is not a physical location but represents an advanced stage of awareness or 'realization' and, thus, an advanced stage of *being*, as all changes in awareness in essentially spiritual entities are, from the perspective of Tradition, changes in their being. The 'ascension' of the 'serpent energy' (or 'serpent power,' as others have referred to it⁸) of *Kundalini* is, likewise, not a passage through *physical* locations. As Eliade points out, the *cakras* (*chakras*) are not anatomical locations (though they are often identified as such) but "transphysiological...'centers' [which] represent yogic states."⁹

---

6   Mircea Eliade, *Yoga: Immortality and Freedom*, 234–235.
7   René Guénon, *The King of the World*, 47.
8   See Arthur Avalon (Sir John Woodroffe), *The Serpent Power: The Secrets of Tantric & Shaktic Yoga* (New York: Dover Publications, Inc., 1974 [originally published by Luzac & Co., London, 1919]).
9   Mircea Eliade, *Yoga: Immortality and Freedom*, 234.

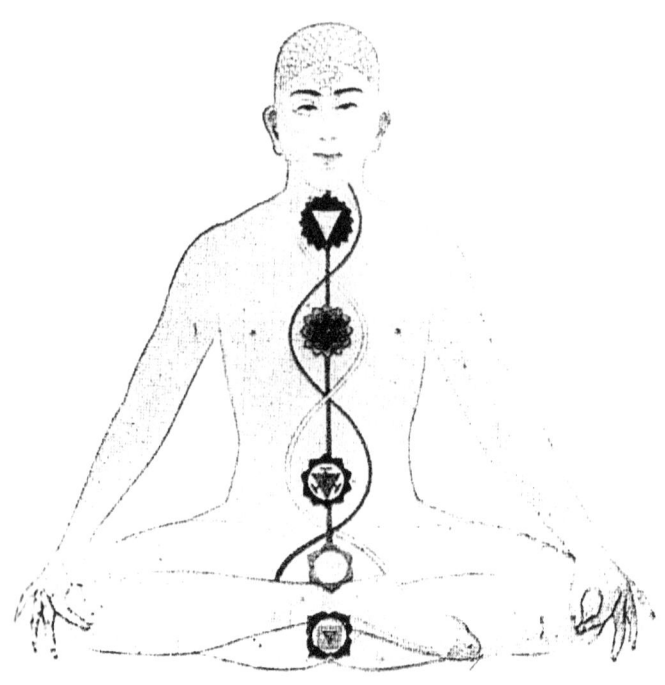

1. The cakras

Fig. 12.1. *The cakras*[10]

In modern times, *yoga* is popularly thought of as a form of exercise or meditation, the purpose of which is to effect in the practitioner a state of physical health and psychological 'well-being.' In *Man & His Becoming According to the Vedanta*, however, Guénon defines 'yoga' in accordance with the ancient South Asian understanding of the discipline as "the intimate and essential union of the being with the Divine Principle…the Universal."[11] 'The being' that Guénon refers to in this definition is not the seemingly 'individual' physical being that undertakes the yogic discipline but the immortal underlying 'Self'

---

10 C. G. Jung, *The Psychology of Kundalini Yoga* (Princeton, New Jersey: Princeton University Press, 1996), Figure 1 after page xlvi.

11 René Guénon, *Man & His Becoming According to the Vedanta*, 31.

(*Atman*) that is the 'ultimate' or 'final' cause of both the practitioner and everything else in the *samsaric* world. According to Guénon in *The King of the World*, the practice of *yoga*, in which the force of *Shakti* reaches the 'third eye,' should culminate in "the restoration of the 'primordial state', in which man recovers the 'sense of eternity', thereby attaining...'virtual immortality.'"[12] This event which is catalyzed by the practice of *yoga* constitutes, metaphorically speaking, the 'ascension,' or 'rising' as I shall term it, of the serpent force of *Kundalini* 'up' the spinal column, which latter serves to symbolize the 'World Axis' that is analogously represented by the rod/staff/cross/tree in other traditional figurations.[13] It would seem that the wings that are sometimes represented in symbolic figurations of *Kundalini* are included in order to indicate more clearly such 'ascension' or 'rising' to other, 'higher,' states of being, although the spinal column itself already makes manifest this possibility (see fig. 12.2).

---

12 René Guénon, *The King of the World*, 47.
13 In *Aion: Researches into the Phenomenology of the Self*, C. G. Jung expresses the ancient writer Hippolytus's belief that "the Gnostics identified the serpent with the spinal cord and the medulla." C. G. Jung, *Aion: Researches into the Phenomenology of the Self*, 233. We may speculate that this direct identification of the serpent with the spinal cord, rather than with the 'energy' or 'force' that flows up the spinal cord, is based upon an incomplete and confused understanding by some Mediterranean peoples of the Hindu symbolism relating to the *Kundalini* energy. According to C. W. King, for example, the Gnostics were interested in a special kind of "supernal and celestial knowledge," although much later than the Hindus were. Charles William King, *The Gnostics and Their Remains: Ancient and Medieval* (London: David Nutt, 1887 [republished in 2008 by Forgotten Books]), 17. King also remarks, in the same passage that the above quotation is drawn from, that "Gnosis was the name given to what Porphyry calls the Antique or Oriental philosophy, to distinguish it from the Grecian systems," thus providing more reason to consider the possibility of a connection between the Gnostic system and the 'Hindu Doctrines.'

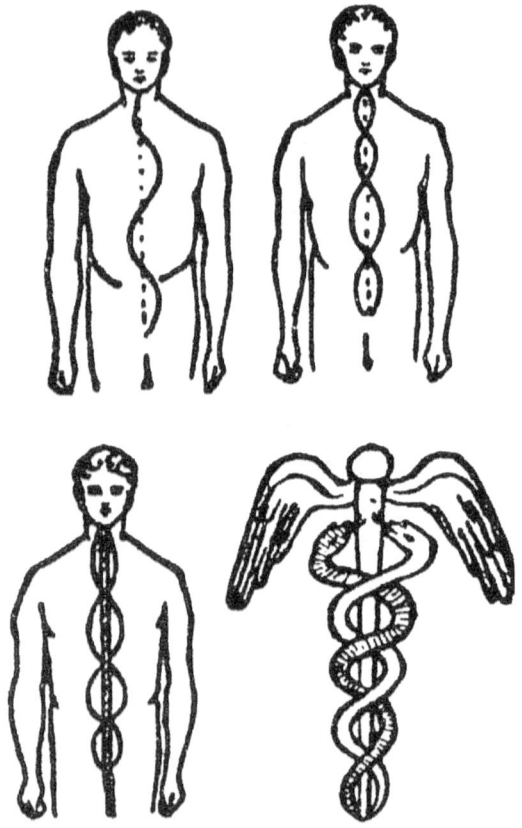

Fig. 12.2. *The Chakras*, C. W. Leadbeater, 1927[14]

It seems fairly clear from the exposition provided by Guénon and Eliade that *Kundalini* serves as a 'mediating' factor, a 'messenger' of sorts, between: 1) the human (and perhaps other beings) as it exists in the 'coils' of *samsara* and 2) the human as it has 'realized' what Guénon calls the 'virtual immortality' of the 'Self'/*Atman*. This 'virtual immortality,' according to Guénon in *Man & His Becoming According to the Vedanta*, consists of the 'virtually perfect' knowledge possessed by those *still living* beings that are on the path to

---

14 Alexander Roob, *Alchemy & Mysticism*, 334.

videha-mukti, "liberation when 'out of bodily form'" that is "obtained in an immediate manner at the moment of death."[15] The knowledge possessed by these 'virtually immortal' beings, according to Guénon, is only 'virtually perfect' because they have not yet died and achieved the 'perfect immortality' of 'liberation' (*moksha*).[16] The 'movement' of the *Kundalini* energy/force in such 'virtually immortal' 'migrating' beings is, as I describe it, a 'message' from, or 'mediation' of, *Brahman/Atman*, the ultimate reality underlying all 'individual' existence and the *maya* of *samsara*. Although *yoga* is a traditional means of effecting 'union' with *Brahman*, it is not a sufficient cause of such 'union.' Many individuals practice *yoga* without ever realizing 'union' with the divine 'Principle.' As the Bhagavad-Gita 7:3 states, "One person in many thousands may seek perfection, yet of these only a few reach the goal and come to realize me." The 'matter' of *Shakti*, specifically, must be acted on in order to allow *Kundalini*'s 'uncoiling' toward the 'third eye.' Like the draconic 'guardians of immortality' encountered by both Herakles and Jason in Greek myth, *Kundalini* must be 'defeated,' one might say, in order to attain the 'treasure' of the 'primordial state' of 'virtual immortality.' A 'quest' of sorts must be undertaken by the *yoga* practitioner, not, I would argue, unlike those undertaken by Jason and Herakles. Like the beech tree in the wood of Colchis, the spinal column serves as the *Axis Mundi* around which the serpent/dragon resides in a state of inactivity until the 'quester,' the seeker of 'Self,' the *yogin*, arrives and 'defeats' it. Guénon describes this 'dragon-slaying' as an event of 'restoration' by which 'virtual immortality' is attained. Eliade argues that, for traditional man, Marduk's defeat of the draconic Tiamat, as a 'creation out of chaos,' is the prototype for the traditional

---

15   René Guénon, *Man & His Becoming According to the Vedanta*, 160.
16   Guénon contrasts the path of *videha-mukti* with that of *jivan-mukti*, the latter of which describes the state of 'liberation' (*moksha*) "obtained by the *yogi* during his actual lifetime...by virtue of Knowledge no longer only virtual and theoretical but fully effective, that is to say by genuine realization of the 'Supreme Identity.'" René Guénon, *Man & His Becoming According to the Vedanta*, 160.

idea of healing. In *The Sacred and the Profane*, as we have noted, Eliade contends that "by symbolically becoming contemporary with the Creation...the sick man becomes well because he begins his life again with its sum of energy intact."[17] For each author, respectively, restoration and healing denote a return to that 'completeness' that pre-exists any degradation. *In illo tempore*, "in those days" of the Creation, according to Eliade, the 'real' was undiluted and uncorrupted. A person 'contemporary with' the Creation is 'reactualized,' for Eliade: 'healed.' For Guénon, by achieving this state of 'virtual immortality,' the person is 'restored' to her/his 'primordial state.' S/he has, as Genesis 1 states, 'separated' what Guénon, Eliade, and others have described as the primordial chaotic 'waters' of 'possibility'/potentiality that exist before any 'Creation'/'manifestation' (actualization, definition, or formation) has occurred.

The serpent/dragon that is depicted, or described, as being 'defeated' by a god or hero (or ruler in some cases, as we shall see) in traditional art and myth is symbolically equivalent to what Guénon terms in *The Multiple States of the Being* the totality of the 'chaoses' of 'formal' and 'non-formal' 'possibilities.' These two 'chaoses,' he argues, are symbolized in "various traditional doctrines" as, respectively, the 'Lower Waters' and the 'Upper Waters.'[18] "In a general way," according to Guénon, "the 'Waters' represent Possibility understood as 'passive perfection', or the universal plastic principle, which, in Being, is determined as 'substance' (the potential aspect of Being)." Genesis 1:6–7 well illustrates this traditional conception:

> And God said, 'Let there be an expanse in the midst of the waters, and let it separate the waters from the waters.' And God made the expanse and separated the waters that were under the expanse from the waters that were above the expanse. [ESV]

---

17 Mircea Eliade, *The Sacred and the Profane*, 105.
18 René Guénon, *The Multiple States of the Being*, 67.

In 'creating' this 'separation' of 'the waters,' God creates, by acting on the 'passive perfection' of one undifferentiated realm of 'Possibility,' two realms of 'possibility'/potentiality, those possibilities existing 'above the expanse' and those possibilities existing 'under the expanse.' The 'expanse' that 'separates' the two 'new' realms of possibilities or 'chaoses' is, in Genesis 1:8, 'Heaven.' 'Heaven' is, thus, a particularization of the 'action' of the metaphysical Principle that is called 'God' in Genesis. In the 'Far-Eastern' version of Tradition also, we shall see that 'Heaven' is a particularization of the *Tao*, for Guénon the Far-Eastern version of the Principle. In that context, Guénon contends that "the consideration of these two chaoses ...is indispensable for the comprehension of...the Far-Eastern symbolism of the Dragon." I argue, more specifically, that the dragon—the serpent in general, as the dragon symbol is a particularization of the symbolism of the serpent—represents the potentiality, indefinitude, and formlessness that the 'chaotic waters' symbolize in all versions of Tradition.[19] Both serpent/dragon and 'waters' are, furthermore, symbolic in Tradition of that which must be 'overcome' in order for creation/manifestation/'realization' of the 'Self'/*Atman* to occur. This explains why both the Hebrew "Spirit of God...hovering over the face of the waters" in Genesis 1:2 [ESV] *and* the Babylonian Marduk's creation of the cosmos by means of defeating the serpentine Tiamat are versions of the same traditional explanation of the 'manifestation' process/event. For Eliade, this creation/manifestation event/process is, as we have seen, a type of 'reactualization' in the same manner that the traditional healing of a sick individual was conceived to be. It is a 'regeneration' or 'rebirth' of the cosmos, whether on the macrocosmic or microcosmic level, and never an *ex nihilo* event. *Kundalini yoga*, considered as Guénon's 'restoration' of the 'primordial state' or 'recovering' of 'virtual immortality,' is therefore a form of the 'creation' process of 'mediation'/'messaging' that constitutes traditional 'healing.' Like the ancient Babylonian

---

19 René Guénon, *The Multiple States of the Being*, 68.

akitu ceremony and the creation/manifestation of the cosmos that it repeats, according to Eliade, *Kundalini yoga* is, I propose, a 'mediator'/'messenger' of 'healing' *as* 'reactualization'/'regeneration' /'rebirth.' It is for this reason that it is traditionally symbolized by means of the serpent.

Restoration of 'the being' to a state of 'completeness' or Reality is, according to both Eliade and Guénon, the traditional definition of 'healing.' The caduceus, therefore, was a traditional symbol of 'healing' *as* the 'mediating' of 'contrariety.' As I argued in Chapter 11, when one thinks of 'contrariety' one thinks in terms of dichotomies. Good is contrary to evil, light is contrary to darkness, health is contrary to sickness. In Genesis 3, the 'contrary' serpent manifests its nature as that aspect of reality that allows room for 'alternatives.' The caduceus, by means of its two serpents, similarly represents the "kingdom of the living" as an 'alternative' to the "realm of the dead," for the 'migrating' being. Because Hermes/Mercury was a 'messenger' between gods and humans, this 'mediation'/'messaging' signified a bringing together of *two* 'states' of being, one Real and the other (the human state) lacking in reality. In general, all forms of healing attempt to resolve two kinds of 'contrariety' or 'conflict': 1) the kind that arises *within* 'the being' and 2) the kind that arises *between* the being and the 'outside world.' From the 'enlightened' perspective of *Atman/Brahman*, however, these two *apparently* different kinds of 'conflict' are not different because 'the being' is actually *Brahman* and *nothing* exists 'outside of' *Brahman*. *Kundalini yoga* is but one traditional method of 'healing' in this broad sense that purports to resolve both kinds of 'conflict' by effecting a re-'union' between the apparent 'individual,' which is lacking in reality, and *Atman/Brahman*, which is completely real.

The Serpent, 'Healing,' and Knowledge/Wisdom

To achieve the kind of 'healing' that is spoken of here, a change of 'state' is necessary for the being who desires it. *Kundalini yoga* is a discipline and practice that allows for such a change. Like any discipline, however, it is based upon acquisition of a specific kind of *knowledge*. *True* healing, in the high philosophical sense of the term spoken of by the sages of old, from the Vedic *rishis* to Socrates and Jesus, is the healing of 'un-wisdom' or *ignorance*. This particular kind of ignorance is constituted by 'separation' from the divine Source of all being, whether this be termed God, *Brahman*, the 'Principle,' or the Form of the Good. In traditional thought, there is an intimate connection between a more 'holistic' kind of 'healing' that seeks to create 'union' between the 'seeking' being and its metaphysical Source and the knowledge/wisdom that is required for this task. The serpent symbol is often an aspect of the symbolism that expresses this 'holistic' wisdom/healing.

In the New Testament, there are two major references to either healing or wisdom in connection with serpent metaphors and similes. We have already written in Chapter 7 of the 'axial' symbolism of both the rod and the cross, and the connection expressed in John 3:14 between Jesus on the cross and Moses's 'copper serpent' described in Numbers 21. In Matthew 10:16, however, Jesus instructs his disciples to "be wise as serpents" when they go out into 'the world.' [ESV] This instruction is given by Jesus to his disciples, I argue, because he knew the serpent to be the traditional symbol of 'holistic healing' that I refer to. Like Asklepios, Quetzalcoatl, and shamans from around the world, Jesus is a 'holistic healer' who is 'wise' in the traditional sense of someone who is capable of healing, not only the body, but the entire *metaphysical* 'Self' in the *Vedantic* sense. This can be seen in Jesus's ability to not only heal the leprous and blind, but to 'cast out' demons (Luke 11) and 'forgive sins,' creating thereby a more 'positive' psychological or spiritual state in his 'patients.' Throughout the Gospels, Jesus trains his disciples to be 'as serpents' — *like him*, that is, who is compared to a serpent in John 3 — in order to 'save,' or 'heal' in the traditional sense, those individuals who have 'fallen' into sin and thereby become 'separated' both physically and *metaphysically* from their source, God. Jesus, as he himself states according to John 14:6, is the 'way' to ('mediator' of) God: "I am the way, and the truth, and the life. No one comes to the Father except through me." [ESV] As such, Jesus serves 'as [a] serpent' in the traditional symbolic sense. He preaches the traditional 'holistic' version of 'healing' in John 3:3 also when he tells the Pharisee Nicodemus, "Truly, truly, I say to you, unless one is born again he cannot see the kingdom of God." [ESV] This 'rebirth' that Jesus speaks for is the 'reactualization' that Eliade writes of as being equivalent to 'creation,' whether on a macrocosmic or microcosmic level. To be 'born again,' from the 'archaic' perspective, is to be 'created' again. 2 Corinthians 5:17 expresses this nicely in stating, "Therefore, if anyone is in Christ, he is a new creation." [ESV]

In speaking of Jesus's 'casting out' demons we refer to a form of 'illness' that was by no means considered by traditional peoples due to 'physical causes.' 'Spirit (or demon) possession' was, and is, considered by Christians, Confucians, Taoists, and shamanic cultures around the world — among others — a primarily *spiritual* disorder which only a certain kind of *knowledge* of a transcendent Source of existence may 'heal.' The rite of exorcism still practiced by the Catholic Church is the most well-known contemporary example of this ancient traditional belief.[20] The 'wisdom of the serpent,' however, lies in the capacity for renewal, whether this be called 'rebirth' (being 'born again'), 'regeneration,' 'reactualization,' 'reincarnation,' 're-creation,' or '*healing*.' In his book titled *Genesis 1–11*, Claus Westermann recognizes that one of the major traditional interpretations of the serpent is as an "animal that brings wisdom and life and advances knowledge in a number of ways."[21] Like Jesus and his apostles, the serpent and its wisdom are 'in' the world but animated *by* the metaphysical 'Principle' (God) that sustains 'the world' and manifests there. Charlesworth notes in *The Good and Evil Serpent* that "the serpent as a symbol of shrewdness

---

20   At the time of this writing, there are still training courses on exorcism offered by the Vatican.

21   Claus Westermann, *Genesis 1–11: A Continental Commentary*, trans. John J. Scullion S. J. (Minneapolis: Fortress Press, 1994 [originally published in 1974 by Neukirchener Verlag, Neukirchen-Vluyn]), 237.

and wisdom is found in the Jewish apocryphal works...as is clear in the Septuagint rendering of Genesis 3:1."[22] According to the ESV translation of Genesis 3:1, "the serpent was more *crafty* than any other beast of the field that the LORD God had made." (My emphasis) The 'shrewdness' or 'craftiness' aspect of the serpent's wisdom may be a reference to the inevitable corruption of a 'higher' knowledge once it is 'converted,' so to speak, by 'the world.' In Matthew 10:16, Jesus perhaps attempts to temper the human part in this 'conversion' process — its impulse to adulterate the divine wisdom/knowledge that he has shared — when he says to his disciples that "I am sending you out as sheep in the midst of wolves, so be wise as serpents *and* innocent as doves." [ESV] (My emphasis) In Matthew 10:20 he then reemphasizes the point by stating to them that "it is not you who speak, but the Spirit of your Father speaking through you." [ESV] One way to interpret both of these quotations is to see Jesus as telling his apostles that they must be on their guard to not adulterate his *Spiritual* (metaphysical) teaching by adding in their own *human* 'wisdom/knowledge.' They must remember, in other words, that they are not 'wise *men*' but 'wise *serpents*': 'messengers' and 'mediators' of the healing/wisdom of *God*.

The connection between the serpent symbol and the idea of wisdom, specifically, in ancient cultures receives, ironically from our perspective, an interesting treatment by one of Guénon's favorite subjects for criticism, the co-founder of Theosophy Helena Blavatsky. In *The Secret Doctrine*, Blavatsky states that

> "Serpent" and "Dragon" were the names given to the "Wise Ones," the initiated adepts of olden times. It was their wisdom and their learning that were devoured or assimilated by their followers....When the Scandinavian Sigurd is fabled to have roasted the heart of Fafnir, the Dragon, whom he had slain, becoming thereby the wisest of men, it meant the same thing. Sigurd had become learned in the runes and magical charms; he had received the "word" from an initiate of that name, or from a sorcerer, after which the latter died, as many do, after "passing the word."....The *Nagas* of

---

22 James H. Charlesworth, *The Good and Evil Serpent*, 356.

the Hindu and Tibetan adepts were human *Nagas* (Serpents), not reptiles. Moreover, the Serpent has ever been the type of consecutive or serial rejuvenation, of IMMORTALITY and TIME.[23]

Blavatsky also notes that "[i]n every ancient language the word *dragon* signified what it now does in Chinese — (*lang*) i.e., 'the being who excels in intelligence' and in Greek...'he who sees and watches.'"[24] We will follow up on some of these associations referenced by Blavatsky in later chapters.

Kundalini, Uraeus, Circle and Sun

There are numerous associations between the serpent and wisdom as knowledge-of-Spirit, or a holistic 'health' that is constituted by 'realization,' that appear in cultural artifacts from around the world. Terence Duquesne notes in "Raising the Serpent Power: Some Parallels between Egyptian Religion and Indian Tantra" that in Tantra,

> a system of spiritual practice of which there are closely interrelated Hindu and Buddhist strands [,]...the body is regarded as having a kind of collateral circulation in the form of two 'arteries', *ida* and *pingala*, one of which is red and one white, which may be regarded as two snakes. These are connected to a number of 'circles' (*cakra*) one of which, located at the brow, is designated *ajna* or 'gnosis'. This is precisely the site of the *uraeus* on the Egyptian royal diadem.[25]

---

23 H. P. Blavatsky, *The Secret Doctrine: The Synthesis of Science, Religion, and Philosophy Vol. I. — Cosmogenesis*. (London: The Theosophical Publishing Company, Limited, 1888), 404.

24 H. P. Blavatsky, *The Secret Doctrine: The Synthesis of Science, Religion, and Philosophy Vol. II. — Anthropogenesis*. (London: The Theosophical Publishing Company, Limited, 1888), 210.

25 Terence Duquesne, "Raising the Serpent Power: Some Parallels between Egyptian Religion and Indian Tantra," *Journal of Comparative Literature and Aesthetics*, XXVI, nos. 1–2 (2003): 109–110.

The "system of spiritual practice" referred to in this quotation is closely related to that which is symbolized in depictions of *Kundalini* in *Hatha-yoga*. Both systems, however, as Duquesne intimates, are expressed by symbolisms that share important traits with the 'ascending,' or 'rising,' ancient Egyptian *uraeus*. In *The Cobra Goddess of Ancient Egypt*, Sally B. Johnson makes the etymological argument that "'uraeus'...the Latinized form of the Greek 'ouraios', [was] undoubtedly taken from the Egyptian word...translated 'the Risen One.'"[26] Both *Kundalini* serpent and Egyptian *uraeus* are 'risen' serpents. Beyond this, however, both are associated with versions of the, so to speak, 'divine feminine.' Johnson states, for example, that "the cobra goddess, symbol of life, order, and legitimate kingship, appears as 'a rearing serpent' in ancient Egyptian art from its inception."[27] *Kundalini*, also, as previously noted, is a form of *Shakti* energy that is always associated in South Asian culture with such *goddesses* as *Sarasvati*, *Lakshmi*, and *Parvati*.[28] Based in part upon Duquesne's observations, I argue that the common elements of 1) 'rising,' 2) feminine, 3) serpent, and 4) life/health/wisdom in the symbolisms of the South Asian *Kundalini* and the Egyptian *uraeus* reveal that they both express a single underlying traditional meaning.

I contend that, like the serpentine/draconic 'guardians' of *moksha*/immortality that were 'defeated' by Herakles and Jason in Greek myth, and like the *Kundalini* energy that must be 'awakened' in order for the spiritual seeker to attain the prize of 'virtual immortality,' the *uraeus* served in ancient Egypt as an interactive 'mediator' that both 'guarded' the Pharaoh from those mortals who came into his presence but that also 'guarded' *them* from his 'divine bearing' (see fig. 12.3). It is commonly known that the ancient Egyptian Pharaoh was

---

26 Sally B. Johnson, *The Cobra Goddess of Ancient Egypt: Predynastic, Early Dynastic and Old Kingdom Periods* (London and New York: Kegan Paul International, 1990), 5.
27 Sally B. Johnson, *The Cobra Goddess of Ancient Egypt*, 3.
28 René Guénon, *Introduction to the Study of the Hindu Doctrines*, 160.

considered to be divine. According to Johnson, he wore the representation of the "divine-royal cobra" as a symbol of an "omnipotent goddess." This "cobra goddess," Johnson argues, which was represented by the *uraeus*, "remained an effective symbol of royal-divine protection throughout pharaonic times."[29] The belief in the divinity of certain humans, or the possibility of certain humans 'realizing' divinity is, of course, not a uniquely Egyptian idea. It is expressed equally in both the Egyptian symbolism of the *uraeus* as well as in that of the Hindu, or Tantric, *Kundalini*. Divinity and the 'risen' serpent are connected in both of these cases, as well as in cases from other religious traditions. Duquesne states that one of the *cakras* of Tantra "is designated for [the state of]…*ajna*," which Duquesne equates with the Greek *gnosis*, a special kind of knowledge whereby one 'realizes' his/her divinity.[30] Duquesne notes that "in the course of Tantric meditation, awareness [*gnosis*] is achieved when *kundalini*, the 'serpent power' is activated." This 'awareness'/'gnosis,' I argue, is equivalent to what Guénon describes as "the restoration of the 'primordial state', in which man recovers the 'sense of eternity', thereby attaining…'virtual immortality.'"[31] The Egyptian Pharaoh thus provides us with a well-known traditional example of one who achieved 'awareness'/*gnosis* and, therefore, enjoyed 'virtual immortality' during his earthly existence. This 'virtual immortality' would become 'actual' upon his physical death.

---

29 Sally B. Johnson, *The Cobra Goddess of Ancient Egypt*, 4–6.
30 Terence Duquesne, "Raising the Serpent Power: Some Parallels between Egyptian Religion and Indian Tantra," 110.
31 René Guénon, *The King of the World*, 47.

Fig. 12.3. The Mask of Tutankhamen, JHC Collection[32]

To the four elements of 1) 'rising,' 2) feminine, 3) 'serpent power,' and 4) life/health/wisdom that are represented in the symbolisms of both the Egyptian *uraeus* and *Kundalini yoga*, a fifth element must be added: the circle. Although in *The King of the World* Guénon describes the *chakras* through which the serpent force of *Shakti* 'ascends' as 'wheels,'[33] we will here appropriate Duquesne's translation of 'cakra'

---

32 James H. Charlesworth, *The Good and Evil Serpent*, 85.
33 René Guénon, *The King of the World*, 47.

as 'circle.'[34] In "Raising the Serpent Power," Duquesne contends that the site of 'awareness' that is achieved "when *kundalini*, the 'serpent power' is activated" is represented in Tantric iconography by the *circle*. Similarly, in discussing human esoteric anatomy according to *Kundalini yoga*, Eliade describes the 'cakras' as "transphysiological... *'centers'* [which] represent yogic states."[35] (My emphasis) As M. Oldfield Howey observes in *The Encircled Serpent*, the conjoining of the symbolism of the serpent with that of the circle goes far beyond South Asia, as does the general idea of the *uraeus*. He argues that

> [a]mong the most interesting and prevalent symbols of Ophiolatry is the hierogram of the Circle, Wings and Serpent, known as the Uraeon, or Uraeus. It is a prominent feature in the hieroglyphics of Persia, Egypt and Mexico, and has been found, though more rarely, in China, Hindustan, Asia Minor, Greece and Italy....It is beyond doubt that this triple emblem is a symbol of the Deity.[36] (See figs. 12.4–8.)

In *The Good and Evil Serpent*, Charlesworth more modestly notes that "[t]he use of the uraeus to represent the serpent extended far beyond the borders of Egypt."[37] In Howey's estimation, "the circle [symbolizes only] the solar disk" in all examples of the *uraei*.[38] He makes no reference to 'cakras.'

---

34 Terence Duquesne, "Raising the Serpent Power: Some Parallels between Egyptian Religion and Indian Tantra," 110.
35 Mircea Eliade, *Yoga: Immortality and Freedom*, 234.
36 M. Oldfield Howey, *The Encircled Serpent*, 1.
37 James H. Charlesworth, *The Good and Evil Serpent*, 229.
38 M. Oldfield Howey, *The Encircled Serpent*, 1. The two following illustrations from *The Encircled Serpent* that refer to 'Azon, the Persian god' are seemingly equivalent to, or variations on, the *fravashi* or 'guardian spirit' of Zoroastrianism that, according to John Bowker in *World Religions*, "represents the essence of god within people." John Bowker, *World Religions* (New York, New York: DK Publishing, Inc., 1997), 13.

Fig. 12.4. The Uraeon (Egyptian)

Fig. 12.5. From the ruins of Naki Rustan

Fig. 12.6. A Chinese Uraeon

Fig. 12.7. Azon, the Persian god (after Kaempfer)

Fig. 12.8. Azon, the Persian god[39]

In depictions of the Egyptian Pharaoh, specifically, the circle usually tops the 'risen' cobra, as is represented in the illustration below of Thothmes III reproduced from William Ricketts Cooper's *The Serpent Myths of Ancient Egypt* (see fig. 12.9). Cooper states that Thothmes wears "the sacred crown of Osiris; beneath it, and above the claft or plaited head-dress, is fixed the jewelled uraeus."[40] I shall argue that Howey's rather popular interpretation of the circle as symbolizing the 'solar disk,' or the sun more generally, signifies a comparatively shallow level of the circle's traditional symbolic meaning, both in the *uraeus* as well as in other cases of traditional circle/sphere symbolism.

---

39 M. Oldfield Howey, *The Encircled Serpent*, 1, 2, and 4.
40 William Ricketts Cooper, *The Serpent Myths of Ancient Egypt*, 7.

Fig. 12.9. Thothmes III. Wearing the sacred crown of Osiris[41]

Along with serpent and circle symbolism, there is also an 'eye' symbolism present both in the pharaonic *uraeus* and in South Asian representations of *Kundalini*. In *The Cobra Goddess*, for example, Johnson refers to an Egyptian myth in which an "eye magically transformed itself into a rearing cobra with expanded hood" for the god Atum which, later, the god "promoted…to the front of…[his] face, so that it could rule the whole world."[42] Atum, as Clark relates in *Myth and Symbol in Ancient Egypt*, was the 'High God' *Re* in its form as the sun, "the Complete One," or "the complete and all-containing one," who is identified in Egyptian tradition as the 'High Hill' or "the world-mound rising out of the Primordial Ocean."[43] Consistent with

---

41 William Ricketts Cooper, *The Serpent Myths of Ancient Egypt*, 7.
42 Sally B. Johnson, *The Cobra Goddess of Ancient Egypt*, 6.
43 R. T. Rundle Clark, *Myth and Symbol in Ancient Egypt*, 37–38.

the traditional motif of the serpent in juxtaposition with an 'axial' symbol, such as the mound, Atum is revealed by Clark in *Myth and Symbol* to be depicted, in some representations, "as a mongoose, a snake-destroying animal."[44] The mongoose is both a perennial 'enemy' of the snake as well as being appropriately 'axial' with its long, cylindrically shaped body. The 'rearing cobra' that is referred to by Johnson is the *uraeus* that is represented on the brows of Pharaohs in much Egyptian art. As we know, however, the 'third eye' that is referred to in *Kundalini yoga* is also located on the human brow and symbolizes one of the *chakras* that is 'opened' by the *yogin* who has, as Guénon puts it, 'aroused' the 'serpent force' within.[45] The varied translations of *chakra* as 'circle' and 'wheel' are important in this context because, in the case of the pharaonic *uraeus*, the symbolism of the circle symbolizes not only the sun's disk, as Howey contends, but the sun's 'wheel-like' *movement* through the heavens and the idea of the perfection of the circle that the sun, among all physical things, manifests most perfectly. The traditional symbolism of the wheel with its uniquely circular movement, perhaps most famously represented in the Buddhist 'wheel of dharma' that represents the spiritual progressions and regressions of the 'migrating' being, has been a symbol of 'return' since very ancient times. Although Howey emphasizes that the circle in the *uraeus* symbolizes *only* the solar disk that represents "the visible embodiment or outermost manifestation of the Divine,"[46] this is, from the perspective of Tradition, only the superficial and exoteric meaning of the *uraeus*' circle component. More deeply, the circularity of the 'solar disk' symbolizes, I argue, the Pharaoh's 'rising' *as yogin*, or the Egyptian equivalent of that state of being, through the various *chakras* (circles), the various levels of the *samsaric* "indefinite series of cycles of manifestation" that are represented by the sun's 'wheeling' (circular)

---

44   R. T. Rundle Clark, *Myth and Symbol in Ancient Egypt*, 53.
45   René Guénon, *The King of the World*, 47.
46   M. Oldfield Howey, *The Encircled Serpent*, 1.

movement. Furthermore, the so-called 'solar disk' symbolizes, in a broadly traditional sense, the successfully 'realized' or 'aroused' *yogin*/Pharaoh that has 'ascended' to the divine realm or 'state' of which the *disk* of the sun, in particular, is the 'visible embodiment.' In the terms of my overall argument, the state of *matter* as a particular kind of awareness of *samsara*, as well as Guénon's *samsaric* "indefinite series of cycles of manifestation" itself, is symbolized in the pharaonic *uraeus* by both the serpent and the sun's disk *considered as a wheel*. Brahman, alternatively, the 'Principle' or Spirit, or in this case the Egyptian god Atum-*Re*, is symbolized in the pharaonic *uraeus* by the sun's disk *considered as the perfect figure of the circle*. The merging of these two meanings into the one 'compound symbolism' of the *uraeus* in representations of the Egyptian Pharaoh indicates that ruler's status as an 'individual' *become-one-in-'union'-with* (*yoga*) the divine metaphysical 'Principle,' Atum-*Re* in this case.

In depictions of *uraei* found around the world, as Howey also notes, wings of various kinds are often represented. Wings were most likely, for pre-modern peoples, the clearest means of symbolically communicating the idea of 'rising'/'ascent.' For this reason, we may presume that they were also thought by traditional peoples the most obvious way to symbolize the metaphysical 'ascension'/'rising' of the *Kundalini* force of *Shakti* through the *chakras* (the 'circles'). As Howey relates, wings are symbolically juxtaposed with both serpent and circle in representations of *uraei* in China, Asia Minor, Persia, Mexico, and other locales around the world, as well as Egypt. I argue that there is a common traditional meaning underlying the symbolic combination of 'serpent-circle-wings' and that of 'serpent-staff/rod/tree/cross,' as the components of 'wings' and axial symbols, such as the staff, both indicate connection to a 'higher' state of being. Manly Hall remarks in *The Secret Teachings of All Ages* that "winged serpents represent the regeneration of the animal nature of man or those Great Ones in whom this regeneration is complete."[47] Though Hall does not pursue this, the 'regeneration' that he refers to always comes from a metaphysical/divine Source in traditional societies, such as the ancient Egyptian and South Asian, since 'regeneration,' or 'healing' in the general sense, was thought by such societies to be a 'reactualization' of the creation that is caused *only* by the metaphysical/divine. What Hall calls 'Great Ones' are the 'yogins' of all traditional societies, whatever such individuals may have been actually called, who have 'realized' their divinity or achieved 'union' (*yoga*) with a 'higher' mode of being symbolized by wings in Hall's example but by a circle(s) or axial symbols in other cases. Perhaps Blavatsky's '"Wise Ones,' the initiated adepts of olden times" are the same.

It is obvious that there was a common symbolic association in traditional civilizations between the 'serpent-and-axis' (staff/rod/tree/cross) and the idea of the divine just as there was between the idea of the divine and the serpent-with-circle and the serpent-with-wings, respectively. Sometimes, all of these symbols — axis, circle, and wings — are present in traditional figurations of the serpent/dragon. Connecting the symbolism of 'axis' and *uraeus*, specifically, in *The Serpent Myths of Ancient Egypt*, Cooper states that

> [a]s the emblem of divine goodness, the crowned Uraeus, resting upon a staff, was one of the most usual of the Egyptian standards, and the serpent upon a pole, which Moses, by divine direction, upheld to the Israelites in the wilderness, has been supposed to have been either an adaptation, or imitation, of the well-known pagan symbol. Again, when once the Uraeus had been associated with the idea of divinity, the Theban priests, rightly desiring to ascribe the gift of life and the power of healing to the Deity alone, significantly enough twined the serpent around the trident of Jupiter Ammon, and the staff of Thoth, or Hermes Trismegistus, the author of medicine, to imply the source from which that subordinate demigod's

---

47 Manly P. Hall, *The Secret Teachings of All Ages: An Encyclopedic Outline of Masonic, Hermetic, Qabbalistic and Rosicrucian Symbolical Philosophy* (New York, New York: Jeremy P. Tarcher/Penguin, 2003), 146.

virtues were derived. From this, in the later periods of her history, Egypt remitted to Greece...the traditional caduceus, or serpent scepter of Cyllenius and Aesculapius.[48]

According to Cooper, the Egyptian 'crowned Uraeus,' like the Rod of Asklepios and the caduceus, represents the 'Deity's' "gift of life and... power of healing." As we have argued, this more 'holistic' idea of 'healing,' which Cooper reveals as being embraced by Egyptian, as well as Greek, culture expresses a connection with the divine.

It is specifically the axial symbol, and not the serpent, that is representative of 'Deity' in all of the cases that Cooper refers to in the above quotation. In the case of the *uraeus*, or 'rising serpent,' however, we must note that the depicted serpent is not only 'risen' but both "resting upon a staff" and 'crowned' as well. As we have already speculated in connection with the symbolism of the *anima mundi*,[49] this 'crown' aspect, when juxtaposed with a serpent/dragon, is yet another indication of 'Deity,' or the metaphysical/Spiritual element, represented in traditional serpent/dragon symbolism. In those cases of serpent/dragon symbolism in which there is no 'axis' present, it is the serpent's 'risen' configuration that represents 'Deity' (the 'Principle') — *unless* there appears a circle. I argue that, in the latter case, it is both the 'risen-ness' of the serpent *and* the symbol's circle element that represents the Spiritual component of the compound symbol. The circle in Tradition, however, is not always *directly* representative of divinity. Guénon argues in *The Great Triad* that "in ancient symbols... [the] double spiral is sometimes replaced by two sets of concentric circles, drawn around two points which...represent the poles."[50] In *Symbols of Sacred Science*, however, Guénon adds that "what all traditions designate as the 'Pole'" symbolizes "the highest spiritual power active

---

48 William Ricketts Cooper, *The Serpent Myths of Ancient Egypt*, 9–11.
49 See Chapter 9.
50 René Guénon, *The Great Triad*, 35.

in the world."[51] The 'Pole' or 'poles' may, thus, in line with Guénon's statements on the nature of "the indefinite series of cycles of manifestation," be understood to represent in Tradition the metaphysical 'Principle' around which manifestation 'circulates.' If this is the case, then the circle in such symbolisms only represents the outward 'manifestation' of the divine Principle or 'Deity.' As such, the circle does not *directly* symbolize the divine, though it does imply its presence in the same way that a perfect geometrical circle implies the existence of its central point or 'pole.'

In the form of the 'solar disk,' specifically, the circle that is juxtaposed with the serpent and wings in the Egyptian *uraeus*, as well as in other *uraei*, symbolizes the *external* 'manifestation' of divinity (the 'Principle'). In Howey's words, the 'solar disk' is the "outermost manifestation of the Divine."[52] In *The Cult of the Serpent*, however, Mundkur connects the serpent symbol with Egyptian solar *and* eye symbolism when he states that "[i]n Egypt, the special powers of the serpent derive from the same divine substance as that of the fiery sun, the 'fiery Horus eye.'"[53] This remark is reminiscent of Johnson's observation in *The Cobra Goddess* that, in the Egyptian myth of Atum, an eye transforms itself into a 'rearing cobra.' In both cases, the sun/eye is somehow symbolic, in ancient Egyptian thought, of the *Source* of the 'serpent power.' The physical sun in traditional thought is of a similar nature to the natural snake insofar as both are *expressions of* a metaphysical state of being. Hall writes in *The Secret Teachings of All Ages*, however, that in many esoteric traditions "the sun, as supreme among the celestial bodies visible to the astronomers of antiquity, was assigned to the highest of the gods and became symbolic of the supreme authority of the Creator Himself."[54] In Plato's Allegory of the

---

51 René Guénon, *Symbols of Sacred Science*, 107.

52 M. Oldfield Howey, *The Encircled Serpent*, 1.

53 Balaji Mundkur, *The Cult of the Serpent*, 64.

54 Manly P. Hall, *The Secret Teachings of All Ages*, 135.

Cave, possibly an allusion to the pervasive 'rites of initiation' in the ancient world that involved an initiate's 'descent' into, and 'ascent' out of, a real cave, the physical sun is a symbol of the metaphysical 'Form of the Good' that is the source of life and clarity to a being's intellect in a fashion analogous to the physical sun's being a source of life and clarity to a being's body.[55] Plato's cave-dweller in the Allegory 'heals' his soul — causes it to be 'reborn' — by traveling to the 'surface' and *reuniting (yoga)* his soul with its metaphysical Source that is represented by the sun. Just as the serpent 'rises' on the Egyptian *uraeus* toward the disk of the sun, so does Plato's cave-dweller 'rise'/'ascend' from the depths of the 'earth' which, I argue, represent the troglodytes' *samsaric* nature. Upon 'realizing' his destination, the cave-dweller bathes in the presence of the Reality of the Form of the Good. This process, not unintentionally I believe, bears a striking resemblance to the natural snake 'rising'/'ascending' from its 'cave' (hole) in the earth to enjoy

---

55 Plato, *Republic* 7:514–519 in *Plato: Complete Works*, ed. John M. Cooper, 1132–1137. See, for example, *The Cave and the Light* by Arthur Herman, in which Herman states that "[w]hen Plato first dreamed up his allegory, he very probably had in mind an actual cave, which we can still visit today. It's on the island of Eleusis, where it served as the entrance to the sanctuary dedicated to the goddess Demeter. Some fifteen feet deep and forty feet wide, it marked the starting point of the famous Eleusinian mystery rites performed every year by Athenians (very likely including Plato himself) and others from all over Greece, in which initiates made a ritual journey into the underworld and then back again." Arthur Herman, *The Cave and the Light: Plato versus Aristotle, and the Struggle for the Soul of Western Civilization* (New York: Random House Trade Paperbacks, 2013), 563. In his article "Introduction to the Study of Plato," Richard Kraut writes of the 'higher' level of reality of all of Plato's Forms, including the Form of the Good, when he states concerning Plato's Allegory of the Cave that "[t]he shadows cast on the wall of the cave are less real than the objects of which they are the images...and in the same way, when the prisoners progress, leave the cave, and learn to understand the Forms, they recognize the existence of a realm of objects that are more real than anything they saw in the cave." Richard Kraut, "Introduction to the Study of Plato," in *The Cambridge Companion to Plato*, ed. Richard Kraut (Cambridge: Cambridge University Press, 1992), 11.

the warmth of the physical sun that rejuvenates — 'heals' in a holistic sense — its natural life.

Duquesne points to further synchronicity between ancient Egyptian and South Asian serpent symbolism when he remarks that

> [i]n Egyptian religion, the two Merty-goddesses [snake-goddesses who were protectresses of the 'solar barque']⁵⁶ represent a symbolism analogous to that of the red and white snakes of kundalini. The parallelism is particularly striking because the Merty are shown in the form of serpents and symbolize the two royal crowns — one red and one white — and hence the two complementary parts of Egypt.⁵⁷

The elements of goddesses (not gods), snakes, and royalty (which latter implies divinity in ancient Egypt) are again referred to. Duquesne adds that "*[t]he* [Egyptian] *Book of the Dead* contains an invocation to the two snake-goddesses as protectresses of the solar barque,"⁵⁸ combining the elements of goddess, snake, and 'rising'/'ascension,' the latter because one of the functions of the 'solar barque' was to carry the sun on its orbit through the sky. The association among the elements of immortality, rebirth/'renewal,' and serpent may also be seen combined in this spell from the Book of the Dead:

> I am the snake Son-of-Earth the one extended in years
>
> One who sleeps and is reborn every day
>
> I am the snake Son-of-Earth who is at the limit of the earth

---

56 According to Rundle Clark, "[a]t death [every] Egyptian hoped, after many trials and mystic journeys, to reach the divine barque" in which, "as the sun, God sailed across the sky....This was the final beatitude, for it meant immortality in the eternal circuit of the heavenly bodies." R. T. Rundle Clark, *Myth and Symbol in Ancient Egypt*, 71.

57 Terence Duquesne, "Raising the Serpent Power: Some Parallels between Egyptian Religion and Indian Tantra," 110.

58 Terence Duquesne, "Raising the Serpent Power: Some Parallels between Egyptian Religion and Indian Tantra," 110, referring to Book of the Dead Spell 37 (Budge text; 102/6–10).

> I sleep and I am reborn
>
> Renewed and rejuvenated every day.[59]

Comparable to this is the following spell included in the Coffin Texts:

> If you (gods) ascend to the sky as serpents
>
> I shall ascend on your coils
>
> If you (gods) ascend to the sky as cobras
>
> I shall ascend on your brows.[60]

In the latter, the divine element 'the gods' is clearly recognizable, and perhaps the spell presents a choice between 'unenlightened' and 'enlightened' 'ascension,' with 'brows' referring to the 'brow *chakra*' previously mentioned and thus to 'enlightenment.' As we have noted, Duquesne states that the brow "is precisely the site of the *uraeus* on the Egyptian royal diadem."[61] The alternative to 'ascending' "on your brows" presented in the spell is to 'ascend' "on your coils," which I would suggest is actually a reference to '*descent*' into the *samsaric* "indefinite series of cycles of manifestation." The expression 'Son-of-Earth' in the first spell may be an honorific title of a divine bearing as well. A final example of the 'risen' serpent in Egyptian myth is provided by Rundle Clark when he writes of "the great Primeval Serpent, who reared up out of the Abyss at the beginning,"[62] an example also of the serpent in connection with creation/manifestation.

---

59 Cited in Terence Duquesne, "Raising the Serpent Power: Some Parallels between Egyptian Religion and Indian Tantra," 111, Book of the Dead Spell 87 (Budge text; 188/1–5).

60 Cited in Terence Duquesne, "Raising the Serpent Power: Some Parallels between Egyptian Religion and Indian Tantra," 111, Coffin Texts III 61 (spell 175).

61 Terence Duquesne, "Raising the Serpent Power: Some Parallels between Egyptian Religion and Indian Tantra," 109–110.

62 R. T. Rundle Clark, *Myth and Symbol in Ancient Egypt*, 238.

'Copper Serpent' and Crucified Christ in Connection with the *Uraeus* and *Kundalini*

In Chapter 7, we discussed Moses's 'copper' serpent and the crucified Christ in connection with Guénon's description of 'the being's' 'migration' through "the indefinite series of cycles of manifestation." I argued there that in both cases the 'risen' serpent, whether on a pole in the 'wilderness' or symbolizing the *body* of Christ on the cross at Golgotha, is used as a means to convey the traditional idea of 'healing' as 'reconciliation' with a metaphysical Source, God in the case of the Bible. In his book *John*, G. R. Beasley-Murray claims that "[t]o the lifting up of the snake on a pole that all may live corresponds the lifting up of the Son of Man on a cross that all may have eternal life."[63] The 'reconciliation' accomplished by such 'lifting up' is, in both cases, equivalent to what I have described as the traditional 'holistic' idea of 'healing,' equivalent to the traditional idea of 'wisdom' expressed so succinctly in Plato's Allegory of the Cave.

In Numbers 21:4–9 it is stated that, not long after Moses delivered the Israelites from their enslavement in Egypt,

> [f]rom Mount Hor they set out by the way to the Red Sea, to go around the land of Edom. And the people became impatient on the way. And the people spoke against God and against Moses, "Why have you brought us up out of Egypt to die in the wilderness?" ....Then the Lord sent fiery serpents among the people, and they bit the people, so that many people of Israel died....So Moses prayed for the people. And the Lord said to Moses, "Make a fiery serpent and set it on a pole, and everyone who is bitten, when he sees it, shall live." So Moses made a bronze serpent and set it on a pole. And if a serpent bit anyone, he would look at the bronze serpent and live. [ESV] (See fig. 12.10.)

---

63 G. R. Beasley-Murray, *John* (Waco, Tex., 1987), 50.

Fig. 12.10. *The Brazen Serpent*, Gustave Doré, 1883[64]

The 'fire' or 'heat' element mentioned here is common to Egyptian and South Asian *Kundalini* serpent symbolism as well as to Hebrew serpent symbolism. As we have seen, Cooper argues in *The Serpent Myths of Ancient Egypt* that

> the crowned Uraeus, resting upon a staff, was one of the most usual of the Egyptian standards, and the serpent upon a pole, which Moses, by divine direction, upheld to the Israelites in the wilderness, has been supposed

---

64 The Holy Bible: King James Version, Barnes & Noble edition (New York: Barnes & Noble, Inc., 2012), 201.

to have been either an adaptation, or imitation, of the well-known pagan symbol.⁶⁵

Insofar as the solar disk of the Egyptian *uraeus* represents the sun, thereby combining a 'risen' element (the 'risen' serpent) with a 'fiery' element (the sun), this 'crowned Uraeus' seems to be a combination of both the 'fiery' serpents of Numbers 21 *and* the 'copper serpent' raised by Moses to counteract their poison, although we shall see in a later chapter that the 'fiery' element associated with traditional circle/sphere symbolism as well as 'axial' symbolism has, at a deeper level, nothing to do with the sun. Symbolically parallel, however, to the imagery of the Egyptian *uraeus* and Moses's staff/rod is the 'awakening' of the 'serpent force' of *Kundalini* that is described in Hindu tradition. In *Yoga: Immortality and Freedom*, Eliade observes that

> [t]he awakening of the *kundalini* arouses an intense heat, and its progress through the *cakras* is manifested by the lower part of the body becoming as inert and cold as a corpse, while the part through which the *kundalini* passes is burning hot.⁶⁶

'Fire' or 'heat' of a 'divine' intensity is also associated in Christian symbolism with the serpent. In John, as we've seen, Christ is symbolized by a snake. He is also, however, described in Luke 3:16 as having power over 'fire,' as when John the Baptist proclaims that "I baptize you with water, but he who is mightier than I is coming.... He will baptize you with the Holy Spirit and fire." [ESV] The Christ, "he who is coming," is also described as the 'Son of Man' in John 3:13: "No one has ascended into heaven except he who descended from Heaven, the Son of Man." [ESV] The expression 'Son of Man' refers to a prophecy in Isaiah which, Christians believe, anticipates the future return of Jesus Christ subsequent to his crucifixion. For the author of John, however, as Charlesworth notes in *The Good and Evil Serpent*,

---

65 William Ricketts Cooper, *The Serpent Myths of Ancient Egypt*, 9.
66 Mircea Eliade, *Yoga: Immortality and Freedom*, 246.

the 'lifting' of the 'Son of Man' which is compared to Moses's lifting of the 'copper serpent' possibly refers to both Jesus's crucifixion *and* his 'ascension' into Heaven.[67] As T. Zahn states in *Das Evangelium des Johannes*, "[T]he lifting up is to be understood as the elevation into heaven, the return of Jesus from the earthly world to the otherworldly realm of God."[68] This rules out the possibility that the 'risen-ness' of Christ refers only to his being *physically* lifted up on the wooden cross. It also may indicate that, in his 'risen-ness,' Jesus attains power over the killing or poisonous 'fire' of the serpent-nature of *samsara* that humankind is 'fascinated' by during the current 'age' of the world. The poisonous 'fire' that Jesus 'overcomes' equates with, I suggest, the 'volatile element' described in Western alchemy that must be 'fixed' and removed during the alchemical 'Great Work.' We shall examine this point further in Chapter 14.

Since serpents in Numbers 21 symbolize that which can both kill *and* heal, it may be that the serpent represented in the Egyptian *uraeus* represents the divine Pharaoh's powers to do the same, just as the 'serpent force' of *Kundalini* has the potential to bring destruction *and* 'enlightenment.' Moses's 'copper serpent,' the Egyptian *uraeus* with 'solar disk,' and the *Kundalini* 'serpent power' that rises up through the 'transphysiological centers' that correspond to physical locations along the *yogin*'s spinal column all serve as traditional symbols of contact with a transcendent Source that can protect, 'heal' in a more 'holistic' sense, and expand the consciousness of, those possessing its power. The 'ascending' serpent is in all cases 'risen' only by divine 'participation,' whether this be the strength of Yahweh, the 'enlightened' 'state' of *Atman/Brahman*, or the authority declared by Pharaoh when "he assumes the sacred asp of Amun-Ra, and wears the basilisk upon

---

67   See pp. 377–380, for example, in James H. Charlesworth, *The Good and Evil Serpent*.
68   T. Zahn, *Das Evangelium des Johannes* (Wuppertal, 1983 [reprint of 1921: 5th and 6th ed.]), 204.

his crown," as Cooper says.[69] When the 'fiery' serpents of Numbers 21 kill the Israelites and the 'risen' serpent heals them, we may presume that the 'fiery' serpents are earth-bound or *horizontal*. As mentioned earlier in connection with Christ's power over 'fire,' the 'fiery' serpents of Numbers 21 traditionally symbolize the killing, or poisonous, serpent-nature of physical existence, *samsara*. The 'risen' serpent is, in contrast, *vertical*. In his homilies on the Fourth Gospel, Augustine stated that "[j]ust as those who looked on that [copper] serpent perished not by the serpent's bites, so they who look in faith on Christ's death are healed from the bites of sin."[70] Like the 'copper serpent,' the 'Son of Man,' master of 'fire' and so of 'fiery' serpents, I would argue, heals by his 'risen-ness'; it is just a question of whether the manner of 'healing' effected is more physical or more Spiritual (metaphysical).

In both John 3 as well as Numbers 21, there are allusions to sin and the need for God's 'healing' of sinners. In Numbers 21:7, 'the people' tell Moses, "We have sinned, for we have spoken against the LORD and against you." [ESV] There is no clean separation between physical and Spiritual healing in that text. In John, however, there is *only* Spiritual healing. Perhaps the absence of 'fiery' serpent imagery in that text, along with Jesus's mastery of 'fire' described in Luke 3:16, speaks to this. A more important difference between John 3 and Numbers 21, however, is the fact that, out of Jesus and Moses, only Jesus is represented as *both* a 'messenger'/'mediator' of the divine and divine *himself*, after the fashion of Hermes and Mercury. Moses is only the first. Perhaps the author of John knew of the cross-cultural truth expressed in the symbolism of the 'divine messenger' when he identified the 'risen' Jesus *not* with Moses, but with Moses's 'copper serpent' staff. In *The Good and Evil Serpent*, Charlesworth notes that "according to Numbers 21, the upraised copper serpent signifies not only the power

---

69 William Ricketts Cooper, *The Serpent Myths of Ancient Egypt*, 7.
70 Augustine, "On the Gospel of John," 12:11; the quotation is from *NPNF1 (Nicene and Post-Nicene Fathers, Series 1) 7* (T. & T. Clark, 1886–1900 and Hendrickson Publishers, 1996), 85.

of God to heal; it also symbolized the presence of God."[71] From this we may presume that by his being 'raised' on the cross, Jesus, like the 'copper serpent,' traditionally symbolizes the 'presence of God.' Moses, although still a prophet of God, and thus one who speaks for God, does not *symbolize* God's 'presence' because, unlike Jesus, Moses is not a party to the 'risen-ness' of the axial symbol itself.

The general message in both Numbers 21 and John 3 is that 'healing' in the traditional 'holistic' sense originates from a transcendent, metaphysical, Source. It may be the case that John 3 more explicitly describes the human need for *metaphysical* 'healing' by its emphasizing the concept of 'eternal life.' Numbers 21, however, clearly indicates that 'the people' need to look *upward* toward Heaven, God, and the 'risen serpent' in order to acquire 'healing' and 'life' in a more 'holistic' sense. This 'large' sense of 'healing' and 'life' ('rebirth,' 'reactualization,' reincarnation, renewal, regeneration, 're-creation') is what is symbolized, transculturally, in the various figurations of the 'risen' serpent that we have discussed: the 'serpent power' of *Kundalini* in Hinduism, the *uraeus* in ancient Egypt, the caduceus and Rod of Asclepius in ancient Greece and Rome, the 'Feathered Serpent' Quetzalcoatl in ancient Mesoamerica, and the biblical examples of Moses's 'copper serpent' and Jesus on the cross just discussed. In all of these cases, the presence of a divine power or energy is symbolized by 'risen-ness' — whether it be the axial imagery of a staff, pole or cross, or the human spinal column, or the 'rearing' serpent of the *uraeus* — or by the symbolism of *wings*, such as one finds in some versions of the caduceus, Quetzalcoatl in his very name, and the Egyptian *uraeus* and other *uraei*. The cases of traditional circle symbolism that manifest in both the solar disk that is part of the Egyptian *uraeus* as well as the *chakras* of *Kundalini yoga* also refer to the 'risen-ness' that indicates divinity or its potentiality. These examples express belief in a traditional idea of 'healing' that is predicated on 'contact' with the divine

---

71 James H. Charlesworth, *The Good and Evil Serpent*, 391.

or Heaven — with 'higher states' of being, in general. This 'healing' offers the 'cure' of metaphysical 'realization' by means of 'the being' 'identifying' with *Brahman*/God/Atum, etc. 'Unrealized' beings are 'sick' insofar as they are *ignorant of*, or 'unwise' to, the 'Principle' which they are truly 'one' with. Their 'unwisdom' must be 'healed' by their being 'risen' into — 'identified' with — the divine presence. And this requires the appropriate instrument for the 'sick' individual to conjoin itself to: a pole, a staff, a cross, a tree, a spinal 'column,' wings, the upward movement of the sun, etc. The 'serpent nature' of such individuals must be 'nailed,' as Christ's *body* was to the cross, to the ultimate *Source* of that derivative, cyclical, nature in order for 'matter' to be formed, order to be created out of 'chaos,' and potentiality to be actualized. Ultimately, such wisdom/'healing' consists in the individual being's recognition that indefinite cyclical rejuvenation, as represented (on a lower symbolic level) by the serpent in Tradition, is *not* true immortality, though it appears to be so to the being that is 'fascinated' by *samsara*, the 'chaotic' "indefinite series of cycles of manifestation."

The Buddhist Variation of Wisdom and 'Healing' as 'Enlightenment': The 'Risen' Serpent in Buddhist Art and Myth

There are many examples in South Asian art and mythology that connect the symbolism of the 'risen' serpent with the traditional ideas of wisdom and 'healing.' These ideas are often conjoined in the experience of 'enlightenment' that is believed to characterize the being called the 'Buddha.' According to Buddhist sources, the historical 'Buddha,' Siddhartha Gautama of the Sakya clan of northern India who lived during the sixth century BCE, is often depicted in traditional Buddhist art juxtaposed with one, or several, serpents 'rearing up' behind him.[72] In appearance, such representations are

---

72 According to Buddhist sources, "Gautama Siddhartha was born in 563 BC, of royal descent, into the Sakya clan, in Kapilavastu, a hilly principality at the

akin to other figurations of the 'rising' or 'ascending' serpent that we have considered: the Egyptian *uraeus*, the South Asian *Kundalini*, the Roman Rod of Asklepios, and the Hebrew 'copper serpent,' among others. On a symbolic level, and just like the listed examples as well as others, such as the cases of Quetzalcoatl and Jesus Christ, examples of Buddhist art that juxtapose the Buddha with a 'risen' serpent suggest a state of affairs similar to the 'union' (*yoga*), in the Hindu sense, of the 'migrating' being with its metaphysical Source, *Brahman*. This, as we shall examine, contradicts the alleged words of Siddhartha, the historical Buddha, as he is recorded as having claimed that he neither sought nor 'experienced' metaphysical truth. The goal of *yoga*, however, 'union' with the divine, in the traditional Hindu *darshana* of that name, is achieved by the 'migrating' being's 'realization' of its 'identity' with its metaphysical Source. I argue that this is what Siddhartha is represented as having achieved in those artworks depicting him in meditation with a 'rising' serpent 'sheltering' him. Like the Egyptian Pharaoh, the Greek Hermes and the Roman Mercury, Moses, Jesus, Quetzalcoatl, and others, Siddhartha is depicted in Buddhist art and mythology as that 'individual' who has become a 'controller' of the 'serpent power' by means of 'realizing' a state of 'identity' with that which is called *Atman/Brahman* in the Hindu tradition.

The source of much of the art depicting the Buddha with a 'rising' serpent that 'shelters' him is, according to Heinrich Zimmer in *Myths and Symbols in Indian Art and Civilization*, "an event that is supposed to have occurred shortly after Gautama's attainment of enlightenment": the protection of the Buddha by a 'Serpent King,' Muchalinda.[73] As Zimmer tells the tale, after having "fathomed the

---

foot of the Himalayas, in the north of India....Having resolved to renounce the world in order to discover a solution to human suffering, Gautama left his family and princely life and became an ascetic." Ramakrishna Puligandla, *Fundamentals of Indian Philosophy*, 37.

73 Heinrich Zimmer, *Myths and Symbols in Indian Art and Civilization* (Princeton, New Jersey: Princeton University Press, 1972), 66.

mystery of dependent origination," a keystone of Buddhist thought, the newly formed Buddha meditates under three great trees in succession: the 'Bo-tree,' or 'Tree of Enlightenment'; "a great banyan tree" called 'The Tree of the Goatherd'; and "The Tree of the Serpent King, Muchalinda."[74] It is under the third tree, appropriately named, that

> Muchalinda, a prodigious cobra, dwelt amongst the roots. He perceived, as soon as the Buddha had passed into the state of bliss, that a great storm cloud had begun to gather, out of season. Thereupon he issued quietly from the black abode [of the hole that he dwelt in] and with the coils of his body enveloped seven times the blessed body of the Enlightened One; with the expanse of his giant snake-hood he sheltered as an umbrella the blessed head. Seven days it rained, the wind blew cold, the Buddha remained in meditation. But on the seventh, the unseasonable storm dispersed; Muchalinda unloosed his coils, transformed himself into a gentle youth, and with joined hands to his forehead bowed in worship of the savior of the world.[75] (See fig. 12.11.)

In the Buddhist view, according to Zimmer, the serpent symbolizes "the bondage of nature." In Buddhist art, for example, "there is a special Buddha-type that stresses... [the] supreme harmony between the savior who has overcome the bondage of nature and the serpent who represents that very bondage."[76] This 'type,' or symbolic 'figuration' as we would say, represents according to Zimmer, "a special modification of a traditional Hindu naga formula...[and] figures conspicuously in the Buddhist art of Cambodia and Siam."[77] The 'naga,' which we shall soon consider in greater depth, are serpentine "genii superior to man... [that] inhabit subaquatic paradises, dwelling at the bottom of rivers, lakes, and seas, in resplendent palaces."[78] Zimmer argues that, although the 'Buddha-type' that consists of a depiction of the

---

74 Heinrich Zimmer, *Myths and Symbols in Indian Art and Civilization*, 66–67.
75 Heinrich Zimmer, *Myths and Symbols in Indian Art and Civilization*, 67.
76 Heinrich Zimmer, *Myths and Symbols in Indian Art and Civilization*, 66.
77 Heinrich Zimmer, *Myths and Symbols in Indian Art and Civilization*, 66.
78 Heinrich Zimmer, *Myths and Symbols in Indian Art and Civilization*, 63.

meditating Buddha 'protected' by a hooded serpent "does not appear among the art works of India proper...the legend that explains it forms a part of the earliest Indian Buddhist tradition and is accorded a prominent place in the orthodox canon preserved by the venerable Buddhist community of Ceylon."[79]

Fig. 12.11. *Buddha Meditating on the Naga Mucalinda*, Cambodian, late eleventh-twelfth century, Musée Guimet, Paris[80]

---

79   Heinrich Zimmer, *Myths and Symbols in Indian Art and Civilization*, 66.
80   Marilyn Nissenson and Susan Jonas, *Snake Charm*, 47.

The contention by Zimmer that the serpent in Buddhism symbolizes the "bondage of nature" is roughly equivalent to Guénon's argument that the serpent in Tradition symbolizes "the indefinite series of cycles of manifestation" or *samsara*, since *samsara*, as we've contended, is a term referring to the essential 'flux' that characterizes 'nature' and is, in *Vedanta*, that which casts a veil of ignorance (*avidya*) over those 'migrating' beings 'trapped' within its illusions. The notion that the 'Buddha-type' 'protected' by Muchalinda's hood is a "savior who has overcome the bondage of nature" is, I argue, a special case of my more general contention that, in *all* traditional art and myth, there are individuals akin to Siddhartha who are represented and described as having 'overcome' the 'chaos' of "the indefinite series of cycles of manifestation" by means of 'realizing' their 'identity' with what is called *Atman/Brahman* in *Vedanta* and the 'Principle,' more generally, in Tradition. I add, however, that the specific case of Buddha-with-Muchalinda, which consists of the conjunction of: 1) Siddhartha's enlightenment under the Bo-tree and 2) his 'protection' by the 'Serpent King' Muchalinda under the latter's eponymous tree, is an example of what I term the Spiritualization of *matter* which is represented in traditional serpent symbolism in several other cultures around the world. Cases of Spiritualization that are, in a broadly traditional sense, symbolically equivalent to that represented by the 'Buddha-with-Muchalinda' 'type' found in the ancient art of Cambodia and Siam include: 1) the 'opening' of the 'third eye' described and depicted in *Kundalini yoga*, 2) the 'rearing' serpent of the pharaonic *uraeus*, 3) Moses's 'raising' of the 'copper serpent' in the 'wilderness,' 4) the crucifixion of Christ, and 5) the Rod of Asklepios, as well as many other symbols of 'risen-ness' or 'ascension' juxtaposed with the serpent/dragon.

As Puligandla observes in *Fundamentals of Indian Philosophy*, Buddhists have always believed that the 'historical Buddha,' Siddhartha Gautama, "resolved to renounce the world in order to discover a solution to human suffering," and that "the overall emphasis of his teaching is on…the conquest of suffering."[81] The historical Siddhartha is thought by Buddhists to have become 'Buddha,' or 'enlightened,' therefore, when he "attained *nirvana*…the state in which one is completely free from all forms of bondage and attachment, having overcome and removed the cause of suffering."[82] Because there is such an emphasis in Buddhism on 'overcoming suffering,' Siddhartha is often called "the great physician."[83] *Nirvana*, however, as Puligandla points out, is not *only* a state in which bondage and suffering are overcome, as he observes that

> it is also the state of perfect insight into the nature of existence. He who has attained *nirvana* has once and for all freed himself from the fetters that bind man to existence. He has perfect knowledge, perfect peace, and perfect wisdom.[84]

This statement is relevant to my argument because it speaks to the essentially metaphysical, and thus traditional, perspective of Buddhism, which doesn't confine itself to making merely practical claims about how to 'conquer' suffering, but speaks freely about the "nature of existence," 'freedom,' and 'perfect insight,' as Puligandla points out. More generally, the Buddhist ideal of 'enlightenment' encompasses wisdom and 'healing' as the 'overcoming' of suffering in a fashion consistent with how wisdom and 'holistic' healing are, as I have argued, interconnected in other symbolic expressions of Tradition. In 'realizing' the state of being called *nirvana*, however, Buddhists believe that Siddhartha achieved not only "a solution to human suffering" but also "perfect knowledge, perfect peace, and perfect wisdom." At the same moment, therefore, that he 'conquered suffering,' it is widely believed by Buddhists that Siddhartha 'attained enlightenment.'

---

81 Ramakrishna Puligandla, *Fundamentals of Indian Philosophy*, 37 and 39.
82 Ramakrishna Puligandla, *Fundamentals of Indian Philosophy*, 47.
83 Ramakrishna Puligandla, *Fundamentals of Indian Philosophy*, 39.
84 Ramakrishna Puligandla, *Fundamentals of Indian Philosophy*, 47.

According to Buddhist doctrine, "perfect knowledge...and perfect wisdom," 'enlightenment,' is equivalent to 'healing' when that term is defined as the 'overcoming' of the cause of 'suffering.' Also according to Buddhist doctrine, however, Siddhartha Buddha achieved, as Puligandla puts it, a "state of perfect insight into the nature of existence" and thereby complete freedom "from all forms of bondage and attachment." The term 'existence' used by Puligandla, which appears in Buddhist texts and discussions in general, seems to refer to either: 1) 'life' as humans *usually* experience it or 2) the state of affairs that leads to what humans normally perceive as 'suffering.' Since Siddhartha, however, is alleged to have often claimed to *not* have metaphysical, or 'universal,' knowledge but only experiential knowledge, it must be the case, based upon his own words, that the "state of perfect insight into the nature of existence" that he achieved was really only 'insight' into the experiential characteristics of 'existence,' *not* into the essence of existence, existence *itself* that is. For to have perceived the essence of existence *itself* Siddhartha would have had to 'experience' something 'beyond' empirical experience, which is always and only knowledge of Particulars. The same goes for Siddhartha's allegedly achieving *perfect* 'insight' into the nature of existence since 'perfection' is not an object of empirical experience any more than 'existence' is. Due, then, to Siddhartha's apparent aversion to metaphysical explanations, it would appear that 'original' Buddhism is inconsistent with the, according to Guénon, essentially metaphysical worldview of Tradition.

There is a major problem with the Buddhist worldview that has been left to us. This problem consists of the idea that one such as Siddhartha could both: 1) 'achieve enlightenment' and 2) *only* acquire enlightenment by means of accumulating and analyzing empirical data, or experiences. To hold both beliefs, however, is to render the idea of 'enlightenment' meaningless. More specifically, to employ only empirical perception and the methods of empirical observation and scientific thinking in order to understand 'existence' can only illuminate the empirical *level* of existence. From his allegedly anti-metaphysical perspective, therefore, Siddhartha himself could only have gained "perfect insight," as Puligandla puts it, into the *empirical level* of existence. He could not have, based upon his own philosophy, understood 'existence' *itself* since 'existence's' metaphysical (universal) essence lies beyond the limitations of empirical experience, which is always of particular objects and events. Along the same lines, Siddhartha could only have "freed himself from the fetters that bind man to existence" insofar as he 'freed himself' from that which humans, in general, *perceive* to be the 'fetters' of 'existence,' not from the 'fetters' of 'existence' *themselves*. For to have truly freed himself from the 'fetters' of 'existence' themselves Siddhartha would first have had to *understand* 'existence' itself in its essence rather than simply in its empirical manifestations. This, however, would require more than the always *limited* number of empirical experiences that serve as the basis for conclusions drawn in the empirical sciences. In general, from the perspective of his allegedly anti-metaphysical outlook, Siddhartha could only have 'conquered suffering,' acquired 'perfect insight,' and 'freed himself' from the 'fetters' of 'existence' if these terms and expressions are defined based upon only the limited understanding of 'existence' that is provided by means of empirical knowledge. To do even these things, however, would have required of Siddhartha that he know 'perfectly' how humans *in general* conceive of 'existence,' how they, in general, *perceive* themselves to be 'bound' to existence, and how they, in general, experience 'suffering.' From the perspective of empirical science, however, there is no way in which to collect the kind of data that would have provided Siddhartha with such knowledge, since such a collection process would presume the ability to observe and record the actions of *all* humans at *all* times.

The above analysis raises the question that Kant asked over two centuries ago: 'What *is* Enlightenment?' In Kant's essay with that title, his answer is that "Enlightenment is man's release from self-imposed tutelage. Tutelage is the inability to use one's natural powers without direction from another."[85] From the traditional perspective, 'achieving enlightenment' entails the existence of, and the 'achievement' of, objective truth, as well as the necessity that there exists a 'true nature' of 'existence.' Insight into objective truth and the 'true nature' of 'existence,' however, requires a 'short-cut' through the accumulation of an always limited number of empirical observations and the inferences that are based upon these observations. Such a 'short-cut' is necessary to any 'enlightenment' worthy of the name because the methodology of basing 'knowledge' upon a process of accumulating empirical observations and analyzing them is both *never-ending* and *incomplete*. *If*, therefore, Siddhartha actually became 'enlightened' in an objective sense, then he must have discovered a metaphysical foundation by means of which to understand, not hypothesize about, 'perfection,' and by means of which to judge, evaluate, and transcend the 'usual' human experiences of 'suffering,' 'fetters,' and 'existence.' This means of achieving true 'enlightenment' must have been for Siddhartha, and always *is* for all humans, that metaphysical 'intuition' of the Source of existence that conditions *all* experience. The popular Buddhist beliefs, therefore, that Siddhartha in his 'enlightenment' experience transcended *all* human limitations, or that he experienced 'nothingness' — as Buddhists are so fond of saying — are only meaningful if interpreted through the lens of the traditional metaphysical paradigm. Because of this, it is flatly *irrational* for Buddhists to claim that Siddhartha could both, at the same time, disavow metaphysics *and* believe in 'nothingness' or in the 'transcendence' of 'suffering.' If we are, then, to take seriously Siddhartha's alleged contention that he did not indulge in metaphysics, we must presume that in his claim to having achieved *nirvana* what he meant is that he *directly intuited*, rather than speculated on abstractly, something that is 'beyond empirical experience' in the terms of what humans *in general* experience. This, however, is

---

85 W. T. Jones, *Kant and the Nineteenth Century: A History of Western Philosophy*, second edition revised (Fort Worth: Harcourt Brace Jovanovich College Publishers: 1975), 7.

still a validation of metaphysics, albeit not of the speculative kind, as it confirms the existence of a 'higher' reality that is 'beyond' the (level of) reality that is experienced by humans *in general*. If Siddhartha did 'directly intuit' that aspect of reality that is 'beyond' normal human experience, however, then we may fairly say that he achieved what is called in Hindu tradition *yoga*, 'union' with the divine/metaphysical reality called *Brahman* in *Vedanta*. For 'direct intuition' of the metaphysical is really just another description of *yoga* ('union'). It is, from the traditional perspective, the only means of discerning the *essence* of all things, whether it be 'life,' 'suffering,' 'healing,' or the 'wisdom' that allows *actually* 'enlightened' individuals to know what 'existence' *really* is, to experience existence's *essence* as that which is "completely free from all forms of bondage and attachment."[86] This 'union' (*yoga*) with the metaphysical reality that allowed for Siddhartha's *actual* 'enlightenment' is, I argue, what is portrayed in traditional Buddhist depictions of Siddhartha and the 'risen' serpent. From the traditional perspective, there is no other kind of 'enlightenment,' since there is no empirical knowledge that reveals that either *all* forms of 'attachment' lead to 'suffering' or that *all* forms of 'attachment' should *all* be 'overcome.' There is, likewise, no *completely* experiential knowledge that tells us what 'existence' is. Claiming otherwise is, ironically, in either of these cases, and by definition, a metaphysical claim itself that is based upon *universalization*. For, as Guénon argues, universal claims *are* metaphysical claims.

The Symbolism of the Buddha with *Naga*

My argument that Siddhartha's 'enlightenment' must be of a metaphysical nature in the sense of a 'direct intuition' of a state of being that is somehow 'beyond' those perceived in 'usual' human experience, is important to our overall argument because it puts the foundations of Buddhism, and thus of its art and mythology, squarely within the

---

86 Ramakrishna Puligandla, *Fundamentals of Indian Philosophy*, 47.

category of Tradition as Guénon defines it. It provides, more specifically, both: 1) a basis for contending that Siddhartha's 'enlightenment' experience is consistent with the traditional notion that true enlightenment is of a *metaphysical* 'Principle' beyond all empirical data and 2) a more complete understanding of the story of Siddhartha's encounter with a being of South Asian art and myth known as the *naga*.

The *naga* are not only giant serpentine beings with a proclivity for aiding budding bodhisattvas, as one might conjecture from the narrative of Siddhartha and Muchalinda related above. In *Myths and Symbols*, Zimmer states that

> [n]agas are genii superior to man. They inhabit subaquatic paradises, dwelling at the bottom of rivers, lake, and seas, in resplendent palaces studded with gems and pearls. They are keepers of the life-energy that is stored in the earthly waters of springs, wells, and ponds. They are the guardians, also, of the riches of the deep sea — corals, shells, and pearls. They are supposed to carry a precious jewel in their heads.[87]

In this quotation, a symbolic association is revealed among *naga*, 'water,' and the varied 'contents' (like pearls) of 'watery' places such as rivers, lakes, and seas. Elsewhere, Zimmer notes that "serpent kings and queens (*naga, nagini*), personify...and direct...the terrestrial waters of the lakes and ponds, rivers and oceans."[88] The *naga, as* 'genii,' are, according to Zimmer, 'forces' *of* the 'waters'[89]; and he notes that "in Hindu mythology the symbol for water is the serpent (*naga*)."[90] These facts indicate an important symbolic connection between the 'spiritual' 'state of being' that is called 'Buddha' and the symbolism of the 'force' ('spirit') of 'water,' the latter of which is symbolically identified with the serpent in both Buddhist art as well as other traditional art. Furthermore, the symbolic connection that is revealed

---

87 Heinrich Zimmer, *Myths and Symbols in Indian Art and Civilization*, 63.
88 Heinrich Zimmer, *Myths and Symbols in Indian Art and Civilization*, 59.
89 Heinrich Zimmer, *Myths and Symbols in Indian Art and Civilization*, 59.
90 Heinrich Zimmer, *Myths and Symbols in Indian Art and Civilization*, 37.

in representations of the Buddha-with-*Naga* is to be expected in any traditional setting since the three elements of serpent, Spirit/'force,' and 'water' are present in other traditional cases of serpent symbolism that we have already looked into, such as the case of Gilgamesh and the serpent who 'stole' immortality in *The Epic of Gilgamesh* and the example of the 'waters' of creation in Genesis 1. Recalling Guénon's argument in *The Multiple States of the Being* that the 'waters' are symbolic in Tradition of 'the two chaoses,' Eliade's contention that the serpent/dragon symbolizes 'chaos' in traditional myth and art, and the traditional belief that 'creation'/'manifestation' is the forming, defining, and actualizing influence of *Spirit*, it is clear that the symbolism of 'water,' serpent, and Spirit in Tradition is pervasive.

According to Zimmer, representations of 'Muchalinda-Buddha' are expressions of the symbolism of 'antagonistic principles' and their 'reconciliation,' an interpretation very much in line with the general understanding of serpent symbolism's representing 'dichotomies' such as 'good and evil.' Zimmer claims in *Myths and Symbols* that

> [i]n this legend [of Muchalinda sheltering the newly 'enlightened' Buddha] and in the images of the Muchalinda-Buddha a perfect reconciliation of antagonistic principles is represented. The serpent, symbolizing the life force that motivates birth and rebirth, and the savior, conqueror of that blind will for life, severer of the bonds of birth, pointer of the path to the imperishable Transcendent, here together in harmonious union open to the eye a vista beyond all the dualities of thought.[91]

Again, this is similar to my more general claim, based in Guénon's observations, that the serpent in Tradition symbolizes 'nature' or the *samsaric* state of *matter* that is constituted by fixation on the 'chaotic' character of "the indefinite series of cycles of manifestation." Zimmer's "life force that motivates birth and rebirth" is rather an abbreviation, however, of the more pervasive cyclical system that Guénon discusses, and which goes beyond the 'birth and rebirth' of 'life,' which seems to

---

91 Heinrich Zimmer, *Myths and Symbols in Indian Art and Civilization*, 67–68.

be what Zimmer is limiting his remarks to. In my argument, of course, any being that 'overcomes' "the indefinite series of cycles of manifestation" is more than a "conqueror of that blind will for life" and more than a "pointer of the path to the imperishable Transcendent." S/he is one who has 'conquered' the state of manifestation or *matter itself*, of which the "will for life" is only one among many other elements. However, it must be admitted that the expressions "the life force that motivates birth and rebirth" as well as "the bondage of nature" are passable *approximations* of *samsara* or "the indefinite series of cycles of manifestation"; and if such is what the *naga* Muchalinda symbolizes in representations of Buddha-with-*Naga*, then Muchalinda's 'sheltering' of the Buddha symbolizes the 'sheltering' *by samsara* of wisdom/healing *itself*, 'enlightenment,' in the person of Siddhartha Gautama.

Based upon the foregoing, I argue that the *naga* Muchalinda's 'sheltering' of the Buddha in the representations discussed symbolizes, in Tradition, the 'alignment' of *samsara*, the latter represented by the 'watery' *naga*, with Siddhartha's new 'enlightened' state of being. This 'alignment,' symbolic of a vertical 'rising' or 'ascension' of the serpent (*naga*), indicates a bringing up from the 'bottoms' of the lakes, rivers, and seas inhabited by the *naga* all of those pearls, jewels and other 'treasures' that have been forgotten there by all 'unrealized' or 'unenlightened' beings. Such 'alignment' hearkens back, however, to the imagery of the 'World Axis,' and, thus, the metaphysical 'Principle' that it symbolizes. Because of this, the representation of the *naga* Muchalinda's 'sheltering' of the newly 'enlightened' Buddha, *as* a vertical 'rising' figuration of the World Axis, symbolizes Siddhartha's successful 'Spiritualization' or 'ascension' to 'higher' states of being. This Spiritualization includes, by means of Spirit's 'evolution' into *matter*, specifically by means of Siddhartha's own 'personal' advanced state of awareness, the Buddha's 'recovery' of all those 'treasures' of wisdom/healing that have been lost and obscured at the bottom of the 'waters of chaos' — the *samsaric* flux of formlessness, indefinitude, and potentiality that obscures all metaphysical realities. This implies, however, that such 'sheltering' representations of the Buddha-with-*Naga* are meant to communicate an essentially *metaphysical* element in representing the 'alignment' of the 'natural' state of *samsara* represented by the *naga* with the 'enlightened,' or 'realized,' state of being represented by the Buddha. The symbolic vertical 'alignment,' thus, of a serpent/ *naga* (*samsara*) with Buddha ('Principle') symbolically indicates the influence of the metaphysical (the 'Principle,' or 'Transcendent,' as Zimmer calls it) over "the indefinite series of cycles of manifestation" — the influence of Spirit over the state of *matter*. As such, the general symbolism of the Buddha-with-*Naga* has the same traditional symbolical import as: 1) *Kundalini* 'rising' up the spinal column, 2) the 'rearing' Egyptian *uraeus*, 3) the caduceus or Rod of Asclepius, 4) Moses's 'copper serpent,' and 5) the 'risen' Christ of John 3, as well as all other figurations of 'rising' serpents/dragons that will be considered involving wings or other symbols of 'ascent,' such as the sun and fire. All indicate Spiritualization or 'enlightenment' as that state of being that consists of both wisdom *and* a more 'holistic' kind of 'healing.'

CHAPTER 13

The Serpent and Sacred Stones

Shesha/Ananta and the *Devas* and *Asuras*: The 'Churning of the Sea' in the *Ramayana*

In arguing in *The Symbolism of the Cross* that the serpent in Tradition symbolizes the 'dual action,' or 'polarization,' of a single metaphysical force, Guénon appeals to what he contends is another expression of the so-called 'Hindu Doctrines,' the *Ramayana*. The *Ramayana*, along with the *Mahabharata*, is one of two major 'epics' of ancient Hindu literature which, according to Radhakrishnan and Moore in *A Source Book in Indian Philosophy*, "deals with the conflict of the Aryans with the then natives of India and of the penetration of the Aryan culture."[1] In *The Symbolism of the Cross*, Guénon refers to an episode of the *Ramayana* known as the 'Churning of the Sea' in order to reveal in that text yet another example of traditional metaphysics and the traditional belief in the 'migration' of the being through the 'multiple states of the being,' as Guénon understands it. This, however, entails his analyzing the traditional axial symbolism of 'sacred stones,' in this case manifested as a 'polar mountain,' as well as the traditional symbolism of the serpent. On this subject, Guénon states in the relevant passage that

---

1   Sarvepalli Radhakrishnan and Charles A. Moore, eds., *A Source Book in Indian Philosophy*, 99.

> [t]he serpent is found coiled not only round a tree, but also round a number of other symbols of the 'World Axis', and especially the mountain, as is seen in the Hindu tradition in the symbolism of the 'churning of the sea'. Here the serpent *Shesha* or *Ananta*, representing the indefinitude of universal existence, is coiled around Meru, the 'polar mountain', and is pulled in opposite directions by the *Devas* and the *Asuras*, who correspond respectively to the states that are higher and lower than the human; we thus obtain either the benefic or the malefic aspect, according to whether the serpent is regarded from the side of the *Devas* or that of the *Asuras*. Again, if the meaning of the latter is interpreted in terms of 'good' and 'evil', we then get a clear correspondence with the two opposed sides of the 'Tree of Knowledge'.[2]

In his reference to "states [of being] that are higher and lower than the human," and in his comparison of the 'good and evil' aspects of the *Hebrew* 'Tree of Knowledge' to the *Hindu* beings called *Devas* and *Asuras*, it can be clearly seen that Guénon once again purports to discern a fundamentally metaphysical, and transcultural, symbolic paradigm underlying the particular stories and symbolic figurations of specific cultures. For Guénon, the Hindu narrative of the Churning of the Sea, like the Hebrew narrative of Genesis 3, expresses broadly traditional concepts in an attempt to transmit the most fundamental truths of Tradition. In this chapter, however, we will examine the Hindu narrative, and other figurations, specifically with a view to understanding the traditional symbolism of 'sacred stones' in connection with the traditional symbolism of the serpent/dragon.

The narrative of the 'Churning of the Sea' in the *Ramayana* begins when an evil sage named Durvasas curses the *Devas* (the Hindu gods) after discovering that a gift he had recently given to the king of the *Devas*, Indra, had been, as William Radice states in *Myths and Legends of India*, "damaged and dishonoured."[3] The effect of Durvasas's curse

---

2 René Guénon, *The Symbolism of the Cross*, 123-24.
3 William Radice, *Myths and Legends of India* (London: The Folio Society, 2001), 60.

is that, as Radice relates, "not just Indra but all the other gods too" should be condemned "to lose their tireless, divine vigour and become as puny as mortals."[4] The resultant weakness of the *Devas*, according to Radice, "gave an opportunity to the Asuras, a race…whose name means 'anti-god' and who are therefore a negation of everything the gods stand for" to mount "a massive armed assault on heaven."[5] In response to this aggression, the enfeebled *Devas*, after appealing to no avail for aid to the, presumably more powerful and non-cursed, gods *Siva* and *Brahma*, approached the god *Vishnu* with their problem. As Radice describes it:

> When Indra and the other gods marched up to Vishnu, [however,] he was asleep — comfortably ensconced on the massive serpent Ananta whose coils form his bed. The gods broke into a loud chorus to wake him, singing his thousand names, and in due course he graciously opened his eyes. 'What has brought you all here?' he asked; and the gods told him of the disaster of Durvasas's curse, their loss of energy and immortality, and the threat now posed to them by the Asuras.[6]

After meditating on their problem, Vishnu advised the anticipant *Devas*,

> 'Only if you drink from the sea of milk that surrounds me — from the ambrosia that secures immortality — will your energy be restored. But at present it is too placid to be effective: it must be churned and energized, and how can you do that in your present pathetic state? No ordinary churning-stick will do: the whole Mandara mountain must be lifted and twirled. And the only beings who can do that are the Asuras themselves, your bitter enemies!'[7]

---

4 William Radice, *Myths and Legends of India*, 60.
5 William Radice, *Myths and Legends of India*, 60.
6 William Radice, *Myths and Legends of India*, 60–61.
7 William Radice, *Myths and Legends of India*, 61.

The dubious solution proposed by Vishnu to the *Devas* to their apparently insoluble problem consisted, in its specifics, in their persuading the hated *Asuras* to help the *Devas* with the churning of the 'sea of milk' by promising them, in exchange, a drink of the resulting 'energized' ambrosia. And so it all came to pass. As Radice relates,

> [w]eak though the gods still were, they combined forces [with the Asuras] to catch Vasuki, a serpent who lived in the underworld....Stretching out in a long line along the whole length of the snake, they laboriously coiled him round the mountain, to use as a churning rope.[8]

Through a trick by Vishnu, however, the placement of the two groups of enemies proved beneficial to the *Devas* and detrimental to the *Asuras*; for the *Asuras* were placed at the head-end of the serpent Vasuki, where they "found they were breathing hot, poisonous breath from his huge, hissing mouth—and this had the effect of weakening them." In opposition, the *Devas* were placed at the tail end of the serpent, and there, as Radice relates, became "invigorated by the fresh, ambrosial breezes that blew from the ocean of milk. With each pull, they grew stronger....So the gods grew stronger, the Asuras grew weaker, and with the balancing of their power the churning proceeded evenly and effectively."[9]

There are a few superficial discrepancies between Guénon's appropriation and Radice's rendition of the *Ramayana* narrative of the Churning of the Sea that require clarification before proceeding. First, the serpent that Guénon calls *Shesha* or *Ananta* in *The Symbolism of the Cross* is called *Vasuki* in Radice's *Myths and Legends*; second, the 'polar mountain' that the serpent is coiled around in the narrative is called Meru by Guénon but Mandara by Radice; and third, Guénon refers to the Hindu gods by their proper name, *Devas*, whereas Radice merely refers to 'the gods.' These variations, although perhaps somewhat confusing to the casual reader, are unimportant to both Guénon's

---

8   William Radice, *Myths and Legends of India*, 61.

9   William Radice, *Myths and Legends of India*, 62.

use of the Churning of the Sea narrative in *The Symbolism of the Cross* and to our present purpose here, which is to understand the serpent symbolism in that narrative and its relationship to the traditional symbolism of 'sacred stones,' or 'mountains' in this case. Whether the name of the serpent in the *Ramayana* narrative of the Churning of the Sea is *Shesha, Ananta*, or *Vasuki*, the important thing for our purposes is that there is only *one* serpent in that narrative. Since Guénon argues that the *Devas* and *Asuras* "correspond respectively to the states that are higher and lower than the human," one might have assumed that there would be *two* serpents in the tale of the Churning of the Sea which correspond, respectively, to the two states of being represented by the *Devas* and *Asuras* — just as there are two serpents represented in the symbolisms of the caduceus and the *amphisbaena* that are, according to Guénon, used in those symbols to represent the 'higher and lower states' and, more specifically, the 'benefic and malefic aspects' of existence. Apparently for Guénon, however, the 'benefic and malefic aspects' of the single serpent *Shesha/Ananta* (*Vasuki*) in the tale are sufficiently represented by the opposition of the *Devas* and *Asuras* that is symbolized by means of their tug-of-war 'team coiling' of the serpent *Vasuki* by means of the axial Mount Meru (Mount Mandara, for Radice). This 'team coiling' by the *Devas* and *Asuras* also symbolizes, however, for Guénon, the 'dual action' or 'polarization' of a single metaphysical force (the 'Principle') that is itself symbolized by the axial Mount Meru (Mount Mandara, for Radice).

Guénon states in *The Symbolism of the Cross* that the serpent *Shesha/Ananta* serves not only as an aid in revealing the 'benefic' and 'malefic' aspects of existence but, in particular, as a means of representing "the indefinitude of universal existence." The expression "the indefinitude of universal existence" is used here by Guénon in a fashion synonymous to his many uses of the expression "the indefinite series of cycles of manifestation." When Guénon argues that the serpent *Shesha/Ananta* symbolizes "the indefinitude of universal existence" in the narrative of the Churning of the Sea, therefore, by his own definition of *samsara* he also argues that the serpent in that narrative symbolizes the flux-like state of "the indefinite series of cycles of manifestation." As a consequence, when Guénon refers to "the indefinitude of universal existence" in the specific case of the Churning of the Sea narrative, I understand him to mean the 'indefinite' flux that exists 'between' any two states, or 'qualities,' of being in the 'multiple states of the being.' This is the case because the serpent *Ananta/ Shesha* in the narrative of the Churning of the Sea literally 'stands between' the 'competing' *Devas* and *Asuras* in the same way that the flux of "the indefinitude of universal existence" 'stands between' dichotomous 'qualities,' such as 'good and evil' or 'hot and cold,' that have an indefinite number of grades of 'opposites' existing 'between' them. More specifically, the two qualities, or 'states,' that Guénon calls 'benefic' and 'malefic,' are 'separated' by the flux of "the indefinitude of universal existence" because there are an indefinite number of grades of beneficence and maleficence 'standing between' the two objective poles of these states/qualities. The relevant 'states,' for Guénon, that we call 'qualities' in the case of the Churning of the Sea narrative that the *Devas* and *Asuras* represent are, therefore, respectively, the 'benefic' and 'malefic' states/qualities of being. As I alluded to earlier, this portion of the narrative reminds one of a 'tug-of-war,' with the 'rope' being the serpent that 'stands between' the two 'teams' of *Devas* and *Asuras*. It is, therefore, *samsara* as "the indefinite series of cycles of manifestation," or equivalently "the indefinitude of universal existence," that 'stands between' the 'benefic' and 'malefic' 'states of being' that are represented by the *Devas* and *Asuras*.

The serpent *Ananta/Shesha* in the 'Churning of the Sea' may also be seen to symbolize that which 'stands between' particular 'states of being' when these states are considered to be 'individual' animate beings. More specifically, *Ananta/Shesha*, as symbolic of the *samsaric* flux, may be considered to be symbolic of that which 'stands between' the particular 'states of being' that are called 'migrations' of 'the being' (*Brahman*) by Guénon, in addition to symbolizing that which 'stands between' those particular 'qualities' such as 'beneficence' and 'maleficence' that Guénon also thinks of as 'states of being.' This is the case because, as Radice says, *Vasuki* (*Ananta/Sesha*) represents that which in the Churning of the Sea narrative 'secures immortality'; and whatever it is that 'secures immortality' makes possible a 'migration' of 'the being' from one 'state of being' to another, specifically, a 'migration' from the state of mortality, in general, to the state of immortality. More concisely put, it is *through* 'migration' that immortality may be 'secured,' but 'migration' itself must be *through* the serpentine *samsaric* flux which 'stands between' the general states of mortality and immortality. In Guénon's interpretation of the Hindu Doctrines there is, as we have seen, a potential in the 'migration' process for an 'individual' being to move 'upward' to 'higher' states of being (the states represented by the *Devas*, according to Guénon) or 'downward' to 'lower' states of being (the states represented by the *Asuras*). What we may call the 'serpent power,' symbolized by *Vasuki/Shesha/Ananta* in the Churning of the Sea narrative, makes 'migration' possible. This 'serpent power' is the 'indefinitude' of the *samsaric* flux that may be 'tapped into' and 'controlled' by 'migrating' souls (*jivatma*) as the means for their achieving 'release' (*moksha*) from *samsara*. Thus an aspect of *samsara*, indefinitude, is employed to achieve release *from samsara*. *Moksha*, however, as 'release' from *samsara*, necessitates passing 'through' *samsara*, "the indefinitude of universal existence," that 'stands between' the 'benefic' and 'malefic' 'states of being' that are represented by the *Devas* and *Asuras*. By means of the 'serpent power,' the *Devas* achieve in the narrative of the Churning of the Sea, if not *moksha*, at least a state of being that is 'closer' to *moksha*.

In Chapter 8 we discussed the role of the serpent/dragon as "the guardian of certain symbols of immortality, the approach to which it forbids."[10] It was observed there, however, that the serpent or dragon only *appears* as a guardian to that 'migrating' being that seeks to

---

10 René Guénon, *The Symbolism of the Cross*, 124.

escape (*moksha*) the *samsaric* "indefinite series of cycles of manifestation." *Moksha*, we argued, was symbolized by the legendary 'dragon's treasure' that is so often depicted and described in traditional art and myth; the serpent/dragon is only a 'guardian' in the sense that it represents that which obstructs the 'hero's' quest of 'release': *samsara*. But *samsara*, we noted, is only an 'obstruction' or 'guardian' to those 'seekers' who have, through their own *karma*, kept themselves from the 'treasure' that they seek, 'identification' or 'realization' of *Brahman* (the Principle). In the narrative of the Churning of the Sea, the serpent *Vasuki/Ananta/Shesha* represents, I suggest, a 'tool' for the seeker of *moksha* or immortality to employ in his quest, for it is *used* by the *Devas* in their hopes of, as Radice puts it, 'securing' immortality and 'restoring' their energy. In this sense, the 'tool' that is *Vasuki/Ananta/Shesha* in the narrative of the Churning of the Sea is like the dragons in the myths of Hercules and Jason insofar as it can also, if used improperly, 'obstruct' the achievement of immortality and the acquirement of renewed energy (possibly *moksha*). And this is exactly what it does for the *Asuras*. To repeat the quotation from Radice: "the Asuras, at Vasuki's head-end, found that they were breathing hot, poisonous breath from his huge, hissing mouth — and this had the effect of weakening them."[11] Perhaps 'Adam and Eve' and Gilgamesh, like the *Asuras*, 'misused' their respective serpentine 'tools,' whereas the *Devas* 'used' theirs properly. The 'serpent power,' so it seems, may be used for better *or* worse.[12] Although it 'obstructed' 'Adam and Eve's' old 'sense of eternity,' it facilitated renewed energy and 'secured' immortality for the *Devas*. Perhaps it is the case that the serpent/dragon more often

---

11   William Radice, *Myths and Legends of India*, 62.

12   In the *Metamorphoses*, Ovid tells that when Perseus beheaded the Gorgon Medusa, "the fleet-winged steed Pegasus and his brother were born then, children of the Gorgon's blood." This narrative combines the elements of 'verticality' (the 'fleet-*winged* steed Pegasus') and 'indefinitude' (the serpentine Gorgon) to show how the 'serpent power' may be 'used' to bring good out of evil. Ovid, *The Metamorphoses of Ovid*, trans. Mary M. Innes (Harmondsworth, Middlesex, England: Penguin Books Ltd., 1955), 115.

appears as a 'guardian' in art and myth rather than as a facilitator because most individuals who seek immortality or *moksha* fail to achieve that which they seek. As the *Katha Upanishad,* one of the paragons of Tradition according to Guénon, says: "sharp like a razor's edge…is the path, difficult to traverse." [*Katha Upanishad* I: 3:14] Because of this, it may be the case that the merely 'indefinite' and 'contrary' nature of what the serpent/dragon symbolizes in Tradition overwhelmingly *appears*, to most seekers, as pure 'guardianship.'

The Serpent, the Mountain, the *Omphalos*, and Sacred Stones

Along with the serpent *Shesha/Ananta/Vasuki*, the 'polar mountain' that is variously named Meru and Mandara also serves the *Devas* in their quest to 'secure' immortality and renew their energy in the *Ramayana* narrative of the 'Churning of the Sea.' Like the 'Tree in the Midst,' the 'polar mountain' is, for Guénon, a common variant of the World Axis that symbolizes the metaphysical Principle in the traditional art and myth of many cultures. Eliade agrees, connecting the Hindu variant of the symbol to the idea of 'polarity' in *Patterns in Comparative Religion* when he states that "in Indian mythology Mount Meru rises up in the centre of the world; above it the Pole Star sends forth its light."[13] Along with "the Meru of the Hindus," Guénon mentions other examples of the "'polar mountain', which, under various names, exists in almost all traditions."[14] Examples include, according to Guénon, "the *Alborj* of the Persians, as well as *Montsalvat* of the Western legend of the Grail; there are also the mountain *Qaf* of the Arabs and the Greek *Olympus*, which in many ways have the same significance."[15] In *Patterns in Comparative Religion*, Eliade also lists *Sumbur* of the Uralo-Altaic peoples, the Iranian *Haraberazaiti*,

---

13 Mircea Eliade, *Patterns in Comparative Religion*, 100.
14 René Guénon, *The King of the World*, 55.
15 René Guénon, *The King of the World*, 55.

and Mounts *Tabor* and *Gerizim* in Palestine as examples of the 'polar mountain,' noting generally that

> [m]ountains are often looked on as the place where sky and earth meet, a "central point" therefore, the point through which the *Axis Mundi* goes, a region impregnated with the sacred, a spot where one can pass from one cosmic zone to another.[16]

Not all 'polar' regions are necessarily mountainous, however, although they all do, according to Guénon, indicate a "region…that, like the Terrestrial Paradise, has become inaccessible to ordinary humanity."[17] The most familiar example of this to Westerners is the Garden of Eden, which according to Genesis 3:24 was guarded by 'cherubim' "and a flaming sword that turned every way to guard the way to the tree of life" after 'Adam and Eve's' expulsion.

The 'polar mountain,' as a mountain, is composed of stone. Because of this, the traditional symbolism of the 'polar mountain' is, for Guénon as well as for Eliade, just a more majestic example of the traditional symbolism of 'sacred stones' and carries essentially the same meaning, for traditional peoples, as various other kinds of stones. Eliade states in *Patterns in Comparative Religion*, however, that in traditional or 'archaic' societies, "stones are venerated precisely because they are not simply stones but hierophanies,"[18] manifestations of the 'sacred' that take place "in some historical situation."[19] For Eliade, insofar as stones, or mountains, symbolize "the place where sky and earth meet," they are "manifestations of the sacred." As we argued in Chapter 3, however, Eliade's idea of 'hierophany' is equivalent to Guénon's idea of the 'manifestation' of the 'Principle,' since both the Principle and the 'sacred' are metaphysical realities that reveal themselves in the physical realm of 'nature' and exercise there an actualizing,

---

16 Mircea Eliade, *Patterns in Comparative Religion*, 99–100.
17 René Guénon, *The King of the World*, 55.
18 Mircea Eliade, *Patterns in Comparative Religion*, 13.
19 Mircea Eliade, *Patterns in Comparative Religion*, 2.

defining, and formative, influence. The 'polar mountain,' for Guénon, is but another variant of the World Axis which is itself symbolic of the Principle, but it is a variant that falls under the symbolism of *stones* specifically. There are, therefore, various *kinds* of 'sacred stones,' and their variations, according to Guénon, that are described and depicted in Tradition that serve the purpose of symbolizing the hierophany of the World Axis or 'center' of the world.

In *The King of the World*, Guénon argues that "one of the most remarkable…symbols in ancient traditions that represent[s] the 'Center of the World'" is the *Omphalos*,[20] and that "the physical representation of the *Omphalos* was generally a sacred stone."[21] Guénon contends that

> [t]he symbol of the *Omphalos* could be situated in a place that was simply the center of a determined region, the spiritual center of course, rather than the geographical one, although in certain cases the two might coincide; in cases where the latter held true, this was because, for the people who inhabited the region in question, the place concerned was truly the visible image of the 'Center of the World', just as the tradition proper to that people was only an adaptation of the primordial tradition, expressed in a form that best fitted its mentality and its conditions of existence.[22]

According to Joseph Fontenrose in *Python*, *Omphalos* means 'navel' in Greek and is

> a word that was often associated with the earth: [the Greek city of] Delphi, claiming to be earth's navel — i.e., central point — symbolized its claim by means of a stone *omphalos*, and other places that made the same claim also had their *omphaloi*.[23]

---

20 René Guénon, *The King of the World*, 56.
21 René Guénon, *The King of the World*, 57.
22 René Guénon, *The King of the World*, 57.
23 Joseph Fontenrose, *Python: A Study of Delphic Myth and Its Origins*, 109.

Guénon supplements Fontenrose's claims in *The King of the World* that *Omphalos* "in Greek…means 'umbilicus' or 'navel', but [adds that] it also designates in a general way all that is central, and in particular the hub of a wheel."[24] This latter association is important, according to Guénon, "because the wheel is everywhere a symbol of the world accomplishing its rotation around a fixed point."[25] It is also, however, reminiscent of the 'wheel-like' 'convolutions of the serpent' about the 'Tree in the Midst' that Guénon writes of, and the "indefinite series of cycles of manifestation" whose 'center' is the World Axis. Other similar symbolisms include the representations of the *samsaric* "indefinite series of cycles of manifestation" by means of the 'wheel of *dharma*' and the 'chakras' ('wheels') of *Kundalini yoga*.

Like the 'sacred', or 'polar', mountain and the Tree of Life in Genesis 3, the *Omphalos* symbolizes for Guénon the World Axis or 'Center of the World.' As we argued previously, however, the World Axis, as the *metaphysical* 'center' of the world, is also the source of Life considered in a 'larger' meta-physical, and thus meta-organic, sense. The case that we specifically elaborated on was the Edenic Tree of Life as World Axis. In this connection, it should be observed that both the navel and the umbilicus that, according to Guénon, are symbolized by the stone *Omphalos*, are 'connectors' to life, since the umbilical cord is a means of sustaining life from mother to child and the last physical connection between them once the child has been born. Similarly, the World Axis that is sometimes symbolized by the *Omphalos* represents that 'place' of passage by means of which the being is capable of 'migrating' from one 'state of being' to another. Marija Gimbutas makes a similar, although wholly organic, interpretation of the symbolism of the *Omphalos*, as well as the symbolism of ancient Western European megaliths, when she argues in *The Language of the Goddess* that

---

24 René Guénon, *The King of the World*, 56.
25 René Guénon, *The King of the World*, 56.

> [d]uring the Neolithic [Age], graves and temples assumed the shape of the egg, vagina, and uterus of the Goddess or of her complete body. The megalithic passage graves of western Europe quite probably symbolized the vagina (passage) and pregnant belly (*tholos*, round chamber) of the Goddess. The shape of a grave is an analogue of the natural hill with an omphalos (stone symbolizing the navel) on top, a universal symbol of the Earth Mother's pregnant belly with umbilical cord, as recorded in European folk beliefs.[26]

Reading between the lines, Gimbutas compares here the forms of 'passage' taken: 1) from pre-birth to life by individual living beings (a pregnant belly), 2) from death to whatever lies beyond death by individual deceased beings (the grave), and 3) from pre-nature to nature by life in general by means of "the Earth Mother's pregnant belly" that is represented, according to Gimbutas, by means of land in the form of a natural hill forming the *tholos* or 'round chamber' mentioned. We will disagree with most of the interpretation that Gimbutas provides here in the next chapter.

The *Beith-El*, the *Omphalos*, and the Oracle of Delphi

One of the most conspicuous textual examples of traditional stone symbolism is the biblical narrative of the Hebrew patriarch Jacob, son of Isaac, and the 'ladder' between Heaven and Earth that he dreams of while journeying from Beersheba to Haran:

> Jacob left Beersheba and went toward Haran. And he came to a certain place and stayed there that night, because the sun had set. Taking one of the stones of the place, he put it under his head and lay down in that place to sleep. And he dreamed, and behold, there was a ladder set up on the earth, and the top of it reached to heaven. And behold, the angels of God were ascending and descending on it! And behold, the LORD stood above it and said, "I am the LORD, the God of Abraham your father and the God of Isaac. The land on which you lie I will give to you and to your offspring.

---

26 Marija Gimbutas, *The Language of the Goddess*, xxiii.

Your offspring shall be like the dust of the earth, and you shall spread abroad to the west and to the east and to the north and to the south, and in you and your offspring shall all the families of the earth be blessed. Behold, I am with you and will keep you wherever you go, and will bring you back to this land. For I will not leave you until I have done what I have promised you." Then Jacob awoke from his sleep and said, "Surely the LORD is in this place, and I did not know it." And he was afraid and said, "How awesome is this place! This is none other than the house of God, and this is the gate of heaven."

So early in the morning Jacob took the stone that he had put under his head and set it up for a pillar and poured oil on the top of it. He called the name of that place Bethel, but the name of the city was Luz at the first. Then Jacob made a vow, saying, "If God will be with me and will keep me in this way that I go, and will give me bread to eat and clothing to wear, so that I come again to my father's house in peace, then the LORD shall be my God, and this stone, which I have set up for a pillar, shall be God's house. And of all that you give me I will give a full tenth to you. [Genesis 28:10–22, ESV]

The biblical tale of 'Jacob's Ladder' overflows with axial imagery. There is mention of stones, a pillar, and a ladder, all traditional axial symbols according to Guénon and Eliade. It is a stone that Jacob sleeps on when he has his revelatory dream and a stone (the same stone, in fact) that Jacob sets up as a pillar to commemorate the location of his 'divine' experience at that location, which he names 'Bethel,' meaning 'House of God.' In the time between his sleeping on the stone and later setting it up as a commemorative pillar, however, Jacob dreams of a 'ladder' that connects two very different realms of existence: Heaven and Earth. "Ascending and descending on" this 'ladder,' in Jacob's dream, are 'angels of God' who use it to travel from one of the two mentioned realms to the other, and back again.

In *Symbols of Sacred Science*, Guénon argues, in accordance with the transcultural metaphysics of Tradition, that "Jacob's ladder extends from the heavens to the earth, and therefore throughout all degrees of universal existence."[27] He adds that, like the *Devas* in the narrative of the 'Churning of the Sea' in the *Ramayana*, the angels in Genesis 28, like all angels, are "representations of higher states."[28] In *The King of the World*, however, Guénon skips over 'Jacob's ladder' and draws attention to the symbolism of the stone that Jacob slept on when he had his dream of the 'ladder' and the pillar that this stone later becomes, connecting stone and pillar both to the symbolism of the *Omphalos*. Guénon contends there that

> [t]he physical representation of the *Omphalos* was generally a sacred stone, commonly called a 'baetyl', a word that seems to be none other than the Hebrew *Beith-El*, or 'House of God', the name given by Jacob to the place where the Lord appeared to him in a dream.[29]

Guénon argues that "the name *Beith-El* applies not only to the place but to the stone itself," quoting Genesis 28:22: "And this stone, which I have set up as a pillar, shall be God's house."[30] The stone that Jacob slept on, therefore, when he dreamed of angels 'ascending and descending' a 'ladder,' symbolizes, according to Guénon, the 'House of God,' which we may presume corresponds to the metaphysical 'center' of the world in traditional thinking since God is Spirit (metaphysical) from that perspective. Eliade substantially agrees with this assessment in *Patterns in Comparative Religion* in stating that "the stone on which Jacob lay sleeping was a *bethel* and was placed 'in the middle of the world', for it is there that the union of all the cosmic regions takes place."[31] This being the case, what is called 'Jacob's Ladder' is, traditionally speaking, a hierophany of the World Axis by means of which the physical and metaphysical realms, Earth and Heaven in the Bible, meet and 'communicate' in a broad sense. The stone that Jacob

---

27 René Guénon, *Symbols of Sacred Science*, 52.
28 René Guénon, *Symbols of Sacred Science*, 53.
29 René Guénon, *The King of the World*, 57.
30 René Guénon, *The King of the World*, 58.
31 Mircea Eliade, *Patterns in Comparative Religion*, 107.

sleeps on when he has his dream of the 'ladder,' insofar as this 'baetyl' is an axial symbol, only doubly confirms the intent of the narrative of Genesis 28 to communicate broadly traditional information about the nature of the World Axis and metaphysical reality in general. The 'ascending and descending' of the angels observed by Jacob would seem to also confirm Guénon's more general contention that there exists, 'at' the World Axis, a means by which beings can 'migrate' among 'the multiple states of the being.'

There is no explicit serpent or dragon imagery in the narrative of 'Jacob's Ladder.' Concerning the *Omphalos* stone, however, which Guénon argues is a sacred stone of the same order as the *Beith-el* slept upon by Jacob, Guénon observes in *The King of the World* that

> [s]ometimes, and notably on certain Greek *Omphaloi*, the stone was encircled by a serpent; this serpent is also found coiled at the base or at the summit of certain Chaldean boundary-stones, which should be considered true 'baetyls'. Moreover, the symbol of the stone...is in a general way closely connected with the symbol of the serpent, and the same holds true for the symbol of the egg, notably among the Celts and the Egyptians.[32]

In this quotation, Guénon proposes a broadly traditional symbolic link between serpent, stone ('baetyl,' specifically), and egg symbolism in ancient cultures, since he refers not only to the use of such symbols by the geographically close Babylonians ('Chaldeans') and Egyptians, but to their use by the widespread, and much further western living, Celts as well. On the *Omphalos* stone, in particular, Guénon notes in *The King of the World* that "the *Omphalos* that is best known is the one in the temple at Delphi, which was quite certainly the spiritual center of all ancient Greece."[33] In *Symbols of Sacred Science*, he argues that

---

32 René Guénon, *The King of the World*, 59.
33 René Guénon, *The King of the World*, 57. Guénon states on the same page that "[t]here were other spiritual centers in Greece, but they were more particularly reserved for initiation into the Mysteries, such centers as Eleusis and Samothrace, whereas Delphi had a social role concerned directly with the entirety of the Hellenic collectivity."

the serpent *Python* has a particular connection with Delphi, called in ancient times *Pytho*, sanctuary of the Hyperborean Apollo; whence the designation *Pythoness* [or *Pythia*], and also the name Pythagoras itself, which in reality is a name of *Apollo*, 'he who guides the *Pythoness*' that is, the inspirer of her oracles.[34] (See fig. 13.1.)

Guénon elaborates on the interchangeability of 'egg' and *Omphalos* (stone, more generally) when he remarks in the same book that "the *Omphalos* could also be represented in the form of...an ovoid...the ovoid form relating directly to...the 'World Egg.'"[35] As we have already seen, the 'World Egg,' as Squier and Guénon both remark upon, is commonly represented with the serpent or dragon in Tradition as what I have termed a 'compound symbol.' The connection between stone and egg that Guénon affirms in *The King of the World*, therefore, implies that there is a symbolic link between the stone, the *Omphalos* specifically, and the serpent, if the stone may be substituted as a symbolic equivalent to the egg in traditional figurations of the serpent or dragon with the 'World Egg.'

Fig. 13.1. *The Omphalos of Delphi*, Buffie Johnson[36]

---

34 René Guénon, *Symbols of Sacred Science*, 174.
35 René Guénon, *The King of the World*, 59.
36 Buffie Johnson, *Lady of the Beasts*, 149.

In *Patterns in Comparative Religion*, Eliade confirms the traditional symbolic link between stones and serpents when he discusses the so-called 'snake-stone' and contends that "in many places, precious stones were thought to be fallen from the heads of snakes or dragons."[37] Eliade adds that

> [t]he belief that precious stones come from snakes' spittle covered a very wide area, from China to England. In India it was thought that the *nagas* carried certain magic, shining stones in their throats and heads. When Pliny declared that *dracontia* or *dracontites* was a stone formed of the brains (*cerebra*) of dragons, he was only giving a rationalization of beliefs that originated in the East. The rationalizing process is marked even more clearly with Philostratus[38] who says that the eye of some dragons is a stone of "blinding brilliance", endowed with magic powers; he adds that sorcerers, when they had adored reptiles, cut off their heads and take out precious stones.[39]

Eliade relatedly remarks in *Patterns in Comparative Religion* that the first-century-BCE Roman scholar "Varro mentions a tradition that the *omphalos* was the tomb of the sacred serpent of Delphi, Python: *quem Pythonis aiunt tumulum.*"[40] And, of course, to further buttress the argument for the transregional presence of the 'compound symbolism' of stone/egg/'center of the world'/dragon/serpent, we need only mention the numerous medieval European tales of dragons hoarding both gold and precious stones (jewels or gems). The "dragon's treasure" of the early medieval Anglo-Saxon poem *Beowulf* that includes "a gem-studded goblet" — a goblet studded with precious *stones* — is one

---

37 Mircea Eliade, *Patterns in Comparative Religion*, 441.
38 Philostratus was a Greek sophist of the Roman imperial period (c. 170/172 — 247/250 CE).
39 Mircea Eliade, *Patterns in Comparative Religion*, 442.
40 Varro, *De Lingua Latina*, vii, 17. Marcus Terentius Varo (116–27 BCE). Mircea Eliade, *Patterns in Comparative Religion*, 231–32.

example.[41] A second example is the Norse tale of the dragon Fafnir who "dwelt in a cave atop a pile of fabulous treasure" that assuredly included precious *stones* and was, furthermore, inside of a *mountain*.[42]

Serpents, 'Angels,' and 'Polarized Currents'

The serpent, or that which it represents in Tradition, makes its presence known in the Genesis 28 narrative of 'Jacob's Ladder' even though there is no explicit serpent imagery there. For the symbolic elements of the *Axis Mundi* that are present in Genesis 28 — 1) baetyl, or 'sacred stone,' 2) 'ascending and descending' angels, and 3) *Beith-el*, or 'House of God' — *combine* to reveal the traditional belief, expressed so thoroughly by Guénon in his works, that 'migration' of the being through "the indefinite series of cycles of manifestation" and into the various 'multiple states of the being' is possible at the World Axis, or 'center' of the world.

There is a long tradition of associating, and even identifying, serpents/dragons with the beings that are called 'angels' in the Abrahamic religions of Judaism, Christianity, and Islam. In Isaiah 6:1-2, the prophet has a vision in which he claims that

> I saw the Lord sitting upon a throne, high and lifted up; and the train of his robe filled the temple. Above him stood the seraphim. Each had six wings: with two he covered his face, and with two he covered his feet, and with two he flew. [ESV]

The 'seraphim' referred to in Isaiah have been traditionally identified as 'angels' for hundreds of years, although there has been disagreement on what exactly an 'angel' *is*. In *Serpent Symbolism in the Old Testament*, scholar Karen Randolph Joines contends that

---

41 Seamus Heaney, trans., *Beowulf: A New Verse Translation* (New York London: W. W. Norton & Company, 2000), 151, ix of the *Introduction* and verses 2217-2221.

42 Doug Niles, *Dragons: The Myths, Legends, & Lore* (Avon, Massachusetts: Adams Media, a division of F+W Media, Inc., 2013), 117.

"the Seraphim [in Isaiah] are probably winged serpents drawn from Egyptian royal and sacral symbolism. In Egypt winged serpents represent sacral sovereignty whether of the pharaoh or of the gods."[43] (See fig. 13.2.)

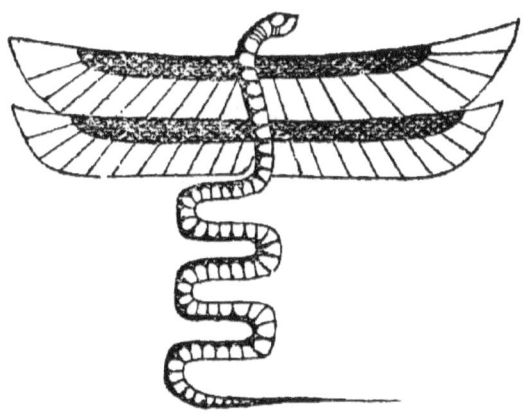

Fig. 13.2. *Four-winged serpent, Chnuphis or Bait*[44]

Joines observes that "Isaiah twice speaks of a *saraph me opheph*, a 'flying serpent' (14:29; 30:6)," and "Isaiah clearly conceives of a *saraph* as capable of flying, therefore of having wings. So it does in the inaugural vision. *A saraph is a serpent*, and for Isaiah it may have wings."[45] Joines later points out that

> [u]nless Isaiah uses [the term] *saraph* indiscriminately to designate different creatures, thereby departing from the sole Old Testament meaning of the word, the Seraphim are winged serpents. That Isaiah would do so seems improbable. Numbers 21:4–9 is from the Elohistic source of the Pentateuch usually dated between 850–750 B.C. Deuteronomy is generally agreed to have been discovered about 622 B.C. The dates of Isaiah are about

---

43 Karen Randolph Joines, *Serpent Symbolism in the Old Testament: A Linguistic, Archaeological, and Literary Study* (Haddonfield, New Jersey: Haddonfield House, 1974), 43.

44 William Ricketts Cooper, *The Serpent Myths of Ancient Egypt*, 12.

45 Karen Randolph Joines, *Serpent Symbolism in the Old Testament*, 45.

equidistant from these dates. Due to the probability that Deuteronomy was redacted long before its discovery, perhaps no more than fifty years separate the earliest and the latest [use] of *saraph* in the Old Testament. Fifty years is a short period of time for a word completely to change meanings.[46]

We have already seen the winged serpent represented in certain depictions of the Egyptian and other *uraei*, as well as in traditional alchemical representations of the *anima mundi*. The 'compound symbol' of 'serpent-with-wings' is rather more pervasive than many other figurations of the serpent symbol in Tradition. It shouldn't be surprising, therefore, to see manifestations of it in the books of the Bible. In *Serpent Symbolism in the Old Testament*, however, Joines argues that, in attempting to determine the identity and meaning of the so-called 'standing Seraphim' in Isaiah, there is "almost no secondary aid…forthcoming in their identification and significance,"[47] although Joines then goes on to mention several interpretations anyway, such as T. K. Cheyne's idea that they represent "serpent-like lightning" and Franz Delitzsch's contention that they are "winged dragons."[48] In the Christian tradition, specifically, the beings that are called 'Seraphim' in Isaiah are repeatedly identified as 'angels,' beings that are metaphysically, though not morally, 'higher' than humans because of their essentially meta-corporeal nature. In the last section of the first part of the *Summa Theologica*, the "Treatise on the Divine Government," the thirteenth-century medieval theologian and philosopher Thomas Aquinas discusses the question "Of the Angelic Degrees of Hierarchies and Orders." There Aquinas relates, based upon the verse from Isaiah (6:3) which states that "[t]he Seraphim cried to one another," that

---

46 Karen Randolph Joines, *Serpent Symbolism in the Old Testament*, 45.
47 Karen Randolph Joines, *Serpent Symbolism in the Old Testament*, 42.
48 Karen Randolph Joines, *Serpent Symbolism in the Old Testament*, 42–43, quoting T. K. Cheyne, *The Prophecies of Isaiah* (London: Kegan Paul, Trench, and Company, 1884), I, 39, and Franz Delitzsch, *The Prophecies of Isaiah* (Edinburgh: T. and T. Clarke, 1889), I, 180.

"there are many angels in the one order of the Seraphim."[49] Aquinas notes shortly afterward, however, that "our knowledge of the angels is imperfect, as Dionysius says," a reference to the putative fifth-century theologian and philosopher Dionysius the Areopagite and his extensive work on angels called the *Celestial Hierarchy*.[50]

Joines points to the presence of a possibly more pervasive angel-serpent connection in the Bible that goes beyond Isaiah when she refers to the interpretation of the 'Seraphim' as serpents in the apocryphal work of *Enoch*. Joines relates that

> [a]pparently, the author of I Enoch felt that the Seraphim were serpents. I Enoch 20:7 mentions the angel Gabriel 'who is over Paradise and the serpents…and the Cherubim.' In I Enoch 71:7 the Cherubim and the Seraphim appear together as guardians of the throne of the Lord of Spirits, and in I Enoch 61:10 they appear together among the host of God. It appears highly probable that in I Enoch 20:7 'serpents' has replaced 'Seraphim.'[51]

In R. H. Charles's translation of Enoch, the passage in that work referred to by Joines describes Gabriel as "presiding over" 'Ikisat' (serpents), rather than over other supposed 'angels' like himself.[52] According to Joines, "Charles says that these serpents are winged and identical with the Seraphim in Isaiah."[53] Since Gabriel is himself described as 'winged' in biblical tradition, and is in league with

---

49 St. Thomas Aquinas, *Summa Theologica*, Volume One, trans. Fathers of the English Dominican Province (New York, New York: Benziger Bros., 1948), Pt. 1, Q. 108, Art. 3.

50 St. Thomas Aquinas, *Summa Theologica*, Volume One, Pt. 1, Q. 108, Art. 3, referring to the sixth chapter of Dionysius the Areopagite, *Works* vol. 2 (1899). "The Celestial Hierarchy," or *De Coelesti Hierarchia*, has been dated to c. the fifth century CE, thus eight hundred years prior to Aquinas's composing the *Summa Theologica*. In *A Dictionary of Angels*, Gustav Davidson defines 'Seraphim' as "the highest order of angels in the pseudo-Dionysian hierarchic scheme and generally also in Jewish lore." Gustav Davidson, *A Dictionary of Angels, Including the Fallen Angels* (New York: The Free Press, 1967), 267.

51 Karen Randolph Joines, *Serpent Symbolism in the Old Testament*, 44.

52 R. H. Charles, *The Book of Enoch* (Oxford: The Clarendon Press, 1898), 92.

53 Karen Randolph Joines, *Serpent Symbolism in the Old Testament*, 55.

these other serpent-beings that he 'presides over,' perhaps he also is a 'serpent' of some sort himself.

David Keck argues in *Angels & Angelology in the Middle Ages* that the Hebrew and Greek equivalents of 'angel' — *mal'akh* and *aggelos*, respectively — "mean literally messenger."[54] This is, of course, reasonable to believe, since the beings that these terms refer to serve as 'messengers of God' throughout the Bible, albeit in different ways. We spoke in Chapter 11 of the symbol known as the caduceus and its connection with the messenger *par excellence* of the ancient Greek and Roman gods, Hermes/Mercury. Like the 'angels' of the Abrahamic tradition that are described in Judaism, Christianity, and Islam as well, the caduceus is, in many of its representations, 'winged.' This actually seems to be a common feature of traditional 'messengers' in general as they are depicted and described in traditional art and myth, such as Hermes/Mercury and the 'angels' of the God of Abraham, whether they be Jewish, Christian, or Muslim. In the story of 'Jacob's Ladder' in Genesis 28, the activity that the 'angels' are engaged in, 'ascending and descending' Jacob's 'ladder' to and from Earth and Heaven (see fig. 13.3), would seem to indicate that these beings are 'conveying' *something* between these two 'places' or 'states.' What else, after all, do messengers do? The angels in the narrative of 'Jacob's Ladder' are moving from Heaven to Earth and back again, from the realm of the divine to the realm of mortals, and back again.

Although Guénon does not explicitly mention it in *The King of the World*, I infer that 'Jacob's Ladder' is another traditional figuration of the 'polarized' forces, or 'currents,' that Guénon discusses in some of his works — the 'malefic' and 'benefic' influences that surround the World Axis or 'center' of the world. In *The Great Triad*, Guénon argues that

> these same two forces are also depicted in different though fundamentally equivalent ways in other traditional symbols, particularly by two helicoidal

---

54 David Keck, *Angels & Angelology in the Middle Ages* (New York and Oxford: Oxford University Press, 1998), 28.

lines coiling in opposite directions around a vertical axis, as is seen for instance in…the two serpents of the caduceus.[55]

Fig. 13.3. *Jacob's Dream*, Gustave Doré[56]

---

55   René Guénon, *The Great Triad*, 33.
56   The Holy Bible: King James Version, Barnes & Noble edition, 50.

As we have seen, Guénon discusses "the dual action of a single force" and the "two forces produced by its polarization" in his discussion of those "symbols of 'duality' in unity" that we considered in Chapter 10, the Androgyne, the *yin-yang*, the double spiral, and the 'World Egg.'[57] The symbolism of 'Jacob's Ladder' in Genesis 28 is, I argue, symbolically equivalent to these "symbols of 'duality' in unity" from a broadly traditional perspective. In consequence, whatever divine power it is that the 'angels' referred to in Genesis 28 are bringing down to Earth, this power is, when translated into Guénon's understanding of Tradition, the 'descending' current of the metaphysical 'single force' that has different names in the different cultural manifestations of Tradition. It is, more specifically, the '*descending*' 'helicoidal line' that Guénon refers to in the above quotation. As we have said before, the Hebrew 'God' Yahweh is but one among many cultural variants of the 'single force' called the 'Principle' by Guénon that is termed *Brahman* in South Asia and *Tao* in East Asia.

In the narrative of 'Jacob's Ladder,' traditional serpent symbolism is replaced by 'angel' symbolism. I do not propose to show here how, or why, this 'replacement' occurred, but I do argue that, since 'angels' are described in both the Old Testament and the New Testament as 'messengers' of God, they are the *biblical* (Abrahamic) version of the metaphysical 'currents' that 'descend' from, and 'ascend' to, the metaphysical 'Principle' that is given different names in different manifestations of Tradition. Like the 'ascending' and 'descending' currents that, according to Guénon, connect the various 'multiple states of the being' in traditional thought, 'angels' serve in the Abrahamic tradition as the means of 'messaging' or 'mediating' the metaphysical Principle's power and influence throughout all of the 'multiple states of the being' and throughout all of "the indefinite series of cycles of manifestation." This, as we have seen, is what is symbolized, according to Guénon, by the two *serpents* of the caduceus insofar as they too represent, as

---

57 René Guénon, *The Great Triad*, 32.

Guénon says, two "helicoidal lines coiling in opposite directions around a vertical axis." In the case of 'Jacob's Ladder,' however, 'angels' replace the, I believe, older symbolism of serpents in representing the two 'helicoidal lines,' and they convey God's 'guidance' and 'commands' between only two 'states of being,' Heaven and Earth, rather than among 'the multiple states of the being.'

Supposing an identity between serpents and 'angels' in the Bible, and specifically in the narrative of 'Jacob's Ladder,' is not an interpretive stretch, both for the reasons already adduced but also because the serpent/dragon is employed in both Jewish and Christian tradition to symbolize so-called 'fallen angels.' This is most prevalent in the Book of Revelation. In Revelation 20:2, Satan, the 'adversary' of God who is interpreted in Christian tradition as the 'fallen angel' Lucifer, is described as "the dragon, that ancient serpent, who is the devil." [ESV] Figure 13.4 is the nineteenth-century French artist Gustave Doré's depiction of the Apostle John's vision described in Revelation 12:1–3:

> And there appeared a great wonder in heaven; a woman clothed with the sun, and the moon under her feet, and upon her head a crown of twelve stars:
>
> And she being with child cried, travailing in birth, and pained to be delivered.
>
> And there appeared another wonder in heaven; and behold a great red dragon, having seven heads and ten horns, and seven crowns upon his heads. [KJV][58]

---

58 The specific placement of moon and sun in this symbolism are of great importance in understanding the overall esoteric meaning of Revelation, but we shall not address this topic here. See also Revelation 12:13–17 and 16:13.

Fig. 13.4. *The Crowned Virgin: A Vision of John*, Gustave Doré[59]

As Gustav Davidson observes in *A Dictionary of Angels, Including the Fallen Angels*, however, "Lucifer ('light giver') [was] erroneously equated with the fallen angel (Satan) due to a misreading of Isaiah 14:12: 'How art thou fallen from heaven, O Lucifer, son of the morning'....[and] the name Lucifer was applied to Satan by St. Jerome and other Church Fathers."[60] In Jewish tradition, Lucifer is the "light

---

59 The Holy Bible: King James Version, Barnes & Noble edition, 1331.

60 Gustav Davidson, *A Dictionary of Angels, Including the Fallen Angels*, 176. The ESV translation of Isaiah 14:12 is: "How you are fallen from heaven, O Day Star,

giver," or "Shining One" in Isaiah 14:12, a being considered favored by God and possessed of 'higher' knowledge, as were the other 'angels' to various degrees according to the Book of Enoch.

Satan himself, however, whether identified with Lucifer or not, is considered as both a 'dragon' and a leader of 'angels' in the 'war of angels' that is described in Revelation 12:7-9:

> Now a war arose in heaven, Michael and his angels fighting against the dragon. And the dragon and his angels fought back, but he was defeated, and there was no longer any place for them in heaven. And the great dragon was thrown down, that ancient serpent, who is called the devil and Satan, the deceiver of the whole world — he was thrown down to the earth, and his angels were thrown down with him. [ESV]

If we may presume that a certain level of symmetry holds in this passage, it may be argued that, since Michael is the leader of the 'good' angels and is himself an 'angel,' then Satan ('the dragon'), as leader of the 'fallen angels,' is also an 'angel.' But then Satan is a 'dragon' as well. Perhaps we may conclude from this 'double identity' of Satan in Revelation as both 'angel' *and* 'dragon' that the ascription of 'dragon' to Satan, in this context, implies that Satan should be thought of by the reader of Revelation as a 'serpent *among* serpents.' From the perspective of Guénon's understanding of traditional metaphysics, this implies that Satan is to be considered, according to Revelation, as a stronger than usual 'malefic' current in the universal process of the manifestation of "the indefinite series of cycles of manifestation." The reference in the same passage of Revelation to the two 'states' of Heaven and Earth should also be noted in the general context of the traditional idea of 'descending' and 'ascending' currents that Guénon writes of. The idea of going (being 'thrown,' in this case) 'down' is similarly relevant and occurs in Revelation 20:1-2, as well as Revelation 12, as follows:

---

son of Dawn!"

> Then I saw an angel coming *down* from heaven, holding in his hand the key to the bottomless pit and a great chain. And he seized the dragon, that ancient serpent, who is the devil and Satan, and bound him for a thousand years. [ESV, my emphasis]

The substance of Guénon's remark in *The Great Triad* that the two forces, or 'currents,' that result from the 'polarization' of a 'single force' "are also depicted in different though fundamentally equivalent ways in other traditional symbols" can be readily seen in Revelation based upon the passages from that text that I have provided. Although there is no explicit stone symbolism associated with the 'dragon' of Revelation, as there is with the 'angels' of Genesis 28 and the narrative of 'Jacob's Ladder,' it may be that the combination of the elements in Revelation 20:1–2 of a 'bottomless pit,' a 'great chain,' and the binding of Satan for a very long period of time, 'a thousand years,' are, together, meant to convey the idea of God's permanence and immutability which are also symbolized by the stone, mountain, and other traditional symbolic figurations of the 'World Axis.'

Sacred Stones Considered Transculturally

In *The King of the World*, Guénon describes the stone that Jacob slept on in Genesis 28 as a 'baetyl,' a word that Guénon argues is traditionally used to refer to 'sacred stones.' According to Guénon, the baetyl that Jacob slept on "seems to be none other than the Hebrew *Beith-el*, or 'House of God', the name given by Jacob to the place where the Lord appeared to him in a dream."[61] As Genesis 28:22 states, "And this stone, which I have set up as a pillar, shall be God's house." [ESV] Guénon argues, therefore, as noted previously, that "the name *Beith-El* applies not only to the place [where Jacob had his dream] but to the stone [that he slept on] itself."[62] For Guénon, therefore, the 'baetyl,' or 'sacred stone,' is, or symbolizes, the *Beith-el* or 'House of God.' In

---

61 René Guénon, *The King of the World*, 57.
62 René Guénon, *The King of the World*, 58.

Symbols of Sacred Science, however, as we have already noted in part, Guénon states,

> The 'baetyl' properly speaking represents the *Omphalos*, and as such is a symbol of the 'Center of the World,' which quite naturally is identified with the 'Divine abode.' This stone could take diverse forms, notably that of a pillar....In all cases, the 'baetyl' was a 'prophetic stone', a 'stone that speaks', that is, a stone that gave out oracles, or near which oracles were given, thanks to the 'spiritual influences' of which it was the support; and the example of the *Omphalos* of Delphi is very characteristic in this regard.[63]

As a place of oracles, 'spiritual influences,' as well as being a 'stone that speaks,' we may conjecture that Jacob's 'baetyl,' the *Beith-el*, was also a place of visions or penetrating dreams. Dreams have traditionally, in many cultures, been believed to be the source of prophetic knowledge. After his 'dream' of the 'ladder,' Jacob has a vision of God, in which God tells him of his *future* increase. Jacob experiences, or is given, a prophecy, in other words. In Genesis 32:24–31, we find Jacob 'wrestling' with a man who is identified in Jewish and Christian tradition as an 'angel,' and saying afterwards that "I have seen God face to face."[64] Again, there is some form of 'mediation' or 'messaging' between Jacob in his earthly 'state' of existence and God (the Spiritual or metaphysical reality) and it is called 'angel.' It should be noted that Jacob is unusually interactive with the 'messengers' of God that are termed 'angels' in Judaism and Christianity, in comparison to most other biblical characters. Translating this into the terms of Guénon's interpretation of Tradition, we may say that Jacob is, therefore, unusually interactive with the 'currents,' or 'malefic' and 'benefic,' influences that surround the 'World Axis.'

---

63   René Guénon, *Symbols of Sacred Science*, 168.

64   The Holy Bible: King James Version, Barnes & Noble edition 32:30. In the Douay-Rheims Version of the Bible, a note to Genesis 32:24 states that "[a] *man*, etc. This was an angel in human shape....He is called *God*, ver. 28 and 30, because he represented the person of the Son of God." The Holy Bible: Douay-Rheims Version. Charlotte, North Carolina: Saint Benedict Press, 2009.

If we look at the narrative of the patriarch Jacob through the lens of Greek mythology, specifically through the lens of the tale of Apollo and the Delphic dragon *Python*, several broadly traditional motifs may be recognized. In the Greek myth, there is the Delphic *Omphalos* stone; in the Hebrew narrative, there is the *Beith-el* ('baetyl') stone. In the Greek myth, there is the dragon/serpent *Python*; in the Hebrew narrative, there are beings called 'angels' that may be derived from, or equivalent to, based upon Joines's arguments, the serpentine 'Seraphim' of Isaiah. In the Greek myth, the action takes place at the location of a stone that is part of an 'oracular shrine,' according to Fontenrose[65]; in the Hebrew narrative, as Guénon points out, the *Beith-el* ('baetyl') stone that Jacob sleeps on when he has his dream of the 'ladder' to Heaven is "a 'prophetic stone', a 'stone that speaks',...a stone that gave out oracles."[66] In the Hebrew narrative, the patriarch Jacob has a potent dream and is given a prophecy by the Hebrew God Yahweh; in Greek tradition, the priestesses known as *Pythoness* that are oracles at the Delphic temple are subject to influences emanating from the area of the temple that cause them to have visions by which they give prophetic utterances.[67] Like Delphi, *Beith-el* — the place of the 'stone' ('baetyl') — is a place of both visions and prophecy, or 'oracles.' It is, according to Guénon, a place of divine 'currents' and 'benefic' and 'malefic' 'influences' that 'descend' from, and 'ascend' to, the metaphysical 'Principle' that is symbolized by various kinds of axial imagery in traditional cultures. In Genesis 28, the *Beith-el* stone, I argue, symbolizes the Hebrew God Yahweh because it symbolizes the World Axis that is sometimes represented by sacred

---

65 Joseph Fontenrose, *Python: A Study of Delphic Myth and Its Origins*, 13.
66 René Guénon, *Symbols of Sacred Science*, 168.
67 The priestess at Delphi was named 'Pythoness' or 'Pythia' after the serpent *Python* that was, according to Greek legend, killed by Apollo. Apollo himself likewise came to be known as 'Pythagoras' because it was "'he who guides the *Pythoness*', that is, the inspirer of her oracles." René Guénon, *Symbols of Sacred Science*, 174.

stones in Tradition. At the Greek oracle of Delphi, it is the oracular *Omphalos* stone that symbolizes the World Axis, and, thus, the metaphysical source that influences, for the ancient Greeks, the visions of the *Pythoness*. Both are 'centers' of the world, traditionally speaking, and, in Eliade's terms, 'hierophanies.' In the narrative of the *Beith-el* stone and 'ladder' of Genesis 28, as well as in the myth of the Delphic dragon and its defeat near the *Omphalos* stone by Apollo, however, it is specifically *serpent* imagery, although obscured in the first case as I have noted, that is traditionally used to symbolize the 'currents' or 'influences' that Guénon speaks of. For, in the first case, I hold that the supposed 'angels' are merely derivative representations of the 'Seraphim' referred to in Isaiah that are *serpents* of some kind. Because of this, both Delphi and *Beith-el* are, in the terms of my thesis, places of the Spiritualization of *matter*, places of the forming, defining, and actualizing of the 'chaos' of nature that Guénon describes as "the indefinite series of cycles of manifestation." They are, thus, places of the 'overcoming' of the 'serpent power.'

From a broadly traditional perspective, the 'messengers' that are called 'angels' in the biblical narrative of 'Jacob's Ladder' are, because they are messengers, meant to be overlooked by the reader of that narrative. For, in the conveyance of a message, it is the message that is meant to be focused on, *not* that which conveys the message. In other words, the reader of Genesis 28 is meant to focus, not on the 'angels,' but on that which such 'messengers' convey: the 'Word' of God. For the *Beith-el*, or 'baetyl' is, as Guénon argues, a "stone that speaks." What it speaks *through*, in Genesis 28, are called 'angels.' The *Beith-el* stone is also the 'House of God,' however, and so the so-called 'angels' are merely the *means* by which the 'House of God' — the presence of God, that is — is communicated throughout the various 'multiple states' of "the indefinite series of cycles of manifestation," the 'state' of earthly existence, specifically, in Genesis 28. This 'Word' of God, just like the words of a 'natural language,' conveys information. It conveys the specific information, to those who, like Jacob, come 'near' to the metaphysical 'center' of being that is God (the Principle), that *Spirit* is the source of all of those 'currents' or 'forces' — "the indefinite series of cycles of manifestation" — that tie together and provide order to the different 'states' of being. The 'Word' of God is conveyed by the 'messengers' called 'angels' in Genesis 28. I argue, however, that this 'Word,' as the intuition of the metaphysical order of reality, was similarly conveyed, in a broadly traditional sense, at the Greek temple of Delphi by the *Pythoness*. This is because the *Omphalos* stone at the Greek temple was also, traditionally speaking, a 'center' where the divine presence most completely manifested, a place, as Guénon says, "near which oracles were given."[68] Like the *Pythoness* at ancient Delphi, by means of his dreams or visions the patriarch Jacob of Genesis 28 was considered a 'prophet' in the sense of one who is qualified to 'speak' God's 'Word.' More traditionally phrased, Jacob was able to *interpret* the metaphysical reality that Guénon terms the 'Principle' but which is called Yahweh, *Brahman*, *Tao*, and many other names in Tradition.

The place of the axial 'ladder' that Jacob dreams of and names 'Bethel' (*Beith-el*) was, according to Genesis 28:19, called *Luz* in Hebrew. (ESV) In *The King of the World*, however, Guénon argues that "the Hebrew word *luz*… [has] many different meanings." One of these, Guénon contends, is

> the name given to an indestructible corporeal particle, symbolically represented as an extremely hard bone, to which the soul, after death, remains linked until the resurrection. As the kernel contains the germ and the bone contains the marrow, so this *luz* contains the virtual elements necessary for the restoration of the being….*Luz*, being imperishable, is the 'kernel of immortality' in the human being, just as the city that is designated by the same name is the 'abode of immortality': this is where the power of the 'Angel of Death' stops in both cases. It is a sort of egg or embryo of the immortal; it may also be compared with the chrysalis from which the butterfly emerges, a comparison which exactly conveys its role with respect to the resurrection.

---

68 René Guénon, *Symbols of Sacred Science*, 168.

The *luz* is said to be located toward the lower end of the spinal column; this might seem rather strange, but becomes clear when it is compared with what the Hindu tradition says about the power called *Kundalini*, which is a form of *Shakti* immanent in the human being. This force is represented by the figure of a coiled snake in a region of the subtle body corresponding precisely to the base of the spinal column; this at least is the case in the ordinary man, but by means of practices such as those of *Hatha-Yoga*, it is aroused, uncoils, and ascends through the 'wheels' (*chakras*) or 'lotuses' (*kamalas*)...to reach finally the region corresponding to the 'third eye', that is, the frontal eye of Shiva. This stage represents the restoration of the 'primordial state', in which man recovers the 'sense of eternity', thereby attaining what we have elsewhere called 'virtual immortality'.[69]

The Hebrew *luz*, according to Guénon an 'indestructible corporeal particle' that is an 'imperishable' 'kernel of immortality,' is also the original name of the place that Jacob renamed *Beith-el*, or 'House of God.' This 'kernel of immortality,' however, is, according to Guénon, located in the same location in humans, if we take "toward the lower end of the spinal column" to be equivalent to "the base of the spinal column," as the force known in the Hindu tradition as *Kundalini* is (in the 'subtle body'). Because of this, and since *Kundalini* "is represented by the figure of a coiled snake," the Hebrew *luz* seems strangely similar to the Greek *Omphalos* stone, since, as Guénon observes, "sometimes, and notably on certain Greek *Omphaloi*, the stone was encircled by a serpent."[70] In other words, the transcultural symbolic association of serpent-stone-immortality, or serpent-stone-metaphysical, since immortality is a characteristic of the metaphysical, seems to hold again in the case of the Hebrew *luz*, once appropriate substitutions are made. At the beginning of this chapter, we argued for a particular symbolic connection between serpent and stone (in the form of 'polar mountain') symbolism in the *Ramayana* narrative of the 'Churning of the Sea.' We then proposed that the 'angels' of Genesis 28, the

---

69 René Guénon, *The King of the World*, 46–47.
70 René Guénon, *The King of the World*, 59.

narrative of 'Jacob's Ladder,' are symbolically equivalent to serpents, and that these 'serpents' symbolize those 'currents' which, according to Guénon, 'descend' from, and 'ascend' to, the metaphysical reality of God that is represented by the *Beith-el* stone. I contend here that the 'indestructible corporeal particle' or 'extremely hard bone' that is, according to Guénon, the Hebrew *luz*, is symbolically equivalent to most all 'sacred stones' of Tradition, such as the *Beith-el* of Genesis 28, the 'polar mountain' of the *Ramayana* narrative, and the *Omphalos* stone of the ancient Greek temple at Delphi. Furthermore, since the *luz* exists, according to Guénon, at the very location in humans where the Hindu 'serpent power' of *Kundalini* is found (in the corresponding 'subtle body'), this is further confirmation of a transcultural symbolic association, present here in Hindu and Hebrew and Greek traditions, of a serpent-stone-immortality/metaphysical symbolism. The immortality/metaphysical element, again, refers to the 'Principial' element of Yahweh or *Brahman*, for example. We may hypothesize that the Greek version of this 'compound symbol,' the *Omphalos* that is a "stone encircled by a serpent," portrays this transcultural 'compound symbolism' more completely than do the Hindu and Hebrew versions, since the symbolism of the Hebrew *luz* leaves out the serpent component of the symbol and the symbolism of the Hindu *Kundalini* leaves out the stone component.

There is, in the symbolism of the Hebrew *luz*, the Hindu *Kundalini*, and the Greek *Omphalos*, a transcultural layering of symbolism in connection with the symbolic elements of stone, serpent, and the metaphysical/immortal. Based upon this layering, we argue that the force that is represented by the nexus of 'angels' and 'ladder' in Genesis 28 is equivalent to the 'serpent power' that is represented by the *Kundalini* serpent in the Hindu tradition, and to the 'visions' of the *Pythoness*, who is named after the serpent *Python*, that are associated with the *Omphalos* stone of ancient Greece. In my opinion, the Hindu figuration is directly pedagogical in its fairy tale bearing; the Hebrew version is layered with symbolical substitutions and strives for poetic allegory; and the Greek figuration is streamlined for simplicity. For Guénon, this stands to reason, since the 'Hindu Doctrines,' for him, exemplify "an entirely metaphysical doctrine," while the Hebrew text, being of a "religious mode," is "mingled with other heterogeneous elements,"[71] and has its intellectual elements mixed with "the presence of a sentimental element affecting the doctrine itself, which does not allow of its preserving an attitude of entirely disinterested speculation."[72]

---

71 René Guénon, *Introduction to the Study of the Hindu Doctrines*, 56.
72 René Guénon, *Introduction to the Study of the Hindu Doctrines*, 81.

CHAPTER 14

The Symbolism of the Serpent in Menhirs and Mounds

The connection between traditional serpent and stone symbolism goes far beyond the narratives of the Jews, the religious beliefs of the Greeks, and the epics of Hinduism. It can also be discerned, for example, in the ancient landscape artworks of Western Europe and North America. Based upon observations made by Guénon and Eliade, as well as other considerations to be mentioned, I argue in this chapter that serpent and stone symbolism are sometimes conjoined in the configurations of Western European megalithic complexes as well as pre-Columbian North American earthen mounds.[1] In this chapter, we shall look at one example of each: the Avebury Cycle in Wiltshire, England, and the so-called 'Ohio Serpent Mound' of Adams County, Ohio.

---

1   According to A. Service and J. Bradbery in *The Standing Stones of Europe*, "[t]he word megalith comes from the Greek, and means a great stone. It is commonly used of any structure built of large stones, usually set upright in the earth, and dating from 5000 to 500 BC in western Europe." Alastair Service and Jean Bradbery, *The Standing Stones of Europe: A Guide to the Great Megalithic Monuments* (London: Weidenfeld & Nicolson, 1979; with new material and revisions in 1993 by Alastair Service), 10.

Megaliths as 'Sacred Stones' and the Element of Time

In *The King of the World*, Guénon argues that

> [t]he stone representing the [Greek] *Omphalos* could take the form of a pillar like the stone of Jacob, and it is quite probable that among the Celtic peoples certain 'menhirs' [large stones set vertically into the ground²] had the same significance; and the oracles were uttered close by these stones, as at Delphi, which is easily explained by the fact that they were considered to be the dwelling-place of the divinity, the 'House of God' being moreover quite naturally identified with the 'Center of the World'....It should be added that the *Omphalos*, although usually represented by a stone, sometimes took the form of a mound or sort of tumulus, which again is an image of the sacred mountain.³

Based upon Guénon's argument that megalithic menhirs "had the same significance" as both the Greek *Omphalos* and Jacob's *Beith-el* stone, I contend that, where such stones exist in serpentine configurations, or where earthen mounds (as forms of stone) are employed to represent the serpent, there exists traditional axial symbolism that identifies the 'Center of the World' where the metaphysical 'Principle' manifests most completely. The Avebury Cycle in Wiltshire and the Serpent Mound of Adams County, Ohio are, respectively, specific examples of these cases. Sites such as these, I propose, express the traditional symbolism of the 'polarized' 'currents'/'forces'/'influences' that Guénon argues are symbolized by the serpent/dragon in Tradition and that emanate from the 'World Axis.'

The traditional symbolism of the serpent/dragon is, as we have seen in the cases of Jacob's *Beith-el* stone, the oracle of Delphi in Greece, and Mount Meru in the *Ramayana* narrative of the 'Churning

---

2   Mircea Eliade, *A History of Religious Ideas Volume 1: From the Stone Age to the Eleusinian Mysteries*, trans. Willard R. Trask (Chicago: The University of Chicago Press, 1978), 114.

3   René Guénon, *The King of the World*, 58–59.

of the Sea,' transculturally associated with 'sacred stones' and the concept of prophecy. Although the prophecy element is perhaps more evident in the first two examples, it should be remembered that, in the narrative of the Churning of the Sea, the god Vishnu *predicts* for the *Devas* what is required for them to overcome the evil sage Durvasas's curse and the threat posed by the *Asuras*. As Radice puts it in *Myths and Legends of India*, Vishnu states,

> 'Only if you drink from the sea of milk that surrounds me — from the ambrosia that secures immortality — will your energy be restored. But at present it is too placid to be effective: it must be churned and energized, and how can you do that in your present pathetic state? No ordinary churning-stick will do: the whole Mandara mountain must be lifted and twirled. And the only beings who can do that are the Asuras themselves, your bitter enemies!'[4]

By being associated with prophecy, traditional serpent symbolism is necessarily also associated with time, since the concept of prophecy is predicated on the awareness, and objectification, of time. We know of the serpent symbol's more direct link with time from our examination of the *ouroboros*. In the cases of Jacob's *Beith-el* stone, the oracle at Delphi, and Mount Meru, however, there is a specific convergence of: 1) stone (as the *Beith-el*, *Omphalos*, and Mount Meru, respectively) symbolizing the 'World Axis' and 2) time in terms of the importance of predicting the future. In Genesis 28:13–14, God is described as predicting the future when he tells Jacob that he will be the source of many 'offspring' and 'descendants'; and the very purpose of the Greek oracle at Delphi was to speak, under the 'god's' influence, of *future* events — conveyed by means of prophetic visions and oracular speech. In all three cases, therefore, of *Beith-el*, *Omphalos*, and Mount Meru, is symbolized the more nuanced temporal idea that the future can be controlled in some sense, and that time is something that one need not be a victim of.

---

4   William Radice, *Myths and Legends of India*, 61.

We have seen the connection between the serpent and cyclical time in Guénon's arguing that the serpent in Tradition symbolizes "the indefinite series of cycles of manifestation." Although the word 'time' is not usually employed by Guénon in his discussion of this concept, the passage of time is necessarily presupposed in any cyclical series of events. According to Guénon, around the eternal and immutable World Axis, the "indefinite series of cycles" of time progresses and the 'migrating' beings caught up in those cycles (in *samsara*) 'migrate' indefinitely. This cyclical 'swirling' is represented, according to Guénon, by the traditional symbolism of the serpent entwined about an axial figure of some sort, whether it be a tree, a rod, or a stone of some kind, such as a mountain. In *The Masks of God: Occidental Mythology*, Joseph Campbell refers to

> the dark mystery of time…the force of the cosmic order itself…the force of the never-dying serpent, sloughing lives like skins, which, pressing on, ever turning in its circle of eternal return, is to continue in this manner forever, as it has already cycled from all eternity.[5]

For Guénon, the metaphysical 'Principle' that is symbolized by the 'center,' or World Axis, is the ultimate source of Campbell's "dark mystery of time…the force of the never-dying serpent." For Guénon, temporality is but a 'state' of eternity, just as any particular manifestation of *Brahman*, such as the human state, is but a state of being of the eternal *Atman*/'Self.'[6]

In *A History of Religious Ideas*, Eliade states that, in the symbolism of western and northern European Neolithic megalithic monuments, "the rock, the slab, the granite block reveal duration without

---

5   Joseph Campbell, *The Masks of God: Occidental Mythology*, 24.
6   Similarly, an individual ego is merely a limited state of the *Atman*. It must be kept in mind that, for Guénon, the physical manifestation that we call a 'human being' is only an *incomplete* particularization of the complete being that is, in *Vedanta*, called *Brahman/Atman*: 'the being.' 'Human being' is a *state* of 'the being.'

end, permanence, incorruptibility—in the last analysis a modality of *existing* independently of temporal becoming."[7] Stone, in other words, according to Eliade, was chosen by the ancient traditional peoples of Europe in the building of their great monuments in order to indicate a meta-temporal, and thus metaphysical insofar as physical reality is temporal, reality. If, however, the ancient Neolithic communities that built these megalithic monuments are taken to be proponents of Tradition as Guénon and Eliade define the term, then they, like all traditional societies, had a notion of the 'World Axis' that symbolizes metaphysical reality. I argue that, like Jacob's *Beith-el* stone, the *Omphalos* of Delphi, and Mount Meru in the *Ramayana*, the stones that compose the great megalithic monuments of western and northern Europe are 'sacred stones' that represent the World Axis and, thus, symbolize the metaphysical 'Principle' of Tradition. In studying these monuments, observers should expect to see serpent symbolism in connection with the 'sacred stones' composing such ancient megalithic structures, whether representationally on individual stones or by means of the serpentine patterns created by the stones in their composing the larger structures that they are a part of. In the present chapter, we will examine the latter, structural, form of symbolism. In the second section of the chapter, however, we will recall Guénon's contention that "the *Omphalos*, although usually represented by a stone, sometimes took the form of a mound,"[8] and examine a product of the ancient North American 'Mound Builder' culture who in some of their works of art, I argue, used earthen mounds in place of 'sacred stones' to represent the serpent and to symbolize its traditional, transcultural, meaning. We will discuss this last possibility when we consider the serpent symbolism of the 'Ohio Serpent Mound.'

In *A History of Religious Ideas*, Eliade discusses the hypothesis that a Neolithic 'cult of the dead' existed in western and northern Europe

---

7   Mircea Eliade, *A History of Religious Ideas Volume 1*, 115.
8   René Guénon, *The King of the World*, 58–59.

in which megalithic structures, such as Stonehenge and Carnac, played a large role. He argues in that book that "the megalithic cult of the dead appears to include not only a certainty of the soul's survival [after death] but, above all, confidence in the power of the ancestors and the hope that they will protect and help the living."[9] He contends that

> in the megalithic religions, the sacrality of stone is chiefly valorized in relation to postexistence....What characterizes the megalithic religions is the fact that the ideas of perenniality and of continuity between life and death are apprehended through the exaltation of the ancestors as identified, or associated, with the stones....Megaliths have a relation to certain ideas concerning existence after death. The majority of them are built in the course of ceremonies intended to defend the soul during its journey into the beyond; but they also insure an eternal postexistence, both to those who raise them during their own lifetime and to those for whom they are built after death. In addition, megaliths constitute the unrivaled connection between the living and the dead; they are believed to perpetuate the magical virtues of those who constructed them or for whom they were constructed, thus insuring the fertility of men, cattle, and harvests. In all the megalithic cultures that still flourish, the cult of the ancestors plays an important part... [and] in the megalithic-type cult of the dead, genealogies play an important part....Menhirs are sometimes found decorated with human figures;...the stylized figures depicted on the walls of dolmens, together with the small idols excavated from the megalithic burial places of Spain, probably represent the ancestors.... [And] the surfaces of the dolmens and menhirs of Iberia and western Europe also display other magico-religious signs and symbols — for example, the image of a sun with rays, the sign of the ax (peculiar to storm gods), the snake, symbol of life, associated with figures of the ancestors, the stag, etc.[10]

It is easy to see why stones should be selected to represent the "continuity between life and death," as Eliade puts it. In James A. Michener's novel *Centennial*, which dramatizes the course of American westward

---

9   Mircea Eliade, *A History of Religious Ideas Volume 1*, 116.
10 Mircea Eliade, *A History of Religious Ideas Volume 1*, 124, 123, 117, and 120.

expansion in the nineteenth- and early twentieth centuries around the town of Centennial, Colorado, Michener has the Indian Gray Wolf tell his adoptive son Lame Beaver that "only the rocks live forever."[11] If not literally forever, it is known scientifically that, at least in the physical universe, rocks 'live' longer than any human, animal, plant, or virus. Compared to other familiar earth-bound objects, then, the rocks do "live forever." But the connection that Eliade also argues to have existed between the "continuity of life and death" and a so-called 'cult of the dead,' or 'cult of the ancestors,' in megalithic societies is easily imagined as well, at least for any person aware of the fact that s/he exists because her/his parents, grandparents, great-grandparents, and on back down the line *also* existed, and procreated. The existence of genealogies recorded either orally or in written form by cultures all around the world implies a very potent past awareness of such genetic continuity. It implies also, however, an awareness of cycles of life in general and, thus, an awareness of *time* as it is traditionally (cyclically) conceived of.

Along with all of this talk of life, death, fertility, and ancestors — along with the implication of time always passing by means of descendants turning into ancestors and life turning into death — and near the end of the long quotation from Eliade produced above, Eliade observes that the image of the *snake* is represented on the surfaces of certain megalithic structures in Europe. Eliade only fleetingly mentions the snake in his listing of other images that appear on the ancient stones, such as the sun, ax, and stag. However, as we have already seen, the symbolism of the 'solar disk' is symbolically connected with the symbolism of the serpent in ancient Egypt, and the traditional symbolism of the circle, of which the 'solar disk' is one form, is connected with other traditional figurations of serpent symbolism, such as that of the *ouroboros* that we discussed in Chapter 9. In a later chapter, we will discuss more carefully the traditional

---

11   James A. Michener, *Centennial* (New York: Random House, Inc., 1974), 119.

symbolism of the ax, mentioned so briefly by Eliade here, as a variant of the so-called 'thunderweapon' that is, along with the tree, rod, cross, and 'sacred stone,' a variation of the World Axis that is, for both Guénon and Eliade, as well as for others, often juxtaposed with the serpent symbol in Tradition.

Serpent Symbolism in the Megaliths: The Avebury Cycle of Wiltshire, England

One of the most striking of the megalithic structures of Western Europe is Avebury, or the 'Avebury Cycle,' so-called due to its location in Avebury parish, Wiltshire, England. Like the well-known 'Stonehenge,' also located in Wiltshire, Avebury is a megalithic 'henge,' according to Palmer and Lloyd in their *Archaeology A — Z*,

> [a] monument or temple used for religious rites…a roughly circular area of ground, bounded by a ditch with a bank outside it, often enclosing a stone or wooden circle or circles.[12]

In *The Avebury Cycle*, Michael Dames discusses the general context of the megalithic configuration at Avebury:

> The monuments in Avebury parish, Wiltshire, make up the most important Stone Age group in Britain. Included in the complex are remnants of two stone avenues, the biggest known henge enclosure, Europe's tallest artificial hill, and England's largest prehistoric tomb….The Avebury monuments deal with order as experienced by a farming community…. In a typically preliterate fashion, the body-architecture of the Avebury monuments served practical needs (growing food, burying the dead, etc.) and also enabled these matters to be viewed as aspects of a supernatural metabolism….What did a farming people care about, if not the relationship between earth and sky, worked out in the cyclical progression of the

---

12   G. Palmer and N. Lloyd, *Archaeology A — Z* (London: Frederick Warne, 1968), 109.

seasons, each different in character, like the Avebury monuments, yet each, like them, linked to its neighbors?[13]

Dames then proceeds in more detail, arguing that Avebury represents by means of its two large 'avenues' of menhirs, 'Beckhampton' and 'West Kennet,' two giant snakes (see fig. 14.1).[14]

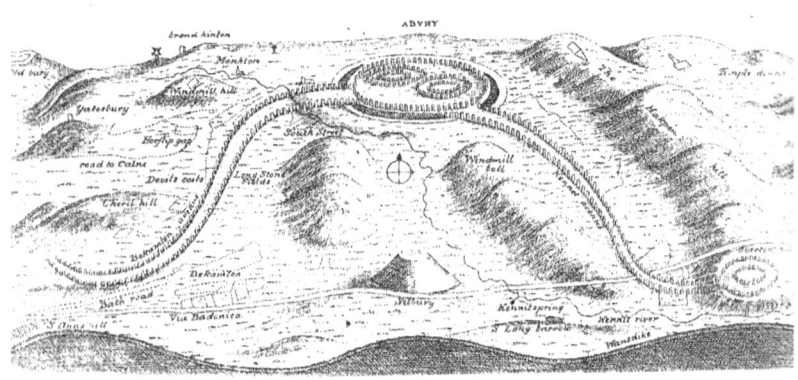

Fig. 14.1. Engraving of Avebury, W. Stukeley, 1743[15]

Dames states that several writers have argued that the 'peculiar meanders' of the two avenues have often been called 'serpentine' and 'sinuous.' He notes, however, that these same authors rejected the avenues' actually representing a serpent, or serpents, using such phrases as 'cannot be taken seriously' when considering that thesis.[16] According to Dames,

---

13 Michael Dames, *The Avebury Cycle* (London: Thames and Hudson Ltd, 1977), 9, 11–12.
14 Michael Dames, *The Avebury Cycle*, 83.
15 William Stukeley, *Abury Described* (London: 1743), reproduced in Michael Dames, *The Avebury Cycle*, 82.
16 Michael Dames, *The Avebury Cycle*, 82–83.

[t]here has been one previous written attempt to consider the overall meaning of the Avebury monuments — made in 1743 (before the birth of archaeology), by the antiquarian, Dr William Stukeley.[17]

In *Abury Described*, according to Dames, Stukeley argues, "based upon fieldwork which he had completed twenty years earlier," that Avebury "imitated the figure of a [single] snake as drawn in the ancient hieroglyphics."[18] According to Stukeley, Dames says, something called the 'Sanctuary' represented the head of the snake "and the two avenues (Beckhampton and West Kennet)...[made] a single body three miles long, on which was threaded the Avebury henge, at a point midway between head and tail."[19] (See fig. 14.1.) According to Dames, "[t]he avenues are seen to meet at Avebury henge, in Stukeley's engraving, with the Beckhampton avenue on the left, and the West Kennet avenue extending from the Sanctuary."[20] The 'Sanctuary,' according to S. Piggott in his *West Kennet Long Barrow Excavations*, was "the temporary storage place for [the] offerings" related to rituals that allegedly took place at Avebury.[21]

In opposition to Stukeley's hypothesis that Avebury by means of its configuration of menhirs represents one serpent, Dames argues that Avebury represents by means of its two avenues *two* serpents. More specifically, Dames argues that the West Kennet avenue in particular "represents a snake on its way from hibernation in the Sanctuary to copulation at the henge,"[22] focusing on this avenue in part because, as he says,

---

17 Michael Dames, *The Avebury Cycle*, 12.
18 Michael Dames, *The Avebury Cycle*, 12, and William Stukeley, *Abury Described*, 33.
19 Michael Dames, *The Avebury Cycle*, 82.
20 Michael Dames, *The Avebury Cycle*, 82.
21 Stuart Piggott, *The West Kennet Long Barrow Excavations, 1955-6* (London: Her Majesty's Stationary Office: 1962), 75.
22 Michael Dames, *The Avebury Cycle*, 85.

the West Kennet avenue has always retained enough stones above ground to place its existence beyond dispute.... [whereas] the same cannot be said of its counterpart, which had lost all but one of its regular members by 1730.[23]

The relative lack of material evidence at Avebury has caused many researchers to doubt not only Stukeley's conclusions but his original fieldwork, maps, and drawings. According to Dames, however, the extant evidence is compelling enough to confirm Stukeley's general impression of the overall serpentine design of Avebury, although again Dames believes that Stukeley misinterpreted the number of snakes represented by the structure.[24] Dames, in fact, goes so far as to speculate that the "stone rows, cursuses [long and narrow bank and ditch enclosures] and avenues [of Avebury] were probably all designed as monumental snakes," although he retains his thesis that Avebury primarily represented only two serpents.[25]

Along with the symbolism of the serpent, circle symbolism is also conspicuously present at Avebury in the forms of both the henge that makes up the center portion of the complex as well as the 'Sanctuary' or 'head' of (one of) the supposed serpent(s). Stukeley describes Avebury henge as being at the midway point between the head and the tail of one giant megalithic serpent that constitutes the entire Avebury complex. Dames, on the other hand, as we have seen, describes the henge as existing midway between two serpents, the two named avenues.[26] (See the center portion of fig. 14.1.) Avebury henge itself, however, contains *multiple* circles. According to Dames, there is

---

23 Michael Dames, *The Avebury Cycle*, 138.
24 Michael Dames, *The Avebury Cycle*, 138.
25 In *The Neolithic Cultures of the British*, Stuart Piggott describes 'cursuses' as "certain extremely long and narrow bank and ditch enclosures. The largest known examples have a width of 250–350 feet between the parallel ditches with internal banks." Stuart Piggott, *The Neolithic Cultures of the British Isles* (Cambridge University Press, 1954), 65. Michael Dames, *The Avebury Cycle*, 92.
26 Michael Dames, *The Avebury Cycle*, 82.

a so-called 'Great Outer Circle' measuring 1,305 feet in diameter and two major inner circles called the 'North Circle' and the 'South Circle' which measure, respectively, 320 feet and 340 feet in diameter.[27] (See fig. 14.2.) There is also an 'Inner North Circle,' and, in Stukeley's illustration from 1743, there appear to be *secondary* inner circles within both the 'North Circle' and the 'South Circle.'[28]

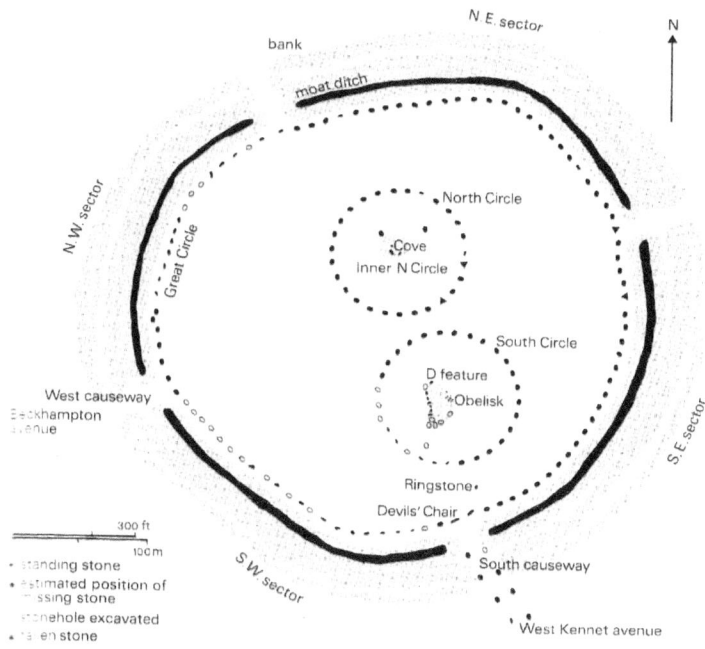

Fig. 14.2. *Plan of Avebury (after I. F. Smith)*, Peter Bridgewater[29]

I argue that the prominent circle symbolism of the Avebury complex expresses the same traditional meaning as that which is expressed in other examples of traditional circle symbolism found in juxtaposition to the serpent/dragon. Examples of such include the 'World'/

---

27 Michael Dames, *The Avebury Cycle*, 117.
28 Michael Dames, *The Avebury Cycle*, 82.
29 Michael Dames, *The Avebury Cycle*, 115.

Mundane Egg with serpent or dragon and the 'solar disk' that is often represented as part of the serpentine *uraeus* of ancient Egypt and other ancient cultures. The meaning of the traditional circle is, as we have seen most explicitly in the case of the 'World,' or Mundane, Egg, the presence of the divine or metaphysical in its relationship to that which the serpent/dragon represents for Guénon: *samsara*, 'nature,' or "the indefinite series of cycles of manifestation." It is also the case, however, that traditional circle symbolism often appears without any accompanying overt representation of the serpent or dragon in such cases as the Chinese *yin-yang* symbol and the symbolism of the 'double spiral' that Guénon discusses in *The Great Triad*, both of which we have already examined. In these cases also, the circle symbolizes the presence of the divine or metaphysical. With respect to the symbolism that Guénon calls the 'double spiral,' specifically, as we have noted in part in Chapter 12, he states in *The Great Triad* that

> [i]n ancient symbols this double spiral is sometimes replaced by two sets of concentric circles, drawn around two points which again represent the poles;....they are the higher and the lower states relative to the human state, or the cycles antecedent and consequent with respect to the preceding cycle....but the double spiral indicates in addition the continuity between the cycles; it can also be said that it represents things in their 'dynamic' aspect, whereas the concentric circles represent them rather in their 'static' aspect.[30]

Based upon this interchangeability or 'replaceability' argued for by Guénon between the double spiral and concentric circles, I contend that the 'North' and 'South' circles that are included within the larger 'Great Outer Circle' of Avebury's henge represent the traditional meaning, as Guénon expresses it, of "two sets of concentric circles" that is equivalent in meaning to the so-called 'double spiral.' E. G. Squier's remarks in his 1851 *The Serpent Symbol, and the Worship of the Reciprocal Principles of Nature in America* would seem to support

---

30 René Guénon, *The Great Triad*, 35–36.

this interpretation to at least some degree. He observes concerning the 'Great Outer Circle' at Avebury that "within this grand circle were originally two double or concentric circles, composed of massive upright stones: a row of large stones, one hundred in number," adding that "Stukeley supposes the entire structure [of Avebury] to correspond to the sacred hierogram of the Egyptians, the circle or globe, the serpent, and the outspread wings."[31] Also in 1851, Squier states that "there are a number of other monuments in the British islands, less imposing it is true than that of Abury [Avebury], but of a similar character."[32]

I mentioned at the outset of this chapter the connection between the serpent symbol and the concept of time, quoting Joseph Campbell's reference to "the dark mystery of time…the force of the cosmic order itself…the force of the never-dying serpent." In his discussion in *The Great Triad* of the symbolism of the 'double spiral' and the 'two sets of concentric circles,' Guénon argues that both symbolisms correspond, in his theory of "the indefinite series of cycles of manifestation," to "the higher and lower states relative to the human state, or the cycles antecedent and consequent with respect to the preceding cycle."[33] If the symbolism of concentric circles is symbolically equivalent to that of the 'double spiral,' however, then that symbolism must also be, at least roughly, equivalent to the symbolisms of the *yin-yang*, Androgyne, and 'World Egg,' the symbols of 'duality' in unity that I discussed in Chapter 10. If that is the case, however, then, since Guénon argues that all of these symbols represent the 'dual action' of a single 'cosmic force,' or 'dual currents' emanating from and returning back to this force, the symbolism of concentric circles must also symbolize this 'dual action.' The 'double spiral,' however, as we noted from

---

31 E. G. Squier, *The Serpent Symbol, and the Worship of the Reciprocal Principles of Nature in America*, 235.

32 E. G. Squier, *The Serpent Symbol, and the Worship of the Reciprocal Principles of Nature in America*, 236.

33 René Guénon, *The Great Triad*, 35.

an earlier quotation by Guénon, "indicates in addition the continuity between the cycles" or between the states (of existence) of the 'migrating' being. From this we may conclude that both the 'double spiral' and 'concentric circles,' insofar as the two symbolisms 'correspond' to "the indefinite series of cycles of manifestation" and the "continuity between the cycles" of existence, and also insofar as traditional peoples conceived of time cyclically, are, for Guénon, symbolic of both time *and* those 'dual currents' that emanate from, and return to, the metaphysical source of time: the 'Principial' force. Since, however, according to Guénon, the 'double spiral' and 'concentric circles' symbolize the cyclical continuity that connects the processes of the 'evolution' and 'involution' of beings, the 'double spiral' and 'concentric circles' symbolize time itself as it is understood in Tradition. This is because time is, according to this traditional symbolism, the 'dual' movement between 'evolution' (manifestation of the metaphysical Principle) and 'involution' (return to the metaphysical Principle).[34] Put colloquially, it 'takes time' for a being (the metaphysical Principle) to become manifest and it 'takes time' for a being (the metaphysical Principle) to become 'unmanifest' — to 'appear' and 'disappear,' as it were. The seemingly unending ('indefinite,' to be precise) process by which metaphysical reality manifests and 'withdraws' from manifestation is what time *is* for traditional humans, based upon Guénon's insights. Being born and dying are simply examples of this 'dual' process in the particular state of being called 'nature.'

In *The Avebury Cycle*, Dames connects the symbolism of Avebury with "the cyclical progression of the seasons," asserting that "the great snake is associated with the springtime journey between death and renewal."[35] However, to symbolize renewal, the progression of the seasons, and the distinctness of the seasons, such as spring, is to both symbolize and be aware of time. Spring, summer, fall, and winter are

---

34 René Guénon, *The Great Triad*, 36.
35 Michael Dames, *The Avebury Cycle*, 11–12; 91.

discrete temporal intervals, perhaps not as precisely definable as a minute or an hour or a day, but nonetheless possessing fairly quantifiable boundaries. I argue that the 'North' and 'South' circles of the Avebury Cycle, along with their various inner circles, represented, in their discreteness and separateness for traditional peoples, the discreteness and separateness of the 'natural' cycles of existence, such as those that Guénon refers to in a general sense when he writes of "the indefinite series of cycles of manifestation." More specifically, the circles of Avebury symbolized for those traditional peoples who employed the 'technology' that *is* Avebury Cycle the binaries, or dichotomies, of the 'natural' cycles that are known as 'dying' and 'being born' (or reborn/renewed) *and* the yearly (solar) cycle that was a recognized *quadripartite* (*two* multiplied by itself) progression of four seasons: spring, summer, fall, and winter. Based upon this reasoning, I conclude that the design of Avebury communicates, to those possessing the requisite esoteric knowledge of its symbolic elements, the revelation that there existed a form of awareness, or understanding of reality, among those who used Avebury 'correctly' that is essentially different from any form of awareness that tends to recognize reality as merely a 'flux,' or that tends to 'blend' together all 'natural' events and processes into a 'unity' or homogenous whole.

On this point, the 'North' and 'South' circles of Avebury are, importantly, *not* connected or 'blended' into Guénon's 'double spiral.' This absence of a represented 'blended' connection between the exactly *two* sets ('North' and 'South') of concentric circles at Avebury that, we can imagine, *might* have been constructed by their builders to form what Guénon describes as a (singular) 'double spiral,' is, I argue, indicative of an awareness by the peoples who built and used the Avebury Cycle of the *discreteness and separateness* of the seasons and of the *discreteness and separateness* of the dying and birthing processes — the *non*-homogeneity of these processes, that is. More specifically, the absence of a represented 'blended' connection between the two ('North' and 'South') concentric circles at Avebury after the fashion of Guénon's 'double spiral' indicates an awareness by the traditional peoples who used Avebury of the discreteness of *time itself* and of time's essentially 'dual' nature, in the sense that duality' is the most basic form of division or non-unity—even though the 'double spiral' also symbolized for traditional peoples, according to Guénon, the 'dual action' of a single 'cosmic force.' This awareness by traditional peoples of the nature of time as composed of discrete and separate 'units' constituted for them an awareness that time is something that may be abstracted from any *particular* life, or earth, cycles without need of referring to such particular cycles, or to *any* particular kinds of cycles, in order to understand time. Although Guénon, therefore, argues for the symbolic equivalence, for traditional peoples, of the 'double spiral' and concentric circles, I contend that, although these two symbols were seen by traditional peoples as 1) being equivalent in terms of their both being symbols of 'duality in unity' expressing the 'dual action' of a single 'cosmic force,' and 2) equivalently, expressing the forces of 'evolution' and 'involution' from and back to the metaphysical 'Principle,' that the traditional usage of concentric circles, as is revealed at Avebury, indicated a further level of abstraction of that kind of symbolism which pushed the symbolism further in the direction of indicating 'duality' and further away from indicating unity. As such, the symbolism of concentric circles, specifically those at Avebury, reveals a radical change in the human awareness of reality from a more 'animalistic' awareness of a homogenous 'flux-like' state to one in which 'duality,' or abstract discreteness, is appreciated. Another way to say this is that Avebury's symbolism reveals how humans went from being: 1) instinctually *responsive* to their environment to 2) analytically *objectifying* of, and *active* in, their environment. The change that I'm imagining is illustrated in the opening sequence of the film *2001: A Space Odyssey*, in which a group of pre-human primates encounters an advanced alien technology that somehow stimulates and 'activates' in them their latent capacity for tool, and specifically weapon, use.³⁶ The thesis presented in *2001* is that these pre-human primates 'evolved' into modern humans by means of the intervention of some extraterrestrial intelligence. I make no such argument here, but I do argue that different phases of traditional art from around the world indicate different steps in the 'evolution' of human consciousness, with this 'evolution' leading in the direction of increased awareness of 'difference.'³⁷ This increased awareness of 'difference' may be described as a movement of consciousness away from awareness of 'unity' and towards awareness of 'duality.'

With the particular kind of awareness of time that is expressed by means of the symbolism of the Avebury Cycle comes a particular understanding of fertility and sexuality. The three –, time, fertility, and sexuality –, are intimately linked in archaic/traditional cultures in general because the cycles of life, such as the return of grasses and leaves after winter, or the regular mating rituals of animals, or the regular menstruation of women, all serve as means of marking the passage of time and of pinpointing other events important to traditional peoples. In parallel to his contention that the largescale structure of Avebury represents serpent*s* (plural) moving toward copulation, then, Dames also suggests that humans used the Avebury complex for ceremonies that included human mating rituals. Focusing on a portion of the West Kennet Avenue of Avebury that he terms "the avenue's neck," Dames argues that

---

36 *2001: A Space Odyssey*, directed by Stanley Kubrick (Metro-Goldwyn-Mayer, 1968).

37 At this, our particular moment in world history, it may be necessary to point out that the apogee of the awareness of 'difference' that I write of is awareness of the uniqueness of the *individual*, not of any 'race' or 'gender' or political 'tribe,' or other superficial 'identity.' This perspective, that in which the substantiality of the individual excels that of *any* group 'identity,' is the Aristotelian perspective, of which the Lockean perspective is a later Western iteration.

[t]he puzzling knots in the avenue's neck can be unraveled by the realization that the avenue reptile, in common with the young people in procession along its length, was probably about to mate.[38]

The mating of the two serpents represented by the Avebury Cycle was, according to Dames, mirrored by the ritual mating of the humans who employed Avebury Cycle in ancient times. In traditional societies, however, the mating ritual is, ideally, if there is no other ritualistic purpose to the copulation, always meant to be consummated in *marriage*. In *The Serpent Symbol in the Ancient Near East*, Leslie S. Wilson remarks on the widespread connection between serpent symbolism and both mating and marriage when he states that "it seems that, from earliest times, the serpent was regarded as the symbol of fertility and life renewal. There are multiple accounts of the role of *naga* (cobra) in Indian wedding ceremonies."[39] If we are looking for transcultural motifs in Tradition, this connection between serpent symbolism and Indian marriage ceremonies referred to by Wilson raises the question of whether the Avebury Cycle is connected, not only with mating, but with marriage.

Dames answers affirmatively to this question and offers a cross-cultural parallel of his own when he states that

[t]he avenue snakes [at Avebury], equal in length and girth, wind their way towards a circular marriage dais [the henge] which lies between them. They are a summary of the total life force of bride and groom. In this, they resemble the most popular form of painted icon found in the Roman household shrines, known as Lararia….The altar over which the serpents met sometimes contained an egg. In many instances the serpents' tails spring from the ground or from a circular plate equivalent to the Sanctuary. Incorporated into the design one often finds a goddess: Luna, the Roman moon goddess, has been identified; so has Isis-Fortuna, and we may suppose that the Avebury henge made sense to some Roman visitors

---

38 Michael Dames, *The Avebury Cycle*, 105.
39 Leslie S. Wilson, *The Serpent Symbol in the Ancient Near East*, 13.

for whom the snakes and wedding ring theme served as a closely related purpose.[40]

After completing his comparison of ancient Roman and British marriage rituals and the connection between marriage and serpent symbolism in both of those cultures, Dames further notes that,

> [i]n vestigial forms, both the spirit and the iconography of avenues and henge were maintained at English rural weddings until about 1750, where silk stockings took on the role of the avenue snakes, and a shallow bowl, or posset of sack, stood for the henge-vulva.[41]

Dames thus argues that the ancient symbolism expressed at Avebury not only makes it into modern times in a meaningful way but that, more particularly, the source of the symbolic imagery of rural marriages in eighteenth-century England lies in marriage ceremonies that Dames proposes took place at the Avebury Cycle perhaps thousands of years earlier.

On the subject of the connection between ancient human conceptions of the bonding of the sexes in general and the symbolism of the serpent, Dames remarks that "of all the world's animals, none has featured more consistently in human fertility symbolism than the snake, irrespective of whether the culture ascribes a positive or negative value to carnal knowledge."[42] As we have seen in our discussions of Marija Gimbutas's and Buffie Johnson's statements on ancient serpent symbolism, for example, many authors remark upon the association between serpent symbolism and fertility or sexuality.[43] Eliade, for

---

40 Michael Dames, *The Avebury Cycle*, 141. We see in this quotation another example, this time Roman, of the symbolic serpent/egg connection that we examined in Chapter 10, and which we shall soon examine in one of its North American appearances, the 'Ohio Serpent Mound.'
41 Michael Dames, *The Avebury Cycle*, 142–43.
42 Michael Dames, *The Avebury Cycle*, 143.
43 See Marija Gimbutas's *The Language of the Goddess* and Buffie Johnson's *Lady of the Beasts* for example.

example, in *Patterns in Comparative Religion*, argues for an archaic linkage of fertility and snake symbolism by means of the powers attributed to the moon by archaic humans:

> The moon then can also be personified as reptile and masculine, but such personifications ...are still fundamentally based on the notion of the moon as source of living reality, and basis of all fertility and periodic regeneration. Snakes are thought of as producing children; in Guatemala, for instance, in the Urabunna tribe of central Australia (who believe themselves to be descended from two snakes which travelled about the world and left *maiaurli*, or "the souls of children" wherever they stopped), among the Togos in Africa (a giant snake dwells in a pool near the town of Klewe, and receiving children from the hands of the supreme god Namu, brings them into the town before their birth). In India, from Buddhist times (cf. the Jatakas), snakes were held to be the givers of fertility....The snake has a variety of meanings, and I think we must hold its "regeneration" to be one of the most important.[44]

Eliade concludes from these examples that "what emerges fairly clearly from all this varied symbolism of snakes is their lunar character — that is their powers of fertility, of regeneration, of immortality through metamorphosis."[45] In reading this quotation, one is immediately reminded of Dames's mention of the Roman moon goddess Luna whose image, he states, was incorporated alongside much serpent imagery into the decoration of ancient Roman household shrines. This ancient and transcultural relationship between moon and serpent symbolism only further goes to show the transcultural (traditional) connection between serpent symbolism and the traditional idea of time since the moon has, seemingly, for all of the ages of man been considered one of the greatest means of measuring temporal intervals, and also known to be intimately related to the intervals of various natural and biological processes, such as the menstrual cycle of women.

---

44 Mircea Eliade, *Patterns in Comparative Religion*, 167–68.
45 Mircea Eliade, *Patterns in Comparative Religion*, 169.

Dames, in consonance with the perceived connection by traditional peoples between fertility and celestial bodies, the moon specifically, asserts,

> So the [Avebury] henge North and South Circles, and the features they contain, were probably intended as a reflection of the sun and moon. For, as Rice Homes [sic] puts it, 'our Neolithic forefathers, like other savages, saw sun and moon as living beings'. Stukeley was right to label the inner circles 'Solar' and 'Lunar' on some of his Avebury plans.[46]

Immortality conjures the notion of time and so does anything to do with the moon's or sun's cycles, at least for traditional peoples. The serpent's shedding of its skin, however, is a regular cyclical process just like the indefinite return of the various phases of the moon. The serpent's regular shedding of its skin could have been seen by traditional peoples as an event similar in nature to the changing phases of the moon. Because of its regenerative nature and the cyclicity of that regenerative nature, the serpent, like the moon, is an obvious choice for any symbolism relating to fertility and time. In *Patterns in Comparative Religion*, Eliade describes the snake as "being immortal because it is continually reborn, and therefore it is a moon 'force', and as such can bestow fecundity, knowledge (that is prophecy) and even immortality."[47] In Eliade's remark, we notice a return to the association between serpent and prophecy that was present at the ancient temple of Delphi with its serpent 'Python' and its prophetic 'Pythoness'. There is also, however, a three-vectored convergence at Delphi of serpent and stone (in the form of the *Omphalos*) symbolism with the idea of time, or prophecy more specifically, as well. But this is exactly what we see in interpreting the purpose of the megalithic structure at Avebury by simply substituting *prediction* for *prophecy*. We have already

---

46 Michael Dames, *The Avebury Cycle*, 135.
47 Mircea Eliade, *Patterns in Comparative Religion*, 164, referring to T. Rice Holmes, *Ancient Britain, the Invasions of Julius Caesar* (Clarendon Press, 1907), 116.

examined what we believe to be indications of a changing awareness, by the archaic peoples who built and originally used Avebury, of time. This 'new' awareness of time characterizes time as abstract discreteness and separateness, and goes beyond the need to look to any *particular* kind of cyclical system, any 'material' example of such, like the cyclical return of the phases of the moon, to understand it. What we add here is that, along with this new understanding of time as something measuring discrete intervals beyond the observation of 'natural' cycles, the peoples who built and originally used Avebury applied this new understanding of time for purposes of *prediction*. As others have argued, the great megalithic henges of western and northern Europe were likely giant instruments for calculating the passage of time as well as predicting events that were deemed important to the cultures that used these 'instruments.' We, therefore, do not intend to present this old thesis in new clothing but, rather, to point out that the temporal element in general, whether tied to prediction and an awareness of the discreteness of the seasons and of the events of birth and death, as in the case of the megalithic Avebury, or tied to prophecy, as in the case of Delphi with the *Omphalos*, is connected, in Tradition, with *stone*.

As we have seen in Chapter 13, 'sacred stones' are connected symbolically with the serpent in traditional cultures. This is because traditional 'sacred stones,' like Mount Meru in the *Ramayana*, or the *Omphalos* at Delphi, are figurations of the 'World Axis' that symbolizes the metaphysical 'Principle' that is, for Guénon, the source of all existence; and the serpent represents "the indefinite series of cycles" that 'coil' about the Axis. The traditional symbolic connection between stone and time exists in places like Avebury and Delphi not only because, as Eliade claims, "the rock, the slab, the granite block reveal duration without end, permanence, incorruptibility — in the last analysis a modality of *existing* independently of temporal becoming,"[48]

---

48 Mircea Eliade, *A History of Religious Ideas Volume 1*, 115.

but because stone is symbolically linked with the *serpent* in Tradition. The serpent is symbolic of time in traditional cultures, however, only insofar as the idea of time in such cultures is based, originally, upon the observations of celestial movements and events and the *prediction* of those movements and events. In general, the western and northern European henges seem to have been, for traditional peoples, either symbolic of, or predictive of, celestial bodies and their movements across the sky—the sun and moon, in particular; and the serpent is traditionally associated with both of these celestial bodies. In an article entitled "Medicine Wheels and Plains Indian Astronomy" that was included in the anthology *Astronomy of the Ancients*, John A. Eddy said of Stonehenge, for example,

> For more than a hundred years, the secret of its alignment with the summer solstice...has been known. Other aspects of the monument's construction are more controversial, such as the claim that it was used to predict lunar eclipses. But Stonehenge does not stand alone; there are at least 900 other structures like it, though not all so grand and megalithic, throughout the British Isles. Many of them have been studied, and by and large their alignments demonstrate an early interest in astronomy.[49]

The Avebury Cycle, which like Stonehenge stands in Wiltshire, England, falls into this same class of ancient structures. In *The Sun and the Serpent: An Investigation into Earth Energies*, Hamish Miller and Paul Broadhurst poetically tie together all of the elements of serpent, fertility, celestial bodies, and the notion of 'duality' or 'opposites' that betrays the same level of abstract thinking that is involved in perceiving *discrete time* when they state that

> [t]he entire edifice [of Avebury] was a marvelous image of Natural alchemy, the fusion of opposites. The raw energy of the Earth was the serpent,

---

49 John A. Eddy, "Medicine Wheels and Plains Indian Astronomy," in *Astronomy of the Ancients*, ed. Kenneth Brecher and Michael Feirtag (Cambridge, Massachusetts and London, England: The MIT Press, 1979), 1.

fertilized by the opposing cosmic forces of Sun and Moon, concentrated in the great circle, the generative organ of the whole complex.[50]

This assessment, with its references to 'Natural alchemy,' 'the fusion of opposites,' and Sun and Moon, is reminiscent of the symbolism of the Hermetic (alchemical) Androgyne that is both associated with 'marriage' and often represented with a serpent, a dragon, or both (see fig. 10.3).

The Ohio Serpent Mound

The so-called 'Serpent Mound' of southern Ohio is perhaps the world's largest earthen representation of a serpent. In *The Moundbuilders: Ancient Peoples of Eastern North America*, George R. Milner describes "this deservedly famous earthwork" as a

> long, low embankment [that] snakes its way down a narrow ridge. The tail forms a tight spiral, and the other end widens to join an oval embankment, commonly interpreted as the head, although some have thought the snake is swallowing an egg.[51] (See fig. 14.3.)

---

50   Hamish Miller & Paul Broadhurst, *The Sun and the Serpent: An Investigation into Earth Energies* (Cornwall, England: Pendragon Press, 1989), 102.

51   George R. Milner, *The Moundbuilders: Ancient Peoples of Eastern North America* (London: Thames & Hudson Ltd., 2004), 79.

Fig. 14.3. Ohio Serpent Mound, Courtesy of the Ohio Historical Society (P396, B4, F2, E3)[52]

Little is known of the creation and age of the Ohio Serpent Mound, with Milner stating as recently as 2004,

> Surprisingly little work has been done at the Serpent considering the attention the earthwork has received. Recently even the dating of the site has been brought into question. Long thought to be an Adena site [c. 1000 BCE to c. 500 BCE] based upon slim evidence, a couple of radiocarbon dates

---

52 George R. Milner, *The Moundbuilders*, 80.

from a small excavation raise the possibility that the earthwork might be no more than a thousand years old.[53]

About a hundred years before Milner published *The Moundbuilders*, E. O. Randall, in his 1907 book *The Serpent Mound, Adams County, Ohio*, examined in detail the characteristics of the Serpent Mound, as well as various interpretations of its meaning. Remarking upon the general ubiquitousness of serpent symbolism among the so-called 'Mound Builders' of pre-Columbian North America, Randall noted in his book that

> [c]ertain it is that the serpent was a well nigh [sic] common symbol or object with the Mound Builders. The snake effigy…is found in various localities of the mound building territory. They exist in Ohio, Illinois, Minnesota, Wisconsin and Dakota….The Mound Builders of the Mississippi Valley were serpent worshippers. The Ohio serpent [however] is the greatest, most accurate and distinctively representative[54] and now the most perfectly preserved of all the snake mounds. When it was built will doubtless always be a matter of conjecture and dispute; certainly it existed centuries ago.[55]

Randall subsequently quotes a Dr. Daniel Wilson, who he describes in his book as "a most learned English authority on archaeology and author of 'Prehistoric Man,'" as stating that "[t]his singular monument

---

53   George R. Milner, *The Moundbuilders*, 79. According to Milner, "[t]he name Adena comes from an estate in Ohio where a large mound was dug about a century ago. For the most part it refers to Early Woodland sites in the middle Ohio River Valley." Milner argues that "[s]ocieties classified as Early Woodland had appeared by the opening centuries of the first millennium BC, and they lasted for the next 500 or more years." George R. Milner, *The Moundbuilders*, 54.

54   Presumably, when Randall states that the Ohio Serpent Mound is the "most accurate and distinctively representative…of all the snake mounds," he means that it most accurately, of all of the snake mounds, represents the natural snake.

55   E. O. Randall, *The Serpent Mound, Adams County, Ohio: Mystery of the Mound and History of the Serpent, Various Theories of the Effigy Mounds and the Mound Builders* (Columbus, Ohio: The Ohio State Archaeological and Historical Society, 1907 [Published by Forgotten Books, 2012]), 52 and 55.

stands alone,...it has no anologue [sic] among the numerous basso-relievos [sic] wrought on the broad prairie lands of that region. It is indeed altogether unique among the earthworks of the New World and without a parallel in the Old."[56]

Although the 'tight spiral' that is formed by the 'tail' of the depicted serpent gives one pause, especially in light of Guénon's emphasis on the symbolism of the spiral and the 'double spiral' in Tradition and all that these symbols imply, arguably the most interesting feature of the Ohio Serpent Mound is the fact that it 'holds' what appears to be some sort of oval object in its mouth. Many researchers have wondered what this object represents. Randall quotes a Prof. James Fergusson, "another famous authority in archaeology," as stating "in his volume on 'Rude Stone Monuments in All Countries,' published in London in 1872," that "it seems to represent an action — the swallowing of something, but whether a globe or a grave is by no means clear."[57] Randall also quotes the aforementioned Dr. Wilson as stating of the Serpent Mound that

> [t]his elevated site has been cut to a conformity with an oval circumvallation on its summit, leaving a smooth external platform ten feet wide, with an inclination towards the embankment on every side. Immediately outside the inner point of this oval is the serpent's head, with distended jaws, as if in the act of swallowing what, in comparison with its huge dimensions, is spoken of as an egg, though it measures 160 feet in length.[58]

More suggestively, Squier, whom we referred to before, says of the Serpent Mound in *The Serpent Symbol, and the Worship of the Reciprocal Principles of Nature in America* that

> it is clearly and unmistakably, in form and attitude, the representation of a serpent, with jaws distended, in the act of swallowing or ejecting an oval

---

56 E. O. Randall, *The Serpent Mound, Adams County, Ohio*, 56.
57 E. O. Randall, *The Serpent Mound, Adams County, Ohio*, 57.
58 E. O. Randall, *The Serpent Mound, Adams County, Ohio*, 55–56.

figure, which we shall distinguish, from the suggestions of an analogy, as *An Egg*. Assuming for the entire structure a religious origin, it can be regarded only as the recognized symbol of some grand mythological idea. What abstract conception was thus embodied, or what vast event thus typically commemorated, we have no certain means of knowing.[59]

Randall also refers to a related remark made by Squier and a certain 'Davis,' whose first name is not provided, on the Serpent Mound in their book *Ancient Monuments of the Mississippi Valley*. There, according to Randall, Squier and Davis observe that "the neck of the serpent is stretched out slightly curved, and its mouth is opened wide as if in the act of swallowing or ejecting an oval figure which rests partially within the distended jaws."[60]

Squier extends his analysis of the oval, or supposed 'egg,' held by the Serpent Mound in *The Serpent Symbol, and the Worship of the Reciprocal Principles of Nature in America* under an examination of the 'Mundane [or 'World'] Egg' that appears in a variety of artworks from around the world. Squier contends, as we discussed in some depth already in Chapter 10, that

> the ['World'] *Egg* became associated with man's primitive idea of a creation. It aptly symbolized that primordial, quiescent state of things which preceded their vitalization and activity, — the inanimate chaos, before life began, when 'the earth was without form and void, and darkness was upon the face of the deep.' It was thus received in the early cosmogonies, in all of which the vivification of the *Mundane Egg* constituted the act of creation.[61]

---

59 E. G. Squier, *The Serpent Symbol, and the Worship of the Reciprocal Principles of Nature in America*, 145.

60 E. O. Randall, *The Serpent Mound, Adams County, Ohio*, 64–65, referencing E. G. Squier, *Ancient Monuments of the Mississippi Valley* (Washington DC: Smithsonian Books, 1998 [originally published in 1848]).

61 E. G. Squier, *The Serpent Symbol, and the Worship of the Reciprocal Principles of Nature in America*, 146.

Squier supports his remarks with various examples, saying, for instance, that

> [w]e have...the egg, representing Being simply, Chaos, the great void from which, by the will of the superlative Unity, proceeds the generative or creative influence; designated among the Greeks as "*Phanes*," "Golden-pinioned *Love*," "The Universal Father," "Egg-born Protagoras" (the later Zeus or Jupiter); in India as "*Brahma*," the "Great Parent of Rational Creatures," the "Father of the Universe;" and in Egypt as *Phtha*, the "Universal Creator."
>
> The Chinese, whose religious conceptions correspond generally with those of India, entertained similar notions of the origin of things. They set forth that chaos, before the creation, existed in the form of a vast egg, in which were contained the principles of all things. Its vivification, among them also, constituted the act of creation.
>
> In these opinions many other nations of the ancient world, the Egyptians, the Assyrians, the Phoenicians, and the Indo-Scythiac nations of Europe, participated.[62]

Squier also references George Stanley Faber favorably, who argued in *The Origin of Pagan Idolatry* that

> [t]he ancient pagans in almost every part of the globe were wont to symbolize the World by an egg. Hence this hieroglyphic is introduced into the cosmogonies of nearly all nations....The symbol was employed to represent not only the Earth, but likewise the Universe in its largest extent: though I am inclined to believe, that in its primary application the Earth alone was intended.[63]

All of the above quotations from Squier are reminiscent of Guénon's study of the serpent and the 'World Egg' as presented in *The Great*

---

62 E. G. Squier, *The Serpent Symbol, and the Worship of the Reciprocal Principles of Nature in America*, 148–149.

63 George Stanley Faber, *The Origin of Pagan Idolatry Ascertained from Historical Testimony and Circumstantial Evidence*, Vol. I (London: A. J. Valpy, Tooke's Court, Chancery Lane, 1816), 175.

Triad. As we have already discussed, Guénon argues in that work that there are various symbols of "duality in unity," such as the Androgyne, *yin-yang*, 'World Egg', double spiral, and serpent, that represent a single 'cosmic force' which became/becomes 'polarized,' and thus 'dual,' by the 'manifestation'/creation process. As Guénon puts it, "we may thus speak either of the dual action of a single force...or of two forces produced by its polarization."[64] Squier's thesis concerning the World Egg in *The Serpent Symbol, and the Worship of the Reciprocal Principles of Nature in America* is very similar to Guénon's interpretation of the traditional meaning of the symbolism of the serpent-with-egg in the terms that both authors believe that this 'compound symbol' represents the existence of some form of fundamental 'duality' or 'dichotomy' in the universe. As Squier puts it, "we may regard the compound symbol of the serpent and the egg...as an illustration of the doctrine of the reciprocal principles, which...enters largely into the entire fabric of primitive philosophy and mythology."[65] By 'reciprocal principles,' Squier has in mind 'active' and 'passive' principles that, together, allow for the event of cosmic creation. He states,

> We claim to have shown that the grand conception of a Supreme Unity, and the doctrine of the reciprocal principles, existed in America in a well defined and easily recognized form. Our present inquiry relates to the symbols by which they were represented in both continents.... [T]he sun came to symbolize the active principle, the vivifying power; and...obviously the egg symbolized the passive elements of nature. That fire should be taken to be the physical, of what the sun is the celestial emblem, is sufficiently apparent....But how the serpent came to possess, *as a symbol*, a like significance with these, is not so obvious. That it did so, however, cannot be doubted.[66]

---

64 René Guénon, *The Great Triad*, 32.

65 E. G. Squier, *The Serpent Symbol, and the Worship of the Reciprocal Principles of Nature in America*, 154.

66 E. G. Squier, *The Serpent Symbol, and the Worship of the Reciprocal Principles of Nature in America*, 154.

In these remarks, Squier ultimately arrives at an equation of the traditional symbolism of the sun with that of the serpent, as he is arguing that both sun and serpent represent the 'vivifying power,' or 'active' principle, of the two 'reciprocal principles of nature.'

In *The Great Triad*, however, Guénon, in speaking of the 'two forces' produced from the 'polarization' of a single metaphysical force, remarks that the two serpents of the caduceus convey "the general symbolism of the serpent in its two opposite aspects."[67] These two 'aspects,' however, are manifestations of Guénon's singular metaphysical 'Principle,' and so exist *within* the manifested state of being (within creation, that is) as dichotomies, such as birth and death, and beneficence and maleficence.[68] However, because these two 'aspects' of manifestation that are represented, for Guénon, by the two serpents of the caduceus exist 'within' manifestation (within the physical realm, roughly put), they *cannot* represent the 'active' principle of nature, as Squier believes, because, according to Guénon, the 'active' principle is *meta-physical*. The truly 'active' Principle that manifests, according to Guénon's understanding of traditional thought, *as* 'nature' is always a metaphysical reality which is represented by the various figurations of the 'World Axis,' such as the rod, tree, cross, etc. Such figurations of the World Axis are never symbolized by the serpent but often juxtaposed *with* the serpent. The traditional symbolism of the serpent, therefore, never symbolizes the metaphysical or divine itself, but, on the contrary, merely represents *how* the divine/metaphysical reveals itself in 'nature'/*samsara*/*matter*/"the indefinite series of cycles of manifestation." Charlesworth states in *The Good and Evil Serpent* that "in Egypt the uraeus had solar significance, and in some Greek magical papyri Helios (the sun) was often portrayed as a serpent."[69] I argue that this figuration that he refers to doesn't imply the *serpent's*

---

67 René Guénon, *The Great Triad*, 33.
68 René Guénon, *The Great Triad*, 31.
69 James H. Charlesworth, *The Good and Evil Serpent*, 235.

divinity but, rather, the serpent's traditional role as that which best *expresses* divinity in the 'lower,' terrestrial, realm of 'nature.' Although the symbolism of the sun, as a form of the symbolism of the divine circle, represents divinity across cultures, and therefore represents the 'active' principle that manifests *in* 'nature,' it is the serpent's role, expressed in the traditional symbolism of the serpent, to merely 'absorb' the sun's (the divine's) power 'passively.'[70] It is, thus, that the serpent's 'immortality' is of a 'derivative' kind, as it is merely that of cyclical rejuvenation in the physical world.

For Guénon and Squier, the 'World,' or 'Mundane,' 'Egg' traditionally symbolizes a 'passive' element that is acted upon by an 'active' element traditionally symbolized by the serpent. As we have seen, however, the 'Word' of John 1:1 that, according to Guénon, 'produces manifestation' represents not the 'active' power in the creation process but the *means* by which creation is affected, two things that are not any more equivalent than Aristotle's efficient and material causes.[71] In medieval European alchemical imagery relating to John 3:14, the Word that is identified with Christ in John 1:1 is depicted as a serpent crucified on a cross, with this imagery also alluding to Moses's raising of the serpent in the wilderness that is described in Numbers 21. In *Alchemy & Mysticism*, Alexander Roob reproduces an illustration of a crucified serpent taken from the alchemist A. Eleazar's *Uraltes chymisches Werk*, itself taken from a fourteenth- or fifteenth-century codex created by the alchemist Nicolas Flamel (see fig. 14.4). Roob says of the illustration that

---

70 James Charlesworth relates the well-known fact that, like other cold-blooded creatures, "the snake must receive its warmth from the sun or the earth." James H. Charlesworth, *The Good and Evil Serpent*, 242. Thinking symbolically, we should ask whether these two sources of 'warmth,' sun and earth, represent what I call the 'dilemma' of *matter*: 1) to be formed, defined, actualized, etc. by the celestial realm (represented by the sun) or 2) to 'fall' further into formlessness, indefinitude, and potentiality (represented by the earth).

71 René Guénon, *The Great Triad*, 33.

[t]he serpent that Moses nailed to the cross...is a symbol of the healing power of the Mercurial elixir, the crucified Christ (John 3, 14). Pseudo-Eleazar calls this snake the "powerful king of nature" who heals the whole world....But before it can become effective, the primaterial poisonous body must be dismembered and the volatile spirit fixed with a golden nail.[72]

Fig. 14.4. Untitled (Crucified Serpent)[73]

Flamel's illustration, like much alchemical imagery, alludes to passages from the Bible. In the present illustration, the imagery alludes to both Numbers 21 and John 3:14 in that it depicts the nailing of a

---

72 Alexander Roob, *Alchemy & Mysticism*, 329.
73 A. Eleazar, *Uraltes chymisches Werk*, Leipzig, 1760, in Alexander Roob, *Alchemy & Mysticism*, 329.

serpent to a cross in order to represent, as Roob puts it, the 'healing' of the 'whole world.' Such metaphysical 'healing' is, of course, what Christians believe that Christ came to earth for. In the spirit of John 3:14, Flamel's illustration presents the serpent as the *means* of the creation/manifestation process, just as Jesus on the cross was the means of salvation and a 'new' creation in Him *as* God for Christians. I contend, however, that Jesus did not take on the role of God as Creator of the universe because Christ on the cross is not equal to God the Creator in Its metaphysical 'completeness' — God as pure Spirit. "The primaterial poisonous body" that God took on to 'become' Jesus disallows such an equivalency between Christ on the cross and God the Creator. In the alchemical illustration that I referred to, it is the 'Word' of God in John 1:1, and *not* God Itself, that is depicted as a serpent nailed to a cross, just as Jesus, also as the 'Word,' was nailed to the cross. In John 1:1, it is stated that it was, specifically, "in the beginning," not at some other time, that the Word was "with God" and "was God." And John 4:24 tells us that "God is spirit." Therefore, at the time of 'the beginning,' but at no other specified time, we are told that the Word was equivalent to spirit. [ESV] It is implied, therefore, that the Word is not necessarily *always* (equivalent to) spirit. God's manifestation in human form, specifically in the form of the *avatar* known as Jesus Christ, 'begot' a being that was, according to Christian doctrine, *not* pure spirit but *both* God (Spirit) *and* man at the same time. Like the theological interpretation of Jesus's crucifixion, therefore, I argue that the serpent in Flamel's illustration is depicted as being reintegrated, or reconciled, with the 'Godhead' after its sojourn into the physical world. This 'reintegration' is depicted, in the case of the serpent, by its being fastened by the 'golden nail' of God back into a metaphysical/spiritual state of being, just as Jesus is reintegrated into the Godhead, according to Christian theology, by his crucifixion on Calvary.[74]

---

74 See Chapter 8 for a discussion of the symbolism of 'gold' and 'golden.'

The crucified physical nature, or body, of Jesus of Nazareth was, like the serpent represented as nailed to a cross in Flamel's art, a 'passive' vessel for the 'active' Principle that is called 'the Lord God' or *Yahweh* in the Bible; for it is always, and only, the 'unmixed' metaphysical 'Principle' that is 'active.' It is, therefore, not the *serpent* in Flamel's alchemical imagery that represents the 'active' power of creation, as Squier and Guénon argue in other cases of serpent symbolism, but the axial symbol: the cross. It is the crucified serpent, like the crucified Christ, that is the *means* of the creation/manifestation process, whether this be the creation of the universe or the creation of a 'new' man by a sort of metaphysical 'healing' of the spirit. Jesus of Nazareth, before his crucifixion, is, in alchemical language, 'contaminated' with a 'poisonous body' that has not yet been 'dismembered' by the purifying crucifixion which will allow the Spirit of God to extricate, or 'separate,' itself from the 'natural' world after its sojourn there. According to Guénon, it is also the *dragon* that, like the serpent, represents in Tradition only the conditions (the 'locus of possibles'[75]) for creation and not the 'active' force of creation that actualizes those conditions. The 'healing' that is affected in the cases of the alchemical crucifixion and the crucifixion of Jesus is, as we have seen in connection with the ancient idea of healing represented in the Rod of Asklepios, a form of creation by archaic man. Although Guénon's metaphysical 'Principle,' the divine, is often represented by using the axial imagery of the 'World Axis,' such as the cross, this Principle is, as we have seen, also represented by the traditional symbolism of the *circle*. I argue that the so-called 'oval,' or 'egg,' that is represented in the Ohio Serpent Mound is a symbolic variation of the traditional 'divine circle.'

As I have already stated, there is a dualism inherent in the symbolism of the serpent/dragon, but it is not the dualism of so-called 'active' and 'passive' principles of nature. This is because, as we have seen, the 'active' element in serpent (and dragon, as we shall soon see)

---

75 René Guénon, *The Multiple States of the Being*, 68.

symbolism is always represented by variations of the 'World Axis,' and the World Axis symbolizes the metaphysical 'Principle.' The serpent/dragon, by contrast, usually symbolizes in Tradition something entirely 'passive,' *matter* as I define it: the potential, indefinite, and formless flux of *samsara*. The oval object depicted in the mouth of the so-called 'Serpent Mound' of Adams County, Ohio, is, as Squier observes, an egg. It is, as Squier contends, *the egg*, the 'World Egg' that may be found in various traditional myths and artworks from around the world. What is equally significant to the Serpent Mound's representing a serpent-with-egg, however, is that the Serpent Mound is a *mound*. According to Guénon, the mound is a traditional representation of the *Omphalos*, which is itself "an image of the sacred mountain."[76] Since the 'sacred mountain' is a symbol of the 'World Axis,' the Ohio Serpent Mound qualifies, from Guénon's perspective, as an example of traditional axial imagery. Of the three components (mound, serpent, and oval/egg), it is the mound component, specifically, of the Ohio Serpent Mound that represents the 'active principle' (the metaphysical 'Principle') in creation/manifestation. It is *not*, as Squier argues, the serpent that symbolizes the 'active principle.' The serpent element of the Ohio Serpent Mound, in opposition, symbolizes the 'passive' element, or 'means,' by which creation/manifestation occurs. Randall notes that the Serpent Mound lies upon the crest of a 'high ridge' of a "sharp, jutting bluff" that "overhangs Brush Creek, whose waters wash its base."[77] This nearness of the Serpent Mound to water confirms my contention that the serpent represented there symbolizes 'passivity,' or in my terms potentiality, indefinitude, and formlessness, because, as we will see, the serpent/dragon is frequently associated in Tradition with water as a 'symbolic synonym' for 'passivity' or potentiality.

There are three primary traditional symbolic elements exhibited in the Ohio Serpent Mound: 1) the mound, 2) the serpent, and 3) the

---

76 René Guénon, *The King of the World*, 59.
77 E. O. Randall, *The Serpent Mound, Adams County, Ohio*, 8–9.

oval/egg. According to Guénon, however, the symbolism of the oval is symbolically derivative of the traditional symbolism of the circle, a 'version' of the circle, one might say. I agree with Squier's argument that the Ohio Serpent Mound represents the 'World Egg' by means of the oval-shaped object that it 'holds' in its mouth, and that, since the World Egg is traditionally associated with the event or process of creation/manifestation, the Ohio Serpent Mound also somehow represents creation/manifestation.[78] I disagree with Squier, however, in terms of the *manner* by which the Ohio Serpent Mound communicates the traditional idea of creation/manifestation. On one level, a more superficial level, it is more consistent, in looking at other figurations of the traditional serpent symbol, to interpret the Ohio Serpent Mound as symbolizing not the event of potentiality being actualized but the event of potentiality emerging from potentiality, one *kind* of potential emerging from another kind of potential, in other words. Although accurate, I think, this is only a superficial interpretation of the meaning of the Serpent Mound in terms of what most viewers today would take to be its salient features: the serpent shape and the egg shape. If one looks more deeply into the symbolism of the Serpent Mound, one sees, as I noted earlier, the mound *itself* symbolizing the actualizing ('active') force out of Squier's two 'reciprocal principles of nature.' One also sees, however, the serpent and the 'egg' that the serpent 'holds,' together, symbolizing the 'passive' force of Squier's two 'principles.' I argue that both 'egg' *and* serpent symbolize, together, the 'passive' element (in Squier's terminology) that is 'vivified' or 'vitalized,' not by the serpent, as Squier argues, but by that element which both 'egg' and serpent have in common: the mound out of which they are constructed. Like a tree, or a rod, or a cross, or a stone, this mound out of which the Ohio Serpent Mound was constructed symbolizes the 'World Axis' or 'cosmic force' that is, according to Guénon, 'polarized' into two forces. In the case of the Ohio Serpent Mound, these

---

78 E. G. Squier, *The Serpent Symbol, and the Worship of the Reciprocal Principles of Nature in America*, 146.

two resultant 'passive' forces are symbolized by the serpent and the 'egg.'

Squier repeatedly states in *The Serpent Symbol, and the Worship of the Reciprocal Principles of Nature in America* that the 'World Egg' represents 'chaos,' and he applies this interpretation to the 'egg' of the Ohio Serpent Mound. In doing so, Squier seems to accede that the serpent and 'egg' in Tradition are symbolically synonymous since the serpent is itself so often associated in Tradition with 'chaos.' Again, however, the serpent and the 'egg' represented in the Ohio Serpent Mound symbolize *two kinds* of potentiality or 'passivity.' The difference between these two kinds of potentiality or 'passivity' that are symbolized by the serpent and the egg of the Ohio Serpent Mound is that the serpent there symbolizes what I shall call the *essentially* 'chaotic' (formless, indefinite, and potential), as it does in much other traditional art and myth, while the 'egg' symbolizes the *relatively* 'chaotic,' or, equivalently, the 'imminently actualized.' Because of this, the 'egg' in the Serpent Mound symbolizes a state of being that is intermediate between that which the mound represents and that which the serpent represents. The 'message,' then, of the Ohio Serpent Mound could be phrased thusly: from the pure potential of *chaos* (the serpent) emerges the *relatively* clear and imminent potential (the egg) for revealing metaphysical order (the mound itself). Another way to say this is: from "the indefinite series of cycles of manifestation," from *samsara* — from the state of *matter*, specifically — emerge beings that are capable of development but that are not yet *fully* actualized; and these beings have the potential to discern metaphysical order. Still another way to express the Serpent Mound's 'message' is: from that which is continually changing — 'oscillating' between the two extremes of an indefinite number of dichotomies — comes that which still has potential but which is tending toward actualization and the revelation of *complete* actualization. More simply put: from the serpent emerges the egg, but only against the backdrop of that which 'contains' them both. The mound that represents the metaphysical 'Principle' is already there, for it is the Principle's 'polarization' that allows for the emergence of, first, serpent and, then, 'egg.' Guénon's 'Principial' order, although it may not, like the mound, reveal itself explicitly at first, is still prior to the serpentine 'chaos,' and it 'stands beneath' ('embedded' and 'hiding' to those who do not look at the whole picture) the development of 'chaos' from "the indefinite series of cycles of manifestation" to the 'imminently actual' that is symbolized by the 'World Egg.'

In our earlier discussion of the serpent *Shesha/Ananta* and the 'sacred mountain' from the *Ramayana* narrative of the 'Churning of the Sea,' we described the serpent as that which 'stands between' — like a rope in a tug-of-war — the states of being that are represented by the *Devas* and the *Asuras* in the 'Hindu Doctrines.' When we discussed the idea of the serpent/dragon as guardian, we also, similarly, interpreted its 'guardianship' more explicitly as a role of obstruction to her/him who would seek to extricate her/himself from *samsara* and 'nature.' I argue that the serpent that is represented in the Ohio Serpent Mound has the same traditional meaning as the serpent *Shesha/Ananta* does in the Hindu story of the Churning of the Sea and that the dragon Ladon does in the Greek tale of Herakles and the golden apples. In all three cases, the serpent/dragon symbolizes that which is *nothing in particular* but which *may be* either of two opposing alternatives. These two alternatives are: 1) a tool for achieving 'enlightenment'/*moksha*/immortality and 2) an obstruction to achieving 'enlightenment'/*moksha*/immortality. For such is what the state of being that I term *matter* is. The serpent and oval/egg represented in the Ohio Serpent Mound is commonly interpreted in one of two ways: 1) the serpent is ejecting an oval/egg from its mouth or 2) the serpent is swallowing an oval/egg.[79] My contention, however, is that the Serpent Mound symbolizes *both*, for it symbolizes the potential of the serpent to *either* 'eject' *or* 'swallow' the 'egg.' If, therefore, the oval that is 'held' in the mouth of the serpent that is represented in the Ohio Serpent Mound is indeed

---

79 E. G. Squier, *The Serpent Symbol, and the Worship of the Reciprocal Principles of Nature in America*, 145.

representative of the 'World Egg' of Eurasian myth and art, then that Serpent Mound symbolizes the potential for 'the world,' or 'nature,' to both: 1) be manifested and 2) fall back into oblivion. In other words, the serpent may, potentially: 1) 'eject' the 'egg,' in which case 'the world' will emerge from 'chaos' and begin to 'actualize,' or 2) 'swallow' the 'egg,' in which case the world will be 'consumed' by 'chaos' (the 'egg' will be consumed by the serpent). I shall call this the *macrocosmic* interpretation of the symbolism of the Ohio Serpent Mound.

There is also, I contend, a *microcosmic* interpretation of the traditional meaning of the Ohio Serpent Mound. On this interpretation, however, the two varieties of potentiality/'passivity' that are symbolized by the serpent and 'egg' are not characteristic of existence in general but of the (any) individual being that is 'migrating' through "the indefinite series of cycles of manifestation." 'Microcosmically,' the Ohio Serpent Mound symbolizes the potentialities of: 1) the individual being's emergence from *matter*/"the indefinite series of cycles of manifestation"/*samsara*/'chaos' and its attainment of *moksha*/immortality and self-'realization,' and 2) the individual being's 'fall' into the state of *matter*, as I define it: the *samsaric* "indefinite series of cycles of manifestation" in its chaotic aspect. The path of 'migration' in both cases, which I argue is "the indefinite series of cycles of manifestation," is represented by the serpent. In *The Symbolism of the Cross*, Guénon claims, as we have noted previously, that "the traversing of the different states is represented in some traditions as a migration of the being in the body of a serpent."[80] This is a nearly synonymous contention to Freidel et al.'s claim in *Maya Cosmos* that "human souls find the bodies of their newborn owners by traveling along the serpent's gullet."[81] In another context, the authors of *Maya Cosmos* also argue that the Maya 'Vision Serpent' "was the embodiment of the path to and from the Otherworld, and ancestral figures were often shown leaning out of

---

80 René Guénon, *The Symbolism of the Cross*, 122.
81 Freidel, Schele and Parker, *Maya Cosmos*, 195–96.

its open jaws to communicate with their descendants."[82] (See figs. 14.5 and 14.6.) In Chapter 9, I noted Freidel et al.'s contention that Maya 'Vision Serpents' were "symbols of the path along which supernaturals traveled on their way to being manifested in this world," concluding from this that such 'Vision Serpents' were, in a broadly traditional sense, symbols of the South Asian concept of the 'migration' of the being into different states of being.[83] I further proposed that, since a 'supernatural' being is one that exists, in its completeness, beyond ('super' or 'meta') the 'natural' order, such a being is equivalent to the *Atman* in *Vedanta* that can 'migrate' into various 'states of being,' or, as Freidel et al. claim, 'manifest in this world.'

---

82 Freidel, Schele and Parker, *Maya Cosmos*, 140.
83 Freidel, Schele and Parker, *Maya Cosmos*, 195–196.

Fig. 14.5. *The Rearing Vision Serpent*[84]

Fig. 14.6. *K'awil merged with a Vision Serpent*[85]

---

84 Freidel, Schele and Parker, *Maya Cosmos*, 198.
85 Freidel, Schele and Parker, *Maya Cosmos*, 196.

There are many examples in Mayan art, such as those provided above, of humanoid figures emerging from "the serpent's gullet," or "leaning out of its open jaws," as Freidel et al. describe the event.[86] The Mayan idea that is apparently expressed by these illustrations of, as Freidel et al. put it, 'traveling' to the 'Otherworld' sounds very much like Guénon's idea of the 'migrating' being's 'traversing' the 'multiple states of the being.' I argue that such Mayan illustrations of 'Vision Serpents' express, although in a different medium and in a different style, the same content as the serpent-with-'egg' that is depicted in the Ohio Serpent Mound. *Microcosmically*, these figurations of so-called 'Vision Serpents' symbolize, like the Ohio Serpent Mound, the potentialities of: 1) the individual being's emergence from "the indefinite series of cycles of manifestation"/*samsara*/'chaos' and its attainment of *moksha*/immortality and self-'realization,' and 2) the individual being's 'fall' into the state of *matter*, as I define it: the 'chaotic' *samsaric* "indefinite series of cycles of manifestation." *Macrocosmically*, these figurations symbolize, again like the Ohio Serpent Mound, the potential for 'the world,' or 'nature,' to either be: 1) created/manifested or 2) 'consumed' by 'falling' back into oblivion. In the cases of Maya 'Vision Serpents,' however, the so-called 'World Egg' that is represented by the oval-shaped object in the serpent's mouth is 'replaced' by a humanoid figure.[87] This humanoid figure represents the 'migrating' being, which may, or may not, be a human. This manner of symbolism employed by the Maya may be a reflection of the idea that each particular 'migrating' being encompasses the whole world *in itself*, perhaps in a manner similar to that of Gottfried Leibnitz's so-called 'monads,' in his view the most basic substances constituting all of existence, each of which

---

86 Also of note on this subject are Eliade's thoughts in *The Sacred and the Profane* on "the initiatory symbolism and ritual of being swallowed by a monster." Mircea Eliade, *The Sacred and the Profane*, 195.

87 I make no claim here as to whether the serpent with 'World Egg' or the 'Vision Serpent' with humanoid figure is the older symbolism.

perceived and reflected all of the other 'monads.'[88] Whatever the specific reasons for the equivalency between the symbolisms of 'egg' and humanoid figure, I argue that, in the same way that the serpent may, potentially, 'eject' or 'swallow' the 'egg' in the figuration of the Serpent Mound, the serpent that is represented in illustrations of Maya 'Vision Serpents' may 'eject' or 'swallow' the represented humanoid figure. And, again, the meaning that is symbolized by this representation consists of the two potentialities that: 1) in the serpent's 'ejecting' the humanoid figure 'the world' will emerge from 'chaos' and begin to 'actualize,' or 2) in the serpent's 'swallowing' the humanoid figure the world will be 'consumed' by 'chaos' (the 'human' will be consumed by the serpent).

---

88 "Gottfried Wilhelm Leibniz was born at Leipzig [Germany] in 1646....The idea of the universe as a harmonious system in which there is at the same time unity and multiplicity, coordination and differentiation of parts, seems to have become a leading idea, probably the leading idea, of Leibniz, at a very early age.... 'There must be simple substances, since there are compound substances, for the compound is only a collection or *aggregatum* of simple substances.' These simple substances, of which all empirical things are composed, are called by Leibniz 'monads'....Leibniz may have been said to have conceived the monad on an analogy with the soul. For each is in some sense a spiritual substance.... But each one, being gifted with some degree of perception, mirrors the universe, that is, the total system, in its own way." Frederick Copleston, *A History of Philosophy Volume IV: Modern Philsophy from Descartes to Leibniz* (New York, New York: Doubleday, 1960), 264, 266, and 296- 297, quoting Leibniz's *Monadology*.

CHAPTER 15

The Dragon and the Orb

The East Asian, or 'Far-Eastern,' Dragon

The *lung*, or East Asian dragon, is the most iconic of the symbols of traditional, or 'old,' China. Representations of it have continuously appeared on buildings, coins, vases, utensils, clothing, and weapons in East Asia for five thousand years. L. Newton Hayes records in his 1922 book *The Chinese Dragon* that

> [t]he first appearance of the true dragon, according to the records of what is considered to be authentic Chinese history, occurred some forty-six centuries ago, during the reign of Huang Ti, or Hsuan Yuan, the third of the five great rulers. We are told that after this personage had reigned one hundred and eleven years a large dragon appeared and took him to heaven upon his back. Since that day dragons have been seen in every dynasty and by hundreds of witnesses, as Chinese history abundantly attests.[1]

Although usually associated in popular culture with China specifically, the East Asian, or 'Far-Eastern' as Guénon calls it, dragon also appears in the traditional art of other East Asian nations, such as Japan, North and South Korea, Vietnam, Cambodia, Thailand, and Indonesia. Dragon symbolism is older than many other kinds of traditional serpent symbolism; and the dragon *is*, I argue, a symbolic variation

---

1 L. Newton Hayes, *The Chinese Dragon* (Shanghai: Commercial Press, Ltd., 1922), 11.

of the traditional 'simple' serpent. Ancient Chinese and Japanese descriptions of the dragon, however, provide it with the characteristics of various animals, with a special emphasis on the horse in Chinese texts. According to Marinus Willem de Visser in *The Dragon in China and Japan*,

> Wang Fu ["who lived at the time of the Han dynasty," 206 BCE-220 CE] says: "The people paint the dragon's shape with a horse's head and a snake's tail. Further, there are expressions as 'three joints' and 'nine resemblances' (of the dragon), to wit: from head to shoulder, from shoulder to breast, from breast to tail. These are the joints; as to the nine resemblances, they are the following: his horns resemble those of a stag, his head that of a camel, his eyes those of a demon, his neck that of a snake, his belly that of a clam (*shen*...), his scales those of a carp, his claws those of an eagle, his soles those of a tiger, his ears those of a cow. Upon his head he has a thing like a broad eminence (a big lump), called *ch'ih muh*....If a dragon has no *ch'ih muh*, he cannot ascend to the sky".[2]

Any child, however, who looks at any illustration of an East Asian dragon will most likely note first the serpentine qualities of the dragon, and these above all else. De Visser states that

> [t]he connection between the snake and the dragon is evident from the description of the so-called *t'eng-she*...a wingless serpent, "which can cause the clouds to rise, and, riding upon them, can fly a thousand miles. It can change into a dragon. Although there are males and females, they do not copulate. Their cry forbodes pregnancy". And Koh Hung states that "tortoises turn into tigers and snakes into dragons". In the *Yiu-yang tsah tsu* we read: "Dragons and snakes are considered by the learned class to be related".[3]

Also:

---

2   Marinus Willem de Visser, *The Dragon in China and Japan* (New York, New York: Cosimo, 2008 [originally published in 1913]), 70 (and 66 for bracketed note).

3   Marinus Willem de Visser, *The Dragon in China and Japan*, 75.

An Appendix of the *Yih king* says: "The hibernating of dragons and snakes is done in order to preserve their bodies". Here we see dragons and snakes being closely connected and regarded as belonging to the same kind of animals. Also in later times the same fact is to be observed.[4]

General Relationship between the Serpent/ Dragon and the Circle/Sphere

In many representations of the 'Far-Eastern Dragon,' there is depicted a circular/spherical object that is either: 1) held in one claw of the dragon, 2) held in the mouth of the dragon, or 3) simply placed in front of the figure of the dragon (see fig. 15.1). What exactly this circular/spherical object is, no one seems able to prove. It has been called an 'orb,' a 'ball,' a 'spiral,' a 'pearl,' and even Earth's moon.

Fig. 15.1. Plate, Ch'ing Dynasty, Yung-cheng period, 1723–1735, Mr. and Mrs. Myron S. Falk, Jr.[5]

---

4   Marinus Willem de Visser, *The Dragon in China and Japan*, 38.
5   Hugo Munsterberg, *Dragons in Chinese Art*, 58.

I argue in this chapter that traditional representations of the 'Far-Eastern,' and specifically Chinese, dragon-with-'orb'[6] parallel the symbolism of: 1) the serpent-with-'egg' that is found, for example, in the so-called 'Ohio Serpent Mound' and 2) the serpent-with-humanoid figure (which is very often a serpent-with-humanoid *head*) that is found in Maya 'Vision Serpents.' This symbolic parallelism consists in the fact that all three figurations are composed of a serpentine creature combined, or juxtaposed, with a circular, oval, or spherical object. There is a striking consonance of subject matter and composition expressed by all three of these wide-spread cultural figurations, one in Asia, one in North America, and the third in Central America, the last two of which are separated from the first by both the largest of the earth's oceans and, most probably, hundreds if not thousands of years between their respective originations and that of the Far-Eastern Dragon. The *superficial* symbolic grammar of Far-Eastern dragon symbolism is, it is noted, not equivalent to the superficial symbolic grammar of Pre-Columbian American serpent symbolism in terms of specifics. A sphere or an 'orb' is not an oval or an 'egg' or a human head. Being gripped in a dragon's claw is not resting in a serpent's open mouth. *Substantially*, however, depictions of the East Asian dragon-with-'orb' are equivalent in both subject matter and formal composition to the Ohio Serpent Mound with 'egg' as well as to Maya 'Vision Serpents' with humanoid heads or humanoid figures protruding from their mouths. This overall symbolic equivalence is no historical accident.

We have already briefly considered the symbolism of the dragon-with-'orb' in Chapter 10 in discussing what I have called 'symbols of duality in unity.' In that chapter, I discussed the East Asian philosophical idea of *Tao* in connection with Guénon's claim that the "Far-Eastern symbolism of the Dragon…correspond[s] in a certain way to the Western theological conception of the Word as the 'locus

---

6 For the most part, I shall refer to the circular/spherical object often found in depictions of the East Asian dragon as an 'orb.'

of possibles."⁷ I argued there, with respect to Guénon's claim, that insofar as the Far-Eastern Dragon symbolizes the 'locus of possibles' which the metaphysical 'Principle' may act *through*, it also symbolizes the 'possibles' (potentiality) that the *Tao* in its 'actionless' way 'acts' through. I further contended that the 'Word,' insofar as it serves as the means of revealing or making manifest the metaphysical Principle in the symbolism of the serpent-with-'egg,' and insofar as the serpent and the dragon are roughly equivalent symbolisms, which Eliade explicitly affirms, also serves by means of the Far-Eastern dragon-*with*-'orb'/'ball'/'pearl'/'spiral'/'moon' to reveal the *Tao*. This last is in accordance with both: 1) Guénon's contention that the *Tao* is the 'Far-Eastern' version of the 'Principle' and 2) my contention that the dragon-with-'orb'/ball/pearl/spiral/moon is the 'Far-Eastern' version of the serpent-with-'egg' or serpent-with-head.

In Chapter 10, we noted that in *The Great Triad* Guénon speaks of the Egyptian god *Kneph* being "represented by the form of a serpent producing an egg from its mouth...an image of the production of manifestation by the Word."⁸ In *Perspectives on Initiation* he says the same:

> Among the ancient Egyptians, *Kneph* in the form of a serpent produces the 'World Egg' from his mouth (which implies an allusion to the essential role of the Word as producer of manifestation).⁹

We also noted in Chapter 10 that in *The Reign of Quantity & the Signs of the Times*, Guénon further remarks that "the Far Eastern Dragon… [is] a symbol of the Word," thus allowing that the symbolisms of the serpent and the dragon may serve the same symbolic function.¹⁰ Since both serpent and dragon are traditional symbols of the Word for

---

7   René Guénon, *The Multiple States of the Being*, 68.
8   René Guénon, *The Great Triad*, 33.
9   René Guénon, *Perspectives on Initiation*, 296.
10 René Guénon, *The Reign of Quantity & the Signs of the Times*, 205.

Guénon, they both symbolize for him the 'production of manifestation.' But *how* exactly do serpent and dragon symbolize 'production' for Guénon? For, it may be presumed that 'production' always refers to the *will* or *intent* behind 'production' and that, therefore, this is what the serpent/dragon symbolizes in Tradition. There are, however, latent or passive elements in any process of production just as there are active or willful elements. It is useful to recall Squier's more complex version of Guénon's above statement, that "according to the mystagogues, KNEPH…was represented as a serpent thrusting from his mouth an egg, from which proceeds the divinity Phtha, the active, creative power."[11] For in this quotation, Squier very clearly attributes the 'active'/'creative' element *not* to the serpent, and not even to that which emerges from the serpent's mouth, the 'egg,' but to that which, as he says, 'proceeds' from the 'egg.' The active *"producer* of manifestation," as Squier interprets the same imagery examined by Guénon, is symbolized not by the serpent but rather by something else. Since the serpent is still an integral part in the traditional imagery that symbolizes the *overall* 'production' process, however, it may be *taken* to symbolize the entire process.

In traditional symbolic figurations of the serpent/dragon with circular/spherical object, it is not, I argue, the serpent/dragon but rather the circular/spherical object that symbolizes the *'producer* of manifestation' in its 'active' aspect. In Squier's example of the god KNEPH and the 'egg,' the serpent, although it symbolizes 'production,' does not symbolize the actual *'producer* of manifestation' because it only 'produces' the 'egg,' and the 'egg' does *not* traditionally symbolize 'manifestation.' It is, however, *from* the egg that "the active, creative power" (Phtha) that *actively* 'produces manifestation' emerges. The serpent in the figuration of the serpent-with-'egg' is, therefore, *not* symbolic of "the active, creative power." Neither is the 'egg' symbolic of this power. What the 'egg,' or oval more specifically, traditionally

---

11 E. G. Squier, *The Serpent Symbol, and the Worship of the Reciprocal Principles of Nature in America*, 150.

symbolizes, according to Guénon, is a 'differentiation' of what the circle/sphere traditionally symbolizes. Although, therefore, the serpent/dragon symbolizes for Guénon the 'Word' and the "production of manifestation," this does not imply that it symbolizes the "active, creative" *element* in the "production of manifestation." As I previously suggested in connection with the Ohio Serpent Mound, the serpent does not symbolize *any* 'active' element in the manifestation/creation process but, rather, along with the oval/'egg' that it 'holds' in its mouth, one of two kinds of *potentiality*. Neither, in the same way, does the 'Word' of John 1:1 refer to an 'active' 'producer' but, rather, only to that which provides the *means* for 'production.' The serpent/dragon as 'Word,' therefore, for Guénon, merely provides the *means* by which the "production of manifestation" ('creation,' in John 1:1) 'proceeds' because the serpent/dragon 'produces' only the 'egg' from which the "active, creative" element emerges. In this sense, serpent and 'egg' traditionally symbolize *two forms of potentiality* necessary to 'actualize' or 'produce'/create manifestation. As argued near the end of Chapter 14, the serpent traditionally symbolizes an '*essentially* chaotic' (formless, indefinite, and potential) kind of potentiality, and the 'egg' traditionally symbolizes a '*relatively* chaotic' kind of potentiality.

'Polarization' of the Principle and Symbolic Differentiation of Circle/Sphere Symbolism

According to Guénon's interpretation of traditional symbolism, some symbols are variations of other symbols, the prior of which I call 'modifications' of the latter. In *Symbols of Sacred Science*, for example, again as noted in Chapter 10, Guénon argues that the sphere in traditional thought is considered to be "truly the primordial form, while the egg corresponds to a state already differentiated, deriving from the preceding form by a sort of 'polarization' or splitting of the center."[12] The circle, the sphere, and the oval are closely related geometrical

---

12 René Guénon, *Symbols of Sacred Science*, 212.

figures. Although in mathematics the circle is a special case of the ellipse ('oval'), according to Guénon the oval is a traditional variation (a 'modification') of the circle, the latter of which is the 'primordial form.' The circle, for Guénon, traditionally represents the 'center' that is symbolically equivalent in Tradition to the 'World Axis.' As the 'center' and the World Axis symbolize in Tradition the metaphysical Principle, so thus does the circle (or sphere). The 'egg' is a version of the oval, and therefore, like the oval, represents for Guénon in Tradition a 'polarization' of the 'center.' Like the oval, the 'egg' is a symbolic 'differentiation' of the circle. Unlike many representations of the Far-Eastern Dragon, which represent a circular or spherical object (an 'orb'), the Ohio Serpent Mound represents an oval object often interpreted as an 'egg.' The oval-shaped human heads that are represented in Maya 'Vision Serpents' are, I suggest, symbolic 'differentiations' that are roughly equivalent symbolically to the oval/'egg' in Tradition. As a 'polarization' of the 'center,' the 'egg'/head represents in Tradition a 'polarization' of that which abides at the 'center,' the 'Principle.'

We have seen Guénon employ the concept of 'polarization' when he describes the event of manifestation as the polarization of the 'unity' of the metaphysical 'force' ('Principle') into two 'currents'/'forces' that connect the various 'multiple states of the being.' We have not discussed *why*, however, the singular metaphysical Principle, the Source of all existence according to Guénon, 'polarizes' itself—why the original 'oneness' becomes 'duality,' and thus 'multiplicity.' This question was addressed at length by the third-century Neoplatonic philosopher Plotinus in his *Enneads*, a work based in large part upon what Eliade has described as the eminently *traditional* philosophy of Plato. In the 'Fifth Ennead' I.7, Plotinus discusses "the 'Intellectual-Principle' [that] stands as the image of The One," the latter of which, according to Plotinus, is the completely metaphysical source of all existence:

The Intellectual-Principle stands as the image of The One, firstly because there is a certain necessity that the first should have its offspring, carrying onward much of its quality, in other words that there be something in its likeness as the sun's rays tell of the sun. Yet The One is not an Intellectual-Principle.[13]

The 'image' and 'offspring,' as Plotinus describes them, of 'The One' is what he calls the 'Intellectual-Principle.' According to Plotinus, therefore, the discerning and dividing 'Intellectual-Principle' that makes 'dual' what is originally 'one,' by means of its discursive powers, is *not* original but is 'engendered' "simply by the fact that in... [The One's] self-quest it has vision: this very seeing is the Intellectual-Principle."[14] If we take Guénon's 'Principle' to be equivalent to Plotinus's 'One,' which I think is justified, then on Plotinus's interpretation the former 'polarizes' its 'oneness' into 'dual' 'currents' or 'forces' in order to fulfill the 'self-quest' of 'Self'-understanding. In the terms of this book, we may translate this to say that metaphysical Reality 'becomes' physical reality (specifically, the state of *matter*) in order to better understand what the meta-physical is. Roughly equivalent to this process is *Brahman*'s 'becoming' 'the multiple states of the being' as it 'migrates' through "the indefinite series of cycles of manifestation."

I have argued that the serpent does not symbolize an 'active' element in traditional representations of creation/manifestation, such as the Ohio Serpent Mound, but rather symbolizes, along with the oval/'egg' that the serpent 'holds' in its mouth, a kind of potentiality. The particular kind of potentiality that the serpent symbolizes in such figurations is what I have called the 'essentially chaotic' aspect of existence that, according to Eliade, many ancient myths represent by means of a serpent/dragon. Similar to Plotinus's 'Intellectual-Principle,' the traditional symbolism of the serpent/dragon represents that element of the creation/manifestation process that introduces

---

13 Plotinus, *The Six Enneads*, trans. Stephen MacKenna and B. S. Page (Chicago: Encyclopaedia Britannica, Inc., 1952), 211 (Fifth Ennead I.7).

14 Plotinus, *The Six Enneads*, 211–212 (Fifth Ennead I.7).

'duality' and multiplicity, thus contrariety and discrimination, into the unity of 'The One,' what Guénon calls the metaphysical 'Principle.' For it is the capacity to discriminate, or to atomize apparent unities into their 'parts,' that typifies 'intellect.' I argue that the 'polarization' of the original 'One,' or metaphysical 'Principle,' is the result of the presence of that which the 'chaotic' serpent symbolizes in Tradition, equivalently, Plotinus's 'Intellectual-Principle.' Neither serpent nor 'Intellectual-Principle,' however, is the *final cause* of the 'polarization' of 'The One'; for, just as, according to Plotinus, the 'Intellectual-Principle' only 'carries onward' 'much,' and not *all*, of the quality of 'The One,' and just as the sun's rays only *incompletely* 'tell' of the true nature of the sun, so does the traditional symbolism of the serpent represent only an *incomplete* means of expressing the 'Principle' or 'One.'

In the traditional symbolism of the serpent-with-oval/'egg' that is epitomized in the Ohio Serpent Mound, the serpent symbolizes both Plotinus's 'Intellectual-Principle' that is the 'offspring' of 'The One' as well as Guénon's 'polarization' of the 'Principle.' Just as, according to Plotinus, "the sun's rays tell of the sun" — the manifested, in other words, 'tells of' that which it manifests — "the indefinite series of cycles of manifestation" (specifically *matter*) that is symbolized by the serpent 'tells of' (is an incomplete expression of) the metaphysical 'Principle' (Plotinus's 'One'). For a traditionally raised or trained person, therefore, to 'see' the serpent symbol is to see *through* the serpent symbol to that which it 'tells of,' just as the sun's rays 'tell of' the sun: the Principle or 'One' that is represented in Tradition not only by 'axial' figures such as the tree, rod, or mound, but also by the sun. I argue, however, that it is more specifically the disk or circle (or sphere) of the sun that, for Guénon, more accurately than the 'egg' and other symbolic 'differentiations,' symbolizes the metaphysical 'Principle'/'One.' The oval/'egg' that appears in traditional figurations of the serpent-with-oval/'egg,' therefore, as a 'differentiation' or 'modification' of the circle/sphere, only represents, as Guénon says, an 'already differentiated' expression of the 'Principle'/'One'. For, again, as Guénon argues in *Symbols of Sacred Science*, it is the sphere (equivalent, I suggest, to the circle in two-dimensional representations) in traditional thought that "extending equally in all directions from its center, is truly the primordial form, while the egg corresponds to a state already differentiated, deriving from the preceding form by a sort of 'polarization' or splitting of the center."[15]

The combination of 'egg' and serpent in traditional art and myth symbolizes the two following ideas as it promises the two corresponding symbolic eventualities: 1) potentiality in its aspect of imminent production/manifestation/'creation,' *an egg about to hatch*, and 2) potentiality in its 'chaotic' aspect, *a serpent about to strike*. The first is an only *relatively* 'chaotic' form of potentiality because it is *initially* actualized in production/manifestation/creation. The second is an *essentially* 'chaotic' form of potentiality because it is *initially* actualized in destruction. The hatching egg *initially* leads to life whereas the striking serpent *initially* leads to death. Perhaps counterintuitively for moderns, that which *appears* to hold more power in representations of the serpent-with-'egg,' the serpent, is, because most 'derivative' of the three elements of serpent, 'egg,' and 'active' power within the 'egg,' actually *least* powerful. Guénon argues that the 'egg' in Tradition symbolizes a 'successive phase' of the sphere in terms of what he calls the "cosmogonic process."[16] A further 'successive phase,' I would argue, is symbolized in Tradition by the essentially 'chaotic' serpent. In applying Guénon's interpretation of the sphere and oval/'egg' in Tradition to the Ohio Serpent Mound, therefore, the oval/'egg' that the serpent 'holds' in its mouth in that figuration is symbolically 'derivative' of whatever it is that represents the 'World Axis' in that figuration. It turns out, however, that there are two elements of the Ohio Serpent Mound that represent the 'World Axis' and, thus, both symbolize the

---

15 René Guénon, *Symbols of Sacred Science*, 212.
16 René Guénon, *Symbols of Sacred Science*, 212.

metaphysical 'Principle.' These two 'axial' elements are: 1) the *mound itself*, which represents the 'active,' 'Principial,' element of production/creation and 2) the oval/'egg,' which represents the *relative concealment* of the 'Principle' in the world of manifestation by means of the *imperfection* of the egg (oval) *as* a 'derivation' of the circle/sphere. The oval/'egg' of the Ohio Serpent Mound is, therefore, in its 'distortion' of the circle/sphere, indicative of the metaphysical Principle's relative 'hiddenness' in manifested existence. This is also reflected, I suggest, in the South Asian belief that *Brahman* is 'hidden' in *samsara* until revealed by the 'migrating' being's 'realization' of the *Atman/Brahman* equivalency. One may ask why, however, the circle/sphere appears in some traditional art, such as the Ohio Serpent Mound, in its 'derivative' 'egg'/oval form, 'hiding' the 'Principle,' but in other traditional art in its 'primordial form,' *revealing directly* the 'Principle' in, for example, representations of the Far-Eastern Dragon with 'orb.' This we shall examine in due course.

The Serpent/Dragon and the Moon

One reasonable inference as to the meaning of the symbolism of the circle/sphere that is juxtaposed with the dragon in much traditional East Asian art is that it symbolizes the moon. Since the phases of the moon and the snake's shedding of its skin are, as previously mentioned, both paragons of cyclicity in Tradition, this is not a surprising thesis. Both the phases of the moon and the snake's shedding of its skin were immediate and pervasive phenomena in the lives of traditional/archaic humans who were attuned to, and embedded in, natural processes. In *Patterns in Comparative Religion*, Eliade observes that "what emerges fairly clearly from… [the] varied symbolism of snakes is their lunar character…their powers of fertility, of regeneration, of immortality through metamorphosis."[17] Marija Gimbutas discusses

---

17   Mircea Eliade, *Patterns in Comparative Religion*, 169.

sphere/moon/serpent symbolism and its antiquity in more detail in *The Language of the Goddess*:

> We learn that both a sphere and a snake coil may represent the full moon. Opposed crescents with a snake coil in the middle, or opposed crescents alone, depict the moon cycle and are frequently encountered on stones.... The wavy lines of a winding serpent appear to measure time; each turn is a counting of the lunar calendar....Such peculiarly winding serpents are encountered not only on Irish megalithic stones, but are also engraved on antler artifacts of the northern European Mesolithic and on the 5th millennium B.C. ceramics of east-central Europe. This argues that time reckoning may well have been accomplished by a similar method in all parts of Europe....The full moon is represented by a spiral or snake coil....Winding serpents, circles, and arcs appear as symbols of renewal with possible lunar configurations.[18]

Gimbutas also states that "possible lunar cycles as symbols of renewal are engraved on curbstones of Knowth,"[19] an ancient megalithic mound site in Ireland.[20] Although Eliade mentions rather laconically that "the snake is an animal that 'changes,'"[21] the serpent, as well as the moon, is a type of metamorphic being that, more particularly, *cyclically returns*. Although mammalian molting of hair/fur and avian molting of feathers are also cyclically 'returning' processes, they were not, I would suggest, as dramatic to traditional/archaic peoples as the snake's shedding of its skin. The snake and the moon, therefore, perhaps more than any other physical beings or phenomena, conjure in the human imagination the concepts of both regeneration and immortality as the results of *transformation*. This has probably led, for the most part, to their being united in some ancient symbolisms. Such

---

18 Marija Gimbutas, *The Language of the Goddess*, 286–87.
19 Marija Gimbutas, *The Language of the Goddess*, 286.
20 Service and Bradbery argue in *The Standing Stones of Europe* that the mound site at Knowth dates to the fourth millennium BCE. Alastair Service and Jean Bradbery, *The Standing Stones of Europe*, 209–213.
21 Mircea Eliade, *Patterns in Comparative Religion*, 168.

combination, however, does not imply that the circle/sphere ('orb') that is so often traditionally represented with the serpent/dragon always, or even usually, symbolizes Earth's moon. As we have seen, and as we shall continue to discuss, it does not.

The Serpent's/Dragon's Traditional Association with the Control of 'Water'

In addition to its common association with the moon, the serpent/dragon is also, as we have alluded to in previous chapters, traditionally associated with water. As with the moon, this is a symbolic association that is extremely ancient. In *The Language of the Goddess*, Gimbutas states that

> [t]he association of the snake with water or stream symbols is visible in ceramic decoration from c. 5500 B.C. on. This symbolism is expressed in isolated snakes, coils, or interlocked snake spirals painted above striated, stabbed, and criss-cross lines or adjacent to parallel lines and meanders.... Such portrayals convey that, as a symbol of life energy, the snake emerges from the waters.[22]

In *Studies in Early Chinese Culture*, former Assistant Professor of Chinese Literature at the University of Chicago Herrlee Creel states that "there is good reason to suppose that at least a part of the origin of the dragon came from some aquatic animal. That it was closely associated with water from a very early period is unquestionable."[23] Eliade argues more generally in *Patterns in Comparative Religion* that snakes and dragons in traditional mythologies are

> the emblems of water; hidden in the depths of the ocean, they are infused with the sacred power of the abyss; lying quietly in lakes or swimming across rivers, they bring rain, moisture, and floods, governing the fertility

---

22 Marija Gimbutas, *The Language of the Goddess*, 125.
23 Herrlee Glessner Creel, *Studies in Early Chinese Culture: First Series* (Wakefield, Massachusetts: The Murray Printing Company, 1938 [Reprinted by Kessinger Legacy Reprints]), 238.

of the world. Dragons dwell in the clouds and in lakes; they have charge of thunderbolts; they pour down water from the skies, making both fields and women fruitful.[24]

Eliade also remarks that

> [i]nnumerable legends and myths show snakes or dragons governing the clouds, dwelling in pools and keeping the world supplied with water. The link between snakes and springs and streams has been kept to this day in the popular beliefs of Europe. In American Indian iconography, the serpent-water connection is very often found; for instance, the Mexican rain-god, Tlaloc, is represented by an emblem of two snakes twisted together; in the same Borgia Codex a snake wounded by an arrow means rainfall.[25]

According to Enrique Florescano in *The Myth of Quetzalcoatl*, "[t]he Plumed Serpent [of the Americas] almost always appears within an aquatic medium, surrounded by lilies, sea conches, Mexican emeralds, and seeds, all symbols of fertility."[26] Similarly, in *The Snake Dance of the Hopi Indians*, Earle R. Forrest describes the 'Snake Dance' as

> an elaborate series of prayers to their [the Indians'] gods, principally to the Plumed Serpent, to send life-giving rain to save their corn and peaches, beans and squashes, and other crops that mean life to the Hopis. Rattlesnakes, bullsnakes, gartersnakes, and any snakes they can capture are believed to be messengers that will carry the prayers of this desert tribe to the gods of the underworld to send rain, and to inform their deities that the Hopis still live in the old way of their ancestors.[27]

In all of these examples, the serpent/'water' association is linked in traditional societies to the ideas of fertility and life. The traditional

---

24 Mircea Eliade, *Patterns in Comparative Religion*, 207.
25 Mircea Eliade, *Patterns in Comparative Religion*, 170. The Borgia Codex is an Aztec manuscript made of animal skins that contains ritual, divinatory, and astronomical information.
26 Enrique Florescano, *The Myth of Quetzalcoatl*, 4.
27 Earle R. Forrest, *The Snake Dance of the Hopi Indians* (New York, New York: Tower Publications, Inc., 1961 [originally published by Westernlore Press]), 8.

idea of 'life,' however, is not simply equivalent to biological processes. Eliade's observation that "you always find dragons appearing as guardians of the rhythms of life whenever the power by which the [ancient Chinese] Hsia dynasty ruled was growing weak, or undergoing a rebirth"[28] implies a larger idea of 'life' that includes political and other artificial accoutrements of the human State.

According to Eliade, it is the moon that, symbolically, ties together the ideas of fertility, immortality, and, by extension, time in Tradition, all of which are traditionally associated with the serpent/dragon. Eliade argues that "the whole pattern is moon-rain-fertility-woman-serpent-death-periodic-regeneration," although, in referring to C. Hentze's *Objets rituels croyances et dieux de la Chine antique et de l'Amérique*, he reduces this pattern to a 'Moon-Snake-Rain' symbolism.[29] Eliade states that "Hentze's researches have quite conclusively proved that this symbolism is based on the fact that the moon supplies the rains."[30] Eliade and others have argued, however, that the serpent/dragon has been identified in traditional societies not only as a 'supplier' of rain but, more generally speaking, as a 'controller' of 'water.' In *The Evolution of the Dragon*, G. Elliot Smith, of whom we have spoken before in a previous chapter, states that

> [t]he attributes of the Chinese and Japanese dragon as the controller of rain, thunder and lightning are identical with those of the American elephant-headed god....It is identified with the Indian Naga....In China and Japan… the dragon is…not only the controller of water, but the impersonation of water and its life-giving powers.[31]

---

28 Mircea Eliade, *Patterns in Comparative Religion*, 208.
29 Mircea Eliade, *Patterns in Comparative Religion*, 170–171, referring to Carl Hentze, *Objets rituels croyances et dieux de la Chine antique et de l'Amérique* (Antwerp: Anvers, Editions 'De Sikkel', 1936).
30 Mircea Eliade, *Patterns in Comparative Religion*, 171.
31 G. Elliot Smith, *The Evolution of the Dragon*, 107.

Based upon this connection between serpent/dragon and 'water' in general, we shouldn't be surprised if we see the moon and the serpent/dragon depicted together in traditional East Asian art. This may, then, cause some to conclude that the 'orb' that is sometimes depicted with the Far-Eastern Dragon must represent the moon. Some, like Eliade, may surmise that the 'orb' represents what the moon *itself* symbolizes in limited contexts, cyclicity. However, although superficially inviting, such hypotheses necessitate reconciling Guénon's interpretation of the circle/sphere as a traditional symbol of the metaphysical 'center' or 'World Axis' with the idea that the circle/sphere is a symbol of that which is the very antithesis of the immutability and trans-temporality represented by the World Axis: the moon or cyclicity.

One wonders whether traditional peoples thought one or another of the serpent/dragon and the moon was the 'true controller' of rain/water, while the other of the two was more of an 'intermediate controller.' It is known that in performing their 'Snake Dance,' the Hopi Indians of the American Southwest danced in a circle holding snakes, by means of which they 'asked' their god, the divine 'Plumed Serpent,' to "send life-giving rain."[32] The Hopi seem to have believed that the presence of snakes in combination with, specifically, *circular* dancing was a means by which rain ('water') can be conjured. In considering such examples, it may seem to the modern reader that what traditional peoples wished to control in 'controlling the waters' is the chemical compound that is two parts hydrogen and one part oxygen, since, from a 'materialistic' (in the Hobbesian sense) perspective, most biological 'life' requires water to survive. In interpreting the traditional symbolism of 'water,' however, one should always ask not what the practical use of H_2O is to humans or to 'life' in general, but what the traditional *meaning* of 'water' is. For whatever is depicted as

---

32   Earle R. Forrest, *The Snake Dance of the Hopi Indians*, 43–46 and 8. In another example of the snake/water connection, C. G. Jung notes in *Aion* that "the Naassenes…considered Naas, the serpent, to be their central deity, and they explained it as the 'moist substance.'" C. G. Jung, *Aion*, 199.

being 'controlled' in traditional figurations of 'water' is *not* equivalent to H_2O. Even from the allegedly physicalist perspective of the ancient Presocratic philosopher Thales of Miletus, 'water' is not referred to as simply some physical 'stuff.' Aristotle, after all, contends that Thales believed 'water' to be the 'principle' of *all* things, imputing to it a metaphysical, rather than a physical, identity.[33] In *The Ancient City*, Numa Denis Fustel de Coulanges similarly discusses the ancient Greek and Roman understanding of 'fire' as something more than a physical substance. De Coulanges expounds upon the Greek and Roman "worship of the sacred fire":

> Let us remark, in the first place, that this fire, which was kept burning upon the hearth, was not, in the thoughts of men, the fire of material nature. What they saw in it was not the purely physical element that warms and burns, that transforms bodies, melts metals, and becomes the powerful instrument of human industry. The fire of the hearth is of quite another nature. It is a pure fire, which can be produced only by the aid of certain rites, and can be kept up only with certain kinds of wood. It is a chaste fire; the union of the sexes must be removed far from its presence....Thus the hearth-fire is a sort of a moral being; it shines, and warms, and cooks the sacred food; but at the same time it thinks, and has a conscience; it knows men's duties, and sees that they are fulfilled.[34]

In *The Multiple States of the Being*, Guénon argues, as we noted in part in Chapter 12, that

> [t]he totalities of formal possibilities and of non-formal possibilities are what the various traditional doctrines symbolize by the 'Lower Waters' and the 'Upper Waters' respectively; in a general way and in the most extended sense, the 'Waters' represent Possibility understood as 'passive perfection',

---

33 G. S. Kirk, J. E. Raven, and M. Schofield, *The Presocratic Philosophers*, 2nd ed. (Cambridge, United Kingdom: Cambridge University Press, 1957, 1983), 89, fragment 85.

34 Numa Denis Fustel de Coulanges, *The Ancient City: A Study on the Religion, Laws, and Institutions of Greece and Rome* (Baltimore and London: The Johns Hopkins University Press, 1980 [originally published in 1864]), 23.

or the universal plastic principle, which, in Being, is determined as 'substance' (the potential aspect of Being).[35]

In *The Sacred and the Profane*, Eliade agrees that "the waters symbolize the universal sum of virtualities; they are *fons et origo*, 'spring and origin,' the reservoir of all the possibilities of existence; they precede every form and *support* every creation."[36] Based upon these quotations, it would seem that, insofar as both of them 'control' 'water,' the serpent/dragon and the moon, separately and in combination, symbolize in Tradition the 'control' of 'possibilities'/'virtualities' in general. But Eliade also contends that "the rain and the snakes are not merely things that follow the rhythms of the moon, but are in fact of the same substance," implying that, since they are all of the 'same substance,' rain ('water'), snakes, and moon are also *all* symbolic of 'possibilities'/'virtualities.'[37] If this symbolic equivalency holds among serpent/dragon, moon, and rain/'water,' then it would also seem that not only are the moon and the serpent/dragon 'controllers' of 'water,' but that 'water' is a 'controller' of 'water,' or that all three are *symbols* of the 'control' of 'water,' the 'control' of 'possibilities'/'virtualities,' that is. For now, we may conclude from this that neither the moon, the serpent/dragon, nor 'water,' by itself, symbolizes the 'controller' of 'possibilities'/'virtualities,' although each of them is symbolically associated with the idea of 'possibilities'/'virtualities' in Tradition. If serpent/dragon, moon, and 'water' all symbolize 'possibility'/'virtuality,' however, another way to say this is that all three symbolize 'indefinitude,' because what is not yet actual, what is potential, *possibility*, is indefinite. Because of this equivalency, serpent/dragon, moon, and 'water' would also, in the terms of my argument, symbolize that which is 'chaotic': the perception, from the level of the state of *matter*, of "the indefinite series of cycles of manifestation"/*samsara*. In *The Multiple*

---

35 René Guénon, *The Multiple States of the Being*, 67.
36 Mircea Eliade, *The Sacred and the Profane*, 130.
37 Mircea Eliade, *Patterns in Comparative Religion*, 171.

States of the Being, Guénon describes the two 'Waters,' "the totalities of formal possibilities and of non-formal possibilities," as 'chaoses.'[38] I argue, therefore, based upon the traditional symbolic equivalency among 'water,' 'chaos' (the dragon), and the moon, that traditional peoples believed that to 'control' the 'Waters,' "the totalities of formal possibilities and of non-formal possibilities," is to control 'chaos.' By the terms of my argument, however, to control 'chaos' is to control "the indefinite series of cycles of manifestation"/*samsara*, specifically by controlling the state of *matter* in which *samsara* is perceived *as* chaos. To control the 'Waters,' therefore, is, traditionally speaking, to control "the indefinite series of cycles of manifestation"/*samsara*/'chaos.' Since the serpent/dragon in Tradition generally symbolizes "the indefinite series of cycles of manifestation"/*samsara*/'chaos,' to 'control' the 'Waters' is to 'control' the serpent/dragon.

East Asian Dragon, South Asian *Naga*, and Moon/Ball/Pearl/Spiral

As I mentioned before, there are several interpretations of the identity of the circular/spherical object that is depicted in sculptures and illustrations of the East Asian, or 'Far-Eastern,' dragon. The moon, ball, pearl, and spiral all figure prominently in the art and myth of the 'Chinese Dragon,' in particular. If the Chinese Dragon is a symbol of the 'Waters' that represent the traditional idea of 'possibility'/'chaos,' according to Guénon, and the serpent/dragon also represents for him the traditional idea of *samsara* as "the indefinite series of cycles of manifestation," I argue that the circle/sphere that is so often juxtaposed with the 'Chinese Dragon' represents Guénon's metaphysical 'Principle' and, more specifically, 'Heaven' in Chinese thought. We have already noted in a previous chapter the traditional association of the circle/sphere with the concepts of divinity and the metaphysical in connection with the Egyptian and other *uraei*. If, however, the

---

38 René Guénon, *The Multiple States of the Being*, 67–68.

circular/spherical object that is often associated with the Far-Eastern or Chinese dragon does symbolize the divine/metaphysical/'Heaven,' then, as 'pure actuality,' like Aristotle's 'Prime Mover,' it is the true 'controller' of the serpent/dragon and the 'Waters'/'water' of 'possibility'/'virtuality'/'chaos.'

The symbolism of the East Asian, or 'Far-Eastern,' dragon-with-'orb' appears in various cultural *realia* of traditional China, including paintings, sculptures, architecture, and clothing. In *The Religious System of China, Vol. 6*, the Dutch sinologist J. J. M de Groot describes, for example, the dragon-ornamented religious dress of certain ancient Chinese 'Wu-ist' priests, whom he describes as "seers and soothsayers, exorcists and physicians; invokers or conjurers bringing down gods at sacrifices."[39] According to de Groot, there were, and are, different specialized classes of 'wu' in China: "soothsaying wu, exorcising wu, and sacrificing wu," as well as others.[40] Among these classes, the *sai kong*, "who almost exclusively occupy themselves with sacrificial work and exorcising magic," is of particular interest to us because of the ritual dress which they wear.[41] According to de Groot, "the *sai kong* are wont to don a special vestment while performing religious work."[42] De Groot states that

---

39 Of the 'Wu-ist' priests, de Groot states that "[t]he wu have ever remained what they probably were from the night of time: men and women possessed by spirits or gods, and consequently acting as seers and soothsayers, exorcists and physicians; invokers or conjurers bringing down gods at sacrifices, and performing other sacerdotal functions, occasionally indulging also in imprecation, and in sorcery with the help of spirits." J. J. M. de Groot, *The Religious System of China: Its Ancient Forms, Evolution, History and Present Aspect. Manners, Customs and Social Institutions Connected Therewith, Vol. 6, Book II: Of the Soul and Ancestral Worship* (Republished by Kessinger Publishing, LLC, www.Kessinger.net [all volumes originally published between 1892–1910 by E. J. Brill, Leyden, Netherlands]), 1212.

40 J. J. M. de Groot, *The Religious System of China, Vol. 6*, 1243.

41 J. J. M. de Groot, *The Religious System of China, Vol. 6*, 1244.

42 J. J. M. de Groot, *The Religious System of China, Vol. 6*, 1264.

This ritual dress is highly significant, and is therefore worthy of attention and description. The principle article of it, always worn at ceremonies of the highest order, is a so-called *kang i*, which...is worn at the presentation of offerings or during the celebration of sacrificial masses, the main object of which always is to call down the gods, that they may enjoy the offerings and requite the givers with blessings.[43]

On some such vestments are depicted dragons. De Groot describes one vestment in detail:

We notice...rolling waves, representing the oceans which encompass the continent of the world on all sides. Beaten by these waves, this continent rises as a pile of mountains, the summit in the centre of which is Mount T'ai or the Principal Mountain, in Shantung, nominally the highest peak in the world. On the left and right, a large dragon rises high above the billows, in an attitude denoting a soaring motion towards the continents; these animals symbolize the fertilizing rains, and are therefore surrounded by gold-thread figures which represent clouds, and some which resemble spirals and denote rolling thunder. Above the dragons we see the sun and the moon, each as a gold disk showing respectively a crow and a rabbit which is pounding medicines, those luminaries being, according to old philosophy, inhabited by these animals; around them, too, we see embroidered clouds, and stars....There is also a broad border of blue silk around the neck, stitched with two ascending dragons which are belching out a ball, probably representing thunder.[44]

Along with the two 'belching dragons,' there is also depicted on the vestment de Groot describes the 'axial' Mount T'ai, the 'Principal Mountain' in Shantung, as de Groot calls it. The description of this mountain as 'Principal,' and its depiction with two dragons, would seem to identify the combination of mountain and dragons as an example of Guénon's 'World Axis' and the two 'currents,' often symbolized by serpents in Tradition according to Guénon, that 'coil' about

---

43 J. J. M. de Groot, *The Religious System of China*, Vol. 6, 1264.
44 J. J. M. de Groot, *The Religious System of China*, Vol. 6, 1265, Plate XVIII (unclear).

it. De Groot remarks on a similar vestment "of the same character, but with somewhat different ornamentation," upon which "an oblong piece of blue silk, embroidered with two dragons which belch out a ball, as also with a continent and waves over which they soar, is stitched in the middle of the gown, both on the back and the front."[45] The action of 'water,' waves, that is, is depicted in both cases. The photographs provided by de Groot of the two vestments are obscure and their referred-to details indistinguishable, probably due to age. In the book *Snake Charm*, however, Marilyn Nissenson and Susan Jonas include a photograph (see fig. 15.2) of a similar article of clothing, an imperial court robe from the Qing dynasty, c. 1644–61, that depicts one large dragon and many smaller dragons with what appear to be several flaming 'balls'/'spirals' in between them.[46] De Groot contends that both the 'ball' that is 'belched out' by one or both of the dragons in such figurations, as well as the 'spirals' depicted on one of the vestments that he refers to, represents thunder. Both 'ball' and 'spiral,' as we have noted, are descriptions that have been given to the ubiquitous circle/sphere ('orb') that appears in depictions of the traditional Far-Eastern Dragon. Since these 'balls' and 'spirals' are put in the context of dragons that are represented with the action of 'water' — waves, that is — and since, as de Groot argues, dragons in East Asia are "animals [that] symbolize the fertilizing rains," I argue that they represent on the vestments worn by the 'Wu-ist' priests the idea of 'controlling' 'the Waters' of 'possibility'/'chaos.' This signifies the control by such priests of the 'possibilities'/'chaos' of 'nature.' The traditional idea of the 'control' of 'possibilities' is, furthermore, what we also see represented by serpent and circle/sphere imagery in other manifestations of Tradition, such as the Hopi 'snake dance.'

---

45   J. J. M. de Groot, *The Religious System of China*, Vol. 6, 1266, Plate XIX (unclear).
46   Marilyn Nissenson and Susan Jonas, *Snake Charm*, 80–81.

Fig. 15.2. Imperial court robe, back. Chinese. Qing dynasty, c. 1644–61, The Metropolitan Museum of Art, New York[47]

In *Dragons in Chinese Art*, Hugo Munsterberg provides several photographs of traditional Chinese depictions of dragons with the so-called 'ball' or 'spiral.' Figure 15.1, produced earlier in this chapter, is a photograph of a Ch'ing dynasty plate from c. 1723–1735. Figure 15.3 (below) is a photograph of a 1623 Ming dynasty tray.

---

47 Marilyn Nissenson and Susan Jonas, *Snake Charm*, 80–81.

Fig. 15.3. Tray, Ming Dynasty, Tien-ch'i period, 1623[48]

In *The Dragon in China and Japan*, de Visser, quoting de Groot, refers to the 'ball' and 'spiral' in depictions of the 'Chinese Dragon' as both being representations of 'the rolling of thunder':

> As to the ball, "belched out by the two dragons", this reminds us at once of the Dragon festival on the 15th day of the first month; the ball carried in front of the dragon on that day might be also explained in the same way, i.e. as thunder belched out by the dragon, and not as the sun, pursued by him....The ball between the two dragons is often delineated as a spiral, and in an ancient charm represented in Koh Hung's [book] *Pao P'oh-tsze* (17th century) "a spiral denotes the rolling of thunder from which issues a flash of lightning". "In the sign expressing lightning, the projecting stroke signifies the flash; therefore its effect as a charm is indefinitely increased by lengthening that stroke so that it looks like a spiral which at the same time represents the rolling of thunder".[49]

Speculating on the interchangeability of 'ball' and 'spiral,' de Visser asks,

> Is the ball, so often seen in connection with the dragon, and often represented as a spiral emitting flames or as a ball upon which something like a spiral is delineated, identical with the spiral, denoting thunder?[50]

---

48 Hugo Munsterberg, *Dragons in Chinese Art*, 53.
49 Marinus Willem de Visser, *The Dragon in China and Japan*, 103–104.
50 Marinus Willem de Visser, *The Dragon in China and Japan*, 105.

A late nineteenth-century bronze dragon in front of the Hall of Preserved Elegance in the Forbidden City clearly shows the flames coming off of a 'ball' with a spiral pattern that the dragon clutches in its right claw (see fig. 15.4). In this case, as in others, it is hard to imagine that what is being represented is the moon or a pearl.

De Visser observes that "the most frequent and apparently the most ancient representation" of the East Asian Dragon with 'ball'/'spiral' is of

> *two dragons* flying with open mouths towards a ball or spiral between them....The artists, especially those of later times, often varied this subject, so that we sometimes see more than two dragons rushing upon one ball, or one dragon trying to swallow it or having caught it with his claw; sometimes there are even two balls and only one dragon.[51]

An early Ming dynasty stone carving of this figuration can also be found in the Forbidden City, at the back of the Hall of Preserving Harmony (see fig. 15.5). The 'ball' is at the very top of the carving between the two dragons represented. Unimpressed with the hypothesis that the dragons in such depictions are attempting to 'belch out' the 'ball,' de Visser argues that

> their [the dragons'] whole attitude, on the contrary, indicates their eagerness in trying to catch and swallow it. Moreover, how can two dragons belch out one ball? And the dragon of the festival constantly follows the ball with his mouth, apparently in order to swallow it.[52]

Such speculation again reminds one of the serpent-with-'egg' that is represented in the Ohio Serpent Mound.

---

51 Marinus Willem de Visser, *The Dragon in China and Japan*, 106.
52 Marinus Willem de Visser, *The Dragon in China and Japan*, 106.

Fig. 15.4. Bronze in front of the Hall of Preserved Elegance, 1884, the Forbidden City[53]

As we argued in the case of that figuration, however, the symbolism of the Far-Eastern Dragon represents the dragon's *potential* to *either* swallow *or* 'belch out,' as de Visser says, the 'ball'/'spiral.' Before addressing this subject, however, we must consider the other mentioned variations of that mysterious circular/spherical object that is so often depicted with the dragon in traditional East Asian art.

---

53   Hu Chui, *The Forbidden City: Collection of Photographs by Hu Chui* (Bowers Museum of Cultural Art, 1998), 60.

Fig. 15.5. Stone carving at the back of the Hall of Preserving Harmony, early Ming Dynasty, the Forbidden City[54]

The pearl, again, is one guess as to what is so often depicted in figurations of the Far-Eastern Dragon. Various Chinese writers in ancient times relate stories in which dragons are in some way connected to pearls. De Visser states, for example, that

> [a]ccording to *Chwang tsze* a "pearl of a thousand pieces of gold...is certainly to be found in a pool of nine layers (i.e. very deep) under the throat of a *li-lung* or 'horse-dragon'". The *Shuh i ki* (sixth century) states that socalled dragon-pearls are spit out by dragons, like snake-pearls by snakes. In the *Lung ch'ing luh* we read about a dragon which in the shape of a little child was playing with three pearls before the entrance of his den. When a man approached he fled into the cavern and, reassuming his dragon form, put the pearls in his left ear. The man cut off the ear, in order to take possession of the pearls, but they vanished together with the dragon himself.
>
> Another legend tells about a man who was very fond of wine and from a female *sien* [magical being/creature] in the mountains obtained a pearl which she said [was] to be kept by the dragons in their mouths in order to replace wine.[55]

---

54 Hu Chui, *The Forbidden City*, 17.
55 Marinus Willem de Visser, *The Dragon in China and Japan*, 88.

De Groot writes of so-called 'Thunder-pearls' "which dragons have dropped from their mouths, and which may thoroughly illuminate a whole house during the night," thus connecting the element of thunder with pearls in addition to 'balls' and 'spirals.'[56] De Visser states that

> [t]he Chinese themselves, however, mostly call the ball a *'precious pearl.'* We find it explained this way in Boerschmann's highly interesting work on *P'u t'o shan*, where a gilt ball of glass is said to hang from the center of the roof of the Great Hall of the Buddhist temple Fa (h)-yu-sze ("Temple of the Rain of the Law"), while eight dragons, carved around the surrounding "hanging pillars", eagerly stretch their claws towards the "pearl of perfection".[57]

Reflecting on this artifact, de Visser argues that "we may be sure that the Chinese Buddhists, identifying the dragon with the Naga, also identified the ball with their cintamani or precious pearl which grants all desires. The question rises [sic]: 'Was the ball originally also a pearl, not of Buddhism but of Taoism?'"[58]

As de Visser intimates in his question, there is a close parallel between the symbolisms of the 'Far-Eastern,' or Chinese, dragon and the South Asian *naga*. We have already examined the connection between the symbolism of the *naga* and the ancient ideas of healing and wisdom in our discussion of the Buddha and the "prodigious cobra" Muchalinda. However, as with the symbolism of the Far-Eastern Dragon and that of the Hopi 'snake dance,' the symbolism of the South Asian *naga* is closely connected with the traditional symbolism of 'water.' In *Myths and Symbols in Indian Art and Civilization*, as noted in Chapter 12, Heinrich Zimmer states that "in Hindu mythology the

---

56 J. J. M. de Groot, *The Religious System of China: Its Ancient Forms, Evolution, History and Present Aspect. Manners, Customs and Social Institutions Connected Therewith, Vol. 5, Book II: Of the Soul and Ancestral Worship* (Republished by Kessinger Publishing, LLC, www.Kessinger.net [all volumes originally published between 1892–1910 by E. J. Brill, Leyden, Netherlands]), 867.

57 Marinus Willem de Visser, *The Dragon in China and Japan*, 107.

58 Marinus Willem de Visser, *The Dragon in China and Japan*, 107.

symbol for water is the serpent (*naga*)."⁵⁹ In this proposition, there is a layering of symbols in which one traditional symbol, namely the serpent/dragon/*naga*, symbolizes *another* traditional symbol, namely 'water.' As we have seen in Guénon's *The Multiple States of the Being*, 'water,' or the 'Waters,' in Tradition symbolizes "the totalities of formal possibilities and of non-formal possibilities," which we have reduced to 'possibility.' Combining Zimmer's and Guénon's contentions, we argue that the serpent/dragon/*naga*, like 'water,' symbolizes 'possibility' in Tradition, which we further equate with 'potentiality.' Because we also agree with Guénon's identification of 'possibility' and 'chaos' in his interpretation of the traditional symbolism of 'the Waters' in *The Multiple States of the Being*, we further contend that both the serpent/dragon/*naga and* 'water,' in traditional modes of symbolism, may be taken generally to symbolize 'possibility,' potentiality, and 'chaos' equally. The serpent's/dragon's symbolization of 'chaos,' supported by Eliade, we have most recently indicated in our examination of the Ohio Serpent Mound, where we identified 'chaos' as being equivalent to one of two kinds of 'possibility'/potentiality. The other kind of 'possibility'/potentiality, which I termed 'imminent actuality,' we proposed to be symbolized by the oval/'egg.'

In further expounding upon the nature of the *naga* and its connection with 'water' in South Asian tradition, Zimmer makes the following assessment (which we provided in Chapter 12 also, but examined from a different angle):

> Nagas are genii superior to man. They inhabit subaquatic paradises, dwelling at the bottoms of rivers, lakes, and seas, in resplendent palaces studded with gems and pearls. They are keepers of the life-energy that is stored in the earthly waters of springs, wells, and ponds. They are the guardians, also, of the riches of the deep sea — corals, shells, pearls.⁶⁰

---

59   Heinrich Zimmer, *Myths and Symbols in Indian Art and Civilization*, 37.
60   Heinrich Zimmer, *Myths and Symbols in Indian Art and Civilization*, 63.

Similar to the dragon-with-pearl motif in East Asian tradition, Zimmer refers here to a *naga*/pearl motif in South Asian tradition. In the latter case, however, the pearl is more clearly put into the context of the realm from which it derives: 'water.' Zimmer writes of "serpent kings and queens (*naga, nagini*)...personifying and directing the terrestrial waters of the lakes and ponds, rivers and oceans,"[61] but he also writes of them as "keepers of the life-energy that is stored" in 'water.' In a specifically Buddhist context, Zimmer writes of the serpent as that which represents, more generally, "the bondage of nature...the life force that motivates birth and rebirth."[62] Transitioning from the Buddhist perspective to a more broadly South Asian perspective, Zimmer argues, in connection with traditional serpent symbolism, that

> [a]ccording to the Indian view...there exists an ever threatening countercurrent, antagonistic to the trend of evolution, which periodically halts, engulfs, and takes back what has already been given form. This force is represented in classical Hindu mythology under the guise of the giant serpent power of the world abyss.[63]

In Guénon's terms, this "counter-current, antagonistic to the trend of evolution" that swallows up all forms and, in Zimmer's terms, 'motivates' their 'birth and rebirth' by means of the process of the 'migration' of 'the being' (*Brahman*), is the process of 'involution' first discussed in Chapter 7, the process by which beings 'return' to their 'Principial' Source. 'Evolution,' from the traditional (Guénon's) perspective, however, is actually the more 'threatening' process, to use Zimmer's word, as it is the process by which beings ('the being') 'migrate(s)' *away from* their (its) source and into the serpentine "indefinite series of cycles of manifestation." Therefore, although Zimmer's information here is useful to our purpose, he has, in his analysis of that information, gotten

---

61 Heinrich Zimmer, *Myths and Symbols in Indian Art and Civilization*, 59.
62 Heinrich Zimmer, *Myths and Symbols in Indian Art and Civilization*, 66 and 67.
63 Heinrich Zimmer, *Myths and Symbols in Indian Art and Civilization*, 78.

the true South Asian, and thus traditional, perspective on this matter exactly backwards. The serpent does, in a sense, represent the 'life-force' insofar as it symbolizes 'nature.' But it also symbolizes, roughly speaking, 'evolution,' *not* 'involution,' *not* the "threatening counter-current, antagonistic *to* the trend of evolution," since 'evolution,' according to Guénon, is the process by which 'the being' that perceives itself as 'separate' moves 'away from' the 'Principle' (*Brahman*) that is its Source. That 'movement' is what the "indefinite series of cycles of manifestation"/*samsara* is. 'Nature,' as we have argued, is more precisely defined as the 'migrating' being's *interpretation* of this 'movement' when 'the being' is in human form.[64] The 'taking back,' however, as Zimmer puts it, of "what has already been given form" is, traditionally speaking, *not* something 'threatening.' It is actually the highest good, from the perspective of a metaphysical understanding of existence. For *Brahman* is beyond all 'forms' and more real (more defined, actual, and 'formed,' in a higher sense) than any of them.

When Zimmer describes *nagas* as "guardians…of the riches of the deep sea" and he identifies the serpent as the "ever threatening counter-current, antagonistic to the trend of evolution," he identifies the serpent, in a general sense, whether as simple serpent or as *naga*, as a sort of 'obstruction.' In doing so, and in spite of his error of interpretation noted in the previous paragraph, he argues in consonance with my own contention that the serpent-as-guardian is more accurately described in traditional art and myth as the serpent-as-*obstruction*. Zimmer's statement describing the serpent as symbolizing "the bondage of nature…the life force that motivates birth and rebirth" is, if we leave out the 'trend of evolution' discussed above, consistent with my thesis that the serpent/dragon symbolizes the formless, indefinite, potential aspect of existence: *samsara* in the South Asian tradition, and what I have called *matter*. Zimmer also describes the serpent as a 'keeper' of the life-energy in 'water,' but again

---

64 The meaning of 'nature' and its dependence upon 'human being' is more fully discussed in Chapter 9.

the alleged serpent-as-guardian is not a guardian or 'keeper' *per se* but an obstruction that *serves as* a 'guardian' from the perspective of those beings ('the being' in specific states of being) that desire that which the serpent stands in the way of: *moksha*/immortality. The serpent/dragon symbolizes *samsara*/*matter* because it is *samsara*/*matter* that obstructs — 'guards' — *moksha*/immortality. In Zimmer's terms, we could say that *samsara*/*matter*, in its near equivalency to 'nature,' is that which "periodically halts, engulfs, and takes back what has already been given form." And this statement would be true *in the sense that* the flux of *samsara* has, by definition, no discernible form. From a more rigorous traditional perspective, however, the 'higher formless' that is the metaphysical 'Principle' (*Brahman*) is what *ultimately* "takes back what has already been given form," as it is the Source of *samsara*.

To Control 'Water' Is to Control 'Possibilities'

An important distinction must be made here between 'water' and "the life-energy *in* water" (my emphasis), as Zimmer puts it. In *Patterns in Comparative Religion*, Eliade states that pearls are "born of the moon," and thus "they have a share in its magic powers."[65] He describes the pearl as "a 'cosmological centre' bringing together the prerogatives of moon, woman, fertility, and birth," adding, however, that "pearls are filled with the germinative force of the water in which they were formed," and thus are "born of the waters."[66] According to Eliade, therefore, the pearl is traditionally considered as born of both the moon *and* 'the waters.' De Visser, in his discussion of 'the dragons and the ball' examined earlier, after a stretch of indecisiveness, seems to epiphanize what it is that the "spiral-shaped ball" so often depicted with the Far-Eastern Dragon represents:

> The moon! ....Would it be absurd to represent dragons trying to swallow the moon? Not in the least, for the dragons are, as we have seen above, the

---

65 Mircea Eliade, *Patterns in Comparative Religion*, 439.
66 Mircea Eliade, *Patterns in Comparative Religion*, 439.

clouds, and the ancient Chinese may easily have fancied that these dragons, quickly approaching and covering the moon, actually devoured it. When they did so, the fertilizing rain soon trickled down upon the thirsty earth, a great blessing to mankind. For this reason they might be represented so often trying to swallow the moon, namely as a symbol of fertilizing rains. Owing to the close connection between the moon and the water, the moon, having been swallowed by the dragon, might have been believed to strengthen the rain-giving power of the latter. The dragon of the festival, persecuting the moon, might be carried along the streets in order to cause rain by sympathetic magic.[67]

The pearl, the earth's moon, and 'water' are, no doubt, closely connected symbolically to the symbolism of the dragon-with-'orb.' This does not mean, however, that the 'orb' directly symbolizes either a pearl or the moon. *If*, as de Visser argues, the Far-Eastern Dragon is "trying to swallow the moon," and *if* pearls are "born of the moon" and act as "a 'cosmological centre' bringing together the prerogatives of moon, woman, fertility, and birth," as Eliade says,[68] and *if* the 'ball'/'spiral' with two dragons denotes thunder,[69] and *if* we remember de Groot's 'Thunder-pearl' which connects the pearl with 'water' through the association of thunder, it may *seem* that 'ball,' 'spiral,' pearl, and moon are symbolically interchangeable in traditional art and myth, or at least in Asian art and myth. After his epiphany that the 'orb' represents the moon is over, however, de Visser admits that "difficult points in the moon theory are the red color of the ball and its spiral-shaped form."[70] In the very next sentence, however, de Visser rapidly dissolves his own doubts when he observes that "[i]f it is a pearl, however, representing the moon or at least closely connected with it, the red colour may mean the lustre of this brilliant, fiery gem." He argues that

---

67 Marinus Willem de Visser, *The Dragon in China and Japan*, 106.
68 Mircea Eliade, *Patterns in Comparative Religion*, 439.
69 Marinus Willem de Visser, *The Dragon in China and Japan*, 105.
70 Marinus Willem de Visser, *The Dragon in China and Japan*, 108.

> [t]he spiral is much used in delineating the sacred pearls of Buddhism, so that it might have served also to design those of Taoism; although I must acknowledge that the spiral of the Buddhist pearl goes upwards, while the spiral of the dragon is flat.
>
> We know the close connection of dragons and pearls in both religions. This connection is quite logical, for the masters of the sea are, of course, the possessors and guardians of its treasures. When the clouds approached and covered the moon, the ancient Chinese may have thought that the dragons had seized and swallowed the pearl, more brilliant than all their pearls of the sea.

These are, however, all mere suppositions.[71]

I have stated earlier that the East Asian dragon's 'orb' does *not* represent the moon. I shall also say, however, that it does not represent a 'pearl' either. *If*, however, the 'orb,' the alleged 'ball'/'pearl'/'spiral'/'moon' that is traditionally depicted in representations of the Far-Eastern Dragon (the 'Chinese Dragon,' specifically), does represent the moon, and if the moon is the 'controller of water,' and if the serpent/dragon is also the 'controller of water,' as we have considered, then the compound symbolism of dragon-with-'orb' would seem to symbolize the idea that 'water' can be 'controlled.' *How exactly*, however, is this 'control' symbolized by these two elements, moon and dragon, combined into *one* 'compound symbol'? De Visser's claims, which he admits are "mere suppositions," do not make clear that the circular/spherical object depicted in representations of the Far-Eastern Dragon represents the moon. And I find his argument that "the red colour [of the 'orb'] may mean the lustre of" the pearl as a "brilliant, fiery gem" not persuasive at all. The spiraling pattern of the 'orb' and the flames that seem to leap off of it in some depictions reveal no clear reference to either moon or pearl (see fig. 15.4).

One might suggest that both dragon/serpent/*naga* and 'orb,' whatever the latter is, represent in traditional cultures the 'control' of H_2O. De Visser's contention that dragons, as clouds, cause fertilizing rains

---

71 Marinus Willem de Visser, *The Dragon in China and Japan*, 108.

to "trickle down" seems to identify the dragon, as much as the 'orb' that may be the moon controlling the tides or the pearl found at the bottom of the sea, as a 'controller' of physical water.[72] On the other side of the world, the circular Hopi Snake Dance provides similar support of this hypothesis: "Humans want rain! See how they wish for it by representing a snake and the moon and a pearl!" in other words. For it is easy to conclude that, ultimately, what humans, like any life form, desire most is that which extends their physical life. Water, those ancient block-headed rascals realized, allows them to live longer, and we innately scientific moderns cannot but nod and knowingly presume and proclaim that such archaic individuals put *all* of their artistic energy into representing that which they observed with their senses and desired with their bodies: H_2O. The problem with this 'commonsense' approach, however, is that, as Guénon repeatedly advises the modern reader of his books, traditional symbols *never* symbolize physical realities and they *always* symbolize metaphysical realities. A representation of water (H_2O), therefore, doesn't symbolize water (H_2O) *itself*. It symbolizes something metaphysically 'higher' than water which the appearance of physical water best communicates.

Based upon Guénon's contention that the 'upper' and 'lower' 'Waters' of Tradition symbolize 'possibility,' as well as other observations made in this chapter, I argue that the dragon-with-'orb' in East Asian art and myth symbolizes the idea that 'possibilities' can be 'controlled.' More specifically, both physical phenomena and human activity can be 'controlled' by those New Men who are aware of the limits of 'life' as other humans perceive it and as they once perceived it. This contention does not entail that the dragon and 'orb' *separately* symbolize the 'control' of 'possibilities' in that compound symbolism, for the combination of the two symbols is significant, especially if we assume that each of them can, as discussed above, be interpreted to symbolize the same thing. We discussed before Guénon's proposition

---

72 Marinus Willem de Visser, *The Dragon in China and Japan*, 106.

that the "Far-Eastern symbolism of the Dragon...correspond[s] in a certain way to the Western theological conception of the Word as the 'locus of possibles.'"[73] I contend that the serpent/dragon that is represented in East Asian figurations of the dragon-with-'orb,' like the 'Word,' symbolizes a *means* of 'control' of 'water,' but not a *cause* of its 'control.' The 'orb' that is represented with the dragon, alternatively, is that which symbolizes the *cause* of the 'control' of 'water' ('the Waters'), and, thus, 'control' of 'possibility.' The 'orb' symbolizes this 'control' because it represents the 'primordial' circle/sphere that symbolizes the metaphysical 'Principle' in Tradition. In Chinese tradition, specifically, the figure of the circle, the sphere in three dimensions, is traditionally identified as representing a reality that exists beyond the terrestrial or 'earthly' realm. De Groot says, for example, that "according to ancient philosophy, expressed in the writings of Liu Ngan, 'Heaven is round and Earth is square...the Tao of Heaven is roundness, and that of Earth squareness.'"[74] According to ancient Chinese belief, Heaven rules Earth. The circle, therefore, which represents Heaven, represents *rule* in traditional Chinese symbology. I argue, therefore, that the 'orb' that is depicted on the dragon-ornamented *sai kong* that is worn by 'Wu-ist' priests, as well as on other traditional 'Far-Eastern' works of art, symbolizes the 'control' of the dragons that are also depicted on that vestment with the 'orb.' In all of these works of art, I contend that the traditional symbolic meaning of the dragons portrayed is equivalent to that of the 'waters,' insofar as the dragon traditionally symbolizes the watery 'chaos' of 'possibility'/potentiality that is the *samsaric* "indefinite series of cycles of manifestation," or *matter*. It is the 'orb' that, in turn, symbolizes 'actualization' of that pure potentiality/'possibility' since 'Heaven' actualizes the potentiality of the Earthly 'Waters' in traditional Chinese thought.

---

73 René Guénon, *The Multiple States of the Being*, 68.
74 J. J. M. De Groot, *The Religious System of China*, Vol. 6, 1264.

The Dragon: 'Water,' 'Possibility,' 'Chaos,' *Matter*

The circle/sphere, as a symbol of the 'center' according to Guénon, traditionally serves as a 'symbolic synonym' for axial symbols such as the tree, rod, and cross. In the case of the Ohio Serpent Mound, the oval-shaped object in the serpent's mouth is an allusion to the traditional symbolism of the circle/sphere and, thus, an allusion to the metaphysical 'center' or 'Principle' in Tradition. The serpent in that earthen sculpture represents potentiality in the form of 'chaos,' which I equate with Guénon's idea of 'possibility' when he discusses the 'formal' and 'informal possibilities' as the 'two chaoses.' The same analysis applies in the case of the Maya 'Vision Serpent' in which a humanoid head (or head and torso), which is roughly circular/spherical, is depicted as protruding from the mouth of a serpent (Figure 15.6 provides another interesting Chinese parallel.[75]). This figuration, as noted before, is another allusion to, or representation of, the metaphysical 'center'/'Principle.' In both cases, that of the oval/'egg' depicted in the Ohio Serpent Mound and that of the humanoid head/torso depicted in Maya Vision Serpents, there is represented the possibility of *either* a 'birth' of a being (the metaphysical 'Principle') from the potentiality/'possibility' of 'chaos' *or* the 'swallowing' of that being back into chaos. Since, as Eliade claims, the serpent/dragon symbolizes 'chaos' in Tradition, I conclude from this that the Far-Eastern (Chinese, specifically) dragon-with-'orb' symbolizes the

---

75 Figure 15.6 depicts a dragon facing left connected to a humanoid figure facing right, of which Munsterberg states, "[T]his jade carving...shows the dragon supporting and upholding a human figure who should be looked upon as a sky deity or a divine ancestor of the Chou people." Hugo Munsterberg, *Dragons in Chinese Art*, 17. Although the humanoid figure is not protruding from the mouth of the dragon, on first glance the image greatly resembles in general form the Maya 'Vision Serpent.' If the humanoid represented is indeed, as Munsterberg suggests, a 'sky deity,' this only makes more persuasive the idea that there exists a symbolic kinship between the two representations, since the 'sky deity' with his 'thunderweapon' is the 'axial' 'opposite' in Tradition of that which the serpent/dragon symbolizes.

potentiality/'possibility' for the 'birth' of the metaphysical 'center' or 'Principle' *from* 'chaos'/'possibility'/potentiality. This hypothesis holds if the dragon's 'orb' is seen as representative of the 'center'/Principle ('Heaven,' in Chinese tradition) in the same manner that the oval/'egg' in the Ohio Serpent Mound, as well as the humanoid head/torso in depictions of Maya Vision Serpents, is seen as an imperfect (because oval, not circular) *allusion to* the 'center'/Principle. If each of these three symbolisms is seen as representing, or alluding to, respectively, the metaphysical 'center'/Principle, then the symbolism of the dragon-with-'orb' is consistent with Guénon's various symbols of 'duality in unity' that represent the 'dual cosmic force' manifested as the 'evolution' and 'involution' of the Principle that is sometimes, according to Guénon, represented by means of two serpents.[76] The 'unity' of the 'orb,' representing the Principle, is manifested in the 'duality of the 'chaotic'/*samsaric* dragon of *matter*. 'Involution' consists in this case in the 'return' of the dragon to its source, represented by the 'orb,' while 'evolution' consists in the dragon's manifesting out of the 'orb.'

---

76 René Guénon, *The Great Triad*, 36.

Fig. 15.6. Pendant Middle Chou Dynasty, c. tenth to seventh century BCE[77]

In the cases of the Ohio Serpent Mound, the Maya 'Vision Serpent,' the 'Far-Eastern Dragon,' and the South Asian *naga*, the power of the metaphysical 'Principle'/'center' that is alluded to in, or represented by, the oval/'egg,' humanoid head/torso, 'orb,' and 'pearl,' respectively, is traditionally represented in these 'compound symbolisms' as being 'held in check' by that which the serpent/dragon/*naga* symbolizes in each case. The symbolism of the pearl in archaic cultures falls into the same category as the oval/'egg,' the humanoid head/torso, and the 'orb,' although it is not, I shall argue, what the Chinese 'orb' represents. The pearl is oval or circular/spherical in shape and, according to Eliade, it is considered to be 'born' of the 'water' in archaic cultures. Applying

---

77 Hugo Munsterberg, *Dragons in Chinese Art*, 17.

Guénon's understanding of 'the Waters' as 'two chaoses' to this observation, the pearl is symbolically 'born' of 'chaos.'[78] Equivalently, therefore, the pearl is 'born' of 'possibilities'/potentiality — "filled with the germinative force of...water," according to Eliade. For 'the Waters,' according to Guénon, "represent Possibility understood as 'passive perfection,' or the universal plastic principle."[79] Now, the serpent/dragon symbolizes 'chaos' insofar as this is the primary *character* of a particular state of awareness, or perception, *of* the *samsaric* "indefinite series of cycles of manifestation." This particular state of awareness/perception — what I have termed *matter* — is what allows for the very existence of the *physical* level of reality that we call 'nature.' Therefore, insofar as the oval/'egg'/head/'orb'/pearl *emerges from* the serpent/dragon/*naga*, this 'compound symbolism' symbolizes the belief that, in some sense, the metaphysical aspect of reality (the 'Principle') comes from the physical aspect of reality (based in awareness of *samsara*). This belief, however, emanates from the perspective of a 'lower' level of 'realization,' for the Principle is, in Tradition, always the ultimate, and 'final,' cause of everything. The mentioned 'compound symbols,' I suggest, symbolize the *impasse* that exists in the relationship between the metaphysical Principle and chaos, whereby neither 'overcomes' the other in the grand cosmic scheme of things, as is represented, for example, in the symbolism of *Yin* and *Yang*. 'Nature,' in other words, never becomes the complete flux of the *samsaric* 'chaos,' but neither does it ever become perfectly formed and divine like the 'Principle.'

Of all of the various circular/spherical symbols connected with the East Asian dragon, the pearl and moon are perhaps the most closely related, symbolically. According to Eliade, pearls are traditionally thought of as being 'born of the moon' and, because of this, "they have a share in its magic powers."[80] As we have said, however, Eliade also

---

78 René Guénon, *The Multiple States of the Being*, 68.
79 René Guénon, *The Multiple States of the Being*, 67.
80 Mircea Eliade, *Patterns in Comparative Religion*, 439.

argues that "pearls are filled with the germinative force of the water in which they were formed" and, thus, are also "born of the waters."[81] The Hindu *naga* and the 'Chinese Dragon' 'guard' what is sometimes *identified as* the moon or pearl — the metaphysical 'center' of all things, that is — in the sense that they *obscure* it. This is what *matter* as potentiality/possibility, formlessness, and indefinitude does as well: it obscures its 'Principial,' actualizing, Source. Both pearl and moon, as we have said, traditionally represent "the life-energy in water." This 'life-energy' that is *in* 'water,' however, is not *equivalent to* 'water.' It is not, in other words, *manifest*; it is *obscured* by 'water' itself. Only the 'water' is manifest. If, however, the serpent/dragon/*naga* is symbolically equivalent to 'water' in Tradition, this means that the 'life-energy' that is *in* 'water' is obscured by the 'guarding' serpent/dragon/*naga*. In Eliade's terms, dragons and snakes are "emblems of water."[82] But this means that that which 'controls' 'water,' the 'life-energy' that resides in the oval/'egg'/'orb'/'pearl,' *comes from* 'water.' And that implies that, in some sense, the metaphysical Principle 'comes from' the 'chaos'/'possibility'/potentiality *of* the *samsaric* "indefinite series of cycles of manifestation": *matter*. But this *only* means that 'realization' occurs *in the midst of avidya* (ignorance). More simply put, it implies that metaphysical Reality (the Principle) is only recognized against the 'backdrop' of the physical, though it is not *caused* by the physical. Since the serpent/dragon/*naga* is symbolically equivalent to 'water,' therefore, the oval/'egg'/'orb'/'pearl' that 'controls' the serpent/dragon/*naga* 'comes from' the serpent/dragon/*naga* in the sense that the latter provides the context in which the 'orb' may be 'realized.'

When we see depictions of the Chinese, or Far-Eastern, dragon 'chasing' the 'orb,' I suggest that such figurations symbolize, in Zimmer's terms, the "giant serpent power of the world abyss"

---

81 Mircea Eliade, *Patterns in Comparative Religion*, 439.
82 Mircea Eliade, *Patterns in Comparative Religion*, 207.

attempting to "take back what has already been given form."[83] This, however, is not, as Zimmer believes, a process 'antagonistic to' evolution, but *is* evolution, as the 'world abyss' that he writes of is not equivalent to the absence of physical manifestation but is, rather, roughly equivalent to the *samsaric* "indefinite series of cycles of manifestation." In the terms of this book, therefore, the Far-Eastern dragon in these representations represents the obscuration, by 'chaos'/*samsara*/*matter*, of the metaphysical order of things. Metaphorically speaking, order (the metaphysical 'Principle') is being 'chased' by 'chaos' in such depictions. Otherwise stated, the 'determinate' is on the verge of being 'swallowed up' into indeterminacy, typified by the flux of *samsara*. When this occurs, the being 'falls' back into forgetfulness and identification with cyclical existence. The answer to the old question posed in the case of the Ohio Serpent Mound concerning whether the serpent there is 'swallowing' the 'egg' or 'ejecting' it is, in the present case, as in that case, *both*. The interpretive rubric that we applied in that case, in other words, applies in the case of the East Asian dragon-with-'orb' as well. Macrocosmically, the Far-Eastern dragon-with-'orb' may represent, like the Ohio Serpent Mound or the Maya Vision Serpent, *both*: 1) 'ejection' of the 'orb' ('ball'/'spiral'/'pearl'), in which case the metaphysical Principle begins to order 'chaos' or 2) 'swallowing' of the 'orb,' in which case the metaphysical order (the Principle) is 'consumed' (obscured) by 'chaos.' *Microcosmically*, in all of these cases: 1) *individuals* may be 'released' from the 'chaotic'/*samsaric* "indefinite series of cycles of manifestation"/*matter* into immortality/*moksha* or 2) *individuals* may 'fall' deeper, or be 'swallowed up,' into the realm of *matter*/'chaos'/*samsara*. The difference between, for example, the oval/'egg' of the Ohio Serpent Mound and the 'orb' of the Far-Eastern Dragon is that, in the former case, the so-called 'World Egg' is a representation of the metaphysical Principle *as it is developing in* 'the world'/ 'nature.' By comparison, the Chinese or Far-Eastern 'orb' is a

---

83   Heinrich Zimmer, *Myths and Symbols in Indian Art and Civilization*, 78.

representation of the *undeveloped* 'center' of existence. The humanoid head/torso represented in depictions of the Maya Vision Serpent falls into the first category with the Serpent Mound.

The Symbolism of the Spiral, and the Chinese *Wang* as Mediator of 'Possibilities'

There is one additional element of the symbolism of the Far-Eastern/ Chinese dragon-with-'orb' that must be addressed: the interpretation of the 'orb' as a spiral. In Chapter 10, we discussed the traditional symbolism of what Guénon terms in *The Great Triad* the 'double spiral.' There we noted Guénon's contention that the so-called 'double spiral' traditionally symbolizes "the dual action of a single force" and "plays an extremely important role in the traditional art of the most diverse countries."[84] According to Guénon, like other symbols of 'duality in unity,' such as the Androgyne and the *yin-yang*, the 'double spiral' "offers an image of the alternating rhythm of evolution and involution, of birth and death, and in a word portrays manifestation in its double aspect."[85] Guénon also discusses in *The Great Triad*, however, the interconnection of the symbolisms of 'the Waters,' the serpent, and the *single* spiral. He argues that

> the serpent is often portrayed as inhabiting the waters....Now these waters are the symbol of possibilities, and their development is represented by the spiral, hence the close association that sometimes exists between this last and the symbolism of the waters.[86]

The coiling and uncoiling of a snake may be reasonably described as a spiraling movement. Thus, when the 'serpent power' of *Kundalini*, "represented by the figure of a coiled snake [,]...is aroused, uncoils,

---

84 René Guénon, *The Great Triad*, 31–32.
85 Elie Lebasquais, "Tradition hellénique et art grec", in the December 1935 issue of *Études Traditionnelles*, quoted in René Guénon, *The Great Triad*, 31.
86 René Guénon, *The Great Triad*, 34.

and ascends through the 'wheels' (*chakras*)," this, also, is a 'spiraling' movement.[87] Like the Hebrew *luz*, which we discussed in Chapter 13, and which Guénon describes as an 'indestructible corporeal particle' located in the area of the human body that corresponds to the force of *Kundalini*, I argue that the 'Far-Eastern' 'orb' symbolizes the metaphysical 'center'/'Principle' that emerges from, and orders, the 'chaos' of 'possibilities' that is represented by both the dragon and 'water.'[88] From the region of the 'migrating' being's anatomy where this 'imperishable' 'kernel of immortality' is located, Guénon argues that *Kundalini* ascends in the 'awakening' being through the *chakras* "that correspond to the various plexuses" to the so-called 'third eye.'[89] By means of this 'ascent,' the 'awakening' being 'recovers,' as Guénon says, the 'sense of eternity.'

In the symbolism of the Far-Eastern dragon-with-'orb,' two primary elements are represented: the 'orb' ('ball'/'spiral'/'pearl'/'moon') and the dragon. Although the circular/spherical object that is a part of this 'compound symbol' is not always clearly representative of a spiral, it *often* is. When it is, the figuration of the Far-Eastern dragon-with-'orb' has in common with the figuration of the South Asian *Kundalini* both of the two primary elements that constitute that 'compound symbol': the spiral and the serpent/dragon. This combination is an ancient one. Gimbutas, whom we referred to before, argues that "the spiral, symbol of energy and cyclic time, appears in the Upper Paleolithic, where it is associated with serpentiforms and horned animals."[90] The spiral is, according to Gimbutas, "both an artistic geometrization and a symbolic abstraction of the dynamic snake."[91] In *Lady of the Beasts*, Buffie Johnson confirms "the ancient relationship of the serpent to the abstract spiral," describing the spiral as "one of the most conspicuous

---

87 René Guénon, *The King of the World*, 47.
88 René Guénon, *The King of the World*, 46.
89 René Guénon, *The King of the World*, 47.
90 Marija Gimbutas, *The Language of the Goddess*, 279.
91 Marija Gimbutas, *The Language of the Goddess*, 279.

motifs in prehistoric art."[92] Johnson contends, similar to Gimbutas, that the 'double spiral,' specifically, "means rebirth or renewal," adducing as evidence the 'double spirals' extant on the represented wombs and vulva of prehistoric statues from the Balkans and Japan.[93] As we have seen, like the 'double spiral,' the serpent/dragon is traditionally associated with 'rebirth,' 'renewal,' fertility, and 'life' in general. Based upon these facts and other considerations to be examined, I argue that the 'Far-Eastern' dragon-with-*spiral*, the latter of which I contend is the true identity of the 'orb,' is a symbolic variation on the prehistoric serpent/spiral symbology that Gimbutas and Johnson refer to. It is, like the South Asian *Kundalini*, broadly symbolic of the interaction of metaphysical order (the 'Principle'/'center') and the 'chaos'/'possibility'/potentiality of the *samsaric* "indefinite series of cycles of manifestation"/*matter*. In *The Great Triad*, Guénon argues that the spiral in Tradition symbolizes the 'development' of 'possibilities'; the 'double spiral,' however, more specifically he contends, symbolizes "the alternating rhythm of evolution and involution, of birth and death, and in a word portrays manifestation in its double aspect."[94] In other words, in the terms of this book, the 'double spiral' symbolizes for Guénon the *actualization* of 'possibilities'/potentiality, whether as: 1) 'evolution' ('development' of 'possibilities' in the manifested realm) *or* 2) 'involution' ('return' of 'the possible' to the unity of the 'Principle'). The 'single spiral' that is depicted in illustrations of the Far-Eastern or Chinese dragon-with-'spiraled orb,' I argue, symbolizes both 'evolution' and 'involution' as well. The fact that there is *only* a 'single spiral,' and not a 'double spiral,' depicted on the 'orb' I see as merely a matter of 'stylistic abbreviation' and not a substantial change in the meaning of the symbolism.

---

92 Buffie Johnson, *Lady of the Beasts: The Goddess and Her Sacred Animals*, 122.

93 Buffie Johnson, *Lady of the Beasts: The Goddess and Her Sacred Animals*, 130–31.

94 Elie Lebasquais, 'Tradition hellénique et art grec", in the December 1935 issue of *Études Traditionnelles*, quoted in René Guénon, *The Great Triad*, 31.

In traditional China, the Chinese Emperor was symbolically associated with the dragon. In *Patterns in Comparative Religion*, Eliade observes that

> [i]n China the dragon — an emblem of sky and water — was constantly associated with the Emperor, who represented the rhythms of the cosmos and conferred fecundity on the earth. When the rhythms were disturbed when the life of nature or of society became troubled, the Emperor knew what he must do to regenerate his creative power and reestablish order.[95]

Guénon explains in *The Great Triad* what the 'royal function' of the Chinese Emperor consisted of "in the Far-Eastern tradition" as well as its symbolism. He relates that the Chinese Emperor was known as the *Wang*, or 'King Pontiff,' adding, however, that

> [i]f *Wang* is indeed King in the proper sense of the word, he is also something else at the same time. Moreover, this follows from the very symbolism of the character *wang*, which is composed of three horizontal lines corresponding respectively...to Heaven, Man, and Earth, united at their centers by a vertical line, for, as the etymologists say, 'the function of the King is to unite,' by which is understood, because of the very position of the vertical line, to unite Heaven and Earth. What this character properly designates is therefore Man insofar as he is middle term of the Great Triad, and envisaged especially in his role as 'mediator' (see fig. 15.7).[96]

Fig. 15.7. The character *wang*[97]

---

95 Mircea Eliade, *Patterns in Comparative Religion*, 208.
96 René Guénon, *The Great Triad*, 106.
97 René Guénon, *The Great Triad*, 106.

The proper and qualified Chinese Emperor, or *Wang*, was considered in traditional China to be a 'mediator' between Heaven and Earth. In traditional China, the harmony of life and civilization was considered to be made possible only by the proper 'mediation' between the influences of Heaven and Earth. To maintain such harmony, however, required a measure of control over 'nature,' and, more specifically, that which represents the 'possibilities' of existence that manifest in 'nature' and that are represented in traditional art and myth by 'water.' As we have argued, the symbolisms of 'water' and dragon are 'symbolically synonymous.' Eliade writes of the symbolic interchangeability in traditional China, specifically, of 'water' and the dragon when he states that "[d]ragons and snakes, according to Tchouang Tseu, symbolize rhythmic life, for the dragon stands for the spirit of water, whose harmonious fluctuations feed life and make all civilization possible."[98] The Chinese Emperor was traditionally considered a 'controller' of 'water' as well as a 'mediator' between Heaven and Earth. Since 'water' is symbolically synonymous with the dragon, however, I argue that the *Wang* (Chinese Emperor) was thought to be a 'controller' and 'mediator' of the dragon as well, or what the dragon symbolized: 'chaos,' 'possibilities'/potentiality, and the *samsaric* "indefinite series of cycles of manifestation." The Far-Eastern Dragon did *not*, therefore, as is often thought, symbolize the Chinese Emperor/*Wang* himself, or his power, in representations of the Far-Eastern or Chinese dragon-with-'spiraled orb' but, rather, represented that which the Emperor 'controlled' and 'mediated.' The 'spiraled orb' is what symbolized the Chinese Emperor/*Wang* and his power. And this is because it was the *Wang* who traditionally: 1) 'controlled' the 'chaotic' 'possibilities' (potentiality) that are represented by both the dragon and 'water' ('the Waters') and 2) 'mediated' the realm of the 'possibilities'/potentiality that lies between Heaven and Earth — the realm of man (humans).

---

98   Mircea Eliade, *Patterns in Comparative Religion*, 207.

Man (humankind) is that which, in traditional China, stands between Heaven and Earth and completes the 'Great Triad' after which Guénon's book is named. The only *particular* human who was capable of fully 'mediating' between those two realms, however, was the *Wang*. According to Guénon, the *Wang* possessed what was called in traditional China the 'mandate of Heaven' (*T'ien ming*), and it was this 'mandate' that empowered the *Wang*, or 'Universal Man,' as Guénon calls him, to provide and sustain the mentioned tripartite harmony.[99] As Guénon states,

> If therefore the *Wang* is essentially 'Universal Man,' the one who represents him and fulfills his function must...be effectively identified with the 'Middle Way' (*Chung Tao*), that is to say with the axis itself, whether that axis be represented by the pole of the chariot, by the central pillar of the *Ming T'ang*, or by any equivalent symbol....He is the 'regulator' of the cosmic order as well as the social order...and when he fulfills the function of 'mediator' it is really all men that fulfill it in his person; thus, in China, the *Wang* or Emperor alone was able to accomplish the public rites corresponding to that function, and especially to offer the sacrifice to Heaven which is the very type of these rites, for it is here that the role of 'mediator' is affirmed in the most evident way....Moreover, one is really *Wang* only if he possesses the 'mandate of Heaven' (*T'ien ming*), by virtue of which he is legitimately recognized as the Son of Heaven (*T'ien Tzu*).[100]

Reminiscent of the *bodhisattva* in Buddhist tradition, who is capable of connecting and communicating with the various levels of reality or 'heavens,' the Chinese Emperor/*Wang* was thought to serve as a 'bridge' between Heaven and Earth. Again appealing to axial imagery, Guénon argues that the *Wang* was thought to receive the 'mandate of Heaven' only "along the [vertical] axis considered in its descending direction" that connected Heaven and Earth, the latter being the dwelling place of humans:

---

99 René Guénon, *The Great Triad*, 109.
100 René Guénon, *The Great Triad*, 107–109.

According to a symbolism common to most traditions, this [vertical] axis is also the 'bridge' that connects Earth to either Heaven, as here, or the human state to the supra-individual states, or even the sensible world to the suprasensible world; it is always the 'World Axis', but viewed sometimes in its entirety or only in one of its parts.[101]

According to Guénon, this axial symbolism is even present in the Chinese character *wang*, stating that "the parts of the character that properly refer to Man, which includes the vertical line plus the middle horizontal line (since the upper and lower lines represent Heaven and Earth), form a cross, which is the very symbol of 'Universal Man.'"[102] In *The Symbolism of the Cross*, 'Universal Man' denotes for Guénon that being that has achieved "the effective realization of the being's multiple states."[103] More specifically:

the conception of the 'Universal Man' will apply in the first place to the sum total of the states of manifestation; but it can be rendered still more universal, in the fullness of the true meaning of that word, if it is also extended to the states of non-manifestation, and hence to the complete and perfect realization of the total being.[104]

An understanding of the ontological status of the *Wang* in traditional China is necessary to understanding why the 'orb' depicted in representations of the 'Chinese Dragon' has the appearance of a spiral (see fig. 15.4). For Guénon, the *Wang*/Emperor is the East Asian expression of 'Universal Man,' a transcultural concept for him.[105] The *Wang*/Emperor symbolized for traditional Chinese people, like the tree, rod, and cross did for traditional peoples in other cultural variations of Tradition, the 'World Axis.' Like the Jain "*tirthankaras* (ford-makers)," according to S. M. Bhardwaj and J. G. Lochtefeld,

---

101 René Guénon, *The Great Triad*, 109.
102 René Guénon, *The Great Triad*, 107.
103 René Guénon, *The Symbolism of the Cross*, 12.
104 René Guénon, *The Symbolism of the Cross*, 13.
105 René Guénon, *The Great Triad*, 107.

"the teachers who build the 'fords' to make it possible for humans to cross the ocean of rebirths," the *Wang* was both 'bridge' and 'bridge builder' to 'Heaven.'[106] As Guénon proposes, "one could further state that this 'bridge', by which communication with the higher states, and through them the Principle itself, is made possible, can only be truly established by one who is himself effectively identified with it."[107] Like Jacob's 'ladder' in Genesis that connected Earth and Heaven by means of 'angels,' the *Wang* served the traditional Chinese as the 'mediator' of the 'influences' or 'currents' that descended from Heaven to Earth, as well as of the petitions and prayers that ascended from Earth to Heaven.

We know from Guénon that the dragon, in its association with the Chinese Emperor, is necessarily also associated with the 'World Axis' "by which communication with the higher states, and through them the Principle itself, is made possible." And we know from Eliade that "the dragon stands for the spirit of water, whose harmonious fluctuations feed life and make all civilization possible."[108] Again, however, this is the *spirit* of 'water' (the spirit of 'possibility,' which is 'actuality') that is symbolized by the 'orb' that the dragon 'chases,' holds, or is simply represented near. Eliade states that the Emperor/*Wang* "conferred fecundity on the earth," and this was accomplished through his bringing Heaven and Earth *together.* By bringing these two states of being together, I argue that the *Wang* was believed to facilitate (to 'actualize') the transmission of the life-giving 'Waters,' or 'possibilities,' of Heaven *to (on)* Earth. When the 'fluctuations' of 'water' (of what is 'possible') were harmonious, 'life' in a *higher* sense and civilization were possible; and it was the Emperor, in his role as communicator with the "higher states, and through them the Principle itself," which made

---

106 Surinder M. Bhardwaj and James G. Lochtefeld, "Tirtha," in *The Hindu World*, ed. Sushil Mittal and Gene Thursby (New York and London: Routledge, 2004), 498.

107 René Guénon, *The Great Triad*, 110.

108 Mircea Eliade, *Patterns in Comparative Religion*, 207.

such 'life' and civilization possible. 'Water' does, of course, also have a literal meaning here. Human beings in the natural world require, and desire, H_2O. According to Guénon, however, from the traditional perspective, the physical derives from the meta-physical: Earth comes from Heaven. Because of this, the event of physical rain is, traditionally speaking, a result of 'control' over the *metaphysical* 'Waters,' the 'chaoses': *possibilities*.

The *Wang*, the *true* Chinese Emperor, 'mediates' between the 'possibilities' of Heaven and the *actualities* of Earth. Like the 'Word'/*Logos* of the ancient Greek version of Tradition, the *Wang* is the 'locus of possibles,' the 'place' out of which, and into which, 'possibilities' flow. Although he does neither, the *Wang* seems to 'ascend' to Heaven, like the winged dragon, and he seems to 'descend' to the depths of the Earth, like the lowly chthonic snake. In actuality, the *Wang* only 'controls' these realms as their 'mediator,' but the symbolically heterogeneous dragon represents the differences between the two realms that the *Wang* 'controls.' What the *Wang* itself is, is of the essence of that which the 'orb'-*as-spiral* represents. De Visser, as we have seen, asks,

> Is the ball ['orb'], so often seen in connection with the dragon, and often represented as a spiral emitting flames or as a ball upon which something like a spiral is delineated, identical with the spiral, denoting thunder?[109]

Our answer to this more specific question is 'yes,' and it is to an examination of the traditional symbolism of 'thunder' in connection with the traditional conception of the metaphysical 'center'/'Principle' that is symbolized by the circular/spherical 'orb' that we now turn.

---

109 Marinus Willem de Visser, *The Dragon in China and Japan*, 105.

CHAPTER 16

The Spiral, the 'Thunderweapon,' and the *Swastika*

'Spiraled Orb,' *Wang*, and 'Thunder'

The 'Far-Eastern' or Chinese 'spiraled orb' that is so often depicted in illustrations of the dragon-with-'orb' is a symbol of the metaphysical 'center'/'Principle' in Tradition. With its spiral representation, the Chinese 'orb' both: 1) 'stylistically abbreviates' the 'double spiral' that Guénon argues is a symbol of "the alternating rhythm of evolution and involution, of birth and death...manifestation in its double aspect," and 2) symbolizes the power in traditional China of the Chinese Emperor or *Wang*.[1] The *Wang*/Emperor is associated with the symbolism of the dragon-with-'spiraled orb' *not* because he is symbolized by the dragon, but rather because he is symbolized by that which 'controls' the dragon or is the source of its power: the spiraled 'orb' that symbolizes the metaphysical 'center'/Principle. The dragon's 'holding' of the 'spiraled orb' in its mouth, or in one of its claws, or the 'orb's' simply being near the dragon, I suggest, represents *not* the dragon's power over the 'orb' but the dragon's 'fascination' with or *by*, to be more exact, the 'orb.' This depicted 'fascination' is a 'play' on, and reversal of, the ancient belief in the serpent's 'fascination' of its prey,

---

1   René Guénon, *The Great Triad*, 31.

discussed in previous chapters, which facilitates consumption of its prey. The 'fascination' of the dragon by the 'spiraled orb,' however, is a 'message sent' that the order of 'nature' symbolized by the serpent/dragon does not reign supreme in the overall order of the cosmos. Far from 'nature' being capable of 'fascinating' Spirit in some ultimate sense, it is rather Spirit that 'fascinates' 'nature' and that allows 'the (migrating) being' that has become (temporarily) 'fascinated' by 'nature' to extricate itself from the state of *matter* that it has 'fallen' into.

We have discussed previously Guénon's contention that the serpent symbol in Tradition is one of several ancient symbols of 'duality in unity.' The so-called 'double spiral' that symbolizes for Guénon the two processes of 'evolution' and 'involution' is another. Evolution and involution, for Guénon, respectively describe the two 'directions' of the metaphysical Principle's 'movement' in the 'manifestation'/'creation' process of what I term the state of *matter*: 1) 'manifestation' of the metaphysical Source of being in *samsara*, leading to the perception by temporal beings (such as humans) of 'the world' or 'nature' and 2) 'return' to the metaphysical Source of being of all manifested beings. Based upon Guénon's contention that the 'double spiral' symbolizes in Tradition the 'alternating rhythm' of this two-part process, I argue that the *single* spiral that is often depicted on the Chinese 'orb' *also* symbolizes, as a 'stylistic abbreviation' of the 'double spiral,' *both* of the processes of 'involution' and 'evolution.' As alluded to in Chapter 15, this 'single spiral' symbolizes the Chinese idea of 'Heaven' (*T'ien*) or of *Tao* as cultural variations of the metaphysical 'Principle'/'center' and indicates, in a general sense, 'Heaven's'/*Tao*'s (the metaphysical Principle's/'center's') 'action' or 'influence' on Earth in terms of both: 1) *manifesting* 'Heaven' (the 'Principle') on Earth (in 'nature') and 2) *reincorporating* Earthly realities into the metaphysical 'Principial' order. In accordance, however, with Guénon's contention that the *Tao* is the East Asian expression of the metaphysical Principle, and also in accordance with the traditional Chinese belief that the *Tao*'s 'action' is, according to the principle of *wu-wei*, 'action-less,' it must be recognized that the 'action' of 'Heaven' or the *Tao*/'Principle' of East Asian tradition is actually 'action-less.' In the case of the *Wang*, or Chinese Emperor, therefore, who expresses the 'mandate of Heaven' on Earth, the '(single) spiraled orb' that symbolizes his power is, likewise, symbolic of 'action-less' force, since, as Confucius says, the "ruler who governs his state by virtue" is like the motionless north polar star.[2] It is, nevertheless, the case that the *Wang*, like the *Tao* or like Heaven, is, according to East Asian tradition, that ultimate cause in the universe that, like Aristotle's 'Unmoved Mover,' compels all action by being the 'final cause' of, and 'inspiration' for, that action.

It may be said that the 'Far-Eastern'/Chinese dragon represents the 'opposite' of what the 'spiraled orb' represents. Rather than symbolizing the 'Principial' *Tao* or 'Heaven,' the dragon thus symbolizes that which is 'governed' by Heaven/*Tao*/*Wang*: 'Earth,' or, more accurately perhaps, the 'earth-ly': 'nature.' In line with my thesis, however, 'Earth' ('nature') only becomes objectified and 'separate' from the perspective of 'the being' as the latter exists in the state of *matter*. This interpretation of the meaning of the serpentine dragon in Tradition is consistent with Guénon's contention that the simple serpent symbol represents "the indefinite series of cycles of manifestation" or *samsara* in the 'Hindu Doctrines.' The 'Chinese Dragon' is merely, I contend, a more complex expression of the reality that the simple serpent represents. With, as we saw in the last chapter, its radically heterogeneous body, the dragon simply represents more explicitly than the simple serpent the indefinite and 'formless' aspect of *samsara* or *matter*. The 'compound symbolism' of the dragon-with-'spiraled orb' is symbolic of the Chinese Emperor's, or *Wang*'s, 'action-less' 'mediation' of the

---

2   It would, strictly speaking, be inaccurate from the traditional Chinese perspective to employ the term 'action' here without quotes since, like the north polar star that Confucius discusses in connection with the "ruler who governs his state by virtue," the metaphysical 'center' only influences by *being* what it is — by its *essence*, *not* by its 'action.' Confucius, *The Analects*, in Wing-Tsit Chan, trans., *A Source Book in Chinese Philosophy*, 22.

'Principial' force of Heaven on Earth, Spirit *in matter* in my terms, since the *Wang* is the 'middle term' of 'the Great Triad' and, as 'Universal Man' according to Guénon, "identified with the 'Middle Way' (*Chung Tao*), that is to say with the [World] axis itself."[3] As such, it is the *Wang*'s function to both: 1) ensure that all manifested (Earthly) beings under its power continue to 'turn upward toward,' or appreciate, their metaphysical Source (*Tao*/Heaven), as well as to 2) remind all such beings that they must eventually 'return,' or 'involute,' as Guénon says, to that Source. Such 'appreciation' is accomplished, I argue, by means of the *Wang*'s imposition, upon both himself and his people, of the Confucian 'moral virtue' of traditional China called *li* that consists of divinely sanctioned religious rituals and the time-honored rules of social etiquette. The meaning of *li*, which derives from an age much earlier than the one in which Confucius himself lived, is simply, as Huston Smith says in *The World's Religions*, "the way things should be done."[4] The traditional Chinese Emperor/*Wang* that I contend is symbolized by the 'spiraled orb' perfectly embodies *li* according to the traditional perspective. In so doing, the *Wang*'s 'royal' presence, as well as the 'spiraled orb' that represents the metaphysical power of this presence, represents 'evolution' and 'involution' as the processes by which *li* both: 1) manifests Heaven on Earth, and 2) aids Earthly entities in their 'return,' in both mind and spirit, to Heaven (the 'Principle'/*Tao*). As 'Universal Man,' the *Wang*'s divine duty or 'mandate,' the 'Mandate of Heaven' acting *through* him, is to bring all humans under his (its) power to an expression, and appreciation, of the 'Universal' or metaphysical. In the Chinese manifestation of Tradition, such expression and appreciation is an expression, and appreciation, of 'Heaven.' The imposition of *li* by the *Wang* upon his people and himself is, symbolically, the 'defeat' of the dragon, the defeat of the 'chaotic' and *samsaric* "indefinite series of cycles of manifestation" by means of 'fascinating'

---

3   René Guénon, *The Great Triad*, 107.
4   Huston Smith, *The World's Religions* (New York, NY: HarperCollins, 1958), 174.

the dragon: numbing and disciplining the 'natural' instincts of man through the practice of 'virtue.'

As we have seen, both de Groot and de Visser entertained the idea that the 'orb' depicted in illustrations of the Far-Eastern/Chinese dragon is a depiction, not merely of a 'ball' with a 'spirally' decoration, but of a specific spiral symbolism that is meant to represent the force of thunder. De Groot, for example, in describing the priestly *sai kong* vestment, refers to that vestment's depiction of "dragons which are belching out a ball, probably representing thunder" as well as 'figures' that "resemble spirals and denote rolling thunder."[5] Traditionally, according to Guénon, thunder, or the thunder*bolt* specifically, served as an axial symbol, a figuration of the 'World Axis' that symbolizes the 'Principle'/'center.' In *Symbols of Sacred Science*, in a chapter entitled 'Symbolic Weapons,' Guénon states that, traditionally, "the thunderbolt…is held to represent a twofold power of production and destruction," the power that Guénon generally attributes to *all* axial symbols.[6] 'Production' and 'destruction' are, for Guénon, variations on the processes of 'evolution' and 'involution' earlier referred to. As a symbol of the power of the *Wang*/Emperor, therefore, I contend that the 'spiraled orb' that represents the force of 'thunder,' whatever that might ultimately mean, symbolizes, and even 'advertises,' the *Wang*'s possession of the powers of both 'production' and 'destruction' as particularizations of his more extensive powers of 'evolution' and 'involution.' Because the 'spiraled orb' that represents the *Wang*'s 'control' over the powers of 'production' and 'destruction' also represents his 'control' over what the dragon symbolizes, the dragon-with-'spiraled orb' *in total* represents the *Wang*'s 'control' over the 'chaos' of 'possibilities,' Guénon's 'two chaoses.' This 'control' consists in the *Wang*'s power to both 'produce' ('evolve') *and* 'destroy' ('involute') 'possibilities.'[7] As

---

5 J. J. M. de Groot, *The Religious System of China, Vol. 6*, 1265, Plate XVIII (unclear).
6 René Guénon, *Symbols of Sacred Science*, 176.
7 René Guénon, *The Multiple States of the Being*, 68.

such, the *Wang* is that being that is 'master of what is possible' for the average human. This is because he is, as Guénon states, the 'Universal Man' and so, he who 'controls' the categories ('universals') of existence.

In the last chapter, we saw that 'evolution' and 'involution' are both forms of 'actualization.' 'Involution,' considered as synonymous with 'destruction,' is as much a form of 'actualization' of 'possibilities' as is the 'evolution' ('production'/'creation'/'manifestation') of the 'possible' into the manifested world.[8] This is because 'involution' is the 'actualization' of manifested existence's potential to go '*back into*' the state of 'possibility' from which it originally derived. The 'involution' (or 'destruction') of manifested existence is, therefore, in its 'return' to metaphysical potentiality (the indefinite set of all 'possibilities') a kind of 'actualization.' I have argued, along with Eliade, that the serpent/dragon represents the 'chaos' of 'nature' that, from the perspective of the state of *matter*, *obscures* ('guards') the Principle from manifested beings to various degrees. In *The Reign of Quantity & the Signs of the Times*, as we have repeatedly noted, Guénon states that "the Far-Eastern Dragon... [is] really a symbol of the Word" of 'creation' ('manifestation'/'production'/'evolution').[9] In *Symbols of Sacred Science*, however, he adds that the Word has, like the "twofold power of production and destruction" that he argues that the thunderbolt represents in Tradition, a "double power as creator and destroyer."[10] If, then, the Word has a "double power as creator and destroyer," and

---

8   The term 'destruction' is a bit misleading, as it implies total annihilation. The process of 'involution' in fact, however, according to Guénon, preserves all possibilities that are necessary for any possible 'future' 'actualizations.' In *The Christ of India*, Abbot George Burke similarly notes with respect to the Hindu god Shiva, as expressive of "God (Ishwara) in His aspect of Dissolver and Liberator...[, that he is] often mistakenly thought of as 'destroyer.'" Abbot George Burke (Swami Nirmalananda Giri), *The Christ of India: The Story of Original Christianity* (Cedar Crest, New Mexico: Light of the Spirit Press, 2018), 82.

9   René Guénon, *The Reign of Quantity & the Signs of the Times*, 205.

10 René Guénon, *Symbols of Sacred Science*, 174.

the Far-Eastern Dragon, as Guénon contends, symbolizes the Word, then it would seem that, insofar as he is associated with the dragon, the *Wang* has a "double power as creator and destroyer" as well. The *Wang*'s association with the traditional symbolism of the 'double spiral' by means of the 'spiraled orb,' and thus his association with the force of 'thunder,' confirms this power. The *Wang*, therefore, like the 'Word,' is, I argue, a 'mediator' or *means* by which the metaphysical 'Principle'/'center'/*Tao*/Heaven: 1) 'creates' (manifests/produces) the 'Principial' reality *in* the 'natural' state of being called 'Earth' (in the state of *matter*, more specifically) in traditional China, and 2) 'destroys' all on 'Earth' (all in the state of *matter* that the *Wang* is able to facilitate, more specifically) that is not found harmonious with the 'mandate of Heaven.' The imposition of *li* is the application of these two powers in the civilized realm *specifically*.

It is important to note that Guénon sometimes writes of only the 'creative' power of the 'Word' and not of its 'destructive' power. For example, he says that "[c]reation is the work of the Word" but says nothing of 'destruction' being part of its 'work.'[11] This would seem to imply that, for Guénon, the dragon as a "symbol of the Word" is only a symbol of 'creation' ('production'): the manifestation of the 'Principle' in those 'possibilities' constituted by "the indefinite series of cycles of manifestation." In *The Great Triad*, however, Guénon argues, as we have seen, that the

> waters are the symbol of possibilities, and their development is represented by the spiral, hence the close association that sometimes exists between this last and the symbolism of the waters.[12]

We have proposed, however, that the 'close association' between the symbolism of 'the waters' and that of the 'spiral' is actually one of diametric opposition. For 'the Waters' is 'symbolically synonymous' with

---

11   René Guénon, *Symbols of Sacred Science*, 9.
12   René Guénon, *The Great Triad*, 34.

the Far-Eastern/Chinese dragon, whereas the 'spiral,' in its connection with both the circular/spherical 'orb' and the force of 'thunder,' is symbolic of the metaphysical Principle/*Tao*/Heaven. Neither, by itself, can symbolize the complete event of 'creation' *or* 'destruction.' If the 'Chinese Dragon' and 'the Waters' are 'symbolically synonymous,' however, and 'the Waters' represent 'possibilities'/'chaos,' and the 'spiral' represents, as Guénon argues, the 'development' of 'possibilities,' then the entire symbolism of the dragon-with-'spiraled orb' that is connected with the *Wang* (Chinese Emperor) symbolizes the 'development' of the 'possibilities' of *both* 'creation'/'manifestation' *and* 'destruction'/'return.' The source of this 'development' of 'possibilities,' however, is the metaphysical Principle that is symbolized by the 'spiraled orb.' And the 'Word' is *not* the 'Principle' but, rather, the 'means' or 'mediator' by which the Principle 'acts' in the state of 'nature' or *matter*. Guénon's contention that "[c]reation is the work of the Word," therefore, is only meaningful in the sense that the Word provides the 'means' or 'possibility' for, not the impetus for, 'creation.' On this interpretation, the dragon as symbolic of the Word symbolizes the *means* of 'creation' and 'destruction,' while the dragon as symbolic of 'the Waters' represents the 'possibility' (potential) that always exists for 'creation' and 'destruction.' From this perspective, the 'spiraled orb' symbolizes the 'influence' of the metaphysical 'center' in 'developing': 1) the 'possibility' (potential) *and* 2) the 'means,' of 'creation' and 'destruction.' Guénon's contention that "the Far-Eastern Dragon... [is] really a symbol of the Word" of 'creation' is, thus, only a half-truth, and for two reasons: 1) because the 'Word' is a 'means' and 'mediator' of *both* 'creation' *and* 'destruction,' and 2) the 'Far Eastern Dragon' symbolizes 'creation' and 'destruction' only insofar as it symbolizes 'the Waters' of 'possibility' (potentiality) that allows for the 'action' of the Principle that 'actualizes' 'creation' and 'destruction.'

Recalling Eliade's observation that "the [Chinese] Emperor... represented the rhythms of the cosmos and conferred fecundity on the earth," it would seem that, if one 'half' of the traditional 'double spiral' symbolizes 'evolution' and the other 'half' symbolizes 'involution,' then the Emperor/*Wang* was more closely associated in traditional China with the 'evolutive' half of the 'double spiral,' the half that represented *natural* 'birth' and the 'creative' side of things in which 'possibilities' are 'actualized' by manifesting in the physical realm of 'nature' (and, more specifically, in the state of *matter*). On this interpretation, the 'half' of the 'double spiral' — the 'single spiral' — that is represented on the figuration of the dragon-with-'spiraled orb' would traditionally symbolize those things associated with 'evolution,' such as biological life, 'fecundity,' as Eliade says, and 'creation,' rather than with 'involution,' *physical* death, and 'destruction.' As Eliade states,

> When the rhythms were disturbed when the life of nature or of society became troubled, the [Chinese] Emperor knew what he must do to regenerate his creative power and reestablish order.[13]

Eliade does not, after all, mention the Chinese Emperor's/*Wang*'s 'regenerating' his 'destructive power' to 'reestablish order.' To 'control' the dragon/'Waters' of 'possibility'/'chaos,' however, the *Wang*/Emperor must have been thought by traditional Chinese people to be able to 'control' 'possibilities'/'chaos' *in general*, not just the 'possibilities' of 'creative' 'manifestation.' But, in order to have such 'control,' the *Wang* must have also been believed to have power over the *Source* of 'possibilities'/'chaos,' which, according to Tradition, is the *meta*-physical state that traditional Chinese people called 'Heaven.' In having this totalizing power, traditional Chinese people must have believed that the *Wang* had power over, not merely the 'actualization' of 'possibilities' in the manifested realm of 'nature,' but power over the 'actualization' of the 'possibilities' of 'return' to the metaphysical Source: to 'Heaven.'

In Tradition, it is only from the 'Principial' perspective, the metaphysical perspective of Yahweh or *Brahman* or the *Tao*, for example,

---

13   Mircea Eliade, *Patterns in Comparative Religion*, 208.

that what is 'possible' or 'chaotic' can be objectively defined. He who 'controls' what is 'possible,' therefore, determines both: 1) what 'chaos' and 'order' *are* and 2) whether 'chaos' or 'order' shall reign in the manifested (physical) realm of 'nature.' Such an individual, because he 'mediates' the 'influence' of 'Heaven' (the metaphysical) on 'Earth,' 'controls,' as Eliade says, the "rhythms of the cosmos" and the balance of harmonious and disharmonious influences upon his land and among his people. This control of 'the Waters' of 'possibility'/potentiality was attributed by traditional peoples to all proper sovereigns of the ancient world. The Chinese Emperor/*Wang* is but one example. In *The Evolution of the Dragon*, G. Elliot Smith states that

> In the earliest records from Egypt and Babylonia it is customary to portray a king's beneficence by representing him initiating irrigation works. In course of time he came to be regarded, not merely as the giver of the water which made the desert fertile, but as himself the personification and the giver of the vital powers of water.[14]

These 'vital powers of water' mentioned by Smith are reminiscent of Eliade's identification of the 'Chinese Dragon' as symbolic of the "*spirit* of water, whose harmonious fluctuations feed life and make all civilization possible."[15] In both cases, it is the *essence* of something called 'water' that is drawn attention to. Smith further argues that "the original dragon was a beneficent creature, the personification of water, and was identified with kings and gods."[16] As we have contended, however, the dragon was only 'identified' in Tradition with "kings and gods" because it represented that aspect of existence that 'received' the formative, defining, and 'actualizing' (Spiritualizing) influence of the metaphysical Principle that *uses* "kings and gods" to 'Spiritualize' the 'natural' state of *matter*, the 'chaotic' and *samsaric* "indefinite series of cycles of manifestation." Often, this formative, defining, and

---

14 Sir Grafton Elliot Smith, *The Evolution of the Dragon*, 4.
15 Mircea Eliade, *Patterns in Comparative Religion*, 207.
16 Sir Grafton Elliot Smith, *The Evolution of the Dragon*, 4.

'actualizing' — Spiritualizing — influence was traditionally symbolized by something called the 'thunderweapon,' which, we may say, was an expression not of 'the Waters,' but of the *spirit* of 'the Waters.'

The Meaning of the 'Thunderweapon' and the Gods Who Wield It

In *The Myth of the Eternal Return*, Eliade analyzes the meaning of the "act of Creation" in Tradition by interpreting the South Asian narrative of the cosmogonic battle between the god Indra and the serpent Vrtra. He argues,

> [t]he serpent symbolizes chaos, the formless and nonmanifested. Indra comes upon Vrtra undivided (*aparvan*), unawakened (*abudhyam*), sleeping (*abudhyamanam*), sunk in deepest sleep (*susupanam*), outstretched (*asayanam*). The hurling of the lightning and the decapitation [of Vrtra] are equivalent to the act of Creation, the passage from the nonmanifested to the manifested, from the formless to the formed. Vrtra had confiscated the waters and was keeping them in the hollows of the mountains.[17]

The narrative of Vrtra's battle with Indra that is encapsulated in this quotation contains the two traditional symbols of 'chaos'/'possibility' that we have often discussed: serpent/dragon and 'water'/'the Waters.' According to both Eliade and Guénon, Vritra, a serpent/dragon of Hindu myth, traditionally symbolizes 'chaos.' For Guénon, 'the Waters' of 'chaos' are, as we have discussed, 'possibilities'; for Eliade, they are 'virtualities.' The narrative of the battle between Indra and Vrtra as a whole, therefore, has to do with 'possibilities'/'virtualities' and the 'struggle' to 'actualize' them. Eliade describes Vrtra as 'confiscating' 'the waters,' thereby preventing those 'possibilities' represented by the 'waters' from 'actualizing.' The serpent Vrtra, however, as a symbol of 'chaos,' is *also* a symbol of 'possibilities,' and so in its act of 'confiscation' the narrative seems to tell us that *one kind* of 'possibility' (that represented by the serpent) is preventing the 'actualization' of *another*

---

17 Mircea Eliade, *The Myth of the Eternal Return*, 19.

kind of 'possibility' (that represented by 'the waters'). In the event, however, it seems that the first kind of 'possibility' is unable to 'actualize' as well. The narrative, therefore, seems to metaphorically communicate to the traditional reader/listener steeped in the knowledge of traditional symbolism, the idea that, until Indra 'slays the dragon,' *all* 'possibilities' — the totality of Reality or of 'the world' — will fail to 'actualize'. And this 'failure' will, the narrative seems to say, continue to occur as long as one *kind* of 'possibility'/'chaos' 'confiscates' *another* kind of 'possibility'/'chaos'. In such a situation, 'the world' will remain in a state of complete 'possibility'/potential or 'warring possibilities,' just as long as the 'possibility'/'chaos' that is represented by Vritra 'confiscates' the 'possibility'/'chaos' that is represented by 'the waters.' And this is just because the *kind* of 'possibility' that is represented by Vrtra has overstepped the bounds of what, traditionally speaking, it *should* 'become' ('actualize as'). From the perspective of Vedic Hinduism, specifically, that which the serpent Vrtra represents in the narrative is shown there to have 'transgressed' the 'natural' cosmic order known in the Vedas as *Rta*. To put the matter more simply, Vrtra's continued 'confiscation' of 'the waters' 'transgresses' the *rule* of *Rta*. And this state of 'transgression' of *Rta*, or of its other cultural equivalents[18] such as *Tao* in East Asia, is, I argue, what traditional peoples believed would occur if the god/hero/ruler, such as Indra in the present case, failed to 'slay the dragon' and thereby *properly* order/'actualize' 'chaos'/'possibilities' and 'release the waters.' As de Visser states in *The Dragon in China and Japan*, "the time is wrong for a dragon to appear, when the Son of Heaven [the Chinese Emperor/*Wang*] does not walk in the Tao, thus throwing into disorder both the Tao of Heaven and men."[19] Indra's 'releasing of the waters,' for traditional peoples, thankfully for them, avoids this 'unnatural' transgression and allows

---

18 I consider the idea of *Rta* to be a roughly equivalent conceptual precursor to the idea of *Brahman*. It is thus that *Rta* stands as a 'cultural equivalent' to *Tao* and God/Yahweh.

19 Marinus Willem de Visser, *The Dragon in China and Japan*, 50.

for those 'possibilities'/potentiality to be 'actualized' that are in accordance with the divine rule of *Rta*, or, in the case of 'old' China, the *Tao*. This task of 'release,' however, we must note, is only accomplished by Indra by means of the expediency of his 'hurling lightning.' This action of 'hurling lightning' is, I contend, a traditional figuration of the symbolism of the 'thunderweapon' and its capacity to 'release the waters.'

In order to 'release the waters' of 'possibility'/potentiality that are in accord with the cosmic rule of *Rta*, the god Indra must, we are told in the narrative, 'hurl lighting' at, and thereby behead and slay, the serpent Vrtra. Such a task, however, requires Indra's control of what the early twentieth-century archaeologist Christian Blinkenberg has called the 'thunderweapon.'[20] Guénon, although he doesn't use the term 'thunderweapon' in *Symbols of Sacred Science*, refers to 'thunder stones' symbolizing lightning, as well as the different kinds of stone weapons employed by ancient gods and heroes that, he argues, symbolize the force of lightning. He states:

> The truth is that 'thunder stones' are stones which symbolize lightning; they are nothing but prehistoric flint axes....The stone axe is the stone that shatters and splits, and this is why it represents the lightning bolt.... [T]he stone axe of Parashu-Rama and the stone hammer of Thor are really one and the same weapon, and this weapon is, moreover, the symbol of lightning.[21]

According to Guénon, the various weapons used by Thor, Rama, and other ancient gods are, like the cross, rod, and tree, figurations of the 'World Axis' that symbolize in Tradition the metaphysical 'Principle' and 'center' of the world. The so-called 'thunderweapon,' therefore, in general terms, served in the traditional worldview to symbolize each of these gods' privileged connection to the metaphysical realm and his 'divine mandate' to convey the power of Heaven to Earth. When,

---

20 Christian Blinkenberg, *The Thunderweapon in Religion and Folklore*.
21 René Guénon, *Symbols of Sacred Science*, 169–170.

therefore, the god Indra 'releases' the 'waters' of 'possibility' and thereby 'actualizes' potentiality in accordance with *Rta*, it is not really he who accomplishes this, although he is chosen as a sufficient conduit for the purpose, but the force of lightning or thunder, the 'thunderweapon,' that 'acts' through him. This 'thunderweapon' that embodies the force of thunder embodies the force of the metaphysical 'Principle' that is 'from' Heaven, and is equivalent, I argue, to what Eliade calls the "spirit of water" and what G. E. Smith calls "the vital powers of water" because it is that which 'actualizes' 'water'/'the Waters.' That is, it 'actualizes,' or, in my terms, Spiritualizes 'possibility,' and the latter characterizes *samsara* or the state of *matter*.

The 'spiraled orb' that is depicted in figurations of the 'Far-Eastern' dragon-with-'orb' represents, like the so-called 'thunderweapon' that is depicted with ancient gods such as Thor or Rama, the force of 'thunder' which is an expression of the power of the metaphysical 'Principle'/*Tao* or 'Heaven.' 'Lightning,' as an expression of the force of 'thunder,' is 'symbolically synonymous' with 'thunder' and, thus, equally expressive of the power of the 'thunderweapon.' The traditional meaning of the 'thunderweapon,' therefore, is, I contend, equivalent to that of the 'thunder spirals' that are depicted with Chinese dragons on various works of art from old China, such as the priestly *sai kong* vestments discussed in the last chapter. Wherever traditional figurations of the 'thunderweapon' or 'spiraled orb' are found, therefore, they symbolize the 'actualization' of the 'chaos' of 'possibilities' that is symbolized by the serpent/dragon and 'the Waters'/'water.' There are, however, as we have previously outlined, two kinds of 'possibilities' that may be 'actualized' according to the traditional paradigm: 1) those 'possibilities' that are 'actualized' by the 'creative' process of 'evolution,' and 2) those 'possibilities' that are 'actualized' by the 'destructive' process of 'involution.' In the case of the Vedic god Indra's decapitation of the serpent Vrtra discussed earlier, the specific kind of 'possibilities' that are emphasized by Eliade as being 'actualized' are those of evolution, or 'creation,' that lead to the formation of the cosmic order out of 'chaos.' In the case of the symbolism of the 'Far-Eastern' or Chinese dragon-with-'spiraled orb,' however, the 'possibilities' to be 'actualized' — *expected* by traditional Chinese people to be 'actualized,' that is, by the *Wang*— are those of *both* evolution *and* involution, those of 'creation'/'manifestation' *and* 'destruction'/'return.' The 'development,' as Guénon puts it, of both kinds of 'possibilities' is, then, symbolized by the 'spiraled orb' that itself symbolizes the force of 'thunder' and, thus, the power of the metaphysical Principle or 'Heaven.' What I have termed the 'single spiral' that is depicted on the 'spiraled orb,' and which is a 'stylistic abbreviation' of the 'double spiral,' indicates this 'duality' of 'possibilities,' as does, according to Guénon, the 'thunderweapon's' characteristic of 'two-sidedness' that we shall soon examine. The 'development' of 'possibilities' that is symbolized by the 'spiral component' of the 'spiraled orb' in particular is, metaphorically speaking, equivalent to the 'thunderweapon's' capacity to 'fascinate' the dragon that symbolizes *samsara*/'nature'/*matter*/'possibilities.' This 'fascination' of the dragon by the 'spiraled orb,' I contend, is traditionally represented by means of the dragon's tightly holding in one of its claws the 'spiraled orb' that represents the force of the 'thunderweapon' and, so, represents the power of the metaphysical Principle/*Tao* or 'Heaven.' It is, therefore, the case that the Chinese Emperor's/*Wang*'s traditional identification with the dragon-with-'spiraled orb' symbolizes his believed responsibility by traditional peoples for *both* 'sides' of what the 'double spiral' represents: 'creation'/'evolution'/'manifestation' *and* 'destruction'/'involution'/'return.' As Guénon argues, the 'thunderweapon' is usually depicted in Tradition as 'two-sided' in order to represent this 'dual' power.

It is well known that, experientially, lightning 'anticipates' thunder. Lightning is, so to speak, a sign, or outward manifestation, of the force and power of thunder. If an observer looks at the relevant part of the sky, he will see a lighting strike well before he hears the thunder associated with it. For any being that observes a clear lightning strike, it is hard to imagine a better means of representing the nature of the connection that traditional peoples believed existed between what they called Heaven and Earth: which is that, to a much greater degree, energy is transmitted *from* Heaven *to* Earth, and not so much the reverse. I have argued that, by means of its circular/spherical shape and its depiction of the 'single spiral,' the Far-Eastern, or Chinese, 'spiraled orb' represents the force of 'thunder,' the 'thunderweapon' that, in Tradition, symbolizes the power of the metaphysical Principle or 'center.' Both the 'spiraled orb' and the 'thunderweapon,' in other words, traditionally symbolize that power by which the metaphysical Principle is both manifested in ('evolves'), and is later wrested away from ('involutes'), the 'chaos' of 'possibilities'/potentiality that is traditionally represented by both the dragon/serpent and 'the Waters'/'water.' This 'creative' and 'destructive' process is illustrated in many ancient 'creation myths' in which a hero or god struggles with, and usually defeats, a serpentine/draconic foe in order to bring the cosmos into existence. After the pattern of Indra's defeat of Vrtra in the *Rig Veda*, the myths of various other ancient cultures describe gods with traits similar to Indra employing various versions of the 'thunderweapon' to vanquish a foe similar to Vrtra. In *Symbols of Sacred Science*, for example, Guénon states:

> It is known that Apollo killed the serpent *Python* with his arrows, just as, in the Vedic tradition, Indra kills *Ahi* or *Vritra*, the counterpart of *Python*, with the *vajra* which represents the thunderbolt; and this comparison leaves no doubt whatsoever as to the original symbolical equivalence of the two weapons in question.[22] (See fig. 16.1.)

---

22 René Guénon, *Symbols of Sacred Science*, 173.

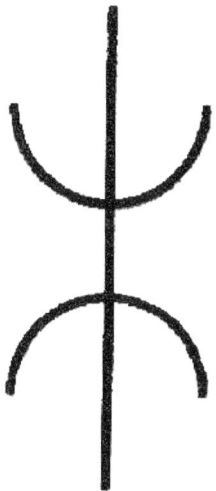

Fig. 16.1. *The Double Vajra*[23]

According to Guénon, Indra's version of the 'thunderweapon,' the *vajra*, is a device that represents lightning in Tibetan Buddhism and that is connected with the Masonic symbolism of the 'mallet,' a version of the hammer, that goes back to the guilds of medieval Europe and perhaps to more ancient times. Guénon states in *Symbols of Sacred Science* that

> the English Masonic historian R. F. Gould thinks that the 'mallet of the Master'...originates from the hammer of Thor. In addition, the Gauls had a 'God of the mallet', who figures on an altar discovered at Mainz; it would even seem that this is the *Dis Pater*, whose name is very close to that of *Zeus Pater* [Ju-piter]....Thus the mallet appears...as a symbolic equivalent of the *vajra* of the Eastern traditions.[24]

For Guénon, therefore, the *vajra*, the 'mallet,' the hammer, 'arrows,' and various other 'two-sided' weapons are all symbolic of (as Guénon labels it) the 'thunderbolt,' and, because of that, are so many

---

23 René Guénon, *Symbols of Sacred Science*, 317.
24 René Guénon, *Symbols of Sacred Science*, 171.

figurations of the 'World Axis' that symbolizes the metaphysical Principle or 'center' of the world. Guénon summarizes his position in *Symbols of Sacred Science*:

> Returning to the various weapons that represent the 'World Axis', we must make the important observation that although not always so, very often they are either double-edged or have a point at each end. The latter instance, like the *vajra*...must clearly be referred back to the duality of the poles considered as two extremities of the axis....As for the double-edged weapons, since their duality is marked along the axis, we must see in them a more direct allusion to the two currents that are represented in another way by the two serpents entwined around the staff or caduceus....The sword itself may generally be considered as a two-edged weapon; but a still more striking example is the double axe, which pertains particularly, although not exclusively, to Aegean and Cretan symbolism, that is, to pre-Hellenic symbolism. Now the battle-axe...is quite specifically a symbol of the thunderbolt, and as such is thus a strict equivalent of the *vajra*; and the comparison of these two weapons therefore clearly shows the fundamental identity of the two forms of symbolism we have mentioned, of double-edged weapons and of weapons with two points.[25]

Blinkenberg makes a similar argument for the 'thunderweapon's' transcultural pervasiveness when he contends,

> As in Tibet, so in Japan, Buddhist mythology and art endow many supernatural beings with the thunderweapon. One of these figures... [is] the demon Fudo-mio-o....The thunderweapon of Tibet and Japan is...only a slightly altered form of the Hellenistic keraunos as depicted, amongst other places, on the altar of Pergamon.[26] (See figs. 16.2, 16.3, and 16.4.)

---

25 René Guénon, *Symbols of Sacred Science*, 174–75.
26 Christian Blinkenberg, *The Thunderweapon in Religion and Folklore*, 46–47. 'Keraunos' is the Greek term for 'thunder' or 'thunderbolt.'

Fig. 16.2. Japanese statuette, with pedestal, National Museum[27]

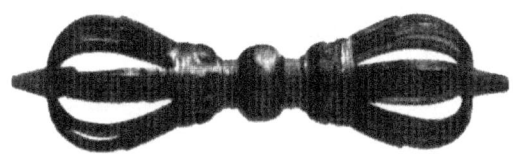

Fig. 16.3. Tibetan thunderweapon (*dorje*) of bronze, National Museum[28]

---

27 Christian Blinkenberg, *The Thunderweapon in Religion and Folklore*, 47.
28 Christian Blinkenberg, *The Thunderweapon in Religion and Folklore*, 45.

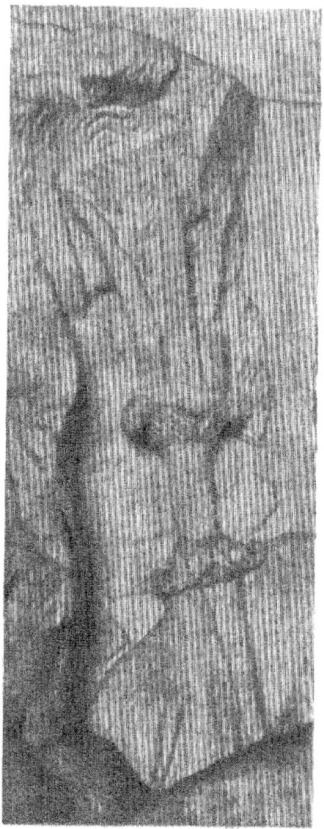

Fig. 16.4. Classical Greek Thunderweapon (*keraunos*) on the altar-relief from Pergamon. Photographed from the cast in the Royal Collection of Casts, Copenhagen[29]

According to Guénon, the 'dual' character of the various versions of what Blinkenberg calls the 'thunderweapon' that is indicated by such weapons' 'double-edged-ness' or 'double-pointed-ness,' although it refers to the "duality of the poles considered as two extremities of the [World] axis," is "a more direct allusion to the two currents" or 'forces'

---

29 Christian Blinkenberg, *The Thunderweapon in Religion and Folklore*, 48.

that emanate from that which symbolizes the metaphysical Principle.³⁰ As with other symbols of 'duality in unity' for Guénon, this version of traditional 'duality' symbolism symbolizes for him the "double force, itself single in essence, but with apparently opposite effects in its manifestation, resulting from the 'polarization' that conditions the latter."³¹

In discussing the particular version of the 'thunderweapon' known as the *vajra*, Guénon notes that

> [t]he *vajra*, beyond the meaning of 'thunderbolt', also has that of 'diamond', which immediately evokes ideas of indivisibility, inalterability, and immutability; and indeed, immutability is really the essential characteristic of the axis around which all things revolve, and which does not itself participate in the revolution.³²

This etymological analysis of *vajra* that is provided by Guénon is well known among scholars and laymen both, as the *Vajrayana* 'way' of Buddhism is usually translated as either the 'diamond way' or the 'way of the thunderbolt.' The translation of *vajra* as 'diamond,' however, as Guénon points out, "immediately evokes ideas of indivisibility, inalterability, and immutability," ideas that are descriptive of the traditional 'Principial' reality that is represented by figurations of the 'World Axis.'³³ By recalling the various 'compound symbols' of the serpent entwined around a staff or tree discussed earlier, one can immediately see the juxtaposition in such symbolisms of "indivisibility, inalterability, and immutability," represented by the staff, with that which is *not* indivisible, inalterable, and immutable: the always changing and rejuvenating serpent. The symbolism of the 'simple' serpent in general, as representing the two 'currents' that 'entwine' about the

---

30 René Guénon, *Symbols of Sacred Science*, 174.
31 René Guénon, *Symbols of Sacred Science*, 174.
32 René Guénon, *Symbols of Sacred Science*, 176.
33 René Guénon, *Symbols of Sacred Science*, 176. The word 'diamond' is derived from the Greek *adamas* which means 'unyielding.'

World Axis, would seem to represent, for Guénon, the 'all things' that he mentions in the above quotation revolving around the World Axis. The tales and depictions of gods such as Indra fighting serpentine/draconic foes such as Vrtra with their 'thunderweapons,' I argue, are merely more dynamic figurations of this same symbolism. And the 'thunderweapon,' again, like the tree, rod, staff, and sphere, is therefore a figuration of the immutable 'center' of existence which, by wielding it, the gods also wield, as Guénon describes it, the "twofold power of production and destruction" that emanates from the 'center,' of which the 'power of life and death' is "just another particular application."[34] Although Eliade's description of Indra's defeat of Vrtra that we examined earlier focuses only on the 'productive'/'evolutive'/'creative' side of the god's action, this in no way implies the absence in his *vajra* of the 'involutive' power of 'destruction,' for all instances of 'creation' are,

---

34 René Guénon, *Symbols of Sacred Science*, 176. The 'twofold power of production and destruction' associated with the generic 'thunderweapon' is commented on by David Snellgrove in his *Indo-Tibetan Buddhism*, where he discusses the symbolism of the *vajra* in terms of the "Buddhist meaning of the Sanskrit word" and its usage in *Vajrayana* Buddhist ritual. Snellgrove states: "The vajra as an instrument plays an essential part in all Vajrayana ritual, where it is used in conjunction with a bell, of which the handle is a half-vajra. Treated thus as a form of duality, the vajra represents the active principle, the means toward enlightenment and the means of conversion, thus the actual Buddha-manifestation, while the bell represents the Perfection of Wisdom, known as the Void (sunyata)." David Snellgrove, *Indo-Tibetan Buddhism: Indian Buddhists and Their Tibetan Successors* (Boston: Shambhala, 2002), 131–32. In the terms of my thesis, and in accordance with Guénon's analysis, the *vajra* indeed serves as "the means toward enlightenment," as Snellgrove puts it, because it symbolizes the force of the metaphysical 'Principle' that is 'active' in comparison to the latent character of the 'chaotic' and formless, indefinite, potentiality of that cyclical state of being that I term *matter*. Based upon the reasoning that supports this inference, it is possible that the 'bell' that is associated with the *vajra* in Tibetan Buddhism, because the former represents the so-called 'Void,' also represents the sort of potentiality/'possibility' and 'chaos' that I term *matter*, the latter of which is symbolized by the serpent/dragon and, in accordance with Guénon's understanding of 'chaos' and 'possibility,' 'the Waters'/'water' in Tradition.

as the 'two-sidedness' of the 'thunderweapon' clearly reveals, also, and necessarily, instances of 'destruction.'

'Sky Gods' and the 'Thunderweapon'

The 'thunderweapon' is the weapon of choice not only of those ancient gods and heroes who battled and defeated serpentine or draconic beasts, but also of the members of a transcultural group of beings known by researchers as 'sky gods.' Along with the South Asian god Indra, this group includes the Greek Zeus, the Roman Jupiter, the Norse Thor, and others. Eliade states in *Patterns in Comparative Religion*, for example, that Zeus, "the supreme divinity of the Greek pantheon," whose "weapon was the thunderbolt," was a 'sky god.'[35] Jupiter, however, as 'Dyaus Pitar,' or 'Zeus Pater,' is, as Eliade mentions, widely accepted to be the Roman 'equivalent' of Zeus and, "like all sky gods, Jupiter punished with thunderbolts."[36] In *The Sacred and the Profane*, Eliade adds that Zeus and Jupiter both "still preserve in their names the memory of the sacredness of the sky" and that, although they are "not identified with the sky," they live there, "manifested in meteorological phenomena — thunder, lightning, storm, meteors, and so on."[37] As 'Zeus Pater,' Zeus has also often been thought of as the "archetype of the patriarchal head of the family," the 'Father' of the other gods and 'Creator' in some sense. In *Patterns in Comparative Religion*, however, Eliade clarifies that

> [t]his "creative" element is very marked in Zeus, not on the cosmogonic level (for the universe was not created by him), but on the bio-cosmic level: he governs the sources of fertility, he is master of the rain. He is "creator" because it is he who "makes fruitful"....And his "creation" depends primarily on what the weather does, particularly the rain.[38]

---

35 Mircea Eliade, *Patterns in Comparative Religion*, 78.
36 Mircea Eliade, *Patterns in Comparative Religion*, 78–79.
37 Mircea Eliade, *The Sacred and the Profane*, 120–121.
38 Mircea Eliade, *Patterns in Comparative Religion*, 79. In *The Ancient City*, Fustel de Coulanges notes that 'pater' "contained in itself not the idea of paternity, but

As 'master of rain,' Zeus is, in the terms of our argument, a 'controller' or 'releaser' of 'water'/'the Waters' of 'possibility.' But this means that he is also a 'controller' of that which the serpent/dragon symbolizes in Tradition since the dragon is 'symbolically synonymous' with 'water'/'the Waters.' He exercises this 'control,' I contend, by means of his 'thunderbolt,' a variation on the 'thunderweapon.'

In *Symbols of Sacred Science*, Guénon argues that

> the thunderbolt is the principal attribute of *Zeus Pater* or *Ju-piter*, the 'father of gods and of men', who strikes down the Titans and the Giants with thunderbolts, just as Thor and Parashu-Rama destroyed their equivalents with weapons of stone.[39]

This theme of ancient gods defeating 'Titans' or 'giants' with variations of the 'thunderweapon' is nearly as pervasive as the theme of their using the 'thunderweapon' to defeat a great serpent or dragon. In *Gods and Myths of Northern Europe*, for example, H. R. Ellis Davidson, who received her Ph.D. for a thesis on beliefs about the dead in Old Norse literature, states that the thirteenth-century Icelandic scholar Snorri Sturluson "tells us that the Aesir proclaimed [Thor's] hammer Mjollnir was the greatest treasure which they possessed, since it enabled them to hold Asgard secure against the giants."[40] Like Guénon, Davidson contends that Mjolnir is a variation of a weapon used by the heroes

---

> that of power, authority, majestic dignity....When the ancients, invoking Jupiter, called him *pater hominum deorumque*, they did not intend to say that Jupiter was the father of the gods and men....The same title of *pater* was given to Neptune, to Apollo, to Bacchus, to Vulcan, and to Pluto." Fustel de Coulanges, *The Ancient City*, 81–82.

39 René Guénon, *Symbols of Sacred Science*, 170.

40 H. R. Ellis Davidson, *Gods and Myths of Northern Europe* (London: Penguin Books, 1990 [first published in 1964 by Pelican Books]), inset information, 24 and 80. Snorri Sturluson was a thirteenth-century Icelandic chieftain, politician, historian, saga writer, scholar, and poet. The Aesir is the name of the principle pantheon of Norse gods; the secondary pantheon is called the Vanir. Asgard is one of the 'nine worlds' in Norse mythology and home of the Aesir.

and gods of not only northern Europe but various other ancient cultures to battle 'monsters' in general:

> The hammer-shaped weapon [of the ancient northern Europeans] is similar to the double axe of antiquity, which also represented the thunderbolt, and which was shown in various forms in temples of the ancient world. Among the early Germanic peoples the god Donar, Thor's predecessor, was considered to resemble Hercules, the mighty male figure armed with a club who battled against monsters, and part of the resemblance was evidently due to the weapon which the god carried. This identification was accepted by the Romans, and there are inscriptions to Hercules from the Roman period, raised by the German soldiers in western Europe. Tacitus [the ancient Roman historian] tells us that the praises of Hercules used to be chanted by the Germans as they went into battle, and that they believed he had visited them.[41]

The Greek semi-divine hero Hercules[42] was not a 'sky god,' but he was, as we have seen in Chapter 8, a dragon slayer. In fact, *all* of the 'sky gods' that we have considered, and shall consider, were serpent/dragon slayers, although not all dragon-slayers were 'sky gods.' The Norse god Thor and the Indian Rama, like Zeus and Jupiter, gods of "tempest and combat" according to Eliade, were 'sky gods.'[43] 'Hurling lightning' at the serpent Vrtra by means of his *vajra*, Indra was a 'sky god' as well. It is significant, therefore, in discerning the meaning of the 'thunderweapon' in Tradition that all of these 'sky gods' did battle with a great serpent or dragon. As noted in part in Chapter 5, Fontenrose similarly states that

> [e]very god has his enemy, whom he must vanquish and destroy. Zeus and Baal, Coyote and Ahura Mazda, Thor and the Lord of Hosts, are alike in this: that each must face a dreadful antagonist. Apollo's enemy was the great dragon Python, whom he had to fight and kill before he could establish his temple and oracle at Delphi....Mankind's myths, legends, and

---

41 H. R. Ellis Davidson, *Gods and Myths of Northern Europe*, 82.
42 As we have already seen, Hercules is also known as Herakles.
43 Mircea Eliade, *Patterns in Comparative Religion*, 80–81.

folktales are filled with tales of gods and heroes who encounter and defeat dragons, monsters, demons, and giants.[44]

Although the ancient gods and heroes of myth and legend fought and defeated apparently different kinds of opponents, the most prominent of their foes was the serpent/dragon. In *The Sacred and the Profane*, Eliade states that, *not* the giant or the 'monster' in Tradition, but

> the dragon is the paradigmatic figure of the marine monster, of the primordial snake, symbol of the cosmic waters, of darkness, night, and death — in short, of the amorphous and virtual, of everything that has not yet acquired a 'form'. The dragon must be conquered and cut to pieces by the gods so that the cosmos may come to birth.[45]

There are, however, several variations on the 'thunderweapon' that can accomplish this 'cutting to pieces.' In *Occidental Mythology*, Joseph Campbell observes, similar to Davidson, that

> [i]n Tacitus's day…Thor was identified with Hercules; but in later Germano-Roman times, the analogy was rather with Jove [Jupiter]. Jove's Day in the Latin world…became Thor's Day (Thursday) among the Germans. Thor's hammer, accordingly, was identified with the fiery bolt of Zeus….The bolt of Jove, moreover, is cognate both in meaning and in origin with the *vajra*, "diamond," "lightningbolt," of the Mahayana Buddhist and Tantric Hindu Iconographies.[46]

The 'fiery' nature of Zeus's (thunder) 'bolt' is, we shall argue, an important clue as to the meaning not only of the force of 'thunder' but of the 'spiraled orb' that represents this force in depictions of the Chinese dragon-with-'orb.' Campbell continues, however:

> For…the lightningbolt is the irresistible power of truth by which illusions, lies, are annihilated; and again, more deeply read, the power of

---

44 Joseph Fontenrose, *Python: A Study of Delphic Myth and Its Origins*, 1.
45 Mircea Eliade, *The Sacred and the Profane*, 48.
46 Joseph Campbell, *The Masks of God: Occidental Mythology*, 480.

eternity through which phenomenality is annihilate. Like a flash of initiatory knowledge, lightning comes of itself and is followed by the roar and tumult of awakening life and rain — the rain of grace. And the idea of the diamond, too, has point in this connection; for as the lightning shatters all things, so does the diamond cut all stones, while the hard, pure brilliance of the diamond typifies the adamantean quality both of truth and of the true spirit.

The two ideas of lightning and diamond, then, which are combined in the Indian vajra, may be readily applied to the hammer of Thor. We have already noted a relationship between this sign and the great Mithraic lion-serpent man, Zervan Akarana. It is the weapon of Shiva and of the Solar Buddha Vairochana, the fiery bolt of Jove, and now, the mighty hammer of Thor. It is also the Cretan double ax of the Bull Sacrifice, and the knife in the hero Mithra's hand with which he slew the World Ox.[47]

The above statements by Guénon, Eliade, Davidson, Fontenrose, Campbell, and Zimmer point to the idea that, for traditional peoples, the 'thunderweapon' symbolized an incomparably powerful reality that is uniquely capable of revealing 'form' or truth, or establishing a new 'order' by means of 'annihilating' the 'illusion' that is traditionally symbolized by the serpent/dragon. This 'annihilation,' such peoples believed, took place by means of 'producing'/'creating'/'manifesting' a 'higher' order of some kind in the physical world that could express itself just as clearly in the creation of a temple as in the creation of the cosmos as a whole. The illusions of darkness, death, and the 'chaos' of *samsara* that are represented by the serpent/dragon in Tradition could only be overcome, according to traditional belief and the content of much traditional myth and art, by means of the 'sky god's' employing his 'fiery' 'thunderweapon' to vanquish the serpent/dragon. For it was

---

47 Joseph Campbell, *The Masks of God: Occidental Mythology*, 480–81. In *The Art of Indian Asia*, Heinrich Zimmer similarly calls the *vajra* "the weapon of or substance of adamantean truth and reality, compared with which all other substances are fragile." Heinrich Zimmer, *The Art of Indian Asia*, Vol. I (India: Motilal Banarsidass, 1983), 194.

only the 'two-sided' 'thunderweapon,' or rather that which it represents, the metaphysical Principle (Spirit), which like a bolt of lightning from the heavens could brilliantly illuminate the illusory terrestrial world of *matter* or "the indefinite series of cycles of manifestation"/ *samsara*. This event of 'illumination' was both 'creation' *and* 'destruction,' 'evolution' *and* 'involution.' For illusion must be destroyed or 'annihilated' before truth can be revealed or 'created.' This 'two-sided' event, therefore, is what all versions of the two-sided 'thunderweapon' effect. More explicitly, in the terms of my argument, all versions of the 'thunderweapon' 'actualize' the 'watery' realm of 'possibility'/ potentiality, the state of *matter* that is traditionally symbolized by the serpent/dragon, by both destroying illusion and 'creating' (revealing, more specifically) truth/reality. This 'two-sided' event of 'revelation,' however, only occurs completely in the event of the 'migrating' being's complete 'identification' with *Brahman* (the 'Principle').

The Norse god Thor's hammer Mjolnir is one example of the 'thunderweapon's' symbolizing the two-fold 'actualization' process of 'production'/'creation'/'manifestation'/'evolution' *and* 'destruction'/ 'return'/'involution' that we have discussed, and which is represented by the 'two-sidedness' or 'double-sidedness' of many versions of the 'thunderweapon.' According to Joseph Campbell, Thor is called in Scandinavia 'The Defender of the World.'[48] 'The World,' however, as we have argued most specifically in our examination of the symbolism of the *anima mundi*, is traditionally constituted by means of the human *perception* of the 'Principle's' manifestation in *samsara*/"the indefinite series of cycles of manifestation." The human perception of the manifestation of the Principle in *samsara*/"the indefinite series of cycles of manifestation" we have *also* labeled 'nature.' 'The World,' or 'nature,' however, is traditionally constituted, as we have also argued, by 'opposites': birth and death, good and evil, light and darkness, etc. As 'Defender of the World,' therefore, Thor is, according to Norse

---

48 Joseph Campbell, *The Masks of God: Occidental Mythology*, 479.

myth as a version of Guénon's Primordial Tradition, he who, along with his 'thunderweapon' Mjolnir, 'defends' the proper balance of the 'opposites.' In *Gods and Myths of Northern Europe*, for example, in discussing the northern European symbolism of the hammer, of which Mjolnir is probably a late version, Davidson states,

> We know that the hammer was raised to hallow the new-born child who was to be accepted into the community, and it seems also to have been used at funerals, since at [the god and son of Odin] Balder's death it was fetched to hallow the funeral ship before this was set alight. When Thor feasted on his goats, he made the sign of the hammer over the bones and skin in order to restore them to life. In this new life given by the god, we can see a possible significance in the use of the hammer at sacrifices and funerals.[49]

The hammer in northern Europe, in other words, was, traditionally, symbolically associated with the 'opposites' of both life *and* death. Davidson also relates that "Thor was the sender of lightning and the god who dealt out both sunshine and rain to men."[50] Again, we see a reference to Thor's power over the 'opposites' of 'nature' ('the World'). Thor's greatest challenge, however, "his most terrible adversary," as Davidson puts it, "is the World Serpent, who lies coiled round the earth."[51] There are multiple versions of the tale of conflict between Thor and the so-called 'Midgard Serpent.' As Davidson notes, however, some versions of the tale have Thor defeating the Serpent while others leave the result of the contest undecided.[52] One popular version has a giant named Hymir rowing Thor deep out into the sea in order to fish for the Serpent, the latter of which he soon catches on his fishing line. In this version of the encounter, Davidson states that, after pulling the Serpent up on his line, Thor and the 'monster' stare

---

49 H. R. Ellis Davidson, *Gods and Myths of Northern Europe*, 80 and 35.
50 H. R. Ellis Davidson, *Gods and Myths of Northern Europe*, 83.
51 H. R. Ellis Davidson, *Gods and Myths of Northern Europe*, 89.
52 H. R. Ellis Davidson, *Gods and Myths of Northern Europe*, 90.

fiercely into one another's eyes. At this terrible sight, Hymir was panic-stricken, and as Thor raised his hammer, he [the giant] cut the line. The serpent sank back into the depths of the sea, and Thor in anger knocked the giant overboard and waded back to shore. Whether he struck off the serpent's head before it sank, or it still lies coiled round the earth, Gangleri [one of the characters the poet Snorri Sturluson uses to tell the story] was unable to discover.[53] (See fig. 16.5.)

Fig. 16.5. *Thor Battering the Serpent of Midgard*, Henry Fuseli, 1790, Royal Academy of Arts, London[54]

---

53 H. R. Ellis Davidson, *Gods and Myths of Northern Europe*, 35.
54 Marilyn Nissenson and Susan Jonas, *Snake Charm*, 36–37.

Davidson relates that "the mother of Thor was said to be Earth herself, and in the earliest skaldic verse he is described in phrases meaning 'son of Earth.'"[55] This association of Thor with the Earth combined with his status as a 'sky god' who commands the power of the 'thunderweapon' would, in addition to his traits already mentioned, seem to further confirm Thor's status as a being possessing power over the 'opposites of nature,' a being that is capable of *both* forms of 'actualization' that we have discussed, 'destruction'/'involution' and 'creation'/'evolution.' In consonance with this view, Davidson states that "in his association with the natural world, Thor was...both destroyer and protector."[56] As a 'controller' of 'water' (in the form of rain) and a foe of the 'World/Midgard Serpent,' but at the same time a dealer of 'sunshine,' I argue that Thor is traditionally identified as one who both 'controls opposites' and 'actualizes' 'possibilities.' As such, Thor was a bestower of 'life' in the 'higher,' metaphysical, sense that we have discussed. In *Symbols of Sacred Science*, Guénon observes that "it is known that the traditional doctrines establish a direct relationship between 'Light' and 'Life.'"[57] In *Perspectives on Initiation*, Guénon states that "the first word spoken at the starting-point of manifestation is the *Fiat Lux* [allowance/'creation' of light] by which the chaos of possibilities is illuminated and organized."[58] Thor wields the 'thunderweapon' Mjolnir that, like the bolt of lightning, provides illumination where it is otherwise dark. He also 'controls' 'sunshine' and 'rain,' both essential material elements to most biological life. As Davidson notes, however, "none of the [Nordic] poems make it clear whether the battle between the god [Thor] and [the Midgard Serpent] monster was a conclusive one," or at least, according to Snorri Sturluson's prose account, "Thor does not slay the serpent until the great final battle, when he himself

---

55 H. R. Ellis Davidson, *Gods and Myths of Northern Europe*, 84.
56 H. R. Ellis Davidson, *Gods and Myths of Northern Europe*, 84.
57 René Guénon, *Symbols of Sacred Science*, 318.
58 René Guénon, *Perspectives on Initiation*, 292.

perishes along with his adversary."[59] Whether he is victorious or not, however, the tale of Thor's battle with the 'World Serpent' illustrates that conflict that all 'migrating' beings are, according to Tradition, believed to experience, the conflict between themselves and the force of *samsara* that, according to the Hindu version of Tradition, takes place throughout all the *yugas*, or ages, of 'the World.' It is the 'battle' that plays out during the lives of all those beings 'trapped' within the earthly 'coils' of the serpentine "indefinite series of cycles of manifestation," a battle that never ends for each 'migrating' being until he, as Davidson puts it, "perishes along with his adversary" and, as I argue, achieves *moksha*, 'identity' with the metaphysical 'Principle.' In those cases, however, in which the serpent/dragon is depicted or described in the myths as being clearly defeated by the hero or god, I contend that immortality, or, more precisely, *moksha* is depicted or described as being achieved. In such cases, the metaphysical/divine Principle is 'infused,' or, in Eliade's terminology, 'hierophanizes' into the state of *matter* in a more complete sense than it usually does in the cases of continual manifestation of the Principle in *matter* that constitute 'nature'/'the World.' Symbolically in Tradition, this 'infusion' or 'hierophanization' is the *strike* of the lightning-, or thunder-, bolt, the truly *willful* wielding of the 'thunderweapon' by the heroes and gods of old.

The 'Spiraled Orb' and the *Swastika*

The 'thunderweapon,' like the rod, staff, tree, cross, and 'orb' (circle/sphere) in Tradition, symbolizes the metaphysical or divine 'Principle' by which the formless, indefinite, and potential ("confused and obscure") aspect of reality is formed, defined, and 'actualized.'[60] The 'thunderweapon,' therefore, like the other traditional symbols listed,

---

59 H. R. Ellis Davidson, *Gods and Myths of Northern Europe*, 90.
60 In employing the expression "confused and obscure," I again refer to the Hindu state of *tamas* discussed in previous chapters.

symbolizes that aspect of reality that 'creates'/'manifests'/'produces'/ 'evolves' *and* 'destroys'/'returns'/'involutes.' That which is the 'object' of these 'dual' processes/events of 'creation' and 'destruction' is the state of being that I term *matter*. The 'thunderweapon,' therefore, in the terms of this book, symbolizes the power of 'Spiritualization' that reveals the essentially Spiritual (metaphysical) 'Principle' *by means of* the 'natural' state of being that I call *matter*. The gods of myth and legend, such as Thor, Zeus, and Indra, like the traditional Chinese Emperor/*Wang*, are, however, not 'Spiritualizers' *per se* but rather the *qualified conduits* ('currents') for the 'coursing' of the power of Spiritualization into that realm of being that is variously called Earth, 'nature,' or 'the World.' The 'single spiral,' as I have termed it, that is depicted in illustrations of the 'Far-Eastern' dragon-with-'orb,' as a 'symbolic abbreviation' of the 'double spiral' that Guénon argues symbolizes the 'dual force' of 'evolution' and 'involution' ('creation' and 'destruction'), represents the force of 'thunder.'

I propose that what I call the 'single spiral' is similar in appearance, and synonymous in meaning, to another traditional symbol examined by Guénon: the *swastika*. Although usually associated by moderns with its mid-twentieth-century usage in Germany, the *swastika* is, as Guénon observes in *Symbols of Sacred Science*, "one of the most widespread of all symbols, seen nearly everywhere, from the Far East to the Far West, for it exists even among certain indigenous peoples of North America."[61] In *The Symbolism of the Cross*, Guénon states that the *swastika* is "one of the most striking forms of the 'horizontal' cross…found in the most diverse and widely separated countries, and from the most remote periods….In antiquity this sign occurs among the Celts and in pre-Hellenic Greece."[62] Davidson similarly observes in *Gods and Myths of Northern Europe* that

---

61 René Guénon, *Symbols of Sacred Science*, 65.
62 René Guénon, *The Symbolism of the Cross*, 62–63.

[t]he swastika, or hooked cross, is a sign found in many regions of the world and known from remote antiquity. It was [more specifically] very popular among the heathen Germans, and appears to have been associated with the symbol of fire [;]....it may have arisen from the use of the hammer or axe to represent thunder, which was accompanied by fire from heaven.[63] (See fig. 16.6.)

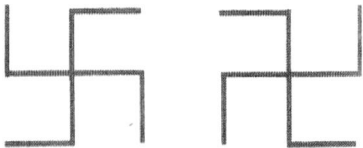

Fig. 16.6. *The Two Directions of the Rotation of the Swastika*[64]

Although Thor was the Norse 'thunder god,' Davidson notes that the Germanic Anglo-Saxons "worshipped the thunder god under the name of Thunor." Both versions of the 'thunder god' were traditionally connected with the symbolisms of the hammer *and* the *swastika*. Davidson relates, for example, that "both the swastika and the hammer symbol are found on stones bearing early runic inscriptions in Norway and Sweden, and some of these call on Thor to protect the memorial and place of burial."[65] These observations and connections show that an understanding of the traditional symbolism of the *swastika* is extremely relevant to an understanding of the traditional symbolism of the 'thunderweapon.' I suggest that, because the *swastika* was symbolically connected in Tradition with the 'thunderweapon,' understanding the symbolism of the *swastika* is also extremely relevant to understanding the traditional meaning of the Chinese 'spiraled orb' because the 'spiraled orb's' meaning is, as I have argued,

---

63 H. R. Ellis Davidson, *Gods and Myths of Northern Europe*, 83.
64 René Guénon, *The Great Triad*, 32.
65 H. R. Ellis Davidson, *Gods and Myths of Northern Europe*, 83.

equivalent to the meaning of the 'thunderweapon.' Both symbols represent the force of 'thunder' that symbolizes in Tradition the power of the metaphysical 'Principle.' Davidson points out, however, that some versions of the 'thunderweapon,' such as the axe and the hammer, since they were traditionally symbolic of the power of 'thunder,' were also symbolic of that which accompanies 'thunder': "fire from heaven." But the *swastika*, she says, also "appears to have been associated with the symbol of fire." For Guénon, *all* of the various versions of the 'thunderweapon,' as well as the *swastika*, were considered in Tradition 'symbolically synonymous' insofar as they were all 'polar' symbols like the 'World Tree.' The cross also, as we have stated repeatedly, is an axial or 'polar' symbol, and both Davidson and Guénon observe that the *swastika* is a form of the cross — the 'hooked cross,' as Davidson calls it. Guénon states that "in the West, it was anciently one of the emblems of Christ, and it even remained in use as such down to nearly the end of the Middle Ages."[66] He further observes, similar to Davidson, that the *swastika* and other 'polar' symbols are also similar in the sense that that which they symbolized was traditionally thought to have a 'fiery' nature. In *Symbols of Sacred Science*, for example, Guénon states that the 'World Tree' has an "igneous nature" and "lightning is of an igneous or luminous nature."[67] We have already seen that in Luke 3:16 Jesus, who is always associated with the axial symbolism of the cross, "will baptize you with the Holy Spirit and fire." [ESV] More generally, Guénon argues that "the 'World Axis' is always regarded more or less explicitly as luminous....Plato, for example, describes it as a 'luminous axis of diamond', which, precisely, links it directly...to one of the aspects of the *vajra*, since the latter means both 'thunderbolt' and 'diamond.'"[68] Around the 'World Axis,' however, swirl the 'dual currents' of the 'cosmic force' that go ever to

---

66 René Guénon, *The Symbolism of the Cross*, 63.
67 René Guénon, *Symbols of Sacred Science*, 318.
68 René Guénon, *Symbols of Sacred Science*, 318.

and from the 'Principial' Source of "the indefinite series of cycles of manifestation." In *The Great Triad*, Guénon connects the symbolism of the *swastika* with that of the 'double spiral' that represents these 'dual currents.' Repeating in part some things that we already know, he states that

> the two spirals [of the 'double spiral'] can be considered as the indication of a cosmic force acting in opposite directions in each of the two hemispheres…the points around which the two spirals coil being the two poles. It can be seen at once that this is closely related to the two directions of the rotation of the *swastika* since this essentially represents the same revolution of the world around its axis but viewed respectively now from one of the poles, now from the other.[69] (See figs. 16.7 and 16.8.)

Figs. 16.7 and **16.8.** *The Double Spiral* and *The Two Directions of the Rotation of the Swastika*[70]

There is, thus, a connection here implied by Guénon between 'polar' symbols such as the *swastika* and versions of the 'thunderweapon' that symbolize the metaphysical Principle and 'fire.' More explicitly, there is the implication that the metaphysical 'Principle' is, itself, 'fiery' in its nature. This 'fiery' quality, however, has not so much to do with

---

69 René Guénon, *The Great Triad*, 31–32.
70 René Guénon, *The Great Triad*, 31–32.

heat as with light, since Guénon argues that "the flash of lightning is one of the most common symbols of 'illumination,' understood in the intellectual or spiritual sense."[71] This 'illumination,' in the terms of the 'Hindu Doctrines,' is the event of the 'migrating' being's (*Atman*'s) 'realization' of its 'identity' with *Brahman* (the 'Principle'). Based upon Guénon's contention that the symbolism of the *swastika* is 'closely related' to that of the 'double spiral' that is itself symbolic of the 'dual force' of 'involution' and 'evolution,' I argue that the *swastika* is, like the '*single* spiral' depicted on the Chinese 'orb,' a 'stylistic abbreviation' of this 'dual force.' It is, therefore, like the 'Far-Eastern' 'spiraled orb,' equivalent in meaning to the 'thunderweapon' that was used by ancient gods, heroes, and rulers to do 'combat' with that which the serpent/dragon symbolized. If successful, the god's/hero's/ruler's 'victory' yielded his 'illumination' and the 'identification' of the *Atman* in his person, or in his entire kingdom or empire, with the eternal *Brahman/Tao*, etc. This 'illuminatory identification' was traditionally represented by the 'fiery' nature of: 1) in the case of ancient heroes and gods, the 'thunderweapon,' and 2) in the case of the Chinese Emperor/ *Wang*, the 'spiraled orb.'

The symbolic equivalency that traditionally exists among the 'spiraled orb,' the 'thunderweapon,' and the *swastika* explains the reason for the oft-observed red coloring of the Chinese 'spiraled orb'-with-dragon that de Visser supposes in *The Dragon in China and Japan* to be a reference to the "brilliant, fiery" lustre of a pearl.[72] De Visser even states that "[d]evastation caused by lightning was believed to be the result of sacred fire, sent by Heaven to stop dragon fights."[73] In this statement, it is admitted by de Visser, albeit indirectly, that the force of Heaven, which I argue is symbolized by the force of 'thunder' represented by the 'spiraled orb,' is that which can 'control' what the dragon

---

71 René Guénon, *Symbols of Sacred Science*, 318.
72 Marinus Willem de Visser, *The Dragon in China and Japan*, 108.
73 Marinus Willem de Visser, *The Dragon in China and Japan*, 48.

symbolizes. To Davidson's observations that "the swastika...appears to have been associated with the symbol of fire" and that the Germans believed that thunder "was accompanied by fire from heaven," may be added Joseph Campbell's contention in *Occidental Mythology* that "Thor's hammer...was identified with the fiery bolt of Zeus."[74] In all of these quotations, the referred-to authors agree that there is a link between a divine or 'heavenly' fire and either: 1) the 'thunderweapon' or 2) the *swastika*. I argue for both propositions and, based upon them, contend that de Visser's supposition that the Chinese 'orb' represented the 'fiery' lustre of a pearl is only 'half right.' De Visser's supposition is only half right because, although I do not believe that the Chinese 'orb' represents the 'fiery' appearance of a *pearl*, it does, in its red coloring, represent *fire* of a certain special kind. In *Symbols of Sacred Science*, Guénon, as we have seen, states that the *swastika* "does have a certain relationship with fire," although it is not, he says, as some have supposed, a 'solar sign,' or, if it is, this is "only accidentally and in an indirect way."[75] The 'fiery' red 'spiraled orb' of the traditional 'Chinese Dragon' is, thus, as a 'stylistic abbreviation' of the 'double spiral,' equivalent in meaning to the traditional symbolism of the *swastika*. The differences between the 'single spiral' and the *swastika* are, again, merely stylistic; the *swastika* is but a more articulated, precise, or 'squared,' figuration of the 'single spiral' that is represented on the 'orb' depicted with the 'Chinese Dragon.' Because of this 'symbolic equivalency' between the 'single spiral' and the *swastika*, I argue that the *swastika*, like the 'orb,' symbolizes what Guénon calls the "vivifying role of the Principle in relation to the cosmic order."[76] For the *swastika*

---

74 H. R. Ellis Davidson, *Gods and Myths of Northern Europe*, 83, and Joseph Campbell, *Occidental Mythology*, 480.

75 René Guénon, *Symbols of Sacred Science*, 64.

76 René Guénon, *Symbols of Sacred Science*, 64.

is, according to Guénon, "not a figure of the World but really of the action of the Principle with respect to the World."[77]

In wielding the 'thunderweapon,' or the '(spiraled) orb,' therefore, the gods, heroes, and rulers of the ancient world wielded the force of 'thunder,' that metaphysical, 'heavenly,' force that is also traditionally represented by means of the *swastika*. In *Revolt Against the Modern World*, traditionalist Julius Evola describes the 'fulgurating power' of the ancient ruler, the "great calm that conveys the feeling of an irresistible superiority....The greatness [that] immediately evokes the feeling of a transcendent force that is already mastered and ready to spring forward; or the marvelous and yet frightful sense of the *numen*."[78] This 'fulgurating power,' I argue, is the power that courses through Thor, Zeus, Apollo, Indra, Hercules, and other traditional heroes and 'sky gods,' as well as the Chinese Emperor/*Wang* and, according to Evola, other imperial and sovereign rulers. Such individuals, however, did not actually 'wield' the power or force of 'thunder' that is symbolized by the 'thunderweapon,' the 'spiraled orb,' and the *swastika*. Rather, they were *wielded by* the 'fulgurating power' of the force of 'thunder.' The ancient gods' double-edged (like Indra's *vajra*) or double-pointed (like Apollo's arrows) or double-surfaced (like Thor's Mjolnir) 'weapons' were, therefore, expressions of the, as Guénon describes it, "double force, itself single in essence, but with apparently opposite effects in its manifestation, resulting from the 'polarization' that conditions

---

77 René Guénon, *Symbols of Sacred Science*, 64. "As for the word *swastika* itself," Guénon states, "it is derived from the *su asti*, a form of benediction, which has its exact equivalent in the Hebrew *ki-tob* of Genesis. Regarding the latter, the fact that it is found repeated at the end of the account of each of the 'days' of the Creation...seems to indicate that these 'days' are assimilable to so many rotations of the *swastika*, or, in other words, complete revolutions of the 'world wheel.'" René Guénon, *The Symbolism of the Cross*, 64.

78 Julius Evola, *Revolt Against the Modern World*, trans. Guido Stucco (Rochester, Vermont: Inner Traditions International, 1995 [originally published by Edizioni Mediterranee-Roma in 1969]), 19.

the latter."[79] As the primary receptacles in the human realm of the metaphysical force that lies behind 'nature,' the gods, heroes, and rulers of the ancient world were the primary transmitters of Tradition in that world. But this force that produces *and* destroys, births *and* kills, hallows the new-born child *and* commemorates the newly dead, all for the purpose of maintaining order in the midst of 'chaos,' only courses through the gods, heroes, and rulers of traditional societies in the manner described by Evola because these individuals prove, for reasons inscrutable to mortals, the best vehicles for disseminating the truth of the 'Principle' in 'nature'/'the World.' This 'truth' of the metaphysical Principle is always and exclusively, from the traditional perspective, that which gives the *only* objective form that there is in the midst of the formless, the only objective definition in the midst of indefinitude, and the only real actuality in the midst of the overwhelming human awareness of infinite 'possibilities'/potentiality — 'the Waters' of 'chaos' where the serpent/dragon abides.

In Norse myth, Thor attempts multiple times to 'lift up' the Midgard Serpent. Davidson states that, on his fishing expedition with the giant Hymir, "Thor had to exert all his divine strength" to 'haul up' the monster.[80] On another adventure, Thor struggles "to lift the serpent in the form of a great grey cat."[81] Both of these 'tests' are indicative of the 'migrating' being's struggle to 'actualize' the potential of what it *currently* is, to form and define it, into that which it *really* is: the *Atman/Brahman* of Hindu tradition. In the case of his fishing expedition, Thor is 'hauling' the serpent 'up' from the depths of the sea — 'the Waters' of 'possibility.' But in both stories, and in all such stories as these, Thor's actions epitomize the actions of the eternal questing warrior that is depicted and described in the art and myth of many ancient cultures. They are the actions of Joseph Campbell's 'hero

---

79 René Guénon, *Symbols of Sacred Science*, 174.
80 H. R. Ellis Davidson, *Gods and Myths of Northern Europe*, 35.
81 H. R. Ellis Davidson, *Gods and Myths of Northern Europe*, 139.

with a thousand faces,' the archetypal actions that, I contend, symbolize, from the traditional perspective, the *whole life* of *every* 'migrating' being who struggles to achieve 'identity' with the metaphysical 'Principle,' or, in *Advaita Vedanta*, achieve the 'identity' of *Atman* and *Brahman*. Campbell states in *Occidental Mythology*,

> Against the symbol of...the force of the never-dying serpent, sloughing lives like skins, which, pressing on, ever turning in its circle of eternal return, is to continue in this manner forever, as it has already cycled from all eternity, getting absolutely nowhere...the warrior principle of the great deed of the individual who matters flung its bolt.[82]

It is this 'bolt' referred to by Campbell, the 'thunderbolt' or 'thunderweapon,' or 'spiraled orb' or *swastika*, I argue, or that which it more properly represents, the force of 'thunder,' or *Brahman/Tao*, or the *essence* of 'Heaven,' or Guénon's 'Principle,' that makes both the "individual who matters" *actually* matter and his "great deed" *in-deed* great. But this greatness stems, ultimately, from that which the hero/god/ruler strives *for*. In the case of Thor, according to Davidson, it is "for mankind, and for the precarious civilization which men had wrested from a hard and chaotic world." Any civilization, however, that is worth 'migrating' through the cycles of *samsara* to construct is, necessarily, predicated on man's 'realizing' his 'actualized' 'identity' with his metaphysical Source.

---

82 Joseph Campbell, *The Masks of God: Occidental Mythology*, 24.

Conclusion

Those who love wisdom must investigate many things.

— Heraclitus, from Clement, *Miscellanies*

As man ascends the ladder uniting effect with cause, he approaches ever closer to conscious realization of Source.

— Manly P. Hall, *Lectures on Ancient Philosophy*

Thus the highest truths, not communicable or transmissible in any other way, can be communicated up to a certain point when they are, so to speak, incorporated in symbols which will no doubt conceal them for many, but which will manifest them in all their brilliance to those with eyes to see.

— René Guénon, *Symbols of Sacred Science*

The Serpent Symbol's Identification with 'Life'

I have argued that the serpent/dragon symbolizes what I term *matter* in traditional art and myth, a *state of being* that consists of a particular kind, or level, of awareness of what Mircea Eliade terms 'chaos' and what René Guénon terms "the indefinite series of cycles of manifestation," the Hindu *samsara*. 'Chaos' and 'indefinitude,' as employed respectively by these two authors, are descriptions of a particular perspective on, or *perception* of, existence that accompanies that state of the 'migrating' being in which it is (*feels*) 'trapped' in *samsara*. In terms of the 'Hindu Doctrines,' *Vedanta* specifically, this perspective or 'state' is one in which Reality is seen to be, or feared to be, an "indefinite series of cycles of manifestation," whether these cycles be celestial or terrestrial. It is, thus, that what I argue to be the 'old' idea of 'life' consisting in complete identification with cyclical existence, which has no inkling of the meta-physical, is, from the 'new' state of *matter* that is 'realized' by the New Man, something to be 'overcome' and, in some cases, later 'managed' or 'controlled.'

As we may interpret from art, literature, religion, and philosophy, humans have, from very remote times, identified 'life' with cycles. In our discussion of the Avebury Cycle of megaliths in England, for instance, it was argued that fertility, and thus 'life,' played a prominent role in both the design and use of that structure. But Avebury had celestial associations as well, with its purported representations of, and possible 'tracking' of, both the moon and the Sun. Many researchers now believe that all, or nearly all, stone and wooden henges in Europe were astronomical devices employed by ancient peoples to track or predict the movements, the *cycles*, of celestial bodies. This assessment seems also to apply to at least some ancient 'mounds' as well, with James Charlesworth stating, for example, that "some experts believe that the [Ohio] Serpent Mound is aligned with the summer solstice sunset and perhaps with the winter solstice sunrise."[1] There are many other cases of a historical connection between the serpent, or serpent symbolism, and the idea of 'life.' In *The Cult of the Serpent*, Balaji Mundkur states that "the Arabic word *hayat*, 'life,' is cognate with, and hence glorifies, none other than, *hayya*, 'serpent.'"[2] In *The Good and Evil Serpent*, Charlesworth adds that

> [i]n Arabic, *hayya* means 'snake', *hayy* denotes 'living,' and *hayah* indicates 'life.' In Persian, *hayat* denotes 'life' and *haiyat* indicates 'serpents (the

---

1 James H. Charlesworth, *The Good and Evil Serpent*, 238.
2 Balaji Mundkur, *The Cult of the Serpent*, 70.

plural of *haiyat*).' In Syriac, *h wa* is the verb 'to be,' but *hayye* signifies 'life,' and *hewya* denotes 'snake.'[3]

Although all of these are 'Middle Eastern' etymological examples, we have already seen that serpent *symbolism* was widely employed in other cultures to express the ideas of fertility, birth, and 'creation' as 'rejuvenation' and 'rebirth,' all ideas that imply the more general concept of biological 'life.' In *The Language of the Goddess*, for example, Marija Gimbutas states that "the snake is life force, a seminal symbol, epitome of the worship of life on this earth."[4] Such examples are of what I have called the 'old,' cyclical, idea of 'life.' In the process of human development, however, specifically in the origination of the state of awareness that I call *matter* which emerged only in *some* humans, I propose that these New Men wondered at the completeness of the 'old' cyclical notion specified. They asked, as the Beatle George Harrison once famously did, "What *is* life?"[5]

Prehistoric artifacts that represent the so-called 'Goddess,' which was apparently always associated in prehistoric societies with fertility, are very often anguine (pertaining to serpents or snakes) in form. In *The Language of the Goddess*, Marija Gimbutas includes numerous illustrations of the so-called 'Snake Goddess.' Examples of this motif in her book include: 8,000-year-old artifacts from Neolithic Crete and the Aegean islands, a 6,600-year-old artifact from Romania, and a 6,500-year-old artifact from Yugoslavia (see figs. C.1-C.4). Gimbutas describes these, and similar, figures with phrases such as: "ophidian/human hybrid Snake Goddess," "limbs are snakelike," "snakelike legs," "arms wind around the shoulders like snakes," "they have the characteristic long snake mouth," "hands depict profiled snake heads," etc.[6]

---

3   James H. Charlesworth, *The Good and Evil Serpent*, 250.
4   Marija Gimbutas, *The Language of the Goddess*, 121.
5   George Harrison, vocalist, "What Is Life," by George Harrison on *All Things Must Pass* (EMI, 1970, vinyl).
6   Marija Gimbutas, *The Language of the Goddess*, 126.

Why, however, was the snake associated with the 'Goddess,' a figure of 'feminine powers' in prehistoric, as well as historic, art? Although we possess no written documentation to corroborate modern interpretations of prehistoric art, it is reasonable to suggest that, for any observer, historic or prehistoric, the most salient features of either the, specifically, *biological* life of a snake *or* of a woman prominently include rejuvenation, rebirth, and cyclicity. A woman gives birth, not a man; a woman menstruates, not a man; a woman lactates, not a man. A snake sheds its skin *periodically*, and, because of this, *rejuvenates* itself. All of these 'mysteries' (to prehistoric humans) have specifically *cyclical* components in terms of: 1) their duration, as with the nine-month gestation period in humans that leads to (re-) birth, and 2) their periodic recurrence, as with a woman's menstruation 'cycle.' Although it may seem a rather unorthodox claim, I submit that prehistoric humans, at least in some cases, 'identified' human mothers, specifically those who have just given birth, with a snake's *skin* and identified the snake *itself* (which has just shed its skin) with the newborn human child. Like the snake that has just shed its skin, the newborn child was seen to 'shed' its mother.

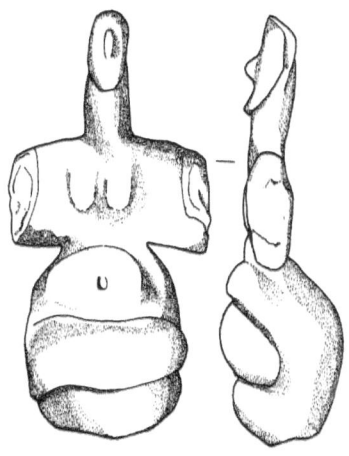

Fig. C.1   Fig. C.2

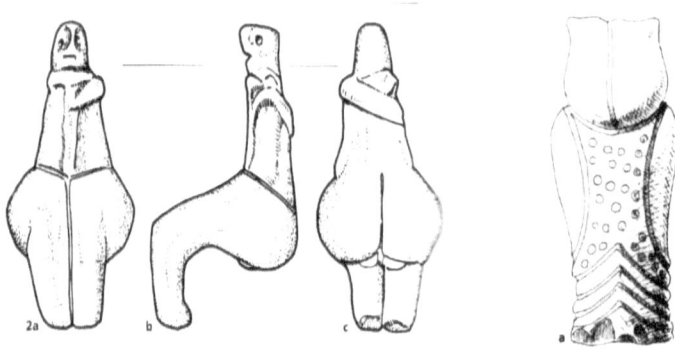

Fig. C.3 **Fig. C.4**

Figures C.1–C.4. *Untitled* Snake Goddess figurines. Fig. C.1: marble sculpture, c. 6000–5500 BCE, Amorgos or another Aegean island; Fig. C.2: clay figurine, 6000–5500 BCE, Kato Ierapetra, S. Crete; Fig. C.3: terra-cotta, 4800–4600 BCE, Cucuteni (Traian Dealul Fintinilor, NE Romania); Fig. C.4: c. 4500 BCE, Vinca (Beletinci, N. Yugoslavia)[7]

As Buffie Johnson points out in *Lady of the Beasts*, "Megalithic and Neolithic imagery introduces many goddesses to the world in snake form. The goddesses tend to be striped….and are often shown with infants in their arms."[8] Johnson draws attention, for example, to a "Neolithic painted terra-cotta figurine of seated mother with child" of which she states that "[s]tripes on the enthroned Madonna suggest a Snake Goddess."[9] She also refers to a fourth-millennium-BCE "[s]erpent-headed Madonna from Ur, suckling her infant."[10] (See figs. C.5 and C.6.) Representations such as these, I believe, are not merely means of identifying the mother's fertility with the snake's nature, but means of representing the newborn human child as the *object* of rebirth/rejuvenation, that which has 'shed' the 'old' life of the mother.

---

7   Marija Gimbutas, *The Language of the Goddess*, 126 and 128.
8   Buffie Johnson, *Lady of the Beasts*, 125.
9   Buffie Johnson, *Lady of the Beasts*, 374 and 125.
10 Buffie Johnson, *Lady of the Beasts*, 137.

Because, however, both mother *and* child are represented with anguine features in prehistoric art, I argue that this art represents the ubiquitousness of cyclical existence, the eventual and necessary 'shedding' that will happen to the newborn in due time just as it happened to its mother when it was born. Such prehistoric art represents and reveals prehistoric peoples' belief that the cyclical 'serpent power' of rejuvenation or rebirth was conveyed from mother to child. As Johnson points out, however, "the serpent deity is not intrinsically a Mother Goddess. Motherhood is not an indwelling characteristic, only one of her many functions."[11] Fertility and rejuvenation, thus, should not be identified exclusively with 'motherhood.' Neither, however, should they be identified exclusively with femininity but, rather, with *cyclicity*, although this manifests perhaps most visibly in the *feminine* powers of re-production. It is, more basically, I argue, the element of *life itself*, perhaps manifest most clearly in the feminine powers of reproduction, that the serpent symbolized for early humans, *not* the female form or specifically feminine capacities.

Fig. C.5

Fig. C.6

---

11 Buffie Johnson, *Lady of the Beasts*, 124.

Fig. C.5. *Neolithic painted terra-cotta figurine of seated mother with child*, early fifth millennium BCE, Sesklo, Greece, courtesy of the National Archaeological Museum, Athens[12]

Fig. C.6. *Serpent-headed goddess with child*, fourth millennium BCE, Iraq, courtesy of Ministry of Culture and Information, State Organization of Antiquities and Heritage, Baghdad, Republic of Iraq[13]

The 'Overcoming' of Cyclicity: The Redefining of 'Life'

The idea of 'life' for early humans was the idea of renewal and rejuvenation, to the extent that early humans *identified* their 'individual' selves with the 'cyclicity' that renewal and rejuvenation exemplify. Johnson notes that

> [t]he spiral, one of the most conspicuous motifs in prehistoric art, often covers the breast or sex of a divinity. As noted, it is as old as the [Upper Paleolithic] Siberian Aurignacian era [43,000–28,000 BP] and appears throughout the world on tomb and threshold stones. Doubled, it means rebirth and renewal.[14]

Serpent and spiral overlap as traditional symbols of 'duality in unity,' as we have seen in Guénon's analysis of those symbols in *The Great Triad*. In historic times, however, for Guénon, both symbols come to represent the 'currents' or 'forces' that Guénon argues are believed in traditional societies to be conveyed between the profane (or terrestrial) and the divine (or celestial) realms by means of the 'action' of the metaphysical Principle. The double spiral is a symbol of both 'manifestation'/'evolution' and 'return'/'involution.' For prehistoric humans, however, 'manifestation' is accomplished by means of physical

---

12 Buffie Johnson, *Lady of the Beasts*, 125.
13 Buffie Johnson, *Lady of the Beasts*, 137.
14 Buffie Johnson, *Lady of the Beasts*, 130.

birth and vegetal renewal. Life itself, for such humans, is 'manifestation,' whether it be the birth of another human or animal, the budding of plants and trees in the spring of the year, or the predictable lunar, solar, and astral cycles. Early humans 'identified with' that element of 'manifestation' for a very long time. It is, perhaps, impossible now to know for how long. And then, at some point, perhaps not long after the beginning of what we term 'historical' times, they didn't. Art and myth reflect this change of consciousness. Instead of representing humans, mothers and children specifically, *as* serpents, it begins to depict and describe humans 'combating' serpents, whether rhetorically (as in Genesis 3) or physically (as in the narratives of the gods Apollo, Zeus, Indra, Thor, Krishna, and others). There is also a corresponding change in the human attitude toward 'life' that moves humans (at least some of them) from simply 'identifying' with life's processes to *questioning* those processes, 'debating' them, struggling against them, 'fighting' them. The "indefinite series of cycles of manifestation" begins to seem 'chaotic' to humans, something that needs to be formed, defined, and 'actualized': Spiritualized. More than simply indicating a movement from a religion of the 'Mother Goddess' of fertility to a worship of the 'heroic' in *man*, as Campbell and others have contended, the imagery of the 'combat myth' between gods/heroes/rulers and serpents/dragons indicates an essential change in human awareness of the 'human situation.' It is not enough, humans began to think, to simply go on serving as yet another 'natural' instrument that perpetuates 'nature' by means of the tools of cyclical rejuvenation (the sexual organs) that are 'built into' humans and that require no *willful* 'creation' on the part of humans. With the dawn of the narratives of 'combat' with the serpent/dragon, therefore, humans became aware that they are *more* than 'nature,' *more* than "the indefinite series of cycles of manifestation," which *now*, in contrast to 'before,' humans perceive as *separate* from themselves. 'Nature,' the human perception of *samsara*, has, in the 'evolved' human consciousness, I argue, become something that is a 'trap' that must be 'escaped' from: *moksha*. The identification, therefore, of the serpent only with 'life' in the biological sense is a very old identification, remembered in symbols although not necessarily in human *consciousness*. 'Life' becomes something much more seen through the lens of what Fontenrose calls the 'combat myth.' The Midgard serpent that encircles the world in Norse mythology and that abides in 'water,' like so many other mythical serpents, is contended with by Thor because Thor's hammer Mjolnir represents a 'new' principle by means of which 'the World' ('nature') can be ordered anew and seen in a new light. This new ordering principle, in opposition to the old ordering principle, is a *metaphysical* principle that transcends the, from the perspective of the New Man, suffocating 'encirclement' ('ouroboros') that has been perpetuated on humans until the *historical* 'moment' of Thor's (or Zeus's, or Apollo's, or Indra's, etc.) 'victory' over "the indefinite series of cycles of manifestation." All of these 'sky gods' or 'thunder gods,' or heroes and rulers of Tradition, are, I contend, indicative of a new age, a new way of perceiving *samsara*, and, so, 'nature.' The 'combat myth' in art and mythology is thus a revelation of this new 'level' of consciousness facing its adversary: the old obsession with life as something biological rather than Spiritual. Satan, "the god of this world" in 2 Corinthians 4:4, is described in Revelation 12:7, 13:4, and 20:2 as both a dragon and a serpent: "Michael and his angels fighting against the dragon"; "and they worshipped the dragon"; "And he seized the dragon, that ancient serpent, who is the devil and Satan, and bound him for a thousand years…so that he might not deceive the nations any longer, until the thousand years were ended." [ESV] In Revelation, Satan is the antagonist, or 'enemy,' of God, that one who *stands in the way of* ('guards') complete 'actualization' of the divine 'plan.' But so it is with every mythical 'dragon' or, more generally, 'monster' or 'giant' that represents the 'worldly' or 'material' level of existence, the 'chaos' of "the indefinite series of cycles of manifestation" that the hero, prophet, or savior must face down and defeat in order that a 'higher,' more *unified*, caliber of divinity, such as Christ, may better form, define, and 'actualize' the indefinitudes and potentialities of the 'duality' of the state of *matter* and the dichotomies of 'nature' or 'the World.'

The symbolism of the Rod of Asclepius implies that 'healing' is a possibility in 'the World,' that there exists an 'ascending' force/current that may be 'co-opted' in order to pause, or overturn, the ever-'swallowing' (like the serpent) force of *samsara*. The 'Plumed Serpent' Quetzalcoatl was known in Mesoamerican lore to be a great educator and civilizer, one who transmuted life as he found it and actually changed some of its motives and machinations. In *The Encyclopedia of Ancient Mesoamerica*, for example, Bunson and Bunson argue that Quetzalcoatl "revolutionized Toltec society, banning human sacrifices, corruption and cruelty," concluding that "[i]n all [Mesoamerican] cultures, Quetzalcoatl was considered the bridge between humans and the divine, between humans and animals, and between humans and the stars."[15] As such, he was aptly named the 'Plumed Serpent,' since he truly, like a bird, 'lifted up,' just as a 'sky god' should, the serpentine 'natural' "indefinite series of cycles of manifestation" to 'Heaven' and 'problematized' 'life.' This, I argue, allows Quetzalcoatl to be classified with those other gods, heroes, and rulers of the world of Tradition who, in accordance with the 'new age' of man that recognized 'life' as something *more* than biological, laid siege to the 'serpent power' in order to master it. Like these others, Quetzalcoatl 'problematized' 'life' by making humans aware of the limitations of what *they* considered to be 'life,' as well as of its non-inclusiveness of Reality. Like Buddha, Jesus, and the Jain *tirthankaras*, Quetzalcoatl provided a 'bridge' to a new 'way' of 'life.' Isaiah 40:3 states, "In the wilderness prepare the way of the LORD; *make straight* in the desert a highway for our God." (My emphasis) [ESV] John 1:23 states, "I am the voice of one crying out in the wilderness, '*Make straight the way of the Lord*,' as the prophet Isaiah said." (My emphasis) [ESV] Siddhartha Buddha, in his 'enlightenment' experience, 'straightened out' the "prodigious

---

15 Margaret R. Bunson and Stephen M. Bunson, *Encyclopedia of Ancient Mesoamerica* (New York, NY: Facts on File, Inc., 1996), 217.

serpent" Muchalinda who represented, by means of his encircling coils, the indefinite circle of 'natural' generation and corruption in 'nature' or 'the World.' Therefore, in the same way that in the ancient Near East the prophets Isaiah and John, and in ancient South Asia the historical Buddha, worked to 'straighten' out 'life' *as* humans had been conditioned by their 'migration' into the cycles of manifestation to *interpret* it, so did Quetzalcoatl work to 'straighten out' 'life' as it was then defined at the time of his appearance in ancient Mesoamerica.

Of course, not all who per chance encounter the essence of "the indefinite series of cycles of manifestation" are up to the task of 'transcending' the cyclical order of 'nature.' It is not clear, for example, as we discussed in Chapter 16, whether, in Norse myth, Thor ever defeats Jormungandr (the Midgard Serpent). Some versions of the narrative claim that he does, some that he doesn't. And it is a 'close thing' in other cultures as well, as in the Hindu myth describing the god Krishna's conflict with the 'snake king' Kaliya, who, along with his "swarms of red serpent warriors…sprayed Krishna with their poison…bit him with mouths running with venom, and…fettered his limbs with their coils" before Krishna, finally, as "the navel of the universe, the support of the gods, the creator, destroyer, and guardian of the worlds" defeated them all (see fig. C.7).[16] In other traditional myths, the serpent/dragon actually *does* get the better of his 'opponent.' Examples of this are both: 1) the 'subtle' serpent's deception of 'Adam and Eve' in Genesis 3 and 2) the opportunistic snake's theft of the 'herb of immortality' from Gilgamesh in *The Epic of Gilgamesh*. These are cases of what I classify as the 'failure to Spiritualize,' for in such cases the god/hero/ruler fails to 'overcome' the state of *matter* and 'identify' with the metaphysical Principle (God in Genesis 3; 'immortality' in *The Epic of Gilgamesh*).

---

16 Heinrich Zimmer, *Myths and Symbols in Indian Art and Civilization*, 83–85.

Fig. C.7. *Lord Krishna Dancing with Seven-Headed Cobra*, sixteenth century, courtesy of the Board of Trustees of the Victoria & Albert Museum, London[17]

In the terms of the *Vedanta*, the dual-natured being termed 'Adam and Eve' and Gilgamesh, although they were both on the verge of final 'escape' (*moksha*), 'fall' back into *samsara*. 'Adam and Eve' is distracted by the 'chaos' of the serpent, Gilgamesh by the 'chaos' of 'water.' The

---

17 Marilyn Nissenson and Susan Jonas, *Snake Charm*, 47.

opportunity provided to both 'migrating' beings by the metaphysical reality described as the 'Principle' to discover, or confirm, their 'identity' with, in the *Vedanta*, *Brahman*, to confirm, in the case of the being 'Adam and Eve,' its metaphorical 'walking with God,' is squandered. It is ignored due to the 'fascinating' power of the serpent (the distraction of "the indefinite series of cycles of manifestation").

The Management and Control of 'Life'

At a certain point in history, perhaps after a 'critical mass' of humans endured the mental struggles consequent upon the dawning awareness that there is a Reality beyond 'nature,' a group of New Men, masculine gods, heroes, and rulers, reached a state of being in which they came to believe that 'nature' ('chaos') might be managed or controlled. At this pivotal moment in history, at least some humans gradually came no longer to 'identify' their inner being with biological life and the 'natural' "indefinite series of cycles of manifestation," as they once did. At this time, the very idea of the system of "the indefinite series of cycles of manifestation" represented to these New Men merely an *aspect* of a 'higher,' somehow more real, reality. The old idea of life that was exemplified in the various cycles of 'nature,' and that seemed to encompass *everything* for such a long span of human history, was now, because it could be, systematically 'put in its place' as merely an imperfect reflection of a 'higher' meta-physical Reality. The new order of Being, which was beyond the "indefinite series of cycles of manifestation," beyond physical birth and death, and beyond all of the endless repetition that seemed to lead "absolutely nowhere,"[18] had, from the perspective of the New Men, to be 'managed,' and could now *also* be conceived by such beings, at least in principle, as 'controllable.' Only certain gifted individuals, however, the New Men thought, could compellingly introduce the concept of the metaphysical 'Principle' to the people, those who had not achieved independent

---

18 Joseph Campbell, *The Masks of God: Occidental Mythology*, 24.

'realization,' a concept which, so it seemed, not everyone could appreciate. These gifted individuals, in their 'profession' of the new idea of 'life,' were 'professionals' at persuasively linking, in the minds of the public, the meta-cyclical (metaphysical) Reality with the cyclical (physical/'natural') course of events. These 'professionals,' as I call them, came to acquire various names and titles, depending upon the epoch or culture in which they arose, such as shaman, priest, prophet, messiah, 'enlightened' one, 'wise' one, king, Emperor, and Pharaoh. These 'professionals' would, I argue, become the 'mediators' between the 'newly discovered' metaphysical, or 'Heavenly,' realm, and the physical/'natural,' or 'Earthly,' realm of the 'old' religion. They, more abstractly, would become the 'mediators' of 'duality' or, more specifically, of the dichotomies of existence: health and illness, good and evil, order and 'chaos,' 'actuality' and 'possibility'/potentiality, Spirit and matter.

The Chinese Emperor/*Wang* and the Egyptian Pharaoh, both associated in Tradition with the symbolism of the serpent/dragon, are examples of the New Men who 'ruled' the new society that was organized around 'connecting' Heaven to Earth and, more abstractly, 'reconciling' the meta-physical and physical realms. Both the Chinese Emperor and the Egyptian Pharaoh were considered 'divine,' or 'semi-divine,' beings by their peoples, and, thereby, capable of serving as 'mediators' between the celestial and terrestrial realms. This, as we saw in Chapter 15, is the meaning of the symbolism of the *Wang*, who was the 'Universal Man' and the 'Son of Heaven' (*T'ien Tzu*). Both Emperor and Pharaoh were 'priest-kings' over their people, individuals who possessed both of the traits of, as Guénon terms them, 'spiritual authority' and 'temporal power.'[19] In the ancient world, there are numerous examples of 'spiritual authority' and 'temporal

---

19 René Guénon, *Spiritual Authority & Temporal Power* (Hillsdale, NY: Sophia Perennis, 2001 [originally published in French as *Autorité spirituelle et souvoir temporel* by Les Éditions de la Maisnie, 1929]).

power' resting in the same set of hands. In *The Ancient City*, Fustel de Coulanges states that, in ancient Greece,

> every tribe...had its religious chief, whom the Athenians called the king of the tribe. It was also necessary that the city religion should have its supreme priest. This priest of the public hearth bore the name of king.... This sacerdotal character of primitive royalty is clearly indicated by the ancient writers....The principle office of a king was...to perform religious ceremonies. An ancient king of Sicyon was deposed because, having soiled his hands by a murder, he was no longer in a condition to offer sacrifices. Being no longer fit for a priest, he could no longer be a king....Homer and Virgil represent the kings as continually occupied with sacred ceremonies. We know from Demosthenes that the ancient kings of Attica performed themselves all the sacrifices that were prescribed by the religion of the city....The case was not at all different with the Roman kings. Tradition always represents them as priests.[20]

In ancient Greece and Rome, according to Fustel de Coulanges, "[m]en saw in [a king]...the man without whose aid no prayer was heard, no sacrifice accepted."[21] Although the Chinese Emperor/*Wang* and the Egyptian Pharaoh were admittedly different in many ways from the ancient Greek and Roman royalty described by Fustel de Coulanges, they were nevertheless of the same general category of 'priest-king.' In all cases, this 'professional' at offering sacrifices and performing religious ceremonies, who at the same time served as the divine archetype on Earth for his people, was 'mediator' between the cyclical realm of 'nature' and the metaphysical realm of 'Heaven.' Communication with the divine, or metaphysical, realm in order to invoke its power or beg its leniency was the prerogative of the New Man thought of as 'ruler.'

The serpent/dragon, as I have argued previously, symbolized in Tradition that aspect of reality that the New Man as 'ruler' was set to rule. On the connection between kingship and the serpent symbol as

---

20 Numa Denis Fustel de Coulanges, *The Ancient City*, 166–67.
21 Numa Denis Fustel de Coulanges, *The Ancient City*, 170.

depicted in ancient art, Charlesworth remarks that "the 'king' or ruler [was often] protected or framed by serpents." For example:

> From Mesopotamia come mythological scenes in bas-relief on a steatite basin... [that] depict a man holding two serpents that are larger than he.... Assyrian seals depict a serpent, thus representing godly and kingly powers and protection....For the Egyptians the uraeus, an aroused cobra or asp, was placed in royal palaces and on the heads of Pharaohs to symbolize their godly and kingly powers. It is thus no surprise to see on Tutankhamen's throne winged serpents rising majestically from the back.[22]

Moving to ancient Greece and Rome, Charlesworth notes that "in myths, especially in the Greek and Roman world, the divine kings were depicted as serpents or had serpent features."[23] In Virgil's *Aeneid*, Charlesworth adds,

> Laocoon was a priest of Apollo, but he offended the gods by breaking his vow of celibacy. Apollo then sent two massive serpents to crush him and his two sons, Antiphas and Thymbraeus (Melanthus), as he, as was his duty, was preparing to sacrifice a bull to Poseidon.[24] (See fig. C.8.)

It is interesting from the perspective of traditional symbolism as we have interpreted it that, in this last case, there are exactly *two* (a 'duality' of) serpents sent to destroy someone who is sacrificing to Poseidon, since the latter is the god of the seas and the symbolism of 'water' in Tradition is symbolically interchangeable with the symbolism of the serpent/dragon. It is almost as if the punishment of the Trojan Laocoon and his sons constitutes yet another case of the 'Materialization' that I have spoken of, since, by sacrificing to Poseidon, Laocoon and his sons are aligning themselves with the power of 'the Waters' of 'possibility'/potentiality, the 'chaotic' "indefinite series of cycles of manifestation" that constitute natural 'life' and

---

22 James H. Charlesworth, *The Good and Evil Serpent*, 238.
23 James H. Charlesworth, *The Good and Evil Serpent*, 238.
24 James H. Charlesworth, *The Good and Evil Serpent*, 149.

that are the very antithesis of 'actualization' or Spiritualization, such as, for example, Gilgamesh also discovered when he failed to achieve 'immortality.'

Fig. C.8. *Hagesander, Polydorus, and Athenodorus*, The Laocoon Group, discovered in 1506 on Esquiline Hill, probably first century BCE or first century CE, Vatican Museum, Rome[25]

All of these cases, however, are not to be confused with the cases of Jason (of Golden Fleece fame) or Herakles and his many 'labors' and

---

25 Marilyn Nissenson and Susan Jonas, *Snake Charm*, 36.

the serpent 'guardians' that they both contended with, which we discussed in Chapter 8. For these cases, like the cases of Thor and the Midgard Serpent and Indra and the serpent Vritra, are cases of the New Man's 'struggle' with that which the serpent/dragon traditionally symbolizes, *not* cases of 'rule' by the New Man over that which the serpent/dragon traditionally symbolizes. As I proposed earlier, these cases of 'struggle' and 'rule' are revealed in traditional serpent/dragon art and narrative as indicating two separate, yet continuous, phases in the transmutation of human nature from that kind of being that 'identifies' with 'nature,' and that defines 'life' as something biological or 'natural,' to that kind of being that 'identifies' itself with something *beyond* (meta-physical) 'nature'/biology and that, likewise, redefines 'life' as something *meta*-biological/physical.

I argued in Chapter 12 that, in his alleged claim to having achieved the unconditioned state of *nirvana*, Siddhartha Gautama (the Buddha) necessarily claimed *metaphysical* 'enlightenment.' Siddhartha's alleged 'enlightenment' experience was, either directly or indirectly, according to Buddhist sources, the culmination of many years of anguish and struggle. Nevertheless, his 'attaining *nirvana*' fits more snugly into the category of 'control and management,' or 'rule,' of "the indefinite series of cycles manifestation" (the state of *matter*) than it fits into the category of 'struggle' or 'combat' with the state of *matter*. When the "prodigious cobra" Muchalinda slithers up to protect Siddhartha from the elements of 'nature,' the rain and storm and sun, etc., it approaches a being that has already undergone 'struggle' and, thus, has already 'defeated the serpent.' It is, in fact, the 'new' state of being that Siddhartha has *already* achieved when Muchalinda arrives to 'shelter' him that is actually the force/power that compels Muchalinda (symbolizing *samsara* and/or 'nature') to slither 'up' in the first place. For, recall that Muchalinda is an example of that transcultural traditional symbolic figuration that we have termed the 'risen serpent' in Chapter 12, and, as such, partakes of the general meaning of that symbolism. Already known as "the great physician"[26] by the time that Muchalinda arrives, Siddhartha has finished the process of 'healing' himself and will now, according to Buddhist tradition, soon begin the work of 'healing' all future Buddhists to the degree that they impose his methods upon the *matter* of their 'natural' selves in order to *metaphysically* form, define, and 'actualize' that *matter*. We must remember, however, to think of the traditional 'healing' that the Buddha allegedly effects in both himself and others in the ancient manner of healing-as-'resurrection,' which is not a process of remedying the ailment or injury of a sick, but still alive, individual, but rather, as we discussed in Chapter 12, a *rescuing* of life (in the form of an individual person or animal) *from* the realm of the dead which s/he has *already* entered. This is most clearly evident in the case of the Greek Asklepios, or the Roman Asclepius, but it is also exactly how Jesus of Nazareth became known as the 'great healer' of the New Testament.

Jesus of Nazareth, whether in the more obvious, to modern eyes, case of freeing Lazarus from the grave, or in the more mundane, again to modern eyes, healing of a leper, was always, from the perspective of Tradition, effecting *rebirth*. More generally, however, by his bestowing a new covenant (the 'New Testament') to humankind, Jesus introduced a new *kind* (or level) of 'healing' into the world, one in which a 'higher' degree of form, definition, and 'actuality' manifests in something that is, from the perspective of this 'new testament,' relatively form-less, in-definite, and potential: human sinners. This 'new covenant' that was, according to Christians, presented to *all* of the people of 'the World' by Jesus and his apostles also involved 'actualizing' the potential of the 'old covenant' (the 'Old Testament') that was, from the perspective introduced by Jesus, 'waiting' to be 'actualized' for a larger audience. The description in Revelation 20:2 of Jesus's future defeat of the 'dragon' by means of his angel "coming down from heaven," as well as Jesus's self-imposed crucifixion (alchemical transmutation) of

---

26 Ramakrishna Puligandla, *Fundamentals of Indian Philosophy*, 39.

the 'serpent nature'[27] described in John 3:13–15, are both evidence of the power of "he who descended from heaven." [ESV] For, like the Chinese *Wang*, the Jesus that is described in John is a 'mediator' of the divine or metaphysical and, thus, 'speaks for' (as the 'Word') God.

In Exodus 7:1–2, Moses and his brother Aaron similarly 'speak' for God when they encounter the Egyptian Pharaoh:

> And the LORD said to Moses, 'See, I have made you like God to Pharaoh, and your brother Aaron shall be your prophet. You shall speak all that I command you, and your brother Aaron shall tell Pharaoh to let the people of Israel go out of his land.' [ESV]

Immediately after being "made like God to Pharaoh," Moses, and his brother Aaron, are given by God the 'serpent power':

> So Moses and Aaron went to Pharaoh and did just as the LORD commanded. Aaron cast down his staff before Pharaoh and his servants, and it became a serpent. Then Pharaoh summoned the wise men and the sorcerers, and they, the magicians of Egypt, also did the same by their secret arts. For each man cast down his staff, and they became serpents. But Aaron's staff swallowed up their staffs. [Exodus 7:10–12, ESV]

This passage from Exodus describes (although the Torah, in general, claims to abhor magic) a sort of 'wizard's duel' between two groups, each of which proclaims its superior control over the *samsaric* "indefinite series of cycles of manifestation" that is symbolized by the serpent/dragon in Tradition and which the metaphysical 'Principle' forms, defines, and 'actualizes': Spiritualizes. Otherwise stated, both "the magicians of Egypt" and the group of 'magicians' consisting of Moses and Aaron claim to speak for, and control, the state of *matter*, and each group of magicians reveals the extent of its respective power over the state of *matter* by the means of revealing its control over the serpent staves of its 'opponent.' According to Exodus 7:12, however,

---

27 I refer here to the alchemical transmutation of the *samsaric* flux of Jesus's body discussed in Chapter 9.

Moses (with the aid of Aaron) was the greater 'wizard' in the contest, that is, the greater manipulator of *samsara* (the state of *matter*), since his brother Aaron's serpent staff 'swallowed up' the serpent staves of the Egyptian magicians (see fig. C.9).

Fig. C.9. *Moses and Aaron before Pharaoh*, Gustave Doré[28]

Later in the Torah, however, in Numbers 21:8-9, Moses switches from prophet to 'healer,' as we have already seen in our Chapter 7:

> And the LORD said to Moses, 'Make a fiery serpent and set it on a pole, and everyone who is bitten, when he sees it, shall live.' So Moses made a

---

28 The Holy Bible: King James Version, Barnes & Noble edition, 93.

bronze serpent and set it on a pole. And if a serpent bit anyone, he would look at the bronze serpent and live. [ESV]

Here again, although as 'healer' rather than prophet in this case, Moses serves as a 'mediator' of the divine will, a mediator of that singular metaphysical force that is, according to Guénon, 'polarized' into two 'currents' that are often symbolized by means of the serpent in Tradition.

The Serpent Symbol, Shamanism, DNA, and 'Duality'

Whether speaking for the metaphysical/divine, or channeling its power to 'heal' and impose order on the 'chaotic' cyclical level of existence, he who possesses the 'serpent power' 'manages and controls,' to a certain degree, the state of being that I term *matter*. The ancient 'profession' of shamanism is one example of a discipline or practice that I contend was developed by the New Man to 'mediate' between Heaven (the metaphysical) and Earth (the physical/'natural'). The shaman is, as mentioned in Chapter 6, a figure that is very often associated in many traditional cultures with serpent symbolism. The anthropologist Jeremy Narby in his book *The Cosmic Serpent: DNA and the Origins of Knowledge* describes his 1985 field trip to the Quirishari community in the Peruvian Amazon's Pichis Valley. There, Narby discusses his meeting with the indigenous Ashaninca people and learning of the "hallucinatory world of ayahuasqueros": shamans.[29] In the course of his conversations with a particular 'ayahuasquero' named Carlos Perez Shuma, Narby relates that Carlos informed him of the cryptic fact that "the mother of Ayahuasca," the hallucinatory substance taken by Quirishari shamans to induce a 'trance state,' "is a snake."[30] As we have mentioned previously, the shaman is everywhere on Earth a 'healer'

29　Jeremy Narby, *The Cosmic Serpent: DNA and the Origins of Knowledge* (New York, New York: Jeremy P. Tarcher/Putnam, 1998), 1.
30　Jeremy Narby, *The Cosmic Serpent*, 34.

of sorts, but also, according to modern-day shamans themselves, such as Carlos, a being that is capable of 'communicating' with the divine, metaphysical, or 'celestial,' level of reality. Shamans accomplish their so-called 'celestial journeys,' according to Eliade in *Shamanism*, by means of what he describes in that book as 'archaic techniques of ecstasy.'[31] The two, 'healing' and 'techniques of ecstasy,' according to Eliade and others, go hand in hand, since 'healing' is accomplished in shamanic societies by means of these 'techniques of ecstasy.' In their article "On the Serpent Cult and Psychoactive Plants," Balaji Mundkur, whom we mentioned before, and medical anthropologist Marlene Dobkin de Rios state that "generally, the shaman uses drug plants to open communication with supernatural realms, to heal, to harm his client's enemies, and to harness resources within himself for particular social ends."[32]

In *The Cosmic Serpent*, Narby observes that, although "not all of the world's indigenous people use hallucinogenic plants," it is a common experience for those who do ingest ayahuasca to see, on their 'journeys,' *snakes or dragons*.[33] Often, these visions are recorded. This 'observation' of "snakes or dragons" by shamans while they are in ecstatic trance states is connected with the Mesoamerican focus on 'Vision Serpents' that we discussed briefly in Chapters 9 and 14. Balaji Mundkur's remark from *The Cult of the Serpent*, which we quoted in Chapter 6, that the snake is "the one common, forceful element that surfaces amidst the great variety of animals in Western Hemispheric myths and religions" seems relevant here.[34] In *Supernatural: Meetings*

---

31 Mircea Eliade, *Shamanism*, 200.
32 Marlene Dobkin de Rios and Balaji Mundkur, "On the Serpent Cult and Psychoactive Plants," *Current Anthropology*, 18, no. 3 (Sep., 1977), 556.
33 Jeremy Narby, *The Cosmic Serpent*, 41.
34 Balaji Mundkur, *The Cult of the Serpent: An Interdisciplinary Survey of Its Manifestations and Origins*, 25. See also Balaji Mundkur, "The Bicephalous 'Animal Style' in Northern Eurasian Religious Art and Its Western Hemispheric Analogues [and Comments and Reply]," *Current Anthropology* 25:4, August-October 1984, 451.

with the Ancient Teachers of Mankind, catastrophism and ancient civilization researcher and author Graham Hancock relates that

> [g]igantic rearing 'vision-serpents' with the bodies of huge snakes and human heads are a repeated theme of Mayan art of all periods...[and] are frequently presented in contexts that leave little doubt that altered states of consciousness were involved, since associated human figures are often shown smoking or otherwise consuming hallucinogens, or self-torturing—another tried-and-tested shamanic technique for inducing visions.[35] (See figs. C.10 and C.11.)

Dobkin de Rios and Mundkur add in the above-cited article that "scholars are in general agreement that, in areas of the New World where serpents are rendered in art, such plants were used ritually."[36] Narby himself notes in *The Cosmic Serpent* that, after taking ayahuasca, *he* saw "enormous fluorescent snakes"[37] and then recounts anthropologist Michael Harner's record, after taking ayahuasca, of his 'meetings' with "dragon-like creatures who explained that they were the true gods of this world."[38] In *The Way of the Shaman*, Harner claims that his meetings with 'dragon-like creatures,' as well as other visions that he experienced, "emanated from 'giant reptilian creatures' resting at the lowest depths of his brain"[39] who showed him "how they had created life on the planet [Earth] in order to hide within the multitudinous forms and thus disguise their presence [from an unspecified enemy who sought their destruction]."[40]

---

35 Graham Hancock, *Supernatural: Meetings with the Ancient Teachers of Mankind* (New York, New York: The Disinformation Company, Ltd., 2007), 349.
36 Marlene Dobkin de Rios and Balaji Mundkur, "On the Serpent Cult and Psychoactive Plants," 556.
37 Jeremy Narby, *The Cosmic Serpent*, 51.
38 Michael Harner, "The Sound of Rushing Water," *Natural History Magazine* 77, no. 6 (1968): 28–29 in Jeremy Narby, *The Cosmic Serpent*, 53.
39 Jeremy Narby, *The Cosmic Serpent*, 55.
40 Michael Harner, *The Way of the Shaman*, 5.

Fig. C.10. *The Rearing Vision Serpent*[41]

Fig. C.11. *K'awil merged with a Vision Serpent*[42]

---

41 Freidel, Schele and Parker, *Maya Cosmos*, 198.
42 Freidel, Schele and Parker, *Maya Cosmos*, 196.

In *The Cosmic Serpent*, Narby takes account of Harner's incredible conclusions. Harner states: 1) "I learned that the dragon-like creatures were thus inside all forms of life, including man," and 2) "In retrospect one could say they were almost like DNA, although at that time, 1961, I knew nothing of DNA."[43]

Serpents are intimately tied to shamanic experiences, especially in the indigenous cultures of Mesoamerica and South America. These experiences, in which the 'supernatural,' as Hancock refers to it, is communicated with, are examples of the 'event of Spiritualization' that is first referred to in the Introduction to this book. The event of Spiritualization is one of three kinds of 'hosts' of Spiritualization, the other two kinds of hosts that I have specified and defined being 'profession'/'personality' and 'place.' In the age of the New Man who has drawn into question the old idea of 'life,' the limitations of this old form of 'life' are articulated in the ancient symbolisms of the 'heroic' art and myth of the age of gods, heroes, and divine rulers. In this art and myth, the New Man is depicted, in various ways in the different cultures of the ancient world, as Spiritualizing—forming, defining, and 'actualizing'—the 'chaotic' "indefinite series of cycles of manifestation" that is the conceptual articulation of the New Man's understanding of his old 'life.' Spiritualizing 'personalities'/'professions,' 'events,' and 'places' of Spiritualization are the *means* by which the New Man's newly discovered 'celestial' meta-physical archetype of order is 'mediated' in the terrestrial physical realm of 'nature' or 'the World.' In the case of the shaman, in particular, the 'techniques of ecstasy' that were employed five hundred years ago by Mesoamerican shamans, and that *are* employed today among South American shamans, are, in the terminology of this book, 'events of Spiritualization.' This is the case, I argue, because shamans of the Americas, as well as in other regions of the world, employed, and employ, a 'supernatural' knowledge to 'heal' and bind their villages and tribes that, they believe, is

---

43 Jeremy Narby, *The Cosmic Serpent*, 55, quoting Michael Harner, *The Way of the Shaman*, 5.

acquired from a realm that exists 'beyond' the 'natural' physical world. These 'archaic' peoples, as Eliade calls them, believed, and believe, that it is only by means of what Eliade describes as the 'event' of shamanic 'ecstasy' that a 'supernatural,' or 'Spiritual,' influence can be employed by a shaman after his/her 'journey' in order to form, define, and 'actualize' the physical world within which s/he and the members of her/his community spend their waking lives. As I have stated, this knowledge that archaic peoples believe comes from the effects of an 'ecstatic' vision or 'journey' to the 'supernatural' realm that is imparted to a shaman's tribe or village by the shaman is an example of what I term the Spiritualization of the state of *matter*, the *samsaric* "indefinite series of cycles of manifestation" in its 'chaotic' aspect that is, from the perspective of the human form of being, interpreted as 'nature.'

According to Eliade, traditional 'healing' in 'archaic' cultures in general is able to "restore the 'communicability' that existed *in illo tempore* [in the 'original time'] between this world and heaven."[44] Humans possessing this 'restorative' capacity in some archaic societies are called 'shamans,' or the equivalent of this term. As Piers Vitebsky notes in *The Shaman*, "the word 'shaman' comes from the language of the Evenk, a small Tungus-speaking group of hunters and reindeer herders in Siberia [and]…was first used only to designate a religious specialist from this region."[45] The cosmic 'flight' of the shaman allows for the kind of knowledge obtained in the 'supernatural' realm that accomplishes 'healing' in the traditional sense. This form of 'healing' is, as J. Schouten contends in connection with the Babylonians and Egyptians, a 'resurrection' of life from the realm of the dead.[46] Jane Harrison, as we noted in Chapter 11, describes traditional 'healing' as a form of 'reincarnation.' In *Themis*, she identifies Hermes, the ancient Greek 'mediator' between the divine and mortal realms, as "the very

---

44 Mircea Eliade, *Shamanism*, 486.
45 Piers Vitebsky, *The Shaman*, 10.
46 J. Schouten, *The Rod and Serpent of Asklepios*, 10. See Chapter 11 of this book.

daimon of reincarnation."[47] I have, more generally, described traditional 'healing' in this book as that 'actualization' of potential that was thought by traditional peoples to occur, although on different scales, in the same fashion in both the medical healing of a person and the 'creation' of the cosmos. The shaman's capacity for cosmic 'flight,' as it is sometimes called, to the supernatural/metaphysical realm, therefore, accomplishes, as Eliade argues in *The Myth of the Eternal Return*, "the actualization of the cosmic Creation, exemplary model of all life, that it is hoped... [will] restore the physical health and spiritual integrity of the patient."[48] 'The patient,' for archaic shamans, is usually one or more members of his/her tribe or village *or* the village as a whole.

Moses, Siddhartha, and Jesus all served the same purpose in their 'ministries': that is, as metaphysical, as well as physical, 'healers' in the traditional sense who 'brought down' from the metaphysical or 'supernatural' level of existence a 'new order' or 'way' of being for humans to 'follow.' Whether it was the 'Ten Commandments,' the 'Eight-Fold path,' or the 'Gospel,' the result was procured, I argue, by means of inducing a trans-human state of consciousness similar to that induced by shamans in archaic societies. Because of their positions as both 'healers' *and* exceptionally 'enlightened' beings who were 'closer' than normal humans to a 'higher' reality (God, for example), Moses, Siddhartha, and Jesus were, appropriately, associated with serpent/dragon symbolism. Along with Quetzalcoatl, the great Mesoamerican 'civilizer' that we discussed in Chapter 11, all three religious figures are, in the terms of my argument, Spiritualizing 'personalities' that 'host' the 'event' of Spiritualizing (forming, defining, and actualizing the state of *matter*) in a fashion very similar to the way in which I argue that the Spiritualizing 'professions' of shamans, Pharaohs, Emperors, and priest-kings do. Both categories of 'hosting' the act of Spiritualization, Spiritualizing 'personalities' as well as Spiritualizing

---

47 Jane Ellen Harrison, *Themis: A Study of the Social Origins of Greek Religion*, 295.
48 Mircea Eliade, *The Myth of the Eternal Return*, 82.

'professions,' are traditionally associated with serpent/dragon symbolism because both categories define individuals who represent or embody the 'overcoming' of *matter/samsara/*"the indefinite series of cycles of manifestation" by means of an appeal to a 'higher' influence that provides greater form, definition, and 'actuality' in the 'lower' physical/'natural'/terrestrial world. In the cases of both Spiritualizing 'personalities' and Spiritualizing 'professions,' it is 'management' and 'control' of the 'lower' 'serpent power' of the state of *matter*, and thus the body, that is operative. The difference between the 'management' and 'control' that is exercised by Spiritualizing 'personalities' like Moses, Jesus, and Siddhartha, in contrast to Spiritualizing 'professions' like the priest-king, the shaman, the Chinese *Wang/*Emperor, and the Egyptian Pharaoh, is that 'management and control' are *systematized* in the cases of the 'professions' rather than being *idiosyncratically introduced* in novel forms, as they are by 'personalities' such as Moses, Jesus, and Siddhartha.

In Chapter 9, we noted Freidel et al.'s contentions in *Maya Cosmos* that "Vision serpents...were symbols of the path along which supernaturals traveled on their way to being manifested in this world" and that "human souls find the bodies of their newborn owners by traveling along the serpent's gullet."[49] It is particularly the case, in Mayan 'Classic-period imagery,' that according to Freidel et al., the 'Vision Serpent' "was the embodiment of the path to and from the Otherworld, [with] ancestral figures...often shown leaning out of its open jaws to communicate with their descendants."[50] These quotations describe the serpent as representing for the Maya a 'path' of some kind between the terrestrial ('this') world and the 'supernatural' (let us say 'metaphysical') 'Otherworld.' Human souls or 'supernaturals,' for the ancient Maya, 'travelled along the serpent's gullet' in order to "find the bodies of their newborn owners" or become "manifested in the world." If this

---

49 Freidel, Schele and Parker, *Maya Cosmos*, 195-96.
50 Freidel, Schele and Parker, *Maya Cosmos*, 140.

is the case, then for the Maya 'human souls'/'supernaturals' can exist separately from their bodies. Furthermore, such souls/'supernaturals' can *use* 'the serpent' (its 'gullet,' specifically) in order to emerge from the 'Otherworld' into the physical world and 'find' their bodies or become 'manifested.' In the terms of this book, this means that 'human souls,' for the Maya, are able to define, form, and 'actualize' (Spiritualize) the "bodies of their newborn owners." They are, in other words, able to 'Spiritualize' the state of *matter*. We have noted Harner's claim in *The Way of the Shaman* that "giant reptilian creatures" showed him, while in an ayahuasca-induced 'vision,' how they "created life" on earth and also told him that they "were thus inside all forms of life." It would seem that, in referring to 'life,' what these 'dragon-like creatures' encountered by Harner were referring to was biological existence on Earth. However, as we have just seen in the Mayan cosmology that is presented in *Maya Cosmos*, biological life ultimately derives from what the Maya termed the 'Otherworld,' the place where souls or 'supernaturals' come from. From the ancient Mayan perspective, however, there was a means by which the souls/'supernaturals' of the 'Otherworld' could 'travel' into the physical/'natural' world: altered states of consciousness. These 'altered states' were associated by the ancient Maya of five hundred years ago, as they are by the shamans of Peru today, with *serpents*. As we have seen from Hancock's book *Supernatural*, "gigantic rearing 'vision-serpents'" are often depicted in Mayan art with human figures who are either "smoking [,]...consuming hallucinogens, or self-torturing."[51] All three of these techniques are known to 'induce visions' that, from the shamanic perspective, indicate the realization of "altered states of consciousness." It is in just such 'visions' or 'altered states,' however, that so-called 'vision-serpents' that once *were* seen by ancient Mayan shamans *are*, according to Narby, seen by Peruvian Ashaninca shamans today. In both cases, these so-called 'vision-serpents' are the means by which

---

51   Graham Hancock, *Supernatural*, 349.

'souls' or 'supernaturals,' a meta-physical reality, 'travelled along the serpent's gullet' (as Freidel et al. put it) in order to 'manifest in this world' and quicken their corresponding bodies. In the terms of my argument, the bodies thus quickened — *biological organisms* or 'life,' that is — were formed, defined, and 'actualized' (Spiritualized), in the Mayan cosmology, by "supernaturals [meta-physical realities] travel[ling] on their way to being manifested in this world."

In *The Cosmic Serpent*, Narby relates that the ayahuasquero/shaman Carlos Perez Shuma told him that "the spirits of nature communicate with human beings in hallucinations and dreams — in other words, in mental *images*."⁵² Narby states, and we must agree, that "[t]his idea is common in [what he calls] 'pre-rational' traditions. For instance, [he relates,] Heraclitus said of the Pythian oracle (from the Greek *puthôn*, 'serpent') that it 'neither declares nor conceals, but gives a sign.'"⁵³ Beyond Heraclitus's contention that the Pythian oracle "gives a sign," which is in itself indicative of the importance of symbols in ancient Greece, Narby's reference to 'the spirits of nature' in connection with 'hallucinations and dreams' inspired by the Pythia is reminiscent of our own discussion of the serpent Python that was, according to legend, defeated by the Greek god Apollo. More generally, Narby's reference to 'spirits' communicating with humans by means of hallucinations and dreams is reminiscent of the connection between serpent symbolism in traditional societies and the idea, widely believed in in those societies, of communication with 'the gods.' Whether they are called 'the gods' or the 'spirits of nature,' in traditional societies, such meta-physical beings are believed to be able to communicate with humans. In such societies, however, there are only certain special individuals, 'mediators' and 'messengers,' who possess the capacity to communicate with these meta-physical 'gods' and 'spirits' in order to

---

52 Jeremy Narby, *The Cosmic Serpent*, 97.
53 Jeremy Narby, *The Cosmic Serpent*, 97, quoting Charles H. Kahn, *The Art and Thought of Heraclitus: An Edition of the Fragments with Translation and Commentary* (Cambridge: Cambridge University Press, 1979), 43.

communicate to the rest of mankind the 'will' of the meta-physical, or 'supernatural,' realm of being. Hermes was the 'messenger of the gods' in ancient Greece; Mercury had the same function in ancient Rome. The serpentine caduceus staff carried by both indicated their status as 'messenger' and 'mediator' of 'the gods,' as we discussed in Chapter 11. As with the Maya 'vision-serpents' and the 'dragon-like creatures' encountered by Harner while on ayahuasca, it seems that the serpent/dragon in ancient Greece and Rome indicated both the 'event' of 'mediation' and 'messaging' between the 'spirits' or 'gods' (the metaphysical in general) and humans, as well as the 'personality' that was qualified or 'chosen' for the 'profession' of 'mediation' and 'messaging.' In both cases, that of the two forms of 'vision-serpents' in the Americas, and that of Hermes/Mercury with his serpentine caduceus staff in ancient Greece, the serpent was a symbol of contact with, specifically 'mediation' and 'messaging' of/from, the 'supernatural.' It was, and still is with the Peruvian Ashaninca, symbolic of, whether in art, myth, or the 'visions' of humans, the *matter* by means of which Spirit (God/*Brahman*/Atum-Re/'the gods'/'the spirits') 'manifests' or 'creates.'

Wherever it is found, what is called 'shamanism' employs the serpent/dragon symbol to symbolize the 'control and management' of *matter*/*samsara*/"the indefinite series of cycles of manifestation" that constitutes physical, or biological, 'life.' As I earlier outlined, this 'control and management' of *matter*, the perceived 'lower' level of 'life' by the New Man, is the third of three stages of an 'evolving' human awareness of ultimate human 'identity.' In the first stage, humans 'identified' with the biological aspect of their own being, the 'cyclical' aspect of their being that they also recognized in the forces of 'nature.' In the second stage of human 'development,' however, this 'old' idea of 'life' was, as I have contended, conceptualized in the changing awareness of the New Men — who were represented in ancient art and myth as the heroes, gods, and rulers of old — as the state of *matter* (the 'chaotic' "indefinite series of cycles of manifestation") that exists before 'articulation' by self-aware Spirit. At the prehistoric level of consciousness, preoccupied as it was with 'fertility,' biological rejuvenation, and cyclicity, there was, I argue, no question of something 'external' or 'different' that 'actualized' or quickened the whole process of 'nature' or 'the World.' After a time, however, for reasons unknown, this primitive idea of 'life,' in the minds of some humans, turned into something to be questioned and 'problematized.' Thus emerged the phase of human existence that I have characterized as the 'combat,' or 'struggle,' with *matter/samsara/*"the indefinite series of cycles of manifestation," portrayed and described in ancient art and the 'combat myths' of Indra and Vritra, Apollo and Python, Zeus and Typhon, and many others. At some point, however, this phase of 'struggle' or 'combat' was modified by yet another modification in the 'evolution' of self-consciousness, at least in some humans, and the encounter with 'the serpent power' of the 'old life' came to be thought of, by the New Men, as something not just to be fought with in order to hold it at a distance from, and not let it be confused with, the true essence of human nature, but something to be 'managed' and 'controlled.' In this new 'age' of humans came into being, beyond the seemingly randomly occurring 'personalities' of a Zeus, or of an Indra, or of a Thor, in different places around the world, a systematized production of 'professionals' to 'manage and control' the 'serpent power' that the first stage of New Men, the heroes and 'gods,' had identified and begun to separate themselves, and all humanity with them, from. This age included, along with the origination of the 'professionals' known as 'shamans,' the origination of other cultural variations on the same idea: priest-kings, Pharaohs, and Emperors.

In *The Way of the Shaman*, Harner opines that "[i]n retrospect one could say [that] they [the dragon-like creatures that he saw] were almost like DNA."[54] Today, based upon empirical inductive science, humans hypothesize that what is called 'DNA' (deoxyribonucleic

---

54 Michael Harner, *The Way of the Shaman*, 5.

acid) serves as a sort of 'blueprint' or 'program' that guides the development and survival of biological 'life,' at least on Earth.[55] One of the ways that DNA does this, scientists believe, is by means of those biological organisms who 'host' DNA, and whose 'development' is largely 'determined' by DNA programming, 'adapting' to changes in their 'environment.' DNA is, according to this hypothesis, necessarily interactive with its environment in a fashion conducive to DNA's *substantial*, although not superficial, continuation in the same 'form.' In *The Cosmic Serpent*, Narby thus observes that

> DNA is a master of transformation....The cell-based life [that] DNA informs made the air we breathe, the landscape we see, and the mind-boggling diversity of living beings of which we are a part. In 4 billion years, it has multiplied itself into an incalculable number of species, while remaining exactly the same.[56]

Several researchers have remarked upon the particular *shape* of the DNA molecule since it was discovered in the second half of the twentieth century. The molecular biologist Christopher Wills, for example, wrote that "[t]he two chains of DNA resemble two snakes coiled around each other in some elaborate courtship ritual."[57] (See figs. C.12 and C.13.). The megalithic Avebury Cycle in Wiltshire, England that we discussed in Chapter 14, with its 'coupling' serpents, comes quickly to mind. With its 'two chains,' the serpent-like DNA molecule is, structurally, a *dual* entity constituting an 'engine of adaptation' that has continuously, for around 4 billion years we're told, spewed forth

---

55 "Deoxyribonucleic acid, a self-replicating material which is present in nearly all living organisms as the main constituent of chromosomes. It is the carrier of genetic information. Each molecule of DNA consists of two strands coiled round each other to form a double helix, a structure like a spiral ladder." http://en.oxforddictionaries.com/definition/dna. Accessed at 9:34 am on 9/28/2019.

56 Jeremy Narby, *The Cosmic Serpent*, 92.

57 Christopher Wills, *Exons, Introns, and Talking Genes: The Science Behind the Human Genome Project* (Oxford: Oxford University Press, 1991), 36.

the indefinite multiplicity of biological organisms *and* their 'environment' that we see on Earth.

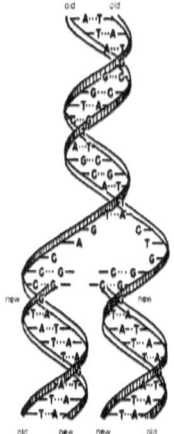 

Fig. C.12. Untitled (The Double Helix)⁵⁸   **Fig. C.13.** The DNA double helix represented as a pair of snakes⁵⁹

Along with the serpent's 'forked' tongue and dual hemipenes, the recognized 'double helix' structure of the DNA molecule adds another interesting twist to the association of the serpent in traditional art and myth with the concepts of 'duality,' the dichotomies of 'the World,' and the 'old' idea of 'life' that was embraced by humans before the appearance on the scene of world history of the New Man. Much of the art and architecture of traditional societies from around the world represents the 'duality' symbolism of the traditional serpent symbol by depicting *exactly two* serpents. Within the terms of my argument, such representations may indicate either of two things: 1) the society that created the relevant art/architecture is advertising its *embracing* of the 'old' idea of 'life' as the *samsaric* "indefinite series of cycles of

---

58 Jeremy Narby, *The Cosmic Serpent*, 89, from James D. Watson, *The Double Helix: A Personal Account of the Discovery of the Structure of DNA* (London: Weidenfeld and Nicolson, 1968), 165.

59 Jeremy Narby, *The Cosmic Serpent*, 92, from Christopher Wills, *Exons, Introns, and Talking Genes*, 37.

manifestation" or 2) certain elements of the society that created the relevant art/architecture are advertising its *overcoming* of the 'old' idea of 'life.' Although we have already analyzed several examples in ancient art of traditional serpent 'duality' symbolism, such as 1) the Egyptian representation of the two-headed snake called the 'provider of attributes,' 2) the Mediterranean symbolism of the caduceus that is always represented with *two* snakes, and 3) the ancient British 'dual' 'serpentine' avenues of the megalithic structure at Avebury, there are many more to be found and from entirely different geographical locations. The following illustration reproduced from 'Middle American' civilization expert Herbert Spinden's *A Study of Maya Art* of a Mayan 'ornamental niche in façade' at Uxmal (in present-day Yucatan, Mexico), for example, shows *three pairs* of 'twin' serpents (see fig. C.14) and is yet another example of traditional serpent 'duality' symbolism.[60] There are, in fact, many ancient Mayan examples of serpent 'duality' symbolism in the art and architecture bequeathed to the world by that ancient Mesoamerican culture. In *Chichen Itza: The City of the Wise Men of the Water*, anthropologist Roman Pina Chan notes, for example, that the structure at Chichen Itza (in present-day Yucatan, Mexico) named 'El Caracol' (the Observatory) has on its "west front...a staircase...which is bordered by narrow balustrades decorated with [two] intertwined serpents."[61] The façade of the 'Temple of the Tigers,' also at Chichen Itza, depicts 'twin' serpents (see fig. C.15), as do many other Mesoamerican artifacts.[62] Included among the latter, for example, are, as Chan states, "minor details on headdresses...that show two-headed reptile forms," an example of which was found in Yaxchilan (in Chiapas, Mexico) (see fig. C.16).[63] All of the architectural examples cited served, in traditional societies, as what I

---

60 Herbert J. Spinden, *A Study of Maya Art*, 118.
61 Roman Pina Chan, *Chichen Itza*, 59.
62 The Temple of the Tigers was briefly referred to in Chapter 5.
63 Herbert J. Spinden, *A Study of Maya Art*, 60.

have termed 'places' of Spiritualization, places of forming, defining, and 'actualizing' what was once, and for a long time, considered 'life' into something more refined and 'realized.'

Fig. C.14. Ornamental niche on façade, Uxmal, Yucatan, Mexico, the Nunnery, North Range, Catherwood, 1884, pl. 15[64]

---

64   Herbert J. Spinden, *A Study of Maya Art*, 118.

Fig. C.15. Façade of the Temple of the Tigers, Chichen Itza, Yucatan, Mexico[65]

---

65 Roman Pina Chan, *Chichen Itza*, 53.

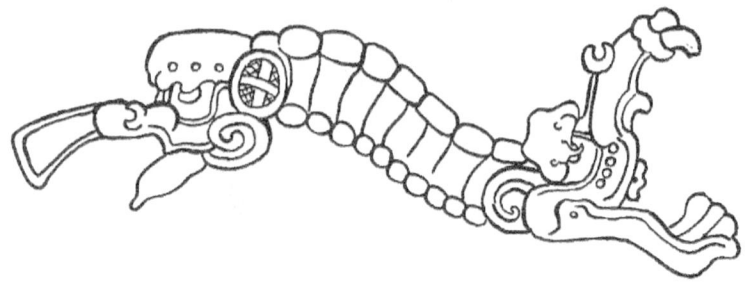

Fig. C.16. Two-headed Dragon, Yaxchilan, Chiapas, Mexico, Lintel 25, Maudslay, II pls. 87 and 88[66]

Lest one think that the 'twin' or 'dual' serpents depicted on these examples of traditional art and architecture are simply aesthetic appropriations of the principle of bilateral symmetry, it is well to recall a particular ancient Egyptian illustration of a two-headed serpent, mentioned above, that was provided in Chapter 6: "The cosmic serpent, 'Provider of Attributes'" (see fig. C.17). In that example, not only 'duality,' but an interesting parallel to the 'double-helix' structure of DNA, is illustrated. As Rundle Clark indicates in the caption to the illustration drawn from his book, 'the cosmic serpent' 'provides attributes.' What *else*, however, does the serpentine 'double helix' of DNA 'provide' in its continual process of 'adaptation'? It would seem that the process of 'realizing' and 'refining' that I mentioned above in defining my concept of 'Spiritualization' is *exactly* what the serpentine 'double helix' of DNA accomplishes, albeit on a purely *biological* level. *If*, therefore, ancient humans were aware of the reality of DNA, of its structure and of its 'purpose,' which I do *not* argue for here, then it is possible that, from this perspective as well as from others already elaborated on, the New Men among them wished to 'improve' upon this 'structure' in order to accomplish a 'higher' purpose that essentially redefines 'life.'

---

66 Herbert J. Spinden, *A Study of Maya Art*, 60.

Fig. C.17. *The Cosmic Serpent 'Provider of Attributes'*[67]

The 'duality' represented by the DNA 'double-helix' that has spawned the "mind-boggling diversity of living beings," perhaps like the ancient architectural examples provided, expresses the nature of 'nature.' In other words, it expresses the nature of the 'chaotic' state of *matter* that is the human *perception* of the *samsaric* "indefinite series of cycles of manifestation" within which 'migrating' beings are 'trapped.' Understanding the 'duality' of existence, which term is short-hand for the indefinite *multiplicity* of *samsara*, shamans (as well as other Spiritualizing 'professions' and 'personalities'), I contend, claimed to 'see' the structure and organization of the old idea of 'life' in the images of serpents and dragons.[68] These latter are, in a sense, as Harner was told in his vision by the 'dragon-like creatures' who came to earth, 'creators' of life on earth. But this is *only* in the sense that the serpents and dragons of traditional (including shamanic) art *symbolize* 'life' in the old (purely biological) sense of the *samsaric* "indefinite series of cycles of manifestation" which the *serpentine* 'double-helix' of DNA is the 'creator' of. The New Men, however, realizing that this biological 'life' is actually derivative of something that exists 'beyond' the

---

67 R. T. Rundle Clark, *Myth and Symbol in Ancient Egypt*, 52.

68 In *The Cosmic Serpent*, Narby actually draws the conclusion that the snakes that shamans see in their 'visions' or 'trances' constitute *direct contact* with the "twisted ladder shape" of the 'double-helix' molecule of DNA. Jeremy Narby, *The Cosmic Serpent*, 88.

physical world (meta-physical), from the 'Otherworld' as the Mayans called it, knew, or *chose*, to *not* 'identify' with what they themselves considered to be a derivative, although widely believed in, expression of 'life.' These New Men included Spiritualizing 'personalities' such as Moses, Jesus, Buddha, Asklepios, Apollo, Thor, and Indra, as well as Spiritualizing 'professionals' such as the traditional priest-kings, Pharaohs, Emperors, and shamans of ancient societies. Shamans — the shamans of Western Amazonia in South America, in particular — realize, for example, that "animate essences...are common to [*but not equivalent to*] all life forms."[69] Their particular 'profession,' based upon their 'ecstatic' experiences, allows them to see the *limits* of the embodiments of 'animate essences,' the limits, that is, of the 'natural' world that merely *manifests* these meta-physical 'essences.'

'Life' Is Something to Be Transcended... and 'Controlled and Managed'

The dissolving, the 'polarization,' as Guénon describes it, of the unity of the metaphysical 'Principle' into *two* currents or forces is reflected, he argues, in the symbolism of 'duality' and 'dichotomies' that appears in traditional art and myth from around the world. The serpent, as we saw in Chapter 10, with its forked tongue and hemipenes, has served in Tradition to symbolize the expression of a divine, or metaphysical, unity by means of the 'duality' of the physical world. In *The Cosmic Serpent*, Narby reveals this traditional 'duality' symbolism in the "theme of twin creator beings of celestial origin" that he finds to be "extremely common in South America, and indeed throughout the world."[70] In that book, Narby finds the connection in South American shamanism among 1) the idea of 'creation,' 2) twin creator beings, 3) common shamanic visions of snakes, and 4) the 'dual' structure of the 'double-helix' of the DNA molecule that serves as the blueprint of life

---

69 Jeremy Narby, *The Cosmic Serpent*, 60–61.
70 Jeremy Narby, *The Cosmic Serpent*, 62.

on earth to be more than simple coincidence. He argues, therefore, in *The Cosmic Serpent* that there exists in the South American shamanic understanding of 'creation' a definite and real connection among 1) the idea of 'life' expressed by the 'dual' 'double-helix' of DNA, 2) 'twin creator beings,' and 3) the 'dual-natured' snake. Quoting the anthropologist and archaeologist Gerardo Reichel-Dolmatoff, Narby draws attention, for example, to the belief in Desana shamanism that

> a large river snake of dark dull colors and an equally large land snake of spectacular bright colors...symbolize a female and male principle, a mother and father image, water and land...; in brief they represent a concept of binary opposition which has to be overcome in order to achieve individual awareness and integration.[71]

This is, of course, yet another example of a traditional, or 'archaic,' culture connecting the idea of 'duality,' and, more specifically, dichotomies, to the symbolism of the serpent.

Narby also argues in *The Cosmic Serpent* that when shamans and others taking ayahuasca see snakes in their trance states it is possible that they are actually seeing 'life' itself insofar as they are directly seeing the DNA 'double-helix.' We noted earlier Christopher Wills' remark that "[t]he two chains of DNA resemble two snakes coiled around each other in some elaborate courtship ritual."[72] Narby states, however, that

> [i]n their visions, shamans take their consciousness down to the molecular level and gain access to information related to DNA, which they call "animate essences" or "spirits." This is where they see double helixes, twisted ladders, and chromosome shapes. This is how shamanic cultures have

---

71 Jeremy Narby, *The Cosmic Serpent*, 57, quoting Gerardo Reichel-Dolmatoff, "Brain and Mind in Desana Shamanism," *Journal of Latin American Lore* 7, no. 1 (1981): 81.

72 Christopher Wills, *Exons, Introns, and Talking Genes*, 36.

known for millennia that the vital principle is the same for all living beings and is shaped like two entwined serpents."[73]

Narby later buttresses this point by noting that DNA is able to "transmit visual information" and that "DNA's highly coherent photon emission accounted for the luminescence of [the] hallucinatory images [seen by shamans], as well as their three-dimensional, or holographic, aspect."[74]

I have argued in this book that, from the traditional perspective of those individuals who have become 'enlightened' as to the true nature of their 'Self' and of the 'chaotic' nature of the *samsaric* "indefinite series of cycles of manifestation" in which they are 'trapped,' 'life,' in the 'old' biological sense, as seen by these New Men, is something to be 'combated,' 'struggled' with, and 'overcome.' The shaman, as noted, is one example of the New Man, a 'professional Spiritualizer' who serves as 'host' for the presence of the metaphysical, the 'higher' Reality, on Earth. Narby notes that "many shamanic peoples use images other than a 'cosmic serpent' to discuss the creation of life, talking particularly of a rope, a vine, a ladder, or a stairway of celestial origin that links heaven and earth."[75] We discussed in some depth the 'stairway to Heaven' called 'Jacob's Ladder' in Chapter 13. Rope, vine, ladder, and stairway are all, from the traditional perspective, figurations of the 'World Axis' or *Axis Mundi* that Guénon and Eliade contend symbolize the metaphysical Source or 'center' of all existence. They are all *also*, I argue, symbolic of the means by which 'life' in the old, limited, biological sense may be 'overcome' or transcended by 'realizing' metaphysical Reality.

In *Shamanism*, Eliade states that

> [b]y crossing, in ecstasy, the "dangerous" bridge that connects the two worlds and that only the dead can attempt, the shaman proves that he is

---

73   Jeremy Narby, *The Cosmic Serpent*, 117.
74   Jeremy Narby, *The Cosmic Serpent*, 125 and 127.
75   Jeremy Narby, *The Cosmic Serpent*, 93.

spirit, is no longer a human being, and at the same time attempts to restore the 'communicability' that existed *in illo tempore* between this world and heaven....Temporarily and for a limited number of persons — the shamans — ecstasy re-establishes the primordial condition of all mankind.... For the shaman in ecstasy, the bridge or the tree, the vine, the cord, and so on — which, *in illo tempore*, connected earth with heaven — once again, for the space of an instant, becomes a present reality.[76]

I argue that the 'bridge,' or 'ladder,' or 'stairway,' or 'vine' that the shaman employs to cross from Earth to Heaven is terrestrial, biological 'life' *itself*, when such 'life' is 'actualized' by the 'enlightened' individual. This is the case because terrestrial 'life,' at least as it is formed, defined, and 'actualized' by 'enlightened' individuals such as shamans and other 'Spiritualizing personalities' and 'professions,' exists as a union or 'mediation' of the 'celestial' and 'terrestrial,' the divine (immortal) and the mortal, the 'upper' and the 'lower' natures. 'Mediating professions' such as the shaman, Egyptian Pharaoh, Chinese Emperor/*Wang*, and priest-kings of ancient Mesopotamia, like the 'mediating personalities' of Jesus, Moses, and Siddhartha Buddha, serve, as I have labeled them, as 'managers' and 'controllers' of the state of *matter* because they know how to properly 'mediate' biological 'life' and its metaphysical Source. Such 'enlightened' individuals show to all other humans the proper 'way' (as Jesus speaks of himself) of a 'higher' metaphysical 'life' insofar as it can be applied to biological life 'on Earth.' It must be remembered, however, that 'Earth,' from the perspective of the 'multiple states of the being,' properly refers, not to the material 'stuff' that the planet Earth is composed of, but to an ignorant *state* of being in which beings believe that physical existence ('nature') constitutes itself and is not the reflection of a 'higher' Reality: the metaphysical Principle/God/*Tao*/*Brahman*.

The 'gods' and heroes of a different age of the world — the *first* of the New Men — Marduk, Indra, Apollo, Zeus, Thor, and others, struggled with their new-found 'separateness' from the old and

---

76 Mircea Eliade, *Shamanism*, 486.

limited *feeling* of biological, terrestrial, 'life' that plants, animals, and unenlightened humans enjoy. In the ancient depictions of their 'combat' with the serpent/dragon, it is sometimes, as in the case of Thor considered earlier, unknown whether these gods and heroes were victorious in their struggle. Many, it seems, *did* finally 'see through,' by means of their 'thunderweapon,' the veil of *maya* that *samsara* casts over 'the World' of the 'unenlightened.' This 'victory' over the serpent/dragon and subsequent 'enlightenment' by the victor, although not always explicitly described in the relevant 'combat myths,' would seem to have still been symbolized in the artistic renderings of these myths by means of the 'dual-natured' 'thunderweapon' wielded by each of the mentioned gods. As Guénon has pointed out, the 'dual' nature of each of the 'thunderweapons,' whether it be a two-pointed arrow, a double-edged sword or ax, a two-sided *vajra*, or a two-faced hammer, *itself* symbolized in Tradition power over the 'duality' symbolized by the serpent that threatens the unity of the metaphysical 'Principle.'

In the case of the 'Spiritualizing personalities' who, I argue, came after the age of the gods and heroes with their 'thunderweapons,' after the age of the dawning awareness of, and psychological 'struggle' or 'combat' with, the older idea of 'life' conceptualized as *matter/samsara*, individuals such as Moses, Buddha, Jesus, and Quetzalcoatl certainly saw through the 'veil' of *samsara* or what I call the state of *matter*. Their mastery over the 'serpent power' that is indicated in the symbolic art of this second age of the New Man, and the narratives of their 'miracles,' 'healings,' and generalized 'civilizing' activities, which, as we have seen, surrounds each of them—Moses, Buddha, Jesus, Quetzalcoatl, and others—is evidence of their 'realization' of the metaphysical Source. Such is also the case, however, of the 'Spiritualizing professions,' for by 'seeing' the serpent insofar as it symbolizes the "indefinite series of cycles of manifestation" that expresses the essence of the old biological 'life,' the shaman, the Pharaoh, the Emperor/*Wang*, and others were able to objectify this limited conception of 'life' and relegate it to its proper, derivative, place in the traditional hierarchy of existence, what Guénon terms the 'multiple states of the being.' In our revealing of the true nature of the 'struggles' and 'combats' of ancient 'gods,' heroes, and 'Spiritualizing personalities' with a dawning 'higher' awareness, as well as the application of such awareness on a civilizational level by the 'Spiritualizing professions' listed, it should be noted that no argument is made that either such metaphysical 'realizations' or the cultural applications made possible by them constitute *necessary* stages in the 'development' of civilization. Nor do Guénon or Eliade make such an argument.

The serpentine 'double-helix' of DNA that Narby tries so hard in *The Cosmic Serpent* to connect to the traditional serpent symbolism of ancient and shamanic cultures would seem, at least for modern people, to symbolize what *they* believe 'life' is. Many so-called 'moderns' 'identify' with this biochemical idea of 'life,' although very few of them actually understand it. In a sense, then, the modern belief that DNA defines 'life' is not very dissimilar from the belief of 'unenlightened' individuals of the pre-modern period that 'life' is basically equivalent to the totality of the various 'natural' cycles—lunar, solar, biological—the *samsaric* "indefinite series of cycles." The worship or adoration of the so-called 'divine feminine' or 'Mother Goddess,' as well as the prehistoric interest in, and depictions of, lunar, solar, celestial, and seasonal cycles, would seem to indicate this 'identification' by early *homo sapiens* with *physical* phenomena. In earlier ages of man's 'evolution,' most humans, like most animals today insofar as they are able to, probably *felt* the various kinds of 'natural' cycles to be as much a part of their 'individual identity' as their own respiration or heartbeat. The 'attachment' to this physical, and limited, variety of 'life' is, I argue, what Thor and Krishna, Apollo and Zeus, Indra and Marduk, and others unnamed most probably, 'struggled' with and 'combated' in their newfound 'realization' that 'natural life' is only a less 'actualized' expression of a 'higher' meta-physical Life. This 'realization' in the lives of such heroes and 'gods' was only later, probably through many generations of intellectual and physical labor, systematized into repeatable methods by means of which the average person could 'identify' with the 'higher' Life and 'realize' metaphysical Reality. Examples of such 'methods of realization,' as I shall call them, were: 1) the ingestion of psychotropic substances, as, for example, present-day shamans ingest ayahuasca, 2) meditational techniques, such as the *yogas* (*jnana, bhakti, karma,* and *raja*)[77] described in the 'Hindu Doctrines,' as well as other (or earlier versions of the) disciplinary practices that the ancient *rishis, yogis,* and Siddhartha engaged in, or 3) 'divine revelations' or 'dispensations,' such as Moses and Jesus allegedly received. It may be the case that 2) and 3) are not actually different but only differ in terms of the information that we currently have on the various individuals that I have classified under these two groupings.

In *The Cosmic Serpent,* Narby provides the following entry for 'serpent' from the *Dictionnaire des symboles*:

> It makes light of the sexes, and of the opposition of contraries; it is female and male too, *a twin to itself,* like so many of the important creator gods who are always, in their first representation, cosmic serpents....Thus, the visible snake appears as merely the brief incarnation of a Great Invisible Serpent, which is causal and timeless, a master of the vital principle and of all the forces of nature. It is a primary *old god* found at the beginning of all cosmogonies, before monotheism and reason toppled it.[78]

---

[77] "*Jnana yoga,* intended for spiritual aspirants who have a strong reflective bent, is the path to oneness with the Godhead through knowledge....The aim of *bhakti yoga* is to direct toward God the love that lies at the base of every heart....The third path toward God, intended for persons of active bent, is *karma yoga,* the path to God through work.... [R]*aja yoga*... [is] designed for people who are of scientific bent, it is the way to God through psychophysical experiments." Huston Smith, *The World's Religions,* 29, 32, 37, and 41.

[78] Jeremy Narby, *The Cosmic Serpent,* 65–66, translated from Jean Chevalier and Alain Gheerbrant, *Dictionnaire des symboles* (Paris: Robert Laffont, 1982), 867–868.

The near-universal association of the symbolism of the serpent in Tradition with the ideas of 'duality'/dichotomies, creation, and 'life' or 'vitality,' is especially clear in Pre-Columbian and contemporary shamanic societies. In Chapter 11, we quoted Charles Phillips's contention in *The Complete Illustrated History, Aztec & Maya* that

> Quetzalcoatl's name has two meanings. In itself, it comprises two Nahuatl words, each of which also has two meanings. *Quetzal* can mean 'green feather' or 'precious' and *coatl* can mean 'serpent' or 'twin.' The elements of the name taken together can therefore mean 'Plumed Serpent' or 'Precious Twin.'....Such dual meaning...demonstrates the concept of duality so characteristic of Mesoamerican deities and religion in general.[79]

In *Histoire de Lynx*, Claude Lévi-Strauss also noted that "[i]n Aztec, the word coatl means both 'serpent' and 'twin.' The name Quetzalcoatl can thus be interpreted either as 'Plumed serpent' or 'Magnificent twin.'"[80] Beyond being known as a great civilizer, as we have already mentioned, Quetzalcoatl was identified in Mesoamerican myth as a 'creator' as well.[81] As we have seen repeatedly, there is a deep association between 'duality' and the symbolism of the serpent in the art and myth of many traditional cultures. We have also discovered, however, a deep association in the most ancient (prehistoric) traditional art between the symbolism of the serpent and an 'older,' cyclical and biological, idea of 'life': the 'vital principle' or 'forces of nature.' According to the anthropologist Jean-Pierre Chaumeil in his *Le chamanisme chez les Yagua du Nord-Est peruvién*, the people of the Peruvian Yagua, a shamanic culture, believe that twins created all living beings.[82] And,

---

79 Charles Phillips, *The Complete Illustrated History, Aztec & Maya*, 184.

80 Claude Lévi-Strauss, *Histoire de Lynx* (Paris: Plon, 1991), 295, from Narby's translation in *The Cosmic Serpent*, 62.

81 Margaret R. Bunson and Stephen M. Bunson, *Encyclopedia of Ancient Mesoamerica*, 217.

82 Jean-Pierre Chaumeil, *Voir, Savoir, Pouvoir. Le chamanisme chez les Yagua du Nord-Est péruvien* (Paris: Éditions de l'École de Hautes Études en Sciences Sociales, 1983), 148–149.

as we have already noted, Narby states in *The Cosmic Serpent* that "the theme of twin creator beings of celestial origin was extremely common in South America."[83] More specifically, Narby points out the connection in Ashaninca mythology between 'trickster twins' and "invisible beings" called *maninkari* that, according to the shaman Carlos, "are found in animals, plants, mountains, streams, lakes, and certain crystals, and who are sources of knowledge."[84] Referring to the anthropologist Gerald Weiss's doctoral dissertation on Ashaninca mythology, *The Cosmology of the Campa Indians of Eastern Peru*[85], Narby states that

> [a]ccording to Weiss, the Ashaninca believe that the most powerful of all maninkari is the "Great Transformer" Avireri, who created life on earth, starting with the seasons and then moving on to the entirety of living beings. Accompanied sometimes by his sister, at others by his nephew, Avireri is one of the divine trickster twins who create by transformation and are so common in mythology.[86]

This association of the ideas of 'duality' (twins), creation, and 'life' in South American mythology seems strangely reminiscent of John Anthony West's words from *Serpent in the Sky* that we quoted in Chapter 6:

> In [ancient] Egypt...the serpent was the symbol for duality...more accurately, for the power that results in duality. And that power is itself dual in aspect; it is simultaneously creative and destructive....When it is realized that the serpent bears both a forked tongue and a double penis, the underlying wisdom of the choice becomes clear.[87]

---

83   Jeremy Narby, *The Cosmic Serpent*, 62.
84   Jeremy Narby, *The Cosmic Serpent*, 24.
85   Gerald Weiss, *The Cosmology of the Campa Indians of Eastern Peru* (Ann Arbor: University Microfilms, 1969).
86   Jeremy Narby, *The Cosmic Serpent*, 106.
87   John Anthony West, *Serpent in the Sky: The High Wisdom of Ancient Egypt*, 58–59.

'Life,' for traditional peoples, according to both Guénon and Eliade, comes from 'beyond' the 'natural' realm of physical/biological existence. I modify this contention by arguing that the 'traditional peoples' referred to are those peoples who 'began with,' and 'followed from,' the New Men who recognized the limitations of the 'old' biological idea of 'life.' This latter was what earlier, 'less evolved,' humans *imagined* (not thought) to be the extent of that concept. According to Guénon, the metaphysical Source of existence that was, I contend, first recognized by New Men such as Indra, Zeus, Apollo, and Thor, 'polarizes' itself, as Guénon puts it, into a 'duality' of currents or forces that manifests *as* the physical world of 'nature.' 'Life' with a capital 'L' becomes 'life' with a lower-case 'l.' It is *diminished* when it 'descends' and it becomes a mere reflection of itself, just as the manifestation of the individual 'ego' in 'nature' or 'the World' is a mere reflection of the eternal 'Self'/ Atman. The serpent symbolizes this 'polarization' and 'duality' because it encapsulates in one form (in its body) both: 1) the anatomical features that express 'duality' (its forked tongue and double penis) and 2) the dependency of physical, terrestrial, 'life' upon a metaphysical, celestial, Source: the snake's requirement of heat from an external source (the sun). This believed dependency in traditional societies of the physical upon the metaphysical, of the snake's 'life' upon the sun's heat, is dramatically illustrated in the equinoctial events that occur every year at the 'place of Spiritualization' called El Castillo, the Temple of the Feathered Serpent, at Chichen Itza in Yucatan, Mexico.[88] This Mayan temple, later appropriated by the Toltecs, has 365 steps (one for

---

[88] The Temple of the Feathered Serpent derives its name from the god to whom it was dedicated, Kukulcan, the Yucatec Maya Feathered Serpent deity who is closely related to the generic Mesoamerican god Quetzalcoatl whom we have already referred to. Because of this, El Castillo is also known as the Temple of Kukulcan.

each day of the year), 91 on each of its four sides plus the platform at its 'summit.'[89] According to nationalgeographic.com,

> [t]wice a year on the spring and autumn equinoxes, a shadow falls on the pyramid in the shape of a serpent. As the sun sets, this shadowy snake descends the steps to eventually join a stone serpent head at the base of the great staircase up the pyramid's side.[90]

This event, which importantly occurs *twice* yearly (a reference, I argue, to the 'duality' of the physical manifestation of the metaphysical Reality), speaks to the great astronomical knowledge possessed by the ancient Maya. It also presents more evidence of the broadly traditional belief that the serpent, the *samsaric* state of *matter*, comes from 'above' and 'descends' from the celestial to the terrestrial just as the shadowy snake 'slithers' down the Temple of the Feathered Serpent to the ground, to *Earth*. This twice-yearly spectacle is meant to inform its viewers, I suggest, that physical or biological 'life,' the *samsaric* state of *matter*, exactly like the ephemeral shadow of the serpent, derives *all* of its substance from the *metaphysical* 'sun.'

Like the serpent that coils about the tree, or about the rod or the staff in traditional symbolism, the 'shadow serpent' at El Castillo symbolized, for the traditional peoples of that region, that aspect of existence that is dependent upon a 'higher' source for its being. In line with this, the Temple of the Feathered Serpent—the physical temple itself—symbolizes both: 1) the physical sun, by means of its exactly 365 steps which are believed by most archaeologists to indicate the duration of a solar year, and 2) the *meta*-physical sun, the traditional metaphysical 'Principle' called God/*Brahman*/*Tao*/Atum-*Re* and other names in the various traditional societies of planet Earth. The symbolizing of the metaphysical Principle by means of the physical sun

---

89 Nationalgeographic.com, *Travel*, "Chichen Itza," November 15, 2010, https://nationalgeographic.com.

90 Nationalgeographic.com, *Travel*, "Chichen Itza," November 15, 2010, https://nationalgeographic.com.

or the 'solar disk' is widespread, occurring not only in ancient Egypt but, perhaps most famously, in Plato's *Republic* where, in the Allegory of the Cave, Plato draws the analogy between the physical sun and the meta-physical 'Form of the Good' that is the Source and cause of everything.[91] As we have discussed at length in Chapter 6, for Guénon and Eliade both, the traditional idea of the metaphysical Principle is often expressed symbolically by means of 'axial' imagery that indicates the meta-physical 'center' of 'the World.' In *The Myth of the Eternal Return*, Eliade states that "[b]eing an *axis mundi*, the sacred city or temple is regarded as the meeting point of heaven, earth, and hell."[92] The most physically permanent human representations of the 'center' on Earth are temples, such as El Castillo. Twice a year at the Temple of the Feathered Serpent the singular metaphysical force that is, according to Guénon, recognized by all traditional societies 'polarizes,' I argue, into the 'earthly' shadow serpent that descends from Heaven to Earth along the face of the great step pyramid. This biannual event thus symbolizes the 'dual' aspect of the 'Principle's' rejuvenation of the 'lower,' terrestrial realm of being from 'above.'

The traditional basis for the *shadow* of a serpent symbolizing the Principial (metaphysical) sun at El Castillo may be found in the snake's most notable characteristic of *ecdysis*, its dramatic skin-shedding. This characteristic, it would seem, is what made the snake such a widespread traditional symbol of time and temporality. In this sense, the serpent serves, as Plato said of time itself in *Timaeus*, as "a moving image of eternity...an eternal image...of eternity remaining in unity."[93] Perhaps more broadly, or more specifically, depending upon how one understands time, the serpent traditionally serves as the paragon of what I term 'regenerative immortality.' The 'regenerative immortality' of the snake, I contend, is, among all things on Earth, that which most

---

91 Plato, *Republic* 7:517b-c in *Plato: Complete Works*, ed. John M. Cooper, 1135.
92 Mircea Eliade, *The Myth of the Eternal Return*, 12.
93 Plato, *Timaeus* 37d in *Plato: Complete Works*, ed. John M. Cooper, 1241.

visibly symbolizes the *actual* immortality of the Heavenly realm that is even more directly symbolized in Tradition by celestial phenomena. In *The Gnostics and Their Remains*, Victorian classicist Charles King argues that "the figure of the serpent is explained as an emblem of the Sun himself for the reason that the Sun is perpetually returning out of, as it were, the old age of his lowest setting, up to his full meridian height as if to the vigour of youth."[94] Unlike the snake, however, the sun as well as the stars, being of the celestial realm, are those things that *directly* symbolize immortality in Tradition. The symbolism of the snake, therefore, does not, as King believes, traditionally symbolize the *physical* sun, but, rather, symbolizes that which the physical sun *also* symbolizes, but in a more faithful manner: the meta-physical 'sun' or 'Principle.' As King points out in the context of Greek mythology, however, — and it seems to be the case on, what I would deem, a less refined level of the Primordial Tradition — "the convolution of the serpents has been selected in preference to anything else [to symbolize the celestial paths of the sun and moon], because of the flexuosity of the course of both these luminaries."[95] This last, however, I feel certain Guénon would argue is an *exoteric* explanation provided by non-initiated individuals, and is, therefore, not properly symbolic. Beyond this, and even worse, King implies, in a general sense in his statement, that ancient symbols may symbolize 'natural' objects or processes. This notion, however, from Guénon's perspective, expresses a fundamental miscomprehension of the meaning and structure of traditional symbolism and Tradition itself. As Guénon states in *Symbols of Sacred Science*,

> Let us here call attention to the error of the modern 'naturalistic' interpretations of ancient traditional doctrines, interpretations which purely and simply reverse the hierarchy of relationships among the different orders of reality: for example, it has never been the role of symbols and myths to

---

94 Charles William King, *The Gnostics and their Remains*, 168.
95 Charles William King, *The Gnostics and their Remains*, 167.

represent the movement of the stars, the truth rather being that in myths one often finds figures inspired by these movements and destined to express analogically something altogether different, because the laws of that movement translate physically the metaphysical principles on which they depend. The lower may symbolize the higher, but the inverse is impossible; besides, if the symbol were not itself nearer the sensible order than what it represents, how could it fulfill the function for which it is destined?[96]

In Tradition, as defined by Guénon and Eliade, I have argued that the serpent/dragon symbolizes a *state* of existence that I have termed *matter*, and that this state encapsulates the 'migrating' being's awareness of his being 'trapped' in the 'chaotic' "indefinite series of cycles of manifestation." The term 'matter' has often, and confusedly I would add, been employed by moderns to refer to a physical 'stuff' which, so they believe, 'constitutes' the universe. In the terms of this book, however, *matter* refers to something more akin to that which Aristotle used the term to refer to: the non-formed, indefinite, potential, non-manifested, aspect of existence. In Guénon's interpretation of the 'Hindu Doctrines,' *matter* refers most closely to "the indefinite series of cycles of manifestation" that 'individual' beings 'migrate' through. In Eliade's *The Myth of the Eternal Return* and *The Sacred and the Profane*, *matter* is synonymous with that which is best described as 'chaos,' that which is nothing definite (nothing formed, defined, or 'actualized') but which *may be* either of any of the 'dichotomies' of existence: good or evil, 'benefic' or 'malefic,' living or dying, productive or destructive, mind or body, as it is that which provides substance *for* the expression of form, definition, and 'actuality.' I have argued that *matter* is symbolized in Tradition by the serpent/dragon. When the 'simple symbolism' of the traditional serpent/dragon has been, as I have termed it, 'modified,' this traditionally indicates the 'Spiritualizing' of the state of *matter*. Examples of such 'modifications' of the 'simple serpent/dragon' symbol from around the world, such as the serpent coiled around a tree, rod, or staff, the 'plumed serpent,' the

---

96 René Guénon, *Symbols of Sacred Science*, 10.

alchemical serpent on a cross, and the dragon with 'orb,' traditionally symbolize the Spiritualizing of *matter* in traditional art and mythology. This Spiritualizing event or 'action,' which is roughly equivalent to both Guénon's idea of 'manifestation' and Eliade's idea of 'Creation,' I have defined as: 1) the forming of the unformed (the clarifying and distinguishing of the 'confused and obscure'), 2) the defining of the indefinite, and 3) the 'actualizing' of the potential/'possible,' all by means of a meta-physical source or 'Principle' that has been variously called God, *Brahman*, *Tao*, Atum, 'The One,' and other names. The various traditional depictions and descriptions of 'combats' with the serpent/dragon, in which a hero or god such as Marduk, Indra, Apollo, Zeus or Thor 'struggles with' and often 'overcomes' the serpent/dragon, symbolize either the Spiritualization event/'action' or the attempt at such.

The "indefinite series of cycles of manifestation," for Guénon an essentially meta-physical system that generates all 'natural' phenomena, can be seen from the perspective of a lower, or less articulated, level of awareness to be symbolized by the serpent or dragon (as Guénon does) because that system indicates *how* Spirit reveals itself in the state of *matter*. Wherever 'personalities,' 'professions,' 'events,' and 'places' are connected in traditional art and myth with the serpent/dragon there exist references to those 'individuals' who, in their 'migration' through "the indefinite series of cycles of manifestation," either 'combated' the *samsaric* cycles or attempted to 'control and manage' them. All such individuals, however, have striven to 'overcome,' 'control,' or 'manage' 'nature,' the 'chaos' that is the state of *matter*, and to 'identify' with something 'beyond' *matter*. 'Identification' *with* the state of *matter*, I have argued, only occurs when humans are incapable of seeing 'beyond' the 'natural cycles' that they are 'trapped' within. Such are what may be called 'old' humans, the 'old men' in contrast to the New Men. In such a state, the 'old men' see nothing beyond the 'indefinite' cycles of: seasonal change; birth-growth-death; the lactating and menstruation of females; the trees shedding their leaves and the animals shedding their fur, feathers, shells, and skin; and the celestial progressions of the sun, moon and stars. However, at some point in what I call the 'evolution' of human consciousness, what is seen by a later version of humanity as a 'lower' definition of 'life' becomes insufficient to the 'new' Spiritual element that is the 'final' cause of the distinctly human element in biological 'life.' At this point, this 'moment' in human being on earth and perhaps in the universe, there comes the age of heroes and 'gods.' The moment of 'struggle' with the 'serpent power' of 'nature' arrives, and the 'new' humans (New Men) begin to see 'beyond' the 'old' 'life,' beyond the 'natural returns' that suffocate any 'actualized' Spiritual being. Individuals with now well-known names, Indra and Thor, Apollo and Zeus, Krishna and Marduk, thus saw 'beyond' and were thus 'actualized.' *Because* they saw deeper and further than other humans, they came to be known as 'gods,' existing radically apart from — 'above,' as 'sky gods' — what was *then* considered 'life.' After another epoch, however, of human Spiritual progression came a third 'moment' of human 'realization' of its true identity. Some of the New Men considered the possibility that *matter* (and thus "the indefinite series of cycles of manifestation"), now seen by them as something 'separate,' could be 'managed' and 'controlled.' Thus, I argue, originated the 'Spiritualizing professions' known now as 'shamans' and 'kings,' 'Pharaohs' and 'Emperors,' and other such 'managers' and 'controllers' — entire *lineages*, that is, of those New Men who were capable of *systematically*, a difference from their predecessors, facilitating interaction between the 'lower,' terrestrial, realm of being and the 'higher,' celestial realm. Such individuals — more likely the masses of people supplicant to them — in their 'mediation' of Heaven and Earth, built mounds, menhirs, temples, and other 'axial' architectural forms in order to 'bring down' the 'force of thunder' and 'raise up' the 'serpent power.'

The architectural examples provided throughout this book are only the embodiments of dim recollections of a much later age, and the original 'places of Spiritualization' were, in line with Guénon's understanding of the Primordial Tradition, constructed by the peoples of the various manifestations of Tradition in locales around the world. The age of the 'Dracontia,' the temples of the worship, not of the serpent, but rather of the serpent's ('nature's') metaphysical *Source*, was born. This original age of New Men, of original human awareness of the meta-physical, did die, however, in the coming of 'newer' men and newer religions that tore down these symbols of the 'older faith.' Rogue 'Spiritualizing personalities' with names such as 'Moses' and 'Aesculapius,' 'Siddhartha' and 'Jesus,' and 'Quetzalcoatl,' were given the garb of serpent symbolism in art and myth and holy texts, although they knew, perhaps, nothing about the ancient and bygone age of 'gods and heroes' and the latter's original 'struggle' with the 'chaos' of the state of *matter*.

Bibliography

'Ali, Abdullah Yusuf. *The Meaning of The Holy Qur'an*. Beltsville, Maryland, U.S.A.: Amana Publications, 1989.

Allen, Douglas. *Structure and Creativity in Religion: Hermeneutics in Mircea Eliade's Phenomenology and New Directions*. The Hague, The Netherlands: Mouton Publishers, 1978.

Anderson, Flavia. *The Ancient Secret: Fire from the Sun*. Wellingborough, Northamptonshire: Thorsons Publishing Group, 1953.

Apostolos-Cappadona, Diane, ed. *Symbolism, the Sacred, and the Arts*. New York: Crossroad, 1986.

Aquinas, Thomas. *Summa Theologica*. Translated by Fathers of the Dominican Province. 5 vols. Notre Dame, IN: Christian Classics, Ave Maria Press, Inc. [Copyright 1948 by Benziger Bros., New York, NY].

Aristotle. *The Complete Works of Aristotle, Volume Two*. Edited by Jonathan Barnes. 2 vols. Princeton, New Jersey: Princeton University Press, 1984.

Sri Aurobindo. *Secret of the Veda*. Twin Lakes, Wisconsin: Lotus Press, 1995.

Avalon, Arthur. (Sir John Woodroffe). *The Serpent Power: The Secrets of Tantric and Shakti Yoga, Being the Sat-Cakra-Nirupana and Paduka-Pancaka*. New York: Dover Publications, Inc., 1974.

Bauchot, Roland, eds. *Snakes: A Natural History*. New York, NY: Sterling Publishing Co., Inc., 2006 [originally published in 1994 by Bordas].

Beasley-Murray, G. R. *John*. Waco, Tex., 1987.

Beowulf: A New Verse Translation. Translated by Seamus Heaney. New York: W.W. Norton & Company, 2000.

Bhardwaj, Surinder M. and James G. Lochtefeld, "Tirtha." In *The Hindu World*, edited by Sushil Mittal and Gene Thursby, 478–501. New York and London: Routledge, 2004.

Bidney, David. "Myth, Symbolism, and Truth." In *Myth: A Symposium*, edited by Thomas A. Sebeok, 3–24. Bloomington and London: Indiana University Press, 1958. [First published in 1955 in Bibliographical and Special Series of the American Folklore Society Volume 5.]

Blackburn, Simon. *Oxford Dictionary of Philosophy, second revised edition*. Oxford: Oxford University Press, 2008.

Blakeslee, Donald J. and Balaji Mundkur. "More on Serpent Cults." *Current Anthropology* 18, no. 1 (March 1977): 116–117.

Blavatsky, H. P. *The Secret Doctrine: The Synthesis of Science, Religion, and Philosophy* Pasadena. California: Theosophical University Press, 1999 [originally published in 1888 by The Theosophical Publishing Company, Limited, London].

Blinkenberg, Christian. *The Thunderweapon in Religion and Folklore: A Study in Comparative Archaeology*. Cambridge: at the University Press, 1911.

Bloss, Lowell W. "The Buddha and the Naga: A Study in Buddhist Folk Religiosity." *History of Religions* 13, no. 1 (August 1973): 36–53.

Booth, Mark. *The Secret History of the World as Laid Down by the Secret Societies*. Woodstock & New York: The Overlook Press, 2008.

Bowker, John. *World Religions: The Great Faiths Explained*. New York, New York: DK Publishing, Inc., 1997.

Briffault, Robert. *The Mothers: The Matriarchal Theory of Social Origins*. New York: The Macmillan Company, 1931.

Buchler, Ira R. and Kenneth Maddock, eds. *The Rainbow Serpent: A Chromatic Piece*. The Hague and Paris: Mouton Publishers, 1978.

Bunson, Margaret R. and Stephen M. Bunson. *Encyclopedia of Ancient Mesoamerica*. New York, NY: Facts On File, Inc., 1996.

Burckhardt, Titus. *Alchemy: Science of the Cosmos, Science of the Soul*. Translated by William Stoddart. Louisville, Kentucky: Fons Vitae, 1997 [originally published in 1960 by Walter-Verlag Ag, Olten].

Burgoyne, Thomas H. *The Light of Egypt: The Science of the Soul and The Stars Vol I & II*. Mansfield Centre, CT: Martino Publishing, 2013.

Burke, Abbot George (Swami Nirmalananda Giri). *The Christ of India: The Story of Original Christianity*. Cedar Crest, New Mexico: Light of the Spirit Press, 2018.

Butterworth, Edric Allan Schofield. *The Tree at the Navel of the Earth*. Berlin: de Gruyter, 1970.

Cameron, Dorothy. "The Symbolism of the Ancestors." *ReVision* 20, Issue 3 (Winter 1998): 6–11.

Campbell, Joseph. *The Hero with a Thousand Faces*. Princeton, New Jersey: Princeton University press, 1972 [originally published in 1949 by Bollingen Foundation, Inc.].

———. *Occidental Mythology: The Masks of God*. New York, New York: Penguin Compass, 1976 [originally published in 1964 by Viking Penguin Inc.].

———. *Primitive Mythology: The Masks of God*. New York, New York: Penguin Compass, 1976 [originally published in 1959 by Viking Penguin Inc.].

Carnoy, Albert J. "The Moral Deities of Iran and India and Their Origins." *The American Journal of Theology* 21, no. 1 (January 1917): 58–78.

Chacornac, Paul. *The Simple Life of René Guénon*. Translated by Cecil Bethell. Hillsdale, NY: Sophia Perennis, 2001 [originally published by Éditions Traditionnelles in 1958 as *La vie simple de René Guénon*].

Chapell, Bryan and Dane Ortlund, eds. *ESV Gospel Transformation* Bible. Wheaton, Illinois: Crossway, 2013.

Chan, Roman Pina. *Chichen Itza: The City of the Wise Men of the Water*. Merida, Mexico: Editorial Dante, 1980.

Chan, Wing-Tsit, trans. *A Source Book in Chinese Philosophy*. Princeton, New Jersey: Princeton University Press, 1963.

Charbonneau-Lassay, Louis. *The Bestiary of Christ*. Translated and abridged by D.M. Dooling. New York, New York: Parabola Books, 1991 [originally published in 1940 by Desclee, De Brouwer & Cie].

Charles, R. H. Charles. *The Book of Enoch*. Oxford: The Clarendon Press, 1898.

Charlesworth, James H. *The Good & Evil Serpent: How a Universal Symbol Became Christianized*. New Haven and London: Yale University Press, 2010.

Chaumeil, Jean-Pierre. *Voir, Savoir, Pouvoir. Le chamanisme chez les Yagua du Nord-Est péruvien*. Paris: Éditions de l'École de Hautes Études en Sciences Sociales, 1983.

Chevalier, Jean and Alain Gheerbrant. *Dictionnaire des symboles*. Paris: Robert Laffont, 1982.

Cheyne, T. K. *The Prophecies of Isaiah*. London: Kegan Paul, Trench, and Company, 1884.

The Chumash: The Torah, Haftaros and Five Megillos with a Commentary Anthologized from the Rabbinic Writings. Edited by Nosson Scherman. Brooklyn, N.Y.: Mesorah Publications, Ltd., 1998.

Chui, Hu. *The Forbidden City: Collection of Photographs by Hu Chui*. Bowers Museum of Cultural Art, 1998.

Clark, R. T. Rundle. *Myth and Symbol in Ancient Egypt*. London: Thames & Hudson Ltd., 1959.

Clarke, Hyde and C. Staniland Wake. *Serpent and Siva Worship and Mythology in Central America, Africa, and Asia and the Origin of Serpent Worship*. New York: J. W. Bouton, 1877 [Reprinted by Kessinger Publishing: www.kessinger.net].

Cohen, Alvin P. "Coercing the Rain Deities in Ancient China." *History of Religions* 17, no. ¾, "Current Perspectives in the Study of Chinese Religions" (Feb. — May, 1978): 244–265.

Cohen, S. Marc, Patricia Curd, and C. D. C Reeve. *Readings in Ancient Greek Philosophy: From Thales to Aristotle*. Indianapolis, Indiana: Hackett Publishing Company, Inc., 1995.

Cooper, William Ricketts. *The Serpent Myths of Ancient Egypt*. Berwick, Maine: Ibis Press, an imprint of Nicolas-Hays, Inc., 2005.

Copleston, Frederick. *A History of Philosophy Volume IV: Modern Philosophy from Descartes to Leibniz*. New York, New York: Doubleday, 1960.

Creel, Herrlee Glessner. *Studies in Early Chinese Culture: First Series*. Wakefield, Massachusetts: The Murray Printing Company, 1938 [republished by Kessinger Publishing, LLC, www.Kessinger.net].

Dames, Michael. *The Avebury Cycle*. London: Thames & Hudson Ltd., 1977.

Davidson, Gustav. *A Dictionary of Angels, Including the Fallen Angels*. New York: The Free Press, 1967.

Davidson, H. R. Ellis. *Gods and Myths of Northern Europe*. London: Penguin Books, 1990 [originally published in 1964 by Pelican Books].

Deane, John Bathurst. *The Worship of the Serpent Traced Throughout the World; Attesting the Temptation and Fall of Man by the Instrumentality of a Serpent Tempter*. London: J. G. & F. Rivington, St. Paul's Church Yard, and Waterloo Place, Pall Mall, 1833 [Republished 2008 by Forgotten Books: www.forgottenbooks.org].

De Groot, J. J. M. *The Religious System of China: Its Ancient Forms, Evolution, History and Present Aspect. Manners, Customs and Social Institutions Connected Therewith*, Vols. 5 & 6, Book II. Republished by Kessinger Publishing, LLC, www.Kessinger.net [all volumes originally published between 1892–1910 by E. J. Brill, Leyden, Netherlands].

Delitzsch, Franz. *The Prophecies of Isaiah*. Edinburgh: T. and T. Clarke, 1889.

De Rios, Marlene Dobkin and Balaji Mundkur. "On the Serpent Cult and Psychoactive Plants." *Current Anthropology* 18, no. 3 (September 1977): 556–558.

Deussen, Paul. *The System of the Vedanta*. Translated by Charles Johnston. Chicago: The Open Court Publishing Company, 1912.

De Visser, Marinus Willem. *The Dragon in China and Japan*. New York, NY: Cosimo, Inc., 2008 [originally published in 1913].

Dudley, Guilford III. *Religion on Trial: Mircea Eliade & His Critics*. Philadelphia: Temple University Press, 1977.

Duquesne, Terence. "Raising the Serpent Power: Some Parallels between Egyptian Religion and Indian Tantra." *Journal of Comparative Literature and Aesthetics* XXVI, nos. 1–2 (2003): 109–117.

Easwaran, Eknath, trans. The Bhagavad Gita. Tomales. California: Nilgiri Press, 1985.

———. trans. The Upanishads. Tomales, California: Nilgiri Press, 1987.

Eddy, John A. "Medicine Wheels and Plains Indian Astronomy." In *Astronomy of the Ancients*, edited by Kenneth Brecher and Michael Feirtag, 1–24. Cambridge, Massachusetts and London, England: The MIT Press, 1979.

Edelstein, E. J. and L. Edelstein. *Asclepius: A Collection and Interpretation of the Testimonies*, 2 vols. Publications of the Institute of the History of Medicine; Johns Hopkins University, Second Series: Texts and Documents 2. Baltimore, Md.: Johns Hopkins Press, 1945.

Eliade, Mircea. *Autobiography Volume I: 1907–1937, Journey East, Journey West*. Translated by Mac Linscott Ricketts. Chicago & London: The University of Chicago Press, 1981.

———. *Autobiography Volume II: 1937–1960, Exile's Odyssey*. Translated by Mac Linscott Ricketts. Chicago & London: The University of Chicago Press, 1988.

———. *The Forge and the Crucible: The Origins and Structures of Alchemy*. Translated by Stephen Corrin. Chicago and London: The University of Chicago Press, 1962.

———. *A History of Religious Ideas Volume 1: From the Stone Age to the Eleusinian Mysteries*. Translated by Willard R. Trask. Chicago: The University of Chicago Press, 1978.

———. "Mephistopheles and the Androgyne or The Mystery of the Whole." In *The Two and the One*, Mircea Eliade. Translated by J. M. Cohen. Chicago: The University of Chicago Press, 1962. [1965 in the English translation by Harvill Press, London, and Harper & Row, Publishers, Inc., New York.] 78–124.

———. *The Myth of the Eternal Return*. Translated by Willard R. Trask. Princeton and Oxford: Princeton University Press, 2005 [originally published in 1954 by the Bollingen Foundation Inc.].

———. "Notes on the Symbolism of the Arrow." In *Religions in Antiquity*, ed. J. Neusner. Leiden: E. J. Brill, 1968, 463–475.

———. *Patterns in Comparative Religion*. Translated by Rosemary Sheed. Lincoln and London: University of Nebraska Press, 1996 [originally published in 1958 by Sheed & Ward, Inc.].

———. *Rites and Symbols of Initiation: The Mysteries of Birth and Rebirth*, Translated by Willard R. Trask. Putnam, Connecticut: Spring Publications, 1994 [originally published in 1958].

———. *The Sacred and the Profane: The Nature of Religion*. Translated by Willard R. Trask. Orlando Austin New York San Diego Toronto London: Harcourt, Inc., 1959 [originally published in 1957 by Rowohlt Taschenbuch Verlag GmbH].

———. *Shamanism: Archaic Techniques of Ecstasy*. Translated by Willard R. Trask. Princeton and Oxford: Princeton University Press, 1964 [originally published in 1951 by Librairie Payot].

———. *Yoga: Immortality and Freedom*. Translated by Willard R. Trask. Princeton and Oxford: Princeton University Press, 2009 [originally published in 1958 by Bollingen Foundation Inc.].

The Epic of Gilgamesh: An English Version with an Introduction. Translated by N. K. Sandars. London, England: Penguin Books, 1960.

Erskine, Thomas. *The Brazen Serpent: or Life Coming Through Death*. Edinburgh: David Douglas, 1879 [Reprinted by Kessinger Publishing: www.kessinger.net].

Evola, Julius. *The Hermetic Tradition: Symbols and Teachings of the Royal Art*. Translated by E. E. Rehmus. Rochester, Vermont: Inner Traditions International, 1995 [originally published in 1971 by Edizioni Mediterranee].

———. *Revolt Against the Modern World*. Translated by Guido Stucco. Rochester, Vermont: Inner Traditions International, 1995 [originally published in 1969 by Edizioni Mediterranee-Roma].

Faber, George Stanley. *The Origin of Pagan Idolatry Ascertained from Historical Testimony and Circumstantial Evidence*, Vol. I. London: A. J. Valpy, Tooke's Court, Chancery Lane, 1816.

Florescano, Enrique. *The Myth of Quetzalcoatl*. Translated by Lysa Hochroth. Baltimore and London: The Johns Hopkins University Press, 1999.

Fontana, David. *The Secret Language of Symbols: A Visual Key to Symbols and Their Meanings*. San Francisco: Chronicle Books, 1994.

Fontenrose, Joseph. *Python: A Study of Delphic Myth and Its Origins*. Berkeley, Los Angeles, London: University of California Press, 1959.

Forrest, Earle R. *The Snake Dance of the Hopi Indians*. New York, New York: Tower Publications, Inc., 1961.

Frazer, James George. *Folk-Lore in the Old Testament: Studies in Comparative Religion, Legend, and Law Vol. 1*. London: Macmillan and Co., Limited, 1918 [Republished in 2012 by Forgotten Books: www.forgottenbooks.org].

———. *The Golden Bough A Study in Magic and Religion, I Volume, Abridged Edition*. New York, New York: Touchstone, 1996 [originally published in 1922 by Macmillan Publishing Company].

Freidel, David, Linda Schele and Joy Parker. *Maya Cosmos: Three Thousand Years on the Shaman's Path*. New York, NY: Perennial: An Imprint of HarperCollins Publishers, 1993.

Frothingham, A. L. "Babylonian Origin of Hermes the Snake-God, and of the Caduceus I." *American Journal of Archaeology* 20, no. 2 (April—June 1916): 175–211.

Fustel de Coulanges, Numa Denis. *The Ancient City: A Study on the Religion, Laws, and Institutions of Greece and Rome*. Baltimore and London: The Johns Hopkins University Press, 1980 [originally published in 1864]).

Gardiner, Alan. "The Personal Name of King Serpent." *The Journal of Egyptian Archaeology* 44 (December 1958): 38–39.

Gardiner, Philip with Gary Osborn. *The Serpent Grail: The Truth Behind the Holy Grail, the Philosopher's Stone and the Elixir of Life*. London: Watkins Publishing, 2005.

Gimbutas, Marija. *The Language of the Goddess*. New York: New York: Thames & Hudson Inc., 1989.

www.Goodreads.com. 'Picasso quotes.' Accessed on 10/28/19 at 3:49 pm.

Gottlieb, Anthony. *The Dream of Reason: A History of Philosophy from the Greeks to the Renaissance*. New York London: W. W. Norton & Company, 2000.

Graves, Robert. *The Greek Myths: 1*. Harmondsworth, Middlesex, England: Penguin Books, Ltd., 1955.

———. *The Greek Myths: 2*. Harmondsworth, Middlesex, England: Penguin Books, Ltd., 1955.

Guénon, René. *The Esoterism of Dante*. Translated by Henry D. Fohr and Cecil Bethell. Hillsdale, NY: Sophia Perennis, 2001 [originally published in 1925 by Éditions Gallimard].

———. *The Great Triad*. Translated by Henry D. Fohr. Hillsdale. NY: Sophia Perennis, 2001 [originally published in 1957 by Éditions Gallimard].

———. "Hermes." *Studies in Comparative Religion* 1, no. 2: 1–4; www.studiesincomparativereligion.com [originally published in 1932 in *Le Voile d'Isis*].

———. *Introduction to the Study of the Hindu Doctrines*. Translated by Marco Pallis. Hillsdale, NY: Sophia Perennis, 2001 [originally published in 1921 by Les Éditions de la Maisnie].

———. *The King of the World*. Translated by Henry D. Fohr. Hillsdale, NY: Sophia Perennis, 2001 [originally published in 1958 by Éditions Gallimard].

———. *Man & His Becoming According to the Vedanta*. Translated by Richard C. Nicholson. Hillsdale, NY: Sophia Perennis, 2001 [originally published in 1925 by Les Éditions Traditionnelles].

———. *The Multiple States of the Being*. Translated by Henry D. Fohr. Hillsdale, NY: Sophia Perennis, 2001 [originally published in 1932 by Les Éditions de la Maisnie].

———. *Perspectives on Initiation*. Translated by Henry D. Fohr. Hillsdale, NY: Sophia Perennis, 2001 [originally published in 1946 by Les Éditions Traditionnelles].

———. *The Reign of Quantity & the Signs of the Times*. Translated by Lord Northbourne. Hillsdale, NY: Sophia Perennis, 2001 [originally published in 1945 by Les Éditions Traditionnelles].

———. "Rites and Symbols." *Studies in Comparative Religion* 4, no. 3 (Summer 1970): 1–3; www.studiesincomparativereligion.com

———. *Studies in Hinduism*. Translated by Henry D. Fohr and Cecil Bethell. Hillsdale, NY: Sophia Perennis, 2001 [originally 1966 by Éditions Traditionnelles].

———. *Symbols of Sacred Science*. Translated by Henry D. Fohr. Hillsdale, NY: Sophia Perennis, 2004 [originally 1962 by Éditions Gallimard].

———. *The Symbolism of the Cross*. Translated by Angus Macnab. Hillsdale, NY: Sophia Perennis, 2001 [originally published in 1931 by Les Éditions de la Maisnie].

Gulyaev, V., S. Ya. Serov, Balaji Mundkur. "On the Cult of the Serpent." *Current Anthropology* 17, no. 4 (December 1976): 742–744.

Hall, Manly P. *Lectures on Ancient Philosophy*. New York, New York: Jeremy P. Tarcher/Penguin, 2005 [originally published in 1929].

———. *The Secret Teachings of All Ages*. New York, New York: Jeremy P. Tarcher/Penguin, 2003 [originally published in 1928 by Philosophical Research Society].

Hamilton, Ross. *The Mystery of the Serpent Mound: In Search of the Alphabet of the Gods*. Berkeley, California: Frog Books, 2001.

Hancock, Graham. *Supernatural: Meetings with the Ancient Teachers of Mankind.* New York, New York: The Disinformation Company, Ltd., 2007.

Hardy, G. H. *A Mathematician's Apology.* Cambridge, England: Cambridge University Press, 1940.

Harner, Michael J. "Jivaro Souls." *American Anthropologist* 64 (1962): 258–272.

———. 'The Sound of Rushing Water.' *Natural History Magazine* 77, no. 6 (1968): 28–33, 60–61.

———. *The Way of the Shaman.* New York: Harper & Row, 1980.

Harris, Stephen L. and Gloria Platzner. *Classical Mythology: Images & Insights.* Mountain View, California: Mayfield Publishing Company, 1995.

Harrison, George, vocalist. "What Is Life," by George Harrison on *All Things Must Pass.* EMI, 1970. Vinyl.

Harrison, Jane Ellen. *Themis: A Study of the Social Origins of Greek Religion.* Cambridge: Cambridge University Press, 1912 [Reprinted by Forgotten Books in 2017].

Haupt, Paul. "The Curse of the Serpent." *Journal of Biblical Literature* 35, no. ½ (1916): 155–162.

Hayes, L. Newton. *The Chinese Dragon.* Shanghai: Commercial Press, Ltd., 1922 [University of Michigan Library reprint: http://www.lib.umich.edu].

Henderson, Joseph L. and Maud Oakes. *The Wisdom of the Serpent: The Myths of Death, Rebirth, and Resurrection.* New York: George Braziller, 1963.

Hentze, Carl. *Objets rituels croyances et dieux de la Chine antique et de l'Amérique.* Antwerp: Anvers, Éditions 'De Sikkel', 1936.

Herman, Arthur. *The Cave and the Light: Plato versus Aristotle, and the Struggle for the Soul of Western Civilization.* New York: Random House Trade Paperbacks, 2013.

Hill, Andrew E. "The Temple of Asclepius: An Alternative Source for Paul's Body Theology?" *Journal of Biblical Literature* 99, no. 3 (September 1980): 437–439.

The Holy Bible: Douay-Rheims Version. Charlotte, North Carolina: Saint Benedict Press, 2009.

The Holy Bible: King James Version. New York, NY: Barnes & Noble, Inc., 2012.

Hooke, S. H., ed. *The Labyrinth: Further Studies in the Relation between Myth and Ritual in the Ancient World.* New York: The Macmillan Company, 1935.

Hooper, Richard. *Jesus, Buddha, Krishna & Lao Tzu: The Parallel Sayings.* New York: Bristol Park Books, 2007.

Hoult, Janet. *Dragons: Their History & Symbolism*. Glastonbury, Somerset: Gothic Image Publications, 1987 [originally published in 1978 as *A Short History of the Dragon*].

Howey, M. Oldfield. *The Encircled Serpent: A Study of Serpent Symbolism in All Countries and Ages*. New York City: Arthur Richmond Company, 1955 [Reprinted in 2005 by Kessinger Publishing: www.kessinger.net].

Hume, David. *An Enquiry Concerning Human Understanding*. New York: Barnes & Noble, Inc. 2004. [Originally published in 1772.]

Hunt, Jr., Wallace E. "Moses' Brazen Serpent as It Relates to Serpent Worship in Mesoamerica." *Journal of Book of Mormon Studies* 2, Issue 2 (1993): 121–131.

Huxley, Aldous. *The Perennial Philosophy*. New York, NY: HarperPerennial, 1944.

Huxley, Francis. *The Dragon: Nature of Spirit, Spirit of Nature*. London: Thames and Hudson, 1979.

Ingersoll, Ernest. *Dragons and Dragon Lore*. New York: Payson & Clarke Ltd., 1928.

Irwin, John C. "The Sacred Anthill and the Cult of the Primordial Mound." *History of Religions* 21, no. 4 (May 1982): 339–360.

James, George Alfred. *Interpreting Religion: The Phenomenological Approaches of Pierre Daniel Chantepie de la Saussaye, W. Brede Kristensen, and Gerardus van der Leeuw*. Washington D.C.: The Catholic University of America Press, 1995.

Jennings, Hargrave. *Ophiolatreia: Serpent Worship, Rites & Mysteries*. (Other editions present the following longer title: *Ophiolatreia: An account of the rites and mysteries connected with the origin, rise, and development of serpent worship in various parts of the world: enriched with interesting traditions and a full description of the celebrated serpent mounds & temples: the whole forming an exposition of one of the phases of phallic, or sex worship*) London: 'Privately Printed', 1889 [Republished in 2008 by Forgotten Books: www.forgottenbooks.org].

Johnson, Buffie. *Lady of the Beasts: The Goddess and Her Sacred Animals*. Rochester, Vermont: Inner Traditions International, 1994.

Johnson, Sally B. *The Cobra Goddess of Ancient Egypt: Predynastic, Early Dynastic and Old Kingdom Periods*. London, England: Kegan Paul International Ltd., 1990.

Joines, Karen Randolph. *Serpent Symbolism in the Old Testament: A Linguistic, Archaeological, and Literary Study*. Haddonfield, New Jersey: Haddonfield House, 1974.

Jones, Scott C. "Lions, Serpents, and Lion-Serpents in Job 28:8 and Beyond." *Journal of Biblical Literature* 130, no. 4 (Winter 2011): 663–686.

Jones, W. T. *Kant and the Nineteenth Century: A History of Western Philosophy*, second edition revised. Fort Worth: Harcourt Brace Jovanovich College Publishers, 1975.

Jung, C. G. *Aion*. Translated by R. F. C. Hull. Princeton, N.J.: Princeton University Press, 1969 [originally published in 1959 by Bollingen Foundation].

———. *Alchemical Studies*. Translated by R. F. C. Hull. Princeton, N.J.: Princeton University Press, 1983 [originally published in 1967 by Bollingen Foundation].

———. *The Archetypes and the Collective Unconscious*. Translated by R. F. C. Hull. Princeton, N.J.: Princeton University Press, 1969 [originally published in 1959 by Bollingen Foundation Inc.].

———. *Mysterium Coniunctionis*. Translated by R. F. C. Hull. Princeton, N.J.: Princeton University Press, 1970 [originally published in 1963 by Bollingen Foundation].

———. *Psychology and Alchemy*. Translated by R. F. C. Hull. Princeton, N.J.: Princeton University Press, 1968.

———. *The Psychology of Kundalini Yoga: Notes of the Seminar Given in 1932 by C. G. Jung*. Edited by Sonu Shamdasani. Princeton, New Jersey: Princeton University Press, 1996.

Kahn, Charles H. *The Art and Thought of Heraclitus: An Edition of the Fragments with Translation and Commentary*. Cambridge: Cambridge University Press, 1979.

Keck, David. *Angels & Angelology in the Middle Ages*. New York and Oxford: Oxford University Press, 1998.

Keener, Craig S. "Brood of Vipers." *Journal for the Study of the New Testament* 28, no. 1 (2005): 3–11.

Kennedy, J. "The Nagas and Serpent-Worshippers in India." *Journal of the Royal Asiatic Society of Great Britain and Ireland* (July 1891): 480–482.

King, Charles William. *The Gnostics and Their Remains: Ancient and Medieval*. London: David Nutt, 1887 [Republished in 2008 by Forgotten Books, www.forgottenbooks.org].

Kirk, G. S., J. E. Raven, and M. Schofield, *The Presocratic Philosophers*, 2nd ed. Cambridge, United Kingdom: Cambridge University Press, 1957, 1983.

Kitagawa, Joseph M. "Primitive, Classical, and Modern Religions: A Perspective on Understanding the History of Religions." In *The History of Religions: Essays on the Problem of Understanding*. Edited by Joseph M. Kitagawa. Chicago: University of Chicago Press, 1967.

Kraut, Richard. "Introduction to the Study of Plato." In *The Cambridge Companion to Plato*, 1–50. Edited by Richard Kraut. Cambridge: Cambridge University Press, 1992.

Kubrick, Stanley. *2001: A Space Odyssey*. Metro-Goldwyn-Mayer, 1968.

Leach, Edmund. *Culture and Communication: The Logic by Which Symbols are Connected, An Introduction to the Use of Structuralist Analysis in Social Anthropology*. Cambridge: Cambridge University Press, 1976.

———. "Structuralism." In *The Encyclopedia of Religion*, 16 volumes, edited by Mircea Eliade, 14:54. New York: Macmillan Publishing Company, 1987.

Lebasquais, Elie. "Tradition hellénique et art grec." *Études Traditionnelles* (December 1935).

Lévi-Strauss, Claude. *Histoire de lynx*. Paris: Plon, 1991.

Lewis, C. S. *The Abolition of Man: Reflections on education with special reference to the teaching of English in the upper forms of schools*. New York, New York: HarperCollins, 1944.

———. *The Chronicles of Narnia*. New York, New York: Barnes & Noble, Inc., 2010.

Lipsey, Roger. *Coomaraswamy, Vol. 3: His Life and Work*. Princeton, New Jersey: Princeton University Press, 1977.

Lloyd-Russell. "The Serpent as the Prime Symbol of Immortality, Has Its Origin in the Semitic-Sumerian Culture." PhD diss., University of Southern California, 1938. Digitallibrary.usc.edu.

Lyle, Emily. "The Hero Who Releases the Waters and Defeats the Flood Dragon." *Comparative Mythology* 1, Issue 1 (May 2015): 1–12.

Macmillan, Malcolm, "Evolution and the Neurosciences Down-Under." *Journal of the History of the Neurosciences* 18:2: 150–196.

Mandt, Gro. "Fragments of Ancient Beliefs: The Snake as a Multivocal Symbol in Nordic Mythology." *ReVision* 23, Issue 1 (Summer 2000): 17–22.

McNamee, Gregory, ed. *The Serpent's Tale: Snakes in Folklore and Literature*. Athens, Georgia: The University of Georgia Press, 2000.

Michener, James A. *Centennial*. New York: Random House, Inc., 1974.

Miller, Hamish and Paul Broadhurst. *The Sun and the Serpent: An Investigation into Earth Energies*. Launceston, Cornwall: Pendragon Press, 1989.

Milner, George R. *The Moundbuilders: Ancient Peoples of Eastern North America*. London: Thames & Hudson Ltd., 2004.

Moberly, R. W. L. "Did the Interpreters Get It Right? Genesis 2—3 Reconsidered." *Journal of Theological Studies*, NS 59, Pt. 1 (April 2008): 22–40

Mobley, Gregory. *The Return of the Chaos Monsters and Other Backstories of the Bible*. Grand Rapids, Michigan/Cambridge, U.K.: William B. Eerdmans Publishing Company, 2012.

Moro, Pamela A. and James E. Myers. *Magic, Witchcraft, and Religion: A Reader in the Anthropology of Religion*, eighth edition. New York, New York: McGraw-Hill, 1985.

Mundkur, Balaji. *The Cult of the Serpent: An Interdisciplinary Survey of Its Manifestations and Origins*. Albany, New York: State University of New York Press, 1983.

———. "The Roots of Ophidian Symbolism." *Ethos* 6, no. 3 (Autumn 1978): 125–158.

Mundkur, Balaji, H.-G. Bandi, Stephen C. Jett, George Kubler, William Breen Murray, Charles R. Wicke. "The Bicephalous 'Animal Style' in Northern Eurasian Religious Art and Its Western Hemispheric Analogues [and Comments and Reply]." *Current Anthropology* 25, no. 4 (August—October 1984): 451–482.

Balaji Mundkur, Ralph Bolton, Charles E. Borden, Ake Hultkrantz, Erika Kaneko, David H. Kelley, William J. Kornfield, George A. Kubler, Harold Franklin McGee, Jr., Yoshio Onuki, Mary Schubert, John Tu Er-Wei. "The Cult of the Serpent in the Americas: Its Asian Background [and Comments and Reply]." *Current Anthropology* 17, no. 3 (September 1976): 429–455.

Munsterberg, Hugo. *Dragons in Chinese Art: March 23 through May 28, 1972*. New York, New York: China House Gallery, 1972.

Murison, Ross G. "The Serpent in the Old Testament." *The American Journal of Semitic Languages and Literatures* 21, no. 2 (January 1905): 115–130.

Narby, Jeremy. *The Cosmic Serpent: DNA and the Origins of Knowledge*. New York, NY: Jeremy P. Tarcher/Putnam, 1998.

Nasr, Seyyed Hossein. *Knowledge and the Sacred*. Pakistan: Suhail Academy, Chowk Urdu Bazar, Lahor, 1988.

Nationalgeographic.com. "Chichen Itza." *Travel*. Last modified November 15, 2010. https://www.nationalgeographic.com/travel/world-heritage/chichenitza.

Neumann, Erich. *The Great Mother: An Analysis of the Archetype*. Translated by Ralph Manheim. Princeton, N.J.: Princeton University Press, 1963 [originally published in 1955 by Bollingen Foundation, Inc.].

———. *The Origins and History of Consciousness*. Translated by R. F. C. Hull. Princeton, N.J.: Princeton University Press, 1954.

Neumann, Franke J. "The Dragon and the Dog: Two Symbols of Time in Nahuatl Religion." *Numen* 22, Fasc. 1 (April 1975): 1–23.

Nicene and Post-Nicene Fathers, Series 1 7. T. & T. Clark, 1886–1900 and Hendrickson Publishers, 1996.

Niles, Doug. *Dragons: The Myths, Legends, & Lore*. Avon, MA: Adams Media, 2013.

Nissenson, Marilyn and Susan Jonas. *Snake Charm*. New York: Harry N. Abrams, Inc., Publishers, 1995.

Ogden, Daniel. *Dragons, Serpents, & Slayers in the Classical and Early Christian Worlds: A Source Book*. New York, New York: Oxford University Press, 2013.

Oldham, C. F. *Sun and the Serpent: A Contribution to the History of Serpent-Worship*. London: Archibald Constable & Co Ltd, 1905 [Reprinted by Kessinger Publishing: www.kessinger.net].

Oldmeadow, Harry. *Journeys East: 20th Century Western Encounters with Eastern Religious Traditions*. New Delhi: Pentagon Press, 2005.

Otto, Rudolph. *The Idea of the Holy: An Inquiry into the non-rational factor in the idea of the divine and its relation to the rational*. Translated by John W. Harvey. London: Oxford University Press, 1923.

Ovid. *The Metamorphoses of Ovid*. Translated by Mary M. Innes. Harmondsworth, Middlesex, England: Penguin Books Ltd., 1955.

Palmer, G. and N. Lloyd. *Archaeology A — Z*. London: Frederick Warne, 1968.

Pals, Daniel L. *Eight Theories of Religion*. New York: Oxford University Press, 2006.

———. *Seven Theories of Religion*. New York, New York: Oxford University Press, 1996.

Panich, Paula. "The Egg Reconsidered." *The North American Review* 281, no. 2 (March — April 1996): 4–5.

Peters, Roderick. "The Eagle and the Serpent; or — The Minding of Matter." *Journal of Analytical Psychology* 32 (1987): 359–381.

Phillips, Charles. *The Complete Illustrated History, Aztec & Maya: The Greatest Civilizations of Ancient Central America with 1000 Photographs, Paintings and Maps*. New York, New York: Anness Publishing Ltd, 2008.

Piggott, Stuart. *The Neolithic Cultures of the British Isles*. Cambridge University Press, 1954.

———. *The West Kennet Long Barrow Excavations, 1955-6*. London: Her Majesty's Stationary Office: 1962.

Pike, Albert. *Morals and Dogma of The Ancient and Accepted Scottish Rite of Freemasonry Prepared for the Supreme Council of the Thirty-third Degree, for the Southern Jurisdiction of the United States and Published by its Authority*. Charleston, 1871.

Plato. *Plato: Complete Works.* Edited by John M. Cooper. Indianapolis/Cambridge: Hackett Publishing Company, Inc. 1997.

Plotinus, *The Six Enneads.* Translated by Stephen MacKenna and B. S. Page. Chicago: Encyclopaedia Britannica, Inc., 1952.

Powell, Corey S. "Relativity versus Quantum Mechanics: The Battle for the Universe." *The Guardian* (Nov. 5, 2015).

Préau, André. "Connaissance orientale et recherche occidentale." *Jayakarnataka* (April 1934).

Pugh, Timothy W. "Flood Reptiles, Serpent Temples, and the Quadripartite Universe: The Imago Mundi of Late Postclassic Mayapan." *Ancient Mesoamerica* 12 (2001): 247–258.

Puligandla, Ramakrishna. *Fundamentals of Indian Philosophy.* New Delhi: D. K. Printworld, Ltd., 2008 [originally published in New York in 1975].

Radice, William. *Myths and Legends of India.* London: The Folio Society, 2001.

Randall, E. O. *The Serpent Mound, Adams County, Ohio: Mystery of the Mound and History of the Serpent: Various Theories of the Effigy Mounds and the Mound Builders.* Columbus, Ohio: The Ohio State Archaeological and Historical Society, 1907 [Republished in 2012 by Forgotten Books: www.forgottenbooks.org].

Reichel-Dolmatoff, G. "Brain and Mind in Desana Shamanism." *Journal of Latin American Lore* 7, no. 1 (1981): 73–98.

Rennie, Bryan S. *Reconstructing Eliade: Making Sense of Religion.* Albany: State University of New York Press, 1996.

Roob, Alexander. *The Hermetic Museum: Alchemy & Mysticism.* Hong Kong, Koln, London, Los Angeles, Madrid, Paris, Tokyo: Taschen, 2006 [originally published in 1997 by Benedikt Taschen Verlag GmbH].

Schouten, J. *The Rod and Serpent of Asklepios: Symbol of Medicine.* Amsterdam London New York: Elsevier Publishing Company, 1967.

Schuon, Frithjof. *Language of the Self: Essays on the Perennial Philosophy.* Bloomington, Indiana: World Wisdom Books, Inc., 1999.

———. *René Guénon: Some Observations.* Hillsdale, NY: Sophia Perennis, 2004 [originally published in French as 'Quelques critiques' in *René Guénon: Les Dossiers H*].

———. *The Transcendent Unity of Religions.* London: Faber and Faber, 1953.

Service, Alastair and Jean Bradbery. *The Standing Stones of Europe: A Guide to the Great Monolithic Monuments.* London: Weidenfeld & Nicolson, 1979.

Shulman, David. "The Serpent and the Sacrifice: An Anthill Myth from Tiruvarur." *History of Religions* 18, no. 2 (November 1978): 107–137.

Skinner, Andrew C. "Serpent Symbols and Salvation in the Ancient Near East and the Book of Mormon." *Journal of Book of Mormon Studies* 10, Issue 2 (2001): 15 pages, digital, no pagination.

Smith, Grafton Elliot. *The Evolution of the Dragon*. London, New York, Chicago, Bombay, Calcutta, Madras: Manchester: At the University Press; Longmans, Green & Company, 1919 [Republished in 2008 by Forgotten Books: www.forgottenbooks.org].

Smith, Huston. *Beyond the Postmodern Mind: The Place of Meaning in a Global Civilization*. Wheaton, Illinois: Quest Books Theosophical Publishing House, 1982.

———. *Forgotten Truth: The Common Vision of the World's Religions*. New York, New York: HarperOne, An Imprint of HarperCollinsPublishers, 1976.

———. *The World's Religions*. New York, New York: HarperOne, An Imprint of HarperCollinsPublishers, 1958.

Smith, Jonathan Z. *Relating Religion: Essays in the Study of Religion*. Chicago and London: The University of Chicago Press, 2004.

Snellgrove, David. *Indo-Tibetan Buddhism: Indian Buddhists and Their Tibetan Successors*. Boston: Shambhala, 2002.

Spinden, Herbert J. *A Study of Maya Art*. New York, NY: Dover Publications, Inc., 1975.

Squier, E. G. *Ancient Monuments of the Mississippi Valley*. Washington, DC: Smithsonian Books, 1998 [originally published in 1848].

———. *The Serpent Symbol, and the Worship of the Reciprocal Principles of Nature in America*. New York: George P. Putnam, 1851 [Republished in 2012 by Forgotten Books: www.forgottenbooks.org].

Strunk, William. *The Elements of Style*. CreateSpace Independent Publishing Platform, 2018. [First published in 1920.]

Stukeley, William. *Abury Described*. London: 1743.

Tiele, C. P. "Religions." In *Encyclopaedia Britannica*, 9th ed. (1884), 20: 358–71.

Tillich, Paul. *Dynamics of Faith*. New York, New York: Harper & Row, Publishers, 1957.

Turabian, Kate L. *A Manual for Writers of Research Papers, Theses, and Dissertations: Chicago Style for Students and Researchers, Ninth Edition*. Revised by Wayne C. Booth, Gregory G. Colomb, Joseph M. Williams, Joseph Bizup,

William T. Fitzgerald, and the University of Chicago Press Editorial Staff. Chicago and London: The University of Chicago Press, 2018.

Van der Leeuw, G. *Religion in Essence and Manifestation: A Study in Phenomenology Volumes 1 & 2*. Translated by J. E. Turner. New York and Evanston: Harper & Row Publishers, 1963 [originally published in 1933 in Tubingen as *Phänomenologie der Religion*].

van der Sluijs, Marinus Anthony and Anthony L. Peratt. "The *Ouroboros* as an Auroral Phenomenon." *Journal of Folklore Research* 46, no. 1 (2009): 3–41.

Vastokas, Joan M. "The Shamanic Tree of Life." *Artscanada* 184–187 (1973/1974): 125–149.

Vitebsy, Piers. *The Shaman: Voyages of the Soul; Trance, Ecstasy and Healing; From Siberia to the Amazon*. London: Duncan Baird Publishers, 2008 [originally published in 1995 by Watkins Publishing].

Vogel, J. *Indian Serpent Lore or The Nagas in Hindu Legend and Art*. London: Arthur Probsthain, 1926 [Reprinted in 2005 by Kessinger Publishing: www.kessinger.net].

Wach, Joachim. *Types of Religious Experience Christian and Non-Christian*. Chicago: The University of Chicago Press, 1951.

Walton, John H. *The Lost World of Adam and Eve: Genesis 2 — 3 and the Human Origins Debate*. Downers Grove, IL: IVP Academic, an imprint of InterVarsity Press, 2015.

Waterfield, Robin. *René Guénon and the Future of the West: The Life and Writings of a 20th-Century Metaphysician*. Hillsdale, NY: Sophia Perennis, 1987.

Watson, James D. *The double helix: A personal account of the discovery of the structure of DNA*. London: Weidenfeld and Nicolson, 1968.

Weber, Max. *The Sociology of Religion*. Translated by Ephraim Fischoff. Boston: Beacon Press, 1963. [First published in Germany in 1922 by J. C. B. Mohr (Paul Siebeck) under the title "Religions-soziologie," from *Wirtschaft und Gesellschaft*.]

Weiss, Gerald. *The Cosmology of the Campa Indians of Eastern Peru*. Ann Arbor: University Microfilms, 1969.

West, John Anthony. *Serpent in the Sky: The High Wisdom of Ancient Egypt*. Wheaton, IL: The Theosophical Publishing House, 1993.

Westermann, Claus. *Genesis 1–11: A Continental Commentary*. Translated by John J. Scullion, S. J. Minneapolis: Fortress Press, 1994.

White, Nicholas P. "Plato's Metaphysical Epistemology." In *The Cambridge Companion to Plato*, 277–310. Edited by Richard Kraut. Cambridge: Cambridge University Press, 1992.

Whitehead, Alfred North. *Process and Reality*. New York, New York: Free Press, 1979.

Widengren, Geo. *The King and the Tree of Life in Ancient Near Eastern Religion*. Uppsala: Uppsala Universitets Arsskrift, 1951.

Wikipedia, the free encyclopedia. "Naga." Last modified 9/18/2011 11:48 am. https://en.wikipedia.org/wiki/Naga.

Wikipedia, the free encyclopedia. "Serpent (symbolism)." Last modified 10/27/2008. https://en.wikipedia.org/wiki/Serpent_(symbolism).

Wikipedia, the free encyclopedia. "Vision Serpent." Last modified 10/27/2008. https://en.wikipedia.org/wiki/Vision_Serpent.

Wilkinson, Loren. "Christ as Creator and Redeemer." In *The Environment and the Christian: What Can We Learn from the New Testament?* edited by Calvin B. DeWitt, 25–44. Grand Rapids, MI: Baker Book House, 1991.

Wills, Christopher. *Exons, Introns, and Talking Genes: The Science Behind the Human Genome Project*. Oxford: Oxford University Press, 1991.

Wilson, Leslie S. *The Serpent Symbol in the Ancient Near East: Nahash and Asherah: Death, Life, and Healing*. Lanham, Maryland: University Press of America, Inc., 2001.

Zahn, T., *Das Evangelium des Johannes*. Wuppertal, 1983 (reprint of 1921: 5th and 6th ed.).

Zimmer, Heinrich. *The Art of Indian Asia*, Vol. I. India: Motilal Banarsidass, 1983.

———. *Myths and Symbols in Indian Art and Civilization*. Edited by Joseph Campbell. Princeton, New Jersey: Princeton University Press, 1972 [originally published in 1946 by Bollingen Foundation].

Index

0–9

2001: A Space Odyssey 394–395, 584

A

Aesculapius/Asklepios 134–137, 155, 176, 266–290, 303, 317, 329–332, 413, 534–542, 556, 572, 587
Alchemy 27–28, 183–184, 217, 231–248, 298, 325, 401–411, 574–587
Allah 202–203
Allegory of the Cave 318–322, 567
Androgyne 244–252, 272, 366, 391–408, 466, 577
angel(s) 354–376, 473, 524, 576–583
anima mundi 216–217, 230–243, 317, 362, 502
Apollo xxxix, 116–136, 195, 276, 358, 372–373, 490–499, 513–531, 546–571
Aquinas, Thomas 362–363, 573
Aristotle 56–70, 174, 223, 235–237, 319, 410, 440–443, 477, 569–581
Atman xxix–xxxvi, 72–83, 107–114, 129–132, 146, 158–231, 257–260, 297–302, 325–332, 381, 419, 434, 511–515, 565
Avebury (Cycle) 135, 378–401, 517, 549, 576
Avidya 106–114, 165–179, 196–215, 227, 332, 464

B

Axis Mundi 127–129, 142–153, 171–195, 243, 299, 351–360, 558–567

Beowulf 359–360, 573
Bhagavad-Gita 70–73, 94, 299
Bhakti xxxv, 17, 73, 562
Blavatsky, Helena 8, 305–316, 574
Blinkenberg, Christian 127–128, 487–494, 574
Book of the Dead 320–321
Brahman xv–xxxix, 71–72, 94–134, 152–244, 257–303, 315–349, 366–381, 431–434, 453–455, 483–486, 502–515, 528, 547, 559–570
Brazen serpent 172, 323, 578–582
Bronze serpent 322, 537
Buddha 328–341, 451, 496–501, 525–534, 556–560, 574–581

C

Caduceus 176, 265–290, 302, 317–327, 341–346, 364–366, 409, 492, 547–551, 579
Campbell, Joseph 125–126, 381–391, 500–528, 575, 590
Chakra/cakra(s) 293–327, 353, 375, 467
Charbonneau-Lassay, Louis 12–14, 140, 216–230, 285–286, 575

Charlesworth, James H. xv, 59, 142, 177–178, 193, 216–218, 304–310, 324–327, 409–410, 517–518, 531, 575
Christ 12–20, 49–52, 140, 171–185, 216–230, 267–292, 304, 322–341, 410–413, 480, 509, 524, 574–575, 590
Chichen Itza 135–138, 551–553, 565–585
Clark, R. T. Rundle 124, 151–153, 218–223, 255–256, 313–321, 554–555, 576
Cooper, William Ricketts 266, 312–326, 361, 576
Copper serpent 172–184, 267, 291–303, 322–341
current(s) 8, 252, 272–286, 360–379, 391–392, 430–431, 444, 473, 492–495, 507–510, 522, 537, 556–565

D

Davidson, H. R. Ellis 498–515, 576
De Groot, J. J. M. 443–459, 479, 576
De Visser, Marinus Willem 424–425, 447–458, 474–486, 511–512, 577
double spiral 244–252, 285, 317, 366, 390–408, 466–489, 507–522

E

Emperor xli, 469–489, 507–513, 529–530, 544, 559–560
Evola, Julius 216, 230–243, 513–514, 578
Evolution xl, 140, 173–185, 215, 240–246, 272–284, 340, 392–395, 438–489, 502–522, 548, 561–588
Exodus (Book of) 71, 535

F

'Far-Eastern' 134, 146, 173, 249–260, 274, 301, 423–490, 507–511
Fatihah 202–204
Fontenrose, Joseph 124–125, 192, 352–353, 372, 499–501, 524, 578

Form(s) xiv–xxxiii, 7–18, 32, 56–111, 127, 158, 170–195, 233–252, 295–302, 319, 331–337, 354, 371–402, 429, 443–454, 480, 492–507, 535–556, 571–584
Frazer, James George 36, 211–215, 579
Fustel de Coulanges, Numa Denis 440, 497, 530, 579

G

Genesis xxxi, 74, 112, 133–215, 227–229, 249–250, 263–305, 339–380, 473, 513–526, 584–589
Gilgamesh 133–135, 153, 207–215, 339–349, 526–532, 578
Gimbutas, Marija 245, 353–354, 397, 434–436, 467–468, 518–520, 579
Gnostic(ism) 297, 568, 583
gold 69, 192–200, 359, 412, 444–450
golden fleece 191–198, 532

L

(Law of Universal) Gravitation 67–68, 88

G

Great Triad, The 72, 173–174, 206, 230–256, 280–285, 317, 364–370, 390–392, 407–410, 427, 461–481, 508–510, 522, 579
Greek myths 191–197, 276, 579
Guna(s) 101, 201–204

H

Hall, Manly P. 62, 315–318, 516, 580
Harrison, Jane Ellen 36, 278, 292, 542–543
Hercules/Herakles 116, 191–207, 299–307, 349, 417, 499–500, 513, 532
Hermetico-alchemical 217, 230–250
Hesperides, Garden of the 191–195, 207

INDEX

Hindu Doctrines xix–xxvi, xl, 7–31, 62–106, 120, 157–158, 196–204, 275, 294–307, 342–348, 377, 417, 477, 511–517, 562–580
History of Religious Ideas, A 379–383, 400, 577
Hopi 437–458, 579
Howey, M. Oldfield 168, 265, 310–318, 582

I

In Illo Tempore xxx, 189–190, 300, 542, 559
Indra xxxix, 116–136, 343–344, 485–533, 548–571
Introduction to the Study of the Hindu Doctrines xx, 7–17, 62–95, 157–158, 294, 307, 377, 580
involution 173–185, 240–246, 272, 392–394, 453–489, 502–522

J

Jacob 71, 143, 354–382, 473, 558
Jacob's Ladder 143, 355–376, 558
Jason (and the Argonauts) 191–200
Jesus xli, 18, 49, 113, 173–185, 267–278, 290–291, 303–305, 324–329, 412–413, 509, 525–544, 556–581
jnana xxxv, 73–77, 204–205, 562
John (Gospel of) 113, 326
Johnson, Buffie 123–124, 194, 245–246, 358, 397, 467–468, 520–522, 582
Joines, Karen Randolph 360–372, 582
Jormungandr 526
Jung, C. G. 28–38, 53, 83, 216, 231–243, 296–297, 439, 583

K

Kaliya 526
Katha Upanishad 350
Krishna 18, 70–72, 94, 116, 523–527, 561–581
Kukulcan xxxix, 565
Kundalini 293–341, 353, 375–376, 466–468, 583

L

Lakshmi 294, 307
Leibniz, Gottfried 422, 576
Lewis, C. S. xxxvii, 90, 584
Luke (Gospel of) 303, 324–326, 509

M

Man & His Becoming According to the Vedanta 17–23, 99–115, 132, 190, 210–213, 227, 273, 294–299, 580
Marduk xxxi, 116–127, 272–279, 299–301, 559–571
Matthew (Gospel of) 267, 303–305
Maya 106–115, 148, 165–182, 196, 210–228, 287–299, 418–430, 460–466, 540–566, 579–588
Metaphysics (the book) 235–237
Moon xxvii, 39–41, 218–221, 367, 396–402, 425–467, 517, 568–571
Moses xxii, 18, 65–72, 172–185, 267–268, 290–303, 316–341, 410–411, 535–544, 556–582
Multiple States of the Being, The 61–62, 97–120, 142–147, 170–174, 201, 228, 256–275, 300–301, 339–367, 413–463, 479, 559–561, 580
Mundkur, Balaji 140–148, 288, 318, 517, 538–539, 574–585
Myth of the Eternal Return, The xvii–xxx, 33–37, 50–69, 102–122, 155, 252, 485, 543, 567–577

N

naga(s) 305–306, 359, 452–454, 583–589
Narby, Jeremy 537–564, 585
Nasr, Seyyed Hossein 22, 93–99, 117–118, 585
Neumann, Erich 229, 585
New Man/New Men xvi, xxviii–xl, 16, 101–123, 150, 190–196, 458, 517–572
Newton, Isaac 67–68, 88–90, 423, 581

O

(Ohio) Serpent Mound xli, 135, 255, 378–382, 397–434, 448–465
Omphalos 350–359, 371–382, 399–400, 414
Orb xvi, xxxviii–xxxix, 89, 119–129, 258–261, 423–515, 570
Ouroboros 153, 216–243, 380–384, 524, 589
Ovid 36, 218, 349, 586

P

Patterns in Comparative Religion 39–64, 127–128, 142–145, 163, 194–195, 208–210, 350–359, 398–399, 434–441, 455–484, 497–499, 578
Pearl 258–261, 425–427, 442–467, 511–512
Perspectives on Initiation 77–78, 255, 427, 505, 580
Pharaoh 307–329, 361, 529–544, 559–560
Pike, Albert 141, 586
Plato xix–xxxiii, 8–24, 78–90, 110, 223, 236, 318–322, 430, 509, 567, 581–590
Plotinus 15, 430–432, 587
Python xxxix, 124–128, 192, 276, 352–359, 372–376, 399, 490–500, 546–548, 578

Q

Quetzalcoatl xxxix, 284–303, 327–329, 437, 525–526, 543, 560–578
Qur'an 202, 573

R

Rajas 204–206, 227–230
Republic (the book) 319, 567
Revelation (Book of) 67–370, 416, 524–534

S

Sacred and the Profane, The xxx–xxxi, 41–65, 101–122, 143–144, 195, 234, 272–279, 300, 421, 441, 497–500, 569–578
Samkhya xix, 32, 99–109, 201–206
Samsara xxv–xli, 101–284, 298–299, 315–349, 381–390, 409–421, 434–442, 454–489, 501–560
Sanchoniathon 141
Sarasvati 294, 307
Sattva 204–206
Schouten, J. 137, 266–290, 542, 587
Schuon, Frithjof 14–22, 587
Shakti 293–315, 375, 573
Shaman/*Shamanism* xl–xli, 43–49, 76, 135–155, 171, 219, 268–269, 290, 303–304, 529–589
Shankara 9, 100
Siddhartha xli, 18, 328–340, 525–544, 559–572
Smith, Grafton Elliot 140, 484, 588
Smith, Huston 22–23, 478, 562
Squier, E. G. 252–261, 358, 390–391, 405–428, 588
Swastika 475, 506–515
Symbols of Sacred Science xxi, 14, 63, 128, 257–262, 317–318, 355–358, 371–374, 429–433, 479–516, 568–580

INDEX 595

Symbolism of the Cross, The xxiii–xxv, 5, 62, 95–106, 130–206, 224–228, 240–244, 263–273, 342–348, 418, 472, 507–513, 580

T

Tamas 99–132, 162, 196–206, 227–228, 273, 506
Tanakh 172
Tao xxv, xxxix, 3, 116, 249–261, 301, 366–374, 426–427, 459, 471–489, 511–515, 559–570
Temple of the Tigers 135–138, 551–553
Thor 125–136, 487–533, 548–571
Thunderstone(s) 127
Thunderweapon xxxviii, 127–135, 262, 385, 460, 475–515, 560, 574
Tiamat xxxi, 125, 272–280, 299–301
Tillich, Paul 52–63, 588
Timaeus xxxiii, 235–236, 567
Torah xxxi, 152–175, 200, 214, 535–536, 575
Treasure 189–210, 299, 349–360, 498
Tree of Life 147–215, 283–291, 351–353, 589–590
Tree of the Knowledge of Good and Evil 133, 147–164, 198–211, 283–291

U

Upanishads xxvi, 11, 116, 158, 181, 577
Uraeus/Uraeon 233, 293, 306–341, 390, 409, 531

V

Veda(s) xx–xxvi, 75, 98–101, 158–159, 486
Vedanta/Vedantic xix–xl, 6–32, 72–134, 146–214, 227–231, 273, 294–303, 332–337, 381, 419, 515–528, 577–580
Vidya 213, 293

W

Wang 424, 466–489, 507–513, 529–544, 559–560
West, John Anthony 150–154, 564, 589
World Axis xxiv, 127–148, 163–171, 184–201, 261–269, 297, 340–385, 400–415, 430–444, 472–496, 509, 558
World Egg xxxviii, 244–272, 358–366, 391, 407–427, 465
World Serpent 503–506

Y

Yahweh xxv–xxxix, 116, 133, 148–166, 182–185, 325, 366–376, 413, 483–486
Yin-yang 126, 244–252, 272, 366, 390–391, 408, 466
Yoga xxi, xxxv, 17, 32–38, 63–77, 94, 293–337, 353, 375, 562–583
Yoga: Immortality and Freedom xxi, 63, 294–295, 310, 324, 578

Z

Zeus 56, 116–136, 407, 491–524, 548–571

OTHER BOOKS PUBLISHED BY ARKTOS

Sri Dharma Pravartaka Acharya	*The Dharma Manifesto*
Joakim Andersen	*Rising from the Ruins*
Winston C. Banks	*Excessive Immigration*
Alain de Benoist	*Beyond Human Rights*
	Carl Schmitt Today
	The Indo-Europeans
	Manifesto for a European Renaissance
	On the Brink of the Abyss
	The Problem of Democracy
	Runes and the Origins of Writing
	View from the Right (vol. 1–3)
Arthur Moeller van den Bruck	*Germany's Third Empire*
Matt Battaglioli	*The Consequences of Equality*
Kerry Bolton	*The Perversion of Normality*
	Revolution from Above
	Yockey: A Fascist Odyssey
Isac Boman	*Money Power*
Ricardo Duchesne	*Faustian Man in a Multicultural Age*
Alexander Dugin	*Ethnos and Society*
	Ethnosociology
	Eurasian Mission
	The Fourth Political Theory
	The Great Awakening vs the Great Reset
	Last War of the World-Island
	Political Platonism
	Putin vs Putin
	The Rise of the Fourth Political Theory
	The Theory of a Multipolar World
Edward Dutton	*Race Differences in Ethnocentrism*
Mark Dyal	*Hated and Proud*
Clare Ellis	*The Blackening of Europe*
Koenraad Elst	*Return of the Swastika*
Julius Evola	*The Bow and the Club*
	Fascism Viewed from the Right
	A Handbook for Right-Wing Youth
	Metaphysics of Power
	Metaphysics of War
	The Myth of the Blood
	Notes on the Third Reich
	The Path of Cinnabar
	Recognitions
	A Traditionalist Confronts Fascism

OTHER BOOKS PUBLISHED BY ARKTOS

GUILLAUME FAYE	*Archeofuturism*
	Archeofuturism 2.0
	The Colonisation of Europe
	Convergence of Catastrophes
	Ethnic Apocalypse
	A Global Coup
	Prelude to War
	Sex and Deviance
	Understanding Islam
	Why We Fight
DANIEL S. FORREST	*Suprahumanism*
ANDREW FRASER	*Dissident Dispatches*
	The WASP Question
GÉNÉRATION IDENTITAIRE	*We are Generation Identity*
PETER GOODCHILD	*The Taxi Driver from Baghdad*
	The Western Path
PAUL GOTTFRIED	*War and Democracy*
PETR HAMPL	*Breached Enclosure*
PORUS HOMI HAVEWALA	*The Saga of the Aryan Race*
LARS HOLGER HOLM	*Hiding in Broad Daylight*
	Homo Maximus
	Incidents of Travel in Latin America
	The Owls of Afrasiab
RICHARD HOUCK	*Liberalism Unmasked*
A. J. ILLINGWORTH	*Political Justice*
ALEXANDER JACOB	*De Naturae Natura*
JASON REZA JORJANI	*Closer Encounters*
	Faustian Futurist
	Iranian Leviathan
	Lovers of Sophia
	Novel Folklore
	Prometheism
	Prometheus and Atlas
	World State of Emergency
HENRIK JONASSON	*Sigmund*
VINCENT JOYCE	*The Long Goodbye*
RUUBEN KAALEP & AUGUST MEISTER	*Rebirth of Europe*
RODERICK KAINE	*Smart and SeXy*
PETER KING	*Here and Now*
	Keeping Things Close
	On Modern Manners

OTHER BOOKS PUBLISHED BY ARKTOS

James Kirkpatrick	*Conservatism Inc.*
Ludwig Klages	*The Biocentric Worldview*
	Cosmogonic Reflections
Pierre Krebs	*Guillaume Faye: Truths & Tributes*
	Fighting for the Essence
Julien Langella	*Catholic and Identitarian*
John Bruce Leonard	*The New Prometheans*
Stephen Pax Leonard	*The Ideology of Failure*
	Travels in Cultural Nihilism
William S. Lind	*Retroculture*
Pentti Linkola	*Can Life Prevail?*
H. P. Lovecraft	*The Conservative*
Norman Lowell	*Imperium Europa*
Richard Lynn	*Sex Differences in Intelligence*
John MacLugash	*The Return of the Solar King*
Charles Maurras	*The Future of the Intelligentsia*
	& For a French Awakening
John Harmon McElroy	*Agitprop in America*
Michael O'Meara	*Guillaume Faye and the Battle of Europe*
	New Culture, New Right
Michael Millerman	*Beginning with Heidegger*
Brian Anse Patrick	*The NRA and the Media*
	Rise of the Anti-Media
	The Ten Commandments of Propaganda
	Zombology
Tito Perdue	*The Bent Pyramid*
	Journey to a Location
	Lee
	Morning Crafts
	Philip
	The Sweet-Scented Manuscript
	William's House (vol. 1–4)
John K. Press	*The True West vs the Zombie Apocalypse*
Raido	*A Handbook of Traditional*
	Living (vol. 1–2)
Steven J. Rosen	*The Agni and the Ecstasy*
	The Jedi in the Lotus
Richard Rudgley	*Barbarians*
	Essential Substances
	Wildest Dreams

OTHER BOOKS PUBLISHED BY ARKTOS

Ernst von Salomon	*It Cannot Be Stormed*
	The Outlaws
Werner Sombart	*Traders and Heroes*
Piero San Giorgio	*CBRN*
	Giuseppe
	Survive the Economic Collapse
Sri Sri Ravi Shankar	*Celebrating Silence*
	Know Your Child
	Management Mantras
	Patanjali Yoga Sutras
	Secrets of Relationships
George T. Shaw (ed.)	*A Fair Hearing*
Fenek Solère	*Kraal*
Oswald Spengler	*The Decline of the West*
	Man and Technics
Richard Storey	*The Uniqueness of Western Law*
Tomislav Sunic	*Against Democracy and Equality*
	Homo Americanus
	Postmortem Report
	Titans are in Town
Askr Svarte	*Gods in the Abyss*
Hans-Jürgen Syberberg	*On the Fortunes and Misfortunes of Art in Post-War Germany*
Abir Taha	*Defining Terrorism*
	The Epic of Arya (2nd ed.)
	Nietzsche's Coming God, or the Redemption of the Divine
	Verses of Light
Jean Thiriart	*Europe: An Empire of 400 Million*
Bal Gangadhar Tilak	*The Arctic Home in the Vedas*
Dominique Venner	*For a Positive Critique*
	The Shock of History
Hans Vogel	*How Europe Became American*
Markus Willinger	*A Europe of Nations*
	Generation Identity
Alexander Wolfheze	*Alba Rosa*
	Rupes Nigra